1971

VERBAL LEARNING
and RETENTION

THE LIPPINCOTT COLLEGE PSYCHOLOGY SERIES

UNDER THE EDITORSHIP OF

Dr. Carl P. Duncan, *Northwestern University*
Dr. Julius Wishner, *University of Pennsylvania*

VERBAL LEARNING
and RETENTION

JOHN F. HALL

Pennsylvania State University

J. B. LIPPINCOTT COMPANY

Philadelphia   New York   Toronto

Preface

During the past decade research in the verbal learning and retention area has grown so rapidly that many individuals believe this material, combined with the substantial body of work which preceded it, should be considered apart from the other areas which typically make up the general learning area. My objective, in keeping with this point of view, has been to review a manageable portion of this experimental work, and write a text which is appropriate for the advanced undergraduate. As with an earlier and more general learning volume, my approach continues to be empirical or functional, with emphasis placed primarily upon an examination of those variables which have occupied the attention of most contemporary investigators.

I have attempted to provide an accurate reflection of the present state of the psychology of verbal learning and retention. Four major types of learning situations have been considered: (1) serial, (2) paired-associate, (3) free recall, and (4) extended serial or contextual. As with my previous text, *The Psychology of Learning,* I have organized my treatment around an examination of those variables which have occupied the attention of most contemporary investigators. Although a stimulus response point of view is prevalent throughout, the work of those investigators who have stressed an organization approach to learning and memory and have used the free recall learning situation has not been neglected. Finally, linguistic variables have also been discussed, particularly in the examination of contextual learning situations.

v

In brief, the approach is primarily an empirical one in which my major concern has been to provide a coherent picture of the major experimental findings gleaned from the experimental literature. Although the approach can be described as a functional one, it is not antitheoretical since one chapter is devoted to an examination of those models which a number of investigators have proposed and which hold promise for a better understanding of verbal learning.

Chapters on transfer, retention, and forgetting are included with considerable attention devoted to the recent experimental work on short term memory.

Carl P. Duncan, coeditor of the Lippincott College Psychology Series, as well as James E. Martin and Frank W. Wicker, have read the complete or portions of the manuscript. I should like to express my thanks for their many helpful comments. Finally, I am particularly grateful to Mrs. Esther Beittel and my wife Jean, for their help in the preparation of the manuscript.

I should like to express my thanks to the many authors as well as the following organizations who very kindly gave me permission to use the figures and tables found in the text: Academic Press, The American Association for the Advancement of Science, *The American Journal of Psychology*, The American Psychological Association, The Archives of Neurology, Brown University Press, Cambridge University Press, *Canadian Journal of Psychology*, The Journal Press, Charles E. Merrill Publishing Company, *Psychological Reports, Psychonomic Science, Quarterly Journal of Experimental Psychology*, and the University of California Press.

John F. Hall

University Park, Pennsylvania
September, 1970

Contents

VERBAL LEARNING
and RETENTION

1　Introduction

Of the many processes that contribute to man's behavior, psychologists regard learning as one of the most important. It is a process that is most pervasive and appears throughout the life span of the individual. Many of the simple responses of the infant are products of learning; similarly the knowledge and skills that first characterize the adolescent and then the adult also arise from the learning process.

The contribution of learning to human behavior, however, is so pervasive that we have chosen to look only at verbal behavior since we believe that most of man's achievements in changing the environment from his early beginnings to the present time must be attributed to his competence and precision in using this response system.

A DEFINITION OF LEARNING: DELIMITING THE AREA OF INQUIRY

A basic problem to be considered prior to our examination of the conditions that influence learning is, what is an acceptable definition of the construct? What is meant by the term *learning?* Many investigators have provided a variety of definitions and the following represents a sampling:

Learning . . . is a change in performance which occurs under the conditions of practice (McGeogh and Irion 1952, p. 5).

Learning is a relatively permanent change in behavior potentiality which occurs as a result of reinforced practice (Kimble 1961, p. 6).

Learning may be defined as the modification of behavior as a function of experience. Operationally, this is translated into the question of whether (and, if so, how much) there has been a change in behavior from Trial n to Trial n + 1. Any attribute of behavior that can be subjected to counting or measuring operations can be an index of change from Trial n to Trial n + 1, and therefore an index of learning (Melton 1963, p. 3).

Learning is a change in human disposition or capability, which can be retained, and which is not simply ascribable to the process of growth. The kind of change called learning exhibits itself as a change in behavior, and the inference of learning is made by comparing what behavior was possible before the individual was placed in a "learning situation" and what behavior can be exhibited after such treatment. The change may be, and often is, an increased capability for some type of performance. It may also be an altered disposition of the sort called "attitude," or "interest," or "value." The change must have more than momentary permanence; it must be capable of being retained over some period of time. Finally, it must be distinguishable from the kind of change that is attributable to growth, such as a change in height or the development of muscles through exercise (Gagne 1965, p. 5).

Learning is a process by which the behavior of an organism is modified by experience. . . . In other words, learning is a process inferred from examination of differences in some overt performance by an organism at two or more points in time (Jung 1968, p. 6).

Learning is a relatively enduring change in behavior which is a function of prior behavior (usually called practice) (Marx 1969, p. 5).

Learning is a relatively permanent process resulting from practice and reflected in a change in performance (Logan 1969, p. 2).

These definitions have much in common; let us examine them in order to extract the essence of what should be contained in a definition of learning.

(1) Learning is posited to be a process taking place within the organism. It is inferred from changes in the organism's performance. This distinction between learning and performance has been generally recognized—we are certainly familiar with individuals who have "learned" material but have been unable to perform under certain circumstances. We shall delay consideration of this learning-performance issue, however, until a subsequent chapter.

(2) It is generally agreed that learning takes place as a result of experience or practice. The contribution of these conditions has been incorporated into the learning definition primarily to differentiate the learning process from certain developmental processes (i.e.,

maturation) that may produce behavior changes without involving a practice component. Hinde (1966), for example, provided a variety of examples in which changes of behavior in animals have taken place independent of experience or practice. Nice (1943) and Barraud (1961) found that young Nibicolous birds appear to beg before they have ever been fed by their parents, make preening movements before their feathers are full-grown, and show a freezing position at the first occasion on which they hear their parents' call of alarm. Obviously these kinds of behaviors cannot be attributed to learning.

A related consideration has to do with the measurement of the behavior change that takes place from one trial to another. Melton (1963) and Jung (1968) pointed out in their definitions of learning that the behavior from which learning is inferred must be examined over two trials in order to ascertain the existence of a change. Underwood (1966) made the same point when he wrote, "We cannot measure performance change without at least two successive measurements—two conditions—and so our operational definition must depend upon two 'trials' of practice for a single group (the two trials constituting the two conditions) with performance on the second being superior to the first" (p. 310). In general, then, two learning trials or their equivalent are necessary so that incremental performance changes can be noted in order to posit that the learning process has been involved in the measured behavior.[1]

(3) We can note that some individuals would designate the learning process to cover only those behavior changes that are of a "relatively permanent" nature. This condition has frequently been included as a part of the learning definition because it is necessary to distinguish those behavior changes that take place as a result of learning from those that might be attributed to fatigue. A typist who begins typing at eighty words per minute but at the conclusion of a sustained period of work is typing just seventy words per minute fulfills the definition of a change in behavior that arises as a result of practice or experience. However, it is generally agreed that such

---

[1] The phrase "or their equivalent" is used to indicate that under certain conditions, only a single trial may be necessary in order for an experimenter to demonstrate that learning has taken place. Under such circumstances, the level of performance of one group on trial n is inferred from the performance of a control group that actually was provided such a trial.

changes do not arise from a learning process but rather come about as a result of fatigue or some postulated inhibitory process. The "relatively permanent" aspect of the definition would eliminate the possibility that this behavior change would be considered a result of the learning process, since a performance level of seventy words per minute would not be "relatively permanent." Presumably, the typist would regain her speed when properly rested.

Some investigators, however, do not believe that all behavior changes that arise from the learning process must be permanent. Some years ago, Woodworth and Schlosberg (1954), in their discussion of the "relatively permanent" aspects of the definition of learning, wrote that the term "relatively" spoils such a definition, for "some things, like telephone numbers, are learned well enough for immediate use but are soon forgotten" (p. 530). More recently, the work that has been done in the area of short term memory also raises a question about this aspect of the definition. What is the nature of this work?

Briefly, a subject is exposed to a trigram (three unrelated letters) for a very short period of time, i.e., one second, following which he is asked to engage in some type of mental activity, i.e., counting backwards by threes for twenty or thirty seconds. He is then asked to recall the trigram. It has been found that frequently the individual is unable to do this. Although such learning behavior could hardly be described as permanent, some investigators have assumed, nevertheless, that the subject learned the verbal unit when it was presented. Thus, Tulving (1968) has assumed that learning, at least the learning of single items, is synonymous with perception. The inability of the subject to subsequently recall the material is due to the fact that he has "forgotten" it during the time in which he was counting backwards. Thus, though the memorial process is considered to be short term, it is assumed that the material has been learned.

It does not seem possible that we can resolve this problem of how permanent the behavior change must be in order for the learning process to be inferred, since it appears that the nature of the controversy is primarily a semantic one. As we shall subsequently note, the distinction between a learning process and a retention or memorial one is arbitrary since the learning of new material obviously involves the remembering of that which has been previously

learned. The placing of emphasis upon a memorial process, however, does emphasize the position that a continuum of behavior
change exists in which at the one end we have changes that are
extremely temporary and at the other end changes that are quite
permanent.

(4) Our last consideration is related to the introduction of
motivational constructs in order to help define the learning process.
It may be noted that Kimble (1961) has made reinforced practice
a condition for learning, stating that some reference must be made
to the reinforcement procedure in order to distinguish learning from
extinction. But a problem is subsequently noted when Kimble acknowledges the difficulty of specifying the conditions that qualify as
reinforcement. This problem is of particular note when we are
working with humans in verbal learning situations and the delineation of reinforcement under such circumstances becomes most
difficult.

Can we arrive at a satisfactory definition of learning? Probably
not one which would have universal acceptance although we believe
the following contains most of the generally accepted aspects of
such a definition:

Learning may be defined as a process which takes place within
the organism and is inferred from specified behavioral changes.
Such changes in behavior (1) are directed towards certain
standards or criteria which have been established, usually by the
investigator and (2) can be related to the necessity of practice or
experience in order to achieve such standards.

As this author has pointed out elsewhere (Hall 1966) the inability of experimenters to come to a completely adequate definition
of learning (or to clearly distinguish between learning and memorial
processes) is not as great a handicap as one might believe. Generally, there is little concern on the part of the experimenter with
looking at a given behavior pattern and attempting to decide
whether or not it has come about as a result of learning or as a
result of some other process, i.e., maturation, fatigue, etc. Rather,
and this has been particularly true in the investigation of verbal
learning, the general procedure has been to provide the subject with
a task in which his change in behavior leads logically to what must

be assumed to be the operation of the learning process. Thus, when a subject is asked to learn a list of words, it is obvious he could not have produced these words before observing them; it is also obvious that after a number of practice trials, he is capable of doing so. It is generally assumed, then, that the process that accounts for such a behavioral change is learning.

This point of view has been expressed quite succinctly by Hilgard (1951) who wrote

a precise definition of learning is not necessary, so long as we agree that the inference to learning is made from changes in performance that are the result of training or experience, as distinguished from changes such as growth or fatigue and from changes attributable to the temporary state of the learner. The experiments themselves define the field ostensively (p. 518).

THE VARIETIES OF VERBAL LEARNING SITUATIONS

In keeping with Hilgard's point of view it seems appropriate to provide a brief description of the various types of verbal situations from which investigators infer the occurrence of learning, or the learning process.

Four kinds of learning situations are used quite frequently: (a) serial learning, (b) extended serial learning, (c) paired-associate learning, and (d) free-recall learning.

SERIAL LEARNING

The serial learning task was first used experimentally by Ebbinghaus (1885) in his now classic study of Memory. As a result of this monumental work, serial learning was the task most frequently used in verbal learning until the early 1950s. With this type of situation, the verbal material is presented in a fixed serial order. The particular order in which each item is presented—i.e., which item is the first in the series, second, third, etc.—is determined randomly, although the experimenter attempts to make sure that there are no obvious associations between adjacent items. For example, if the words *table* and *chair* were used in making up the serial list, they would not be placed in adjacent positions since there is an obvious associative relationship between the two items.

A variety of methods have been used to present the material. A frequently used procedure is the anticipation method. This consists of instructing the subject to associate each item with the subsequent one on the list. Thus, when each item is presented to the subject, it serves as a stimulus or a cue to which the subject must respond with the next item on the list. Exposure time for each item is usually fixed at from one to four seconds per item. Presentation of all the items constitutes a trial.

A second method of presentation is the study-test technique. Lockhead (1962) has termed this the blocking method, while Runquist (1966) has designated it as the recall method. With this procedure, the material is presented item by item (study trial). At the conclusion of the presentation, the subject is asked to recall as many of the items as he can and in their appropriate order (test trial). A second study trial is then presented, followed by a test trial, etc., until the appropriate number of trials are provided.

EXTENDED SERIAL LEARNING

A kind of modified serial learning situation may be provided when the experimental material consists of sentences or prose, rather than a series of units that are of the same form class. Although some writers have considered the learning of prose to be a type of serial learning, it would appear, at least as generally used, that there are fundamental differences between the two situations. First, of course, the typical method of presenting prose material is not in a word by word fashion, but rather in phrases or even sentences. Moreover, each word in the sentence does not serve as a stimulus or a cue for the next word. Secondly, the experimenter does not demand that what is to be learned be the rote recall of what has been presented. Rather the learning of ideas, or the providing of paraphrases, etc., seems central in this type of learning situation.

PAIRED-ASSOCIATE LEARNING

In the learning of serial lists, it may be noted that each item first serves as a response and then as a stimulus or cue for the subsequent item. Since each unit has both stimulus and response characteristics, there is an obvious difficulty in breaking down the serial learning task into clearly identifiable stimulus and response units. As a result, the paired-associate task has in recent years supplanted the serial learning task as the "standard" vehicle among traditional psychologists for studying verbal learning. Briefly, the paired-associate task consists of a series of pairs of items in which one item of the pair serves as a stimulus and the second item as a response. In a sense, the task is not unlike the learning of a vocabulary for a foreign language in which the English word serves as the stimulus and its foreign equivalent the response.

In constructing a list of paired-associates, two precautions are invariably taken. First, as in the serial learning task, the experimenter attempts to make sure that a previously established associative relationship does not exist between any paired-associates. Thus, the words *black-white* would not be used as a paired-associate item unless this kind of associative relationship was of experimental interest to the investigator. Secondly, in order to preclude serial learning of the responses (here the subject could ignore the stimuli and simply learn the responses in a fixed order) the items are not presented in a constant order but their position is changed from trial to trial.

Presentation methods for paired-associate learning include the already familiar anticipation and recall or study-test methods, in addition to a third method that has been termed "prompting." With the anticipation method, the stimulus is presented for a short period of time during which the subject must call out or anticipate the response that had been paired with that stimulus. The response item is then presented along with the stimulus; this provides the subject with the opportunity to see the two items together. Presentation times for stimulus and stimulus-response exposure have varied from one-half second to four seconds and sometimes longer, although two seconds has been probably the most frequently used interval. Thus, a 2:2 procedure means that the stimulus is presented for two seconds followed by the presentation or exposure of both the stimulus and response for two seconds. There is no reason, of course, why the stimulus term cannot be presented for a longer or shorter period than the response term. Some investigators have used 4:2 or 2:4 time intervals rather than the traditional 2:2.

With the recall or study-test method the stimulus and response pair is presented together for a fixed interval of time that constitutes the study trial. The test trial follows and consists of presenting the stimuli, with the individual providing as many of the responses as can be recalled. This test trial is followed by a second study trial, then a second test trial, etc.

A variation of both the anticipation and recall methods has been described as the "prompting" or nonanticipation procedure. The stimulus term is presented alone for a fixed interval, followed by the presentation of the response term, which is then followed by overt practice by the subject of the response term. Since there is no adequate test measure on any trial, test trials must be given after each trial or at selected points, in order to measure performance. This procedure has been used by a relatively small number of investigators, i.e., Cook and Kendler (1956), Cook (1958), Cook and Spitzer (1960), and Sidowski, Kopstein and Shillestad (1961).

FREE-RECALL LEARNING

The last type of verbal learning situation we will present here has been designated free-learning, or more frequently, free-recall learning. The typical procedure consists of presenting a discrete list of verbal items to the subject with a fixed rate of presentation. Following this, a so-called "recall" trial is provided during which the subject is asked to recall as many of the items as he can without regard to order. Most frequently, only a single presentation (study trial) and a single recall (test trial) are provided, although multiple study-test trials may be used.

VERBAL MATERIALS

The characteristics of verbal material will be discussed in greater detail in a subsequent chapter; however, at this point we should like to introduce the topic to the reader. An examination of verbal material used in experimental studies of learning must start with Ebbinghaus (1885) who "invented" the nonsense syllable—two consonants separated by a vowel (e.g., XET) in order to provide himself with verbal material that had the attributes of large numbers of the items readily available, and at the same time had both simplicity and uniform difficulty. This last attribute was presumed since there were no established associations between one nonsense syllable and another.[1]

American investigators have made extensive use of the nonsense syllable or the CVC trigram (consonant-vowel-consonant), as it is now termed. But a variety of other materials have also been used. Consonant syllables or CCCs (i.e., BSV) have been employed, along with other types of three-letter combinations.

Another kind of nonsense material is the paralog or dissyllable, which consists of a two-syllable combination of letters that is pronounceable but bears little resemblance to actual words, e.g., GOJEY.

Many experimenters have considered nonsense material as representing something less than the ideal verbal learning unit. The problem is that virtually all so-called nonsense material is capable of arousing associations in the same way that words or other meaningful units do, and as a result, this type of material cannot be considered to have the unique verbal property that Ebbinghaus believed it possessed. Some investigators (Deese 1961) have suggested that nonsense materials, and in particular the nonsense syllable, or CVC, should be abandoned. There has been little enthusiasm on the part of experimenters for adopting this position although nonsense syllables are not used as frequently as they were a decade ago. One problem in their abandonment has been that a large number of experiments have been conducted using nonsense syllables and many investigators, wishing to extend or amplify the findings obtained in these studies, feel that it is important to continue to use the same kind of material.

Digits, single letters as well as bigrams, words, word couplets, and prose have also been used as units of verbal material. Words, of course, have an advantage in that the relationships that exist among words (e.g., synonyms, antonyms, etc.) provide a semantic dimension that frequently cannot be utilized when using nonsense material.

---

[1] The reader may find it interesting to note that the invention of the nonsense syllable prompted Titchener (1919) to write, "It is not too much to say that the recourse to nonsense syllables, as a means to the study of association, marks the most considerable advance, in this chapter of psychology, since the time of Aristotle" (pp. 380–381).

POINTS OF VIEW

For a long time, verbal learning was studied in the tradition of the British associationists, who had held that the basic verbal unit was an association of ideas. In addition, the conceptual framework that was most frequently adopted was based upon a stimulus-response analysis of behavior.

During the 1950s, significant changes in the study of verbal learning began to emerge. One such change was the increasing awareness that stimulus, response, and association constructs should be conceptualized in ways that were vastly different from those proposed by earlier investigators. For example, present experimenters, in using a particular verbal unit as a stimulus in a paired-associate task, have recognized that the subject might not use the total stimulus as a cue for his response. A stimulus compound consisting of a CVC placed upon a particular colored background may result, at least under certain kinds of experimental conditions, in the subject's ignoring the CVC and using only the color to cue his response. The stimulus, as defined by the experimenter, is known as the nominal stimulus, while that part of the stimulus to which the individual attaches his response is known as the functional stimulus. The process whereby the subject selects only a part of the stimulus provided by the experimenter (functional stimulus) to which to respond, has become known as stimulus selection.

It was also recognized that the subject may transform the verbal response that has been provided by the experimenter. Thus, given the trigram RIV to learn as a response, the subject might "code" this response into the word *river* with the added mental note, "first three letters." During the past decade, many investigators have been looking at the conditions under which coding takes place and how it aids (as well as hinders) the learning of verbal materials.

Finally, it has been recognized that the so-called association between the stimulus and the response may be neither as simple nor as direct as many of the traditional verbal learning investigators had assumed. Some of the contemporary work in this area has been subsumed under the topic of mediation. That is, presentation of a stimulus may have the result that the subject makes an intermediate response that in turn serves as a stimulus for the response that was demanded by the experimenter. For example, if it is necessary for a subject to learn to respond with the word *dog* to the stimulus word *nine,* this association may be mediated by the word *cat.* Here the stimulus word *nine* elicits the mediating response, *cat,* which in turn serves as a stimulus term for the response *dog.* The many experimental demonstrations that such mediating responses play an important role in learning reveal the untenability of earlier approaches to verbal learning—approaches based upon the establishment of simple and direct bonds or associations between a verbal stimulus and its response.

As Underwood (1966a) pointed out, these considerations represent some of the basic aspects of modern associationism as it is being formulated in the verbal-learning laboratory around paired-associate learning.

A second change has come in terms of what Underwood called constituent analysis. Briefly, this type of analysis recognizes that even the so-called simple tasks of serial and paired-associate learning are somewhat more complex than had been previously believed, and that it is necessary to break these tasks down into stages or component parts.

An early example is found in a study by Hovland and Kurtz (1952), who were interested in examining the learning of a series of CVCs. These investigators described the learning of this task in terms of the subject's (1) learning of the response terms and (2) learning the order in which the items appear. Some years later, Underwood and Schulz (1960), and McGuire (1961) provided a somewhat similar type of analysis for the learning of paired-associates. These investigators proposed that the learning of a list of paired-associates consists of a response learning stage (similar to that proposed by Hovland and Kurtz 1952) and an associative or hook-up stage.[1] Thus, the first stage consists of a process through which the responses become available to the subject. For example, prior to the time that a subject could learn to associate the word *vulpine* to the stimulus word *red, sultanate* to the stimulus word *blue,* and *scoria* to *green,* it would be necessary for him to have the

[1] Since these early studies were done, a number of other processes have been postulated to take place as a part of the paired-associate learning task. See Battig (1968) for an excellent description of these processes.

words *scoria, sultanate* and *vulpine* available or accessible in his vocabulary. Once their availability was established, the second stage would consist of learning to attach these words to their appropriate stimuli.

Underwood (1966a), in commenting upon this type of approach to the study of verbal learning, wrote,

There is nothing new in constituent analysis. It typifies the method of approach which sooner or later is seen in almost any experimental discipline. It may be directed by theoretical analysis or by logical analysis. It involves a refinement in the control of independent variables and also a refinement in response measures, both of which indicate a simplification of the experimental task. If a single feature can be used to typify the stage of research in an area at any moment in time, we would typify verbal learning today as being in the stage of constituent analysis (p. 496).

As Underwood further commented, there is the implicit assumption in the breaking down of a given learning task into its constituent parts that these processes can be summed up to produce the whole. At the present time, constituent analysis of the traditional learning tasks has not moved sufficiently far that we can be sure it will be possible to do this in all situations.

Thus, Underwood (1966a) writes,

It will always remain a possibility that a given task, particularly one of some degree of complexity, has emergent properties. We may know all of the constituents and we may "add" these in many, many different ways and still not approximate the behavior on the complex task as it occurs on this task. Most of us would probably resist accepting this final alternative until it seemed absolutely necessary. For to accept it means that constituent analysis becomes a way of studying or discovering lower-level phenomena but these must become ends in themselves if we cannot show with any precision how they enter into the complex phenomenon from which they were extracted. This is not to minimize the importance of discovering these lower-level phenomena, and to identify the subphenomena making up a complex one does achieve some level of understanding of the complex. But in the long run we would be most pleased if the parts of the whole could be successfully combined to produce the whole (p. 500).

The developments described above have taken place within the traditional stimulus-response, associationistic position. Paralleling this evolving tradition, however, has been another point of view, frequently described as the "new look" in verbal learning. Here, emphasis is placed upon a memorial rather than a learning process, with storage and retrieval constructs being posited to play important roles. Simply stated, experimenters have conceptualized the presentation of material in terms of the subject's "storing" such material and subsequently attempting to retrieve the information that has been stored.

As a result of this kind of formulation, storage and retrieval mechanisms have become basic concepts for a number of investigations. Thus, experimenters who have analyzed the storage process believe that the way in which the subject organizes the material that is presented is of primary significance. An experiment that neatly illustrates this position is found in an early study by Bousfield (1953). In this single trial, free-recall learning experiment, subjects were presented with a randomized list of sixty items made up of four fifteen-item categories: (1) animals, (2) names, (3) professions, and (4) vegetables. Immediately following the presentation of these items, the subjects were given ten minutes to list all of the words they could recall. Results indicated that the subjects showed a greater than chance tendency to place items in clusters or groups that contained members of the same general category. From such data, Bousfield inferred an organizing tendency on the part of the subject that he termed "clustering." Since this early study, many subsequent investigators have verified the position that clustering is indeed an important organizational process.

An interesting note is that the single trial, free-recall learning situation lends itself quite well to a storage-retrieval type of analysis. The experimenter who studies such a learning situation, unlike the traditional associationistic experimenter, cannot examine a gradual strengthening of associative bonds, since the stimulus and response items are not clearly delineated and only a single trial is provided.

SUMMARY

Although there has been some problem in providing a definition of learning that is acceptable to everyone, learning has frequently been defined as a process, the existence of which is inferred from behavior changes that are relatively permanent and which comes about as a result of practice or experience. The inability to arrive at a completely acceptable definition of learning is not as great a handicap as one might believe since there has been little concern on the part of investigators with looking at a given behavior pattern to decide whether or not it has come about as a result of learning. Rather, the general procedure has been to use tasks in which changes in the subject's behavior lead logically to what must be assumed to be the operation of the learning process.

Four types of tasks have been used frequently in the study of verbal learning: (1) serial learning, (2) extended serial learning, (3) paired-associate learning, and (4) free-recall learning. With serial learning, the material is presented to the subject in a fixed serial order and the task of the subject is to learn the material as well as its order. A frequently used procedure is the anticipation method, in which each item serves as the stimulus to which the subject must respond with the next item on the list. Each item has both stimulus as well as response characteristics. Extended serial learning tasks consist of sentences or prose; the task of the subject is to learn the ideas, or to provide paraphrases. In the paired-associate task, the subject is presented with a series of paired items in which the first item of each pair serves as the stimulus while the second item serves as the response. Finally, free-recall learning consists of presenting the subject with a list of items, following which the subject is asked to recall as many items as he can but without regard to order.

A wide range of experimental material has been used in the study of verbal learning. American investigators have made extensive use of the nonsense syllable or CVC trigram, but digits, single words, word couplets, and prose have been also used.

A stimulus-response, associationistic analysis has been the most frequently adopted point of view in the study of verbal learning, but recent work has placed emphasis upon the memorial rather than the learning process. This kind of conceptualization places emphasis upon the subject's "storing" of presented material with subsequent attempts to retrieve the information that has been stored. Thus, storage and retrieval mechanisms become basic concepts with this type of analysis.

2 *Measurement and Methodology*

Before proceeding to the examination of the variables that contribute to verbal learning, a few methodological considerations will
be discussed. These have to do with (1) the distinction between
learning, retention, and performance; (2) response measures, or
measures of learning; (3) learning curves; and finally (4) some
variations in procedure.

LEARNING, PERFORMANCE AND RETENTION

LEARNING AND PERFORMANCE

We have defined learning as a process that takes place within
the nervous system and is inferred from changes in the organism's behavior. Everyday observation reveals the inappropriateness
of assuming that learning is always mirrored by performance. We
are all familiar with the student who has studied diligently for an
examination and presumably has "learned" the material only to find
the test-taking situation so traumatic that he is unable to perform
in keeping with his preparation. Inasmuch as he has demonstrated
his learning by appropriate performance the evening before or perhaps only a few hours prior to his taking the test, it would be most
unlikely for him to have "forgotten" the material during this intervening period. Thus, his poor performance in the test situation is
readily distinguished from what it has been assumed that he has
learned.

16

For more than forty years learning theorists have been interested in attempting to distinguish between learning and performance; the works of Hull (1943, 1951, 1952) and Spence (1956) provide the most definitive attempts to make this distinction. These investigators have attempted to determine those variables or conditions that influence learning (or habit), in contrast to those that contribute only to performance. It must be acknowledged that much of the experimental work designed to examine the adequacy of the learning-performance distinction has been done with animals performing in relatively simple learning situations.

Most experimenters in verbal learning have not been concerned with attempting to distinguish between the two constructs. Their lack of enthusiasm for making such a distinction undoubtedly can be traced to the position of McGeoch (1942) who stated that

the distinction between learning and performance is logically valid, but practically and operationally of little importance in a treatment of learning. . . . The only way we can know that learning has occurred is by an observation of successive performances, since *learning is a relation between successive performances*. . . . This does not mean that learning cannot occur without being measured, but only that we can never know that learning has occurred without measurement or observation of some kind. The statement that it can occur without being measured admits the validity of the logical distinction between learning and performance, while the statement that it cannot be known as a scientific datum without being observed or measured denies the operational validity of the distinction. Assertions that motive and effect influence performance but not learning become meaningless in the absence of quantitative demonstration, a demonstration which cannot be made without measurements of performance (pp. 598–599).

A recent plea for making a distinction between learning and performance in verbal learning situations has come from both Adams (1967) and Postman (1968). Postman's distinction between learning and performance in the verbal learning area is similar to that proposed by earlier investigators in that

the course of acquisition is determined by two conceptually distinct sets of factors : (a) the laws governing the establishment of associative dispositions which are assumed to be general principles which remain valid regardless of the specific conditions of practice, and (b) the conditions of performance which determine the activation of these dispositions during practice (p. 557).

In recognizing that there has been little systematic concern in the past by investigators with attempting to identify those determiners of performance as distinguished from the conditions of learning, Postman (1968) wrote that

The reason is perhaps that most conventional experiments on verbal learning are carried out under conditions where instructions, self-instruction and pre-experimental habits all combine to maximize performance of what has been learned. The dependence of behavior on motivational arousal, which has served to bring the distinction between learning and performance into clear focus in the animal laboratory, has rarely become salient in the analysis of verbal processes (p. 556).

Finally, Postman proposed that at least under certain conditions, the transfer situation may be used in helping to distinguish between the two constructs.[1] He pointed out that the performance requirements that are imposed during the learning of a specific task may limit the possibility of determining what it is that the subject is learning; thus, while the subject is meeting the criterion of the learning task, he may be acquiring other dispositions as well which cannot be reflected in his performance. By the same token, although he may fail to meet the criterion of the current task, nonetheless certain kinds of learning may still have taken place. The use of a second (transfer) task may be used to indicate the nature of such learning.

Adams (1967) also emphasized the need for investigators in verbal learning to make the distinction between the two constructs. He took the position that "a scientific approach to memory [learning] must be based on some kind of theory that makes a learning-performance distinction as Hull does, even though the theory is crude, preliminary, and qualitative" (p. 14). More specifically, Adams believes that there must be some basis for believing that habits (rather than performance) are being studied.

The belief may be wrong, in the sense that a definition of habit may be wrong at any given time, but this is a matter of empirical fact that will be corrected in the normal development of psychology as a science. The point is that an experimenter must have ideas about the variables which define habit, and a knowledge of how these variables differ from those defining

[1] Transfer refers to the influence that the learning of one task has on the learning of a second.

other conceptual states, in order to exert experimental control and design experiments which bear on habit and its retention. He must be assured that in observing *performance* he can infer about *learning* (p. 14).

What conclusions can be drawn concerning the viability of making the learning-performance distinction? We are sympathetic with those individuals who have pleaded for the positing of some theoretical structure which, like the Hullian model, will not only make a distinction between the two constructs but will also indicate those variables that contribute to learning in contrast to those that contribute to performance. But the experience of those psychologists working primarily with animals during the past quarter of a century should not be lost upon us. These investigators, in contrast to those interested in verbal learning, have used far less sophisticated subjects and have had considerably better control over their motivational conditions. And yet their work has not led to either the verification of the Hullian distinction between learning and performance nor to other theoretical (or operational) distinctions between the two constructs.

It may be possible that, with some verbal learning tasks, the use of a transfer experiment may be of some help in distinguishing between learning and performance. But the contribution that is provided by this relatively restricted type of situation is a far cry from the theoretical model for which Adams (1967) pleaded. Perhaps it will be necessary for the neurological basis of learning to be discovered before a general and viable distinction can be made. In the meantime, it is probably true that most investigators will continue their experimental work without attempting to distinguish between the two constructs.

LEARNING AND RETENTION

Let us operationally describe what can be indicated as the traditional distinction between learning and retention. A group of subjects is required to learn a list of twelve paired-associates, using the anticipation method with a one-minute interval between trials. Following the reaching of a criterion of one perfect trial, the subjects are asked to return to the laboratory one hour later, at which time they are asked to recall the items they had previously learned. Under such circumstances, the performance of the group during the acquisition trials is believed to reflect the operation of a learning process; the difference between the criterion measure and performance at the end of the hour is used to indicate the amount retained.

But let us look at these operations more carefully. Following the first learning trial, performance on the second and subsequent trials reflects the retention of learning that has occurred on earlier trials. It also reflects the operation of the learning process that takes place on the current trial. Thus, performance on any learning trial except the first reflects not only the operation of the learning process but also retention of material from previous trials. The intertwining of these processes has been long recognized. As Marx (1969) wrote recently, "it is apparent upon reflection that without retention there could be no learning; that is to say, unless the effects of one trial or response persist until the next trial or response, over a period of time, they cannot have the effect upon subsequent behavior that we have identified as learning" (p. 13).

A second aspect of the problem is related to the length of the interval between learning trials and the time interval that is interpolated between the last learning trial and the test for retention. In the example noted, it would have been possible to use a sixty-minute intertrial interval; this would have made the test for "retention" simply another learning trial.

What we are attempting to indicate, then, is the difficulty of making any absolute distinction between learning and retention. But what guides can be used to make the distinction? One answer has been provided by Melton (1963), who pointed out that a change from trial n to n + 1 is considered to be a learning change when the variable of interest is the ordinal number of trial n and not the temporal interval between trial n and n + 1. A change arising from trial n to n + 1 is considered to be a retention change when the variable of interest is the interval itself and/or the events that fill this interval.

This distinction of Melton's (1963) has provided a convenient framework for organizing the studies that have used the traditional multiple trial presentation, and those that have used a learning criterion–time interval–test of retention procedure. The utilization of multiple trials almost invariably means that the investigator is interested in the operation of some variable that manifests itself over the trials provided, thus allowing an examination of the influence of that variable on the learning process. On the other hand, if the experimenter provides for a time interval and particular events to fill the interval between the reaching of the learning criterion and the subsequent performance test, he is interested in a retention or forgetting process.

One difficulty, however, has arisen as a result of two classes of experimental studies that have been identified as (1) single trial free-recall learning and (2) short term retention. With single trial free-recall learning, the investigator is typically interested in the operation of a specific variable on performance, thus placing this type of study in the "learning" study category. However, the use of only a single trial means that there cannot be the investigation of an acquisition process that is typically the hallmark of learning studies. Short term retention studies in which only a single item is presented and performance is measured following "retention" intervals measured in seconds makes this kind of study a radical departure from the traditional retention study.

Although many individuals continue to accept the learning-retention distinction as proposed by Melton (1963), some investigators have distinguished between these two constructs by positing that retention represents the fundamental process associated with behavior change. For example, Tulving (1968) posited that a single item is always "learned" when it is first presented—learned in the sense that the probability of its recall increases from a value near zero prior to the presentation of the item, to unity immediately following its presentation. From this point of view, it would seem that the learning of an individual item is equivalent to its perception since the operations involved in measuring learning and perception are identical. In the multiple item, multitrial type of experiment, Tulving posited that learning refers to the more or less systematic increase in the number of items *retained* over successive trials, and can be described as the slope of the function relating the number of items recalled to the ordinal number of the trial.

Thus, when "learning" is used as a descriptive term in multitrial experiments, it serves as a shorthand expression for the fact that recall increases over trials. To ask why learning occurs, or to ask what processes are involved in learning . . . means to ask why recall scores increase from trial to trial, or what processes are involved in such an increase (Tulving 1968, p. 7).

Murdock (1960) made a similar distinction between learning and retention. Using the free-recall verbal learning study as his model, he suggested that learning be considered the slope of the curve showing the number of correct responses as a function of the number of trials. Such a distinction between learning and retention is analogous, he wrote, to the distinction between velocity and position in mechanics. Just as velocity is the rate of change of position with respect to time, so learning is the rate of change of retention with respect to the number of presentations.

What conclusions can be drawn from the difficulties involved in providing a distinction between learning and retention? One conclusion is that traditional distinctions that have been drawn between learning and retention are arbitrary. Moreover, free-recall learning and short term retention studies reflect basic operations that must be investigated if the complete picture of performance change is to be observed. Whether or not these experiments are believed to measure "learning" or "retention" is not important.

We are faced with the task, however, of providing some organization for the variety of learning and retention experiments that have been conducted. Accordingly, we shall consider performance with multiple-item or infra-span memory material and one or more continuous presentations, as reflecting the learning process. This organization includes the bulk of serial, paired-associate and free-recall learning studies. Our examination of the retention process shall include those traditional retention studies in which an interval of time, usually measured in minutes or hours, has been interpolated between the last learning trial and the test for retention. In addition, we shall also include short term retention studies where the amount of material that is presented to the subject is typically within his memory span and where the test for retention is measured in seconds.

RESPONSE MEASURES

A basic question that arises in any learning experiment is how to measure the subject's performance. In general, performance measures for verbal learning studies have been divided into two general categories: (1) probability of response measures, and (2) latency or time measures. To illustrate these, we can take a hypo-thetical experiment in which a subject is given a paired-associate learning task in which the anticipation method is utilized. During each trial we can measure (1) whether or not the subject correctly anticipates the response term, as well as (2) the time interval be-tween the presentation of the stimulus and the elicitation of the response.

Most frequently, probability measures are used; the two most often-used measures are (1) recall and (2) recognition.[1,2] Let us look at these probability measures in a little more detail.

PROBABILITY MEASURES

Recall: With this response measure, the subject is asked to re-produce or recall the material that has been presented. The number or percentage of responses correct or the number or percentage of errors are used as basic data.

Recognition: Here, the subject must identify material that had been presented on a previous learning trial. The subject is provided with a number of alternatives from which to choose a previously presented item. Two, three, four, or even more alternatives may be provided along with the correct item itself. Another method has been to provide the subject with a large pool of alternatives and have him select the correct ones. As an example, Luh (1922), in an early study, provided subjects with twenty-four nonsense syl-lables from which they were to select the twelve that had been previously presented.

A more recently employed method of measuring recognition is to present the subject with a series of items with the instructions that he is to respond in terms of whether or not the material has been previously presented. Using one variation of this method, Murdock (1965) presented his subjects with six paired-associates consisting of common English words, following which either one

---

[1] The distinction that many investigators have made between learning and retention is noted in the delineation of the response measures. Traditionally, recall and recognition have been designated as retention rather than learning measures. Since the distinction between learning and retention is arbitrary, there is no reason why differences in response terminology should be used.

[2] Other measures have been used, i.e., reconstruction, but their use has been very infrequent.

of the previously presented pairs or a new pair was presented. The subject was required to respond with a yes if he had seen the pair previously, or a no if he had not. Another variation is found in a study by Shepard and Teghtsoonian (1961), who presented subjects with a long series of three-digit numbers, some of which were duplicates of ones that had been presented earlier, i.e., 761, 856, 445, 621, 125, 449, 856, 927, etc. The subject was to respond in terms of whether or not each item had been seen previously (thus making it an "old" item) or had not been seen before (thus making it a "new" item). Subjects were allowed to proceed through the deck of items at their own rate but were not permitted to look back at any earlier item.[1]

It should be acknowledged that recognition test scores are always relative to the characteristics of the alternatives or distractors used. This position that recognition test scores are dependent upon the particular testing conditions has been recognized by virtually all investigators utilizing this method of response measurement. Almost twenty-five years ago, Underwood (1949) wrote, "If we required S to learn a list of adjectives and then placed the adjectives among a group of nonsense syllables, S would probably show very small loss in retention. Obviously the similarity of the test material to the other material is an important variable which determines the recognition score" (p. 512).

A second point is that when the traditional methods of measuring retention are used, scores that are obtained, although corrected for guessing, are related to the number of alternatives provided, a finding supported by the experimental studies of Teghtsoonian (1958), Schwartz (1961), and Murdock (1963), as well as many other investigators. In the study by Murdock (1963), for example, subjects were given lists of twenty words to study for thirty seconds. They were then asked to identify as many of these words as possible when shown a longer list of either 40, 80, 120, or 160 words. The mean proportion of correct responses after being corrected for chance was .56, .54, .44, and .42 for lists of 40, 80, 120, and 160 word alternatives. Analysis of variance indicated

---

[1] These newer methods of measuring recognition have lent themselves to an examination of recognition memory using a signal detection model, as proposed by Swets, Tanner and Birdsall (1961). We shall postpone our examination of this model for a later chapter.

that the differences among groups were significant, thus supporting the position that response scores are a function of the number of alternatives provided, even though appropriate statistical correction may be made.

LATENCY MEASURES

It will be recalled that latency or time measures represent the second of the response indicants. As Runquist (1966) acknowledged, only a small percentage of investigators have used latency measures since "the technical problems of recording latencies are considerable" (p. 515). The use of the latency measure, however, does deserve comment. Osgood (1948) wrote some time ago that the latency measure may be a more sensitive measure of response strength than the mere presence or absence of the correct response; a good example of the correctness of Osgood's position can be found in a recent study by Peterson (1965). In this study, subjects were given twenty trials on a list of ten paired-associates presented on a memory drum. The stimuli were ten consonant bigrams while the responses were the digits 1 through 8. Subjects were permitted as much time as necessary to make a response while the stimulus was being presented (anticipation interval). The latencies of the responses beginning with the first trial following the last error on an individual pair are indicated in Fig. 2–1. Only those pairs for which ten trials beyond the last error were available were used in the analysis. Thus, it can be noted that although all responses were correct there were considerable differences in latency over trials, and it would seem that speed of responding appears to be a measure of the strength of an association that changes gradually over trials.[1]

Studies by Brown and Huda (1961), and Shapiro (1968) have also shown the sensitivity of the response latency measure. In the

[1] It should be noted that all investigators have not been able to obtain these findings. Millward (1964) used a paired-associate task in which two-digit numbers served as the stimuli and the responses were represented by buttons that had to be punched by the subject. Twelve paired-associates were used. An examination of the mean latency for twenty trials for those stimulus-response pairs that were correct after the last error did not reveal a pattern of decreasing time such as that found by Peterson (1965). Rather, latency of responding was just about constant over twenty trials.

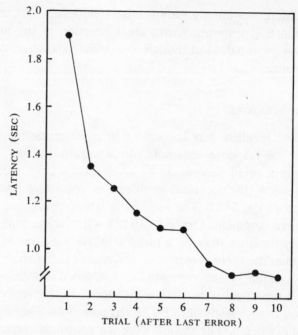

Fig. 2–1. Mean latency for ten trials after the last error in a paired-associate task.

(Adapted from Peterson 1965)

Brown and Huda (1961) study, two groups of subjects learned a list of paired-adjectives to a criterion of three successive error-free trials under either massed or distributed practice. For one group the intertrial interval was four seconds while for the other group it was forty seconds. These investigators found that the response latencies were significantly longer on the criterion trials for the massed group. Shapiro (1968) found that paired-associate response latencies of adult subjects vary inversely as a function of variations in the free association strength of normatively associated word pairs. Thus, in one experiment (experiment 5) three strengths of free associated pairs, high, intermediate, and low, made up the paired-associate list. The mean latency in seconds as a function of trials is indicated in Fig. 2–2. What is interesting about this experiment is that when a probability of response measure has been used, a number of investigators have been unable to find such differences (Haun 1960; Martin 1964; Postman 1962).

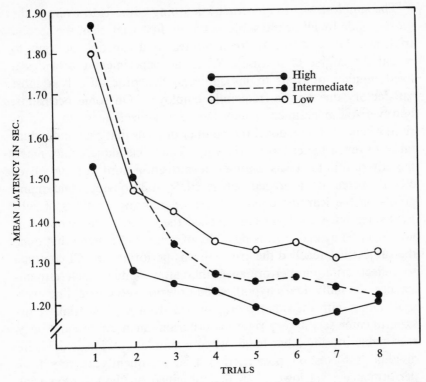

Fig. 2–2. Mean item response latencies per trial for the three strengths of free-associated word pairs.

(Adapted from Shapiro 1968)

LEARNING CURVES

Frequently, investigators are interested in determining how behavior changes throughout the learning trials provided, and one of the most appropriate techniques for obtaining this information is the learning curve. Such curves are plotted by placing trials or the independent variable along the abscissa while performance measures are placed along the ordinate. Although it would be possible to plot individual learning curves in a given experiment, such a project would be not only quite laborious but the individual curves would be quite irregular as well, and the assumed orderliness of the learning process would be obscured. As a result, group curves are used.

The simplest way to construct a learning curve is to average the scores made by all of the subjects on the first trial, then the second trial, etc. These scores are then plotted as a function of trials to reveal the course of learning. When an experimenter provides a fixed number of trials to his subjects, this procedure is a most satisfactory one and is frequently employed. On some occasions, however, the experimenter may have his subjects learn to a criterion; whenever this is done, the number of trials that each individual takes to reach the criterion will vary. Thus, one subject may reach the criterion in ten trials, another in thirteen, a third in twenty-two, etc. If scores are averaged across trials, it is obvious that many points on the learning curve will reflect differing numbers of subjects since once a subject has reached the criterion, his scores will no longer be available. It is possible, of course, to assume that once the subject has reached the criterion, his performance will continue to reflect criterion performance thereafter. Under such circumstances, the individual's hypothesized criterion score would be averaged along with the other scores provided on a given trial. If the experimenter sets a very rigorous criterion, such an assumption is reasonable; on the other hand, when a simple criterion is used, individual subjects on postcriterion trials frequently regress to a performance level lower than that obtained on the criterion trial, and the basic assumption is obviously erroneous. The general result has been that few experimenters use this procedure.

The most frequently used method for constructing a group learning curve when a learning criterion has been used, has been devised by Melton (1936) and is called a successive criterion curve or the trials to criteria curve. With this method, the average number of trials to reach successive criteria, or succeeding numbers of correct responses, is plotted. As an example, we may hypothesize that three subjects, A, B, and C, are asked to learn a serial list of eight adjectives to a criterion of one perfect trial. The protocols are illustrated in Table 2–1. In order to convert a subject's specific learning score into data that can be used to construct the successive criterion curve, we should note the following: Subject A obtained one correct response on the first trial; as a result it took him one trial to reach the criterion of one correct—the first of the successive criteria. Two correct responses were obtained on Trial 2 for subject A so that the second successive criterion was obtained with a

TABLE 2–1

RECORDS FOR THREE SUBJECTS (A, B, AND C) LEARNING
A LIST OF EIGHT ADJECTIVES

	Trials									
	1	2	3	4	5	6	7	8	9	10
Subject A:										
No. Correct Responses	1	3	4	4	6	6	7	8		
Subject B:										
No. Correct Responses	2	4	3	4	5	5	6	6	6	8
Subject C:										
No. Correct Responses	1	4	5	7	8					

(Adapted from Hall 1966)

value of 2. Note that three correct responses were achieved also on Trial 2. Four correct responses were obtained on Trial 3, while five and six correct responses were obtained on Trial 5. Seven correct responses took place on Trial 7 and eight correct responses on Trial 8—the last of the criteria used. When such a conversion is made for all subjects, the mean trials to reach each successive criterion are obtained and the data are then plotted by placing the criterion score on the abscissa and the mean trials to criterion on the ordinate. Table 2–2 illustrates the data that are used to construct

TABLE 2–2

DATA USED TO CONSTRUCT THE SUCCESSIVE CRITERION
CURVE

	Trial on Which Each Successive Criterion Was Achieved							
Subject	*1*	*2*	*3*	*4*	*5*	*6*	*7*	*8*
A	1	2	2	3	5	5	7	8
B	1	1	2	2	5	7	10	10
C	1	2	2	2	3	4	4	5
Total	3	5	6	7	13	16	21	23
MEAN	1.0	1.7	2.0	2.3	4.3	5.3	7.0	7.7

(Adapted from Hall 1966)

the successive criterion curve, while the curve itself can be noted in Fig. 2–3.

A second method, used earlier, for plotting a learning curve when subjects have been run to a criterion was devised by Vincent (1912). The result is called a Vincent curve, although the original procedure outlined by Vincent has been subjected to a number of modifications (Kjerstad 1919; Hunter 1929). The basic procedure can be described as follows: Each individual's learning curve or trials to mastery is divided into equal fractions; performance at these varying fractional intervals is summated, averaged, and then plotted. On the abscissa, equal fractions of learning are used rather than trials, while the performance measure is plotted on the ordinate.

To illustrate the construction of the Vincent curve, we can use the protocols obtained by subjects A, B, and C, as indicated in Table 2–1. Since subject C reached the criterion in just five trials we shall use fifths of learning on the abscissa. This means then that the performance obtained on each of the five trials for subject C will represent successive fifths of the learning period. Since subject B has taken ten trials, every other trial (i.e., trials 2, 4, 6, 8, and

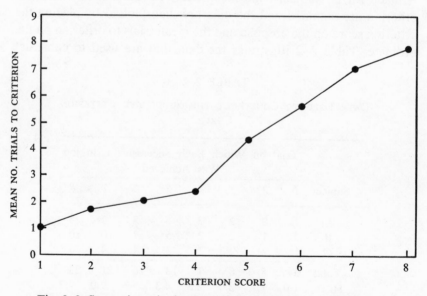

Fig. 2–3. Successive criteria curve derived from data in Table 2–2.
(Adapted from Hall 1966)

10) will represent successive fifths of this subject's learning. Finally, a more complex situation arises for subject A, who required eight trials to reach the criterion. This means that if these eight trials are divided into five equal fractions, each 1.6 trials represents one fifth of the learning curve. The question immediately arises as to how we can obtain a performance measure for fractions of an individual's learning trials. In this case, it means that performance measures would have to be obtained from trials 1.6, 3.2, 4.8, 6.4, and 8.0. The general method of handling this problem has been to assume that trials are continuous and performance increments are uniformly distributed within any trial. Thus, the performance value for subject A for trial 1.6 would be 2.2; 3.2 trials would provide a performance value of 4; the third fifth of subject A's learning curve would be indicated by trial 4.8, which would result in a performance value of 5.6; while the fourth fifth of the learning curve would be indicated by a trial value of 6.4, giving the number of correct response values at 6.4. The fifth fifth of the learning curve would be represented by the criterion score of 8. The data used to construct the Vincent curve can be found in Table 2–3 while the learning curve itself is indicated in Fig. 2–4.

The use of a learning curve is an exceedingly helpful device for depicting differences among the various groups that are employed in an experiment. Too much dependence should not be placed upon these curves, however, as representative of individual behavior. Over the years a large number of individuals (Merrill 1931; Skinner 1938; Sidman 1952; Hayes 1953; Bakan 1954; Estes 1956; Spence 1956) have raised serious questions concerning the use of

TABLE 2–3

PERFORMANCE VALUES ON EACH FIFTH OF LEARNING

	First	Second	Third	Fourth	Fifth
Subject A	2.2	4	5.6	6.4	8
B	4.0	4	5.0	6.0	8
C	1.0	4	5.0	7.0	8
Total	7.2	12	15.6	19.4	24
Mean	2.4	4	5.2	6.5	8

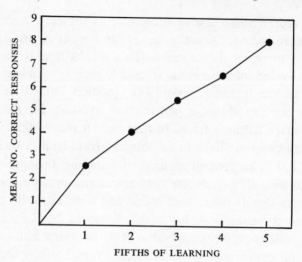

Fig. 2–4. A Vincent curve derived from data in Table 2–3.

the group learning curve. Spence (1956) has written that the "averaging of individual data often produces considerable distortion with the consequence that the group curve does not accurately reflect the individual curves" (p. 60). He has indicated that an alternative procedure for treating data from a group of subjects would be to construct a curve based upon the mean of all "like" or homogeneous subjects. Different criteria have been used for determining whether a subject should be included in the group from which the learning curve was derived. Hilgard and Campbell (1936) classified individual subjects into subgroups on the basis of the shapes of their individual conditioning curves, while Spence (1952) selected subjects on the basis of the similarity of their response measures for the total learning period.

There is no question that group learning curves perform a very useful function for the experimenter; however, a sampling of individual learning curves should be plotted as well. The smoothing of such individual curves may be accomplished by averaging measures on blocks of trials, providing such blocks each contain only a relatively small number of trials. It is then possible to see if individual curves mirror the performance of the group curve. If serious discrepancies are revealed, considerable doubt must be raised concerning the value of the group curve.

PROCEDURAL CONSIDERATIONS

The examination of differences in procedure is not as exciting an area of research as many others and yet it is an integral aspect of any examination of the verbal learning area. One reason for its importance is that if we are to make meaningful comparisons of findings among experiments that have utilized different procedures, it is important that we become aware of the contribution to learning of the procedures themselves. An added gain is that at times such comparisons lead the investigator to new insights about some of the processes that are presumed to operate. In this section, we will discuss differences in learning arising from (1) the method of presentation, (2) constant vs. serial order of presentation of items in the paired-associate learning situation, and (3) mixed vs. unmixed lists.

ANTICIPATION, STUDY-TEST, AND PROMPTING AS METHODS OF PRESENTATION

PAIRED-ASSOCIATE LEARNING

It will be recalled that in our examination of serial and paired-associate learning, the methods of presentation that were described were anticipation, study-test or recall, and prompting. Of these methods, the anticipation procedure was the most frequently employed, at least until the 1960s. Anticipation had had a long history of use with serial learning situations and it was most logical to continue the use of the procedure when paired-associate learning emerged as important in verbal learning. An added consideration was that there appeared to be a kind of similarity between the paired-associate learning situation that utilized the anticipation method and the classical conditioning paradigm.[1]

Finally, it had been commonly assumed that the anticipation method represented the most efficient way to learn an association between two items. The reason for this view was that many of the

[1] In fact, the classical conditioning model has been used to "explain" paired-associate learning. This point of view is discussed in Chapter 9.

basic conditions that investigators had posited to be essential for optimal learning were incorporated into this paradigm. Thus, the almost immediate presentation of the response that followed the subject's anticipatory response provided him with knowledge of results and/or reinforcement. In addition, the subject's overt response represented a kind of recitation technique that Gates (1917), many years before, had indicated facilitated learning.

Beginning in the 1950s, the recall or study-test procedure began to be used with paired-associate learning, perhaps as a result of the frequent use of this method with the free-recall learning situation.

Certain dissatisfactions with the anticipation procedure undoubtedly were also responsible for the fact that investigators began to examine other methods of presentation for use with the paired-associate task. As many experimenters have acknowledged—e.g., Underwood (1964), Battig (1965)—with the anticipation method it becomes impossible at any stage in paired-associate learning to obtain a measure of performance that directly reflects the subject's degree of learning. Each attempted anticipatory response by the subject that provides a performance measure for the experimenter is followed immediately by the presentation of the correct response. The result is that the learning that takes place as a result of the subject's viewing of the correct response cannot be measured until the following trial; thus, any performance measure lags one trial behind the subject's actual state of learning.

With the increased use of the recall method of presentation, a number of investigators became interested in determining how learning varied as a function of each of these methods of presentation. Battig and Brackett (1961) performed one of the early experiments in this area. These investigators used nonsense shapes as stimulus items and two-digit numbers as responses.[1] A 5:5-second presentation was utilized; this meant that for those subjects undergoing the anticipation procedure, the stimulus was presented for five seconds followed by presentation of the stimulus and response for another five seconds. For subjects undergoing the recall or study-test procedure, each stimulus-response pair was presented for five seconds, following which test trials were provided. These test trials

[1] A nonsense shape is a nonrepresentational form that is analogous to the nonsense syllable. A set of points are located randomly in a plane and then joined, usually by straight lines, to provide an outline figure.

consisted of presentation of each stimulus for five seconds, during which time the subject was given the opportunity to make the correct response. Learning was carried out to a criterion of one perfect trial. As Fig. 2–5 indicates, significantly superior learning was obtained for the recall procedure.

Subsequent studies by a number of investigators (Lockhead 1962; Reynolds 1964, 1967; Battig and Wu 1965; Goss and Nodine 1965; and Cofer, Diamond, Olsen, Stein and Walker 1967; Bruder 1969) have provided equivocal findings. Some of these experiments have indicated no differences in performance as a function of the method used while other studies have confirmed the earlier Battig and Brackett (1961) findings that indicated the superiority of the recall method.

Lockhead (1962) and most recently Bruder (1969) have been unable to find differences in learning as a function of the method used. Reynolds (1964) conducted two experiments in which single digits served as stimuli, and high or low pronunciability CVCs were

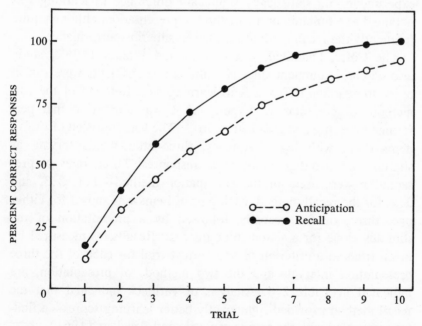

Fig. 2–5. Learning curves representing mean percent correct responses for the first ten trials under the anticipation and recall methods.
(Adapted from Battig and Brackett 1961)

used as the responses. Results from the first experiment revealed no difference between the methods used; in the second experiment, Reynolds found that the recall method was statistically superior to the anticipation method. In a study conducted three years later, Reynolds (1967) was unable to find any difference between the methods.

Goss and Nodine (1965), in their extensive study of paired-associate learning, ran five experiments using CVCs as stimuli and responses, and examined the recall and anticipation methods of presentation as a function of a variety of conditions, namely: the meaningfulness of the stimulus and response members (experiments 7 and 11); similarity of the stimulus and response members (experiment 8); meaningfulness of the stimulus and response members combined with the length of the list and whole or part-whole presentation (experiment 9); and similarity of the stimulus and response members combined with the length of list and whole or part-whole presentation (experiment 10). In almost all of these experiments, no statistically significant difference in learning was obtained as a function of the method of presentation, although quite frequently the recall method resulted in superior performance.

The Cofer, Diamond, Olsen, Stein and Walker (1967) study also deserves comment since six different experiments were run in order to examine differences in learning as a function of the two methods of presentation. Experiment 1 was similar to that performed by Battig and Brackett (1961). The lists consisted of twelve items each, with high frequency, three-letter words serving as stimuli, and two-digit numbers as responses. Three rates of presentation were used for the anticipation method—1:1, 3:3, and 5:5; for the recall method, each pair of items was shown for either one, three, or five seconds, followed by a presentation of the stimulus alone for a similar time interval. Results, as measured by mean trials to a criterion of one perfect trial for each of the three presentation intervals and the two methods of presentation, are indicated in Table 2–4. Analysis of variance indicated that the recall method provided significantly better learning scores—a finding in keeping with the results of Battig and Brackett (1961).

In a second experiment, three levels of intrapair similarity were examined in addition to the two methods of presentation. The mean number of correct responses achieved over twenty trials indicated

TABLE 2–4

MEAN TRIALS TO CRITERION

Experiment 1			
	Presentation Interval		
	1:1	3:3	5:5
Anticipation	32.75	15.00	9.18
Recall	23.06	8.06	5.69

(Adapted from Cofer, Diamond, Olsen, Stein and Walker 1967)

that more correct responses occurred under the recall than under the anticipation method at each similarity level, although the only significant difference between the methods of presentation was found when medium intrapair similarity was used.

Four additional experiments were conducted, in which the researchers examined the two methods of presentation under a variety of other conditions. The findings obtained from these other studies, however, did not provide support for the first two experiments, which indicated that the recall method provides superior learning to anticipation. Nonsignificant differences between the methods were obtained in each case.

It will be recalled that a variation of the anticipation and recall method has been described as the "prompting" procedure. As utilized by Cook and his associates (Cook and Kendler 1956; Cook 1958; Cook and Spitzer 1960) this procedure consists of presentation of the stimulus term, then the response term, followed by overt practice of the response term. Subsequent test trials are then employed to measure learning. Variations of this method have been employed by Peterson and Brewer (1963), and Hawker (1964). Basic to any prompting procedure is the fact that the subject is prohibited from making erroneous responses because the correct response to each stimulus is shown to him before he responds.

When prompting is compared with the anticipation procedure, the results mirror those obtained when anticipation is compared with recall. The findings of Cook and Kendler (1956), Cook (1958), and Cook and Spitzer (1960) all support the superiority of the prompting method; similarly, Sidowski, Kopstein and Shillestad (1961) have shown that English-Russian paired-associates are more rapidly learned with the prompting procedure. On the other hand, there is the suggestion from the studies of Peterson and Brewer (1963), and Hawker (1964) that prompting provides superior learning only during the early part of training. Thus, in the Peterson and Brewer (1963) study, a twelve-item paired-associate task was used in which high frequency nouns served as stimuli and the digits 1 through 12 as responses. Half of the pairs were learned using the prompting method (the stimulus and response pair exposed together, followed by presentation of the stimulus) while half were learned by the anticipation procedure. Following each presentation trial, a test trial was provided in which there was random exposure of the twelve stimulus words and the subject attempted to respond with the appropriate digits. The results obtained for these trials are indicated in Fig. 2–6. It can be noted in this figure that there is a systematic difference between the two procedures for the first five trials, but after that no difference between the groups is apparent.

Hawker (1964) obtained similar findings when using line figures as stimuli and adjectives as responses: prompting appeared to have

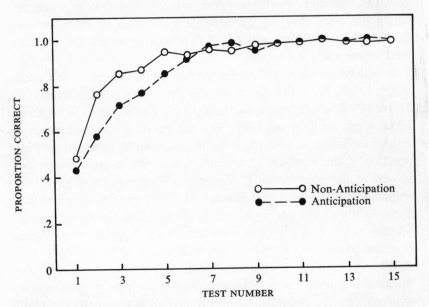

Fig. 2–6. Results obtained by anticipation technique and a prompting technique in paired-associate learning.
(Adapted from Peterson and Brewer 1963)

a facilitating effect during the early part of training but lost its effect as training progressed.

Finally, and to complete the circle, Silberman, Melaragno and Coulson (1961), using connected discourse as their experimental material, were unable to find any difference between the two methods.

What can be concluded from the findings obtained when the varying methods of presentation are compared? We believe that the most general finding indicates that the anticipation method, although purporting to have the advantage of immediate reinforcement, knowledge of results, and the immediate correction of errors, does not result in more rapid learning. In fact, the bulk of the experimental evidence seems to indicate that the recall and prompting procedures will always prove as good as and frequently superior to the anticipation method, although such superiority may not reach statistical significance.

SERIAL LEARNING

Because of the experimenter's inability to delineate clearly the stimulus and response items in serial learning tasks, serial learning studies examining procedural variations have been relatively few. In one study, however, Waugh (1963) examined serial learning using both the anticipation method and the recall method. With the anticipation method, each word was presented for two seconds followed by another two-second interval during which time the subject attempted to anticipate the next word. With the recall procedure, the words were exposed in immediate succession, each for two seconds, and the subjects were required to read each word aloud. Just after the list had been presented, the subject was given two minutes in which to recall the items. Four subjects each learned twenty lists consisting of sixteen monosyllabic English words per list. Ten of these lists were learned by the anticipation method and ten by the recall method. Six trials were provided on each list. The subjects' responses on each anticipation trial were scored in terms of the number of words correctly anticipated; under the recall condition, responses were scored by noting the numbers of successive pairs of words correctly recalled on each trial regardless of the absolute serial position. A word was considered to have been recalled correctly if the response that came before it was the word that actually preceded it on the list. Thus, if the sequence A, B, C, D, E, F was presented and the subject's responses were D, E, A, B, C, F the score would be 3 since three pairs, DE, AB, and BC fulfilled this criterion. Although Waugh found that the anticipation method was superior to the recall method on the first trial (8.5 words vs. 4.5), differences between the two methods were not obtained on subsequent trials.

In a second serial learning study, Battig and Lawrence (1967) examined the anticipation and recall procedures in addition to two other variables.[1] A ten-item list of trigrams served as the material to be learned. When the anticipation procedure was employed, the subject attempted to anticipate each item in the list during the presentation of the immediately preceding item. A four-second presentation rate was used. The recall procedure differed in that the subject made no responses during the actual presentation of the items but attempted to recall the items in order during ten successive blank four-second intervals beginning four seconds after the presentation of the last item. The criterion for the first-list learning was a total of sixty correct responses accumulated over all trials, while the learning of the second list was continued to a criterion of one errorless trial. The results indicated that fewer list I trials were required to reach the criterion using the recall procedure than using the anticipation method; the difference was statistically significant. A significant superiority of the recall method was also obtained in the learning of the second list of items.

The findings Battig and Lawrence obtained with serial learning are in keeping with those obtained with the paired-associate task; all of these studies suggest that either there is no difference among methods or that the recall method is slightly superior. Battig and Lawrence have suggested that the superiority of the recall method most likely reflects the temporal separation of presentation of items for learning from performance measurement, in contrast to the necessity of performing both functions simultaneously under the anticipation procedures.

[1] Neither of these variables is of present concern. One involved starting and ending the serial list with a different item on each trial but otherwise maintaining a constant sequential order; the second involved a comparison of learning a transfer (second) list, with the second-list items consisting of the items used on the first list and arranged either in mirror image reversal order or an unsystematic scrambling of first-list order.

CONSTANT VS. VARIED SERIAL ORDER OF
PRESENTATION IN PAIRED-ASSOCIATE LEARNING

It will be recalled from our brief discussion of paired-associate learning in Chapter 1 that a common procedure utilized by investigators is to have each paired-associate occupy a different position on the list from one trial to another. Such a procedure prevents the subject from learning the task by means of memorizing the responses (which would occur if these appeared in a fixed order) and concomitantly ignoring the stimuli.

The concern about not using a fixed order probably arose from the findings obtained by McGeoch and McKinney (1937) and McGeoch and Underwood (1943), who found that the presentation of paired-associates in a constant serial order, as contrasted with the usual presentation in varied order, resulted in facilitation of learning.

The findings that have been obtained by more recent experimenters investigating the manner in which the paired items are presented confirm these early results, although frequently the difference between the two methods is neither large nor statistically significant.

In one study by Newman and Saltz (1962), three groups of subjects were used. For the constant order, five paired-associate trials were provided in which each S-R pair appeared in the same serial position. A varied group was also given five paired-associate trials; however, the S-R pairs appeared in a different serial position on each trial. Both stimulus and response were presented together. For both groups, a sixth trial was provided which served as the test or retention trial. In this trial, only the stimulus terms were presented—for the constant group, the items were shown in the same order as on the previous five trials, while for the varied group, they were presented in an order different from any of those of the five learning trials. Finally, a third group was used in which the paired items appeared in the same order on all five learning trials but in a different order on the testing trial. For the sixth trial, each stimulus item was presented for ten seconds, during which time it was necessary for the subject to respond. Finally, following this test trial, a free learning-recall trial was provided in which the subject was given sixty seconds to respond with all of the response terms that he could recall. The ten paired-associates were made up by using low association CVCs; the response terms were high frequency words. Results revealed that the two groups whose learning trials were in a constant order learned significantly more responses than the varied group; this was indicated either by the sixth test trial or by the sixty-second free-recall period.

Subsequent studies by Battig, Brown and Nelson (1963), Newman (1966), Rubin and Brown (1967), Wright (1967), Tragash and Newman (1967), Stein (1969), and Wright, Gescheider and Klein (1969) have also indicated that a constant serial position may facilitate paired-associate learning.[1] The Battig, Brown and Nelson (1963) study is a most extensive one. It consisted of five different experiments that investigated a variety of conditions. We can summarize the general findings by indicating that the results support the position that paired-associate learning is significantly facilitated by the use of a constant serial order of presentation. However, these investigators do point out that although the facilitative effect of a constant serial order on paired-associate learning seems to be generalizable across a variety of tasks and procedural conditions, it is also quite small in magnitude and rarely of better than borderline statistical significance.

In examining the mechanism whereby the constant serial position facilitates the learning of paired-associates, Battig, Brown and Nelson (1963) have suggested that the serial position cues offer the subject a wider range of choice as to how each pair can be learned. That is, since the serial position can act as a stimulus in addition to the stimulus that has been paired with the response, the subject can choose between the stimuli, or perhaps combine them— which results in a stimulus compound that is quite unique and in-

---

[1] It should be noted that Martin and Saltz (1963) were unable to obtain findings supporting this conclusion. Their material and procedure was similar to that used in the earlier Newman and Saltz (1962) experiment. In these experiments the response items were the same as those used previously; however, the stimulus items were nonsense syllables, having low intralist similarity in contrast to the high similarity lists that had been used in the earlier study. The procedure consisted of presenting five learning trials, a test trial, five additional learning trials, and a second test trial. The three experimental groups were identical to those used in the Newman and Saltz study. Experimental findings from both studies indicated that a constant serial position did not facilitate the learning of the stimulus-response pairs.

dividualistic. This, in turn, leads to facilitation in the learning of these pairs.

This point of view would suggest that as the learning task becomes more difficult, a constant ordering of the pairs of items in the list would assume greater importance. Studies by Rubin and Brown (1967), Wright, Gescheider and Klein (1969), and Stein (1969) have provided some support for this hypothesis.

Rubin and Brown (1967) examined a constant versus varied order of paired-associate learning as a function of intralist similarity. (A number of investigators have shown that learning is related to how similar the items are that make up the paired-associate list.) In their study, high and low similarity items were used for both stimuli and responses, thus providing both for the constant and varied groups four similarity conditions: high stimulus–high response, low stimulus–low response, high stimulus–low response, and low stimulus–high response. The twelve CVC pairs that served as the experimental material for each of these lists are indicated in Table 2–5. The recall or study-test procedure was used with a five-second presentation rate and all subjects were run to a criterion of

TABLE 2–5

PA LISTS FOR EACH SIMILARITY CONDITION

Lists			
HH	LL	HL	LH
LUW-VAC	CAY-MIJ	LUW-CAY	MIJ-VAC
MOF-VIK	KAS-DOY	MOF-KAS	DOY-VIK
MUW-CIV	TIR-PUQ	MUW-TIR	JOW-CAK
FOW-CAK	YUK-JOW	FOW-YUK	PUQ-KAV
LUF-KAV	VOG-SEB	LUF-VOG	QAD-CIV
WOL-ZAC	REQ-NAL	WOL-NUZ	SEB-ZAC
FOL-KIZ	NUZ-TIX	WOM-JEB	NAL-KIZ
LOM-KAC	JEB-QAD	LOM-REQ	TIX-KAC
FUM-VIZ	SAH-BIP	FUM-SAH	WUF-VIZ
WUF-CIZ	HIV-GER	FOL-HIV	FEN-CIZ
WOM-ZIV	PEX-WUF	WUF-PEX	GER-ZIV
MUL-ZAK	GOC-FEN	MUL-GOC	BIP-ZAK

Note.—A second list for each similarity condition was obtained by reversing the S and R terms for each list.

(Adapted from Rubin and Brown 1967)

TABLE 2–6

MEAN TOTAL ERRORS FOR EACH CONDITION DURING PA LEARNING

	Constant S-Sim				Varied S-Sim		
R Sim	H	L	*Mean*	R Sim	H	L	*Mean*
H	83.4	69.5	76.5	H	199.5	96.5	148.0
L	35.0	49.5	42.3	L	110.1	46.7	78.4
Mean	59.2	59.5	59.4	*Mean*	154.8	71.6	113.2

(Adapted from Rubin and Brown 1967)

two successive errorless trials.[1] Results, as measured by the mean total errors for each condition, are indicated in Table 2–6. It may be noted that there is a large overall superiority of the constant condition over the variable and this difference proves to be a highly reliable one. The largest difference is found under conditions of high stimulus similarity.

Two subsequent studies, by Wright, Gescheider and Klein (1969), and Stein (1969), both investigated the constant versus serial order of presentation as a function of stimulus meaningfulness, a second variable that is related to learning difficulty; the Stein (1969) study also examined rate of stimulus presentation during test trials, another variable correlated with learning difficulty. The results obtained in both studies support the general position we have outlined: as stimulus meaningfulness decreases and rate of presentation increases, a constant order of presentation results in easier learning.

MIXED VS. UNMIXED LISTS

A third procedural consideration of which the reader should be aware has to do with experimental designs that use either mixed or unmixed lists of items. For example, if an experimenter is interested in investigating some characteristics of the material being learned,

[1] Five subjects in the variable condition were unable to reach this criterion within the two-hour session. The data for these subjects through trial forty-three was used in the analysis.

rather than make up a number of lists of items, with the lists varying with regard to this attribute, each of the varying types of material is included within the same list. Thus, in the examination of meaningfulness of material, the mixed list design would call for all of the various kinds of material to be placed within the same list. In contrast is the separate or unmixed list design in which each characteristic level of the material—in this instance, meaningfulness —would be represented by a different list.

It is obvious, of course, that in many experiments it is not possible to use a mixed list design, since many independent variables are not amenable to this kind of manipulation. As we have indicated in our example, generally the mixed list design is used when the experimenter is interested in investigating the characteristics of the material, although as we shall subsequently note, this is not always true.

The basic question that must be asked when the two types of experimental designs are compared is, do they provide comparable findings? There can be no general answer to this question, at least at this time, since—as Runquist (1966) has indicated—there has been little systematic study of the issue. If the materials being investigated interact, the mixed list design is not appropriate to use; but this is an obvious consideration, and what is needed is a systematic examination of the conditions under which the mixed list design is (or is not) appropriate. It should be noted that considerable work has been done in the transfer area—we shall review these experiments in a subsequent chapter.

Unfortunately, all that can be brought to bear on this issue are a few studies in which the investigator has been interested in examining a particular variable as a function of the type of design. Frequently, such studies indicate that the two designs provide comparable findings; in some instances, however, they do not. An example of both findings is found in a study by Reynolds (1964), who used the mixed and unmixed list designs to examine the anticipation and prompting methods of presenting material. In addition, CVC responses of high and low pronunciability were also investigated. In Reynolds' first experiment, using the unmixed list design, he obtained no differences in learning as a function of the different procedures utilized, although he found that the items that were easier to pronounce were also easiest to learn. In a second

experiment, using a mixed list design, Reynolds (1964) found that
the prompting method resulted in significantly better learning than
the anticipation method—a finding in contrast to that obtained in
the first experiment. However, learning continued to be reflected
as a function of differences in pronunciability.

SUMMARY

In this chapter we examined four methodological problems that
have generated considerable interest among experimenters. The first
had to do with distinguishing between learning and retention, and
learning and performance. Inasmuch as performance does not always mirror learning, it has been deemed desirable to distinguish
between these two constructs, since the concern of most learning
psychologists is to determine those variables that influence learning
rather than performance. It does not seem possible at this time,
however, to distinguish between learning and performance.

Performance on any trial reflects not only the learning process
operating on that trial, but also the retention of material from
earlier trials; thus, there is difficulty in making any absolute distinction between learning and retention. Traditionally, these concepts
have been distinguished in that the changes from trial n to n + 1
have been considered learning changes when the variable of interest
is the ordinal number of trial n; while changes arising from trial n
to n + 1 are considered retention changes when the variable of
interest is the interval itself and/or the events that fill this interval.
Difficulties with this distinction arise from free-recall learning
studies in which only a single trial is provided, and short term
retention studies that utilize very short recall intervals between the
presentation of the material and the test for recall.

The second problem area considered was concerned with the
response measures utilized in verbal learning studies. These include
probability of response, and latency or time-related measures. The
two most frequently used probability measures have been: (1)
recall and (2) recognition.

Learning curves provide an excellent graphic device for determining the course of learning throughout the trials provided. Most
frequently, a fixed number of trials are provided for all subjects so

that performance is plotted as a function of trials. There is some problem when a learning criterion is used, since plotting trials on the abscissa would result in differing numbers of subjects being reflected at different points on the learning curve. Successive criterion and Vincent curves have been used to solve this problem.

The last methodological problem area was related to the variety of procedures that have been used in the presentation of the material. Anticipation, recall or study-test, and prompting methods have been employed most frequently. When these procedures are compared, the experimental evidence suggests that there are no differences among the methods, or that there is a slight superiority for the recall and prompting methods. In any event, the purported advantages of immediate reinforcement, knowledge of results, and immediate correction of errors—which presumably accrue to the use of the anticipation method—do not result in more rapid learning through this procedure.

A second procedural consideration was concerned with whether the pairs of items in paired-associate learning should be varied from trial to trial or whether they should have a constant serial position. Some experimental evidence indicated that the use of a constant serial position facilitated the learning of paired-associates, since the subject may use serial position as a cue to which to attach the response, rather than the stimulus with which the response has been formally paired. The last procedural consideration was related to whether a mixed or unmixed design should be used. With the mixed list design, all of the various conditions are represented in the same list of items; with the unmixed list, each condition is represented by a different list. Unfortunately, there is little experimental evidence to indicate whether these different designs would provide similar findings.

3 Characteristics of Verbal Material

In our first chapter, we discussed briefly the kinds of material frequently used in verbal learning experiments. In this chapter, we should like to extend this discussion to a consideration of some of the attributes or characteristics of such material.

Although Ebbinghaus (1885), in inventing nonsense syllables, assumed that they were relatively homogeneous in eliciting associations, Glaze's (1928) work indicated that this assumption was erroneous. Glaze found that different syllables were capable of evoking different numbers of associations. Many subsequent investigators have also found that syllables that differ in association value also differ in their ease of being learned.

The fact that association value could play a role in ease of learning has led many experimenters to examine other association measures, as well as other characteristics or attributes of verbal material.[1] In the following section we shall consider some of these attributes in some detail.

[1] In the last analysis, what might be considered to be an attribute of the material must eventually be related to the operation of some organismic process in the individual. That is, material is not learned more easily because of the characteristics of the material, but because such characteristics reflect or can be related to some organismic process that facilitates learning.

ASSOCIATION VALUE, FREQUENCY, FAMILIARITY AND PRONUNCIABILITY

ASSOCIATION VALUE

The first systematic work to examine the association value of verbal material, and in particular nonsense syllables, was that of Glaze (1928).[1] In this study, fifteen subjects were presented with more than 2,000 syllables. Each syllable was presented one at a time for two or three seconds and subjects were instructed to indicate in a word or two what the syllable meant to them—that is, whether or not it elicited an association. If the stimulus aroused none, the subject was to remain silent. The association value of each syllable was obtained by computing the percentage of subjects who indicated that a given syllable provided some association.

Subsequently, Hull (1933) and Krueger (1934) also examined the association value of nonsense syllables, while Witmer (1935) determined the association value for consonant syllables (CCCs).

Krueger's (1934) procedure was to have his subjects first write the syllable and then note any ideas the syllable aroused. The time allotted for each response was thus considerably longer than what Glaze had provided. Witmer (1935) exposed each syllable for four seconds on a memory drum; the subject was instructed to spell out the syllable and then indicate if it aroused any associations. Hull (1933), on the other hand, had his subjects learn lists of nonsense syllables but at the same time report what each syllable made them think of when it was presented. The subject was not directed to think of associations but if associations did occur he was to report them. Each list (consisting of sixteen items per list) was presented three times to each of twenty subjects. The association index was the number of associations reported for each syllable from the sixty presentations of the material.[2]

[1] A better description of this material would be CVC (consonant-vowel-consonant), since there is considerable doubt that any verbal symbols are truly "nonsense" or without meaning.

[2] A distressing fact has been the frequency with which the items calibrated for association value more than forty years ago have been used in contemporary experiments. Costantini and Blackwood (1968) reevaluated 343 low associations CCCs found in Witmer's (1935) list and striking differences in associative strength for many of the items were noted.

Many investigators have considered operations that measure association as measures of meaningfulness. Thus, McGeoch and Irion (1952) wrote "the meaningfulness of nonsense syllables has been measured by Glaze in terms of the percentage of subjects having associations aroused by each syllable" (p. 469).

Noble (1952) defined meaningfulness also in terms of association value but his measurement operation was different from those we have just reviewed. Defining meaning as a relation between a stimulus and a response, Noble postulated that meanings increase as a simple linear function of the number of S-multiple R connections acquired in a particular individual's history. When this postulation is transformed into behavior, an appropriate index of meaningfulness or *m* is provided by the average number of continued written associations made by a sample of subjects during a specified interval of time—frequently thirty or sixty seconds.

In the original study (Noble 1952), seventy-eight verbal units were obtained by using two-syllable nouns obtained from the Thorndike-Lorge (1944) word frequency count; these were supplemented by eighteen artificial items, making ninety-six items in all. The subjects (N = 119) were presented with one item at a time and given sixty seconds to write down as many words as they could think of which were associated with the stimulus word. Subjects were instructed to respond only to the stimulus words and not to use any other responses as stimuli to which to respond. Thus, if the word *Bob* was presented, and the subject responded with *Hope,* this would be an acceptable response. If his next response, however, was *faith* this would be unacceptable inasmuch as it would be assumed that *faith* was a response to *Hope* rather than *Bob.* Table 3–1 provides the *m* values for the varying verbal units used by Noble.

The reliability of Noble's measure of *m* has been excellent. Utilizing an intergroup correlation method, the reliability of the original *m* scale was .993 (Noble and McNeely 1957). Rocklyn, Hessert and Braun (1957) have reported an average (uncorrected) reliability of .96 for subjects from twenty to sixty-six years of age and of wide educational differences. Other examinations of reliability have been equally as impressive (Noble and Parker 1960; Noble 1961).

Mandler (1955) found that Noble's production method is ap-

TABLE 3–1

LIST OF DISSYLLABLE WORDS (NOUNS) IN RANK ORDER OF INCREASING MEANINGFULNESS (m) AS DEFINED BY MEAN FREQUENCY OF CONTINUED ASSOCIATIONS IN 60 SEC.

Rank	m-Value	Word	Rank	m-Value	Word
1	0.99	GOJEY	37	2.14	STOMA
2	1.04	NEGLAN	38	2.15	GRAPNEL
3	1.05	MEARDON	39	2.19	FLOTSAM
4	1.13	BYSSUS	40	2.26	CAROM
5	1.22	BALAP	41	2.26	NIMBUS
6	1.22	VOLVAP	42	2.28	LEMUR
7	1.24	TAROP	43	2.41	CAPSTAN
8	1.24	XYLEM	44	2.43	PERCEPT
9	1.26	LATUK	45	2.48	LICHENS
10	1.26	QUIPSON	46	2.54	JETSAM
11	1.27	GOKEM	47	2.59	ENDIVE
12	1.28	NARES	48	2.63	TARTAN
13	1.28	ZUMAP	49	2.69	OVUM
14	1.30	POLEF	50	2.73	ROSTRUM
15	1.33	SAGROLE	51	2.76	VERTEX
16	1.34	NOSTAW	52	2.80	BODICE
17	1.39	BODKIN	53	2.89	TANKARD
18	1.50	ULNA	54	3.06	PALLOR
19	1.53	WELKIN	55	3.21	SEQUENCE
20	1.54	ICON	56	3.34	ARGON
21	1.55	KUPOD	57	3.36	RAMPART
22	1.60	DELPIN	58	3.51	JITNEY
23	1.71	ATTAR	59	3.55	ENTRANT
24	1.73	MATRIX	60	3.62	PALLET
25	1.74	DAVIT	61	3.64	NAPHTHA
26	1.78	WIDGEON	62	3.77	PIGMENT
27	1.79	BRUGEN	63	3.91	ORDEAL
28	1.82	KAYSEN	64	4.44	ZENITH
29	1.84	MAELSTROM	65	4.60	YEOMAN
30	1.84	TUMBRIL	66	4.68	QUOTA
31	1.86	RENNET	67	5.10	QUARRY
32	1.90	ROMPIN	68	5.13	EFFORT
33	1.95	GAMIN	69	5.32	UNIT
34	2.09	FEMUR	70	5.33	FATIGUE
35	2.09	LOZENGE	71	5.47	KEEPER
36	2.13	FERRULE	72	5.52	KENNEL

(*Continued*)

TABLE 3–1 (*Continued*)

LIST OF DISSYLLABLE WORDS (NOUNS) IN RANK ORDER OF INCREASING MEANINGFULNESS (*m*) AS DEFINED BY MEAN FREQUENCY OF CONTINUED ASSOCIATIONS IN 60 SEC.

Rank	*m*-Value	Word	Rank	*m*-Value	Word
73	5.61	MALLET	85	7.17	GARMENT
74	5.94	LEADER	86	7.28	VILLAGE
75	5.98	QUARTER	87	7.39	INSECT
76	5.98	REGION	88	7.58	JEWEL
77	6.02	HUNGER	89	7.70	JELLY
78	6.15	ZERO	90	7.91	HEAVEN
79	6.24	INCOME	91	7.95	OFFICE
80	6.57	UNCLE	92	8.12	WAGON
81	6.75	YOUNGSTER	93	8.33	DINNER
82	6.83	TYPHOON	94	8.98	MONEY
83	6.88	CAPTAIN	95	9.43	ARMY
84	7.12	ZEBRA	96	9.61	KITCHEN

(Adapted from Noble 1952)

plicable in obtaining the meaningfulness (*m*) of a list of 100 selected nonsense syllables, while Spreen and Schulz (1966) have used the method in obtaining *m* values for 329 nouns. In this study, all nouns (with a few exceptions) with a Thorndike-Lorge (1944) frequency of 50 to 100 per million words and a length of three or fewer spoken syllables represented the experimental population of material.

In contrast to adult populations, which have been typically used in the various studies examining meaningfulness (*m*), Shapiro (1964) and Mickelson (1969) have both obtained m measures for a variety of words using children as their experimental subjects.

The obtaining of either Noble's measures of meaningfulness (*m*) or Glaze's measure of association value is time-consuming. An alternative procedure for securing these measures has been to use a rating scale in which each subject makes a judgment concerning the number of associations that he believes a given verbal unit will elicit. In a very extensive study, in which the 2,100 possible CVC combinations of the alphabet were used as the experimental material, Noble (1961) had 200 undergraduates indicate the number of associations they had to each of these syllables. The five rating categories were: none, below average, average, above average, and very many.

Three association measures were obtained from the data. One was Glaze's (1928) classical measure, *a*, calculated in terms of the relative frequencies of responses exceeding the none category. A second measure, a', was secured by obtaining mean ratings for each syllable, computed by assigning the ordinal weights 1, 2, 3, 4, and 5 to the five rating categories.[1] The third measure was designated as m'. Here, the rating frequencies of the syllables were transformed into deviates of the normal curve by the method of successive intervals.

Another verbal association measure has been provided by Archer (1960). This method consisted of having subjects view a verbal symbol (CVC) for four seconds on a filmstrip. The subjects were instructed to pronounce each item to themselves and then to ask the following questions: Is it a word? Does it sound like a word? Does it remind me of a word? Can I use it in a sentence? Subjects indicated their judgments on a two-choice IBM answer sheet. They responded yes if they could answer at least one of the four questions in the affirmative, or no if answers to all of the four were negative. The percentage of subjects who made yes responses to each item defined the association value, or meaningfulness, of the material used.[2]

Recently, Vicory and Asher (1966), and Taylor and Kimble (1967) have proposed association measures similar to some of those described above. Vicory and Asher termed their measure "associ-

[1] This type of measurement is used frequently in obtaining associative indices for a variety of materials. Battig and Spera (1962), and Cochran and Wickens (1963) have used it to provide association values for numbers ranging from 0 to 100, while Cochran (1968) has employed it to obtain association values for 251 different colors.

[2] A number of objections have been raised to the measurement operations used by both Noble (in obtaining a' and m') and Archer. Archer (1961) pointed out that Noble's multiple presentation of his syllables (seventy-five items appeared on each sheet of Noble's test booklet) undoubtedly resulted in subjects' making comparisons among the items. In addition, Saltz and Ager (1962), as well as Archer (1961), have objected to Noble's (1961) assigning of weights to the varying scale values, since this assumes that there is an equality of the psychological distances between each value—a questionable point. Noble (1961) wrote that "the novelty of Archer's four questions raises doubt concerning the psychological status of this index of wordness" (p. 518).

ative frequency (AF)"; here the subject writes a tally mark in a booklet for each association evoked to a given verbal stimulus within a ten-second interval. This method has the advantage of rapid administration, while at the same time providing the experimenter with the specific number of associative responses made to each verbal stimulus.

Taylor and Kimble (1967), on the other hand, used a variation of Glaze's procedure to scale 320 five-letter, structurally homogeneous (CVCVC) nouns and paralogs. Following the presentation of an item, subjects were instructed to give their first association as quickly as possible. A number of response measures were obtained. The percentages of subjects responding in less than 2.5 seconds to each item was one of these measures and represents a measure most closely identified with that of Glaze (1928).[1]

The fact that all of the measures that we have described are associative in content might lead one to suspect that many of these measures are highly correlated. Such a suspicion would be correct. Although no investigator has examined the intercorrelations among all of the association measures described, correlations between Glaze's association value and rated number of associations (m'), between Noble's m and rated number of associations (m'), and between Noble's a' and Archer's measure, have ranged from .87 to .95.

OBJECTIVE FREQUENCY

Another dimension of a verbal unit is frequency, defined as the number of times that a given verbal item is found in printed material or as a part of the subject's oral repertoire. It has been assumed that objective frequency reflects the experience that a given subject has had with the material. Frequency values for common English words can be found in the Thorndike-Lorge (1944) frequency count. The authors obtained this count by examining a wide range of printed material and tabulating the frequency with which the various words occurred. The list contains a number of different subcounts, each related to the source that was used. For example, an L count is used to denote sampling from "recent and popular"

---

[1] Other measures obtained include: (1) the number of subjects responding with the most frequent response, (2) the number of other response categories, and (3) the mean latency for all responses.

magazines, while a J count indicates sampling of material obtained from books recommended for boys and girls in grades three to eight. The most frequently used count, however, is a general word count (G), which is a sum of the frequencies obtained from all of the sources of material the investigators examined and which categorizes words on the basis of occurrences per million words examined. Words found 100 times per million or more are given a ranking of AA while words found from 50 to 99 times per million are listed as A. Frequency counts of less than fifty are indicated by their actual number.

In general, the Thorndike-Lorge frequency count has had little critical appraisal, although Rosenzweig and McNeill (1962) have called attention to a number of discrepancies and errors in the count, while more recently, Tryk (1968) listed some general criticisms that can be leveled against this word source. Chief among them are the following: (1) Although Thorndike and Lorge wrote that "the list tells anyone who wishes to know whether to use a word in writing, speaking, or teaching how common the word is in standard English reading matter" (p. x), the count was obtained only from printed material and a basic question can be raised as to whether the count faithfully reflects other modes of expression. (2) There is considerable question as to whether or not the tabulated frequency values reflect accurately contemporary word frequencies. As Tryk writes, "Although the general structure of language is not likely to change markedly in 20 years, drastic changes in usage for individual words can be expected. Since World War II, previously rare and obscure words, such as 'nuclear,' 'missile,' 'stereophonic,' and 'discotheque,' have appeared in the common American vernacular" (p. 171). (3) The count does not provide a continuous and uniform dimension of frequencies, since if a word occurs fifty to ninety-nine times per million occurrences it is given a frequency score of A, while if the frequency is greater than this, the word is given a score of AA.

A more recent word frequency count can be obtained from Kučera and Francis' (1967) Computational Analysis of Present-Day American English. Their sample consisted of 1,014,232 words of natural-language text; up-to-dateness was assured by confining the data to texts first printed in the year 1961. Further restrictions imposed were that the material should be prose, printed in the

United States, written by American writers, and with no more than 50 percent of any selection in dialogue (this automatically excluded drama as well as some fiction). To insure representativeness, 500 samples of approximately 2,000 words per sample were obtained. These samples were distributed among fifteen categories that the authors believed represented the full range of subject matter and prose styles.

The categories and number of selections assigned to each were as indicated in Table 3–2, while a sample of the frequency counts is found in Table 3–3.

In contrast to printed frequency counts, Howes (1966) has provided a frequency count of spoken English. Here, word frequencies were obtained from 250,000 words of spoken discourse recorded between 1960 and 1965. The corpus was composed of fifty interviews of 5,000 words each with forty-one different subjects. Of these, twenty were college sophomores while twenty others were patients at a Veterans Administration Hospital (but were free of cerebral defects and of acute or debilitating diseases). Finally, one

TABLE 3–2

CATEGORIES AND NUMBER OF SELECTIONS USED IN
KUČERA AND FRANCIS'S COMPUTATIONAL ANALYSIS
OF PRESENT-DAY AMERICAN ENGLISH

a.	Press: reportage	44
b.	Press: editorial	27
c.	Press: reviews	17
d.	Religion	17
e.	Skills and hobbies	36
f.	Popular lore	48
g.	Belles lettres, biography, etc.	75
h.	Miscellaneous	30
j.	Learned and scientific writings	80
k.	Fiction: general	29
l.	Fiction: mystery and detective	24
m.	Fiction: science	6
n.	Fiction: adventure and western	29
p.	Fiction: romance and love story	29
r.	Humor	9

(Adapted from Kučera and Francis 1967)

TABLE 3–3

A Sampling of the Kučera-Francis Frequency Count *

69971–15–500	The	6742–15–500	On
36411–15–500	Of	6377–15–499	Be
28852–15–500	And	5378–15–500	At
26149–15–500	To	5305–15–498	By
23237–15–500	A	5173–15–338	I
21341–15–500	In	5146–15–495	This
10595–15–500	That	5133–15–422	Had
10099–15–485	Is	4609–15–495	Not
9816–15–466	Was	4393–15–453	Are
9543–15–428	He	4381–15–490	But
9489–15–500	For	4369–15–500	From
8756–15–500	It	4207–15–492	Or
7289–15–500	With	3941–15–498	Have
7250–15–500	As	3747–15–498	An
6997–15–435	His	3618–15–482	They

* The three sets of figures, separated by dashes, provide the following information: The first figure gives the actual frequency of occurrence of the word in the Corpus. The second figure designates the number of genre subdivisions in which the word occurs (there are fifteen subdivisions found in the Corpus). The third figure provides the number of samples in which the word is found. (The Corpus is composed of 500 samples of roughly equal length.)

(Adapted from Kučera and Francis 1967)

additional patient was interviewed ten times in order to study the stability of word-frequency data for a single individual.

The interview itself placed little constraint on the subject's conversation. He was simply told that the purpose was to obtain a sample of his speech for a statistical study of language and to feel free to talk about anything he pleased. Frequently, it was necessary for the interviewer to start the subject off by asking a very general question such as, "Tell me what brought you to the hospital," or "Tell me about the field you are majoring in"—depending on whether the subject was a hospital patient or a student. Once the subject began talking freely, the interviewer endeavored to say the minimum amount necessary to maintain rapport.

The main table, a sample of which can be found in Table 3–4, reflects the frequency of words that occurred more than once: the

TABLE 3–4

A SAMPLE OF THE HOWES COUNT OF SPOKEN ENGLISH

Word	Total	U	H
A	6038	2514	2549
Abbot	2	0	2
Abide	2	2	0
Abilities	5	4	1
Ability	13	9	4
Able	81	31	41
Abnormal	2	0	2
Aboard	7	1	6
Abolished	2	0	2
About	934	422	423
Above	16	6	10
Abroad	2	2	0
Abrupt	2	0	0
Absence	3	1	0
Absentee	2	1	1
Absolute	2	2	0
Absolutely	8	5	3
Absolves	2	0	2
Abstract	3	3	0
Abused	2	0	0
Abutment	2	2	0
Abutments	3	3	0
Academic	4	3	1
Academy	7	3	4
Accent	5	3	2
Accept	12	6	4
Accepted	16	13	3
Accident	16	0	14

(Adapted from Howes 1966)

first column represents the total number of occurrences of the word in the full corpus of 250,000 words; the second, its frequency in the sample of 100,000 words from interviews with university students; the third, the frequency with which the word appeared among the 100,000 words obtained from the interviews with hospital patients.

Subjective spoken word frequency counts have been obtained by Tryk (1968) who had his subjects provide two estimates indicating how often they (private estimate), as well as an average American (public estimate), used 100 nouns that had been selected from the Thorndike-Lorge (1944) word count. Absolute values were obtained; a subject who estimated that he used word X four times a day, or that the average American used word Y ten times a month, then placed these values on the form that was provided. The correlations obtained between the public and private estimations suggested that the two sets of estimates yielded similar subjective scales of estimated word frequency. The reliability of the ratings obtained by the test-retest method (two weeks between testings) was quite high (.96, .98).

The frequency of three-letter units (trigrams) has been measured by Underwood and Schulz (1960), who used what they have described as the contiguous method. In obtaining this count, the general procedure was to break down all words sampled into successive three-letter units. For example, in the word *learning* the successive trigrams generated were as follows: LEA, EAR, ARN, RNI, NIN, and ING. The general position taken by the authors was that if such a breakdown were made for a large number of words taken from English texts and if all identical trigrams were summed, the result would be a count of the relative frequency with which trigrams occur in the language.

In order to select a sample of English words, the authors took the first five words appearing in each column of the Thorndike-Lorge word count. A total of 2,080 words were thus selected from the almost 20,000 listed on pages 1 through 208 of that volume. Each word was broken down into its contiguous trigrams and the appropriate frequency entry was made for each item. Inasmuch as the words that were used differed in frequency, the frequency value of the words was incorporated into the frequency value of the trigram. For example, if the trigram ARN appeared in the word *barn,* and *barn* was listed by the Thorndike-Lorge count as having occurred forty-five times per million words, the trigram ARN could be tallied as having occurred forty-five times. When ARN appeared as part of the word *darn,* which occurred twelve times per million words, that frequency of twelve would be added to the earlier frequency of forty-five in order to get the total frequency count for that particular trigram.[1]

FAMILIARITY OR SUBJECTIVE FREQUENCY

More than three decades ago Robinson (1932) suggested that acquaintance was an important variable in verbal learning, and a number of investigators have since pointed out that this concept is similar to familiarity (Waters 1939; Hovland and Kurtz 1952; Epstein, Rock and Zuckerman 1960). The operations for producing acquaintance or familiarity can frequently be reduced to those that involve either learning or frequency of presentation. Waters (1939) had his subjects "familiarize" themselves with the material to be learned by reading the items aloud. Hovland and Kurtz (1952) had subjects become "familiar" with nonsense syllables by studying them in a constantly changing order, until they knew each syllable sufficiently well that they could provide the missing letter when it had been omitted in the syllable's presentation.

Lindley (1960) has provided a somewhat different measure of familiarity for trigrams by recording the number of times that the various combinations occur as the first three letters in words found in the Thorndike-Lorge frequency count.[2]

The methods just described are techniques or operations that investigators have used to produce varying amounts of familiarity in their subjects. As might be anticipated, however, familiarity has also been measured by use of the rating scale. Haagen (1949) defined familiarity in terms of the degree to which the meaning and use of a word was known to the judge, taking as the criterion of "greatest familiarity" the immediate recognition and absolute certainty of the meaning and use of the word. A seven-point rating scale was used in obtaining such judgments. Noble (1953), on the other hand, has defined familiarity as "a stimulus attribute which is some increasing function of the frequency of occurrence of a given stimulus" (p. 97). His measurement operation consisted of

[1] It was necessary for the authors to make some decision to change A and AA frequencies into numerical multipliers. Their decision was to use 50 as the multiplier for A words and 100 for the AA words.

[2] Although Lindley's operations are similar to those that have been used to measure objective frequency, Lindley has chosen to define this measure as one of familiarity.

asking subjects how often they had come in contact with certain words. A five-point rating scale was used to describe the frequency of contact and utilized the following descriptions: never, rarely, sometimes, often, and very often. A rating of "never" meant that the subject had never seen or heard or used the word in his life, while at the other extreme, "very often" meant that the subject had seen or heard or used the word nearly every day of his life. This measure may also be described as a subjective frequency measure.

It should be anticipated that familiarization training with verbal material would be reflected in increasing scaled familiarity measures. This general finding has been confirmed by Noble (1954), who chose sixteen items from the low end of his scale of disyllables and presented them for varying frequencies. Items were exposed for either zero, one, two, three, four, five, ten, fifteen, twenty, or twenty-five presentations, and subjects were required to pronounce each item aloud as it was presented. Subjects were then asked to judge the familiarity of the stimuli following such presentation on the rating scale as has just been described. A negatively accelerated curve, as indicated in Fig. 3–1, was obtained with little change in judged familiarity following five presentations.

On the other hand, Riley and Phillips (1959) have shown that a somewhat different type of familiarization training does not influence either the latency or the number of associations (m) which are made to the "familiarized" stimuli. In this study, familiarization training was provided by requiring subjects, who had been exposed

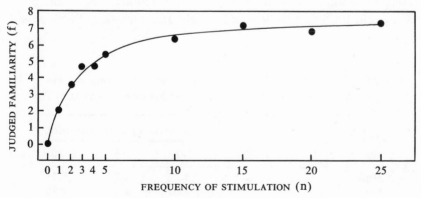

Fig. 3–1. The familiarity-frequency relationship.
(Adapted from Noble 1954)

to only two of the three letters that made up a CVC, to supply the third letter. Following such training, these familiar CVCs, as well as unfamiliar ones (syllables that had not been presented before), were presented to the subjects, who were asked to respond as rapidly as possible with as many words as the syllable reminded them of, for a period of thirty seconds. Neither the median latency of the first response nor the mean number of responses in the thirty-second period revealed differences between the familiar and nonfamiliar syllables.

A subsequent study by Schulz and Thysell (1965) has confirmed as well as extended this general finding that experimentally produced familiarity does not affect meaningfulness, at least as measured by Noble's (1952) production method. In this study, subjects received either zero, five, or twenty one-second familiarization trials with ten disyllables of either high or low meaningfulness (m). Control subjects (zero familiarization trials) received twenty trials of irrelevant familiarization with the digits 0 to 9. The familiarization procedure consisted of presenting each item for one second, during which time the subject was instructed to say that item silently to himself. Following such training, all subjects were given a production test for the determination of m; thirty-second periods were provided, however, instead of the usual sixty seconds.

The means for the number of associations per disyllable produced under the various conditions are indicated in Table 3–5. It can be noted that m fails to be systematically influenced by variations in amount of familiarization. In summary, the findings of Riley and Phillips (1959), and Schulz and Thysell (1965) would

TABLE 3–5

MEANS FOR NUMBER OF ASSOCIATIONS AS A FUNCTION OF THE
AMOUNT OF FAMILIARIZATION AND MEANINGFULNESS

	Amount of Familiarization		
m	0	5	20
High	8.20	8.74	8.11
Low	4.04	4.09	4.50

(Adapted from Schulz and Thysell 1965)

justify a firm conclusion that familiarization does not alter the meaningfulness (at least as measured by Noble's *m*) of isolated verbal material.

PRONUNCIABILITY

The experimental work of Underwood and Schulz (1960) has provided strong support for the position that pronunciability represents an important attribute of verbal material. Their procedure for measuring the pronunciability of verbal material consisted of providing 181 subjects with 178 different three-letter combinations. The subjects were instructed that they were to rate each of the combinations as to the relative ease or difficulty of pronouncing it. A nine-point rating scale was used with the words "difficult" and "easy" anchoring the ends of the scale, while "average" was placed in the middle.

The general scaling procedure to measure pronunciability has been used quite frequently, although five- and seven-point scales have been used in addition to the nine-point scale devised by Underwood and Schulz.

The measurement of ease or difficulty of pronunciability has been extended to latency measures. Lindley and Stone (1967) presented verbal items visually, and pronunciability latency (PL) was measured as the time between the visual onset of the verbal stimulus and the onset of the subject's pronouncing the item. The specific procedure consisted of instructing the subject to pronounce the trigram as soon as it was presented, to be phonetically accurate in the pronunciation, and then to rate the pronunciability of the item on a nine-point scale (Pr). The correlation between PL and Pr was .90; the shorter the time between item onset and the onset of pronunciation, the easier the item was rated to pronounce. The correlation between the Underwood and Schulz Pr values and Lindley and Stone's PL was .83.

DICTIONARY MEANINGS

Saltz and Modigliani (1967) have suggested that another verbal material variable may be the dictionary meanings (dm) of a word.

In the study cited, Webster's New Collegiate Dictionary (1959) was used to determine the number of dictionary meanings for 100 words that were to be later used in a paired-associate task. Meanings the dictionary indicated as obsolete or archaic were not counted.

CONCRETENESS, SPECIFICITY, VIVIDNESS AND IMAGERY

The verbal dimensions we have discussed have been primarily those of: (1) association, (2) objective frequency, (3) familiarity, or subjective frequency, (4) pronunciability and (5) dictionary meanings. It has been recognized, however, that at least some verbal items, particularly nouns, may be more concrete and have greater specificity than others, as well as being more vivid and able to more readily elicit images. Relatively recent experimental work has been directed toward the measurement of these verbal attributes.

CONCRETENESS

Although Stoke (1929) was interested in an abstract-concrete dimension of verbal material, and a number of early investigators were interested in this attribute as it was related to reaction time, Gorman's (1961) examination of this construct appears to be first among contemporary research efforts.

In this study, 1,791 nouns were obtained from the Thorndike-Lorge word count subject to a number of restrictions.[1] Two judges, using a dictionary in order to examine the meanings of these words, then classified them on the basis of (1) concrete—those referenced to objects, material, or sources of sensation that are relatively direct, or (2) abstract—those referenced to objects, material, or sources of sensation that are relatively indirect. Results revealed a high

---

[1] The specific restrictions were as follows: (a) the noun should have a G frequency index higher than six; (b) the noun should not be capitalized, abbreviated, contracted, or hyphenated; (c) the noun should not be a plural of an entry that could be used in the singular; and (d) the noun should not have a substantial nonnoun use.

level of agreement between judges, since agreement as to the appropriate category occurred for almost 96 percent of the words examined.

Recent investigators have used the rating scale to measure this attribute. For example, both Spreen and Schulz (1966), and Paivio, Yuille and Madigan (1968) have used seven-point rating scales. With these scales, words that refer to abstract concepts and cannot be experienced by the senses should receive a low concreteness rating, while words that refer to objects, materials, or persons— where the source of sensation is relatively direct—should be given a high concreteness rating. In the Spreen and Schulz (1966) study, 329 nouns were rated, while Paivio, et al. (1968) examined a sample of 925. The reliability of the ratings has been excellent; Spreen and Schulz reported an *r* of .94 obtained by correlating the scores of one subgroup with those of another.

SPECIFICITY

Another characteristic of verbal material has been posited by Paivio and Olver (1964) as specificity. These authors have considered this attribute to be part of the broader continuum of the concrete-abstract dimension just discussed. In order to examine this attribute, Paivio and Olver (1964) selected thirty-two "general" and thirty-two "specific" nouns with frequencies of forty or more per million, as measured by the Thorndike-Lorge frequency count. This was done by matching a relatively general word (e.g., *furniture*) with a more specific example of its referent class (e.g., *table*).

In a subsequent study, Paivio (1967) demonstrated that it was possible to select words that had the attributes of both concreteness and specificity. Thus, an example of a concrete-general noun would be *tool,* while a concrete-specific noun would be *hammer;* an example of an abstract-general noun would be *emotion,* while an abstract-specific noun would be *grief.*

VIVIDNESS AND IMAGERY

The constructs of vividness and imagery have been also posited to be attributes of verbal material, and the work of Tulving, Paivio and his associates, as well as others, have been instrumental in quantifying these attributes.

Although anecdotal evidence suggests that the vividness of an experience plays some role in its being learned and in its recall, the experimental evidence that was marshalled to support this position, at least until recently, was quite modest. An early study by Bowers (1932) suggested a "distinctiveness" characteristic of single letters; some years later Haagen (1949) found that pairs of adjectives could be rated on their vividness of connotation. Only recently, however, has interest again been aroused in this characteristic of isolated items. Thus, in order to examine the role of vividness in free-recall learning, Tulving, McNulty, and Ozier (1965) selected eighty-two two-syllable nouns, five to seven letters in length, whose Thorndike-Lorge frequency count was between fifteen and nineteen. The authors had subjects rate these words, using a seven-point rating scale, on the ease with which the words would produce a picture, or a visual image.

At about the same time, although stemming from his earlier work with the attribute of concreteness, Paivio and his associates were interested in examining the construct of imagery, an attribute that appears to have much in common with vividness.

Using five- (Paivio 1965) or seven- (Paivio, Yuille and Madigan 1968) point rating scales, subjects were asked to rate nouns as to the ease or difficulty with which they would arouse a mental image. Specific instructions emphasized the point that any word that aroused a mental image very quickly and easily should be given a high imagery rating, while words that aroused mental images with difficulty or not at all should be given a low imagery rating.

In the Paivio, Yuille and Madigan (1968) study, imagery and concreteness values (in addition to meaningfulness) were obtained for 925 nouns; a sampling of these ratings is found in Table 3–6. It may be noted that there are considerable similarities in the ratings between the two constructs; in fact, the authors report an *r* of .83 between the two measures. For some of the words, however, there is a marked discrepancy between the ratings. The authors have found that when the scale value of concreteness exceeds imagery by two or more scale units, these words are char-

TABLE 3–6

Noun	Mean Imagery Rating	Mean Concreteness Rating
Abasement	2.03	2.38
Abbess	2.97	4.78
Abdication	3.57	2.66
Abdomen	6.00	6.83
Abduction	4.93	3.48
Aberration	2.27	2.98
Ability	2.67	2.03
Abode	5.07	6.31
Abyss	5.17	5.40
Accordion	6.50	7.00
Acrobat	6.53	6.38
Adage	2.77	3.63
Admiral	6.20	6.35
Advantage	2.37	2.25
Adversity	2.80	2.73
Advice	3.13	2.08
Affection	4.87	2.18
Afterlife	2.40	1.77
Agility	4.57	2.93
Agony	5.43	3.13
Agreement	3.33	2.93
Air	4.17	5.67
Alcohol	6.47	6.87
Algebra	5.17	4.85
Alimony	4.47	4.87
Allegory	2.13	2.56
Alligator	6.87	6.93
Amazement	4.47	2.18

(Adapted from Paivio, Yuille and Madigan 1968)

acterized by their unusualness, and a number of them have Thorndike-Lorge frequencies of one per million or less. The authors have suggested that the low imagery ratings are attributable to infrequent association with concrete sensory experience. On the other hand, when the scale value of imagery exceeds concreteness by two or more scale units, this type of word frequently has strong emotional or evaluative connotations.

EMOTIONALITY

It seems appropriate to mention that an attribute of verbal material that has interested a few investigators has been related to the affective state or emotionality that the item generates in the individual. In an early examination of this attribute, Noble (1958) used the ninety-six items that he had originally scaled for meaningfulness (*m*) and asked subjects to place each of these disyllables into one of four categories: neutral, pleasant, unpleasant, or mixed. More recently, Silverstein and Dienstbier (1968) had subjects rate 101 two-syllable nouns on a seven-point pleasantness rating scale; the scale categories were: (1) very unpleasant, (2) moderately unpleasant, (3) slightly unpleasant, (4) neutral, (5) slightly pleasant, (6) moderately pleasant, and (7) very pleasant.

ORTHOGRAPHIC DISTINCTIVENESS

One unusual attribute of the isolated verbal unit that has been examined recently is its orthographic distinctiveness. This dimension has been related to the word's physical features. For example, if the words *genie* and *gnome* are considered, although both have approximately the same initial letter and length, approximately the same frequency of occurrence, and similar definitions, gnome would be generally considered to be more orthographically distinctive than genie. Providing very explicit instructions as to what constituted orthographic distinctiveness, Zechmeister (1969) had two groups of subjects rate on a nine-point scale, 150 five-letter, low frequency words for their orthographic distinctiveness and their pronunciability, Overall mean ratings supported the position that these words varied in terms of their structural distinctiveness. It was interesting to note that the correlation between this feature and pronunciability was .61.

In summary, we have described a number of measures that investigators have hypothesized and experimentally demonstrated to be attributes of verbal material. Table 3–7 provides a concise listing of these measures.

But can one state that these measures all reflect different attributes of verbal material? What are the relationships that exist among these measures? This must be our next consideration.

TABLE 3–7

VARYING DIMENSIONS OF VERBAL CHARACTERISTICS

Measure	Frequently Used Symbol	
Association	*a*	Percentage of population indicating that a given verbal item elicits an association, where each item is presented individually. May also be obtained by using a rating scale (see a′) and calculating relative frequencies of responses exceeding the No Association category.
Association	*a′*	Mean ratings of association frequency where: five-, seven-, or n-point rating scale is used. Thus, on a five-point scale: no association = 1; below average = 2; average = 3; above average = 4; very many = 5.
Association	(Archer)	Percentage of population indicating that a verbal item elicits a "yes" response on at least one of four questions all related to whether or not the item seems like a word: Is it a word? Does it sound like a word? Does it remind me of a word? Can I use it in a sentence?
Association	*m*	Number of associations provided by a subject to a verbal unit in a specified amount of time, frequently thirty or sixty seconds.
Association	*m′*	Mean ratings of number of associations a given verbal item is believed to produce; five categories have been most often used. Frequencies may be transformed into deviates of the normal curve by Thurstone-Attneave method of successive intervals.
Frequency	F	Frequency of verbal items (words) as found in some objective word counts (Thorndike-Lorge, Kučera-Francis).

(Continued)

TABLE 3–7 (*Continued*)

VARYING DIMENSIONS OF VERBAL CHARACTERISTICS

Measure	Frequently Used Symbol	
Frequency		Frequency of trigrams as measured by contiguous three-letter combinations obtained from words randomly selected from the Thorndike-Lorge word count compiled by Underwood and Schulz (1960).
Familiarity	f	Frequency with which a subject has come into contact with specified verbal items as measured by rating scale. Five-point scale as used by Noble (1953) employed never, rarely, sometimes, often, very often. Rating frequencies may be transformed into deviates of normal curve.
Pronunciability	Pr	Mean ratings by judges of pronunciability where a five-, seven-, or n-point rating scale is used.
Pronunciability	Pl	The time interval or latency between the onset of the presentation of a verbal item and the onset of the S's voice in pronouncing the item.
Dictionary Meaning	dm	The number of meanings provided a given word as found in a standard dictionary. Archaic meanings are usually not included in the count.
Concreteness	C	Rating by judges using a dictionary in which the word has reference to objects or material in which the source of sensation is relatively direct (Gorman 1961); or mean ratings of degree of concreteness as measured by five-, seven-, or n-point rating scale.
Specificity		Mean ratings by judges as to whether a verbal symbol refers to a referent class, or refers to a member of that class.

(*Continued*)

TABLE 3–7 (*Continued*)

VARYING DIMENSIONS OF VERBAL CHARACTERISTICS

Measure	Frequently Used Symbol	
Vividness or Imagery	V I	Mean ratings by judges as to ease or difficulty with which a verbal symbol will produce a visual picture, or will arouse a mental image as measured by a five-, seven-, or n-point rating scale.
Pleasantness or Emotionality	PL e	Mean ratings by judges as to pleasantness or unpleasantness of a given verbal symbol.
Orthographic Distinctiveness		Mean ratings by judges as to the physical or structural distinctiveness of a word as measured by a nine-point rating scale.

INTERRELATIONSHIPS AMONG THE VARYING MEASURES

A number of investigators have been interested in examining the relationship that exists among many of the measures just discussed. In Table 3–8 we have provided a sampling of the correlations among measures obtained by a variety of investigators. It should be noted, of course, that any correlational value obtained is related to the homogeneity of the material which is used. For example, Hall (1967) has found that the correlation between familiarity or subjective frequency and pronunciability is just .36 if three-letter words comprise the experimental population. If both three-letter words and three-letter nonwords are used, the size of the correlation increases to .75.[1]

[1] Another example of this is found in a dispute between Noble (1961) and Archer (1961). Noble wrote that Archer's association values can be identified most closely with his a' value and reported a correlation of .955 between 120 of Archer's association values and Noble's corresponding a' values. Archer (1961) reported a similar value (.949) when the entire range of values is sampled but pointed out that a more adequate test of commonality would be one that restricted the range of values. Thus, when the range is restricted to 20 percent intervals on his scale, correlations between his values and Noble's are considerably lower, ranging from .32 to .68.

TABLE 3–8

INTERCORRELATIONS AMONG A NUMBER OF VERBAL CHARACTERISTICS:
A SELECTED SAMPLING

	No. Items on Which *r* Is Based	*r*	Reference
1. *Glaze's Association value*			
with rated Number of Associations *m'*)	200	.87	(Hall 1967)
with Familiarity	200	.84	(Hall 1967)
with Underwood-Schulz frequency count	200	.54	(Hall 1967)
with Pronunciability	200	.90	(Hall 1967)
2. *Noble's m*			
with rated Number of Associations	96	.92	(Noble 1963)
with Thorndike-Lorge frequency	925	.33	(Paivio, Yuille & Madigan 1968)
with Familiarity	96	.92	(Noble 1953)
with Pronunciability	329	.29	(Spreen & Schulz 1966)
with Concreteness	925	.56	(Paivio, Yuille & Madigan 1968)
with Imagery	925	.72	(Paivio, Yuille & Madigan 1968
3. *Rated Number of Associations*			
with *m*	96	.92	(Noble 1963)
with Familiarity	200	.88	(Hall 1967)
with Pronunciability	200	.88	(Hall 1967)
4. *Thorndike-Lorge Frequency*			
with *m*	925	.33	(Paivio, Yuille & Madigan 1968)
with Underwood-Schulz frequency count	451	.38	(Hall 1967a)
with Familiarity	48	.85	(Underwood, Ekstrand & Keppel 1965)

(*Continued*)

TABLE 3–8 (*Continued*)

INTERCORRELATIONS AMONG A NUMBER OF VERBAL CHARACTERISTICS:
A SELECTED SAMPLING

	No. Items on Which *r* Is Based	*r*	Reference
5. *Familiarity*			
with Noble's *m*	96	.92	(Noble 1953)
with rated Number of Associations	200	.88	(Hall 1967)
with Thorndike-Lorge frequency	48	.85	(Underwood, Ekstrand & Keppel 1965)
with Underwood & Schulz frequency count	200	.78	(Hall 1967)
with Pronunciability	200	.75	(Hall 1967)
6. *Pronunciability*			
with Glaze association	200	.90	(Hall 1967)
with Noble's *m*	329	.29	(Spreen & Schulz 1966)
with rated Number of Associations	200	.88	(Hall 1967)
with Underwood-Schulz frequency count	200	.37	(Hall 1967)
with Familiarity	200	.75	(Hall 1967)
with Concreteness	329	.30	(Spreen & Schulz 1966)
7. *Concreteness*			
with Noble's *m*	925	.83	(Paivio, Yuille & Madigan 1968)
with Thorndike-Lorge frequency	925	.56	(Paivio, Yuille & Madigan 1968)
with Familiarity	96	.01	(Paivio 1968)
with Pronunciability	329	.30	(Spreen & Schulz 1966)
with Imagery	925	.83	(Paivio, Yuille & Madigan 1968)

(*Continued*)

TABLE 3–8 (*Continued*)

INTERCORRELATIONS AMONG A NUMBER OF VERBAL CHARACTERISTICS:
A SELECTED SAMPLING

	No. Items on Which r Is Based	r	Reference
8. *Imagery*			
with Noble's *m*	925	.72	(Paivio, Yuille & Madigan 1968)
with Thorndike-Lorge frequency	925	.23	(Paivio, Yuille & Madigan 1968)
with Concreteness	925	.83	(Paivio, Yuille & Madigan 1968)
9. *Emotionality*			
with Noble's *m*	96	.57	(Noble 1958)
with Association value (*a'*)	101	.58	(Silverstein & Dienstbier 1958)
with Lorge magazine count	101	.23	(Silverstein & Dienstbier 1958)
10. *Orthographic Distinctiveness*			
with Pronunciability	150	.61	Zechmeister (1969)

Moreover, the relationship between two variables may be curvilinear, and since the Pearsonian *r* is a measure of linearity, the relationship between the two variables may be underestimated.

A scatterplot, of course, will help the investigator determine whether or not a curvilinear relationship does exist between the measures in question. It has the additional value of indicating something about the sensitivity of the measures at the extreme ends of the scale. For example, Noble (1963), and Noble, Sutker and Jones (1968), plotting scaled meaningfulness (*m'*) and association value (*a*) of CVCs, have shown a sigmoidal relationship between these two measures. These authors have pointed out that the association value measure appears to be relatively insensitive at the extreme ends of the scale—a condition, of course, that may impair its usefulness.

In general, however, most investigators, in examining the relationship among the varying measures of meaningfulness, have been content to obtain a Pearsonian *r* among the measures with which they have been concerned. The values presented in Table 3–8 are reflections of this approach.

A casual inspection of these values indicates that the relationships among many of the measures are quite high; thus, it seems obvious that some of them are measuring quite similar (if not identical) attributes. The task at hand is to identify those measures that indicate unique attributes of the isolated verbal item. One solution to this problem has been to use factor analysis. In one study by Frincke (1968), 70 English nouns were randomly selected from the 1,791 nouns comprising a source list previously prepared by Gorman (1961) in her examination of concreteness.[1] It will be recalled that this list includes all noncapitalized nouns in the Thorndike-Lorge word count with G-count frequencies of seven or more occurrences per million words.

The following attributes of these words were examined: (1) Noble's *m*, (2) rated meaningfulness (*m'*), (3) imagery, (4) concreteness, (5) Thorndike-Lorge frequency count, (6) familiarity or subjective frequency; as well as four other characteristics that we have not discussed. These were: (7) estimated trigram frequencies as compiled by Stolurow, Jacobs, and Blomme (1960); (8) word length as measured by number of letters; and (9) word "goodness." (Here two seven-point rating scales were used to evaluate each word. One scale measured the words on a Good-Bad continuum, the other on a Pleasant-Unpleasant continuum. The two ratings for each word were then combined to provide a "goodness" value.) The tenth measure was an evaluative semantic-differential polarity score obtained by rescoring the ratings on the Good-Bad, and Pleasant-Unpleasant scales. Here values from zero to three were assigned according to their distance from the neutral or central position on each scale. These values were then combined and classified as the evaluative semantic value. Reliabilities were obtained for each of the measures and they ranged from .94 to .98.

In addition, a free-recall score was obtained by providing seven trials during which each word was presented for 2.6 seconds. Fol-

---

[1] It should be mentioned that Frincke's (1968) original sample consisted of seventy-four nouns. Frincke found, however, that more than 20 percent of his subjects reported that they had never heard, seen, or used the words: *ado, alder, dory,* or *lynx;* as a result, these words were excluded from the analysis.

lowing each trial, a fifty-second interval was provided. At the conclusion of the seventh trial, the subjects were given ten minutes to write down all of the words they could remember. The free-recall score for each word was obtained by counting the number of subjects recalling that word.

Groups of forty subjects participated in providing the investigator with a given measure of a word attribute.

Factor analysis of the free-recall scores and the varying word attributes revealed two common factors. The first was tentatively identified as meaningful-familiarity, since rated meaningfulness (m') and familiarity loaded highly on it, while moderate loadings of Noble's m and the Thorndike-Lorge frequency count were also found. The second factor was classified as an imagery-concreteness factor, since imagery had a very high loading on this factor.[1]

A second factor analytic study by Paivio (1968) has provided somewhat more complex findings. Thirty different measures were obtained from each of ninety-six nouns comprising his experimental population of words. Although we cannot detail all of the measures that were obtained, these did include paired-associate and free-recall learning scores, Thorndike-Lorge frequency count, meaningfulness (m) as provided by the production method, and ratings on the following scales: ease of imagery, familiarity, abstract-concrete, good-bad, impressive-unimpressive, simple-complex, active-passive, unusual-usual, specific-general, emotional-unemotional, hard-soft, vague-precise, boring-interesting, tangible-intangible, meaningful-meaningfulness, smooth-rough, colorful-colorless, and narrow-wide.

The words used were not randomly selected but had been used in an earlier study (Paivio 1966), in which forty-eight had been classified as "concrete" and forty-eight as "abstract." A variety of subject populations were used to secure the varying measures.

Paivio reported that his factor analysis yielded six factors. The first, and in keeping with Frincke's (1968) findings, indicated a *concrete-imagery* factor, since high loadings were obtained from rating scale scores that measured both the vividness of images formed by each of the words as well as the difficulty with which such images were formed. Surprisingly, a second factor designated as *specificity* emerged, since it had substantial loadings obtained from two rating scales that measured (1) specificity and (2)

---

[1] The author reports that since imagery was highly correlated with concreteness ($r = .92$), the concreteness scale was not included in the factor analysis.

preciseness. (The author had originally thought that these two measures would supplement and contribute to the abstract-concrete attribute.)

No meaningfulness-familiarity factor was obtained. Meaningfulness, as measured by Noble's (1952) *m*, loaded substantially on the first factor, *concreteness-imagery;* familiarity or subjective frequency ratings loaded on a third factor that Paivio termed *familiarity;* a measure of verbal reaction time (which could be conceptualized as a measure of associative strength, not unlike that obtained by Glaze [1928]) contributed to a fourth factor that Paivio hypothesized to be *associative.* Scores obtained from a meaningful-meaningless rating scale contributed to a fifth factor that Paivio identified as *impressiveness,* since it also loaded highly on scores obtained from rating scales used to measure impressiveness, interest, complexity, activity, emotionality, and colorfulness.

Finally, the sixth factor, was identified as a *learning* factor, since it had moderate to substantial loadings on three different learning scores, one obtained from a free-recall task, and the other two from the learning of paired-associates.

Paivio's (1968) findings notwithstanding, we believe that the two attributes of the isolated verbal item that are primarily related to learning are: (1) meaningfulness-familiarity, and (2) concreteness-imagery. It should be recognized, however, that virtually all investigators who have posited an imagery-concreteness factor have used nouns as their experimental material and it remains to be seen whether other types of verbal material (i.e., other parts of speech) have this characteristic. In addition, the role of pronunciability remains obscure since Frincke (1968) did not include it among the measures he used. However, since pronunciability correlates quite highly with (a) Glaze's association values, (b) familiarity, and (c) rated number of associations, there is the suggestion that it is not independent of the meaningfulness-familiarity dimension.

WORD RELATEDNESS

The measurements of the varying characteristics of verbal materials that we have just examined have been obtained when the items have been presented and responded to as single items. And the experimenter, in making up the learning task, has usually made every effort to see that the items that comprise the task are unrelated, thus attempting to preserve the insularity of the individual items.[1]

But in many instances, certainly in everyday situations, the words that make up a list are not unrelated. A grocery list, for example, may include the separate items *milk, butter, cheese, apples, bananas, grapes, peas, beans, corn, doughnuts, pie* and *cake;* however, it can be noted that groups of these items can be related to the larger conceptual categories of *dairy products, fruits, vegetables,* and *pastry.* As a result, some investigators have been interested in examining how tasks in which there is a relatedness among the items, are learned.

What are these measures of relatedness, and how have they been scaled? In this section, we should like to briefly summarize four of those that have been employed most often. The interested reader may consult Marshall and Cofer (1963), Garskof and Houston (1963), and Gentile and Seibel (1969) for additional, less frequently used measures.

1. FREQUENCY OF ASSOCIATION

The cultural or verbal relatedness between two words can be measured by the frequency with which one word occurs as a response to another in a free association test. Free association norms are used to provide this measure. Using the Palermo and Jenkins (1964) norms, for example, we find the stimulus word *white* elicits the following response frequencies from a population of 939 college students: *black* 500, *snow* 190, *dark* 27, *pure* 25, *house* 14, *dress* 12, *color* 11, *clean* 10, *blue* 9, *sheet* 9, etc.

The relatedness of the stimulus and a specific response, R_1, is expressed as a percentage in which the total number of responses is divided into the number of R_1 responses. Thus,

$$\frac{R_1}{N} \times 100 = \text{Percent Frequency of Association}$$

In the example provided, the strength of the WHITE–BLACK pair would be expressed as 53% (500/939 × 100).

[1] There is the general assumption here that the value of an attribute for a given item (i.e., GOJEY having an *m* value of .99) does not materially change when the item becomes part of the larger task.

2. MUTUAL RELATEDNESS (MR)

This measure, developed by Jenkins and Cofer (1957), and Bousfield, Whitmarsh and Berkowitz (1960), like the frequency of association measure, is computed from single response free-association data. Unlike association frequency that examines the relationship between just two words, this index takes into account all of the responses that two words have in common. One important consideration in obtaining MR scores should be noted. In standard free-association test procedures, subjects are instructed to respond with any word that occurs to them, *other than the stimulus word*. However, the MR index makes the assumption that on presentation of the stimulus word, all subjects respond initially by repeating the stimulus word before making their free-association response.

The formula for obtaining an MR score is as follows:

$$\frac{\text{Sum of responses in common to } S_1 \text{ and } S_2}{\text{Total number of responses to } S_1 \text{ and } S_2} \text{ or } \frac{R_c}{R_t} = MR$$

An example of the computation of the MR index for two pairs of words, *oak-pine* and *hand-glove,* is presented in Table 3–9.

3. INTER-ITEM ASSOCIATIVE STRENGTH (IIAS)

The two measures just discussed are applicable only when the relationship between two words is of interest to the investigator. The inter-item associative strength measure (IIAS), however, as developed by Deese (1959), is applicable to larger numbers of words. The IIAS has been defined "as the average relative frequency with which all items in a list tend to elicit all other items in the same list as free associates" (Deese 1959, p. 305).

In order for this measure to be obtained, free associations must be available to each word in the group of words that are being considered. A matrix is set up, with all words in the group listed in row and column form. The percent frequency with which a word in the column is a response to the word on the row is entered in the appropriate cell. (Unlike the MR index, it is not assumed that any word will elicit itself.) The percent frequencies are summed by columns; the sum of the column frequencies is divided by the

TABLE 3-9

COMPUTATION OF THE MR INDEX FOR TWO PAIRS OF WORDS [a]

STIMULI	OAK......PINE		Responses Common to the Two Stimuli (Rc)
Oak	(102)[b]	0	0
Pine	0	(102)[b]	0
Tree	88	70	70
Forest	1	2	1
Shade	2	1	1
Wood	2	5	2
Sum Rc			74

$$\text{MR Index} = \frac{RC}{Rt} = \frac{74}{204} = .363$$

STIMULI	HAND.....GLOVE		Responses Common to the Two Stimuli (Rc)
Hand	(102)[b]	53	53
Glove	17	(102)[b]	17
Finger	20	5	5
Hold	2	1	1
Warm	1	1	1
			77

$$\text{MR Index} = \frac{77}{204} = .377$$

(In this example, it should be noted that the total number of responses made to OAK was 102, and to PINE was also 102, thus totalling 204 responses. Only 93 of those shown to OAK and 74 to PINE have relevance for computation of Mr. since there were no other responses common to the two stimuli.)

(This example indicates how the assumption that the subject's responses to the stimulus word by first saying the stimulus word contributes to the MR index. If this assumption was not made, the total number of responses common to both stimulus words would be 7, and the MR index would be .034.)

[a] These indices were calculated from the single response free-association norms collected by Marshall and Cofer (1963) from 102 students at Brooklyn College.

[b] Implicit responses.

(Adapted from Marshall and Cofer 1963)

TABLE 3–10

MATRIX USED TO OBTAIN INTER-ITEM ASSOCIATIVE
STRENGTH FOR A LIST OF FOUR WORDS
(ENTRIES ARE PERCENTAGES)

	Stimuli			
	Boy	Girl	Woman	Man
Responses				
Boy	—	64	0	9
Girl	76	—	10	4
Woman	0	5	—	67
Man	6	1	57	—
Total	82	70	67	80

$$\text{IIAS} = \frac{82\% + 70\% + 67\% = 80\%}{4} = 74.75\%$$

number of columns and this provides the inter-item associative strength for the group of words.

Table 3–10 provides an example of IIAS computation.

4. TAXONOMIC INDEX

This measure, based on restricted association frequency, attempts to measure associative strength between a class or a category name and specific instances of that class or category. Two procedures for obtaining this information have been used. Cohen, Bousfield, and Whitmarsh (1957) provided subjects with a category name (forty-three category names were provided in all) and then had them list the first four instances of that category that came to mind. A second method, recently used by Battig and Montague (1969), was to read the name of the category and then give subjects thirty seconds in which to write down as many items as they could to be included in that category. Regardless of method, the frequency of occurrence of each response to each category name is summed across subjects, so that a frequency distribution is obtained for each category. An example of this index, obtained from norms provided by Battig and Montague, is provided in Table 3–11.

TABLE 3–11

TOTAL FREQUENCY OF OCCURRENCE OF RESPONSES
GIVEN TO THE CATEGORY "FRUIT"

16. A FRUIT

Response	Frequency	Response	Frequency
1. apple	429	17. watermelon	47
2. orange	390	18. prunes	44
3. pear	326	19. cantalope	31
4. banana	283	20. raspberry	28
5. peach	249	21. pomegranate	23
6. grape	247	22. blueberry	21
7. cherry	183	23. mango	18
8. plum	167	24. avocado	17
9. grapefruit	154	25. fig	16
10. lemon	134	26. raisin	16
11. tangerine	110	27. coconut	12
12. apricot	102	28. nectarine	12
13. pineapple	98	29. berry	11
14. lime	69	30. melon	11
15. tomato	63	31. kumquat	10
16. strawberry	58		

NINE—blackberry, date.
EIGHT—papaya.
FOUR—honeydew.
THREE—olive, persimmon.
TWO—nut, papaw.
ONE—black raspberry, bowl, boysenberry, breadfruit, carpel,
    citrus, core, cranberry, criminal, escarole, food, gooseberry,
    gourd, guava, hard, homosexual, muskmelon, nectar, onion,
    parish, passion fruit, passion melon, people, pickle, pump-
    kin, seed, soft, squash, sunflower seed, sunshine, tangelo,
    vitamins C and D, wrestler.

Note: The sample included 442 subjects. Subjects were permitted to write down as many responses as they could within
a thirty-second period.
(Adapted from Battig and Montague 1969)

If it is desired to express the relatedness of a specific item R_1
to the general category as a percentage, the total number of subjects responding to that category name is divided into the number

of R_1 responses. The norms provided by Battig and Montague (1969), covering fifty-six categories, will undoubtedly be of considerable use to those experimenters who desire to use this measure of word relatedness.

SUMMARY

A variety of attributes or characteristics of single verbal items have been examined. Glaze's (1928) determination of the association value of CVC trigrams was one of the early and classic studies in this area. Noble's (1952) measure of meaningfulness (m), determined by the average number of continued written associations to a specific item over a specified interval of time (frequently thirty or sixty seconds), is perhaps the most frequently used association index at the present time. Other measures that have been used and appear to be related to association value have been objective frequency, familiarity or subjective frequency, and pronunciability.

Another set of measures appears to be related to the ease with which a word can arouse an image. These include measures of imagery, concreteness, vividness, and specificity. Finally, the affective state or emotionality that a verbal item generates in the subject as well as its orthographic distinctiveness represent two other verbal item attributes that have been measured.

Inasmuch as many studies have indicated reasonably high correlations among many of these measures, factor analytic studies have been conducted in an effort to reduce the number of word attributes to clearly independent measures. One such study by Frincke (1968) indicates that most measures reflect one of the following two factors: (1) meaningfulness-familiarity, or (2) concreteness-imagery.

Another area of investigation of the single verbal item has been to obtain measures of word relatedness. A variety of such measures have been developed; four of these were discussed, namely, (1) frequency of association, (2) mutual relatedness, (3) inter-item associative strength, and (4) taxonomic index.

4 The Characteristics of Isolated Verbal Material Related to Learning

It will be recalled that in Chapter 3, we discussed the identification and measurement of a variety of attributes of verbal material. A number of experimental investigations suggest that many of these variables contribute significantly to learning, and in this chapter we should like to examine some of these studies in detail.

ASSOCIATION AND FAMILIARITY MEASURES

SERIAL LEARNING

In an early unpublished study, Melton (1929) reported an inverse relationship between association value of CVCs as measured by Glaze (1928) and difficulty of serial learning.[1] Most subsequent studies that examined the serial learning situation have confirmed this finding.

Experiments by Underwood and Richardson (1956), and Sarason (1957) illustrate the general findings obtained. In the Underwood-Richardson study, two serial lists of ten CVCs per list were constructed. One of the lists consisted of items falling in the 93 percent to 100 percent range of Glaze association values, while the items comprising the other list fell between the 0 to 20 percent as-

[1] Although their results are not directly related to the manipulation of association value, the early published studies of Davis (1930) and Sauer (1930) are supportive of this finding. Both of these investigators demonstrated that serial learning of words was significantly easier than serial learning of nonsense syllables.

84

sociation range. Different groups of students learned each list to a criterion of one perfect trial. The authors found that the list made up of items of high association value required significantly fewer trials to learn (19.27 trials) than the list consisting of low association value CVCs (29.18 trials). Sarason (1957), using longer lists of CVCs (seventeen items per list) and three levels of association value (27 percent, 53 percent, and 80 percent), also found that high association CVCs were significantly easier to learn than lists made up of CVCs consisting of either middle or low association value.

When association value is defined in terms of Noble's m, the findings obtained by a number of experimenters are in accord with those just reported. Representative of this group of studies is one by Noble (1952a), who made up three twelve-item serial lists using his scaled material. The items on the first list had a mean m value of 1.28 (low m), the second list had a mean value of 4.42 (medium m), while the third list had a mean value of 7.85 (high m). Serial anticipation learning was employed using a two-second presentation rate, with all subjects learning to a criterion of one perfect trial. One group of subjects, however, was given a two-minute rest pause during which they were asked to name colors, after reaching a subcriterion of seven correct; the other group was not provided with this interval. Significant differences among groups, as can be noted from Fig. 4–1, were obtained as a function of m level. The subsequent studies of Dowling and Braun (1957), Braun and Heymann (1958), Sarason (1958), Schulz and Kasschau (1966), and Gladis and Abbey (1969), as well as many others, have demonstrated serial learning to be a function of Noble's m level.

As noted in Chapter 3, although the correlation between association value as measured by Noble's production (m) or rating (m') method, and as measured by Glaze (1928) is high, this relationship appears to be sigmoidal in form; thus, it is possible that a certain range of m or m' values may be selected which differ in m value, while the Glaze or a values are approximately equal. Noble, Showell and Jones (1966) have recently examined the contribution of m' on serial learning, when association value was held constant.

Two studies were conducted in which in the first experiment, five lists of ten CVCs were constructed. The mean m' values for each of

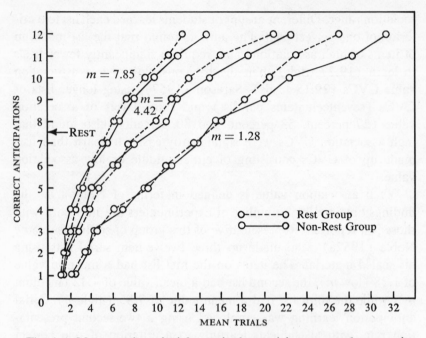

Fig. 4–1. Mean number of trials required to anticipate correctly successive numbers of items with and without a two-minute rest pause of color-naming introduced after reaching the criterion of 7/12 correct. The m parameters denote average meaningfulness of twelve-item lists.

(Adapted from Noble 1952a)

the lists were as follows: 3.31, 3.59, 3.84, 4.09 and 4.37. The mean association a value was 1.00 for all lists. Standard serial anticipation procedures were used, and twenty trials were given to all subjects. In the second experiment, three lists of ten CVCs were constructed with mean m' values of 2.33, 2.79, and 3.36, and the mean association value for all lists .997. The findings from both experiments revealed that ease of learning was a function of m' value. Inasmuch as the mean association value of all lists in each experiment was held constant, the authors have concluded that Glaze's (1928) values cannot be used in lieu of scaled meaningfulness (m') to forecast the learnability of CVCs within this range.

Familiarity appears to contribute to serial learning in much the same way as does association value and meaningfulness. In an early study by Hovland and Kurtz (1952), three different lengths of lists consisting of six, twelve, or twenty-four CVCs were learned under familiarization as well as nonfamiliarization or control conditions. In this study, familiarity was manipulated by presenting a set of items to subjects, one CVC at a time, and changing the order for each run through the set. Familiarization packs were constructed by printing the CVCs individually on 3″ x 5″ cards. Three such packs were constructed in which a dash was substituted for one of the three letters of each syllable. Each letter of a given CVC was omitted in one of the three packs. Familiarization training was continued until the subject responded correctly on all syllables in a single test trial. Following such training, the serial learning task was presented with each item exposed for two seconds. The serial anticipation procedure was used; the criterion was two successive perfect recitations. Table 4–1 indicates the mean number of repetitions required to learn the varying lengths of lists under familiarization and control conditions, while Fig. 4–2 plots the data when the criterion was one perfect trial. In general, then, the effect of prior familiarization with the syllables was to reduce the number of trials to mastery by a moderately constant amount for all lengths of lists. In the case of the shortest list, this amounted to a reduction of approximately half the number of trials required by the ordinary procedure, while with the longer list it amounted to a much smaller proportion.

TABLE 4–1

MEAN REPETITIONS REQUIRED TO LEARN
VARYING LENGTHS OF LIST UNDER
FAMILIARIZATION AND
NO-FAMILIARIZATION
CONDITIONS

Length of List	To 1 Perfect Trial		To 2 Suc. Perfect Trials	
	Famil.	No-Famil.	Famil.	No-Famil.
6	2.2	4.1	3.6	5.9
12	11.4	15.9	14.2	19.5
24	30.2	33.0	38.7	45.9

(Adapted from Hovland and Kurtz 1952)

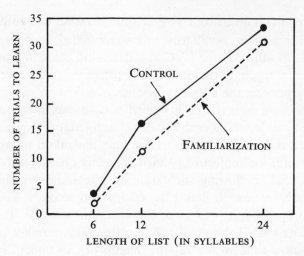

Fig. 4–2. The number of trials to learn to a criterion of one perfect recitation as a function of the length of list under familiarization and control procedures.

(Adapted from Hovland and Kurtz 1952)

Riley and Phillips (1959) obtained findings supporting the Hovland and Kurtz (1952) results. The familiarization training provided by Riley and Phillips was basically similar to that used by Hovland and Kurtz. That is, subjects were required to spell out all three letters of the CVC that was to be used in the learning task, after seeing either the first two or the last two letters. The experimental material consisted of a twelve-item serial list, and CVCs were used which averaged between 19 percent and 22 percent association value. The material was learned to a criterion of one perfect trial. Results, like those obtained by Hovland and Kurtz, indicated the superiority of the group that received the familiarization training.[1]

Noble's (1954, 1955) procedure for providing familiarization training was different from that used by Hovland and Kurtz (1952), and Riley and Phillips (1959). In one of Noble's studies (1955), fifteen items were chosen from the low extremes of his meaningfulness (*m*) and familiarity (f) scales (Noble 1952, 1953). These items had average *m* and f scale values of 1.27 and

[1] It should be recognized that neither Hovland and Kurtz (1952) nor Riley and Phillips (1959) used a group presented with irrelevant CVCs, which would have controlled for warm-up effects.

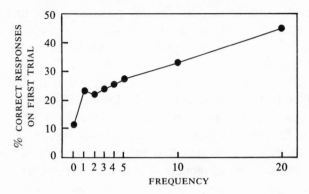

Fig. 4–3. Percentage of correct responses on trial 1 as a function of prior frequency of experience.
(Adapted from Noble 1955)

.44 respectively. Six of these items were selected at random and familiarization training was provided. This training procedure consisted of presenting each item visually (slide projector) and requiring the subject to pronounce the item aloud. The critical items were presented either zero, one, two, three, four, five, ten, or twenty times. Filler items were used so that all subjects had a total of 144 exposures. Following the familiarization training the six items were made into a serial list and were learned to a criterion of two successive perfect trials. Items with different amounts of manipulated frequency occurred equally often at each serial position in the list. Results can be noted in Fig. 4–3, which indicates the percentage of correct responses on the first trial as a function of prior frequency of experience or familiarization.

FREE-RECALL LEARNING

Association value has been also demonstrated to play an important role in free-recall learning. Using the single trial, free-recall learning situation, McGeoch (1930) was interested in examining the contribution of Glaze association values to learning. In McGeoch's first study, twelve lists of items were constructed; each list consisted of ten items. Thus, two lists each were constructed with items obtained from Glaze association values of either 0, 20, 46, 53, 73, or 100. Thirty-six subjects learned one list from each association value level. The general procedure was to have each subject study the list for a two-minute period, which was then followed by a two-minute recall period. Order of list presentation differed among subjects so that the practice effects were equally distributed over all lists. In a second study, thirty-one of the same thirty-six subjects learned another list from each association value, but in this case, the subjects were permitted just one minute to study the list prior to their two-minute recall period. The findings from both studies indicated that the mean number of correct responses increases as a function of increases in association value.

PAIRED-ASSOCIATE LEARNING

In contrast to the serial and free-recall learning tasks, the paired-associate learning situation clearly divides the task into stimulus and response items. Early experimenters considered the stimulus and response as a single unit, and it is not surprising that when paired-associate learning situations are utilized in which the stimulus and the response items both reflect the same association value,

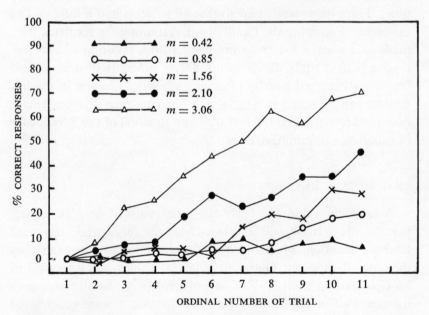

Fig. 4–4. Acquisition curves for single S-R pairs as a function of scaled meaningfulness (*m*).

(Adapted from Noble, Stockwell and Pryer 1957)

the findings should parallel those obtained with serial and free-recall learning.

Studies by Mandler and Huttenlocher (1956), and Noble, Stockwell and Pryer (1957) have demonstrated paired-associate learning to be a function of the meaningfulness of the CVCs used. In the Noble, Stockwell and Pryer (1957) study, for example, a list of 100 CVCs was first scaled for *m'*. Following this, ten pairs of items were selected from this list so that each two pairs of items differed in scaled meaningfulness; the values employed were as follows: .42, .85, 1.56, 2.10, and 3.06. Using a memory drum that presented the pairs at a 3:3 rate, all subjects were given eleven trials. The findings, which can be noted in Fig. 4–4, supported the earlier findings of Mandler and Huttenlocher (1956).

Both Kimble and Dufort (1955), and Noble and McNeely (1957) have extended this general finding to the use of disyllables which had been scaled for *m* in Noble's (1952) early study. The Noble and McNeely (1957) study was a most extensive one, in which eighteen experimental lists were utilized. Ten pairs of items made up each list, and the paired-associates making up any given list had meaningfulness values ranging from .29 to 8.54 in ten approximately equal interval steps. A 3:3 presentation rate was used with subjects who were given twenty trials. The results can be noted in Fig. 4–5, which indicates the difficulty-meaning relationship for the ten groups of paired-associates.

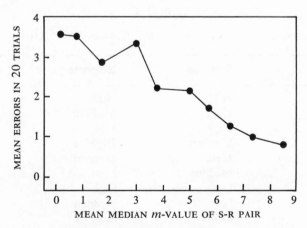

Fig. 4–5. The difficulty-meaning relationship for ten groups of paired associates.

(Adapted from Noble and McNeely 1957)

In the paired-associate learning studies that we have reported, the investigators were primarily interested in relating the verbal material attribute to the stimulus-response item viewed as a unit. Subsequent investigators, however, have been interested in examining the contribution of a given variable to the stimulus and to the response individually. In one of the early studies, Cieutat, Stockwell and Noble (1958) used CVCs and three levels of Noble's (1952) *m*—high, medium, and low—of stimuli and responses (Experiment 2) to make this analysis. Nine different combinations of the *m* values of the stimulus and response syllables were employed; these are indicated in Table 4–2.

Subjects were given twenty trials on one of the experimental lists. Table 4–3 presents the mean performance for each group for each list, and it is apparent that the average difference among groups due to the *m* value of the response is greater than that which can be attributed to the *m* value of the stimulus.

In a second study (Experiment I), Cieutat, Stockwell and Noble (1958) examined four conditions of stimulus and response association value (high-high, high-low, low-high, and low-low); the verbal material used was the disyllables that Noble (1952) had scaled earlier. Eighty subjects, divided into four groups of twenty each, were given twelve trials. The findings, which can be noted in Fig. 4–6, confirm the general position that (1) paired-associate lists with high association value stimuli and high association value re-

TABLE 4–2

VARYING MEANINGFULNESS (*m*) COMBINATIONS UTILIZED

Stimulus	Response
High	High
High	Medium
High	Low
Medium	High
Medium	Medium
Medium	Low
Low	High
Low	Medium
Low	Low

(Adapted from Cieutat, Stockwell and Noble 1958)

TABLE 4–3

MEAN TOTAL CORRECT RESPONSES DURING TRIALS 1–20

Meaningfulness of Stimulus	Meaningfulness of Response			Row Means	Stimulus Difference (High-Low)
	Low	Medium	High		
Low	6.0	16.7	30.5	17.7	
Medium	17.4	31.4	77.5	42.1	23.3
High	21.0	47.2	54.8	41.0	
Column Means	14.8	31.8	54.3		
Response Difference (High-Low)		39.5			

(Adapted from Cieutat, Stockwell and Noble 1958)

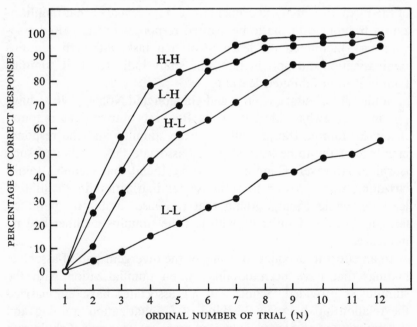

Fig. 4–6. Acquisition curves for lists of ten paired associates as a function of practice (N) in Exp. I. The four S-R combinations of low (L) and high (H) meaningfulness (m) represent the parameter. Each curve contains twenty Ss.

(Adapted from Cieutat, Stockwell and Noble 1958)

sponses are easier to learn than any of the other lists; (2) paired-associate lists with low association value stimuli and low association value responses are most difficult to learn; and (3) the influence of stimulus association value on learning is less than that of response association value. A later study by Kothurkar (1963), which also used items obtained from Noble's (1952) list, obtained findings that confirmed these results. Finally, similar results are obtained when stimulus and response meaningfulness is defined by Glaze's (1928) calibration procedure. L'Abate (1959) formed four conditions of stimulus and response meaningfulness utilizing Glaze's association values, and his findings paralleled those obtained in the previous studies, cited above.

Unlike the contribution of association value, the influence of familiarity on paired-associate learning has provided equivocal findings. Although an early study by Waters (1939) indicated that familiarization training did not contribute to learning, Underwood and Schulz (1960) conducted a study in which the results of two of their experiments (Experiments 1 and 3) revealed that familiarization training with the to-be-learned responses in the paired-associate task facilitated the learning of that task, although stimulus familiarization did not; in fact, one study indicated that stimulus familiarization inhibited learning.

Studies by Cieutat (1960), and Gannon and Noble (1961) have provided somewhat different results. Both sets of investigators found that prior familiarization with both the stimulus and the response members of the to-be-learned paired-associate task facilitated such learning. However, Gannon and Noble found that stimulus familiarization was superior to response familiarization in facilitating learning, while Cieutat found that response familiarity inhibited learning but that familiarity with just the stimulus member had no influence.

In an effort to account for some of the divergent paired-associate findings that have been obtained when familiarization with the stimulus is provided, Schulz and his associates have emphasized the relationship between the kind of familiarization training and the procedures employed in paired-associate learning. Schulz and Tucker (1962, 1962a) hypothesized that when familiarization training requires that the subject pronounce the item as it is presented, and when the subsequent paired-associate task also demands that the subject pronounce the stimulus term (typically this is not done), increasing stimulus familiarization should facilitate paired-associate performance. The reason is that subjects who have been familiarized with the stimulus material are able to pronounce the items very rapidly—the latency of the subject's response grows shorter as the number of familiarization trials increases—and thus, these subjects have a longer effective anticipation interval in the paired-associate task than subjects who were not provided with familiarization training. Since paired-associate learning is directly related to the length of the anticipation interval in the range from 1 to 2½ seconds, the positive influence of stimulus familiarization when the paired-association learning situation requires the subject to articulate the stimulus material is predictable.

On the other hand, the habit of pronouncing the items during familiarization training provides conflict when paired-associate instructions require the subject not to pronounce the stimulus items. Thus, the attempt to inhibit overt articulation of the stimuli during paired-associate learning should decrease the effective length of the anticipation interval, which in turn should make learning more difficult. Finally, if neither familiarization nor paired-associate learning involves articulation of stimulus units, stimulus familiarization should not influence paired-associate performance.

Two studies by Schulz and Tucker (1962, 1962a) have supported this hypothesis. In the first study the investigators provided three amounts of stimulus familiarization training (zero, twenty, or sixty trials), and all subjects were required to pronounce each stimulus unit as it appeared. The material used was disyllabic paralogs, which were chosen from the low end of Noble's (1952) *m* scale. Following familiarization training, seventeen trials on a paired-associate task were provided, in which the familiarized material served as stimuli. One-half of the subjects were required to pronounce each stimulus word during this learning period, but the other half was not. The findings supported the investigators' hypothesis—for the group required to pronounce each stimulus word during paired-associate learning, the mean number of correct responses increased as a function of the number of familiarization trials; for the group not required to pronounce the material, performance decreased as a function of the amount of familiarization. See Fig. 4–7.

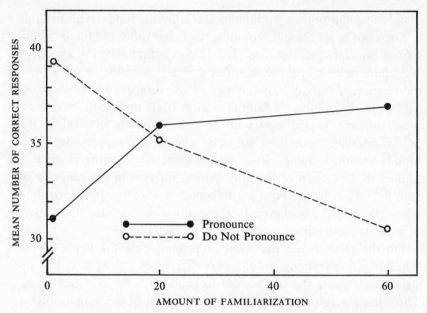

Fig. 4–7. Mean total number of correct responses during seventeen anticipation trials as a function of whether or not the subject was instructed to pronounce the stimulus word and the number of familiarization trials.
(Adapted from Schulz and Tucker 1962)

In the second study, a similar procedure was utilized in which all subjects were required to pronounce the material during stimulus familiarization training. One-half of the subjects were also required to pronounce each stimulus word during paired-associate learning. In this study, the paired-associate learning situation utilized a four-second anticipation interval in contrast to the two seconds used in the previous study (Schulz and Tucker 1962a). According to the experimenters' hypothesis, this long anticipation interval should have eliminated or substantially reduced both the facilitating and inhibiting effects of stimulus familiarization. Again, the findings supported the investigators' hypothesis. Sixty stimulus familiarization trials did not influence the paired-associate performance of either articulating or nonarticulating subjects.

A subsequent study by Schulz and Martin (1964) has further supported the Schulz and Tucker position, as well as providing additional evidence that increases in response familiarity should facilitate paired-associate learning. Subjects were given either thirty trials of relevant-familiarization training, thirty trials of irrelevant-, or zero trials of familiarization training. Trigrams representing four levels of pronunciability were utilized as the experimental material. Familiarization trials consisted of the experimenter's spelling the trigrams while subjects listened silently. A two-minute free-recall trial was given after ten, twenty, and thirty trials of familiarization. On these trials, the subjects spelled as many trigrams as they could remember, while the experimenter recorded their responses. Following such training, subjects learned a paired-associate learning task that consisted of either eight trigram-number pairs (stimulus familiarization condition), or eight number-trigram pairs (response familiarization condition). Fifteen study and test trials were provided, and both types of trials were aurally presented.

The findings revealed that relevant response familiarization resulted in more rapid paired-associate learning than irrelevant response familiarization; on the other hand, there was no difference in learning between the relevant and irrelevant stimulus familiarization groups. It should be noted that in all comparisons, the performancies of groups that were given familiarization training, regardless of whether or not it was relevant, were superior to that of the group for which familiarization training was not provided. Presumably some type of practice effect established during the familiarization training aided the paired-associate learning process.

We have noted that Schulz and Martin (1964) as well as others have found that familiarization of an item facilitates learning when that item serves as a response in the subsequent paired-associate task. A recent study by Kuiken and Schulz (1968) suggests that such facilitation arises from the response availability process. These investigators found that response familiarization trials did not provide any facilitating effect when paired-associate learning was measured using a multiple choice test that presumably eliminated the need for the subject to have the response available.

In summary, although an articulation factor plays a role in determining the contribution of familiarization training, there is some question as to whether or not the diversity of findings noted in this area can be accounted for solely by reference to this variable. Goss and Nodine (1965), Hall (1966), and Jung (1967) have all pointed out that the familiarization paradigm is essentially a transfer situation, in which familiarization training effectively represents task 1, and the subsequent learning situation constitutes task 2. If this analysis is correct, the kinds of interassociations that are formed among the items during familiarization training play an important role in determining whether such training facilitates or inhibits the learning task. Jung (1967), in an excellent review of this area, has concluded that until it is possible to provide some analysis of the characteristics and strengths of the associations that are formed during familiarization training, any attempt to assess the role of familiarity will be most difficult.

OBJECTIVE FREQUENCY

WORD FREQUENCY AND FREE-RECALL LEARNING

Measuring word frequency by the Thorndike-Lorge (1944) word count, and using a multiple trial free-recall learning procedure, Hall (1954) constructed four lists of words, with twenty words on each list. The words selected were seven letters long, and were chosen at random from the Thorndike-Lorge word count. One list consisted of words occurring one per million, the second list 10 per million, the third list 30 per million, and the fourth list 50 to 100 per million. Each list was presented five times, and each word was exposed for five seconds. Following the last presentation, the subjects were given five minutes to list all of the words they could recall. The findings, presented in Table 4–4, reveal a monotonic relationship between word frequency and number of words recalled.

TABLE 4–4

LEARNING AS A FUNCTION OF THORNDIKE-
LORGE WORD FREQUENCY

T-L Frequency Count	Mean Recall
1 per million	12.04
10 per million	13.31
30 per million	15.02
50–100 per million	15.04

(Adapted from Hall 1954)

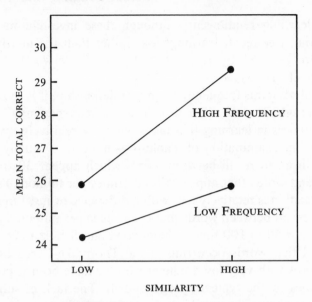

Fig. 4–8. Free learning as a function of conceptual similarity and word frequency.
(Adapted from Underwood, Ekstrand and Keppel 1965)

Underwood, Ekstrand and Keppel (1965), also using the multiple trial free-recall learning situation, have obtained findings supporting the position that word frequency contributes to learning. In one study of a series (Experiment III), lists of twelve high or low frequency words (the lists were also differentiated in terms of being either high or low with regard to conceptual similarity) were used.[1] Three alternate study and recall trials were provided, with each word presented for two seconds during the study trial; a paced recall procedure, also using a two-second rate, was employed. Results are presented in Fig. 4–8; it can be observed that for both high and low conceptual similarity items, the lists consisting of high frequency words were the ones learned most rapidly.

The studies of Bousfield and Cohen (1955), and Bousfield, Cohen and Whitmarsh (1958) have also confirmed the word fre-

---

[1] In this instance, conceptual similarity lists were defined in terms of whether or not the words that made up the list would elicit the same category name. Thus, the high conceptual similarity list consisted of words—i.e., *dog, cat, horse, cow, bear, lion,* etc.—all of which would elicit the word *animal*. Low conceptual similarity lists consisted of words that each would elicit a different category name.

quency-learning relationship, although these investigators used a
single trial, free-recall learning task, rather than the multiple trial
procedure as used by Hall (1954), and Underwood, Ekstrand
and Keppel (1965).

In analyzing this frequency-learning relationship, it is to be noted
that although absolute differences in word frequency may be large,
the differences in learning that takes place are relatively small. For
example, an examination of Table 4–4 indicates virtually no difference in mean recall between words which appear 30 times per
million and words that appear 50–100 times per million. Thus, the
whole function is relatively flat, with a difference of just three words
in mean recall between words that occur once per million and those
which occur 50 to 100 times. Underwood and Schulz (1960) have
suggested that words occurring in the Thorndike-Lorge list, even
those words with very low frequencies, may have been experienced
many times by the typical college student. The lack of substantial
differences among the words used may at least in part account for
the inability of some investigators to confirm the learning-frequency
relationship.[1]

Another possibility is that frequency is not the basic condition
contributing to free-recall learning, but only a frequent concomitant
of another variable. Deese (1960) has presented evidence which
supports the position that inter-item associative strength, rather
than word frequency, is the basic variable. Failures to find a learn-
ing-word frequency relationship may take place when the word lists
used do not reflect the close relationship usually obtained between
word frequency and inter-item associative strength.[2]

FREQUENCY AND PAIRED-ASSOCIATE LEARNING

A number of investigators, i.e., Jacobs (1955), Postman
(1962), Martin (1964), Underwood, Ekstrand and Keppel

[1] For example, Peters (1936) was unable to find a relationship between word
frequency and free-recall learning, although the restricted range of frequencies
he used can undoubtedly account for his negative results. More recently, Dukes
and Bastian (1966), using the multiple trial, free-recall learning situation, found
that low frequency words were learned more rapidly than high. Gorman (1961)
has also obtained findings that indicate that low frequency words are more easily
recalled, as measured by a recognition task, than high frequency words.

[2] The relationship between learning and inter-item associative strength, as well
as other organizational variables, is discussed in Chapter 7.

TABLE 4–5

MEAN NUMBERS OF TRIALS TO CRITERION

R Terms	Stimulus Terms						Over-all Mean
	S_h		S_m		S_l		
	Mean	SD	Mean	SD	Mean	SD	Mean
R_h	10.5	6.3	10.5	40.0	12.1	6.9	11.0
R_m	12.9	6.0	12.2	54.0	15.7	8.8	13.6
R_l	16.2	8.5	11.2	4.0	16.3	6.5	14.6
Over-all Mean	13.2		11.3		14.7		

(Adapted from Postman 1962)

(1965), and Shapiro (1969), all have demonstrated that paired-associate learning is a function of word frequency. As an example of these findings, Postman (1962) constructed nine lists of ten paired-associates per list; the lists represented all possible combinations of high, medium, and low word frequency of stimuli and responses. The words themselves were two-syllable nouns; their frequency was measured by the Lorge magazine count.[1] The anticipation method was used, with learning carried out to a criterion of one perfect trial. Results are presented in Table 4–5. It can be noted that speed of learning increases steadily with increases of word frequency for the responses; speed of learning first increases and then decreases as a function of increases in word frequency of the stimuli. These findings parallel the results obtained when meaningfulness (m) has been varied, in that word frequency makes a greater contribution to the response side than to the stimulus side.

Our discussion has been concerned with word frequency. But what of letter or trigram frequency? Our examination of this area will take us into a consideration of the role of pronunciability as well.

Underwood and Schulz (1960), in their extensive examination

---

[1] The Lorge magazine count is found in the Thorndike-Lorge (1944) listing and represents a word count obtained from magazines that were popular at the time the count was taken. The value of this count is that high frequency words are represented by a numerical value, rather than A or AA.

of meaningfulness, hypothesized that frequency represented a basic dimension of meaningfulness, This position was supported by some of the findings that we reviewed in the previous section, which indicate that learning is related to word frequency. These investigators were interested, however, in examining the contribution of single letter, and of bigram, as well as trigram, frequency to learning. In one experiment (Experiment 9), single letter frequency was determined and two paired-associate tasks were set up in which two-digit numbers were utilized as stimuli while single letters of varying frequency were used as responses. Typical paired-associate procedures were employed, and the material was presented for fifteen anticipation trials at a 2:2 rate. Results indicated that the learning of single letter responses took place as a function of their frequency.

In a second experiment (Experiment 10), a similar procedure was used, except that two-letter responses (bigrams) were employed. Again, two lists were utilized, each consisting of twelve pairs of items. When the mean number of correct responses was tabulated for the fifteen anticipation trials and this was correlated with bigram frequency, the correlation for the twenty-four items was .34. Although this correlation did not differ significantly from zero, the authors did conclude that it was suggestive of a small positive relationship between bigram frequency and learning.

Their next step was to examine learning and trigram frequency as measured by their contiguous method. It was here, however, that their frequency hypothesis broke down, since trigrams of widely different objective frequencies were not learned at different rates. However, the authors frequently found pronunciability to be an excellent predictor of learning. For example in one study (Experiment 11), for thirty-six items obtained from three separately learned lists, the correlation between frequency and mean number of correct responses over fifteen trials was .09. On the other hand, the correlation for pronunciability and mean number correct was .57. In another experiment (Experiment 12), the correlation between pronunciability and correct responses was .76.

As a result, the investigators concluded that

the data . . . point unmistakably toward a conclusion that the frequency with which trigrams occur in words is unrelated to rate of learning these trigrams as responses in paired-associate lists. Apparent positive relationships between frequency and learning were attributed to the relationship between pronunciability and frequency, and when pronunciability was held constant through the use of partial correlations, the "relationship" between frequency and learning disappeared (pp. 188–189).[1]

PRONUNCIABILITY

Underwood and Schulz's (1960) emphasis upon pronunciability as an important variable in learning led some investigators to examine the contribution of this variable in a variety of learning tasks. Thus, Underwood and Postman (1960), using a serial learning task, Schulz and Martin (1964), employing free-recall learning, and DiVesta and Ingersoll (1969), examining paired-associate learning, have all confirmed Underwood and Schulz's (1960) position that pronunciability is related to learning.

To illustrate the nature of these findings, Underwood and Postman (1960), using a serial learning task, constructed two lists of high frequency trigrams (either words or nonwords), and two lists of low frequency trigrams (either words or nonwords). Each list was learned to a criterion of one perfect trial. Inasmuch as all forty-eight items had been rated by subjects on ease of pronunciability, these values were correlated with the total number of correct anticipations for each item during learning. Although the *r* was .28, when the serial position bias was removed, its value increased to .46.[2]

Similarly, Schulz and Martin (1964), in a familiarization study, found that the free recall of a list of eight trigrams was a function of their pronunciability ratings. DiVesta and Ingersoll (1969), who had subjects learn a list of nine pairs of either high or low

---

[1] It must be recognized that Underwood and Schulz (1960) have qualified their position by pointing out that

there are no firm grounds for rejecting the frequency hypothesis in the learning of single letters as responses, highly integrated multiple letter responses, and very poorly-integrated responses; indeed the evidence we have can be interpreted as favorable to the frequency theory. The rather complete breakdown in a theory occurs with multiple-letter units in the broad range between the extremes of well-integrated and poorly-integrated units (p. 280).

[2] We have not discussed as yet the role of serial position on learning; however, it is well known that the position of an item in a serial list, at least in part, determines how rapidly it is learned. Items at the beginning and at the end of the list are learned most rapidly.

pronounceable trigrams, also found that paired-associate learning was related to ease of pronunciability.

A basic problem, however, is that frequently pronunciability is related to other verbal item attributes, so that it is not always clear that this is the critical variable in learning. We shall return to this problem in a subsequent section.

CONCRETENESS

FREE-RECALL AND RECOGNITION LEARNING

Stoke (1929), in an early study, examined free-recall learning as related to three types of words, abstract nouns, concrete nouns, and onomatopes.* Lists of this type of material were constructed and read aloud to three groups of subjects—(1) college students, (2) fifth graders, and (3) sixth graders. Following the presentation, the subjects were asked to write as many words as they could recall. The percentage of the total number of words recalled for the three types of words can be noted in Table 4–6; here it can be seen that concreteness contributes to learning.

A somewhat similar procedure was used by Gorman (1961) in her examination of concreteness, except that recognition was used as the learning measure. In this study, 1,061 nouns were first classified by two judges as to whether they were (1) concrete or (2)

TABLE 4–6

PERCENT OF THE TOTAL NUMBER OF WORDS RECALLED

| | 5th and 6th Grade | | College [1] | |
			Low Coll. Ent.	High Coll. Ent.
Abstract	21.6	24.8	29.0	29.9
Onomatope	31.7	33.8	33.6	34.9
Concrete	46.7	41.2	37.3	35.1

[1] These students were divided into two groups according to high and low college entrance examination scores.

(Adapted from Stoke 1929)

* An onomatope is a word the meaning of which is suggested by its sound.

abstract. Following this classification, 240 items, equally divided between the two classes, were used as the experimental material.[1]

The words were then divided into 8 reading lists of eighteen items per list, and eight corresponding test lists, also consisting of eighteen words per list. On each test list, six words were repeated from the previous reading list while twelve were new words. The general procedure was to have each subject observe each word on the reading list for one second. Following the exposure of the eighteen words that made up the list, the test list was then presented, again with each word observed by the subject for one second. The subject's task was to indicate which of the words on the test list were "old," that is, were previously observed on the reading list. Eight of these reading test presentations were provided in all.

Scores were obtained for each test list by weighting each correct response $+1$, each incorrect response -1, and adding algebraically. Gorman (1961) found that concrete words were significantly more easily recognized than abstract.

PAIRED-ASSOCIATE LEARNING

Studies by Epstein, Rock and Zuckerman (1960), as well as Paivio and his associates have examined the role of concreteness in the learning of paired-associates. Epstein, Rock and Zuckerman hypothesized that concrete nouns would be learned in the paired-associate task more rapidly than other types of verbal material since the subject would find it easier to build these into a unified concept. In a test of this, (1) concrete nouns, (2) abstract nouns, (3) verbs and (4) pictures of concrete nouns were utilized. The materials consisted of two series (A and B) of four lists per series, with each list consisting of six pairs of items. All subjects learned just one series (four lists) of material. The presentation of the varying lists was systematically arranged so that every list followed and preceded every other list an equal number of times. The material used is illustrated in Table 4–7 and Fig. 4–9. Each list was presented for one trial at the rate of one pair of items every five seconds. The subjects read the pairs or gave the name of the de-

[1] It should be mentioned that of the words selected, half of each category was of high and low Thorndike-Lorge (1944) frequency count; however, this is not of primary concern in this section.

TABLE 4–7

MATERIAL USED IN THE PAIRED-ASSOCIATE TASK

Series A	Series B
Concrete Nouns	Pictures
suit—key	suit—key
fish—rug	fish—rug
knee—mask	knee—mask
wood—shirt	wood—shirt
slip—dog	slip—dog
boat—wall	boat—wall
Pictures	Concrete Nouns
house—tree	house—tree
boot—glass	boot—glass
pencil—door	pencil—door
hand—chair	hand—chair
pipe—clock	pipe—clock
book—dog	book—dog
Abstract Nouns	Abstract Nouns
fame—height	death—mood
law—time	mind—greed
truth—grief	luck—norm
peace—fate	pride—age
vice—life	weight—ideal
joy—oath	glee—worth
Verbs	Verbs
sang—walked	bought—hopped
wrote—threw	planned—shook
brings—melts	slept—rang
found—jump	flows—thinks
looks—takes	pour—join
dives—helps	opens—grows

(Adapted from Epstein, Rock and Zuckerman 1960)

Series B

Fig. 4–9. Pairs of pictures used in Series A and B.
(Adapted from Epstein, Rock and Zuckerman 1960)

picted objects aloud under instructions to learn the list in preparation for a test in which they would be asked to supply the missing right-hand item upon presentation of the left-hand item. Following the presentation, the stimuli were rearranged and the test was then given. The number of pairs learned as a function of the type of material presented can be noted in Table 4–8. Pictures, followed by concrete nouns, verbs, and abstract nouns, provided a superior source of material presentation.

Paivio and his associates have also investigated concreteness as a verbal attribute in a series of studies. In one of the earlier studies, Paivio (1963) ran two experiments, the first with grade school children and the second with university students. Both studies employed lists of sixteen adjective-noun or noun-adjective paired-associates. Within each list, eight of the adjectives were paired with concrete nouns and eight with abstract nouns. The general procedure consisted of presenting a single study trial in which the paired-associates were read aloud once. One test trial followed in which the stimulus words were then read aloud at ten-second intervals; subjects were asked to write down the appropriate responses. Stimulus words were presented in a different order from that used in the study trial.

The results of both studies indicated that, regardless of word order, pairs of words that contained concrete nouns were much easier to learn than pairs that contained abstract nouns. This finding can be observed in Table 4–9.

A whole host of subsequent studies have not only confirmed this

TABLE 4–8

NUMBER OF PAIRS LEARNED

	Series A		Series B		Series A & B	
	Number Retained	Mean	Number Retained	Mean	Number Retained	Mean
Pictures	94	3.9	92	3.8	186	3.9
Concrete Nouns	75	3.1	71	3.0	146	3.0
Abstract Nouns	45	1.9	52	2.2	97	2.0
Verbs	55	2.3	56	2.3	111	2.3
N	24		24		48	

(Adapted from Epstein, Rock and Zuckerman 1961)

TABLE 4–9

MEAN NUMBER OF CORRECT RESPONSES TO STIMULI
DURING RECALL TEST AS A FUNCTION OF ADJECTIVE-NOUN
WORD ORDER AND NOUN ABSTRACTNESS

	Noun-Adjective Order	Adjective-Noun Order
Experiment I (N = 136)		
Concrete nouns	5.24	3.92
Abstract nouns	4.06	3.25
Experiment II (N = 120)		
Concrete nouns	5.14	4.10
Abstract nouns	2.51	1.73

(Adapted from Paivio 1963)

finding but also have indicated that concreteness contributes to learning primarily when it is placed on the stimulus side of the paired-associate task. In one such study, Yarmey and Paivio (1965) had subjects learn lists of eight (a) CVC-noun, or (b) noun-CVC paired-associates. Concrete and abstract nouns equated for association value as measured by Noble's *m* were used as stimuli or responses, while high association value CVCs served as the other member of the pair. The varying S-R combinations used were as follows: (1) concrete noun stimuli-CVC responses; (2) abstract noun stimuli-CVC responses; (3) CVC stimuli-concrete noun responses; (4) CVC stimuli-abstract noun responses. The material was learned to a criterion of two successive errorless trials. Results, as measured by the mean number of trials to criterion, are indicated in Table 4–10, from which it can be observed that concrete nouns

TABLE 4–10

MEAN NUMBER TRIALS TO CRITERION

	Stimulus	Response
	Mean	Mean
Concrete	15.6	16.2
Abstract	22.6	15.9

(Adapted from Yarmey and Paivio 1965)

provided superior learning only when they appeared on the stimulus side of the associate; the difference between concrete and abstract nouns was not significant when these were used as responses.

IMAGERY AND VIVIDNESS

In hypothesizing about the processes taking place in the learning of concrete and abstract nouns, Lambert and Paivio (1956) suggested that nouns serving as stimuli in the paired-associate task may act as conceptual "pegs" on which other words may be hung. Moreover, the efficiency of these verbal pegs depends on their capacity to arouse images. It follows that concrete nouns are better able than the abstract variety to produce images and thus promote learning. Imagery was thus conceptualized as an attribute of verbal

TABLE 4–11

EXPERIMENTAL LISTS

High Vividness			Medium Vividness			Low Vividness		
Word	V	M	Word	V	M	Word	V	M
Apron	5.17	4.00	Abode	4.13	4.06	Buyer	2.94	3.93
Balloon	5.63	4.03	Bucket	4.50	3.88	Crisis	2.10	5.23
Bunny	5.23	3.93	Builder	4.00	4.28	Entry	2.08	3.71
Butler	5.79	3.79	Cargo	4.57	4.03	Founder	1.85	3.92
Cabbage	5.32	4.06	Fiber	3.96	3.50	Output	1.50	3.77
Camel	5.79	3.88	Hamlet	4.83	4.03	Patron	2.70	3.50
Chorus	5.63	4.43	Handful	4.36	3.43	Renown	1.33	3.94
Cigar	6.53	4.41	Madame	4.61	4.27	Routine	1.28	4.64
Circus	6.08	4.54	Pebble	4.76	4.15	Rover	2.11	3.30
Comet	5.81	3.96	Porter	4.64	3.79	Rumour	2.20	4.57
Granny	5.00	4.17	Pudding	4.61	4.05	Session	2.86	3.83
Jungle	6.00	4.36	Summit	4.77	4.46	Surplus	1.83	4.43
Lantern	5.43	4.32	Thicket	4.54	3.75	Tariff	1.50	3.61
Rainbow	6.13	4.94	Trainer	4.25	4.19	Topic	1.50	4.03
Runner	5.64	4.61	Veteran	4.07	4.40	Treason	1.50	4.70
Satin	5.42	3.62	Voter	4.32	5.15	Vigour	2.70	4.44
Mean	5.66	4.19	Mean	4.43	4.09	Mean	2.00	4.10

(Adapted from Tulving, McNulty and Ozier 1965)

material (certainly, nouns) and was postulated to make an important contribution to the learning process.

In a recent review of his experimental work, Paivio (1969) wrote that imagery and concreteness "appear largely to be alternative measures of the same variable . . ." (p. 245) and thus can be used interchangeably. As reported in Chapter 3, a sample of 925 nouns on which normative data were available on rated concreteness and rated imagery indicated the correlation between these variables to be .83 (Paivio, Yuille and Madigan 1968); an experimental study by Yuille (1968) also indicated that the effective variable underlying the concreteness effect in paired-associate learning was imagery.

It should be also acknowledged that Tulving, McNulty and Ozier (1965) have been also interested in imagery as a verbal attribute contributing to learning, although in keeping with the earlier work

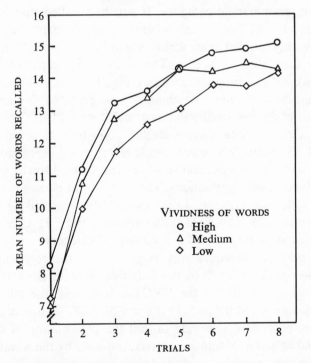

Fig. 4–10. Mean number of words recalled as a function of trials for three lists differing in word vividness.

(Adapted from Tulving, McNulty and Ozier 1965)

of Bowers (1931), and Haagen (1949) they identified this variable as vividness. Tulving et al. constructed three lists (sixteen words per list) that differed in vividness (high, medium, and low) but were equated on meaningfulness. The words used are found in Table 4–11. An eight trial free-recall learning situation was used in which all subjects learned all three lists. On each trial, the material was presented at a rate of one word per second, following which the subject was given sixty seconds to recall as many of the words as possible. Significant differences in recall scores were obtained, and the material rated as most vivid proved the easiest to learn. Fig. 4–10 illustrates these findings.

GRAMMATICAL CATEGORY

We should like to call attention to one final attribute of verbal material, grammatical category. It will be recalled that in the Epstein, Rock and Zuckerman (1960) study, concrete nouns were more readily learned than verbs, which in turn were learned more rapidly than abstract nouns. The noun-verb comparison suggests that perhaps grammatical category might make a contribution to learning; however, few investigators have explored this area.

In one of the few studies in this area, Glanzer (1962) constructed four paired-associate lists, each list consisting of seven English-word–CVC pairs. The seven words on each list represented seven grammatical categories: nouns, adjectives, verbs, adverbs, pronouns, prepositions, and conjunctions. The words were chosen on the basis of the following criteria: (1) they all had Thorndike-Lorge AA frequencies, (2) they were monosyllables, and (3) they could be unambiguously assigned to a grammatical category.

The general procedure was to provide all subjects with twenty successive trials on each of the four lists. Half of the subjects had the words as stimuli and the CVCs as responses; the other half of the subjects learned the pairs in the reverse order. A modified paired-associate procedure was used in that the presentation of each pair consisted of first exposing an asterisk, followed by the stimulus word and then the response word; each item was exposed separately for two seconds.

The mean number of correct anticipations for the word-CVC

and CVC-word paired-associates is indicated in Fig. 4–11. It should be noted that direction of learning was significant with the CVC-word lists eliciting more correct responses than the word-CVC lists. In addition, the effect of grammatical category was significant; nouns and adjectives were learned more rapidly than words in the other grammatical categories. In short, what might be described as content words were learned more readily than function words.

In attempting to account for why function words were at a disadvantage in paired-associate learning, Glanzer (1962) argued that function words are incomplete as units and that in order for them to function efficiently in learning, it is necessary for them to be surrounded by other elements. A second experiment was conducted in which three-term units or triplets served as responses in a paired-associate task. The first and third units were CVCs, while the middle word, which was "framed" by these syllables, belonged to one of

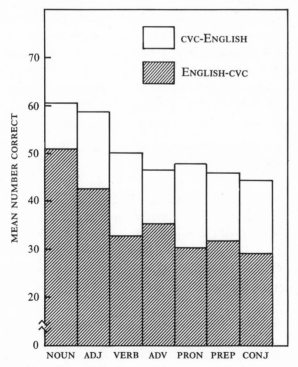

Fig. 4–11. Mean number of correct anticipations for English→CVC and CVC→English paired-associates.

(Adapted from Glanzer 1962)

the grammatical categories previously employed. Results indicated that function words are easier to learn than content words under such circumstances.

Cofer (1967) pointed out that the triplets containing function words used by Glanzer (1962) did not take as long to pronounce as triplets containing content words; moreover, the function word triplets appeared to be easier to pronounce, i.e., compare TAH OF ZUM with TAH CHURCH ZUM. By lengthening the anticipation interval and utilizing shorter content words, Cofer concluded that "the finding that response triplets containing function words are superior in paired-associate learning to triplets containing content words appears to be a rather fragile effect. Manipulating variables designed to afford each kind of unit an opportunity to be spoken more completely has resulted in eliminating the effect statistically" (p. 201).

A recent study by Kanungo (1969) has reaffirmed Glanzer's (1962) findings, demonstrating that content words in contrast to function words are more rapidly learned when they appear as stimuli or responses in a paired-associate task, but are learned less rapidly when framed with CVCs. Why divergent findings are obtained when content or function words are framed with nonsense syllables must await further experimental tests.

INTERRELATIONSHIPS AMONG SOME OF THE VERBAL ATTRIBUTES

In most of the studies we have reviewed, investigators were generally unconcerned with whether a particular verbal attribute they were investigating might be correlated with some other measure. There is an obvious necessity, however, for giving consideration to the relationships among the varying attributes of verbal material, since many of these are highly intercorrelated.

PRONUNCIABILITY, ASSOCIATION VALUE, FREQUENCY, FAMILIARITY AND LEARNING

It will be recalled that Underwood and Schulz (1960), in their extensive examination of the role of frequency in paired-associate learning, concluded that pronunciability was the basic variable which contributed to learning, since they found that when pronunciability was controlled through the use of partial correlations, the relationship between frequency and learning disappeared.

This rejection of frequency and emphasis upon pronunciability stimulated a number of investigators to look at the contribution of pronunciability to learning when other variables have been controlled.

Johnson (1962) was perhaps the first investigator to do this, questioning the Underwood and Schulz (1960) position in terms of how frequency should be measured. Using a *subjective* method of measuring frequency (rather than the contiguous method used by Underwood and Schulz) Johnson reanalyzed some of Underwood and Schulz's data and found that only very small differences in learning could be attributed to pronunciability and that such differences were overshadowed by large differences occurring as a function of frequency. It should be acknowledged, however, that Underwood and Schulz (1960) were aware of the high correlation between learning and subjective frequency, reporting correlations of .69 (Experiment 12) and .68 (Experiment 13) between these two variables.

Lindley and his associates (Lindley 1963; Lindley and Stone 1967), by the judicious selection of items, found it possible to construct lists of trigrams that differed in one variable (pronunciability, association value, or familiarity) but were similar on two others. In the first study, four lists of trigrams, with twelve items per list, were used in a *serial learning task*. The lists were so constructed that by comparing two specific lists, it was possible to assess separately the contribution of one of three variables—pronunciability, association value, or familiarity—to learning. Table 4–12 provides an analysis of the lists that were used, as well as the comparisons made. All lists were presented on a memory drum with items appearing at a two-second rate with a fourteen-second rest period between trials. Lists were learned to a criterion of one perfect recitation or for twenty-five trials, whichever took longer—although subjects were not given a total of more than sixty trials. Lindley found that ease of learning was a function of association value but was not related to either pronunciability or familiarity.

In a subsequent study, Lindley and Stone (1967) extended these findings to the *single trial, free-recall learning situation*. The material used in the previously cited study was employed. Subjects, used as their own control, studied each of the four lists. A study period

TABLE 4–12

CHARACTERISTICS OF THE LISTS USED

List	Association Value	Pronunciability	Familiarity
1	Low	Hard	Unfamiliar
2	Low	Easy	Unfamiliar
3	High	Easy	Familiar
4	High	Easy	Unfamiliar

Note: List 1 vs. 2 examines the contribution of pronunciability.
List 3 vs. 4 examines the contribution of familiarity.
List 2 vs. 4 examines the contribution of association values.

(Adapted from Lindley 1963)

of two minutes per list was provided; following each study period, subjects were permitted two minutes to write down as many of the items as they could recall. Different orders of list presentation as well as different orders of item presentation within the list were used, in order to control for the influence of earlier learning and serial position. Again, findings indicated that learning was primarily related to association value.

In an earlier study, Gibson, Bishop, Schiff and Smith (1964) had also found pronunciability to be inferior to meaningfulness as a predictor of learning in the free-recall learning situation. In this study, the same letters were used to examine both pronunciability and meaningfulness of trigrams—although meaningfulness was of a face validity variety. This was accomplished by using such trigrams as IBM, FBI, or TVA (meaningful) and then rearranging the letters to make an easily pronounceable unit, i.e., BIM, BIF, or TAV. Control trigrams were generated by rearranging the letters still differently, i.e., MBI, IFB, or AVT. Twelve such trigrams comprised the experimental material. Perceptual thresholds were obtained for all trigrams; the trigrams were then presented on filmstrip for three trials. At the end of each trial, subjects were given instructions to recall as many of the items as they could. The free-recall learning curves are provided in Fig. 4–12 and it may be noted that although trigrams that can be pronounced were better recalled than those that made up the control list, the meaningful trigrams were recalled best.

Finally, Braud, Tolin and Holborn (1966), and Hall (1968) were also unable to confirm the importance of pronunciability in the learning of paired-associates. Braud, Tolin and Holborn used as responses the CVCs that Lindley (1963) had employed and which, it will be recalled, differed in pronunciability but were equated with regard to association value and familiarity. The digits 1 through 12 served as stimuli. Four lists of twelve items each were constructed; two contained easy to pronounce CVCs, and two contained CVCs that were difficult to pronounce. The lists were learned to a criterion of one perfect trial or for twenty-five trials, whichever took longer. Results revealed that the lists comprised of easy-to-pronounce items were not learned significantly faster than those lists containing items that were difficult to pronounce. In fact, the mean trials to criterion for the two easy lists was 30.6, and for the two difficult lists was 28.7.

Using a somewhat different procedure to control pronunciability,

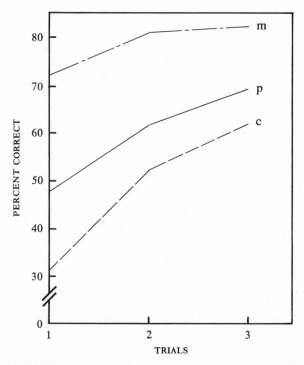

Fig. 4–12. Recall curves for three types of trigrams (meaningful, pronounceable, and control).

(Adapted from Gibson, Bishop, Schiff and Smith 1964)

TABLE 4–13

VARIATION OF WORD FREQUENCY WITH PRONUNCIABILITY HELD CONSTANT

List	Stimulus	Thorndike-Lorge Word Frequency	Response	Thorndike-Lorge Word Frequency
A	Bowl	A	Style	A
B	Bowl	A	Stile	4
C	Bole	1	Style	A
D	Bole	1	Stile	4

(Adapted from Hall 1968)

Hall (1968) held pronunciability constant by using words and their homophones, while the Thorndike-Lorge frequency of these words was varied. The rationale was that if pronunciability was the basic contributor to learning, one should not find differences in learning the pairs of items as a function of frequency. High and low frequency stimulus and response words were used to construct four lists of items, made up of ten pairs each. An example of these can be found in Table 4–13. Here, it can be noted that although each stimulus (and each response) is pronounced the same way, the pairs do vary in word frequency. Typical paired-associate learning procedures were used, with all subjects run to a criterion of two consecutive perfect trials.

The mean number of trials required by each of the four groups to reach the learning criterion was 13.52, 15.24, 18.29, and 24.28 for the H-H, L-H, H-L and L-L lists respectively. Statistical analysis revealed that the differences among groups were significant; these results approximated the findings reported by other investigators (i.e., Cieutat, Stockwell and Noble 1958; L'Abate 1959; Kothurkar 1963) who have manipulated association value or m. In brief, then, word frequency does contribute to learning, even when pronunciability has been controlled.

MEANINGFULNESS (m), FREQUENCY, AND LEARNING

In a continuation of essentially the same approach as we have just described, Saltz (1967), and Saltz and Modigliani (1967) have examined the contribution of Thorndike-Lorge frequency and meaningfulness (m) in the learning paired-associates.

In the first study (Saltz 1967), the influence of these variables was examined when they were manipulated on the stimulus side. Three paired-associate learning experiments were conducted in which m value was held constant and T-L frequency count varied or T-L frequency count was held constant and m value varied. We shall not detail the experimental procedure used other than to point out that common nouns served as responses and subjects were given up to fifteen trials or performance of one errorless trial, whichever occurred first. Using mean number of errors per item, the findings were most unusual in that m and T-L frequency had opposite effects. If m was held constant, increases in T-L frequency resulted in poorer learning; on the other hand, with T-L frequency constant, increased stimulus m resulted in the facilitation of learning. A recent study by Modigliani and Saltz (1969) has confirmed this finding that increases in T-L frequency with m held constant results in increased errors in learning.

In a second study (Saltz and Modigliani 1967) two similar experiments were conducted except that T-L frequency and m were varied on the response side of the paired-associates. Results indicated that with high, constant m levels, increasing T-L frequency resulted in increased learning. Similarly, with constant, high T-L frequency count, increasing m level also facilitated learning. In contrast, with low T-L frequency count held constant, variations in m level were not related to learning; nor did variations in T-L frequency contribute to learning when m level was low.

How can these findings be interpreted? On the response side, inasmuch as both T-L frequency and m operate to produce similar findings, it is possible that both of these variables produce greater response availability or result in easier differentiation among the responses to be learned. Either of these processes would in turn facilitate learning.

It is on the stimulus side, however, that a more complex explanation is needed in order to account for the opposing influences of T-L frequency and m. Saltz (1967) has suggested that "increased T-L frequency of the stimulus item is a factor that produces greater interference with the new response to be acquired" (p. 477). More specifically, by virtue of the fact that a word has been more frequently used, and thus is strongly attached to the responses with which it has been associated, these S-R connections provide more resistance to the establishment of the new S-R relationship demanded by the new learning situation.

On the other hand, the facilitative effect of increased m level on learning is accounted for by the fact that with equal frequency of occurrence, although a stimulus word with a high m has a larger number of associates than one with a low m, the associative strengths between the S and the varying responses are weaker and thus not as likely to produce interference in the learning of the new S-R connection. Table 4–14 attempts to further clarify the relationship between T-L frequency and m and the facilitative and inhibitory effects on learning.

TABLE 4–14

Low T-L Frequency for S_1	High T-L Frequency for S_1
S_1----R_1	S_1----R_1
S_1----R_2	S_1----R_1
	S_1----R_2
	S_1----R_2

In this paradigm, increasing T-L frequency of the stimulus word (m held constant) results in poorer learning. Note that m (number of different responses elicited by S_1) is constant for both high and low frequency stimulus words. However, the greater strength of the S_1----R_1 and S_1----R_2 connections (as indicated by two sets of S_1----R_1, S_1----R_2) has the result that these S-R relationships provide greater interference when the subject has to learn S_1----R_3.

Low m for S_1	High m for S_1
S_1----R_1	S_1----R_1
S_1----R_1	S_1----R_2
S_1----R_2	S_1----R_3
S_1----R_2	S_1----R_4

In this paradigm increasing m (with T-L frequency held constant) results in superior learning. Note that T-L frequency (number in S_1's) is constant for both high and low m groups. However, the low m group's S-R connections are of greater strength, and this provides greater interference when the subject has to learn S_1----R_5.

IMAGERY, MEANINGFULNESS AND LEARNING

At this point, we will pick up our earlier discussion of imagery, since Paivio and his associates have been most interested in examining the relationship of this construct to *m*.

In one of the early studies of the series, Paivio, Yuille, and Smythe (1966) found that when concrete and abstract pairs of items were used, and when these pairs also differed in meaningfulness, high meaningful abstract words were learned more rapidly than low meaningful abstract words; on the other hand, meaningfulness did not contribute to the learning of concrete pairs of items. In contrast to the findings of many of the meaningfulness studies examined earlier, these investigators also found that when meaningfulness did contribute to learning (in the case of the abstract pairs), it was equally effective on both the stimulus and response side of the pair. (It will be recalled that typically, *m* has been found to be more effective when it is varied on the response side of the paired-associate.) This finding was in contrast to the concreteness variable, which appeared to contribute most to learning when it was placed on the stimulus side of the pair.

In a more recent series of studies, and in contrast to the experiment just reported, Paivio (1967) has presented evidence to support the position that when imagery is held constant, *m* does not make any contribution to paired-associate learning. Thus, in the first experiment, examining the learning of paired-associates in which the attributes of meaningfulness and imagery were manipulated, Paivio (1967) reported the correlation between paired-associate learning and stimulus imagery as .54; on the response side, the *r* was .31. The corresponding correlations for stimulus and response meaningfulness (*m*) were .37 and .21. However, in order to determine the relative contributions of imagery and meaningfulness to learning, first-order partial correlations were also computed (I and *m* correlated .69 with the sample of nouns which were used). When *m* was partialled out, the paired-associate learning scores correlated .47 with stimulus imagery and .25 with response imagery. On the other hand, the corresponding partial correlations between paired-associate learning and stimulus *m* and response *m*, with imagery partialled out, were zero.

In two subsequent studies (Smythe and Paivio 1968; Paivio,

Smythe and Yuille 1968), the contribution of meaningfulness and imagery was examined by constructing lists of items in which one of these attributes was left to vary while the other was held constant.

Thus, in one part of the Paivio, Smythe and Yuille (1968) study, two lists of paired-associates were constructed in which, for one list (List I) thirty-two nouns were equated on m; however, sixteen of these were relatively high and the other sixteen low on imagery. The second list (List M) consisted of sixteen high m and sixteen low m nouns; all items were equated on imagery. The nouns that were used appear in Table 4–15 along with the means and standard deviations of I and m scores for the high and low values of each

TABLE 4–15

WORDS USED IN THE TWO PA LISTS

	List I		List M	
	High *I*	Low *I*	High *m*	Low *m*
	ACCORDION	DIFFUSION	ABODE	ABDUCTION
	ACROBAT	DUTY	AFFECTION	BARD
	BOULDER	ECONOMY	CIRCUIT	DERELICT
	BOUQUET	EFFORT	CODE	ENSEMBLE
	CORNER	EMBEZZLEMENT	DRAMA	FATIGUE
	DRESS	IMMUNITY	MALARIA	HENCHMAN
	GENTLEMAN	INTEREST	MILEAGE	HIERARCHY
	GOBLET	MIND	MOLECULE	INSTITUTE
	HONEYCOMB	MIRACLE	PANIC	INTERVIEW
	HOTEL	NECESSITY	POETRY	JEALOUSY
	JUGGLER	PERCEPTION	POLLUTION	LABYRINTH
	LARK	PERJURY	PROSECUTOR	LETTERHEAD
	LETTER	PROMOTION	THEOLOGIAN	MONTH
	MACHINE	QUALITY	TRACTION	NEPHEW
	MONK	SATIRE	VISION	RESIDUE
	PIANIST	SPIRIT	WHALEBONE	ROSIN
I mean	6.36	3.25	4.80	4.77
SD	.22	.14	.24	.25
m mean	5.83	5.71	6.62	4.56
SD	.10	.14	.30	.33
T-L mean	41.63	42.25	14.19	14.25
SD	42.05	41.59	13.53	23.85

(Adapted from Paivio, Smythe and Yuille 1968)

list. (It should also be pointed out that Thorndike-Lorge mean frequencies, which were held relatively constant within each list, are also indicated.) In the two lists, the critical attribute (either I or *m*) was varied factorially on the stimulus as well as the response side of the pairs. Thus, each list contained pairs of items that were (1) high-high, (2) high-low, (3) low-high, and (4) low-low.

According to the general procedure followed, each group of subjects received four alternating study-recall trials, with presentation by a slide projector at a two-second rate for the pairs on study trials. An eight-second rate of presentation for stimuli on recall trials provided time for subjects to write out their responses.

The mean total recall for the four trials as a function of both high and low imagery and high and low meaningfulness is indicated in Fig. 4–13. For List I, with meaningfulness controlled, statistical

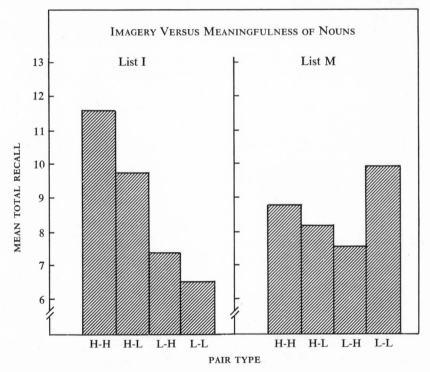

Fig. 4–13. Mean total recall over four trials as a function of high (H) and low (L) values of the stimulus and response attributes of pairs in three PA lists.

(Adapted from Paivio, Smythe and Yuille 1968)

analysis revealed a highly significant effect of stimulus imagery, and a smaller but also significant effect of response imagery. On the other hand, statistical analysis of List M yielded only a significant negative main effect of response *m*. That is, low *m*-low *m* pairs were learned significantly better than either high *m*-low *m* or low *m*-high *m* pairs.

In a subsequent study, Paivio, Yuille and Rogers (1969) have examined the influence of imagery and meaningfulness in free recall as well as serial learning situations. In their first experiment, two twenty-four item lists were constructed, in which one list was comprised of twelve high imagery and twelve low imagery nouns; the mean *m* value was the same in both lists. The second list included twelve high meaningful and twelve low meaningful items; mean imagery value was the same in both lists. Four study-test trials were provided. The results are indicated in Fig. 4–14, where it may be noted that recall is generally better for high levels of either variable, although the difference is greater in the case of imagery. A second experiment, in which four homogeneous lists were used to investigate the influence of these variables, was conducted, and the results confirmed those obtained in Experiment 1.

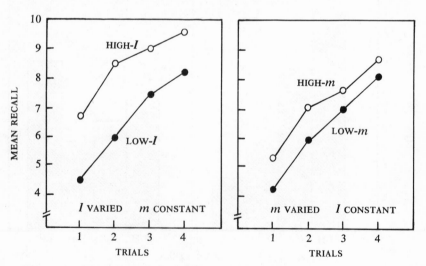

Fig. 4–14. Mean free-recall scores over trials for high and low levels of *I* and *m* in Exp. I.

(Adapted from Paivio, Yuille and Rogers 1969)

Experiment 3 of the series compared the effects of imagery and *m* in serial recall. The four lists used in Experiment 2 were employed and a similar procedure was followed, except that the items of each list were presented in a fixed serial order for five trials, and the subjects were told to write down their responses in the order in which they had been presented. Experiment 4 was similar to Experiment 3 except that somewhat greater control was exercised in instructing subjects to recall the items in order, beginning with the first item; moreover, forward recall was further insured by having the subjects write their responses for a given trial, one response per page, in a twelve-page booklet.

The findings obtained from Experiments 3 and 4 are presented in Fig. 4–15; again the results indicate the superiority of imagery in this type of learning situation.

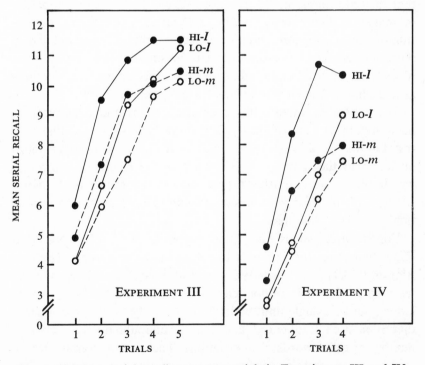

Fig. 4–15. Mean serial recall scores over trials in Experiments III and IV. (Adapted from Paivio, Yuille and Rogers 1969)

CONCLUSIONS

At the present time, there is no widely accepted theory that is able to "explain" how the variety of verbal attributes discussed in this chapter relate to each other, or how they contribute to learning.

One tentative approach in attempting to answer these questions has been proposed by Paivio (1969), who hypothesized the operation of two processes: (1) nonverbal imagery and (2) verbal symbolic processes. Imagery is assumed to be related to the concreteness (or undoubtedly vividness) or image-evoking value of a verbal item, while verbal processes are presumably independent of concreteness but linked to associative measures, i.e., association value, meaningfulness, etc.

Both of these processes function as associative mediators or memory codes in facilitating learning; however, Paivio points out that they are differentially available. Thus, the mediating function of imagery is theoretically coordinate to an abstract-concrete dimension of stimulus meaning that is defined in terms of the directness of sensory reference. The more concrete the stimulus item is, the more likely it is that the stimulus will evoke a sensory image that functions as a mediator, and thus influence learning and memory.

Much greater interest has been aroused by the constructs of meaningfulness and familiarity, and it has been suggested that as a result of the operation of these variables the response becomes more available to the individual. But what is the mechanism through which this is accomplished? One suggestion, found in Mandler (1954), is that these variables contribute to integration or "unitization" of a stimulus item.

For example, let us take three trigrams, i.e., CAT, KNO, and RZQ, that make up part of a list of items to be learned. The first trigram, CAT, is a word. We would also say that this item is integrated in that it is responded to not as a collection of separate letters, but as a single unit, which in turn can be easily pronounced; that it is used frequently; and that it undoubtedly can elicit a number of other words or associations. The second trigram, KNO, is not a word, and so lacks integration on this score. At the same time, however, it can be easily pronounced, is observed as a part of a number of other words that are used frequently (i.e., *know, knowledge,* etc.), and undoubtedly would arouse a number of associations. In short, response integration of KNO would be poorer than that of CAT, but would be better than that of the third trigram, RZQ, which is difficult to pronounce, is seen rarely if at all, and undoubtedly would elicit very few associates.

Our analysis suggests, then, that integration or the unitizing of verbal material is undoubtedly related to the subject's recognition of the item as a word (or not a word), to the frequency with which the item is experienced, to the ability of the subject to pronounce the item, and also to the number of associations that the item elicits. The basic point we would make is that the integration process is multi-faceted—in that a number of variables contribute to the integration or unitization of a verbal item, and at least partial integration can be achieved through the operation of some of these variables.

But in serial learning as well as in the paired-associate task, the integration or response availability process represents just one stage of learning. A second stage is concerned with an ordering process in the case of serial learning, or with an associative phase in the learning of paired-associates. Much of the experimental evidence indicates that the meaningfulness-familiarity attributes contribute to these types of learning situations, although it is not clear how they influence the ordering and associative stages, if indeed they do.

There has been the hypothesis that the reason why high *m* responses contribute to the learning of paired-associates is that the probability is higher that one of these associates may be more likely to elicit a response that serves as a mediator, thus hastening the learning of the associative or ordering stage. Underwood and Schulz (1960) have termed this an associative probability hypothesis, while Glanzer (1962) has given it the name of a grapnel hypothesis. But this explanation has a number of difficulties. A primary one is that the more associations a given unit may have, the greater the possibility that these previously established relationships may interfere with the learning of the new task.

Martin (1968) has recently provided a different explanation as to how stimulus meaningfulness contributes to paired-associate learning. According to Martin, in the paired-associate task the subject makes a perceptual response to the stimulus when it is presented, and this is followed by a functional encoding of the nominal stimulus. Attached to s is the overt response, R. The encoding and associative phases can then be diagrammed as follows:

$$S\text{----}r\text{-}s\text{----}R$$

Martin's major thesis is that with low meaningful material, the possibility exists that such material will produce many more possible encodings by the subject; thus, the relationship between the characteristics of the stimulus material and the number of encodings can be diagrammed as follows:

Thus, whereas S_H can be observed to have only one functional encoding, S_L is seen to have three, only one of which will be assumed to occur on any single trial. We can note, then, the central thesis of Martin's position is that as stimulus meaningfulness varies, there occurs, inversely with meaningfulness, a simultaneous variation in the number of perceptual encoding responses that can be made to those stimuli.

In analyzing the role of familiarity, Martin (1968) has concluded that training does not change the nature of the r-s encodings in such a way as to provide better associative learning. Thus, he states that the characteristics of the encoding are not changed (by familiarization training), "at least not in a way that changes the availability of one alternative encoding relative to another for purposes of incorporation into an overt-response-producing association" (p. 423). Support for such a position is found in the earlier cited study by Schulz and Martin (1964), who showed that thirty stimulus familiarization trials have the same effect on subsequent paired-associate learning, at all levels of stimulus *m*, as do thirty trials of familiarization on trigrams that do not become stimuli in the subsequent paired-associate task.

SUMMARY

Our basic task in this chapter has been to examine how a variety of verbal material attributes influence learning. One area of research has centered on associative indices, so that association value, meaningfulness, objective frequency, familiarity and pronunciability all have been investigated. Considerable evidence has accumulated to support the position that virtually all of these variables facilitate learning regardless of whether the task is of a serial, free-recall, or paired-associate variety. With this latter task, when the stimulus and response items are individually examined, associative strength on the response side appears to make a greater contribution to learning than when such strength is on the stimulus side.

A second area of research has centered in the capacity of a verbal item to arouse an image. The terms "concreteness" or "vividness" have also been used to describe this attribute. These variables also make a contribution to learning, although in contrast to associative indices they appear to have greater influence when they are placed on the stimulus side of the paired-associate, rather than on the response side.

When imagery is contrasted with an associative index such as meaningfulness, in order to determine the relative contribution of each of these attributes to learning, most of the evidence appears to indicate that imagery is the more potent of the two.

5 Similarity and Isolation Effects

The task variable that has generated the greatest amount of experimental work has been the characteristics of the material used— a variable discussed in earlier chapters. The similarity of the material to be learned, as well as its isolation, represent two other conditions that have aroused considerable interest among experimenters. We will turn now to an examination of these.

SIMILARITY

The basic question that must be raised first is how similarity should be defined.[1] Wallach (1958) has provided a number of definitions of similarity; two of these appear particularly relevant for our discussion. The first, derived from Hume (1939), defines

---

[1] In any discussion of similarity, we should be aware of Mandler's (1968) concern about the use of the concept. He points out that

even brief reflection makes it quite clear that "similarity" is not a dimension but must always refer to some other dimension as well. For example, any two words are "similar" to each other in their printed form, in terms of simple light-dark discriminations. Certainly, the word "table" and the word "propinquity" are more similar to each other, as physical stimuli, than either one of them is to a horse. However, most of us would say that "table" and "propinquity" are not similar; that they are not similar in respect to some particular dimension, which usually remains unspecified. Typically, statements about similarity should add the statement "similarity in respect to. . . ." It is what similarity is *about* that is important in discussing the problem of similarity (p. 110).

similarity in terms of common environmental properties, or what has been frequently designated as formal similarity. Stimulus objects or responses that have a large number of common and usually formal environmental properties are judged to be more similar to one another than items that have few such properties in common. Thus, the CVC, RIV, is more similar to RIX than it is to QEW.

Experimenters are now beginning to realize that the number of identical letters in so-called similar trigrams represents only one dimension of formal similarity. A second concern is the position of the identical letters. Runquist and Joinson (1968), and Runquist (1968a) have provided measurements of the rated similarity of CVC trigrams as related to a variety of combinations of letter-position identities. To illustrate the role of position, these authors have found that the identity of the first letter in the trigram was found to be more important in determining rated similarity than identity of either the second or third letter.

One basic advantage of defining similarity in this way is that the experimenter is able to define the concept independently of his experiment. That is, the similarity of material is first determined by reference to this criterion; experiments may then be performed to determine the contribution of similarity to learning.

The difficulty, however, is that in many situations the experimenter is interested in what might be described as semantic similarity; the use of a formal similarity criterion under such circumstances would be of little value. It would be more likely for an individual to perceive *vase* and *urn* as more similar than *vase* and *base,* although in terms of common environmental properties (letters) the latter two words are more similar. Underwood, Ekstrand and Keppel (1965), and Underwood (1966) have used the term "meaningful similarity" to describe this dimension.

A third type of similarity is conceptual similarity (Underwood, Ekstrand and Keppel 1965; Underwood 1966). This refers to the extent to which items represent instances of the same class or category. As an example, in a study conducted by Ekstrand and Underwood (1963), high conceptual similarity was provided by making up a list consisting of the names of twelve nations; the investigators' low similarity list consisted of twelve unrelated words.

Finally, the last type of similarity we will consider is associative similarity, defined in terms of the number of subjects who produce a given response to a stimulus word in a word-association test. To illustrate, in an experiment by Schwenn and Underwood (1968) lists were constructed consisting of eight associated pairs per list. A low associative similarity list involved pairs of words in which between 100 and 200 subjects out of 1,000 tested gave the same primary response. An example of one such pair found on this list would be *music-sound,* in which the word *sound* was given by 161 subjects in response to the stimulus word *music.* A list involving slightly greater associative similarity consisted of pairs of words in which between 200 and 300 subjects out of the 1,000 tested gave the same primary response.

In summary, it may be noted that formal, meaningful, and conceptual similarity have been used in verbal learning studies most frequently, while associative similarity has been employed only sparingly. Results from a study of Runquist (1968) that examined formal, meaningful, and associative similarity suggested that any generalization concerning the influence of stimulus similarity on learning, without reference to the type of similarity manipulated, should be made with caution.

A second general approach, proposed by Wallach (1958), is to define similar stimuli as those that produce common responses. If a subject responds in the same way to two stimuli, although those stimuli may be objectively different, they would be classified as similar. On the other hand, if the subject responds differently to stimuli despite the environmental properties that the stimuli have in common, no such similarity would be inferred. The basic problem, of course, is that this type of definition is circular since there is no way to judge similarity independently of the response that the experimenter is attempting to predict. It might be possible, following the lead of Meehl (1950), who wrote of trans-situational reinforcers, to have trans-situational similarity. Here, one experiment would be used to define similarity in terms of the responses that were obtained. Following the calibration of the varying stimuli in terms of the kinds of responses that were obtained, a second experiment could be run.

SERIAL LEARNING

A number of investigators, i.e., Underwood (1952), Underwood and Richardson (1956), and Underwood and Schulz (1959), have found that the learning of a serial list grows more difficult as the formal similarity of the material increases. To illustrate, in the Underwood and Richardson study, four lists of CVCs were constructed. Two lists were made up of syllables with Glaze association values of 93.3 to 100 percent. The other two lists used syllables with association values of zero to 20 percent. One of the two lists at each level of association value had high intralist similarity (defined as the number of letters that the varying CVCs had in common), whereas the other had low similarity. One hundred subjects learned each list to a criterion of one perfect trial. The authors found that learning was an inverse function of the amount of intralist similarity; the difference in learning between high and low intralist similarity was much greater for lists containing the low association syllables. These findings were confirmed in a study by Underwood and Schulz (1959), who constructed four lists of low association CVCs in which intralist similarity increased from list 1 through list 4. Table 5–1 illustrates the material used in each list. In addition, these investigators were interested in determining whether massed (two-second intertrial interval) or distributed practice (seventeen-second intertrial interval) interacted with the similarity variable. Forty learning trials per list were presented, and sixty subjects learned each list. As Fig. 5–1 indicates, learning was found to be an inverse function of intralist similarity, and the

TABLE 5–1

LISTS OF CVCs USED

List 1	List 2	List 3	List 4
CEF	SIW	GOK	XAZ
DAX	QAS	GUW	ZAX
GAH	QUW	GYK	XEY
MEQ	KOJ	KIG	YOZ
SIJ	BEJ	KEZ	ZUY
TOV	YAB	WUG	YUZ
NUB	YOV	WEZ	XIY
YIL	XEZ	ZIK	ZEY
ZOK	ZIK	ZYW	YIX
WUP	VUX	ZOW	ZOY

(Adapted from Underwood and Schulz 1959)

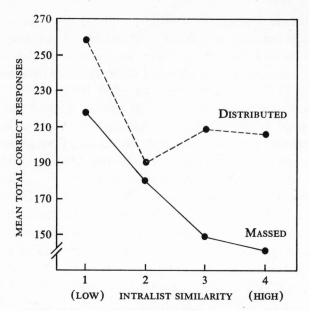

Fig. 5–1. Total correct responses over forty trials as a function of intralist similarity and intertrial interval.
(Adapted from Underwood and Schulz 1959)

massed practice condition provided considerably stronger support for this generalization than the distributed practice condition.

If meaningful similarity is manipulated, with adjectives used as the experimental material, similar findings are obtained. Underwood and Goad (1951) found that the following list of adjectives —*elated, gleeful, carefree, jolly, laughing, happy, pleasant, festive, sunny, blissful, genial, smiling, cheerful,* and *hearty*—was much more difficult to learn than a list of adjectives that did not have this meaningful-synonymity relationship.

FREE-RECALL LEARNING

When formal similarity of the material is manipulated, free-recall findings are controversial, although it is most likely that such learning is impaired by the manipulation of this variable. But let us look at the experimental findings. Horowitz (1961), examining formal similarity, reported findings supporting the position that similarity aids free recall. The material he used consisted of twelve-item lists of trigrams of either high or low similarity. The trigrams in the high similarity list contained only four different letters whereas those in the low similarity list contained twelve. Each list was presented to two groups of secondary school students with one group required to learn the items by the method of free-recall learning, and the other group required to learn the order of the items but not the items themselves. This latter procedure was accomplished by giving the subjects, following each presentation, packets of slips of paper, each sheet of which contained a single trigram. Subjects were instructed to arrange these slips so that the order corresponded to the order in which the original material had been presented. The free-recall procedure was one in which the subjects were instructed to record on answer sheets, in any order, as many of the items as they could recall. Ten presentations of the material were provided, with an ordering or free-recall test following each presentation. Horowitz (1961) found that high intralist similarity facilitated free recall early in the learning although this superiority was lost on later trials. Low intralist similarity, on the other hand, facilitated the learning of the order of the trigrams over all presentations.

Underwood, Ekstrand and Keppel (1964), on the other hand (experiments III and IV), have found that formal similarity hinders free-recall learning. High intralist similarity was constructed by using just five different letters to construct six consonant trigrams, i.e., XQV, XKH, KHQ, VHX, VKQ, HVK. Low similarity items were constructed in which no letters were duplicated, i.e., BQL, FZV, MKC, HSX, RDP, JNW. Presentation rate was two seconds per trigram, while test trials consisted of paced recall; subjects were given two seconds for responding. Ten sets of alternating study and recall trials were provided. In addition, intertrial intervals of either four, fifteen, thirty, forty-five, or sixty seconds were manipulated, and the intertrial interval always occurred after a recall trial.

A comparison of free learning performance over the ten trials for the high and low similarity lists, as indicated in Fig. 5–2, reveals that performance on the low similarity list far exceeded that on the high similarity list—a difference noted on all intertrial intervals, and a finding at variance with that of Horowitz (1961), reported earlier.

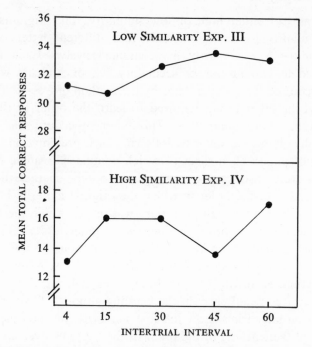

Fig. 5–2. The effect of intertrial interval on free learning with high and low response-term similarity.
(Adapted from Underwood, Ekstrand and Keppel 1964)

Underwood et al. (1964) hypothesized that inasmuch as Horowitz (1961) encouraged his subjects to guess and provided unlimited free-recall time as well, the better performance with the high similarity list might have been due, as Horowitz (1961) also suggested, to the subjects' guessing.[1] Moreover, it was possible for the subjects to discover rules by which some of the trigrams could be generated at recall.

Recent studies by Stimmel and Stimmel (1967, 1968) have also provided some support for the position that formal intralist similarity is negatively related to learning in the free-recall learning situation.

In contrast to the role of formal similarity, a number of investi-

[1] With regard to the paced technique as used by Underwood et al. (1964) versus the unlimited recall time permitted by Horowitz, the study by Underwood et al. (1964), in which sixty-second free-recall periods were provided rather than the pacing method, provided findings that also indicated that the low similarity trigrams were better learned than high.

gators, i.e., Ekstrand and Underwood (1963), Bourne and Parker (1964), Underwood, Ekstrand and Keppel (1965), and Stimmel and Stimmel (1967, 1968) all have shown that free-recall learning may be facilitated when the material to be learned is conceptually similar.

In the Ekstrand and Underwood (1963) study, the low similarity list consisted of twelve unrelated words whereas the high similarity list consisted of the names of twelve countries. The material was presented by a memory drum for three study trials alternated with three test trials. An additional variable was whether the study trials were paced or unpaced. For unpaced recall, subjects were permitted sixty seconds to write down all the words they could remember. The paced recall procedure was as follows: the subject was instructed that he was to recall a single word each time an asterisk appeared in the window of the memory drum but before the next asterisk came into view. Fig. 5–3 presents the mean total of correct responses as a function of type of recall as well as intralist similarity. Both of these variables produced highly significant differences.

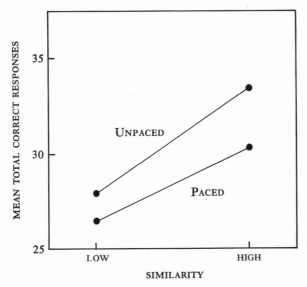

Fig. 5–3. Mean total correct responses as a function of type of recall and intralist similarity.

(Adapted from Ekstrand and Underwood 1963)

TABLE 5–2

LISTS OF WORDS OF HIGH AND LOW CONCEPTUAL
SIMILARITY (HS AND LS) AND HIGH AND
LOW FREQUENCY (HF AND LF)

LS-LF	HS-LF	LS-HF	HS-HF
spleen	camel	captain	dog
possum	possum	cotton	cat
seamen	lynx	leg	horse
lotus	sloth	cow	cow
ottoman	weasel	pistol	bear
calico	chipmunk	sofa	lion
garret	mole	lily	elephant
janitor	gorilla	mansion	rat
hearse	kangaroo	wagon	fox
lance	elk	chimney	rabbit
buttress	muskrat	thunder	tiger
drizzle	moose	engineer	sheep

(Adapted from Underwood, Ekstrand and Keppel 1965)

These findings were confirmed by Underwood, Ekstrand and
Keppel (1965), who used four lists of words: high conceptual similarity, high frequency words; high conceptual similarity, low frequency words; low conceptual similarity, high frequency words; low
conceptual similarity, low frequency words. These are presented in
Table 5–2. Three alternating study and test or recall trials were
presented in which each word was presented at a two-second rate.
A paced procedure was used for recall. Results are indicated in Fig.
5–4.

The demonstration that conceptual similarity of material aids
free-recall learning is an interesting finding, although there is nothing in any of the experimental reports to indicate why this result is
obtained. Wood and Underwood (1967) have suggested at least
two possible explanations for the superior free-recall learning of
conceptually related words. First, the words may tend to elicit each
other directly. For example, in the Underwood, Ekstrand and Keppel (1965) study, it could be that *dog* elicited *cat, cat* elicited *rat,*
etc. A second explanation may be that the words in the list elicit
the same implicit associational responses. How can common im-

plicit associational responses facilitate acquisition? The assumption
that Wood and Underwood (1967) have made is that the common
implicit associational responses produce increased frequency of the
appropriate response via the backward association. The illustration
provided is as follows. Assume that two words, *forest* and *pine*,
occur successively in a list, each eliciting the implicit associational
response *green*. When *pine* is presented, the implicit chain is assumed to be *pine* to *green* to *forest*, with the second association a
backward one. Thus, the response *forest* occurs twice, once when it
is first presented and once when the word *pine* is presented. On
the assumption that the frequency of the response is directly related
to learning, a list in which common implicit associational responses
are elicited should produce faster learning than one in which common implicit associational responses are not elicited. Moreover, it
would follow that in a series of conceptually related words, those
presented first in the series will be better recalled than those presented later, since the first ones will have a greater opportunity of
being elicited by backward associations from the common implicit
associational responses than will the latter ones. In an experiment

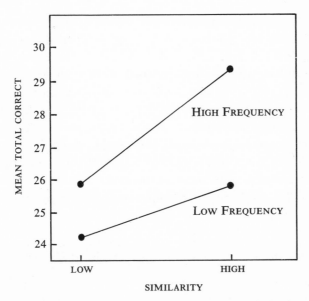

Fig. 5–4. Free learning as a function of conceptual similarity and word
frequency.
(Adapted from Underwood, Ekstrand and Keppel 1965)

designed to examine the role of implicit responses and conceptual similarity, Wood and Underwood (1967) obtained support for this point of view. A subsequent study by Underwood and Freund (1969) has given further support to this general position that conceptual similarity in free-recall learning brings these implicit or rehearsal mechanisms into play.

PAIRED-ASSOCIATE LEARNING [1]

In an early study, Underwood (1951), using lists of paired-adjectives, found that learning was negatively related to the amount of intralist similarity. An examination of the pairs of items that Underwood used in this study reveals that there was no attempt to separate the similarity of the stimulus items from that of the response; in short, the similarity of the stimulus items, of the response terms, and between stimulus and response items was confounded.[2]

Subsequent experimenters, however, have been interested in isolating stimulus similarity effects from those of response similarity; in addition, formal similarity as well as meaningful similarity has been investigated.

Probably the most extensive study of formal similarity was conducted by Goss and Nodine (1965), who conducted a series of experiments (experiments 1, 2, 3, 4, 5, 6, 8 and 10) that investigated the similarity of stimulus and response CVCs under a variety of conditions. In all of these experiments, learning was found to be inversely related to stimulus similarity. Experiment 1 indicates the general procedure of the investigators, as well as providing typical results. In this study, two levels of stimulus similarity were combined with two levels of response similarity; in addition, two levels of association value were also manipulated.[3] The four combinations of high and low similarity of stimulus and response members (high-high, high-low, low-high, low-low), using high association value

[1] Goss and Nodine (1965) have provided an excellent summary of many of the paired-associate learning experiments that have investigated stimulus and response similarity.

[2] An example of the pairs of items used are as follows: *double-soiled; clumsy-twofold; awkward-unclean.*

[3] A third variable that was manipulated, but would merely complicate our presentation without adding anything to the findings, was the occurrence of the presentation of the response member.

CVCs, were combined with four similar combinations of CVCs that had low association values. A mixed list design was used. The anticipation method, employing a 2:2 rate, was employed, and subjects were required to learn the list to a criterion of one perfect trial. The findings are indicated in Table 5–3. These results clearly indicate that learning is related to both stimulus as well as response similarity with material of either high or low association value. A variety of other experimenters have obtained findings in keeping with the conclusion that learning is negatively related to formal stimulus similarity, i.e., Gibson (1942), Underwood (1953), Newman and Buckhout (1962), and Runquist (1968).

It should be noted that an examination of the findings obtained with the *low* association value CVCs in Table 5–3 indicates that response similarity has a greater effect on learning than stimulus similarity. Most experiments, including others in the Goss and Nodine (1965) series, have not provided support for this conclusion. In fact, both Underwood (1953), and Newman and Buckhout (1962) were unable to find that variations in response similarity made any contribution to learning.

TABLE 5–3

MEAN TRIALS TO CRITERION

	Response Similarity		
	Low	High	Mean
High Association Value CVCs			
Stimulus Similarity			
Low	3.8	8.8	6.3
High	12.6	24.2	18.4
Mean	8.2	16.5	
Low Association Value CVCs			
Stimulus Similarity			
Low	12.4	18.0	15.2
High	14.6	28.6	21.6
Mean	13.5	23.3	

(Adapted from Goss and Nodine 1965)

When meaningful similarity is manipulated, the findings are similar to those obtained with formal similarity; that is, they demonstrate that stimulus similarity contributes to poorer learning, while response similarity appears to have no influence. In one such study, Underwood (1953a) conducted six experiments with experimental lists made up of ten pairs of adjectives Each list of items consisted of three groups of words (4-3-3), with synonymity manipulated within each grouping. To illustrate the material used, a high similarity list consisted of: *angry, enraged, pained, wrathful; royal, regal, kingly; double, dual, twofold.* The low similarity list consisted of: *fickle, heedless, fitful, giddy; sickly, bedfast, feeble; complete, perfect, utter.* The various levels of similarity were obtained from a list of adjectives rated for similarity and provided by Haagen (1949). The variations in stimulus and response similarity for the six experiments can be noted in Table 5–4.

In addition to similarity, Underwood (1953a) was also interested in examining the role of four-, thirty-, or sixty-second intertrial intervals. A 2:2 anticipation procedure was used in which learning was carried out to one errorless trial. Findings indicated that variations in response similarity did not influence rate of learning. Variations in stimulus similarity had a complex effect; the medium similarity list proved the most difficult to learn.

A combination of both formal and meaningful similarity material within the same experiment has been investigated by Feldman and

TABLE 5–4

EXPERIMENTS USED IN EXAMINING VARIATIONS
IN STIMULUS AND RESPONSE SIMILARITY

Experi- ment	Stimulus Similarity	Response Similarity
1	low	zero
2	medium	zero
3	high	zero
4	zero	low
5	zero	medium
6	zero	high

(Adapted from Underwood 1953a)

Underwood (1957), and Hawker (1964). In the Feldman and Underwood experiment, seven pairs of items made up each list; CVCs served as stimuli and adjectives as responses. High similarity stimuli were constructed by repeating two consonants four times, while two other consonants were repeated three times, i.e., WEZ, GYK, GOK, KIG, GUW, ZOW, ZYW; for low similarity stimuli, no consonants were repeated. For the responses, high similarity was provided by having a commonality of meaning among all seven words, i.e., *gleeful, genial, pleasant, smiling, blissful, elated,* and *laughing.* For low similarity responses, words were used with little if any commonality of meaning. Four stimulus-response combinations were used: high-high, high-low, low-high, and low-low. The anticipation method, using a 2:2 rate, was used, and learning was continued until the subject attained two successive errorless trials. Results can be found in Table 5–5, where it can be noted that performance varies significantly as a function of both stimulus and response similarity.

The role of conceptual similarity has not been of interest to most investigators. One such study, however, was conducted by Underwood and Schulz (1961a). The results supported the previously reported findings obtained with formal and meaningful similarity materials, namely, that learning is negatively related to both stimulus and response similarity.

In this study (experiment III), four experimental lists were constructed by using four groups of four conceptually related stimuli and/or responses. Thus, list 2 consisted of four groups of four conceptually related responses paired with sixteen nonrelated stimuli. List 3 consisted of four groups of four conceptually related stimuli

TABLE 5–5

MEAN TRIALS TO LEARN

	Responses	
Stimuli	High Similarity	Low Similarity
High Similarity	34.20	28.53
Low Similarity	25.17	15.13

(Adapted from Feldman and Underwood 1957)

TABLE 5-6

PAIRED-ASSOCIATE LISTS USED IN EXPERIMENT III

List 1	List 2	List 3	List 4	List 5
CRUISER-HEAD	HEAD-MEASLES	BOB-HEAD	BOB-MEASLES	BOB-NITROGEN
EMERALD-WALL	BUS-MUMPS	BILL-BUS	BILL-MUMPS	BILL-SPARROW
BLUE-COTTON	KNIFE-POLIO	JOE-KNIFE	JOE-POLIO	JOE-GERMANY
THEFT-BEE	JOHN-CANCER	JOHN-CANCER	JOHN-CANCER	JOHN-CANCER
DOCTOR-BUS	WALL-RUSSIA	COW-WALL	COW-RUSSIA	COW-BLUEJAY
COPPER-TABLE	DOG-FRANCE	DOG-FRANCE	DOG-FRANCE	DOG-FRANCE
DOG-FRANCE	TROUT-ENGLAND	CAT-TROUT	CAT-ENGLAND	CAT-HYDROGEN
GASOLINE-MAPLE	DAISY-GERMANY	HORSE-DAISY	HORSE-GERMANY	HORSE-POLIO
WALTZ-OXYGEN	COTTON-BLUEJAY	RABBI-COTTON	RABBI-BLUEJAY	RABBI-MEASLES
WINE-GEOLOGY	MAPLE-CANARY	BISHOP-MAPLE	BISHOP-CANARY	BISHOP-RUSSIA
TRUMPET-KNIFE	GEOLOGY-SPARROW	MINISTER-GEOLOGY	MINISTER-SPARROW	MINISTER-SULPHUR
APPLE-TROUT	PRIEST-ROBIN	PRIEST-ROBIN	PRIEST-ROBIN	PRIEST-ROBIN
HAT-SECOND	BEE-NITROGEN	RHUMBA-BEE	RHUMBA-NITROGEN	RHUMBA-MUMPS
JOHN-CANCER	TABLE-HYDROGEN	FOXTROT-TABLE	FOXTROT-HYDROGEN	FOXTROT-ENGLAND
FOOTBALL-DAISY	WALTZ-OXYGEN	WALTZ-OXYGEN	WALTZ-OXYGEN	WALTZ-OXYGEN
PRIEST-ROBIN	SECOND-SULPHUR	TANGO-SECOND	TANGO-SULPHUR	TANGO-CANARY

(Adapted from Underwood and Schulz 1961a)

paired with sixteen nonrelated responses. Lists 4 and 5 consisted of four groups of four conceptually related stimuli and four groups of four conceptually related responses; however, the pairing of items that made up list 4 was such that all of the conceptually similar stimulus items were paired with conceptually similar responses. For list 5, the items were paired at random. Finally, list 1 was a control list and consisted of sixteen unrelated pairs. Table 5–6 illustrates the pairs of items that were used for all lists. The anticipation method, with a 2:2 rate, was employed, and each list was presented for fifteen trials. An additional variable that interested the investigators was the examination of massed and distributed practice; the massed practice condition consisted of four seconds between trials while a thirty-second intertrial interval was used for the distributed practice condition.

The findings obtained under both massed and distributed practice conditions are indicated in Table 5–7. It can be noted that these results can be broken down into three groups of values. First, learning was clearly superior for list 1—the list that consisted of all unrelated pairs of items. The second grouping indicates that pairs of items consisting of either conceptually similar stimuli or

TABLE 5–7

MEANS OF TOTAL CORRECT RESPONSES IN LEARNING THE FIVE LISTS
AS A FUNCTION OF MASSED AND DISTRIBUTED PRACTICE

List	Massed Mean	Distributed Mean
1 (Unrelated stimuli and responses)	197.40	197.33
2 (Unrelated stimuli paired with conceptually similar responses)	189.80	175.27
3 (Conceptually similar stimuli paired with unrelated responses)	176.13	187.60
4 (Conceptually similar stimuli systematically paired with conceptually related responses)	157.33	143.40
5 (Conceptually similar stimuli randomly paired with conceptually related responses)	159.20	147.73

(Adapted from Underwood and Schulz 1961a)

responses were learned next most rapidly, while lists 4 and 5, which consisted of both conceptually similar stimuli and responses, were learned least rapidly. In summary, these findings are in keeping with most of the other studies reported in this section—learning is negatively related to increases in similarity of stimuli.

SIMILARITY AND ITS RELATIONSHIP TO STAGES OF PAIRED-ASSOCIATE LEARNING

As we discussed in an earlier chapter, paired-associate learning has frequently been conceptualized in terms of a response learning stage, as well as an associative or hook-up stage. A study by Underwood, Runquist and Schulz (1959) examined how meaningful response similarity contributes to the response learning stage. In this experiment, two lists of ten paired-associates were used in which the stimuli were CVCs of low intralist similarity while the response items were two-syllable adjectives. For one list, the response items were similar in meaning (*cheerful, sunny, carefree, pleasant, gleeful, laughing, happy, genial, jolly, smiling*), while in the other list, the responses were of low similarity or unrelated (*spicy, rounded, hairy, equal, modern, tiresome, fiery, faithful, plastic, guilty*). Three basic conditions each involved paired-associate learning of the high similarity and the low similarity lists, with separate groups learning each list under each condition. In condition I (Control), the subjects learned the paired-associate lists using the standard 2:2 anticipation procedure for fifteen trials. In condition II (Response Learning), the subjects were first provided with response learning: the ten responses were presented in varying orders for five trials, and a recall test was given after each trial. Following this, the subjects were given the standard fifteen trials on the paired-associate list. Condition III was designed to determine the extent of response learning taking place during the paired-associate learning. Various groups were stopped at different points during the fifteen paired-associate learning trials, and were given a single free-recall trial. This response learning was tapped at six points; namely, after one, two, three, five, eight, or thirteen exposures of the paired-associate lists. Inasmuch as each subject was stopped only once, this condition involved six groups for each list. The general free-recall pro-

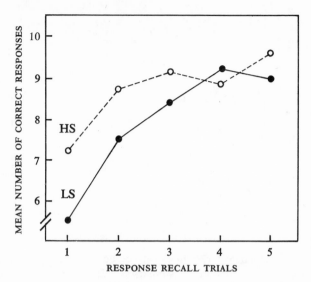

Fig. 5–5. Mean correct responses on each response-recall trial as a function of high similarity (HS) and low similarity (LS).
(Adapted from Underwood, Runquist and Schulz 1959)

cedure consisted of the subject's being given 1.5 minutes to write down all of the responses in the list that he could remember. After this recall period, he was informed that he would not be interrupted again and the standard paired-associate procedure was continued.

The findings from this study were as follows. First, the mean number of correct responses on each of the five response recall trials for the response learning condition (condition II) is shown in Fig. 5–5. Here it can be noted that, initially, the high similarity responses are recalled significantly better than the low similarity responses; although by trial 4, performance is approximately equal on both lists. In general, then, response learning occurs more rapidly for responses of high meaningful similarity than for those of low similarity.[1]

When condition III is examined—in which, it will be recalled, various groups were asked to provide free-recall responses after one, two, three, five, eight, or thirteen paired-associate trials—the

[1] It will be recalled that if we are examining formal similarity, the free-recall findings of Underwood, Ekstrand and Keppel (1964) indicate that low similarity material is learned more rapidly than high.

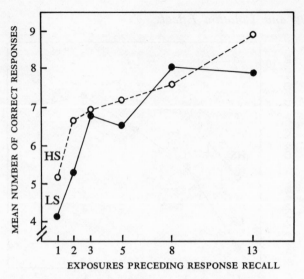

Fig. 5–6. Mean correct responses on response recall during paired-associate learning as a function of similarity (HS vs. LS) and number of exposures preceding response recall.

(Adapted from Underwood, Runquist and Schulz 1959)

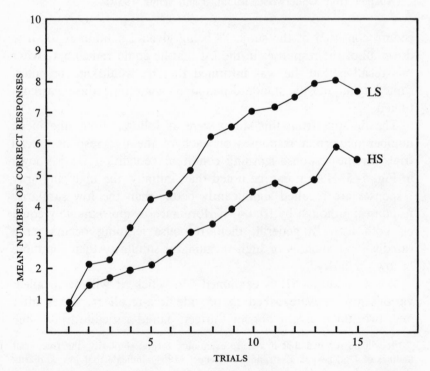

Fig. 5–7. Paired-associate learning as a function of intralist response similarity.

(Adapted from Underwood, Runquist and Schulz 1959)

findings are as indicated in Fig. 5–6. Again, high similarity material results in superior response learning, although there is little difference between the groups after the first few trials.

The acquisition curves for paired-associate learning for the control groups (condition I) are presented in Fig. 5–7. In keeping with the findings obtained in earlier studies, it can be noted that low response similarity resulted in superior paired-associate learning in spite of the fact that high similarity results in superior response learning. Presumably, the highly similar items generate considerable confusion during the hook-up stage, and this more than offsets any temporary gain this condition produces during the response learning stage.

STIMULUS SIMILARITY AND MEANINGFULNESS

A recent concern has been with examining the relationship of similarity to meaningfulness. Underwood (1963) has hypothesized an interaction between stimulus meaningfulness and formal stimulus similarity. Increasing stimulus similarity, he points out, should result in a greater performance decrement when the meaningfulness of the material is low than when it is high. Underwood reasons that when a CVC is of low meaningfulness, it is not attended to as an integrated unit—the subject attends to individual letters. When an item is meaningful, however, the subject perceives the item as a total or integrated unit. Thus, duplication of letters among stimuli, which typically produces increments in similarity, results in more increased similarity among the poorly integrated items than a similar duplication of letters provides for the meaningful units.

For example, consider the following three-item *stimulus* lists of low and high meaningful CVCs:

Low Meaningful Lists			High Meaningful Lists		
1	2	3	1	2	3
ZOK	ZOK	ZOK	BED	BED	BED
YEF	ZIF	ZIK	LOW	BAT	BID
KIJ	ZUR	ZUK	RUN	BUG	BAD

It can be noted that similarity increases from list 1 through list 3 for each level of meaningfulness. It would be predicted that such increases in stimulus similarity would have the result that the low meaningful list would become increasingly more difficult to learn than the high meaningful list, since the identity of letters among the low association lists tends to produce a greater amount of list similarity than the same identity of letters produces among the high association list. Perhaps another way of saying this is that letter identity contributes very little to the similarity of meaningful material, and that when dealing with this kind of material, similarity must be manipulated by means of meaningful or conceptual similarity.

Although Underwood's (1963) analysis seems logical, the early experiments of Goss, Nodine, Gregory, Taub and Kennedy (experiments 1A and 1B, 1962), Nodine (1963), and Goss and Nodine (1965) did not provide support for this position. In fact, both Goss et al. (1962), and Nodine (1963) found that learning difficulty significantly increased with high but not with low association value CVCs as similarity of the material increased from low to high. And Goss and Nodine's (1965) extensive examination of formal similarity and meaningfulness resulted in their stating,

At present, for the particular procedures for specifying meaningfulness, formal similarity of stimulus and response members, and the levels of meaningfulness and similarity employed, there is no convincing evidence of interactions of similarity and meaningfulness of stimulus members, of response members, or of both. This holds for both unmixed and partly mixed lists (p. 148).

Recent studies by Lockhart (1968), and Nelson (1968) suggest, however, that Underwood's position may have some validity. In Lockhart's study, three levels of meaningfulness, i.e., word-CVCs, high m' CVCs, and low m' CVCs, were examined along with three degrees of formal stimulus similarity, defined by number of common letters. The experimental material was obtained by using, for each level of meaningfulness, two different initial consonants, two vowels, and two different final consonants—which produced eight different CVCs when combined. For example, in order to construct the word-CVCs, the initial consonants B, R, the vowels A, U, and the final consonants G, T were used, producing the following words: *bag, bat, bug, but, rag, rat, rug, rut.*

In his examination of similarity, Lockhart has indicated that the eight trigrams that constitute each list may be grouped pairwise into three classes as a function of the number of letters that a given pair has in common, i.e., in terms of their degree of formal similarity. (For example, when *bag* is compared with every other word-CVC for number of common letters, it can be observed that it has two common letters [or degrees of formal similarity] with *bat* and *rag,* just one common letter with *bug, but, rat, rug,* and no common letters with *rut.*) Single-digit numbers served as responses, and the standard 2:2 anticipation procedure was used. Subjects were run to a criterion of two consecutive errorless trials or to a maximum of sixty trials.

The number of errors (corrected for the number of potential errors) made as a function of the meaningfulness of the material as well as the amount of formal stimulus similarity, can be noted in Table 5–8. As can be observed, when word-CVCs are used, the degree of formal stimulus similarity emerges as an irrelevant variable, since the probability of failing to discriminate two words of high formal stimulus similarity is no greater than for stimuli that have no letters in common; in contrast, with CVCs of high and low meaningfulness the relationship between formal stimulus similarity and the distribution of errors is highly significant. These findings, of course, are in accord with Underwood's position.

An experiment by Nelson (experiment 2, 1968) may be also cited to support Underwood's hypothesis. In this study, two paired-associate CVC lists were constructed with high intralist similarity,

TABLE 5–8

MEAN CONFUSION ERROR SCORES AS A FUNCTION OF FSS
AT THREE LEVELS OF MEANINGFULNESS

| List | Degree of Formal Stimulus Similarity No. of Common Letters | | |
	0	1	2
Words	9.56	7.78	9.78
High m'	13.78	11.11	23.22
Low m'	13.89	17.67	30.30

(Adapted from Lockhart 1968)

and with either high or low association value. For each list, similarity was produced by using just two different first letters, i.e., F and Z for the low association CVCs, and two different last letters, i.e., J and Q for the low association list, combined with three vowels, A, E, and I. Thus, the combinations, FAJ, FEJ, FIJ, ZAJ, ZEJ, ZIJ, etc., represented six of the twelve low association, highly similar CVCs. The anticipation method, using the 2:2 presentation rate, was employed, with learning carried out to a criterion of one perfect trial. The data obtained in this experiment were combined with data secured from low similarity, high and low association groups that had been run in an earlier study. When the high and low similarity, low association CVC learning data were compared with the high and low similarity, high association data, results indicated that the difficulty of learning was proportionately greater for the high similarity, low association group—a finding in keeping with Lockhart's (1968) results and with the similarity-meaningfulness interaction proposed by Underwood (1963).[1]

In summary, the experimental findings are equivocal in supporting Underwood's (1963) hypothesis of an interaction between meaningfulness and stimulus similarity. One approach in attempting to reconcile these differences, however, should be an examination of the kinds of material that investigators have used in their high meaningful condition. Although one cannot always determine whether high association CVCs or words have been used, in some of the studies that have reported findings at variance with Underwood's (1963) position, words have not been used, i.e., Goss, Nodine, Gregory, Taub and Kennedy (1962), Nodine (1963), Goss and Nodine (1965). It may be that in order for a trigram to be perceived as a completely integrated unit and thus to negate the influence of formal stimulus similarity, the trigram must be a word. Certainly, the two studies that have supported the Underwood

[1] The complexity of this area is indicated in the findings of Nelson's (1968) first experiment, which did not support the Underwood position. In this study, three levels of association value, three levels of similarity—produced by employing either four, eight, or twelve identical letters—and two conditions of location of the identical letters (either the first or last letter position) were manipulated using typical paired-associate learning procedures. Responses were two-digit numbers. In this experiment, the findings supported the Goss et al. (1962) study, which indicated that when similarity was increased, learning difficulty was proportionately greater under high than under low association value. This was particularly in evidence when the identical letters appeared in the first position.

(1963) position (i.e., Lockhart 1968; Nelson 1968) used words as their high meaningful material.

THE ROLE OF ITEM IDENTITY

At one end of the similarity continuum is identity, and one may ask the question, how does an identical item that serves as a stimulus for one paired-associate and as a response for another paired-associate influence learning?

Umemoto and Hilgard (1961) found that lists containing identical items that serve as both stimuli and responses are more difficult to learn than lists in which unrelated items are used; moreover, such learning appears to be a function of the number of identical units making up the list. The experimental materials consisted of three lists of paired-associates, with each list consisting of eight pairs of CVCs. On list 1, each CVC used as a stimulus was also used as a response; thus, only eight different CVCs were used in making up the list. For example, if RIV-JAF represented one of the paired-associates used, RIV would serve as a stimulus for a second paired-associate, while JAF would be used as a response for the third pair of items. On list 2, only one-half of the eight pairs used had common stimulus and response units, thus resulting in a list composed of twelve different CVCs, as contrasted with eight different CVCs of list 1. In list 3, none of the CVCs making up the eight pairs were repeated, so that sixteen different CVCs were employed. Learning was to a criterion of one errorless trial. The results, as can be noted from Fig. 5–8, indicated that list 3 was the easiest list to learn and list 1 the most difficult. Young (1961) has also obtained findings in keeping with these results.

These findings have been interpreted by the experimenters as being related to the inhibiting effects of backward associations. Thus, when RIV appears as a stimulus, the subject has to learn to respond with JAF; however, the investigators have hypothesized that a backward association is set up also between JAF and RIV. When JAF appears as a stimulus for another pair of items, there is a tendency for it to elicit RIV, which interferes with the learning of the correct response. In the experiment cited, as the number of responses that also serve as stimuli decreases, interfering backward associations also decrease.

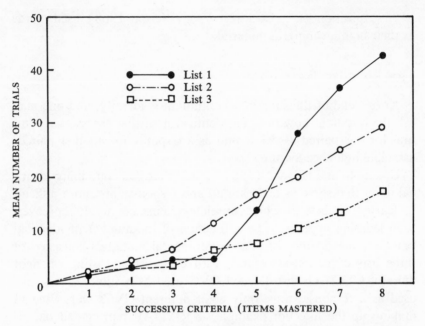

Fig. 5–8. Learning as a function of the number of items that are common to both the stimulus and response. List 1 has all items common to both S and R, List 2 has half of the items in common, while List 3 has none in common.

(Adapted from Umemoto and Hilgard 1961)

Umemoto and Hilgard (1961) have also posited that the use of identical items combined with other items that are similar may result in facilitation rather than inhibition. Such a prediction arises from the position that the backward association produced may facilitate new learning because of a synonymity or association effect. This is illustrated by the situation in which a subject learns the following paired-associates: *faultless*-RIV, RIV-*perfect*. The RIV-*faultless* backward association aids the subject in learning the RIV-*perfect* pair. In a second experiment, these experimenters tested this hypothesis by constructing three lists that varied with regard to the number of identical-similar stimulus and response pairs. As in the previous study, all lists contained eight pairs of items; CVCs and adjectives served as both stimuli and responses. For all lists the same CVCs and adjectives were utilized. For list 1, adjectives and synonyms were used to provide the facilitating relationship that has been just described; i.e., RIV-*perfect, perfect*-RIV, *noonday*-

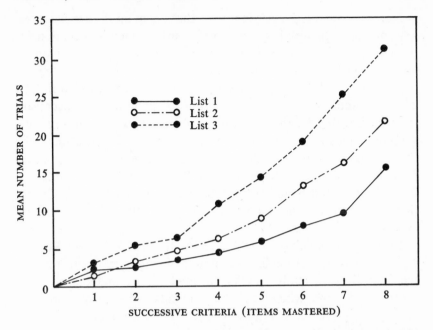

Fig. 5–9. Mean number of trials to successive criteria. In List 1 both members of similar adjective pairs are associated with the same nonsense syllable; in List 2 half the pairs have both members associated with the same nonsense syllable; in List 3 no similar adjective pair has its members associated with the same syllable.

(Adapted from Umemoto and Hilgard 1961)

GID; GID-*midday;* etc. The adjectives used in list 3 were not so paired; i.e, RIV-*perfect; faultless-*ZOT; GID-*vacant;* etc. Finally, one-half of the pairs found in list 1 and one-half in list 3 were used to make up list 2. As Fig. 5–9 indicates, the findings revealed that list 1 was the easiest to learn and list 3 the most difficult— findings in keeping with the investigators' hypothesis.

THE INFLUENCE OF ISOLATED MATERIAL, OR THE VON RESTORFF EFFECT [1]

It has been noted in both serial and paired-associate learning situations, that as either formal, meaningful, or conceptual similarity

[1] An excellent and detailed review of the historical, empirical, and theoretical status of the von Restorff phenomenon has been provided by Wallace (1965).

is decreased among the varying items that make up the experimental material, such material is more easily learned. One explanation for this effect is that as the items become more similar, it grows increasingly difficult for the subject to discriminate among them; that is, there is a great deal of confusability among the items, which in turn leads to difficulty in correctly ordering the material as is necessary in serial learning, or in associating a given response with a specific stimulus (hook-up) as is required in paired-associate learning. The suggestion has been made that if one item was maximally dissimilar from all of the others, that item could be most readily discriminated from the rest and would in turn be more rapidly learned. Operationally, when an item in a list is made markedly different from the others, it is classified as "isolated."

Early workers (Calkins 1894, 1896; Jersild 1929; Van Buskirk 1932) characterized the isolated item as being more vivid; thus, in the Van Buskirk study, a CVC printed in red and placed on a green background, when learned as a member of a list of more conventionally presented CVCs, was recalled better than a corresponding member of a homogeneous list.

A year later von Restorff (1933) found that a two-digit number was learned more rapidly if it was placed among a list of CVCs than if it was placed among a list of other two-digit numbers. In contrast to some American psychologist who had posited that vividness was the primary contributor to this effect, von Restorff attributed her results to the "isolation" of the stimuli. As a Gestalt psychologist, von Restorff posited that an item that is different or "isolated" can be conceived of as a figure, whereas homogeneous material in which the isolated item has been embedded may be conceptualized as the ground. Thus, the figure-ground relationship that occupied an important conceptual position in Gestalt psychology was extended to the learning of verbal material. Most subsequent investigators have referred to the general findings in this area as the von Restorff effect.

Contemporary research has been directed toward examining the von Restorff effect in serial learning and paired-associate tasks.

SERIAL LEARNING

A question that arose almost immediately after the isolation effect was discovered was, how does the rapid learning of the isolated item influence the learning of the remainder of the material? More specifically, is a list that contains an isolated item more rapidly learned than a list that does not contain such an item?

In an early study examining this problem, Jones and Jones (1942) constructed two lists of ten CVCs, in which all of the CVCs in the control list were printed in black. In the experimental list, the seventh CVC was printed in red; all of the others were in black. Subjects were required to learn the material to a criterion of one errorless trial; a week later, they were required to relearn the material to the original criterion. The findings revealed that although the red CVC was more readily learned and better retained than its control, thus confirming the isolation effect, a comparison of the learning and retention of the two *lists* indicated no difference between them.

The serial learning studies of Smith (1949), Smith and Stearns (1949), Newman and Saltz (1958), Jensen (1962), and Roberts (1962) have all confirmed the findings of Jones and Jones (1942) that a *list* containing an isolated item is not learned more rapidly than a homogeneous list.[1]

Another parameter that has been investigated has been the extent or amount of isolation. It would be hypothesized that as the isolated unit becomes more and more similar to the material that surrounds it, it should grow progressively more difficult to learn. In an examination of this hypothesis, Kimble and Dufort (1955) had four groups of subjects learn serial lists of thirteen words that were identical except for the middle one. Twelve words on the list were obtained from Noble's (1952) fourteen most meaningful words. The thirteenth word, which was to occupy the middle position of the serial list and thus be identified as the "isolate," varied in terms of its meaningfulness and ranged from the nonsense word GOJEY through *rampart, kennel,* and *office.* As one can note from Table 3–1 (Chapter 3), GOJEY has an *m* value of .99, *rampart* an *m* value of 3.36, *kennel* an *m* value of 5.52, and *office* an *m* value of 7.95. The word *office* was in the same meaningfulness category as the twelve words that made up the remainder of the list. Statistical analysis revealed that the relative difficulty of learning the "isolated"

[1] It should be acknowledged that in one part of the study conducted by Smith and Stearns (1949), the findings were not in agreement with this general conclusion.

TABLE 5–9

NUMBER OF ERRORS AS A FUNCTION OF THE
SIZE OF THE ISOLATED ITEM

Size of Unisolated CVCs, Inches	Size of Isolated CVCs, Inches			
	2.3 x 4.5	3.3 x 6.4	4.7 x 9.1	6.7 x 13.0
Small (2.3 x 4.5)	15.5	13.2	11.0	7.8
Large (6.7 x 13.0)	11.9	15.5	14.4	21.2

(Adapted from Gumenik and Levitt 1968)

word varied as a function of the meaningfulness of the item, with
GOJEY the easiest to learn, and *office* the most difficult.

Gumenik and Levitt (1968) have also found that learning is a
function of the amount of isolation of the isolated item. In this
study, the serial learning task consisted of nine CVCs projected on
a screen; subjects were given thirty trials with the anticipation
method. The isolated item was projected at one of four sizes, and
each size was a constant fraction of the next largest size. All other
items were projected at one of two sizes, which corresponded to
either the smallest size or the largest size of the isolated item. The
results, as indicated by the mean number of errors for the learning
trials, are presented in Table 5–9 and support Kimble and Dufort's
earlier findings.

In studies examining serial list learning, a common finding has
been that the first and last items of the list are learned most rapidly,
while the middle portion is learned more slowly. The functional
relationship between ease of learning and the serial position of the
items is best described by a bow-shaped curve.[1] A number of investigators have been interested in determining whether isolated
items can play any role in changing this relationship. Both Kimble
and Dufort (1955), and Newman and Saltz (1958) have demonstrated that it is possible to manipulate the shape of the curve by
introducing isolated items into the list. In the Newman and Saltz
study, six thirteen-item serial lists were made up, three of which
each contained an isolated item in the seventh position of the list
(a position that typically results in very poor learning), while the
other three lists were used as controls. Twelve of the words were

[1] For further discussion of this phenomenon, see Chapter 6.

the same as those used by Kimble and Dufort in the study just cited; the isolated words used in the seventh position for the three experimental lists were: GOJEY, NEGLAN, and BYSSUS. For the three control lists, the words used in the seventh position were: *youngster, typhoon* and *office*—words that were comparable in meaningfulness to the nonisolated items. A typical serial anticipation procedure was utilized, in which each item was presented at a two-second rate and the subjects were required to learn the task to a criterion of one errorless trial.

The findings are indicated in Fig. 5–10. As can be noted, the typical bowed serial position curve was obtained for the three lists in which the item placed in the seventh position was similar in meaningfulness to the other items in the list. On the other hand, it can be noted that the isolated item resulted in a sharp (and statistically significant) drop in the error curve.

A logical continuation of this problem has been to determine whether or not there is an interaction between the isolation effect and other serial position effects. For example, does the contribution

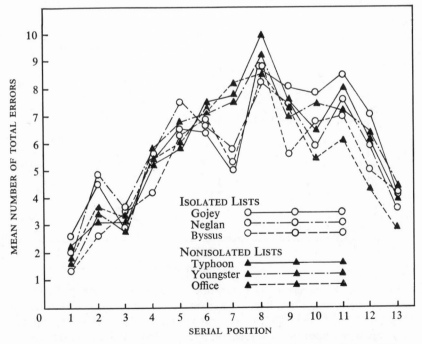

Fig. 5–10. Mean number of total errors as a function of serial position. (Adapted from Newman and Saltz (1958)

of the isolation effect vary as a function of the length of the list or of the serial position of the isolated item? A study by McLaughlin (1966) examined these questions and concluded that this was not the case.

In this study, experimental lists of three, seven, eleven and fifteen

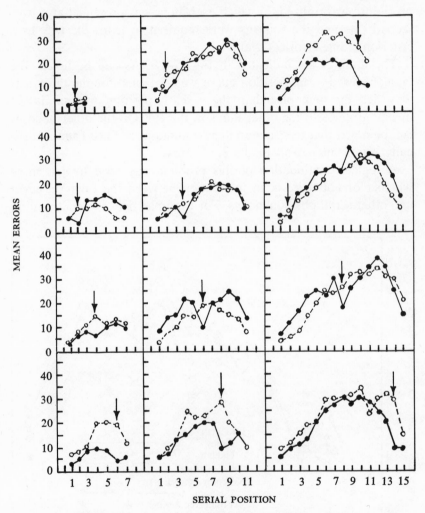

Fig. 5–11. Mean errors as a function of item serial position in three-, seven-, eleven-, and fifteen-item experimental (solid line) and control (broken line) lists. (The I- and CC-item positions are marked by arrows. The number of points represented on each function indicates the length of the series.)

(Adapted from McLaughlin 1966)

CVCs were constructed so that each list included one trigram typed in red, uppercase letters, while the remaining items were typed in black, lowercase letters. The isolated item was placed in the middle position of the three-item list, in either the second, middle or penultimate position of the seven- and fifteen-item lists, and in either the second, fourth, sixth, eighth, or tenth position of the eleven-item list. Control lists, identical in all respects to the experimental lists, except for the characteristics of the isolated item, were also used. Subjects learned the lists using the anticipation procedure with a three-second presentation rate. The learning criterion was three consecutive errorless trials.

The findings are indicated in Fig. 5–11. It can be noted that each isolated item was learned significantly more rapidly (as indicated by fewer errors) than its control item, which was located in the same serial position. No significant first- or second-order interactions were obtained; as a result, the absence of a significant interaction between isolation and the serial position or between isolation and the length of the list suggests that the magnitude of the facilitation did not vary as a function of either of these variables.

A more recent study by Bone and Goulet (1968) has confirmed McLaughlin's (1966) finding of no interaction between the isolation effect and serial position.[1]

THE ISOLATION EFFECT IN PAIRED-ASSOCIATE LEARNING

Inasmuch as the paired-associate learning situation clearly identifies the stimulus and the response, this task has been used frequently to examine varying aspects of the isolation effect.

Erickson (1963) used the paired-associate task to demonstrate that the isolation effect does not need to be related to the structural or absolute qualities of the material but can operate with relationships as well. In this study, a nine-item paired-associate list was constructed in which four pairs of items consisted of three-digit

[1] It should be acknowledged that Bone and Goulet's (1968) statistical analysis of the mean correct responses per trial as a function of serial position did yield a significant interaction; however, when they reanalyzed their data in terms of percentage of facilitation, they obtained no interaction effects. They concluded that the apparent differential facilitation observed when absolute measures were used was undoubedly attributable in a large part to ceiling effects due to very rapid learning of the items placed in the first and tenth positions.

numbers as stimuli associated with consonant syllables (CCCs) as responses, i.e., 217-SWJ. Four other pairs were constructed in which consonant syllables were used as stimuli and associated with three-digit numbers as responses, i.e., CLG-472. The ninth and isolated pair consisted only of consonant syllables. An examination of the list indicated that the stimulus syllable for the isolated item could not be viewed as isolated since four other stimulus items were also consonant syllables. Similarly, the isolated response syllable could not be considered isolated since four other response terms were consonant syllables as well. A standard paired-associate procedure was used with a 2:2 rate and each subject was run to a criterion of one errorless trial or twenty-five trials. Results indicated that relational isolation facilitated the learning of the critical pairs. Thus, a paired-associate item that possessed a unique stimulus-response relationship within the list was learned more rapidly than paired-associate items not possessing this relationship.

Of major concern to a number of investigators who used the paired-associate task has been whether the isolation effect manifests itself on the stimulus or on the response side of the pair.

In an early study by Kimble and Dufort (1955), these investigators assumed that the isolation phenomenon was primarily perceptual; thus, they hypothesized that the isolation effect should manifest itself when the isolated unit was used as a stimulus but not as a response. Although they obtained findings that supported their position, questions have been raised regarding their experimental material as well as interpretation of their data.[1]

The more recent studies of Nachmias, Gleitman and McKenna (1961), and Erickson (1965, 1968) have indicated that isolation effects can be obtained when the isolated item is placed on either the stimulus or the response side, although there is some disagreement as to whether similar or differential effects are obtained. In the Nachmias, Gleitman and McKenna (1961) study, isolation effects, obtained on both the stimulus and response sides, were found

[1] Their selection of the isolated items was most unusual. The verbal materials used represented a continuum of meaningfulness (as measured by Noble's *m* values) rather than isolated items placed among groups of homogeneous items. For example, TAROP and XYLEM represented the isolated items and were placed among the following "nonisolates": *femur, pallor, ordeal, quarry, region, zebra, wagon* and *army*. In addition, Erickson (1965) has raised some questions regarding their interpretation of the experimental findings.

to be about equal. In this study, three types of material were employed: two-digit numbers, nonsense syllables and common five-letter adjectives. Twelve different paired-associate lists were constructed. Six lists were used to examine the influence of stimulus isolation and six lists were used to examine the role of response isolation. Each list consisted of nine paired-associates, seven pairs of a single type of material, and two pairs representing the isolated material. The composition of the lists used is indicated in Table 5–10. Twelve groups of five subjects per group were used. Typical paired-associate procedure was used with all subjects run to a criterion of one perfect trial. The findings, as measured by the mean number of errors in the isolated and nonisolated pairs are presented in Table 5–11. Here it can be noted that the isolation effect appears to operate on both the side of the stimulus and that of the response, and at about the same level.

Erickson's (1965, 1968) recent findings, although also indicating

TABLE 5–10

SCHEMATIC REPRESENTATION OF THE COMPOSITION OF THE
TWELVE LISTS (A = ADJECTIVES; N = NUMBERS;
S = NONSENSE SYLLABLES)

Condition	List	Type of Stimulus Making up List		Type of Response Making up List	
		Isolated	Other	Isolated	Other
Stimulus-Isolation	1	A	S		N
	2	A	N		S
	3	S	A		N
	4	S	N		A
	5	N	A		S
	6	N	S		A
Response-Isolation	7		N	A	S
	8		S	A	N
	9		N	S	A
	10		A	S	N
	11		S	N	A
	12		A	N	S

(Adapted from Nachmias, Gleitman and McKenna 1961)

TABLE 5–11

MEAN NUMBER OF ERRORS IN ISOLATED AND
NONISOLATED PAIRS

Condition	All Errors	
	Isolated Pairs	Nonisolated Pairs
Stimulus-isolation	21.3	28.8
Response-isolation	23.6	33.3

(Adapted from Nachmias, Gleitman and McKenna 1961)

that the isolation effects are to be found on both the stimulus as well as the response side of the pair, revealed that the stimulus effects were greater. In the first (1965) study, eight-item lists were constructed; the stimuli and responses were two-letter consonants, i.e., RV-MB. Erickson isolated the items by having them printed in red, while all nonisolated items appeared only in black; the isolated bigram served as either a stimulus or a response. Erickson (1965) also examined the manner of stimulus exposure. One group was presented the material in the usual paired-associate manner, with a 2:2 rate. With this procedure the stimulus is exposed for a total time of four seconds, the last two of which are contemporaneous with the exposure of the response item. For a second group of subjects, the stimulus shutter closed at the end of the two-second period, just as the response shutter opened to expose the response item for two seconds. This condition is in contrast to typical paired-associate procedure in which the stimulus item is exposed for a longer period than the response. In the examination of isolation effects, however, any difference between stimulus isolation and response isolation might be attributed to the longer exposure time of the stimulus; hence equivalent exposure times were utilized. Twenty-four trials were provided. The results, as measured by the number of mean correct responses per subject per pair over trials 1 through 24, for the isolated and critical nonisolated pairs under conditions of stimulus and response isolation, are indicated in Table 5–12. Fig. 5–12 indicates the mean errors made for the isolated and nonisolated pairs for stimulus and response isolation over the twenty-four trial periods. These data reflect a combining of both

TABLE 5–12

MEAN CORRECT RESPONSES PER *S* PER PAIR OVER TRIALS 1–24
FOR ISOLATED AND CRITICAL NONISOLATED PAIRS UNDER
CONDITIONS OF STIMULUS AND RESPONSE ISOLATION

| | Isolation Condition | |
Response Category	Stimulus Isolated	Response Isolated
Isolated Pair (I)	18.58	13.52
Nonisolated Pairs (N)	9.45	8.67
Difference (I − N)	9.13	4.85

(Adapted from Erickson 1965)

stimulus presentation groups, since it was demonstrated that different stimulus exposure times did not result in significant differences between the groups.

In summary, Erickson found that although the isolation of either a stimulus item alone or a response item alone can facilitate learning, the isolation of the stimulus item produces the greater effect. In addition, the advantage of stimulus over response isolation is not contingent upon the longer exposure time for stimulus items characteristic of the usual paired-associate procedure. A subsequent study by Erickson (1968) has supported these results.

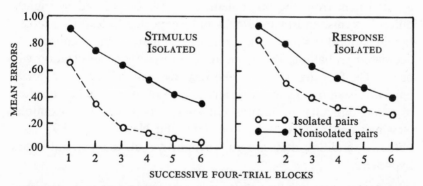

Fig. 5–12. Mean errors per *S* per pair per trial made to isolated and critical nonisolated pairs averaged over four-trial blocks for each isolation condition.

(Adapted from Erickson 1965)

In accounting for why Nachmias, Gleitman and McKenna (1961) did not obtain similar findings, Erickson (1965) posited that the Nachmias et al. results might have been attenuated by the fact that two isolated pairs were used in each list rather than one. It should also be pointed out that the methods for isolating the material in the two studies differed. Erickson used red letters in contrast to the regular black, while Nachmias et al. used different types of material, i.e., two adjectives among seven numbers, two numbers among seven CVCs, etc. It would be interesting to investigate whether the manner in which the material was isolated contributed to the differential findings.

THE ANALYSIS OF ISOLATION EFFECTS

In a study investigating the role of similarity, Gibson (1942) compared the ease of learning different lists consisting of figures paired with nonsense syllables. Her findings indicated that the lists with highly similar stimulus figures were significantly more difficult to learn than the lists that utilized low similarity stimulus figures—a finding in keeping with many of the other stimulus similarity experiments that we have cited. Gibson suggested that stimulus generalization takes place among the stimulus items that make up a list, and as a result, the subject must learn to differentiate among them before learning the individual S-R items. In short, the isolation of an item aids in the differentiation or discrimination of that isolated item from the other items in a list. Or, placed in slightly different terms, an isolated item can be expected to lead to a reduction in within-list stimulus and response similarity, and a consequent decreased probability that stimulus and response generalization will occur. The fact that stimulus and response generalization processes have not been delineated with any degree of exactness has resulted in some difficulty in testing Gibson's hypothesis. For example, Newman and Saltz (1958) and Saltz and Newman (1959) have obtained findings that are not supportive of the generalization hypothesis.[1]

[1] A basic problem with these studies is that the authors have used serial learning situations, and their analysis has frequently been based on the position that a given item acts as the functional stimulus for the next item, which serves as a response. Unfortunately, the problem of identifying the functional stimulus in serial learning has not been solved.

One interesting hypothesis proposed by Waugh (1969) is that when an item is perceptually isolated, it is especially attended to or rehearsed, and as the result of such rehearsal, the item is more rapidly learned. In a test of this position, Waugh conducted a series of free-recall learning experiments in which subjects attempted to recall lists of unrelated words. Some of these words were accompanied by an auditory signal denoting that they were to be especially attended to, thus "isolating" them from the other words on the list. Waugh's findings revealed that instructing a subject to pay special attention to certain arbitrarily designated items made him much likelier to recall those items than he would otherwise, so long as only a few items were so designated. When many items were signaled, however, the probability that any one of them would be retained approached the proportion of items recalled when none was signaled. Moreover, signaled items were retained at the expense of unsignaled ones, such that the total number recalled remained constant regardless of how many were signaled. These latter findings are consistent with typical findings obtained in isolation studies.

As Waugh has written, however, these findings cannot be taken as direct evidence that the von Restorff effect reflects the selective rehearsal of such items; however, they do point out that an item's novelty or significance as such is not necessary for its selective retention. Waugh's experiment would have been more illuminating if her findings had been obtained with a paired-associate task in which both stimuli and response were independently signaled.

In summary, and in keeping with Wallace's (1965) position, there is not as yet an adequate theory to explain the von Restorff phenomenon.

Recent concern has been directed toward examining the isolation effect within the context of the two-stage analysis of paired-associate learning. More specifically, investigators have asked, what is the influence of stimulus and response isolation on (1) the associative stage and (2) the response availability stage?

There has been the suggestion, obtained from the *serial* learning studies of Newman and Saltz (1958), and Saltz and Newman (1959), that the isolation effect may influence the response availability stage rather than the hook-up or associative stage. These experimenters have found that the isolation of an item leads to the facilitation of the free recall of that item, and to significantly more

overt intrusions than those experienced with its nonisolated counterpart. But there is not an increased elicitation of the isolated item
by its appropriate stimulus. There is some question, however, as to
how much help the serial learning situation can provide in analyzing
how paired-associate learning takes place; moreover, the experiments by Erickson (1968) using the paired-associate situation do
not provide support for this point of view.

In the study by Erickson (1965) to which we have previously
referred (p. 164), the author believed that the advantage of stimulus over response isolation resulted at least in part from differential
effects that the stimulus isolate had on the associative stage. Two
experiments were subsequently conducted (Erickson 1968) in
order to examine the validity of this inference.

In experiment 1, the materials, apparatus, and general procedure
used in the earlier study (Erickson 1965) were replicated. In that
study it will be recalled that eight-item lists were constructed, and
the stimuli and responses were two-letter consonants—i.e., RV-
MB. Isolated items were printed in red while all nonisolated items
appeared only in black. Isolated bigrams served as either stimuli or
responses. The anticipation procedure, using a 2:2 rate, was utilized and twenty-four trials were provided. The major difference
between this study and the earlier one, however, was that at the end
of each four trials, the memory drum was stopped and the subject
was required to write down as many of the responses as he could
recall. When the subject indicated that he could recall no more
response items or when one minute had gone by without an entry,
trials were resumed.

Table 5–13 shows the mean correct responses over trials 5
through 24 for isolated and nonisolated pairs under the two conditions of isolation. Fig. 5–13 presents the learning curves for isolated
and nonisolated pairs within each of the conditions of isolation. As
can be noted, stimulus isolation produced a larger effect than
response isolation on anticipation scores, thus confirming the findings obtained in the earlier study. Free-recall learning scores, however, did not reflect this difference. Thus, since isolating the items
appeared not to have any influence on the response availability
stage, the influence of the isolation was assumed to take place at
the associative stage.

In a second experiment, using similar material and apparatus,

TABLE 5–13

MEAN CORRECT RESPONSES PER SUBJECT PER PAIR OVER TRIALS 5–24 FOR
ISOLATED AND CRITICAL NONISOLATED PAIRS UNDER CONDITIONS OF
STIMULUS AND RESPONSE ISOLATION

Response Category	Anticipation Scores		Free-Recall Scores [a]	
	Stimulus Isolated	Response Isolated	Stimulus Isolated	Response Isolated
Isolated pair (I)	16.88	13.31	17.87	17.62
Nonisolated pairs (N)	10.17	9.98	16.12	16.33
Difference (I − N)	6.71	3.33	1.75	1.29

[a] Free-recall scores multiplied by 4 for comparison with anticipation scores.

(Adapted from Erickson 1968)

the procedure was varied slightly by providing each subject with a
3″ x 5″ card on which the eight bigrams that served as response
items were typed in black capital letters in a single four-inch
column. Twelve anticipation trials were provided rather than the
usual twenty-four. In addition, the subject was instructed that after
the first trial, he was to select the correct response item from the
card he was holding. Subjects were given ample time to make their
response inasmuch as the stimulus item remained exposed until the
subject had made a response. At this point, the response aperture

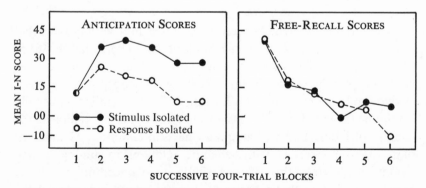

Fig. 5–13. Mean isolation (I–N) score per *S* per trial averaged over four-
trial blocks for each isolation condition.

(Adapted from Erickson 1968)

opened and remained open for two seconds; following this, both apertures closed and the memory drum advanced. The findings obtained in this second experiment replicated those obtained in the first, in that the isolated pairs were learned more rapidly than the nonisolated pairs and the advantage of isolated over nonisolated pairs was greater under the stimulus isolation condition. Thus, because response availability was equal for both the isolated and non-isolated list groups, and differences were still obtained, Erickson (1968) assumed that the associative stage was being influenced by the isolated item.

In general, then, the major implication of the findings of the two experiments is that at least one effect of isolation can be manifested directly as a strengthening of the association between the stimulus and the response of the critical stimulus-response pair.

It would also appear that the advantage of the stimulus over response isolation obtained in the multitrial learning of paired-associate lists is not dependent on increased availability of the critical response item, since in Experiment 2 critical response items were equally available under conditions of stimulus and response isolation, yet an advantage of stimulus over response isolation was maintained in anticipation learning. Rather, the results found in this experiment also support the position that a stronger association between the stimulus and response of the critical S-R pair takes place.

SUMMARY

Two variables that have been investigated in a variety of verbal learning situations have been (a) similarity and (b) isolation. It has been recognized that similarity can be conceptualized along a number of verbal dimensions; formal, meaningful, conceptual, and associative similarity have all been identified. Formal similarity, usually manipulated with CVCs or nonmeaningful material, refers to the number of letters that verbal stimuli have in common. Meaningful similarity is concerned with semantic relationship among words; synonyms illustrate this type of similarity. Conceptual similarity refers to the extent that a group of items represent instances of the same class; so that *rose* and *orchid,* as members of the same class, would be conceptually more similar than *rose* and *dog.* Finally, associative similarity is the extent that a given stimulus word will elicit a common response. Since *king* will elicit *queen* much more frequently—as determined by free association norms—than *music* will elicit *sound, king* and *queen* are considered to have greater associative similarity than *music* and *sound*.

The experimental results have supported the general position that serial learning is hindered by formal and meaningful similarity. Free-recall learning is also hindered by formal similarity but appears to be aided by conceptual similarity.

Paired-associate learning situations have frequently been used, since this type of task enables the investigator to examine the influence of similarity of stimuli independently of similarity of response. Most investigators have found that both stimulus as well as response similarity of either a formal, meaningful, or conceptual nature, inhibits paired-associate learning; however, the similarity variable appears to be more potent when it is on the stimulus rather than the response side of the pair. If paired-associate learning is analyzed in terms of a response learning and associative phase, it has been generally found that response learning is facilitated; the associative phase, on the other hand, is inhibited.

Experimenters have noted that if one item of a list of verbal material stands out from the rest—that is, if by reason of its physical or semantic characteristics, etc., it can be isolated from the other members of the list—this item is learned more rapidly than its control. The effect has been designated as the isolation phenomenon, or von Restorff effect, so named because of one of its early investigators.

The experimental examination of this phenomenon reveals that learning is a function of the degree or amount of isolation; a list containing the isolated item, however, does not enjoy learning superiority over a similar list that does not contain the isolated member. When paired-associate learning tasks are examined, experimental evidence attests to the fact that such learning is facilitated when either the stimulus or the response becomes the isolated unit. Some evidence supports the position that the effect is greater when the stimulus item is isolated rather than the response. With regard to the two-stage analysis of paired-associate learning, experimental studies indicate that the isolation effect makes its primary contribution to the associative rather than to the response availability stage.

6 *Other Learning Variables*

In this chapter we will review a number of other variables that investigators have examined in their search for the conditions that influence the learning process. For the most part, like the characteristics of the material, and similarity and isolation, these variables are related to the task itself, and include stimulus variation and position, as well as temporal considerations. However, we will also discuss some of the work that has been done in examining the motivational conditions of the subject.

STIMULUS VARIATION

Although it is commonly believed that stimulus invariability results in optimal learning, Bevan and his associates have conducted a series of studies in which they have shown that varying the sitmulus leads to a greater amount of learning than occurs when the stimulus remains constant or unchanged.[1]

In the first study, Bevan, Dukes and Avant (1966) addressed themselves to the question, will a subject be better able to recall X if he has been exposed to the sequence X_a, X_a or X_b, X_b rather than to the sequence X_a, X_b? The procedure consisted of using

---

[1] Inasmuch as free-recall learning situations have been used in these studies, some question must be raised as to whether or not the stimulus for any given response can be identified. With this in doubt, the designation of the presented items as stimuli is undoubtedly gratuitous.

slides to present twenty pictures of easily recognizable and identifiable objects, e.g., apples, shoes, etc. Twenty additional slides were presented; half of these were duplicates of the first twenty; each of the remaining ten presented different examples or aspects of the same object. For example, the first series might present such objects as: a man's shoe, a black pencil, a large pair of scissors, a thick book, or a portable typewriter, etc. The second series of items would show half of these objects exactly as they had been presented in the first series; the other half of the series, however, would show different instances of these objects: a woman's shoe, a green pencil, a small pair of scissors, a thin book, a standard typewriter, etc. Following the presentation of the fortieth item, subjects were asked to write down the names of all objects they could recall. Scores for each subject were obtained by subtracting the number of duplicated items recalled from the number of varied items recalled. Although the mean difference (1.27 items) was not large, it was significant, indicating the superiority in memory for varied presentation over sheer repetition.

Experiment 2 was similar to the first except that twenty different common nouns were used as the primary stimulus objects, with variety achieved by using different modifiers, e.g., *pine tree, oak tree, sunny weather, rainy weather,* etc. Following the presentation of the slides, the subjects were asked to write down only the second word, i.e., only the noun. Again, although the difference between the varied and identical presentations was small, amounting to a mean difference of approximately half a word (.54), it was significant. The third experiment run by the authors was much more extensive in that different degrees of variation were introduced. The pictures used in the first experiment were supplemented by providing additional instances to each of the twenty categories so that the following five series, totaling eighty items, were presented:

AAAA—each A item was presented four times in complete, randomized sets of twenty.

AAAB—each B item was presented one time to every three presentations of the A item.

AABB—each B item was presented twice for every two presentations of the A items.

AABC—each A item was presented twice, B once, and C once

ABCD—four complete randomized sets of twenty items each, one composed of A items, one of B items, etc.

The general procedure was similar to that used in the two previous experiments except that three minutes rather than 1½ minutes were permitted for recall. In addition, retention was tested two to four days after presenting the slides and again after a three-week period. Each subject's score was the number of generic stimuli recalled; the findings can be noted in Fig. 6–1. As the authors concluded, the data from each of the experiments indicate that memory

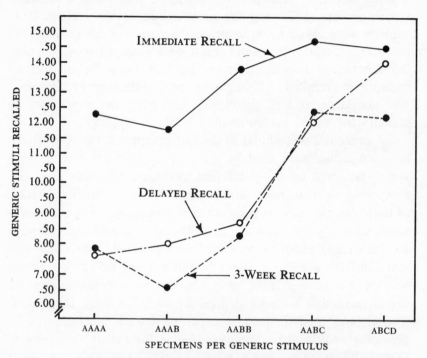

Fig. 6–1. Recall of generic stimuli as a function of the number of specimens representing each generic stimulus: *AAAA*, four presentations of a single specimen for each generic stimulus; *AAAB*, three presentations of one and one presentation of a second specimen; *AABB*, two presentations of two specimens; *AABC*, two presentations of one specimen and one presentation of two other specimens; and *ABCD*, one presentation of four different specimens.

(Adapted from Bevan, Dukes and Avant 1966)

for generic stimuli may be enhanced by varying, in successive presentations, the specimens representing those stimuli. The subject is more likely to recall *shoe* if he is shown one picture of a woman's play shoe and another of a man's oxford than if he is shown the same object twice.

In attempting to explain these findings—the positive effects of variety on memory for generic stimuli—one might hypothesize either an associationistic or a motivational hypothesis. With the associationistic hypothesis, the increased number of associations would enhance the probability of recall because recalling any one of the several items could lead to the recall of the appropriate word, as opposed to the limited conditions of the single associate. A motivational hypothesis would make the advantage of the varied presentation stem from heightened interest or attention.

In a second study, Bevan and Dukes (1967) looked at the kind of variation that was introduced into the experimental situation. That is, in taking their starting point from Thorndike's (1932) concept of belongingness, they hypothesized that if X is presented once with *a* and once with *b*, the variation will be more beneficial in recalling X if *a* and *b* "belong" with X than if they do not. A procedure similar to that of their earlier experiments was used; however, the belongingness aspect of the study was manipulated by pairing adjectives both with nouns to which the adjectives belonged and with nouns to which they did not belong. The experimental design consisted of four groups in which the conditions were as follows: (1) Belonging pairs repeated—*tall tree, tall tree;* (2) Belonging pairs varied—*tall tree, green tree;* (3) Nonbelonging pairs repeated—*round army, round army;* (4) Nonbelonging pairs varied —*round army, sweet army*. Results indicated that the type of variation was important. Consonant with the investigators' initial hypothesis, variation was found to be a more effective agent in recall of the nouns when the adjective varied belonged with the noun to be recalled than when it did not. Thus, variation was most effective when the pairs were high in belongingness, while, in contrast, belongingness exerted no influence upon recall of the nouns under the repeated conditions. Table 6–1 presents these findings.

The "Bevan effect" is a most interesting one and certainly not in keeping with what can be described as a traditional stimulus-

TABLE 6–1

Mean Recall Scores

Conditions	N	Nouns
(1) Belonging pairs repeated	35	10.06
(2) Belonging pairs varied	65	12.35
(3) Nonbelonging pairs repeated	99	10.45
(4) Nonbelonging pairs varied	62	11.16

(Adapted from Bevan and Dukes 1967)

response position, which assumes that optimal learning and minimal forgetting take place when the stimulus conditions remain constant.[1]

The kinds of experimental material that produce this effect, however, must be subjected to further study. Daves and Adkins (1969), employing pictures of the same type of material, i.e., familiar objects, used by Bevan, Dukes and Avant (1966), were able to replicate the findings; on the other hand, experiments by Dukes and Bevan (1967), and Avant and Bevan (1969) did not provide confirmation. In the Dukes and Bevan (1967) study, the task was to associate names with a variety of photographs of individuals, while in the Avant and Bevan (1969) experiment, the stimulus material consisted of nonsense figures, with CVCs used as responses.

STIMULUS POSITION

When a learning task is provided a subject, there is some ordering of the parts that comprise it. Such ordering may be an important part of the task, as in the case of serial learning, or it may be deemed by the experimenter as unimportant, as in the free-recall learning situation. In any event, the fact that the material has been presented in an invariant order in certain types of learning situations has stimulated a great deal of interest among investigators in examining learning as a function of the position of the material.

[1] For example, see McGeoch and Irion (1952), who have discussed altered stimulating conditions as a basic condition for forgetting.

SERIAL LISTS

We can observe that when a list of adjectives or CVCs is learned in serial order, although the material has been previously equated for meaningfulness, etc., the number of correct responses or errors that are made in learning are not equally distributed over the items that make up the list. If the number of errors is used as a measure of performance, a type of bow-shaped curve is obtained, with those items just beyond the middle of the list being the most difficult to learn, and the items at the beginning and end of the list the easiest.

An early study by Ward (1937) demonstrated changes in the serial position curve taking place as a function of varying stages of practice. In the study, twenty-four subjects learned a list of twelve CVCs by the serial anticipation procedure; each item was presented at a two-second rate. Fig. 6–2 reveals the effects of serial position from the first trial, on which only three CVCs were learned, through those trials on which five, seven, nine and eleven items were correct.

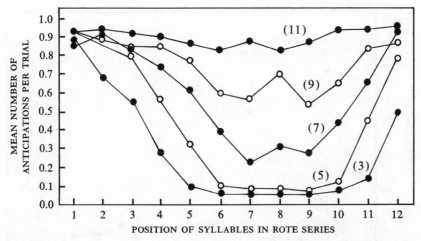

Fig. 6–2. Mean number of correct anticipations at each point in the rote series for five levels of mastery. The individual curves are each marked with the level of mastery represented. Curves are given for levels of mastery of three, five, seven, nine, and eleven correct anticipations, respectively, in a single learning trial.

(Adapted from Ward 1937)

Some experimenters have been interested in determining how certain variables influence the shape of the curve. In one such study, Hovland (1938) showed that the serial position effect appears to be steeper under massed than under distributed practice. Subsequent studies by Hovland (1940) and by Patten (1938) confirmed this finding.

McCrary and Hunter (1953) pointed out, however, that if the *percentage* of total errors is plotted as a function of serial position rather than the absolute values (mean errors)—a measure which is typically used—the shape of the serial position curve does not change. When these authors replotted the data obtained in Hovland's (1938) study, they found that "the striking feature of the percentage plots is that there is essentially no difference in the curves for the different conditions of learning" (p. 132).

In an experiment of their own, McCrary and Hunter had subjects serially learn fourteen CVCs or fourteen familiar names; learning was carried out to a criterion of one errorless trial. Fig. 6–3 provides the serial position curves for syllables and names that are

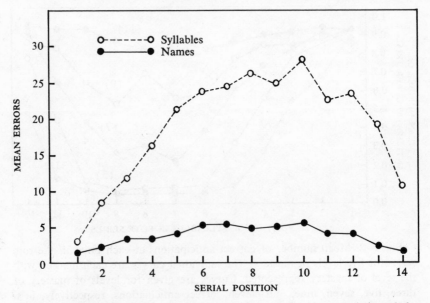

Fig. 6–3. Serial position curves as a function of the characteristics of the material used.

(Adapted from McCrary and Hunter 1953)

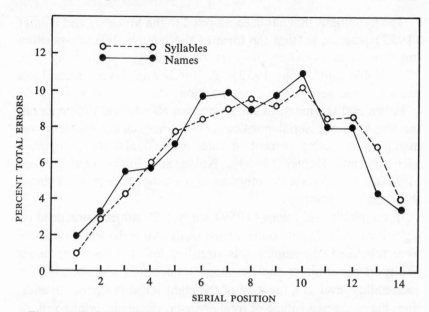

Fig. 6–4. Serial position curves as a function of the characteristics of the material used. Note that the ordinate expresses performance in terms of percentage of total errors.

(Adapted from McCrary and Hunter 1953)

plotted in terms of mean errors, while Fig. 6–4 replots the same data using percentage of total errors made at each serial position. With this latter way of presenting the data, it can be noted that the percentage plots for the two conditions are essentially identical.[1]

---

[1] These findings have given rise to two general observations. Murdock (1960) concluded that since the shape of the serial curve is not a function of the meaningfulness of the material—a variable that contributes to learning, as noted in an earlier chapter—serial position is not a learning variable. Rather, Murdock suggested that the shape of the curve results from the unequal distinctiveness of the items that make up the list.

Jensen (1962), on the other hand, proposed that serial rote learning data may be analyzed into three components: (1) task difficulty—as measured by the number of trials to reach a given criterion; (2) efficiency of learning—as measured by the percentage of errors or correct responses; and (3) relative difficulty of learning the items at the various positions. It is only the third measure, Jensen believed, from which a true serial position curve should be obtained, although he noted that the serial position curve most frequently found in the literature confounds at least two of the above-mentioned components. He suggested a new measure— the Index of Relative Difficulty—as the only satisfactory method of representing the serial position effect. Few investigators have been persuaded by Jensen's arguments to use his Index of Relative Difficulty to plot serial position curves.

The hypothesis that has been ascribed to the McCrary and Hunter (1953) position is "that the form of the *relative* difficulty-position function is an invariant property of serial, verbal learning" (p. 571, Noble and Fuchs 1959). A number of investigators have examined the generality of this position.

Braun and Heymann (1958) were not able to find differences in the shape of the serial position curve when meaningfulness was manipulated (using percent of total errors), and thus supported McCrary and Hunter (1953). Noble and Fuchs (1959), and McManis (1965), on the other hand, have not been able to obtain these kinds of findings.[1]

In the Noble and Fuchs (1959) study, 120 subjects practiced an eight-item serial list of nouns for ten trials. After the learning scores were tabulated, the sample was stratified into five levels of initial ability of the subjects and the mean total errors was obtained for each ability level as a function of the eight serial positions. In addition, the mean percentage of total errors at the eight serial positions was also computed. Statistical analysis of the data indicated that the main effects of initial ability were not significant, although serial position was. The serial position times initial ability interaction was also significant—a statistic that means that the obtained differences in trend among the ability levels could not reasonably be attributed to chance. Thus, a plot of the fast learners (groups 4 and 5) and slow learners (groups 1 and 2) indicated a systematic tendency for the fast learners to make proportionately more errors in the middle of the list, and fewer errors at the beginning and end of the list.

In the McManis (1965) study, forty-five retarded subjects learned serial word lists of three lengths (four, eight, and twelve words) using the serial anticipation method. The findings indicated that the percentage of errors in the middle portions of these lists was a

---

[1] It should be also noted that Underwood and Schulz (1959) observed that the shape of the serial position curve differed for massed and distributed practice. Learning under the massed practice condition gave the classical bowed curve, with the point of maximal difficulty just beyond the center of the list and with learning of the last few items of the list much slower than that of the first few items. Under distributed practice, the curve was almost symmetrical. Very little skew was evident and the last items in the list were learned almost as rapidly as the first items in the list. Although relative difficulty was not measured, it is clear from the description provided that these findings would not be in keeping with McCrary and Hunter (1953).

positive function of the lengths of the lists. That is, the shorter the list, the greater the percentage of errors made in the middle of the list. As the author states, "since the invariance hypothesis would require a prediction of no significant differences in percentage of errors in the middle half of the serial lists of different levels of learning difficulty, it is not supported by the present data" (p. 1088).

Some question must be raised as to whether or not McCrary and Hunter (1953) meant that their findings would have generality over all of the learning or individual difference conditions that might be examined. Although they did state that, "the reduction in mean errors per serial position, although greatest in the middle or just past the middle of the series, will be closely proportional at each position to the total number of errors made" (p. 133), it would seem that they were referring to the studies they had examined, and the statement was not meant to be considered as a basic condition of all serial learning studies.

FREE-RECALL LEARNING

A number of investigators have been interested in the serial position curve that is obtained when the free-recall learning situation is used. Deese and Kaufman (1957) made up two lists of unrelated words randomly selected from the Thorndike-Lorge (1944) word list. One list was ten words long, the other thirty-two. Two groups of subjects learned ten lists of words each; one group learned the ten-item list while the other group learned the thirty-two item list. The presentation of the material was oral, and the words were presented at the rate of one per second. Immediately following the presentation of each list of words, a test for recall was provided. The results for the two lists of words, in terms of mean number of items recalled per list, are indicated in Fig. 6–5.

Subsequent studies by Murdock and Babick (1961), and Murdock (1962) obtained similar findings. In the latter study, Murdock examined serial position effect as a function of the length of the list as well as presentation time. Six groups of subjects each had different combinations of these two variables with lists of ten, fifteen, and twenty words presented at a rate of two seconds per item, and lists of twenty, thirty, and forty items presented at one second per item. Following the presentation of a list, a 1.5-minute

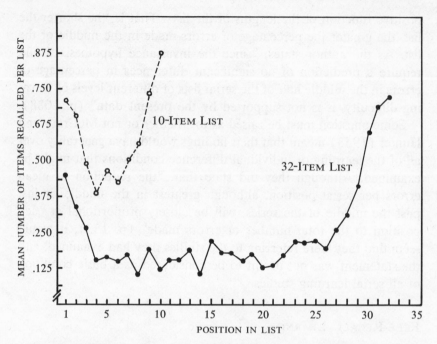

Fig. 6–5. Mean frequency of recall per list per *S* for lists of randomly arranged words as a function of position of items in original lists.
(Adapted from Deese and Kaufman 1957)

recall period was introduced during which the subjects were requested to write down as many of the words as they could remember without regard to the order in which they had been presented. All groups were given twenty lists per session, and four sessions were provided. The serial position curves obtained are indicated in Fig. 6–6. If the general shapes of these curves are examined along with those obtained by Deese and Kaufman (1957), it may be noted that all of them seem to share certain general characteristics—a marked recency effect, a flat middle section, and a primacy effect that is smaller in magnitude than the recency effect. This type of curve, which indicates best learning for items at the end of the list, contrasts with serial anticipation learning, which indicates that the best performance is found for items located at the beginning of the list.[1]

[1] Bousfield, Whitmarsh and Esterson (1958), and Jahnke (1963) were not able to obtain findings that support this general result. Both of these studies indicate that recall of the first items in the list is greater than recall of the final items. However, the recency effect has been obtained so many times in free-recall learning

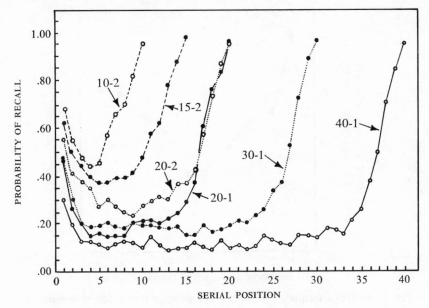

Fig. 6–6. Serial position curves for the six groups.
(Adapted from Murdock 1962)

EXTENDED SERIAL LEARNING

Deese and Kaufman (1957), in addition to examining the effects of serial position for unrelated words, also examined passages of connected discourse. This material, obtained from the World Almanac, was approximately 100 words in length and consisted of ten sentences. The sentences were so structured that by minor rewording they could be presented in different orders. The material was presented orally and subjects were instructed to attempt to remember what they had heard. A test for recall was obtained immediately after the passage had been read. Three passages, each on a different topic, were presented to twenty-seven subjects. The passages were scored by number of correctly recalled statements per position in the paragraph. The serial position curve for this material is indicated in Fig. 6–7. It can be noted that this curve is much like the classical curve for the method of serial anticipation, with the highest

studies that it would appear that the instructions used by these investigators, which emphasized that their subjects were to recall the items in the order in which they were given, were responsible for these anomalous results.

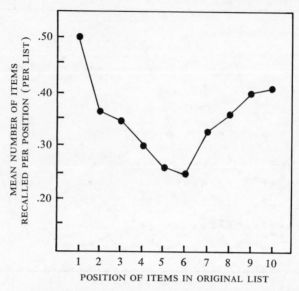

Fig. 6–7. Mean frequency of recall per passage per *S* for statements in textual passages as a function of position of statements in original passages. (Adapted from Deese and Kaufman 1957)

frequency of recall found at the beginning of the list and the lowest frequency of recall just past the middle.

We have noted that connected discourse provides a serial position curve in which the material presented first is best learned; on the other hand, the recall of unrelated items results in a serial position curve in which the last items presented are best recalled. A logical question that follows is whether this change in the serial position curve could be obtained as a function of the sequential structure of ordinary prose. Miller and Selfridge (1950) devised a series of passages that provide orders of approximation to English, and in a second experiment, Deese and Kaufman (1957) used such material in an effort to examine the serial position effect as related to the varying orders of approximation to English.[1] Seven orders of ap-

---

[1] For any given number of words in a passage, the probability that one word will follow another can be assessed; these sequential probabilities provide varying approximations to English. For example, if a ten-word passage is used, zero approximation to English would be obtained by drawing the ten words at random from a dictionary. Higher order approximations would reflect the probability that the second word in the passage could be predicted if the first was known; that the third word in the passage could be predicted if the first two words were known;

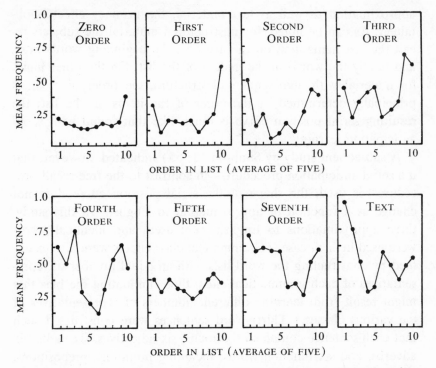

Fig. 6–8. Mean frequency of recall per *S* for items in lists of various degrees of sequential structure (orders of approximation) as a function of position of items in original lists (averaged by groups of five items).

(Adapted from Deese and Kaufman 1957)

proximation and a textual passage were presented to all subjects. The material was read to each subject at the rate of one word per second and the subject was requested to recall as much of the material as he could after the presentation of a given passage. The mean frequency of recall for each subject for the items in the lists representing varying orders of approximation to English is presented in Fig. 6–8. Although the curves are not smooth and there is considerable irregularity in them, a general trend can be noted. Thus, where the approximation to English is at a very low level, it can be noted that a recency effect predominates. As the material approaches textual variety, as indicated by the seventh order of

etc. Chapter 8 can be consulted for a more complete description of the procedures that have been used by investigators to obtain the varying approximations to English.

approximation as well as text material, the primacy effect is obtained. As can be noted, for unstructured material the subjects recall the last items first, on the average, the beginning words next, and finally the words in the middle of the list. On the other hand, for material with high sequential structure, the order of recall is principally determined by the order of the items on the list; the resulting serial position curve is much like that found with serial anticipation learning.

A subsequent study by Simpson (1965) indicated, however, that if a serial anticipation procedure—in contrast to the free-recall procedure—is used, the shape of the serial position curve does not change as a function of approximation to English. In this study, three approximations to English were used, and identical words were used in each case. (Grammatical class effects were also examined by constructing the word lists with an equal number of representatives of each grammatical class, thus eliminating the bias that might result from learning different numbers of representatives of the various classes.) Thirty-word sentences were constructed such that each sentence contained six nouns, six adjectives, six verbs, six adverbs, and six function words, including pronouns, prepositions, conjunctions, and articles. The sentences constituting the highest approximation to English or sentence word order would be as follows: *"During hot afternoons small children often stop quietly to see distant mountains build wildly wonderful cities or think of unusually beautiful people who almost always speak and teach great wisdom."* The medium-approximation word order was obtained by dividing each of the sentences into six successive groups of five words and then ordering the six groups according to the permutations contained in a random 6 x 6 Latin square. A sample from this approximation was as follows: *"Distant mountains build wildly wonderful beautiful people who almost always during hot afternoons small children cities or think of unusually often stop quietly to see, speak and teach great wisdom."*

The lowest approximation word order was obtained by rearranging the sentence word order according to the permutations in a random 30-x-30 Latin square. A sample here would be, *"and almost think unusually hot teach quietly during cities small great stop see of to beautiful build afternoons speak distant wonderful always or children wildly who often people mountains wisdom."*

Three groups of individuals each learned one of the word orders using the method of serial anticipation. Words were exposed individually at a two-second rate. Results, as illustrated in Fig. 6–9, indicate the mean percent errors at each serial position under each of the three approximations to sentence word order. As the author indicates, there is little evidence for differences in general trend as a function of level of approximation to English.

In a subsequent study Simpson (1967), examining only fifteen words arranged in high and low approximation to sentence word order and using a similar procedure, was able to confirm his earlier findings.

In summary, the serial anticipation method appears to produce the traditional bow-shaped curve, regardless of the type of material

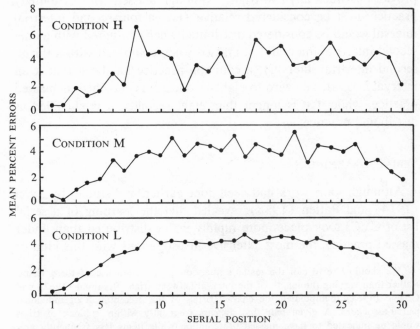

Fig. 6–9. Mean percent errors (n = 60) at each serial position under each of three approximations to sentence word order.
(Adapted from Simpson 1965)

used. Why the typical free-recall procedure yields a different serial position effect must await further research.

TEMPORAL VARIABLES

Although time has frequently been regarded only as a conceptual framework within which events take place, many experimenters have examined the influence of time in a variety of learning situations. Perhaps the most frequently investigated area has been the distribution of practice.

MASSED VS. DISTRIBUTED PRACTICE

The massing or distributing of trials provided in the learning situation generally refers to the length of time that the experimenter provides between any two trials.[1] Although massed (or distributed) practice must be considered relative (i.e., a four-second intertrial interval would be considered distributed when compared with a one-second intertrial interval, but massed when compared with a thirty-second intertrial interval), a common practice has been that if an interval is short, i.e., zero to eight seconds, it is classified as massed practice, while if it is longer than eight seconds, it is classified as distributed practice.

SERIAL LEARNING

Although some work had been done earlier, and studies by Lyon (1914) and Patten (1938) revealed that the learning of a serial list of CVCs took place more rapidly under distributed than under massed practice, the most extensive investigations with this kind of

[1] We should like to call the reader's attention to a second use of these terms. Rather than varying the length of the interval between trials, Bregman (1967) and Greeno (1964) manipulated the characteristics of the presentation of individual paired-associates. A given pair that appears frequently within a block of trials would be indicated to have massed presentation while items less frequently presented would be considered distributed. For example, in the Bregman study, a block of twenty-two presentations of pairs of items consisted of eight presentations of one pair (massed), four presentations of a second pair (intermediately distributed), and two presentations of each of five pairs (distributed).

task were a series of studies by Hovland (1938, 1939, 1940, 1949), and by Underwood and his associates.

Hovland's work was directed toward examining the position that the massing of trials resulted in the building up or accumulation of inhibitory tendencies, which in turn reduced the efficiency of learning. Since inhibition was presumed to dissipate with time, it followed that by distributing trials such inhibition would not accumulate; this, in turn, would increase the efficiency of learning. In his first study, Hovland (1938) had subjects learn lists of CVCs under massed (six seconds between trials) or distributed practice (two minutes and six seconds between trials). The distributed practice condition produced a significant increase in ease of learning as measured by the number of trials necessary to reach a criterion of seven out of twelve correct.

In a second study (Hovland 1940), the massed-distributed practice condition was examined as a function of the length of the serial list. Lists consisting of eight, eleven, or fourteen CVCs were used and again findings indicated that the distributed practice condition was superior for all lengths of lists. In addition, as the lists grew progressively longer, the superiority of the distributed practice condition increased.

Underwood did not work within the same theoretical framework; rather, his studies were more of a functional variety. In an early study Underwood and Goad (1951) were interested in the interaction of the distribution of practice and intralist similarity. In this experiment, lists of adjectives were constructed in which there was either high or low similarity of the material. Intertrial intervals of either two, fifteen, or thirty seconds were utilized. The significant looked-for interaction was obtained with the fifteen- and thirty-second intertrial interval groups showing superior learning when the high similarity list was used. However, no difference was obtained among the varying intertrial interval groups in learning of the low similarity list.

Unfortunately, subsequent studies by Underwood (1952a, 1953b), and Underwood and Schulz (1959) were not able to confirm the interaction between similarity and distribution of practice. Rather, the findings of these studies indicated that distribution of practice results in learning superiority for low similarity as well as high similarity lists.

The role of massed vs. distributed practice has also been investigated using interlist similarity. In one study by Underwood and Richardson (1955) seven lists, each consisting of six consonant syllables, were so constructed that intralist similarity was minimized but interlist similarity was maximized. The first list was learned using a two- or thirty-second intertrial interval. The next five lists were learned with the two-second intertrial interval while the seventh list was learned with either a two-second, one-, two-, or three-minute intertrial interval. The results are indicated in Fig. 6–10, where it can be noted that the distributed practice group was superior on the first list as well as on the seventh.

Finally, an early study by Underwood (1951a) indicated that the distribution of practice continued to reflect the superiority of learning over a number of lists that were learned. In this study, four serial lists of fourteen adjectives per list were learned by either massed (two seconds between trials) or by distributed prac-

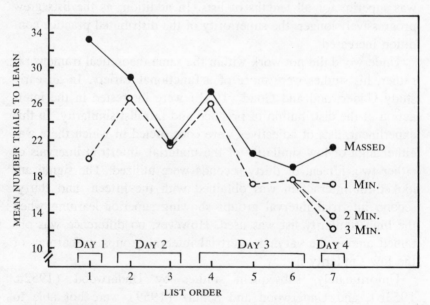

Fig. 6–10. Mean number of trials to attain one perfect recitation on each of the seven lists.

(Adapted from Underwood and Richardson 1955)

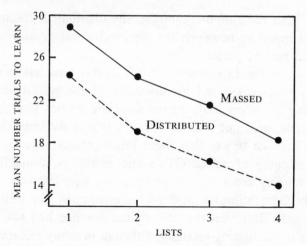

Fig. 6–11. The effect of stage of practice on learning by massed and by distributed practice.

(Adapted from Underwood 1951a)

tice (thirty seconds between trials). Just one list was learned per session. The findings revealed that learning by a distributed practice procedure was consistently more rapid than was learning by massed practice; the difference between the two conditions was constant over all four sessions. Fig. 6–11 presents these findings.

PAIRED-ASSOCIATE LEARNING

Although the experimental evidence is reasonably unequivocal in demonstrating the superiority of distributed practice in the serial learning task, the same conclusion cannot be made for paired-associate learning.

In an early study Hovland (1939), using pairs of CVCs, found that learning did not take place more rapidly under distributed practice than under massed practice; but in a subsequent study (Hovland 1949), positive findings were obtained. In this study, nine pairs of CVCs served as experimental material. The rate of presentation was 1:1 or 2:2 seconds; the massed practice condition consisted of six-second intervals between successive presentations of the list while the time interval for the distributed practice condition consisted of two minutes and six seconds. Learning was carried out to a criterion of two perfect trials. The findings indicated that with both rates of presentation, the distributed practice condition was superior; however, the superiority was greater with the one-second rate of presentation.

The bulk of the experimental work in this area has been conducted by Underwood and his associates. Little would be gained by detailing the many early paired-associate studies that these experimenters carried out in examining the role of the intertrial interval. It will suffice to say that these investigations were concerned with the learning of paired CVCs and adjectives, using intertrial intervals ranging from four seconds to two minutes, with varying degrees of both stimulus and response intralist similarity. Frequently results indicated that distributed practice had some slight advantage in facilitating learning, although in many instances such differences were not statistically significant.

After critically examining the experimental work that had been done until 1960, Underwood (1961) concluded "that a certain amount of response-term interference must be present before DP [distributed practice] will facilitate acquisition" (p. 230). More specifically, when distributed practice facilitates verbal learning the evidence points strongly toward the fact that it does so because of interference operating during the response-learning stage.[1] Underwood hypothesized that as long as interference attained a certain level in the response acquisition stage, its source was irrelevant. Thus, such interference could be derived from formal similarity (duplicating letters among CVCs) or it could stem from habits learned either within or outside of the laboratory.

It was further assumed that when response interference is high, the massing of trials results only in the suppression of the interfering response tendencies. Thus, these tendencies could arise from time to time during the course of learning, to preclude the rapid acquisition of the complete list. Distributing trials on the other hand permitted the error tendencies arising from interfering responses to recover in strength; but with the subsequent occurrence of the correct responses, these error tendencies were extinguished. The extinction procedure was thus hypothesized to represent a more

[1] As the reader will recognize, Underwood's analysis of the influence of distributed practice is based on the Underwood and Schulz two-stage conception of paired-associate learning.

effective elimination of the deleterious effects of the interfering responses than their suppression.

The length of the intertrial interval was considered to be quite critical, however, since if it was too long, weak associative strengths of the correct responses would be forgotten, and the recovery of the incorrect responses would persistently block or replace the correct responses. If the intertrial interval was too short, it might not permit sufficient time for the incorrect response tendencies to recover in strength, and would thus result only in their suppression.

It would serve no useful purpose to present in detail the evidence that Underwood (1961) used to support his position. Part of his point of view was based on the findings of studies that demonstrated that when response competition has been virtually absent, as in the case of verbal discrimination learning studies (Underwood and Viterna 1951; Underwood and Archer 1955), or when responses are common words, and readily available to the subject, distributed practice does not facilitate learning. On the other hand, in a number of studies in which response competition was maximized by having the subjects learn a number of lists (Underwood and Schulz 1961, 1961a), distributed practice did result in superior learning.

A more recent examination of this position by Underwood and Ekstrand (1967) revealed difficulties. Summaries of sixteen single-list experiments (mostly unpublished) that investigated massed and distributed practice under conditions designed to provide varying amounts of response competition are presented in Table 6–2. Only two of the experiments (1 and 9) reveal a statistically significant effect in favor of distributed practice. In addition, the results of nine multiple-list experiments all have indicated that distributed practice inhibits learning.

The failure to find consistent significant differences between massed and distributed practice conditions has led the authors to point out that the distributed practice effect with paired-associate learning is one of extremely small absolute magnitude. They have further suggested that the distributed practice effect may be mediated by some inhibitory state that retards or slows the growth of associative strength, and that such inhibition dissipates during the distributed practice rest interval. Presumably, however, the deleterious effect produced by the inhibitory state is quite small. Further research examining the inhibition explanation must await the devel-

TABLE 6–2

MATERIALS, CONDITIONS, AND RESULTS FOR SIXTEEN EXPERIMENTS ON THE EFFECT OF MASSED AND DISTRIBUTED PRACTICE IN PAIRED-ASSOCIATE LEARNING

Experiment	Materials	Conditions	Mean Total Correct Responses for Varying Intertrial Intervals Seconds			
			4	15	30	60
1 List 1	JH, XV, EY, RZ, CF, MK, QW, DS	Stimuli: 2–9, 15 trials				
2:1			38.17	51.58	41.92	54.17
2:2			60.92	63.17	50.33	70.50
List 2	RQ, YF, OC, MX, AJ, PN, TK, HS					
2:1			46.50	51.58	54.58	63.67
2:2			63.17	78.50	70.83	81.42
2		12 trials	41.37	39.27	43.60	37.67
3 1.5:2	Same as List 1, Exp. 1	12 trials	33.65		40.70	
2:2			43.35		49.40	
4	WX, MF, BW, GV, RZ, HK, DS	Anticipation and study-recall methods used				
		Anticip.	48.91		55.72	
		Recall	49.64		55.72	
5	Same as List 1, Exp. 1	Instructions to minimize or maximize overt errors				
		Min. Errors	59.45		52.60	
		Max. Errors	52.30		55.50	

			Values			
6 List 1	KB, RD, JH, ZG, FX, LV, MU	Color names as stimuli for Lists 1 & 3	43.92		44.08	
2	WB, ND, QH, SG, CX, PV, AU		47.50		40.42	
3	BK, DR, JH, GZ, XF, VL, UM	Animal names for Lists 2 &	46.58		46.08	
4	BW, DN, HQ, GS, XC, VP, UA	4, 10 trials	43.75		47.67	
7 List 1	OCZ, AJU, YFV, HSW, TKD, RQL, PNB, MXG		93.21	98.55	95.36	105.33
List 2	HDU, BPC, XEW, IJF, RNL, TVZ, MGK, YSA	Stimuli: 2–9, 25 trials	98.15	111.52	111.55	115.73
8	XKV, VFK, FVK, KXF	Stimuli: names of colors, 20 trials	20.75	26.95	24.35	29.65
9	DSU, RZI, CFY, XBN, IGW, TPM, OVJ, KHQ	Stimuli: adjectives, 20 trials	37.28		68.72	
10	Same as Exp. 9	20 trials	57.00		60.06	
11	HFG, BVA, XPL, IWD, RZQ, TJU, MKC, YSN	Stimuli: 2–9, 20 trials	52.92		53.00	
12	IRB, IZR, FZI, FBZ, RIF, LFI, BFL, ZIR	Stimuli: two-syllable words, 20 trials	35.30		41.25	
13	Same as List 9	20 trials	72.95		73.95	
14	Stimuli: VHX, XKH, HVK, KHQ, XQV, VKQ	Responses: No. 2–7, 20 trials	54.59		57.27	

TABLE 6-2 (*Continued*)

MATERIALS, CONDITIONS, AND RESULTS FOR SIXTEEN EXPERIMENTS ON THE EFFECT OF MASSED AND DISTRIBUTED PRACTICE IN PAIRED-ASSOCIATE LEARNING

Experiment	Materials	Conditions	Mean Total Correct Responses for Varying Intertrial Intervals Seconds			
			4	15	30	60
15 List 1	Oak-Bob, Oak-Cow, Oak-Waltz, Oak-Ant, Dog-Elm, Dog-Bill, Dog-Bean, Dog-Head, Joe-Cat, Joe-Fir, Joe-Trout, Joe-Iron	Stimuli: names of dwellings, 15 trials	92.20		93.95	
List 2	Double-word response units of List 1 reversed		88.90		94.05	
16	COF-JUL, DAP-BEV, HEB-JUL, GOS-VOR, KAL-BER, CAS-JUL, PID-BEV, LIB-VOR, VIK-JUL	15 trials	78.85		81.45	

Note: The items listed under MATERIALS represent the response terms for all experiments except experiment 14. Stimulus and response terms are indicated in experiment 16. (Adapted from Underwood and Ekstrand 1967)

opment of a procedure or technique for producing large amounts of inhibition in verbal learning.

PRESENTATION TIME

Presentation time usually refers to the amount of time required to present a given item to be learned; total presentation time refers to the total amount of time taken to present an entire list of items. In an examination of the relationship between the amount of learning and presentation time, Bugelski (1962) hypothesized "that in at least some areas of memorization, and under some conditions of presentation, the degree of learning will be a function of total time, regardless of the duration of the individual trials or interitem times" (p. 409). We will now examine this hypothesis as applied to a variety of learning tasks.[1]

PAIRED-ASSOCIATE LEARNING

Bugelski (1962) was the first investigator to spell out the role of total presentation time in learning. In an experimental test of his hypothesis, noted above, his procedure consisted of having five groups of subjects learn eight pairs of CVCs under conditions in which the stimulus syllable was presented for two seconds, and the response syllable was presented for either an additional two, four, six, eight, or fifteen seconds. A two-second interval preceded the presentation of each new stimulus. It may be noted, then, that the total exposure times for the five groups were either six, eight, ten, twelve, or nineteen seconds per pair of items. Subjects learned the syllables to a criterion of two successful anticipations of the complete list. The apparatus did not allow for the elimination of pairs as they were learned; however the total learning times reported are based on the time taken to learn each pair to the criterion. The trials as well as total time to learn for the five different presentation times are shown in Table 6–3. Total times were obtained by multiplying the total number of trials to learn each pair in the series by the presentation time. As might be anticipated, a significant difference was found between trials to learn, with the fastest

[1] An excellent review of the experimental investigations of the total time hypothesis has been provided by Cooper and Pantle (1967).

TABLE 6–3

MEAN TRIALS AND TOTAL TIMES TO LEARN LISTS

Presentation Time	N	Trials, Mean	Total Exposure Time, Mean
6 sec.	20	10.2	61.2
8 sec.	20	8.8	70.1
10 sec.	20	5.8	57.9
12 sec.	20	4.7	56.1
19 sec.	20	3.3	62.2

(Adapted from Bugelski 1962)

learning occurring with the longest presentation times. When the presentation time was multiplied by trials, however, no significant differences were found.

In a second study, Bugelski and Rickwood (1963) permitted subjects to pace themselves and terminate the presentation time for a given item whenever they desired. Thus, the general procedure was to present the stimulus CVC for two seconds, during which the subject could anticipate the response item. The response item would then appear and remain until the subject turned a manual switch that removed the response item; two seconds later the new stimulus item would appear. The mean total time for the subjects to reach a criterion of two successful repetitions of the correct response was 66.5 seconds, and when this value was compared with groups that were run in the earlier study, no difference in total presentation time was obtained.

Findings of studies by Newman (1964), Baumeister and Hawkins (1966), Brewer (1967), and Zacks (1969) all supported Bugelski's hypothesis. Cooper and Pantle's (1967) examination of five other paired-associate studies (Goss, Morgan and Golin 1959; Hovland 1949; Postman and Goggin 1966; Underwood and Keppel 1963; and Wilcoxon, Wilson and Wise 1961) resulted in their stating that the total time hypothesis has had support from these studies as well, although the investigators in question were not specifically interested in testing the total time hypothesis.

One exception to these findings has been noted in a study by Nodine (1965) who used stimulus and stimulus-response durations of .5, 1, 2, and 4 seconds, with subjects learning sixteen CVC trigrams to a $^{15}/_{16}$ criterion. These stimulus and stimulus-response duration times were varied factorially. Nodine found that total learning time showed a significant increase with increasing stimulus durations, and concluded that this variable was not invariant with respect to total learning time.

FREE-RECALL LEARNING

In an extensive examination of the role of presentation time and length of the list in free-recall learning, Murdock (1960) found that the learning of a list of unrelated words, each presented for just a single time, was a linear function of the total time required for presentation of the list. As an example of this finding, Murdock presented (1) a twenty-item list with items presented at a rate of three seconds per item; (2) a thirty-item list presented at a rate of two seconds per item; (3) a forty-item list presented at a rate of 1.5 seconds per item; and (4) a sixty-item list presented at a rate of one second per item. The mean recall scores for the four lists were: 9.3, 9.3, 9.6, and 8.4 words; these performance measures were not significantly different.

In a second study, discussed in our examination of stimulus position, Murdock (1962) presented lists of ten, fifteen, and twenty words at a rate of two seconds per word, as well as lists of twenty, thirty, and forty words presented at a rate of one second per word. Following the presentation of a given list, a short recall period was provided during which the subjects were requested to write down as many of the words as they could remember without regard to the order in which they were presented. An examination of the mean number of words recalled for each of the conditions is found in Table 6–4. It should be noted that groups with the same total presentation time did not differ significantly in mean number of words recalled. That is, no significant differences in mean number of words recalled were found between groups 10-2 and 20-1; between groups 15-2 and 30-1; and between groups 20-2 and 40-1.

Presentation time and free-recall learning was investigated also by Waugh (1967). In keeping with the findings of Murdock (1960, 1962), Waugh found that the number of words recalled from a list increases as a function of the total amount of time taken to

TABLE 6–4

MEAN NUMBER OF WORDS RECALLED

Group	N	Mean
10-2	18	6.39
20-1	16	6.87
15-2	19	8.25
30-1	19	8.82
20-2	15	8.53
40-1	16	8.24

(Adapted from Murdock 1962)

present the list. As a corollary of this finding, she found that the probability that a given word will be recalled increases in direct proportion to the total number of seconds for which it is presented.

SERIAL LEARNING

As Cooper and Pantle (1967) have written, the evidence supporting the total time hypothesis is less impressive in serial learning studies than it is in either paired-associate learning or free-recall learning studies. In fact, the only study that has provided strongly supportive evidence is an experiment by Keppel and Rehula (1965). In this study, a serial list of fourteen adjectives was learned to a criterion of either $\frac{5}{14}$ or $\frac{10}{14}$ under either two- or four-second presentation rates. Although it was noted that performance under the two rates of presentation required different numbers of trials to reach the criterion, there was a constancy in total learning time. In contrast, one part of Braun and Heymann's (1958) study, as well as an experiment by Postman and Goggin (1964), did not support the total time hypothesis.

TOTAL TIME PROCESSES

Cooper and Pantle (1967) suggested that the process that underlies the invariance shown in total learning time may be rehearsal, or repeated representational response (RR) evocation. That is, longer item presentation times permit the subject more rehearsal time for the items he has been instructed to learn.

These authors point out, however, that the amount of time available should be categorized in terms of (1) nominal time—defined simply as clock time, which provides the amount of time potentially available for rehearsal—and (2) effective time, defined as that part of nominal time during which rehearsal actually takes place. It must be recognized that effective time is not always identical to nominal time. Presumably, discrepancies between nominal time and effective time are responsible for the inability of some investigators to find supporting data for the total time hypothesis. Thus, if only the stimulus term is presented for varying time intervals, as provided in the earlier discussed Nodine (1965) study, the response term may not be available to the subject. Regardless of how much time is available, the representational response, or rehearsal, cannot take place.

Or, if the presentation rates are extremely fast or slow, as provided by Johnson (1964), the total time hypothesis may not be supported. Cooper and Pantle (1967) indicated that fast rates impair the production of the correct representational responses necessary for study. Such rapid presentation rates may also result in the subject's being unable to provide mediators that would aid in the learning. Extremely slow rates, on the other hand, simply result in lapses of study—the attention of the subject is diverted to other things with a resultant loss in rehearsal. In short, the authors propose that there are upper and lower limits on presentation rate beyond which optimal study does not take place.

A second factor related to the total time hypothesis is concerned with the characteristics of the task. The authors have hypothesized that tasks that require more "active" operations to sequentially process items already in memory storage are not likely to provide support for the total time hypothesis. Here, the evidence indicates that the total-time relationship holds in those tasks that require only rehearsal or study for mastery, but does not hold for tasks whose minimal requirements exceed simple rehearsal or study.

In summary, Cooper and Pantle propose two criteria for the specification of learning situations in which the total-time hypothesis can be expected to hold: (a) task requirements must not exceed simple rehearsal, and (b) effective rehearsal time must bear a positive and linear relationship to nominal time.

One last point should be made. The recent experiment by Zacks (1969) indicates the necessity for distinguishing between the "nominal" and the "covert" distribution of study time. She has found that the way in which a subject covertly distributes his study time only rarely corresponds directly to the nominal, or experimenter's, distribution of presentation time. That is, regardless of the variety of presentation times that the experimenter may provide the subject, subjects covertly distribute their study time in much the same way. Thus, if items are presented at a fast rate, the subject probably concentrates on a few pairs on each study trial; when a slow rate is used, subjects may rehearse items other than the one that is currently being presented.

MOTIVATION

The construct of motivation, like that of learning, is difficult to define. In general, the concept refers to a state of the organism that incites, impels or supplies the power for action. Like learning, motivation is inferred from changes in the organism's behavior that arise from the manipulation of variables that have been, by common consent, designated as motivational. Traditionally, these variables have been related to certain kinds of physiological states of the organism, i.e., needs, as well as to the conditions that satisfy them, i.e., rewards and/or incentives.

Most of the experimental work that has been done in examining the contribution of motivational variables to learning has consisted of animal studies; relatively few investigators have examined the role of motivation with humans in verbal learning situations. One reason, at least according to Jung (1968), is that in verbal learning studies "the level of motivation can be considered sufficiently high so that it is difficult to manipulate it by experimental treatments such as instructional variations" (p. 22). Postman (1968) made a somewhat similar point when he has stated that "most conventional experiments on verbal learning are carried out under conditions where instructions, self-instructions and pre-experimental habits all

combine to maximize performance of what has been learned"
(p. 556).

Some interesting work has been done, however, and in this
section we will examine a portion of it in some detail. Since the
influence of motivation is generally conceptualized to be independent of the task, we will depart from much of our earlier organization and will not consider the various types of learning situations
separately.

HULLIAN MOTIVATIONAL THEORY

One attempt to examine verbal learning as a function of motivational conditions was provided by Spence who used Hullian
(1943) theory as his frame of reference. In agreement with Hull's
(1943) theoretical formulation, the basic source of action was considered to arise from the physiological need states of the organism.
These needs were the antecedent conditions from which the construct of drive (D) was inferred, which in turn resulted in ener-
gizing appropriate habit patterns (sHr). The formula $D \times sHr =$
performance indicates that motivation is (1) a necessary condition
for the evocation of behavior and (2) independent of learning.

With this formulation, it may be noted that increase in D should
result in increases in performance. One revision of Hull's theory
was made by Taylor and Spence (1952) who noted "that the
theoretical implication of increasing drive level of S will depend
upon the nature of the behavior situation" (p. 61). It was argued
that in situations in which there is only a single response tendency,
an increase in the strength of drive will result in an increase in the
level of performance. In more complex learning situations such
as trial and error or selective learning, in which there are a number
of competing stimulus-response tendencies, the effect of increasing
the level of drive will depend upon this initial response hierarchy
and the relative habit strength of the correct response in the hierarchy. Thus, under certain conditions, particularly when the habit
strength of the correct response is weaker than those of competing
responses, increasing the drive level would be expected to impair
performance. This follows from the assumption that D will multiply
the habit strengths of all responses, correct as well as incorrect, and

thus will increase the amounts by which the excitatory strengths of the incorrect response exceed that of the correct response.

In those experiments that have used verbal learning studies to examine the Taylor-Spence position, the drive level of the subject has not been manipulated in the experimental sense but rather, variations in drive have been provided by selecting subjects with assumed different motivational levels. This general technique was used by Taylor (1951), who assumed that the variations in what can be psychiatrically described as "manifest anxiety" or emotional responsiveness reflect variations in drive level. A test designed to measure anxiety was constructed by first securing approximately 200 items from the Minnesota Multiphasic Personality Inventory and submitting them to clinical staff members with instructions to designate those items they judged to be indicative of manifest anxiety. The sixty-five items on which there was 80 percent agreement or better were selected for the final anxiety scale. In experimental use, individuals who have made extreme scores on the test are designated as "anxious" or "nonanxious" and were recruited as subjects.

Early studies by Montague (1953), and Spence, Farber and McFann (1956) illustrate examinations of the Taylor-Spence theoretical position using serial as well as paired-associate learning situations. In Montague's study three different serial learning tasks, each consisting of twelve CVCs, were constructed in order to manipulate level of difficulty. List 1 used CVCs of high similarity and low association value, which would produce a difficult learning task; list 2, an intermediate difficulty task, used items of low similarity and low association value. The CVCs of list 3 were of low similarity and high association value, which provided an easy task. The difficult list was presented for forty-five trials while the other two lists were presented for just twenty-five. Sixty subjects with anxiety scores of 9 or below (lower 20 percent) made up the nonanxious group, while sixty subjects with scores of 30 or above (upper 10 percent) comprised the high drive level or anxious group. Performance curves plotted for the anxious and nonanxious subjects for each list are shown in Fig. 6–12. It is clear that these findings are in keeping with the general theoretical position proposed by Taylor and Spence (1952)—high drive level subjects were superior on the easy task, low drive level subjects on the difficult task—

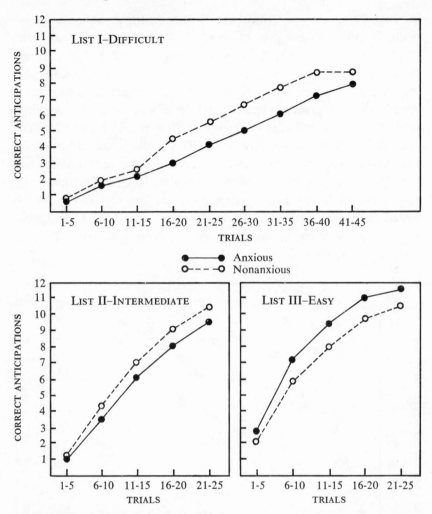

Fig. 6–12. Mean number of correct anticipations per trial over blocks of five trials.

(Adapted from Montague 1953)

although the only statistically significant difference between the anxious and nonanxious groups was on list 3.

In the Spence, Farber and McFann (1956) study (experiment 2), a twelve-item paired-associate list was so constructed that for four of the stimulus-response pairs of adjectives the associative connection between each pair was very high—which would result

in their being easy to learn, i.e., *barren-fruitless, little-minute*—
while for the remaining eight pairs of items, each pair had little
or no associative connection—which would make this a difficult
task, i.e., *arid-grouchy, gypsy-opaque*. Typical paired-associate
learning procedures were utilized with all subjects learning to a
criterion of two errorless trials. Drive level was varied by selecting
subjects who scored either in the upper 20 percent or lower 20 percent of the Manifest Anxiety Scale. The findings are indicated in
Fig. 6–13. The two lower curves represent the performance on
the eight weakly associated word pairs that had strong competing
responses, while the two upper curves are for the four pairs in
which the words were initially highly associated. Like Montague's
(1953) work, these findings are also in accord with the Taylor-
Spence (1952) prediction.

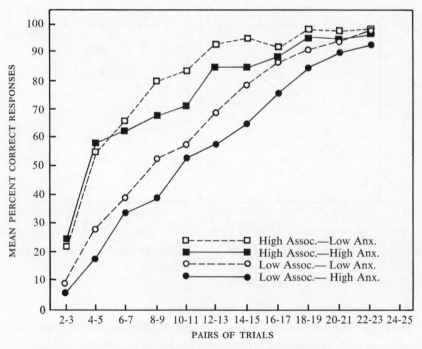

Fig. 6–13. Paired-associate learning as a function of anxiety under conditions of high interpair competition. Word pairs of both high- and low-
association value were interspersed within the same training list, but were
analyzed separately.

(Adapted from Spence, Farber and McFann 1956)

Little would be gained by citing the variety of early serial and paired-associate learning studies that were conducted in order to examine the Taylor-Spence position.[1] As Spence (1958) later wrote of these studies, "the batting average of our theory is fairly high but by no means perfect" (p. 140).

In 1958, Spence called attention to a number of considerations concerning the Taylor-Spence (1952) position as related to verbal learning. First, with regard to the relationship between drive level and performance, Spence pointed out that with difficult tasks, low drive groups should be superior to high during only the early stages of training, following which performance of the high drive group should eventually reach and then overtake the performance of the low drive group. Such a statement indicates that the performance curves for the two groups should be expected to cross. (It should be noted that this prediction was not in accord with the findings obtained in the Montague [1953] and Spence, Farber and McFann [1956] studies that we have just cited.)

Second, Spence indicated that the problems involved in the extension of the theory to complex human learning situations "are quite formidable and that at this stage there necessarily must be considerable amount of trial and error in our theorizing" (p. 140). In this regard, he considered that the serial learning situation was an unsatisfactory task to use since there was little or no knowledge of the relative strengths of competing responses to each of the items on the list.

Finally, he believed that it was evident from the data reported that differences in manifest anxiety scores, if indeed a factor in determining performance on human learning tasks, was a relatively unimportant one. Individual differences in verbal learning ability, he believed, played a much more decisive role.

What can be said regarding the present status of the Taylor-Spence theory as applied to verbal learning situations? First, Spence's (1958) awareness of the lack of contribution of anxiety level to performance has led a number of investigators to accentuate the anxiety effect by combining it with other conditions. For ex-

---

[1] We do not want to give the impression that only verbal learning studies were used in order to examine this theory. Many studies were conducted using classical conditioning and instrumental learning situations. For a review of some of these, see Spence (1964) and Hall (1966).

ample, Spielberger and Smith (1966) obtained findings in accord with the Taylor-Spence position when they combined manifest anxiety with instructions that presumably produced stress on the part of the subjects; the relationship between anxiety and stress was noted by Nicholson (1958), Taylor (1958), and Sarason and Palola (1960).[1]

Thus, it seems that in order to obtain differences in drive level with the manifest anxiety scale, it is necessary to combine this factor with other conditions, to produce stress. An added consideration, however, is that if subjects are already working at a high motivational level when they are performing in verbal learning studies—a condition to which both Jung (1968) and Postman (1968) have called attention—investigators will have difficulty in producing still higher motivational levels.

Secondly, our conceptualization of paired-associate as well as serial learning has been changing so that the newer ways of looking at these learning tasks must be taken into consideration in application of the theory. For example, and as we noted earlier, Underwood and Schulz (1960) contend that paired-associate learning involves two separate habits or stages rather than one (as had been previously assumed by Spence [1958]). Assuming the correctness of the two-stage hypothesis, each paired-associate task must be analyzed in order to determine the contribution of the associative stage (and hence response competition) to the total learning task. Certainly different predictions would be made concerning the influence of high and low drive level, depending on the contribution of each stage to total performance. For example, and as Goulet's (1968) insightful analysis of this problem has indicated, in a paired-associate task where response competition is absent or minimized, high anxious subjects should be superior to low anxious subjects because of the facilitative effects of drive on both stages of learning. In short, it would appear to be much more fruitful to make predictions concerning the influence of drive level on each stage of paired-associate learning rather than in terms of an easy-difficult dimension.

Although Spence (1958) indicated that the serial learning task was inappropriate to use in the examination of the $D \times sHr$ posi-

---

[1] Sarason (1960) has provided an excellent review of empirical findings and theoretical problems in the use of anxiety scales.

tion, since there was little or no knowledge of the relative strengths of competing responses in each of the hierarchies, the work of Spielberger and Smith (1966)—using the serial learning task—is most provocative. These experimenters assumed that response competition at the beginning and at the end of the serial list is minimal, with the result that items at these positions are easier to learn than items located in the middle of the list, where considerable competition prevails. Therefore, these investigators postulated that a high drive group should learn the beginning and end items more easily than low drive subjects; on the other hand, the low drive group should learn the items in the middle of the list most rapidly.[1] In an experimental test of this position, high and low anxious college males were asked to learn, using the serial anticipation method, a serial task consisting of twelve CVCs. A learning criterion of two errorless trials, or a maximum of twenty-five trials, was provided. For one condition, stress conditions were imposed by informing the subjects that there was a relationship between learning ability and IQ; for a neutral condition, subjects were not so informed. The results are indicated in Fig. 6–14, which shows learning curves for the high and low anxiety groups that served under the stress and neutral conditions. As can be noted, although no difference was obtained as a function of anxiety level for the neutral condition, the results did indicate that learning was related to anxiety level when incorporated with stress. When the mean number of correct responses was analyzed as a function of serial position for this second condition, findings indicated that the trigrams that appeared in the "easy" positions in the list, i.e., one, two, three, and twelve, were learned most rapidly for the high anxiety group, while the trigrams which appeared at the difficult positions, i.e., six, seven, eight, and nine, were learned most rapidly for the low anxiety group. See Fig. 6–15. In short, Spence's theoretical position was confirmed when a stress condition was added to differential anxiety levels.

[1] If the assumption that differential response competition is basic to the serial position effect is correct, virtually all of the earlier serial learning studies—i.e., Lucas (1952), Deese, Lazarus and Keenan (1953), Montague (1953), Lazarus, Deese and Hamilton (1954), Saltz and Hoehn (1957), Kalish, Garmezy, Rodnick and Bleke (1958), and Nicholson (1958)—which have attempted to examine learning as a function of drive level, are confounded. It is possible that such confounding has been the principal reason for many of the equivocal findings obtained.

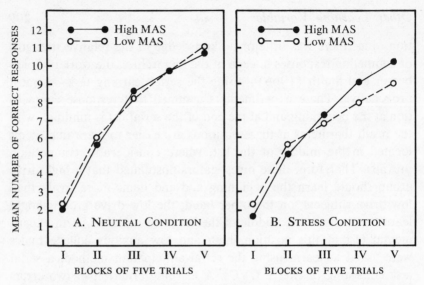

Fig. 6–14. Learning curves for HA and LA Ss: A. The mean number of correct responses given over trial blocks by Ss in the Neutral condition. B. The mean number of correct responses given over trial blocks by Ss in the Stress condition.

(Adapted from Spielberger and Smith 1966)

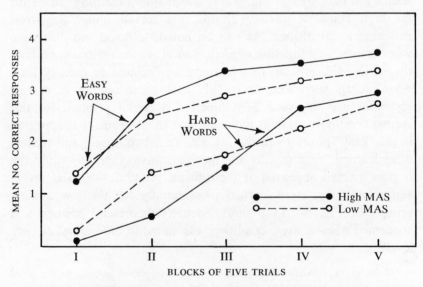

Fig. 6–15. Mean number of correct responses given by HA and LA Ss on successive trial blocks for "easy" and "hard" words. The easy words appeared in serial positions 1, 2, 3, and 12; the hard words appeared in serial positions 6, 7, 8, and 9.

(Adapted from Spielberger and Smith 1966)

AROUSAL

A second motivational area that has interested some experimenters has been designated as activation theory. A basic construct in the theorizing of these researchers has been the concept of arousal.

Although it is difficult to provide a precise definition of arousal, most workers in the area consider it to be an intervening variable related to an organism's energy or excitation level, or to his response intensity. That is, intuitively, one can recognize a crude continuum of arousal expressed by the terms: great excitement, alertness, attentiveness, wakefulness, drowsiness, and sleep. The concepts of motivation, emotion, attention, and vigilance (in addition to many others) have been used as synonyms for the arousal construct. A number of response measures have been used from which some level of arousal is inferred; the most frequently used of these are the galvanic skin response, heart rate, respiration rate, pupillary response, and muscle action potential.

Physiological as well as behavioral approaches to the study of arousal and activation have been made; one of these that has significance for verbal learning situations was provided by Walker (1958; Walker and Tarte 1963). He proposed an interrelationship between arousal, perseverative consolidation, and action decrement; the relevant propositions stemming from his theoretical point of view were as follows (Walker and Tarte 1963):

(1) The occurrence of any psychological event, such as an effort to learn an item of a paired-associate list, sets up an active, perseverative trace process which persists for a considerable period of time. (2) The perseverative process has two important dynamic characteristics: (a) permanent memory is laid down during this active phase in a gradual fashion; (b) during the active period, there is a degree of temporary inhibition of recall, i.e., action decrement (this negative bias against repetition serves to protect the consolidating trace against disruption). (3) High arousal during the associative process will result in a more intensely active trace process. The more intense activity will result in greater ultimate memory but greater temporary inhibition against recall (p. 113).

Although some experimental tests of Walker's (1958) position have been conducted with animals (Walker 1956; Walker 1958;

Walker and Paradise 1958; Walker and Motoyoshi 1962), our primary interest is in the work that has been done with humans, utilizing verbal learning tasks.

In one such experiment, Kleinsmith and Kaplan (1963) used as part of a paired-associate task eight stimulus words that were expected to produce different arousal levels as measured by the subject's skin resistance (GSR). These words were as follows: *kiss, rape, vomit, exam, dance, money, love, swim.* Responses attached to these stimuli were the single digits 2 through 9. A study-test procedure was employed; however, following the presentation of each S-R pair and in order to separate any arousal effects from one set of pairings to the next, two slides containing four colors each were inserted between pairs, and the subject was instructed to name the colors. In order to control for serial order effects, eight different training lists were used; this had the result that the eight stimulus words appeared in each position on the list. Following the presentation of a single trial, a test trial was provided that required the subject to indicate the response following the presentation of the stimulus. This test trial was presented at one of the following intervals: immediately, twenty minutes, forty-five minutes, one day, or one week following the study trial.[1]

In analyzing the data, the authors considered that any drop in the subject's skin resistance occurring within four seconds of the presentation of a given word was an arousal deflection. Each subject's eight GSR deflections were then ranked; the three highest were designated "high arousal learning," and the three lowest, "low arousal learning." Fig. 6–16 indicates the relationship between high and low arousal recall as a function of time of testing. It may be noted that at immediate recall, the numbers associated with low arousal words were recalled five times as often as numbers associated with high arousal words. On the other hand, the capacity to recall numbers associated with high arousal words revealed incremental performance. In summary, the findings are in keeping with Walker's theoretical position that (1) the greater the arousal present when learning is taking place, the stronger the permanent memory, and (2) there is a degree of temporary inhibition of

[1] This study as well as a number of others that will be reported in this section examined what would normally be classified as retention or memory, in addition to learning.

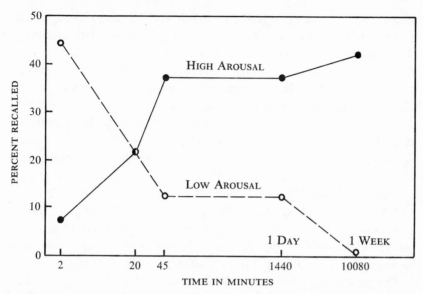

Fig. 6–16. Differential recall of paired-associates as a function of arousal level.

(Adapted from Kleinsmith and Kaplan 1963)

recall that is indicated by poorer recall scores for the high arousal words immediately following the study trial.[1]

In a second and similar study Walker and Tarte (1963), using a separate groups design, constructed different lists of words in order to vary arousal level. Thus, one list consisted of all high arousal words while a second list consisted of low arousal words. A third list was mixed, consisting of four high and four low arousal words. The response items associated with each of the stimulus words were the digits 2 through 9. The materials were programmed in a slide projector, and each slide was exposed for four seconds. The first slide contained the stimulus word, the second slide consisted of both the stimulus and the response items, while the third and fourth slides consisted of four colored squares. Subjects were instructed to speak each word aloud, to say both word and number, and to name the colors in any order. Three groups of subjects learned each list; however, the interval between learning and the recall task was two minutes for the first group, forty-five

[1] It must be acknowledged that Kleinsmith and Kaplan (1963) did not relate their findings to Walker's theoretical position.

minutes for the second, and one week for the third group. The results can be noted in Fig. 6–17 and in part support the findings of Kleinsmith and Kaplan (1963). That is, with low arousal words, the capacity to recall the numbers associated with the stimulus decreases as a function of time, but this does not appear to be true when high arousal words are used. A major difference between the two studies, however, is in the performance of the groups at immediate recall. Although Kleinsmith and Kaplan (1963) found significant differences in favor of the low arousal condition, this was not true in the present study.

Kleinsmith and Kaplan (1964) attempted to confirm their experimental findings by employing CVCs of zero association value as stimuli so that the high and low arousal curves would contain the same items; thus differential behavior in learning could not be explained in terms of qualities unique to the stimuli.

The procedure previously utilized was employed, with six zero-association-value CVCs utilized as the stimulus material (CEF, QAP, TOV, JEZ, LAJ, DAX). Response items were single digits

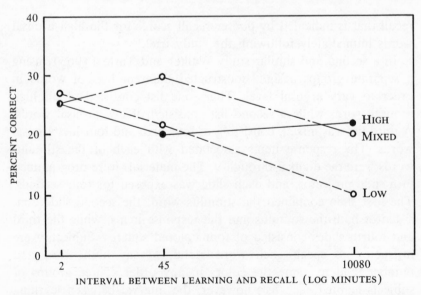

Fig. 6–17. Percent recall for the two homogeneous lists and the mixed list as a function of time. High- and low-arousal words were selected on a priori grounds.

(Adapted from Walker and Tarte 1963)

from 2 to 7. In order to determine the specific arousal effects of each nonsense syllable, skin resistance was recorded during the presentation of the material. Following the single training trial, subjects were tested for recall either immediately, after twenty minutes, or one week later.

In analyzing the data, any drop in the subject's GSR that occurred within four seconds of the presentation of the CVC was considered an arousal deflection. Each subject's six deflections to the stimuli were then ranked. The three highest deflections for each subject were designated high arousal learning while the three lowest were designated as low arousal learning. Fig. 6–18 presents the general findings, and the marked similarity of these results to those obtained in the first study can be noted. Thus, at immediate recall, low arousal learning is significantly greater than high arousal learning; after one week the situation has reversed and high arousal recall is significantly better than low arousal recall.

Findings obtained by other investigators have been generally supportive of the work of Kleinsmith, et al., although there are exceptions. A paired-associate learning study conducted by Ber-

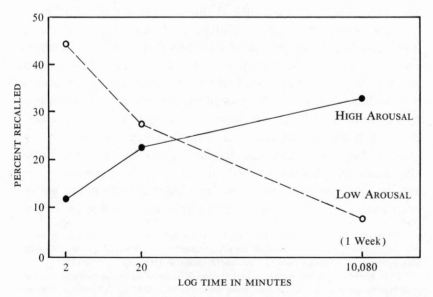

Fig. 6–18. Differential recall of CVC paired-associates as a function of arousal level.

(Adapted from Kleinsmith and Kaplan 1964)

lyne, Borsa, Craw, Gelman and Mandell (1965) is of interest since in one of their experiments (experiment III) these investigators used white noise to induce arousal. The experiment was a complex one involving the examination of a variety of different stimulus terms as well.[1] Disyllabic male first names were used as responses. The general procedure was one in which subjects learned the material under either (1) one of a variety of levels of white noise, or (2) no noise; and recalled the material a day later, also under either of these conditions. Thus, the following conditions were examined: (1) learning under no noise and recalling under no noise, (2) learning under no noise and recalling under noise, (3) learning under noise and recalling under no noise, and (4) learning under noise and recalling under noise.[2]

Results indicated that white noise impaired learning but improved recall as measured twenty-four hours later, a type of finding that had also been obtained by Kleinsmith and Kaplan (1963). It is interesting to note that variations in the level of the intensity of the white noise had no significant effects.

The authors pointed out that their procedure represented two basic departures from other experiments examining arousal. First, arousal was actually manipulated through the use of white noise, whereas other investigators distinguished only between arousal levels based on the magnitude of the GSRs that specific word stimuli evoked. Secondly, the stimuli in these other studies that induced arousal were the stimuli with which the responses to be learned were to be associated; in the present experiment, arousal was raised by a completely independent agent, belonging to a different sensory modality from the material used in the learning process.

A second paired-associate learning study by Berlyne, Borsa, Hamacher and Koenig (1966) also used white noise to induce arousal, and employed the same learning-recall procedure as had been used previously. These investigators were unable to support

[1] More specifically, heterogeneous double stimulus terms that involved the use of two adjectives (i.e., *glassy-crucial*) were compared with homogeneous double stimulus terms (i.e., *crucial-crucial*) and single stimulus terms (i.e., *crucial*).

[2] This general type of experimental design is similar to many animal learning experiments in which investigators have attempted to distinguish between learning and performance. See Kimble (1961) or Hall (1966). Considerable question must be raised, however, as to whether this type of design does distinguish between these two constructs.

the previous finding that white noise had a detrimental effect on learning, but did confirm the earlier conclusion that white noise during training improved recall.

Although Levonian (1966), who used high school students viewing a safety film in a free-recall learning situation, was able to obtain findings in keeping with Kleinsmith and Kaplan (1963); another free-recall study by Maltzman, Kantor and Langdon (1966) was unable to do so. In this latter study, eight high and eight low arousal words, used earlier by Walker and Tarte (1963), were presented in random order, with each word shown for ten seconds. Half of the subjects were given an immediate recall test, while for the other half, a retention test was provided one half-hour after the presentation. Results indicated that the high arousal words revealed superior learning as measured immediately following the presentation of the material, as well as superior retention.[1]

A second theoretical point of view, and one that is older than that proposed by Walker (1958), has been put forth by a number of investigators, i.e., Schlosberg (1954), Hebb (1955). Briefly, an inverted U relationship between level of arousal and performance level or learning has been posited. This relationship is indicated in Fig. 6–19, which Hebb (1955) has provided.

Stennett's (1957) experimental support for this relationship, using a tracking task, encouraged Berry (1962) to examine the relationship in the verbal learning situation. In the Berry study, two experiments were performed; the second one was a replication of the first. Male subjects were presented with thirty pairs of words; each pair was presented just once for ten seconds. Following the study trial, there was a six-minute delay following which the stimulus words were presented for ten seconds each and the subject was required to respond as often as possible. Each subject's GSR was continuously recorded throughout the experimental session.

[1] Kaplan and Kaplan (1968) have pointed out that the Maltzman et al. use of the free recall of familiar words rather than recall of unfamiliar paired-associates represents a major procedural change, and there is little reason to expect the results from the two types of learning situations to be comparable. Thus, they wrote that "free recall of familiar words involves selection of certain material well represented in memory; paired-associate learning presumably involves the formation of new bonds or representations" (p. 291). They have also indicated that the results of research in their laboratory using the free-recall learning situation agree with the Maltzman et al. findings of superior recall for high arousal material.

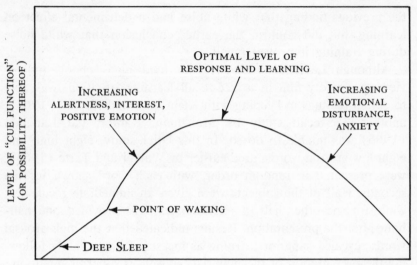

Fig. 6–19. Theoretical relationship proposed to exist between learning and arousal level.

(Adapted from Hebb 1955)

The findings obtained from both experiments suggested that moderate levels of skin conductance, as measured during the first minute of the learning session, were related to superior recall. Thus, the moderately aroused subject was shown to give a superior performance during the recall task, in contrast to subjects who were either highly aroused or only minimally so.[1]

Kleinsmith, Kaplan and Tarte (1963) were interested in attempting to replicate Berry's (1962) findings, since those results were at variance with what Kleinsmith et al. had obtained. The position of these investigators was that since time of recall was such a critical variable, it was possible that the inverted U-shaped function be-

[1] A study by Obrist (1962), using both heart rate and skin resistance as response measures and relating these to the learning of serial lists of CVCs for an extended period of time (thirty-six lists were learned), obtained findings that provided partial support for Berry's (1962) results. For three of five subjects used, a curvilinear relationship in the form of an inverted U was found between one or both performance measures (number of responses correct and latency) and one or both of the autonomic response measures. Obrist's study, which appears to be a model of experimental procedure, does point to the complexity of the relationship between at least some of the responses from which arousal is inferred.

tween learning and arousal was a temporary phenomenon and was not indicative of long term memory. They believed that if a longer recall interval was used in order to avoid the immediate confounding effects of active consolidation, a strong positive relationship between arousal and learning might be expected. The materials and procedures used by Berry were replicated. However, in addition to the six-minute recall group, a one-week recall group was also employed, in order to examine the effect of arousal on long term memory. Results indicated that although the relationship between recall and skin conductance level for the six-minute group was suggestive of the inverted U-shaped relationship as obtained by Berry (1962), data from the one-week recall group indicated a positive relationship between arousal and learning. The correlation coefficient between these two variables was .54, which was significant at the .005 level; the correlation coefficient for the six-minute recall group was .07. In summary, Kleinsmith et al. concluded that although an inverted U-shaped relationship had been demonstrated, it was probably artifactual, because of a failure to consider the effects of the recall interval employed.

Uehling and Sprinkle (1968) were interested in examining the effects of arousal at time of recall only. A ten-item serial list of disyllabic English adjectives was used as the learning task.[1] Serial anticipation procedures were used with a two-second rate of presentation and a four-second intertrial interval, and learning was carried out to a criterion of one errorless trial. Three retention intervals were examined: (1) immediately following learning, (2) twenty-four hours after learning, (3) one week following learning. The first three minutes of the retention period were devoted to the presentation of one of three arousal conditions: (1) instructions to relax, (2) the induction of muscle tension, or (3) bursts of white noise. Following this, all subjects were instructed to recall the words learned in the previous session; subjects were given either five relearning trials or attainment of one errorless trial, whichever came first. Results are indicated in Fig. 6–20; it should be noted that the statistically significant facilitation of recall at twenty-four hours and one week by white noise is consistent with earlier studies reported.

---

[1] The selection of the words was made on the basis of a rating procedure using five semantic differential scales, which were chosen for their apparent relationship to arousal. The ten most neutral words out of fifty rated were used.

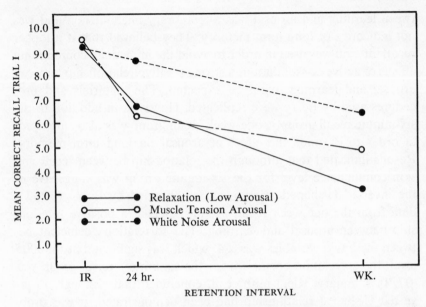

Fig. 6–20. Mean number correct responses on Recall Trial 1 for each arousal condition.

(Adapted from Uehling and Sprinkle 1968)

The apparent difference in recall at one week between the instructions to relax condition and the muscle tension condition, however, was not significant.

The study of Uehling and Sprinkle (1968) is interesting since in their use of muscle tension, they examined a variable that, although having a long history of experimental investigation and an obvious relationship to arousal, has been frequently ignored by contemporary investigators.[1]

One such hypothesis relating muscle tension to learning was suggested by Meyer (1953), who proposed that induced muscular tension facilitates responding "by making the motor system available to an input, and not by operating upon the input" (p. 209). In summary, then, the effect of such tension is not upon the subject's ability to learn but rather upon his ability to respond. As Bourne (1955)

[1] This relationship between muscle tension and arousal can be noted in Uehling and Sprinkle's (1968) discussion of their findings. Thus, they state, "it was reasoned that stimulation from muscle tension even without precise quantification of the degree of tension would be sufficient to produce neurophysiological and behavioral arousal" (p. 106).

wrote, Meyer's theory "can account for changes in magnitude and latency of a response but not for changes in rate of acquisition" (p. 418).[1]

Findings reported by Bourne (1955) are in keeping with Meyer's hypothesis. In this study, subjects were given a single trial in the learning of a list of paired-adjectives under conditions of tension or no tension, and then 0, 30, 60, 120 or 240 seconds later, were given a recall test, also under conditions of tension or no tension. Tension was produced by having the subjects squeeze a hand dynamometer to one-third their maximum exertion level. Results indicated that tension had no influence on the number of adjectives recalled immediately following the presentation of the material; however, as the time interval increased between the presentation of the material and the test for recall, recalling under tension became increasingly superior to recall without tension.[2,3]

SUMMARY

In addition to similarity and the characteristics of the material, learning has been investigated as a function of a number of other task variables as well. These have included (a) stimulus variation, (b) stimulus position, as well as (c) temporal variables that encompass the distribution of practice as well as presentation time.

A series of studies conducted by Bevan and his associates indicated that varying the material presented frequently leads to greater learning than would occur if the material presented were not so varied. Thus, the presentation of a variety of different *shoes* will result in better recall of the word *shoe* than if the presentation had remained invariant.

When a list of items is learned in serial order, a great many

[1] It should be acknowledged that Meyer (1953) assumes that probability of responding represents a measure of learning, while the measures of latency and magnitude reflect only performance.

[2] It will be recalled that Uehling and Sprinkle (1968) were unable to find that tension facilitated recall; they attributed this failure to the fact that their subjects were not instructed to exert any specified amount of tension on the dynamometer used. As a result the amount of muscle tension produced could have been minimal.

[3] All investigators have not been able to obtain findings supporting Meyer's theoretical position. See Sidowski and Nuthmann (1961).

experimenters have found that the number of correct responses is not equally distributed over all of the items that make up the list; rather a bow-shaped curve is obtained. Items at the beginning of the list are learned most rapidly; next, items at the end of the list. If free-recall learning situations are utilized, a type of bow-shaped curve is also obtained, except that the items at the end of the list are easiest to learn, followed by items at the beginning. With both tasks the items in the middle of the list are most difficult to learn.

The influence of time as a variable has been examined in a variety of situations; one of the oldest areas of investigation has been massed versus distributed practice. The experimental evidence appears to be unequivocal in demonstrating the superiority of distributed practice in serial learning tasks. After an extensive review of the work that had been done with paired-associate learning, Underwood and Ekstrand (1967) concluded that the distributed practice effect with this type of task is one of extremely small absolute magnitude. When such an effect is obtained, it may be due to the presence of some inhibitory state that retards the growth of associative strength; such inhibition presumably dissipates during the distributed practice rest interval.

A second temporal area has been the examination of learning as a function of the total amount of time provided. Bugelski (1962) hypothesized that the degree of learning will be a function of the total time involved, regardless of the duration of individual trials. The evidence obtained from paired-associate and free-recall learning situations has been reasonably strong in support of the total time hypothesis. Cooper and Pantle (1967) suggested that the process that underlies the invariance shown in total learning time is probably rehearsal. These investigators proposed two criteria for the specification of learning situations in which the total time hypothesis could be expected to hold: (a) task requirements must not exceed a simple rehearsing of the to-be-learned material, and (b) effective rehearsal time must bear a positive and linear relationship to the amount of presentation time the experimenter provides.

A second area considered in this chapter was motivation. Although not a task variable, motivation has interested some investigators as an important contributor to performance.

Using the Hull-Spence $D \times sHr$ theoretical framework, a variety of experimenters have conceptualized emotional responsiveness as a basic motivational source and have manipulated it in both serial as well as paired-associate learning situations. Work in the area has resulted in the recognition that emotional responsiveness, as measured by the Taylor Manifest Anxiety Scale, must interact with some type of environmental stress in order to provide a substantial increase in the subject's drive level, which in turn is posited to have an important influence in the verbal learning task. In addition, the fact that paired-associate learning is generally conceptualized as consisting of two stages has made it imperative for investigators to consider the influence of drive on each of these stages.

A second motivational topic that has interested some experimenters is the area of arousal. Arousal hypotheses have not been uncommon in psychology. One of the more recent was proposed by Walker (1958), and Walker and Tarte (1963), who hypothesized that high arousal during learning results in a temporary inhibition against immediate recall. A delay in the test for recall, however, results in increased performance or a kind of reminiscence effect. A number of studies by Kaplan and his associates have provided some confirmation of this hypothesis.

7　Organizational Processes

One of the important developments that has taken place in the study of verbal learning over the past decade has been the examination of organizational processes.

Introspective analysis of what takes place when an individual is asked to learn a list of words or paired-associates reveals that frequently there is an attempt to organize the material in such a way that its acquisition and recall will be facilitated. Up until a decade ago, these organizational aids used by the subject were largely ignored by psychologists interested in verbal learning. True, psychologists were aware of the existence of these processes since their own introspective analysis of the learning of a list of items indicated that such processes were utilized; at the same time, however, experimenters did their best to minimize the role of these aids in learning. Thus Woodworth and Schlosberg (1954) wrote in their experimental text,

Such aids in memorizing are naturally regarded with much favor by O, but E would like to be rid of them. They make the learning task less uniform and introduce variability and unreliability into the quantitative results. Besides, E wants to study the formation of new associations, not O's clever utilization of old ones (p. 708).

A somewhat similar point of view was expressed by Miller, Galanter and Pribram (1960), who pointed out that an important reason why associational (and organizational) aids were not studied was that these kinds of reports look hopeless since every subject appears to provide a different way of associating the items.

It is much easier to think in terms of an average subject with normal, but unspecified, associations. It may even be better to do so, because introspections are notoriously unreliable and because there is no assurance that these elaborate translations and groupings and associations by the memorizer are really any help at all (p. 127).

Most contemporary investigators now accept the position that with virtually all learning tasks, the subject organizes the material that is to be learned. Thus, learning and recall are not conceptualized as passive constructs but rather, it is believed, the subject actively brings into play a variety of processes, that have the end result of simplifying and facilitating the learning of the task at hand.

In an early and classic paper demonstrating such an organizational process, Miller (1956) indicated that although the span for immediate memory appears to be relatively fixed at about seven units (or "chunks," as he termed them) the amount of material to be recalled (or learned) can be increased by building larger and larger chunks. That is, the individual can organize or combine a number of small chunks into a larger one, and thus increase the amount of material that can be recalled.

The example Miller used to illustrate this phenomenon was the man just beginning to learn telegraphic code. At first, he hears each dit and dah as a separate chunk, but soon he is able to organize these sounds into letters so that he deals with letters as chunks. After some practice, the letters organize themselves into words, which become still larger chunks. Following this, the telegrapher begins to hear whole phrases. Miller has indicated that as larger and larger chunks emerge in the learning of the code, the amount of the message that the operator can remember increases accordingly.

A second example of the operation of an organizational process is found in a study by Allan (1961). In this study, servicemen were requested to learn a randomized order of the letters of the alphabet. The sequence of the letters was as follows: N A J S T W H I D Q V F Z C E P G O K B X R Y L M U. Each letter was individually placed on an index card; the subject turned over each card and called the letter aloud, until all of the twenty-six letters had been presented. A recall trial followed each presentation. Learning and recall trials continued until each subject was able to recall all of the letters in the order presented. Allan noted that subjects frequently organized the letters into manageable units, and devised meaningful translations of these units. Thus, OK was recalled by some as a slang expression, while HID was simply remembered as a word. QV was recalled by one subject as Queen Victoria, while QVF was recalled by another as a code used in the Navy.

A variety of terms have been used to describe these organizational processes that are presumed to operate. "Stimulus selection," "coding," "mediation," and "clustering" are some of these. We cannot be sure, however, that because different names have been used to describe what the subject appears to be doing, the processes are also different.[1]

PAIRED-ASSOCIATE LEARNING

STIMULUS SELECTION

If a stimulus situation has a number of component (and distinctive) parts and the subject selects just one of these to which to respond, we have the operation of what many investigators have called a stimulus selection process. It is this process that provides the distinction between the nominal and functional stimulus. The paired-associate learning situation represents an excellent experimental situation in which to examine the influence of this process, since it clearly distinguishes between the stimulus and response elements of the task.

Underwood (1963) wrote that the observations that brought his attention to the general problem of stimulus selection were made by Mattocks, a student working under his direction. The experimental situation was one in which subjects learned a paired-associate list consisting of eight pairs of items—trigrams served as stimuli while common three-letter words served as responses. There was no similarity among the trigrams since twenty-four different letters were used in constructing them. Following learning, the subjects were questioned as to how they had formed associations between each pair on the list. The experimenter was surprised when 62 percent of the reports made it clear that the subject indicated

---

[1] For example, Underwood and Erlebacher (1965) have pointed out that stimulus selection may be classed as a form of coding.

that he had used only the first letter of the trigram as the stimulus to which to respond. Although the nominal stimulus consisted of three letters, the functional stimulus for many of the subjects was the first letter of the trigram.

An early experimental demonstration of the stimulus selection process can be found in a study by Underwood, Ham and Ekstrand (1962). The method and procedure they employed was as follows: A compound stimulus consisting of a word or a trigram was placed on a colored background and was paired with a response term consisting of a single-digit number from 2 to 8. The stimulus components that were used can be noted in Table 7–1. Anticipation trials were used with a 2:2 rate; learning was continued until the subjects achieved one perfect recitation of the list. Following such learning, ten transfer trials were provided in an effort to determine what stimulus element the subject had used. For one group, only the background colors were used as stimuli, whereas for a second group only the verbal stimuli (word or trigram) with a homogeneous background were presented. In addition, control groups were utilized in which the transfer task consisted of continued presentation of both verbal and contextual stimuli.

Fig. 7–1 presents the acquisition curves on the transfer trials for both trigrams and words. An examination of that part of the study that utilized words reveals that words as well as colors were used by some individuals as stimuli to which to attach responses. The fact that transfer was greater when words were used as the sole

TABLE 7–1

STIMULUS COMPONENTS USED IN THE LISTS

Words	Trigrams	Colors
GAS	GWS	Red
DAY	DWK	Brown
NEW	NXQ	Yellow
DIE	DHX	Blue
BAD	BWD	Orange
GOT	GVS	Black
BED	BXD	Green

(Adapted from Underwood, Ham and Ekstrand 1962)

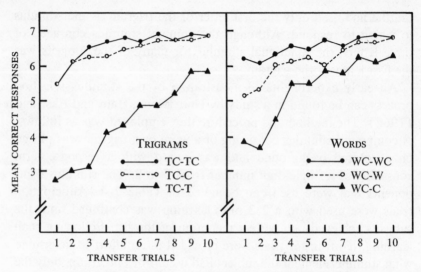

Fig. 7–1. Acquisition curves on the ten transfer trials.
(Adapted from Underwood, Ham and Ekstrand 1962)

stimulus condition than when just colors were presented supports
the position that subjects use words as stimuli for most associations.

It is the findings with the trigrams, however, that provide most interest. When colors were presented alone, virtually complete transfer
resulted, with the performance of the color group only slightly below
that of the control group (which had been provided both the trigram and the color on the transfer tests). Some transfer, however,
could be noted for the group that was provided the trigrams but not
color. Trigrams, at least under certain circumstances, were able to
serve as nominal stimuli.[1]

VARIABLES RELATED TO STIMULUS SELECTION

POSITION, MEANINGFULNESS, DISTINCTIVENESS AND RESPONSE CHARACTERISTICS

It is obvious, then, that stimulus selection is a basic process that
operates in at least some learning situations. Our concern is to
delineate some of the variables that experimenters have found to be
related to its operation.

[1] The Underwood, Ham and Ekstrand (1962) findings have been replicated by
Jenkins and Bailey (1964).

A number of investigators have shown that stimulus selection can be related to the position of the stimulus elements that make up the stimulus compound. We have already noted the tendency on the part of Mattocks' subjects to select the first letter of a trigram as the functional stimulus. A subsequent experiment by Jenkins (1963) confirmed Mattocks' findings. In Jenkins' study, a paired-associate task was used in which trigrams served as stimuli and single digits as responses. Following the learning of the list, the stimulus letters were divided into three groups according to the position they had in the trigram. These single letters were then presented one at a time with instructions to the subjects to recall the appropriate digits. Correct responses to letters from each of the three positions were above chance. As Mattocks had found, the amount of recall was highest to the first letter and lowest to the middle letter.

In a further examination of the role of position as well as meaningfulness in stimulus selection, Cohen and Musgrave (1964) had subjects learn to associate single-letter responses to compound stimuli that consisted of two CVCs each, representing high-high, high-low, low-high, and low-low combinations of degrees of meaningfulness. More specifically, the high CVCs were words, while the low meaningful lists contained CVCs with average association values of 10 percent. Learning trials were carried out to a criterion of two consecutive perfect trials. Following this learning, a transfer task was utilized in which the individual CVCs (components of the training stimuli) were presented singly. Four such trials were provided.

The authors found that for the paired-associates with two low meaningful CVCs as stimuli, there was a significant tendency on the part of subjects to select the first CVC rather than the second to which to attach their response—a finding in keeping with the studies of Mattocks (Underwood 1962) and Jenkins (1963). It should be noted, however, that this tendency to select the first CVC was not present when the compound stimulus consisted of two high association CVCs.

A second finding was that when the stimulus consisted of a low meaningful CVC and a high meaningful CVC, regardless of the position of the high meaningful CVC, testing with only the high meaningful CVC resulted in significantly more correct responses than testing with the low. Presumably, then, there is a tendency on the part of subjects to select stimulus elements that are meaningful—

TABLE 7–2

MEAN NUMBER OF CORRECT RESPONSES TO SINGLE
LETTERS IN TEST LIST

	Position 1	Position 2	Position 3	Group Means
Group 1	4.17 [a]	.91	1.25	2.11
Group 2	1.75	2.58 [a]	.91	1.75
Group 3	2.25	1.25	2.58 [a]	2.03
Position Means	2.72	1.58	1.58	1.96

[a] Red letters.
(Adapted from Rabinowitz and Witte (1967)

perhaps because it is easier to form an association between the
stimulus item and the response.

We have noted that the position as well as the meaningfulness of
a stimulus element within the compound may play a role in the
selection process. As might be anticipated, the distinctiveness of the
element may also be a factor. Rabinowitz and Witte (1967) made
up a paired-associate list composed of CCCs as stimuli and single-
digit numerals as responses. For a given group, the letter in either
the first, second, or third position of the trigram was red, while the
letters in the other two positions were black. When the list had been
learned to a criterion of one perfect trial, the individual letters were
presented and the subjects were required to respond with the appropriate response number. Nonsignificant differences in the rate of
learning the paired-associate list were noted. Within each position
in the transfer test, as Table 7–2 indicates, the subjects responded
correctly more often to those letters that were red in the paired-
associate list.

STIMULUS INTEGRATION

In another examination of the selection process in the paired-
associate learning situation, Postman and Greenbloom (1967)
investigated the contribution of what has been termed stimulus

integration. The authors' experimental procedure consisted of using a list of six paired-associates, in which trigrams served as stimuli and single digits as responses. For one list, however, the stimulus trigrams were difficult to pronounce while for a second list, they were easy to pronounce. Following the learning to a criterion of one perfect recitation, either the first, second, or third stimulus letter was presented; in addition, another group of subjects was given all three letters as a stimulus. The specific procedure consisted of presenting a single letter and dashes in place of the missing letters. The subjects were instructed not only to recall the digit that had been paired with the stimulus but also to indicate the missing trigram letters as well.

Postman and Greenbloom (1967) found that there was little evidence for single-letter cue selection when the stimulus terms were easy to pronounce, a finding subsequently confirmed by Lovelace and Blass (1968). In addition, and in keeping with the earlier findings of Mattocks (Underwood 1963) and Jenkins (1963), the authors found that when the stimulus terms were difficult to pronounce, the selection of stimuli was largely limited to letters in the first position.

These authors posited, then, that stimulus selection may be expected to occur only among functionally discrete units. Inasmuch as the easy-to-pronounce trigrams were well-integrated sequences of letters, the subjects responded to them as single units. Thus, stimulus selection, which would involve the breaking up of a functional unit, took place only sporadically when the easy-to-pronounce trigrams were used. In contrast, the difficult-to-pronounce trigrams were not integrated units and it is reasonable to assume that the subjects initially responded to the letters as discrete elements. This kind of situation appears to be most favorable to the stimulus selection procedure. Moreover, the most economical procedure was for the subjects to select the first letter. The distribution of recall scores as well as postexperimental reports of the subjects indicated that subjects do indeed heavily favor the first letter when they select a single element.[1]

---

[1] Postman and Greenbloom (1967), as well as Steiner and Sobel (1968), call attention to several methodological and interpretive problems that arise in the analysis of stimulus selection. Postman and Greenbloom point out that the correct responses made to single elements on a test of recall do not by themselves consti-

From our experimental findings, it should be concluded that if the nominal stimulus is perceived as an integrated unit, the selection process is minimal. Or as Postman and Greenbloom (1967) hypothesized, the stimulus selection process may be expected to take place only among functionally discrete units.

However, when the nominal stimulus is composed of functionally discrete units, there is the likelihood that the subject will select that element which provides greatest meaningfulness, familiarity, distinctiveness, etc.[1] Moreover, as Harrington (1969) recently demon-

tute evidence for stimulus selection since such responses may be mediated by the reproduction of additional letters. That is, the initial letter presented may possibly give rise to the recall of the second and third letters, which in turn elicit the appropriate response. In these authors' study, a dual criterion was used: only those cases in which the subject failed to reproduce additional letters and yet also gave the correct response were classified as instances of single-letter selection. The authors indicated that this dual criterion must be recognized as a conservative procedure since it is quite possible that some subjects practiced single-letter selection early in acquisition and then proceeded to respond to the remaining elements as well, or perhaps learned additional letters incidentally. Thus the amount of selection that occurred at some time during the acquisition is probably underestimated.

Steiner and Sobel (1968), using a paired-associate learning situation with compound stimuli (word-color pairs), showed intercomponent association formation during the learning trials. That is, these investigators found that following the learning of a paired-associate task in which compound stimuli were used, the subjects were able, using a matching test, to match components of the compound stimuli. More specifically they found that subjects were able to form intercomponent associations (S-S) and to match components on the basis of these associations, rather than associating the two stimulus components by the mediation of the response (S-R-S).

In experiments on stimulus selection, following training on compound stimuli, subjects typically are given recall tests with single components. If intercomponent associations are formed during training, the performance to one component when tested alone may be affected by the level of learning to the other component of the same compound. This process may be anticipated to minimize recall performance differences between selected and unselected components.

[1] A study by Houston (1967) has lent credence to this position. His experimental materials and procedure were similar to those previously employed by Underwood, Ham and Ekstrand (1962). Here, it will be recalled, a trigram and a color formed each stimulus in a paired-associate learning situation. In Houston's study, subjects were given one of four types of learning instructions. One group of subjects (syllable) were told to concentrate on the trigrams as they would be subsequently tested with those items alone. A second group (color) were given the same kind of instructions concerning color. The third group (either) were told that they would be tested with either the colors or the trigrams; while the fourth group (control) were given no special instructions. We cannot detail all of the results; however Houston found that although the syllable group had been instructed that they were going to be tested only on syllables, they were able to respond to color

strated, the selection strategy will also involve the selection of an aspect of the nominal stimulus that is consistently available throughout the list.

In short, the subject attempts to reduce the complexity of the learning task by selecting the stimulus element that will provide a stable mediating response to the nominal stimulus, which in turn will (1) aid the subject in differentiating among the other stimuli that make up the material to be learned, as well as (2) provide for the most efficient response-term association.

One test of this second point is found in a study by Underwood and Erlebacher (1965) (experiment 5), who investigated stimulus variability. The stimuli which these investigators used in their paired-associate learning task were five-letter units that could not be encoded into words. With these materials, the hypothesis was that the rate at which a stable response to each stimulus would be established would be inversely related to the number of different letter orders that were used on the varying learning trials. Thus, for one condition, the order of the letters was invariant from trial to trial, while in a second condition, two different orders of the letters were used; in a third condition, four different orders were examined. In addition, interstimulus similarity was manipulated with the expectancy that the number of different stimulus letter orders would exert more influence on high similarity material than on low.

The materials consisted of the stimulus terms made up of five letters (four consonants and a vowel). For the low similarity lists, eighteen consonants and four vowels were used, while for the high similarity items, only nine consonants and two vowels were used. The stimulus and response terms used are indicated in Table 7–3. Original learning was carried out until the subject correctly anticipated six responses on a single trial. Typical paired-associate instructions were given, although subjects were also informed that the order of the stimulus letters might vary from trial to trial.

The mean number of trials to reach the criterion of six correct responses for each of the six types of lists are indicated in Fig. 7–2. Here it can be noted that stimulus similarity was a highly significant

cues during the test situation almost as well as the color group. Houston (1967) concluded that "the most easily utilized components are probably the ones which are attended to" (p. 513).

TABLE 7–3

EXPERIMENTAL MATERIALS

| Stimuli (one ordering of letters) | | |
Low Similarity List	High Similarity List	Response
OTVBK	BUNTK	GROPE
MXECH	FJANS	WHINE
TPAJS	CNSBA	WAKEN
OGXLR	PBUFK	BLINK
EFKLW	TPSJA	MANLY
PUVJH	KCBPU	STUNG
SBCAN	PCAJT	RIGID
WEZFN	STUFJ	FOCUS

(Adapted from Underwood and Erlebacher 1965)

variable, and that difficulty in learning increased as the number of different orders of the stimulus terms increased. As can be noted, however, most of the change occurred between one- and two-letter orders, with only slight increases in difficulty between two- and four-letter orders.

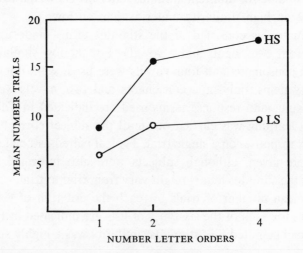

Fig. 7–2. Acquisition as a function of stimulus-term similarity and number of different letter orders of the stimulus terms.

(Adapted from Underwood and Erlebacher 1965)

THE ROLE OF LEARNING

Intuitively, one might expect that learning would influence the selection process in the following way. When the subject is first faced with a learning situation involving compound stimuli, it might take several trials before he discovers that he need not attend to all of the components of the stimulus. Under such circumstances, the selection process should be minimal. As learning trials continue, however, the subject finds that he can discriminate among the stimuli on the basis of just a single component, which results in a selection effect. Finally, as stimuli continue to be presented, the subject may turn his attention to the remaining components of the stimuli and establish associations between these components and the responses.

Although the experimental findings are equivocal, studies by James and Greeno (1967), and Davis, Brown and Ritchie (1968) have indicated that the stimulus selection process may operate in the manner in which we have just described. In James and Greeno's (1967) first experiment, eight compound stimuli were used in which each stimulus consisted of a three-letter word and a CVC trigram. The words had association values of 100 percent while the average association value for the trigrams was 10 percent, according to Archer's (1960) norms. The responses attached to each of these compound stimuli were the digits 1 through 8. Three groups of subjects were each given different amounts of practice. One group (underlearning) was stopped after the trial in which subjects first gave four correct responses. The second group (criterion) was stopped after the trial on which subjects gave correct responses to all eight of the items. The third group (overlearning) of subjects was overtrained—run to a criterion of one perfect trial and then given ten additional trials. The study-test procedure was used during the learning trials. As soon as each subject reached one of the learning criteria, a transfer test was provided. Here, each compound stimulus was split into its two components, and each component was paired with the same response that had been used during the original learning. Thus, the transfer list consisted of sixteen paired-associates—eight pairs with word stimuli and eight with CVC stimuli. Five anticipation trials were provided, in which each component was presented and the subject was required to respond to every item on every trial. After the subject responded, the correct response was shown.

As might be anticipated, the mean number of trials taken by the varying groups to meet the original task criteria was significantly different. The underlearning group (group U) required 5.95 trials, the criterion group (group C) 9.45 trials, while the overlearning group (group O) required 22.45 trials. It is the transfer test, however, that are of primary concern. An examination of the mean number of errors made by each subject on each type of transfer item yields the following findings: when the word stimuli were presented, the means of the error scores for groups U, C, and O were 15.4, 7.8, and 5.5. The authors point out that the significant result involves the use of the CVCs as stimuli. When these were presented, the means of the error scores for groups U, C, and O were 27.2, 24.6, and 17.4. Here, the difference between group U and group C was not significant, but group O differed significantly from both of these groups. Thus, subjects who were trained to a single perfect trial during the original training showed no more transfer to the nonsense components than subjects who were trained to four out of eight correct responses. On the other hand, subjects who received ten overtraining trials on the compound stimulus showed significantly more transfer to the nonsense components. A second experiment was run in which the stimulus word did not always appear on the left during acquisition trials as it had in experiment 1, but appeared equally often on the right and left positions. The results obtained were similar to those obtained in the first experiment. Table 7–4 provides the findings for both experiments. In summary, the authors

TABLE 7–4

MEAN ERROR SCORE

	Experiment I		Experiment II	
	Words	Trigrams	Words	Trigrams
Underlearning	15.4	27.2	16.45	27.65
Criterion	7.8	24.6	7.15	27.75
Overlearning	5.5	17.4	2.15	10.20

(Adapted from James and Greeno 1967)

have interpreted their data as consistent with the hypothesis that the subject actively selects among stimulus components until the list is mastered, but then relaxes this selection response during over-training.

One part of a study by Davis, Brown and Ritchie (1968) has confirmed the James and Greeno findings. Here, a six-item paired-associate list was used in which the stimuli were CCCs with no repeated letters within or between stimuli. The response terms were low similarity CVCs that did not have any letter overlap (BOV, DUT, FAP, KEZ, RYX, SIH). Eight groups of subjects were run and four degrees of learning were investigated; namely, either two. four, or six correct responses on a single trial, or three consecutive errorless trials (6 + 3). The study-test procedure was used during the learning trials. Following the reaching of the appropriate learn-ing criterion, the test for stimulus selection was administered. Here, following the Postman and Greenbloom (1967) procedure, the first letter of each stimulus term was presented, and the subject was instructed to give the missing two letters of the stimulus term and then to spell aloud the three letters of the response term that had been previously paired with that item. The order of exposure of the stimulus letters was varied across subjects within each group and subjects were given unlimited time to respond to each stimulus letter.

The determination of first-letter cue selection requires the appli-cation of the dual criterion—that is, an inability to reproduce miss-ing stimulus letters and the correct recall of the response term on the cue selection test. If there is reproduction of one or both of the stimulus letters when the response is correctly recalled this would suggest that these additional letters could have been used as com-ponents of the functional stimulus. For each subject, correct re-sponses given on the cue selection test were divided into three response categories: S0, S1, and S2, corresponding respectively to zero, one, and two stimulus letters correctly reproduced. Fig. 7–3 shows the mean number of correct responses in each of these cate-gories as a function of the degree of learning. As can be noted, the magnitude of the superiority of the S0 category is essentially the same under the two and four correct response degree of learning (DL) criteria; however, a significant increase is noted in the relative number of S0 responses at DL6 followed by a decrease at DL6 + 3. The authors have interpreted these findings in much the same way

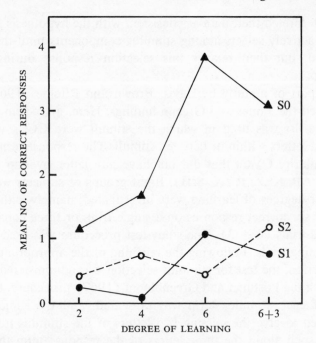

Fig. 7–3. Mean number of correct responses in each recall category as a function of degree of learning.

(Adapted from Davis, Brown and Ritchie 1968)

that James and Greeno (1967) explained their results: As the learning of the list proceeds through initial mastery, increased attention is directed toward the first letters of the stimulus terms. With increased practice, the subjects acquire additional stimulus letters, perhaps as a means of increasing resistance to forgetting.

It should be noted that the second part of the Davis, Brown and Ritchie's (1968) study, as well as experiments by Houston (1967) and Lovelace and Blass (1968), all have been unable to find an interaction between degree of learning and the characteristics of the stimulus selection process. In Houston's study, the Underwood, Ham and Ekstrand (1962) experiment was replicated. In order to manipulate the degree of learning, either one, three, twelve, or twenty anticipation trials were provided. The subjects were then tested for digit recall when either colors, trigrams, or both colors and trigrams were provided. Although Houston was able to confirm the Underwood et al. (1962) finding that color alone was highly effective in eliciting the appropriate responses in the transfer test, and that trigrams presented alone were not nearly as effective, he was not able to obtain an interaction between degree of learning and the type of recall cue. Thus, although the effectiveness of all three types of cues, i.e., color, trigram, and color and trigram, increased as a function of the amount of learning, there was no change in the relative effectiveness of these as the degree of learning increased.

In a similar type study, Lovelace and Blass (1968) conducted four experiments in which the stimuli were six trigrams and the responses were the numbers 3, 4, 5, 6, 8 and 9. The study-test procedure was used. The degree of learning was manipulated by stopping different groups of subjects when they reached a criterion of (a) 50 percent correct on a given trial, (b) one errorless trial, or (c) 50 percent overlearning, which required half again the number of trials to reach the one perfect trial condition. After reaching the criterion, each subject received three test trials. Within each test trial, subjects were presented first-position trigram letters for two trigrams; second-position trigram letters for two other trigrams, and third-position trigram letters for the last two trigrams. In the experiments conducted, three types of trigrams were employed—(1) medium meaningful CCCs, (2) low meaningful pronounceable CVCs, and (3) English word-CVCs. A summary of the results of the four experiments revealed no systematic improvement in the ability of subjects to utilize the second and third positions as effective stimuli when higher degrees of original learning were provided.

It is probably unrealistic to assume that an interaction between the degree of learning and the stimulus selection process will always be found. The kind of stimulus material that is utilized, as well as the general strategy adopted by the subject, would appear to play a role in determining whether or not there would be a change in the selection process as learning progressed.

CODING

When a subject is given verbal material to learn, he may decide to change it into a form that he believes will permit him to perform the task more efficiently. Thus, a trigram such as FML that must be learned as a response to a stimulus may be transformed or coded into the word "FEMALE." The process whereby the subject changes the character of the stimulus or the response, usually into a more meaningful form, is known as coding.[1]

Underwood and Erlebacher (1965) examined the contribution of coding to the learning of paired-associates in a series of studies. In one of these, the authors assumed that a major portion of overall paired-associate learning involves the acquisition of responses as such (response learning stage), and encoding the trigrams into words should facilitate the acquisition of the three letters that make up the trigram. This would follow since the encoded unit has higher meaningfulness than the unit as presented. However, in any examination of coding, the decoding process must be considered as well. If decoding is difficult, the use of the built-in coding system may be inefficient. In an experimental examination of this issue (experiment 3), a paired-associate task was used, in which three-letter response terms were used that permitted one, two, or four decoding rules. The stimulus terms were the numbers 1 through 12 paired randomly with response terms. Lists were presented at a 4:3 second rate—the four-second presentation of the stimulus was used to permit sufficient time for decoding, if this were to occur. All responses were spelled by the subjects. Learning was carried to a criterion of eight out of twelve correct responses on a single trial. Acquisition curves plotted as mean trials to attain successive criteria are indicated in Fig. 7–4; it is obvious that the single decoding rule resulted in significantly faster acquisition.

In the study cited, the coding operation was performed on the responses. In a second study these investigators (experiment 4) were interested in examining the coding of stimuli. Most research has indicated that stimulus meaningfulness does not play an important role in paired-associate learning, so a coding system that

---

[1] In considering a definition of coding, Underwood and Erlebacher (1965) commented that if the representation of a given verbal unit in memory is isomorphic to the unit as presented for learning, no coding has occurred. On the other hand, if the verbal item undergoes certain changes, transformations, additions, subtractions, etc., between the unit as presented, and the unit as it is stored in memory, coding is said to have taken place. Under these circumstances, the reader will note that the stimulus selection process that has just been discussed can be conceptualized as a type of coding.

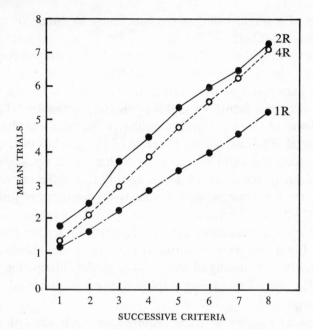

Fig. 7–4. Acquisition of paired-associate lists as a function of number of decoding rules (experiment 3).

(Adapted from Underwood and Erlebacher 1965)

transformed a meaningless stimulus into a meaningful one would probably produce only slight differences in learning. On the other hand, stimulus similarity does play a major role in paired-associate learning; as a result, the authors manipulated this variable in an effort to maximize the influence of coding of stimuli.

Their approach can be illustrated by the following example. Assume a stimulus term in a paired-associate list is an anagram— ESMOK. This anagram can be solved to produce the word *smoke* but whether or not the functional stimulus is *smoke* or ESMOK should make little difference in overall learning since differences in meaningfulness have so little effect on learning. Assume that another stimulus term is EMSUO. The two uncoded stimuli, ESMOK and EMSUO, have very high formal similarity and as uncoded stimuli would be expected to retard learning in contrast with two stimuli with low formal similarity. Such retardation would be accentuated if the order of the letters of each stimulus was varied from trial to trial in order to make stimulus selection (i.e., the

selection of a single letter as the functional stimulus for each trigram) quite difficult.

The experimental procedure consisted of manipulating three
variables. The first variable was whether or not the five-letter
stimulus item could be transformed into a word. A second variable
was the ease or difficulty of making this transformation.[1] The third
variable was the formal intralist similarity that was introduced into
the material. This was varied in terms of the number of duplicated
letters among the eight stimulus items that made up a given list.
Low similarity consisted of using twenty-two different letters to
make up the list while the high similarity list consisted of just eleven
different letters. The response terms for all lists were five-letter
words having a Thorndike-Lorge frequency of ten to twelve per
million. Eight lists were constructed permitting the examination of
these variables. Learning of any list was by the anticipation method
with a 4:2 second rate being employed; the criterion used was one
perfect trial.

The mean number of trials required to reach the criterion for
the varying groups can be observed in Fig. 7–5. First, it may be
noted that stimulus similarity influenced the rate of learning for
all types of lists, and that low stimulus similarity lists proved the
easier to learn. The easy-to-decode variable also was significant;
this effect was produced primarily by the more rapid rate of acquisition of the word solution–easy-to-decode variable than all other
lists. The authors point out that the results are quite clear in
showing that stimulus coding can to some extent be controlled by
the experimenter. However, the coding system appears to have
operated only when it was obvious that the letters, when rearranged, produced a word, and this occurred only when letters
were in the easy order. If the letter order made the anagram a
difficult one to solve, the learning proceeded in much the same
way as it did in the control list where solution was not possible.

---

[1] The authors were aware that this variable does not have the same meaning as
it does for the lists that permit word solutions. However, they point out that "by
ordering the letters to correspond to the easy-solution stimuli of the S [solution]
lists, and also according to the difficult-solution orders, it seemed possible that the
differences in the wordlike characteristics of the stimuli which resulted might influence the learning" (p. 15).

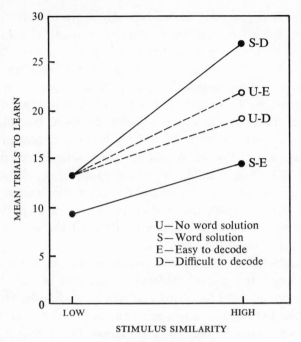

Fig. 7–5. Acquisition of paired-associate lists as a function of stimulus-term similarity and other stimulus-term properties.
(Adapted from Underwood and Erlebacher 1965)

MEDIATION

A third type of organizational process that has been inferred from some paired-associate learning findings is mediation. The concept of mediation was utilized by the early associationists who posited that an association between two terms, which were not directly related themselves, could be mediated by a third term that had no associative relation to the original terms. The positing of mediators permitted these early theorists to deal more easily with complex cognitive processes. Thus, a "new" idea that seemed to occur in the absence of any known associative relationship between that idea and earlier ones could be accounted for on the basis of some association that the "new" idea and an earlier one had in common.

It is, of course, no surprise that subjects, in learning paired-associates, frequently report that they have used mediators. As

Dallett (1964a) wrote, "Ss are typically eager to volunteer information to the effect that the seeking of meaningful mediators is,
indeed, an important part of their learning process" (p. 209).

The basic mediation paradigm is that if A is associated with B,
and C is also associated with B, then A will come to have some
association with C. In an attempt to facilitate the learning of an
A-C relationship in the verbal learning situation, the subject may
provide a covert response, B, which—because it has an already-
established association to A and also to C—facilitates the acquisition of A-C. For example, if the paired-associate, *dog-nine* is to
be learned, many subjects might find that the learning of this
stimulus response relationship could be facilitated by providing the
mediated response *cat*. Here, *dog* would elicit the word *cat* which
would in turn elicit the word *nine*.

Although Reed (1918) investigated mediators more than half
a century ago, the general tendency on the part of verbal learning
investigators up until ten years ago was to studiously avoid them.
During the last decade, however, a number of experimenters have
become interested in their use. Underwood and Schulz (1960),
Clark, Lansford and Dallenbach (1960), and Bugelski (1962)
all have recently reported on the use of mediators by their subjects.
In Bugelski's study, for example, subjects were asked after learning
pairs of CVCs if they had used mediators to help them learn the
pairs. Bugelski reported that with two-thirds (67 percent) of the
items, the subjects indicated that they had made use of some sort
of mediational device.

Five types of mediators were identified: (1) those in which the
subjects would form one word from the two CVCs, e.g., DUP-TEZ
would result in *deputize*. (2) Those in which the CVCs would be
formed into two separate words, e.g., CEZ-MUN becomes *says
man*. (3) Those in which the subject would manufacture or
imagine appropriate phrases or words that would sound like the
syllables, e.g., GEY-NUR becomes *general nurse*. (4) Those in
which the subject would attempt some abstract analysis of the
syllables to get at some lead to the response, e.g., BIH-XIR becomes BI = 2, X = 10. (5) Those in which the subjects would
report some vague association with one part of the combination,
e.g., GAC-QET becomes translated into *tourniquet*. Bugelski further noted that not all pairs aroused reportable mediators and

some mediators were forgotten after being used. Inasmuch as one part of the study manipulated the length of the time that the response was exposed, i.e., two, four, six, eight, or fifteen seconds, an additional finding was that the longer the time interval, the more likely the occurrence of a mediator.

It should be pointed out that the mediators reported by Bugelski were provided by the subjects themselves; following Adams' (1967), we can identify these mediators as natural language mediators (NLM) since they arose from the subjects' previous language experiences.

An experimental investigation of NLMs has been provided by Montague, Adams and Kiess (1966), who were interested in examining (a) meaningfulness and (b) presentation time as variables that would be likely to influence the production of natural language mediators. Their experimental procedure consisted of presenting ninety-six pairs of high or low meaningful CVCs for either fifteen or thirty seconds. Upon presentation of the pair, the subjects were instructed to write each of their natural language mediators on a separate card. Only a single presentation of the material was provided; twenty-four hours later, each stimulus CVC was presented and the subjects were asked to recall not only the CVC response but their NLM for that pair as well. Findings with regard to the operation of meaningfulness and presentation time on the production of natural language mediators are provided in Table 7–5. Here, it can be noted that NLMs significantly increase

TABLE 7–5

MEAN NUMBER OF NATURAL LANGUAGE
MEDIATORS (NLMs) USED IN
ACQUISITION

Presentation Time	m'		Mean
	Low	High	
15	31.1	59.4	45.2
30	50.5	74.7	62.6
Mean	40.8	67.1	

(Adapted from Montague, Adams and Kiess 1966)

both with meaningfulness and presentation time. A second question was related to how mediators influence retention. In examining recall scores, the experimenters were interested in determining whether the mediator used during the original presentation and the recall test was the same (or similar), whether it was different, or whether no mediator was used, in which case it was assumed that the learning was by rote. Table 7–6 shows the proportion of correct recalls in each NLM category for the four experimental groups. Examination of these findings reveals a high correlation between the retention of NLMs and correct responses at recall. Correct recall was quite low, on the other hand, when the mediator was either not the same, or when no mediator was available.

Wood and Bolt (1968) have also demonstrated the facilitative effect on learning with the use of mediators; in this instance, the mediators were based on free association norms. In this study, a paired-associate task was used; stimuli were single letters while responses were high frequency words. An experimental group of

TABLE 7–6

PROPORTION CORRECT RECALLS IN EACH NLM CATEGORY FOR EACH GROUP

Group	NLM Category			Group Total
	Same or Similar	Not the Same	Rote	
L-15	83/182	6/752	57/1946	146/2880
	.456	.008	.029	.051
L-30	154/337	5/1178	72/1365	231/2880
	.457	.004	.053	.080
H-15	339/421	32/1361	93/1098	464/2880
	.805	.024	.085	.161
H-30	666/770	41/1472	73/638	780/2880
	.865	.028	.114	.271
Category Total for All Groups	1242/1710	84/4763	295/5047	1621/11520[a]
	.726	.018	.058	.141

Note.—The proportion is based on the ratio given, which is number correct over number of items in a category for a group.

[a] All items, all groups.

(Adapted from Montague, Adams and Kiess 1966)

subjects was told that they would be given a mediator in order to help them link each of the letter-word pairs. Here, then, the mediating response was externalized in that it was written out and placed in parentheses between the stimulus and the response on each of the study trials provided. The characteristics of each mediating response were that it started with the same letter as the stimulus and was a strong associate of the response. Thus, the stimulus-response pairs: T-*chair;* K-*queen;* and M-*lamb* had the following mediating responses—*table, king,* and *mutton* (i.e., T[*table*]-*chair;* K[*king*]-*queen;* M[*mutton*]-*lamb*). A control group was not provided with these mediators. Subjects received four alternating study and test trials. The mediating response was not, of course, provided on any of the test trials. An examination of the mean number of correct responses for the experimental and control groups for the four test trials can be noted in Table 7–7. Statistical analysis indicated that the mediators significantly facilitated performance. Moreover, the superiority of the mediation group was maintained across the four trials as indicated by the nonsignificant interaction between trials and conditions.

It may be noted that in this experiment, the control group did not have the advantage of being provided a mediator—a variable that the authors believed might have hindered the performance of this group. In an effort to control for this factor, a second experiment was conducted. Two experimental groups were provided mediators; however, these mediators were inappropriate to the task at hand. One experimental group received the same mediating responses as the experimental group had received in experiment I, but the task responses were changed. Here, for example, the medi-

TABLE 7–7

MEAN NUMBER OF CORRECT RESPONSES

	Trials			
	1	2	3	4
Control	3.25	6.25	8.42	10.17
Experimental (Mediating)	5.92	9.50	12.08	13.17

(Adapted from Wood and Bolt 1968)

ators *table, king,* and *mutton* were used in learning the paired-associate pairs, T-*doctor,* K-*sour,* and M-*afraid.* For the second experimental group, the same external responses used in experiment I were used; in this case, the mediators were changed. Thus, the mediators for the pairs, T-*chair,* K-*queen,* and M-*lamb,* were *town, kiss* and *mile.* Control groups learned the two lists without being provided mediators. The experimental procedure used for this experiment was similar to that employed in experiment I except that six study-test trials were provided rather than four.

The results from this second experiment can be noted in Table 7–8. Here it can be observed that the mean number of correct responses for the experimental groups was smaller than for their appropriate controls—a finding obtained over almost all of the test trials provided.

In summary, these findings support the position that the facilitation of learning by the experimental groups in experiment I was dependent upon the preestablished associations between the stimulus and the mediator, as well as between the mediator and the response.

As the reader might have anticipated, investigators have been interested in determining some of the conditions governing the use of mediators. We have already discussed the Montague, Adams

TABLE 7–8

MEAN NUMBER OF CORRECT RESPONSES

	Trials					
	1	2	3	4	5	6
Mediating I [K-(king) Sour]	1.33	3.94	6.11	7.83	9.72	10.78
Control I (No mediators)	2.11	6.44	8.11	8.94	10.00	10.67
Control II [No mediators]	6.33	9.11	10.33	11.83	12.33	13.50
Mediating II [K-(kiss) Queen]	2.56	5.33	7.44	8.56	10.44	11.39

(Adapted from Wood and Bolt 1968)

and Kiess (1966) experiment that investigated the roles of presentation time and meaningfulness. A recent study (experiment II) by Schwartz (1969) indicated that learning is also facilitated by instructions to use verbal mediators. In this study, it was necessary for subjects to learn ten pairs of items. Like Wood and Bolt's (1968) material, the stimuli were letters while the responses were words that could be related to the letter via a mediator, e.g., A-(Apple)-Pie. One group of subjects was instructed that "some subjects find it easier to learn a list of this type by mentally changing the left-hand letter into a word that begins with that letter and is also related to the right-hand word" (p. 2). An uninstructed group was not provided with these instructions. A single-study trial was followed by a recall trial in which the subjects had unlimited time to provide each response. Following the recall test, a matching test was also provided in which all of the responses were listed alphabetically, and the subject had to match the appropriate response with the stimulus. Results indicated that with both measures, the instructed group was superior in terms of the mean number of correct responses recalled.

It is well known that many so-called memory systems use visual images as mediators in order to provide the individual with a "system" that will improve his memory. Studies by Bugelski and his associates have used the paired-associate learning task to experimentally examine images as mediators.

In a study by Bugelski, Kidd and Segmen (1968), three groups of subjects were equated on the basis of their scores in a preliminary learning task. An experimental group then learned to associate the numbers 1 through 10 with ten words, i.e., (1) *bun,* (2) *shoe,* (3) *tree,* (4) *door,* (5) *hive,* (6) *sticks,* (7) *heaven,* (8) *date,* (9) *wine,* and (10) *hen.* This group read this list of rhyming words (list A) and was tested on them until they could recite them without error five times in succession. The subjects were also told that these words could aid them in the learning of a new list of ten words if they picture the words to be learned in some context with the words on the original list. Thus, if the third word on the new list was *bird,* a bird could be pictured sitting in a tree.

One control group was given training similar to that provided the experimental group in that they learned the mnemonic list so it could be repeated for five successful repetitions without error;

however, they were not informed as to how it might be used. A second control group was not told about the list, nor did they receive any learning trials.

The three groups of subjects were then presented with a test list consisting of ten common object names, with instructions to learn to associate these words with their positions in the list (i.e., 1-*car*, 2-*barn*, 3-*mask*, etc.). It should be also noted that each group was divided into three subgroups, and the test list of items was presented at different rates—either two, four, or eight seconds per word. The experimenter then tested for recall by calling out the ten numbers in random order and permitting each subject four seconds during which to respond. Subjects were given two points for each correct response; if a word in the list was recalled, but not to the correct number, a single point was given. The learning scores obtained by the varying groups of subjects are noted in Table 7–9. These values indicate that in the learning of the test list of words, the experimental group had significantly higher learning scores than either control group at both the four- and eight-second presentation rates. The two-second presentation rate, however, resulted in essentially no difference among the groups. The reports of the experimental subjects indicated that they followed the practice prescribed by the experimenter, in that they attempted to mediate the position number with the word to be learned by using the word from the mnemonic list.

In a second study, Bugelski (1968) was interested in examining the influence of images as mediators over a series of six lists. The experimental procedure was similar to that utilized in the previous

TABLE 7–9

MEAN SCORES

Treatment	Presentation Times		
	2 sec.	4 sec.	8 sec.
Experimental Group	8.9	15.9	19.4
Rhyme Control Group	7.8	11.7	12.3
Standard Control Group	8.6	12.5	14.6

(Adapted from Bugelski, Kidd and Segman 1968)

study except that only a single control group (a group not given any training trials in the learning of the mnemonic list) in addition to the experimental group was used. In addition, all subjects were permitted unlimited presentation time. That is, following the presentation of a word, the subject indicated to the experimenter when to present the next one. Following the learning of the first list, the experimenter called out the ten numbers in a random order, and the subject attempted to recall the varying words associated with each number. Two points were provided for each correct response. Following the recall of list 1, five other lists were presented with a recall period following each presentation. The words used can be found in Table 7–10. After the recall of the sixth list, the subjects were asked to recall all of the number one words, then all of the number two words, etc., in order to determine how many of the sixty words were retained. At the completion of the experiment, each subject was asked to describe how he had learned the varying words that made up each list.

Although individual subjects were free to take all of the time they wanted for the number-word association, there were no significant differences in mean time scores between the experimental and control subjects. As Table 7–11 indicates, the experimental subjects were clearly and significantly superior in learning scores for five of the six lists. When total recall scores are examined, a similar

TABLE 7–10

MNEMONIC LIST AND THE SIX WORD LISTS USED IN THIS STUDY

Mnemonic	List 1	List 2	List 3	List 4	List 5	List 6
1-bun	car	dime	pencil	bird	ship	wheel
2-shoe	flag	barn	kite	chair	moon	cigar
3-tree	clock	nail	mask	brick	snake	fan
4-door	book	rat	table	gun	bed	face
5-hive	knife	ball	radio	cat	purse	broom
6-stick	shirt	lamp	stamp	bicycle	glasses	candle
7-heaven	drum	rug	cup	ring	medal	desk
8-gate	scissors	apple	window	hat	hammer	umbrella
9-wine	pen	telephone	soldier	couch	sword	rose
10-hen	ski	airplane	key	magazine	box	garage

(Adapted from Bugelski 1968)

TABLE 7–11

Means for the Experimental (Mnemonic) Group (N = 18) and
the Control Groups (N = 18) in Original Learning and
Subsequent Recall after Learning All Six Lists

	Means					
Group	1	2	3	4	5	6

Original Learning List

Experi-						
mental	18.00	16.00	17.11	17.00	17.56	16.78
Control	12.00	10.00	14.33	12.44	14.33	14.44
t	4.96***	3.29***	1.98****	3.37**	2.62***	ns

Recall from All Six Lists

Experi-						
mental	11.00	9.89	12.67	13.00	13.89	15.67
Control	3.00	3.56	5.11	5.89	8.89	11.89
t	6.83*	3.96*	4.89*	5.55*	3.36**	2.78**

* p = .001
** p = .005
*** p = .01   Means were obtained by multiplying each correct
**** p = .05   response by 2

(Adapted from Bugelski 1968)

finding is obtained except that the difference between the experimental and control groups was significant for all lists. Bugelski (1968) notes that the control subjects had little to say in terms of how they learned individual associations, although they did report trying a variety of schemes, such as rapid rehearsal, attempting to fit the words into a story, etc.

FREE-RECALL LEARNING

Free-recall learning situations have frequently been used as a vehicle for the examination of organizational processes. Inasmuch as the identification of the stimulus with this type of task remains obscure, investigators have centered their attention primarily on associational processes, although the coding process has interested a few experimenters.

CODING

The approach that investigators in this area have taken has been to look at the coding process in free-recall learning tasks in the same way as researchers have examined it in paired-associate learning. That is, how does coding operate to enhance or inhibit free-recall learning? In one such study, Underwood and Keppel (1963a) presented ten trigrams to subjects for five alternate study and recall trials. Each of the ten trigrams could be changed into either of two words by rearranging the letters. For example, UTB could be arranged to spell either *tub* or *but*. One group of subjects were given instructions indicating that these trigrams could be coded into words. A second group remained uninstructed. Within each of these groups, four subgroups were differentiated on the basis of the nature of the correct response demanded by the experimenter. One subgroup was instructed, prior to the first learning trial, that the letters could be written in any order. The second subgroup was instructed that the letters must be recalled exactly in the order presented, to be counted correct. Following the first test trial, this group was reinstructed that on subsequent trials the letters could be written in any order. For the third subgroup the instructions to write the letters as presented held until after the third test trial, at which time they were reinstructed that on subsequent trials the letters could be written in any order. Finally, the subjects in the fourth subgroup were required to write the items on all test trials as they had been originally presented. The results indicated that when the subjects were permitted to recall the letters of each trigram in any order, performance was facilitated if the trigrams were encoded into words. And as might be anticipated, the instructed group was superior to the uninstructed. On the other hand, when the group was required to recall the trigrams as they were presented, the noninstructed group revealed superior performance. The reason for the inhibitory effect of coding was that although the coding process was a simple one, a specific decoding rule had to be learned for each trigram. Thus, if DMA was encoded into *mad* the rule for decoding had to be something like, "Put the first letter third." But, for the trigram SBU, which had been coded into *sub*, a different decoding rule was necessary. Since no single decoding rule could apply to all trigrams, there were numerous possibilities for interference among the decoding rules—which undoubtedly contributed to poorer performance.

In a further study of coding Underwood and Erlebacher (1965) demonstrated that the learning of a list of trigrams was related to the number of decoding rules that had to be applied. More specifically, the twelve-item lists used were so constructed that in one condition (1R) a single decoding rule applied to all twelve trigrams; in the second condition (2R), two decoding rules were needed, each rule applying to six of the trigrams. Finally, in the third condition (3R), four rules were required, each applying to a different group of three trigrams. The general procedure consisted of presenting each trigram at a three-second rate for six study trials, with each study trial followed by a forty-eight second written recall period. Instructions emphasized that the three letters of each trigram should be written in the order presented to be counted correct. In addition, it was pointed out to the subjects that if the letters of each trigram were rearranged, a common word would result. The mean number of correct responses on each of the six trials for the three groups is shown in Fig. 7–6. Subjects in condition 1R were clearly superior to those in the other two groups throughout

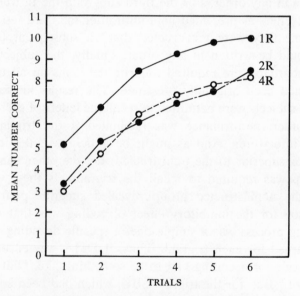

Fig. 7–6. Acquisition as a function of number of decoding rules. (Adapted from Underwood and Erlebacher 1965)

the learning period. Performance under condition 2R and condition 4R showed no differences. The authors concluded that the number of decoding rules appears to be a relevant variable in the free-recall learning of the lists but that its effect is limited to a difference between one rule and two or more.

ASSOCIATIONAL PROCESSES

Stimulus selection, mediation, and coding may be conceived of as reflecting the operation of an organizing process on the part of the subject. As was discussed in the introduction to this chapter, the subject actively utilizes these processes to facilitate learning. Associational processes may be conceived of as having a similar function. That is, the verbal association network that develops as a result of the individual's experience with the language is used to organize the free-recall learning task so as to facilitate its acquisition. Such associational processes have been inferred primarily from the characteristics of the empirical relationships that have been discovered to exist among the words that make up the learning task.

CLUSTERING

One such associational process is known as clustering. Clustering may be defined as a tendency on the part of the subject to organize or group words that (1) belong to a common category, or (2) can be related vis-à-vis free association procedures. As an example of category clustering, although the words *diamond, pearl* and *emerald* might appear as widely separated items in a list of words to be learned, they typically are recalled together. Presumably, the general category "precious stones" would serve as a cue for the subject to recall these items as a group. Similarly, associative clustering would show up when the words *WHITE* and *BLACK* were recalled together although they were not originally presented together.

Bousfield (1953) was one of the early investigators to examine category clustering. In his experiment, subjects were presented with a randomized list of sixty words made up of four fifteen-item categories: animals, names, vegetables, and professions. Immediately following the presentation of the items, subjects were given ten minutes to write down all the words they could recall. Bousfield found that the subjects showed a greater-than-chance tendency to place items in clusters or groups that contained members of the same category. Thus a subject's recall protocol might be as follows: *dog, cat, cow, pea, bean, John, Bob, Joe, Jim, doctor, lawyer, professor, dentist.*

The measure of clustering that Bousfield (1953) and most subsequent investigators have used was repetition ratio (RR). This measure is obtained by dividing the number of consecutive items recalled from the same category by the total number of repetitions possible for the words recalled. (This value is simply the number of words recalled minus one.) Thus, the RR formula is as follows:

$$RR = \frac{r}{N - 1}$$

where N is the total number of words recalled, and is typically contrasted with the value that would be obtained by chance.[1]

Since the varying words forming a cluster may be described in terms of their membership in a general class or category, the name "category clustering" has been given to this type of experimental arrangement. Moreover, since the order of items recalled, as measured by the repetition ratio (RR), corresponds to the cate-

[1] One problem that is connected with this measure is that when more than a single category is represented in the material presented, there is no allowance made for the fact that a clustered response cannot take place in going from one category to another. Thus, this measure is not independent of the number of categories represented by the words recalled. For example, if two lists of twelve words are presented, and one list contains two categories and the second six, a perfect clustering protocol for the first list would provide an RR score of .909

$$\begin{array}{cccccccccc} 1 & 2 & 3 & 4 & 5 & & 6 & 7 & 8 & 9 & 10 \\ (A & A & A & A & A & A & B & B & B & B & B & B), \end{array} \quad (RR = \frac{10}{11} = .909)$$

while a perfect score for the second list would result in an RR score of .545

$$\begin{array}{cccccc} 1 & 2 & 3 & 4 & 5 & 6 \\ (AA & BB & CC & DD & EE & FF). \end{array} \quad (RR = \frac{6}{11} = .545).$$

Moreover, the number of repetitions possible, as indicated by the formula, would be eleven. Alternative clustering measures have been suggested by Bousfield and Puff (1964), and Robinson (1966). The interested reader may consult Shuell (1969) for a further discussion of the difficulties with these varying clustering measures. The problems involved do not appear to be serious, however, since Shuell (1969) reports that the relationship among these varying measures is quite high; the correlations obtained is in the high eighties and low nineties.

gories that were preexperimentally determined, most investigators have inferred that an organizational process is in operation during the presentation and/or recall period. Thus Bousfield (1953) wrote: "The results of this study have indicated that subjects, when given a list of randomly arranged items will in their recall show a greater-than-chance tendency to group the items in clusters containing members of the same general category. This implies the operation of an organizing tendency" (p. 237).

The RR measure, however, does not provide the answer to a second question that has interested many investigators; namely, are more items recalled from a categorized word list than from a control list? In order to answer this question (which could not be answered in the Bousfield study), it is necessary to assemble a list of unrelated words that are matched with those on the categorized word list for word frequency, length, etc. If significantly more words are recalled from the categorized list, it may be inferred that the organizational process has contributed to the superior recall.

An example of utilizing recall scores in this type of study is found in a study by Cofer (1959), who examined the tendency of synonyms to cluster. In this experiment, a synonym list was prepared that was composed of eight groups of five synonyms each. Forty unrelated words were used as a control list, and each control word was selected to match in initial letter and syllabic sound, length, and Thorndike-Lorge (1944) frequency, a word in the synonym list. Items were auditorily presented, and subjects were given five minutes to recall as many of the items as possible. Measuring repetition ratio (RR), Cofer (1959) found that the group given the synonym list revealed significantly more clustering than would be expected by chance, and also more clustering than indicated by the control group.[1] On the other hand, the number of words recalled from each list revealed no difference between the groups.[2]

[1] As the author points out, the control group cannot be scored for clustering in a real sense, but the data were analyzed in terms of the incidences of sequences of words from the same artificial group. The clustering values thus constitute an empirical check on chance values.

[2] Although one might expect repetition ratio and number of words recalled to be highly correlated, since presumably a common organizational process contributes to both, the relationship is not as high as one might anticipate. Cofer, Bruce and Reicher (1966) found that the correlations computed between these

ASSOCIATIVE OVERLAP

Associative overlap, used to identify another aspect of the associational process, has been investigated in a series of studies by Deese (1959, 1960). Deese hypothesized that the number of words recalled in the free-recall learning situation is determined primarily by the associations between the words on the list or their inter-item associative strength. It will be recalled that we discussed the measurement of this variable in Chapter 3.

In Deese's (1959) first experiment, eighteen lists of fifteen words per list were used. Six of these lists consisted of words frequently given as associations to particular Kent-Rosanoff stimuli. Six other lists consisted of low frequency associations to the same six stimuli, while the remaining six lists consisted entirely of words never given as associations to those stimuli. In summary, then, three lists consisting of either high, low, or zero associative (HF, LF, ZF) frequency were constructed from responses made to each of the following stimulus words: *butterfly, slow, whistle, music, command* and *chair*. The procedure consisted of presenting words from each list auditorily, and then permitting the subjects time to write down as many of the words as they could remember.

In order to secure inter-item associative strength for the varying lists, fifty subjects were used to obtain free association norms for the ninety words used in the experiment.

The number of items recalled for each list, along with the inter-item associative strength for each list, is indicated in Table 7–12. It can be noted that within each three-list set, the number of items recalled is related to the strength of the inter-item associations. Moreover, the correlation between the inter-item associative strength and the number of items recalled per list is .88.

It should be acknowledged that increases in inter-item associative strength do not always facilitate learning. In serial learning situations, where correct performance depends on placing the items in correct order, high inter-item associative strength may be detri-

two measures for twelve different conditions examined resulted in r's ranging from –.29 to .64, with a median value of .53. They concluded that the relationship between these variables "is neither invariant nor very high" (p. 860). More recently, Shuell (1969) has supported Cofer, Bruce and Reicher (1966) by reporting an r of .44 between these two variables.

TABLE 7–12

INTER-ITEM ASSOCIATIVE STRENGTH AND MEAN NUMBER OF
ITEMS RECALLED FOR ALL LISTS

List		Inter-item Assoc. Str.	N Items Recalled
Butterfly	HF	28.3	7.9
Butterfly	LF	4.3	6.7
Butterfly	ZF	1.0	5.6
Slow	HF	15.1	6.5
Slow	LF	0.2	5.8
Slow	ZF	2.7	5.8
Whistle	HF	22.8	7.3
Whistle	LF	4.0	5.6
Whistle	ZF	2.3	5.4
Music	HF	20.5	7.7
Music	LF	9.3	6.1
Music	ZF	0.0	5.1
Command	HF	13.0	7.1
Command	LF	0.7	5.6
Command	ZF	0.0	5.2
Chair	HF	17.0	7.8
Chair	LF	2.0	6.6
Chair	ZF	0.0	6.1

(Adapted from Deese 1959)

mental to learning. A recent study by Postman (1967) has demonstrated such to be the case. In this study, serial lists of twelve items
per list were made up in which there was either high or zero inter-
item associative strength among the items. The mean number of
trials to a criterion of one errorless performance was 18.1 for the
high inter-item associative list and 15.4 for the zero inter-item
associative strength list. Although this overall difference was not
reliable, it was found that the middle items in the high list were
significantly more difficult to learn. As Postman has pointed out,
the net effect of inter-item associative strength on acquisition will
depend upon the requirements of the learning task. If reproduction
of the serial order is not required, as in the free-recall learning
situation, preexisting associations among the items serve as mediating links and thus serve to facilitate learning. On the other hand,

when correct performance depends on accuracy of sequential order, the previously established inter-item associations become a source of interference, which in turn makes the learning of the sequential order demanded by the experimenter more difficult.

In a subsequent study by Deese (1960) this investigator confirmed the findings of his first experiment; but more important, he demonstrated that word frequency does not contribute to number of words recalled if inter-item associative strength is controlled. His general procedure consisted of varying word frequency, but at the same time, obtaining inter-item association measures for all of the words used so that the contribution of these two variables to recall could be compared.

In this study, the two principal independent variables were list length and word frequency. Here, ninety lists composed of 12, 25, 50 and 100 items were used. Each list was homogeneous with respect to frequency of usage and was made up of words limited to one of the following ranges from the Thorndike-Lorge (1944) word count: (1) words occurring more frequently than 100 times per million (AA); (2) words occurring between 50 and 100 times per million (A); (3) words between 49 and 21 occurrences per million; (4) words occurring between 20 and 9 per million; (5) words between 8 and 3 per million; and (6) words occurring 1 or 2 times per million. In all, fifteen lists represented *each* of the six Thorndike-Lorge categories. The words were selected by taking every tenth AA and A word in the count and every twentieth word from the lower frequency ranges. These words provided the basic pool of words from which the items actually used in the experiment were chosen by a table of random numbers.

The general procedure was to present each word auditorily at a rate of 1.5 seconds per word. Following the presentation, subjects were provided with answer sheets on which they wrote their recalls.

Free association norms were obtained for all of the words in the list, using a population different from that used for the recall phase of the experiment.

The general findings of the study are presented in Table 7–13. Inspection of the table reveals that inter-word association varies with list length as well as with frequency of usage. These values do not indicate, of course, that inter-item associative strength is the basic variable, since recall scores vary as a function of word

TABLE 7–13

MEAN NUMBER OF WORDS RECALLED AND THE INDEX OF INTER-WORD ASSOCIATION FOR ALL FREQUENCIES
OF USAGE AND LIST LENGTHS

Frequency of Usage	Number of Words in the List							
	12		25		50		100	
	Mean Recalled	Inter-word Assoc. (%)	Mean Recalled	Inter-word Assoc. (%)	Mean Recalled	Inter-word Assoc. (%)	Mean Recalled	Inter-word Assoc. (%)
AA	7.3	1.0	9.0	1.5	13.5	2.8	18.0	6.7
A	6.3	0.0	8.3	0.2	10.7	1.2	14.8	2.0
49–21	5.8	0.0	8.3	0.1	10.7	0.1	12.0	0.2
20–9	6.3	0.0	8.3	0.0	9.5	0.1	12.2	0.2
8–3	5.8	0.0	7.1	0.0	10.7	0.0	11.4	0.0
2–1	5.3	0.0	6.7	0.0	10.3	0.0	11.1	0.0

(Adapted from Deese 1960)

TABLE 7–14

MEAN RECALL FOR ALL LISTS WITH ZERO INTER-WORD ASSOCIATION

Frequency of Usage	Number of Words in the List							
	12		25		50		100	
	Mean Re-called	N Lists	Mean Re-called	N Lists	Mean Re-called	N Lists	Mean Re-called	N Lists
AA	6.7	1						
A	6.3	8						
49–21	5.8	8	7.7	1	9.7	1		
20–9	6.3	8	8.4	3	10.7	1		
8–3	5.8	8	7.1	4	10.3	2	11.4	1
2–1	5.3	8	6.7	4	10.3	2	11.1	1

(Adapted from Deese 1960)

frequency as well. Table 7–14 presents the mean recall scores for all of those lists at each level of frequency of usage and list length that yielded inter-word association indexes of zero. It is these findings that suggest that variation in mean recall as a function of word frequency "is either drastically reduced or eliminated by holding inter-word association constant" (Deese 1960, p. 342).

ASSOCIATIVE CLUSTERING

The contribution of associative strength to clustering is nicely illustrated in a study by Jenkins and Russell (1952). These investigators had subjects recall a list of forty-eight words composed of stimulus and response pairs obtained from the Kent-Rosanoff association norms. The words, of course, were presented in a random order but in their recall, subjects showed a highly significant tendency to group or cluster the items in their stimulus-response or associative sequence. Thus, although a number of words intervened between the presentation of *table* and *chair*, recall protocols indicated that *table* and *chair* were recalled together. Reversed associations, i.e., *chair-table* occurred significantly more frequently than chance pairings but significantly less than the forward sequence.

Subsequent studies by Jenkins, Mink and Russell (1958), and Rosenberg (1966), working with adults, and Wicklund, Palermo and Jenkins (1965), employing children as subjects, have confirmed these findings.

Shapiro and Palermo (1967) were interested in assessing the influence of indirect or mediated associations upon clustering in free recall. To illustrate, consider the triad of words: *income-money-green*. *Income* elicits *money* as an associate and *money* elicits *green* as an associate in a free association test, but *green* is not a free associate of income. The occurrence of mediated clustering may be tested by presenting a list of word pairs like *income* and *green* and observing whether such pairs tend to occur contiguously in free recall. In their first experiment, these investigators found that when the items were presented in randomized order, no clustering was obtained, even though eight study-test trials were provided.

A second experiment that employed the block presentation of the pair members, also for eight trials, revealed that significantly more clustering took place for the experimental group than for control groups and that clustering increased over trials. In addition, the number of items recalled by the experimental group exceeded those by the control group.

OTHER VARIABLES RELATED TO CLUSTERING AND RECALL

As might be anticipated, investigators have been interested in examining a number of variables that they believe are relevant to the examination of clustering and recall, and from which organizational processes have been inferred. Let us consider some of the most important of these.

ASSOCIATIVE STRENGTH

The studies of Jenkins and Russell (1952), and Deese (1959, 1960), which we have already discussed, illustrate that associative processes make important contributions to clustering and free-recall scores.

In a further examination of associative clustering, Jenkins, Mink and Russell (1958) demonstrated that the amount of clustering is a function of the amount of associative strength as measured by frequency of association. In this study, groups of subjects were asked to recall four different word lists; each list was made up of twelve stimulus and response pairs (twenty-four items) obtained from the Kent-Rosanoff association norms. The average associative strength of the stimulus and response pairs varied systematically from list to list. For example, list 1 had the highest associative strength, being made up of such pairs of words as *man-woman*, *table-chair*, *black-white*, etc.; the fourth list, on the other hand, had the lowest associative strength, utilizing such pairs as *cheese-crackers*, *child-baby*, *earth-round*, etc. The words were not used in their paired-order, of course, but were presented in random fashion. Findings revealed a significant tendency to recall the words in their stimulus-response sequence—a finding that confirmed the earlier Jenkins and Russell (1952) study and first illustrated associative clustering. More important, however, was the fact that the average amount of such forward associative clustering was closely related to the average free associative strength of the pairs in each list.

Finally, it should be recognized that clustering can take place even though inter-item associative strength is low as Hudson (1968) recently demonstrated. In order for such clustering to take place, however, it appears to be necessary to provide subjects with information (or instructions) regarding the categories to be used, as well as an opportunity for them to learn the relationship involved.

In this study, four categories were used: *Small, Round, White,* and *Smelly,* with eight words grouped under each category. Thus, under *White,* the following items were used: *milk, chalk, bandage, teeth, ivory, napkin, linen, rice.* Inter-item associative strength indicated an index of .23 percent obtained for each of the four categories. Free-recall learning procedures were utilized, with separate groups being given either one, two, three, four, five, six, seven, or eight presentations of the thirty-two words. However, half of the subjects in each of these groups were given the instructions that the words presented could be categorized and were given the category names; the other half were not given such instructions. Each presentation of the items was in a different random order. Following the last presentation, subjects were given four minutes to write down as many words as could be recalled. The findings are indicated in Fig. 7–7, which depicts clustering as a function of the number of

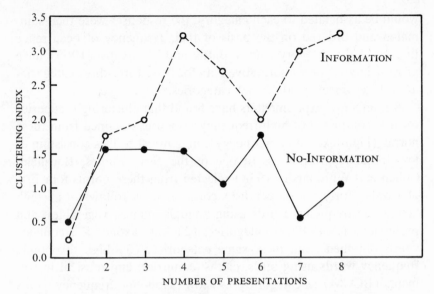

Fig. 7–7. Clustering index as a function of the number of presentations for the Information and No-Information groups.
(Adapted from Hudson 1968)

presentations.[1] Both the information condition as well as the numbers of presentation conditions were significant.

A type of associative strength found in categorized word lists can be measured in terms of taxonomic frequency. It will be recalled from Chapter 3 that here we are measuring the associative strength between a category name or concept, and instances of that category.

Early investigators studying clustering (i.e., Bousfield 1953) were not concerned with this type of associative strength; moreover, the category items used were determined by an intuitive appraisal by the experimenter of what items should be included within a given category. This dependence upon subjective evaluation was eventually replaced by normative data. Cohen, Bousfield and Whitmarsh (1957) secured norms for forty-three different category names by asking 400 students to provide four specific words that they believed

[1] The clustering index used by Hudson (1968) was different from that used by most investigators. This index was adapted from a test of multiple runs provided by Barton and David (1957). It consists of subtracting the expected number of repetitions from the observed number of repetitions and dividing by the appropriate standard deviation. This produces approximately normal standard scores, thus making the chance index of clustering zero.

would be associated to each category; the responses were then summated and ordered on the basis of their frequency of occurrence
to each of the category names. Battig and Montague (1969) have
provided more recent normative data for these forty-three categories
as well as thirteen additional categories.

A number of experimenters have found that clustering is superior
for lists comprised of high frequency responses obtained from these
norms (high taxonomic frequency), in contrast to lists consisting of
low frequency responses. In one of the early studies, Bousfield,
Cohen and Whitmarsh (1958) selected from these norms four lists
of words (forty words per list) constituted as follows: (1) high
taxonomic frequency words using animals, names, vegetables, and
professions (ANVP) as categories; (2) low taxonomic frequency
words obtained from these same categories; (3) high taxonomic
frequency words using birds, cloths, countries, and musical instru-
ments (BCCM) as categories; (4) low taxonomic frequency words
using these same categories. Typical free-recall learning procedures
were used, with each word presented just once for 2.5 seconds. The
results, as presented in Table 7–15, indicate the mean ratios of
repetition (RR), and mean recall scores as functions of the taxonomic means, as well as Thorndike-Lorge frequencies of the
stimulus words. Clustering (as measured by RR), as well as mean
recall, was significantly superior for the two high taxonomic frequency lists.

TABLE 7–15

MEAN RECALLS AND MEAN RATIOS OF REPETITION AS FUNCTIONS OF THE
MEANS OF THE TAXONOMIC AND THORNDIKE-LORGE FREQUENCIES
OF THE STIMULUS WORDS

Stimulus Word List	Geometric Mean of Taxonomic Frequencies	Geometric Mean of T-L Frequencies	Mean Recall	Mean Ratio of Repetition
ANVP-high	74.7	38.9	23.67	.516
ANVP-low	3.5	9.4	17.37	.404
BCCM-high	84.3	13.0	25.99	.574
BCCM-low	4.8	5.6	20.10	.496

(Adapted from Bousfield, Cohen, and Whitmarsh 1958)

A basic problem with this study was that Thorndike-Lorge (1944) frequency was also significantly different between the high and low taxonomic frequency lists. As a result, in a second study by Bousfield, Steward and Cowan (1964) the experimenters examined high and low taxonomic frequency lists with Thorndike-Lorge frequency held constant. The findings replicated the clustering results of the earlier study; on the other hand, recall scores between high and low taxonomic frequency groups revealed no difference. As the authors wrote, "These results imply that while the Thorndike-Lorge frequencies of usage were directly related to the number of items recalled, they were apparently unrelated to the incidence of clustering" (p. 210).

Two years later, Cofer, Bruce and Reicher (1966) also demonstrated (experiments I and III) that lists containing high taxonomic frequency items lead to significantly greater mean repetition ratios than lists consisting of low taxonomic frequency items.

BLOCKED VS. RANDOM PRESENTATION OF ITEMS

Since it would seem that category clustering may depend upon the subject's noting some conceptual relationship among the items presented, any technique or procedure that the experimenter utilizes to emphasize this relationship to the subject should result in improved clustering.

One such procedure is known as block presentation. Here, the experimenter does not present the words in random order; rather, the items that make up a single category are presented contiguously, followed by another block of items, etc., until all of the items are presented.

Studies that have examined blocked versus random presentation have conclusively demonstrated the superiority of the blocked presentation technique (Dallett 1964a; Weingartner 1964; Cofer, Bruce and Reicher 1966; Puff 1966). Puff's study is noteworthy since his examination of blocked presentation extended beyond the typical two-group, randomized-blocked procedure. His material consisted of thirty words—ten words from each of three taxonomic categories. The presentation of these items, at a 2.5 second rate, was arranged so that independent groups of subjects were provided with either zero, nine, eighteen, or twenty-seven category repetitions.

This meant, then, that in the zero condition, the items were randomly presented (no word in the list was ever followed by another word from the same category); while in the twenty-seven repetition presentation, all ten items from one category were presented, followed by ten items from the second category, and then ten items from the third category (blocked presentation). Items so arranged to provide nine and eighteen category repetitions represented partially blocked presentations equally spaced between the two ends of the random presentation-blocking continuum.

Results revealed that both clustering and recall increased as a function of the number of category repetitions.

NUMBER OF CATEGORIES

How is recall influenced by the number of clusters or categories that make up a list? That is, if a list is comprised of forty words, what is the influence on recall if these 40 words are represented by two, four, or eight categories? Bousfield and Cohen (1956) conducted one of the early studies in the area, but the contradictory findings they obtained from two experiments did little to answer the problem.[1]

At the present time, most investigators agree that an important aspect of this question is whether or not the category names are available to the subject during the recall period. Mathews (1954), Tulving and Pearlstone (1966) and Earhard (1967) all of whom

---

[1] In Bousfield and Cohen's (1956) first experiment, naive subjects learned a word list comprised of forty items that were divided into either two, four, or eight categories. Results indicated that the number of words recalled was a function of the number of categories which were used. In their second experiment, replicating the experimental procedures of the first, but using subjects who had participated in clustering experiments previously, opposite findings were obtained—the mean number of words recalled for the eight-category lists was 19.71 in contrast to 23.54 and 25.50 for the four- and two-category lists. These investigators have taken the position that the results of the first study reveal the more general relationship between free recall and the number of categories that make up a list, hypothesizing that the previous experience of the subjects in the second experiment produced a particular set in those subjects to look for word categories—a set that was not present in subjects serving in experiment I. Jung (1968) on the other hand speculated that "One possible reason for the opposed results is that subjects who had learned prior categorized lists might not remember which categories were involved on the latest list. In that situation, the fewer categories used, the easier it would be to remember the categories involved in the most recent list" (p. 156).

have provided category names as part of their experimental procedure have found recall to be a function of the number of categories used.[1]

In Mathews (1954) study, twenty-four words (individual's names) were divided into either two, three, or six categories—with category defined as a profession or occupation, i.e., artist, athlete, scientist, etc. The general procedure was for the subject to first identify each of twenty-four individuals as belonging to one of either two, three, or six categories. Following this, a retention test was provided in which subjects had to recall the names they had previously identified. Retention instructions indicated that if the subjects had forgotten any of the categories, they could refer to a sheet that contained them. Thus, subjects were in a position to use category names as cues for the recall of the individuals' names. Mathews found that subjects who had to identify individuals belonging to six categories recalled significantly more names than those who had to identify individuals belonging to only three. This group, in turn, recalled significantly more names than the group using only two categories to classify the items.

Tulving and Pearlstone (1966), using three different list lengths (twelve, twenty-four, or forty-eight words per list) and three different categorizations (two, three, or six) per list, arrived at similar findings. When recall was cued, the number of words recalled was a function of the number of categories that made up the list.

In both the Mathews (1954), and Tulving and Pearlstone (1966) experiments, the number of items per category did not exceed six; Earhard's (1967) study investigated how the number of items per category, as well as the number of categories that make up the list, influence recall. Eight lists of twenty-four English nouns per list were constructed so that each list could be divided into groups of equal numbers of words that began with the same letter of the alphabet. In this experiment, then, the varying letters of the alphabet served as the cues to be used by the subjects in their free-recall period. The number of items per cue (or category) was as follows: 1/24, 2/12, 3/8, 4/6, 6/4, 8/3, 12/2 and 24/1. Thus,

---

[1] Mention should be made also of a series of studies by Mandler (1967) who, using unrelated items, and having subjects determine their own categories (more than one but no more than seven), found that the number of items recalled was a function of the number of categories used.

list 6/4 contained six words beginning with each of the letters d, f, p, and s. Twenty learning trials were provided; the words were presented at the rate of one word per second. Subjects were instructed that the words in the stimulus list would begin with a restricted number of initial letters. After each trial, a ninety-five second recall period was provided. Each initial letter was presented

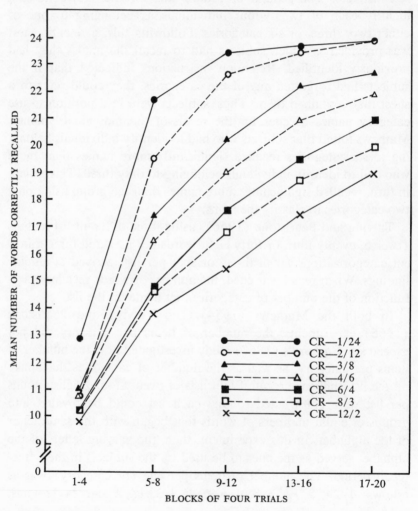

Fig. 7–8. Mean performance scores under CR conditions for successive four-trial blocks. The parameter is the number of items per cue in the stimulus list.

(Adapted from Earhard 1967)

and the subject was instructed to write down as many of the words beginning with that letter as could be remembered prior to going on to the next cued letter. Subjects were also informed that there were equal numbers of words for each letter and that they should distribute their time among the letters as evenly as possible.

In addition to the cued recall instructions, two lists consisting of 1/24 and 24/1 items per cue were learned under free-recall or noncued instructions.

Figures 7–8 and 7–9 provide the major findings of this study. First, as Figure 7–8 indicates, when subjects were provided with the initial letter cues during each recall period, cued-recall varied inversely with the number of words in a category. Thus, subjects attempting to learn twenty-four words belonging to a single category recalled fewer items than if there were two categories consisting of twelve words each; this in turn resulted in poorer recall than if

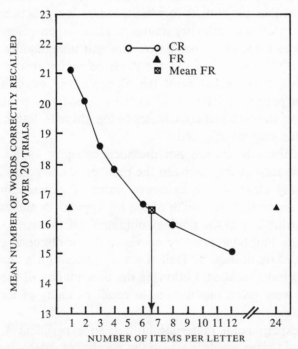

Fig. 7–9. Mean performance over twenty trials under CR and FR conditions as a function of the number of words that begin with the same letter in the stimulus word list.

(Adapted from Earhard 1967)

there were three categories consisting of eight words each, etc. As Figure 7–9 reveals, the two noncued free-recall performances were similar in number of words recalled. (Inasmuch as the subjects were not given instructions about categories, it is reasonable to assume that such instructions did not contribute to the subjects' learning.) In addition, it can be noted that noncued, free-recall performance was similar to cued-recall when there were about six items per cue. With a smaller number of items per cue, cued performance proved superior to free-recall. The author suggested that the efficiency of a cue for retrieval is probably dependent upon the number of items that are related to that cue, and that an efficient strategy for remembering must reflect some compromise between the number of cues used and the number of items assigned to each cue.

It would appear, however, that the generality of these findings revealing noncued recall to be superior to cued-recall when the number of items exceeds eight, remains to be demonstrated. There is considerable question as to whether there is a functional equivalence of letters and category names as cues. When category names are used as cues, more associative strength undoubtedly exists between the category name and the items belonging in that category, than exists between letters of the alphabet and words that begin with that particular letter. And in the last analysis, it may be this associative strength that contributes to the ultimate determination of the relationship investigated.

When the subjects are not provided category names, or cued-recall, the relationship between the number of categories and recall is not very clear. In an extensive series of experiments, Dallett (1964) found that the length of the list appears to make an important contribution to the findings obtained. Of the five experiments conducted, four have primary relevance to our discussion. The general procedure utilized by Dallett was to present on a tape recorder the items to be recalled. Following the presentation of the last item, subjects were given one minute to recall as many of the items as they could.

The experimental materials utilized in experiment 1 consisted of a list of twelve words in which the number of categories used was either one, two, three, four, or six, and all words within a given category were presented contiguously (blocked presentation). Experiment 2 replicated experiment 1 except that the words within a given category were distributed randomly throughout the list. Experiments 4 and 5 were similar to experiments 1 and 2 except that the lists were twenty-four words in length rather than twelve, and the number of categories employed was two, four, six, eight, and twelve. In all experiments, control lists of material were constructed by matching control words with experimental words on the basis of word frequency, number of syllables, and initial letter. A control list, an experimental list, and a control list, in that order, were presented to each group of subjects during a given experimental session.

The results for the four experiments are indicated in Figs. 7–10 and 7–11. These findings suggest that the relationship between recall and the number of categories that make up the list differ for

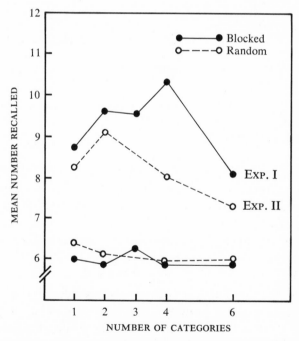

Fig. 7–10. Mean number of items recalled as a function of the number of categories. The upper curves represent performance on the category lists while the lower curves are control-list scores and are keyed to correspond to the category-list curves above.

(Adapted from Dallett 1964)

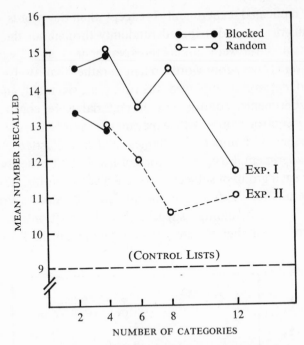

Fig. 7–11. Mean number of items recalled as a function of the number of categories. Experiment IV (open circles) examined 2 and 4; experiment V (filled circles) examined 4, 6, 8 and 12.
(Adapted from Dallett 1964)

different lengths of the list. With a list of twelve words, recall was a curvilinear function of the number of categories, but when the list was increased to twenty-four words, recall increased as the number of categories decreased.

In summary, the experimental evidence supports the position that if cues are provided during the recall period, the number of items recalled is an increasing function of the number of categories provided. On the other hand, if cues are not provided during the recall period, the relationship between recall and the number of categories that make up the list appears to be dependent upon the length of the list. With a long list of items, the findings are opposite to those obtained with cued-recall; that is, recall is inversely related to the number of categories used. On the other hand, with a relatively short list of items, there is a curvilinear relationship between the two variables—recall increases as the number of categories increase, and then decreases as more categories are provided. The conclusions arrived at with noncued (or free) recall must be regarded as most tentative. As a number of investigators have pointed out, a basic difficulty with the experimental findings is the problem of not knowing whether or not the categories provided by the experimenter have actually been used by the subject.

EXHAUSTIVE VS. NONEXHAUSTIVE CATEGORIES

One last variable should be mentioned. Cohen (1963) has called attention to the fact that the words making up a category may be exhaustive whereas at other times the words may form a nonexhaustive category. An exhaustive category may be defined as one in which the number of words contained in the group represent all or nearly all of the words in the category. Thus, the words *north, south, east* and *west* exhaust the members of the category that might be termed cardinal points of the compass. On the other hand, the words *dog, lion, horse,* and *bear* represent members of a nonexhaustive category since they represent only a small sample from a large pool of animal names. Cohen (1963) attempted to determine whether the exhaustive-nonexhaustive dimension was an important one in the free recall of categorized word lists. A second objective was to determine if this variable also contributed to the recall of categories. Four experiments were run, each study employing the same general procedure and material. Lists of seventy words including ten exhaustive and ten nonexhaustive categories of items were presented using typical free-recall learning procedures. Results showed that significantly more words of the exhaustive categories were recalled, indicating that an important variable in the presentation of a categorized word list is whether or not the words exhaust the varying categories that are used. No difference, however, was obtained in the number of categories recalled.

THE ORGANIZATION OF UNRELATED MATERIAL

In the studies we have examined, the experimental material has been so chosen by the investigator to permit the subject to organize it in a particular way. We have noted that the demonstration of category or associative clustering is dependent upon the selection of the particular words that make up the lists to be learned. But what of lists of so-called unrelated words—the type that is typically used with control subjects? Do subjects organize these as well? Tulving (1962) demonstrated that such is the case. He reasoned that words that are organized by the subject would be expected to occur in close proximity in the subject's response pattern, and that the existence of an organizing process could be inferred from the repeated occurrence of these response patterns. Subjective organization under such circumstances then would be defined as the subject's tendency to recall a series of unrelated words in the same order on different trials.[1]

The basic measure used by Tulving is that of second-order sequential organization—that is, the examination of pairs of successive responses calculated over a number of blocks of trials.[2,3]

In his demonstration of the subjective organization that a subject places upon unrelated words, Tulving selected sixteen unrelated words and arranged them in sixteen different trial orders, such that each word appeared just once in each position, and was preceded and followed by each other word just once. Sixteen trials were then provided during which the words were presented at one-second intervals. Following each trial, the subjects were given ninety seconds to write down in any order as many words from the list as they could remember.

We shall not detail the specific procedures used by Tulving to analyze his data; in general, however, the formula is one in which subjective organization is a measure of actual organization relative to the maximum. Maximum subjective organization is indicated by

[1] By unrelated words, Tulving means words among which there is an absence of any experimentally manipulated sequential organization.

[2] Tulving recognized that in addition to second-order organization, it would be possible to examine higher orders as well. He concluded, however, that "within limits of the present method, the second-order SO [subjective organization] is about as useful a measure of sequential organization as that based on any combination of different orders, and more useful than any other single higher-order SO measure" (p. 351).

[3] Measures of subjective organization are not meaningful, of course, when calculated for a single trial, inasmuch as SO is defined in terms of the subject's tendency to recall words in the same order on successive trials.

a value of 1.00 and would be achieved by an individual who re-called all words on all trials exactly in the same order. Zero organi-zation would be one in which the subject recalled each word, and in a different position on each trial.[1] Subjective organization would be seen to be increasing as SO values increase over successive blocks of trials.

Fig. 7–12 provides a clear demonstration that subjects do organize their recall sequentially, even in the absence of any sequential organization in the stimulus list, and that this organi-zation increases systematically with repeated exposures of the material. In brief, then, Tulving demonstrated that even with a series of unrelated words, each subject provides the words with some type of organization. An interesting observation made from these findings is that "a list of completely *unrelated* words is prob-ably as fictional as is a truly nonsensical nonsense syllable" (p. 352).

An examination of Fig. 7–12 indicates that performance as well as subjective organization both increase as a function of trials, and although it may seem plausible that the correlation between these two response variables results from the effect of organization on performance, alternative interpretations are possible. In an effort to show that performance is dependent upon subjective organi-zation, Tulving (1962a) undertook a second study in which two groups of subjects were placed in a free-recall learning situation and asked to learn a list of twenty-two English nouns. All words were five to seven letters in length and no two words had the same first letter. Each word was projected at a rate of approximately 1.5 seconds per word. After the third trial, one group was simply advised to continue (as before) trying their best on each recall trial. The other half of the subjects were told that they should attempt to organize their recall words alphabetically. That is, they should note the first letter of each word on the screen and make an attempt to associate each word with its initial letter. Then when it was time to write the words down, they should go through the

---

[1] The interested reader may consult Bousfield, Puff and Cowan (1964) for a second and somewhat simpler technique for measuring the subjective organiza-tion of unrelated items.

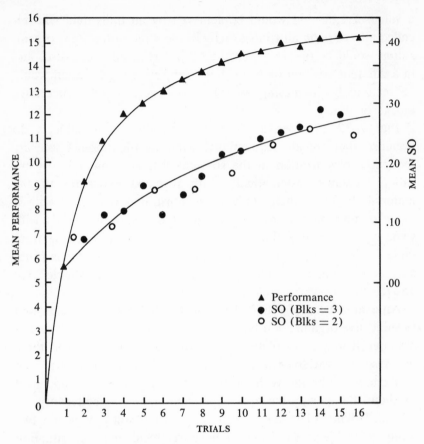

Fig. 7–12. Mean performance (upper curve) and mean SO (lower curve) as a function of trials. (Values of performance are to be read from the left ordinate, SO from the right ordinate.)

(Adapted from Tulving 1962)

letters of the alphabet one at a time and try to remember which word goes with which letter.

The mean number of words recalled as a function of trials for the two groups is indicated in Fig. 7–13. As Tulving indicates, the findings of this experiment leave little doubt that subjective organization is an important determinant of performance in free-recall learning.

The superiority of performance of subjects who organized their recall alphabetically over that of those who used different, apparently less power-

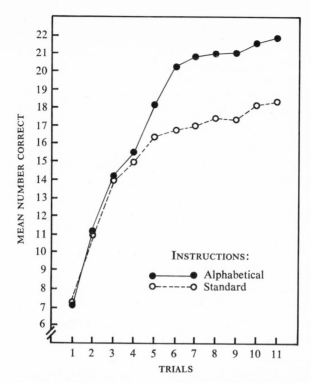

Fig. 7–13. Mean number of words recalled as a function of trials. Each curve is based on an independent group of forty subjects. Immediately preceding trial 4, different instructions were given to the two groups.

(Adapted from Tulving 1962a)

ful methods of organizing was both large and obvious. In the light of this finding it is entirely reasonable to assume that correlations between performance and subjective organization, under conditions where methods of organizing are not under the experimenter's control, reflect nothing more nor less than the same functional relation demonstrated in this experiment (p. 189).[1]

[1] It should be pointed out that a study by Laurence (1966) investigating free-recall learning of six different age groups (five-years, eight-months old; six-years, nine-months; eight-years, one-month; ten-years, six-months; undergraduates; and elderly—ages sixty-eight to eighty-four) found a number of different ways in which subjective organization and performance differ. For example, Laurence found that, in comparing the young adults with the elderly, the elderly subjects produced subjective organization scores not significantly different from those of the younger— a finding in marked contrast to their uniformally lower and significant performance scores.

SUMMARY

An important area of investigation during the past decade has been the examination of organizational processes. Such processes have been acknowledged to play an important role in the learning and retention of verbal material.

When paired-associate tasks are examined, stimulus selection, coding, and mediation emerge as three such organizational processes. Stimulus selection refers to the tendency on the part of subjects to select only a part of the stimulus to which to attend. Thus, in the case where a CVC served as a stimulus in a paired-associate task, the stimulus selection process would be indicated by a subject who chose (or selected) only the first letter of the CVC to which to attach the appropriate response. The first letter may be identified as the functional stimulus, in contrast to the total CVC, which represents the nominal stimulus. A number of variables have been demonstrated to be related to the stimulus selection process. Position, meaningfulness, and in general, the distinctiveness of the component parts of the stimulus, all contribute to determine the aspect of the nominal stimulus to which the subject will attend. Of course, if the stimulus is perceived as a whole, or as an integrated unit, the selection of specific parts of the nominal stimulus is less likely to take place.

A second organizational process investigated in paired-associate learning has been coding. While the selection process is invariably related to the stimulus, the coding process is identified with the response. Thus, if a trigram, FML, must be learned as a response, the subject may code or transform these letters into the word, *female*, in order to aid the learning and/or retention process.

The third organizational process, mediation, refers to the tendency on the part of the subject to link the stimulus and response items that comprise the paired-associate terms with a covert response that has some relationship to both items of the pair. For example, in learning the paired-associate *dog-nine*, a subject might use the mediator *cat* so that *dog* would elicit the word *cat*, which in turn could serve as a stimulus for the to-be-learned response *nine*. In general, it has been shown that learning is facilitated if mediators are used. When such mediators arise as a result of the language habits of the subject, they have been termed, following Adams (1967), natural language mediators (or NLMs).

Organizational processes have been extensively studied with free-recall learning tasks; frequently, these have been of either a coding or associational variety. An important associational process to which a great deal of attention has been devoted is clustering, defined as the tendency to organize the items that make up a list into varying groups, which usually fall into categories having associational or semantic bases. If a list of sixty items, represented by three categories—e.g., the names of animals, vegetables, and professions—were presented to be learned, the subject attempting to recall the items would tend to recall them in clusters of words belonging to particular categories. The associative strength between the category names and the items that make up each category, the number of categories that are used, as well as the characteristics of the categories themselves—e.g., exhaustive or nonexhaustive—have been shown to influence the number of items recalled.

Finally, as Tulving (1962) demonstrated, although the words that make up a list may be unrelated, the subject will provide his own organization in order to aid his recall process.

8 The Characteristics and Learning of Extended Serial Material

The verbal material with which we have been primarily concerned up to this point can be described as isolated items or single units. Even in those cases where pairs of items were utilized, as in the paired-associate learning situation, the experimenter made every effort to see that no relationship had been previously established between the two items.

It is recognized, however, that a great deal of verbal material is neither encountered nor learned in isolation. As a result, some researchers have been interested in measuring some of the characteristics of extended verbal or contextual material, as well as in determining the influence of those attributes on the learning of such material.

It should be acknowledged that this examination of context on learning has taken two directions. The first has been to examine the learning of extended verbal material itself, while the second has been to determine the role of context in the learning of both serial and paired-associate items.

APPROXIMATIONS TO ENGLISH

We recognize that in English sentences, as well as those of other languages, there is not equal probability that any word will randomly follow any other word. For example, if a sentence starts out with the word *the* there is a reasonably high probability that some noun, such as *boy*, *girl*, etc., or an adjective of some variety, will follow the first word. On the other hand, the probability is much lower that a conjunction, an article, or a preposition will follow *the*. If sufficient time and energy were available it would be possible for an investigator to take a large sample of contextual material and tabulate the number of times that any given (single) word found in the sample would follow another. From such data, it would be possible to determine the statistical structure of English for that sample. Moreover, it would be possible to take two-word samples and determine the probability that any given third word would follow the first two. This could then be done for three-word samples, four-word samples, etc.

The probability that one word will follow a second, etc., has been designated as approximation to English. Miller and Selfridge (1950) proposed that for any given number of words in a verbal passage, there are varying approximations to English. With a ten-word passage, for example, zero-order approximation would be obtained by drawing the ten words at random from a dictionary. First-order approximation would reflect the relative frequencies of occurrence of pairs of words while higher orders would reflect trios, quartets, etc., up to tenth-order approximation, which would be obtained from written English (prose).

The measurement operation that Miller and Selfridge (1950) used to obtain the varying approximations to English was to provide a subject with a given number of sequences of words and then have him use these in the construction of a sentence. For second-order approximation, a common word such as *they* was presented to a subject who would be instructed to use the word in a sentence. The word used directly after *they* was noted and then presented to another subject, who was also asked to produce a sentence. Thus, if the first subject made up the sentence, "They went to the base-ball game," the word *went* would be presented to the second subject. The word used directly after the one presented to the second subject would be noted and given to still another subject. This procedure would be repeated until the total sequence of words of the desired length was obtained.

The investigators obtained varying approximations to English for ten-, twenty-, thirty-, and fifty-word passages. They then proceeded to examine the difficulty of learning such material. The procedure consisted of reading a given passage aloud and instructing the subjects to write the words they remembered as nearly in correct order as possible, although order was not used as a criterion for scoring. The results are presented in Fig. 8–1. Surprisingly enough these findings seem to indicate that there is little improvement in learning, as measured by the free-recall learning situation, above fifth-order approximation.

The experimenters' interpretation of the findings was that the learning of multiple units or extended verbal material is dependent upon the presence of familiar, short-range associations among words, and that the varying higher order approximations reflect these short range associations equally well. Sharp (1958), Postman and Adams (1960), and Richardson and Voss (1960), using the

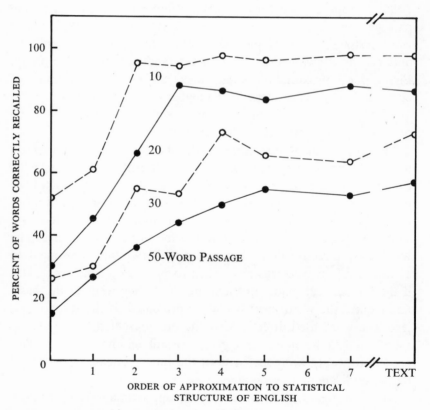

Fig. 8–1. Percentage of words correctly recalled as a function of the order of approximation to the statistical structure of English.

(Adapted from Miller and Selfridge 1950)

same material as that used by Miller and Selfridge (1950), were able to replicate their findings, although Epstein, Rock and Zuckerman (1960) were unable to do so.

Marks and Jack (1952), and more recently Coleman (1963) called attention to the fact that the methodology and materials employed in the Miller and Selfridge study limit the generality of those conclusions. Marks and Jack (1952) pointed out that, first, Miller and Selfridge's scoring method was concerned only with the number of words recalled, regardless of whether the consecutive order of the presented material was followed. Such a procedure permits the subject to form his own associations; thus, the findings may not be attributable to the "short range associations" posited by Miller and Selfridge. Secondly, the textual material used by Miller and Selfridge is somewhat misnamed, in that parts of more than a single sentence appear in the longer lists.

In the Marks and Jack (1952) study, second, third, and fifth orders of approximation were used in addition to textual material. The material used by Miller and Selfridge was lengthened to contain 261 words. These 261 word sequences were then divided into consecutive segments of six-, seven-, eight-, nine-, etc., up to twenty-three-word units. For the textual material, complete sentences of similar lengths were chosen from novels and biographies. The procedure consisted of providing individual testing sessions in which subjects were presented with segments of increasing lengths of material until two consecutive segment "failures" were obtained. A failure was defined as any omission, inversion, or addition of a word or words. The subject's score was the number of words in the longest segment that he was able to recall correctly. The results, as indicated in Table 8–1, clearly indicate that order of approximation significantly affects recall; unlike Miller and Selfridge's (1950) findings, textual material was recalled significantly better than fifth-order approximation. As the authors wrote, when a different measure of retention is used, recall seems to be very much a function of the a priori relative meaningfulness of the material.

Coleman (1963) called attention to additional difficulties with the Miller and Selfridge experiment. In one part of Coleman's study, expert linguists were asked to rank as to grammatical correctness, the varying approximations that had been used in the original study. It was found that the linguists rated those approxi-

TABLE 8–1

NUMBER OF WORDS IN LONGEST SEGMENT CORRECTLY
RECALLED AS A FUNCTION OF ORDER OF APPROXI-
MATION TO STATISTICAL ENGLISH

Order of Approx.	N	Mean	SD
Second	20	7.7	1.5
Third	20	8.4	2.3
Fifth	20	10.0	2.6
Text	20	15.1	3.2

(Adapted from Marks and Jack 1952)

mations from the fifth-order on as deviant from English grammatical rules. As Coleman wrote, "as order of approximation becomes higher, apparently the grammatical constructions gradually
become more awkward and implausible; that is, the subjects do
not agree so well with their verbs, nor the verbs with their direct
objects, nor the modifiers with the words they modify, etc." (p.
241).

Moreover, Coleman (1963) pointed out that the relative complexity of the words used in the varying Miller and Selfridge approximations was not the same. Complexity was defined in this
instance by: (1) the number of uncommon words (all those occurring less than 100 per million) found in the approximation, (2)
the number of syllables obtained for each 100 words in the approximation, and (3) the number of morphemes obtained for each
100 words in the approximation. These findings were in agreement
with ratings obtained by linguists that eighth-order approximation
and prose material were more complex than approximations below
this level.

Coleman then replicated the Miller and Selfridge procedure but
used material in which the prose as well as the varying approximations to English were matched in syllabic length and word
frequency. In addition, recall was scored in correct two-word, three-
word, etc., up to correct seventeen-word sentences. The results,
supporting the Marks and Jack (1952) findings, indicated that
prose was recalled significantly better than the higher order approximations. Moreover, as recall was scored in longer and longer

sequences, the advantages for higher order approximations became greater.

In summary, although the Miller and Selfridge (1950) findings have frequently been accepted as representing a basic finding in the learning of extended verbal material, the work of Marks and Jack (1952), and Coleman (1963) would indicate that the Miller and Selfridge findings have little generality beyond the specific material used and the scoring techniques employed.

SYNTAX AND SEMANTICS

In looking at a typical English sentence, two characteristics can almost invariably be noted. The first is that it makes sense; the second is that varying words occupy relatively specific places in the sentence. These two variables can be identified as: (1) semantics and (2) syntax, and psychologists are indebted to the linguists for indicating the importance of these variables in the learning of contextual material. But let us look at these variables in more detail.

Syntax, as we have just noted, is the orderly arrangement of words that are found in prose. It is recognized that only certain classes of words can be substituted into the various positions in a sentence, so that the choice of a given word at a given location in a sentence is limited to a choice from an appropriate class of words, rather than from the total English vocabulary. As Miller and Isard (1963) wrote,

For a listener to be able to take advantage of these syntactic constraints, however, he must first infer the phrase structure of the sentence. If a sentence is grammatical but so complicated syntactically that the listener cannot easily grasp its phrase structure (e.g., *The race that the car that the people whom the obviously not very well dressed man called sold won was held last summer*), it will be difficult for him to exploit the syntactic rules and he will be unable to use his knowledge of English syntax to simplify his perceptual decision (p. 218).[1]

[1] It is not necessary to discuss in detail the phrase structure of a sentence. Miller and Isard (1963), however, illustrated its description nicely. Briefly, syntactic rules must specify that the sentence, "A boy hit the ball," consists of a noun phrase, "A boy," followed by a verb phrase, "hit the ball." The noun phrase in turn is made up of an article, "A," and a noun, "boy"; the verb phrase consists of a verb, "hit," and another noun phrase, "the ball." Thus, the structural description of the total sentence can be indicated by parentheses, "(a boy) (hit (the ball))," where it is understood that each subunit is of a particular syntactic type.

Semantic constraint also plays a role in limiting the class of words appropriate to a given position in a sentence. "The boy sang a boat" is grammatically correct, but semantically anomalous. A listener might expect to hear that the boy rowed a boat, or that the boy sang a song, but "sang a boat" violates semantic rules known and accepted by speakers of English. "An adequate semantic theory must incorporate a dictionary that lists, for each word (or morpheme) of the language, all of the syntactic functions and all of the senses of that word, plus some indication of the linguistic contexts in which each sense is appropriate" (Miller and Isard, 1963, p. 218).

In summary, linguists working with psychologists have called attention to two variables that will undoubtedly contribute to the learning of extended verbal discourse. We shall now turn to some of the studies in which these constructs have been investigated.

SYNTAX

Epstein (1961) hypothesized that since verbal messages in ordinary usage are encoded according to a set of grammatical rules, the learning of this material may be very different from the learning of a list of independent items, such as a list of nonsense syllables. In a series of studies, Epstein (1961, 1962, 1963, 1967) demonstrated that syntax does play an important role in the learning of extended verbal material.

In experiment I (Epstein 1962), which replicated an earlier study (Epstein 1961), four categories of material—each consisting of two sentences—were presented. The varying types of material can be noted in Table 8–2. Here it can be seen that category 1 contains sentences made up of nonsense syllables in combination with two fuctional words that have no referential meaning. Grammatical tags such as "ed" on verbs in the past tense and "s" on plural nouns have been appended to the syllabic stems in such a way as to simulate the requirements of English syntax. This procedure thus produces a series of nonsense syllables that is readily perceived to have a "grammatical" structure. Category 2 consists of the same material, but with the items arranged in a random, unstructured order. The two remaining categories consist of meaningful words. However, the words are arranged in a meaningless order—although category 3 contains two series of words so ordered

TABLE 8–2

LEARNING MATERIAL FOR EXPERIMENT I

Category	Sentence
1*	(1) A haky deebs reciled the dison tofently um flutest pav.
	(2) The glers un cligs wur vasing un seping a rad moovly.
2	(1) deebs haky the um flutest reciled pav a tofently dison
	(2) cligs seping a wur rad un moovly glers the un vasing
3*	(1) Wavy books worked singing clouds to empty slow lamps.
	(2) Helping walls met eating trees from noisy poor lines.
4	(1) worked clouds slow empty to wavy singing books lamps
	(2) noisy trees walls from lines helping eating poor met

* Note that the "sentences" in this category begin with a capitalized item and end with a period.

(Adapted from Epstein 1962)

as to meet the demands of syntactical structure (category 4 does not).

Subjects, forty-eight in all, were each assigned to learn one of the four categories of material. The procedure consisted of presenting these individuals with one of the sentences within a category for seven seconds with instructions to distribute their attention evenly among the items so that all the items could be learned in the order in which they were presented. Thirty-second recall periods were provided in order to give the subjects time to write down what they remembered. Trials and recall periods were continued until the subject was able to reproduce the sentence without error. Table 8–3 reveals the findings, and it can be noted that the syntactically

TABLE 8–3

SUMMARY OF RESULTS OF EXPERIMENT I
(Both sentences combined for each category)

Measure of Learning	Category 1		Category 2		Category 3		Category 4	
	M	SD	M	SD	M	SD	M	SD
Trials to criterion	7.29	2.87	8.87	3.37	2.62	1.12	3.78	1.87
Errors to criterion	23.95	9.89	35.54	9.48	4.75	2.72	10.00	3.74

(Adapted from Epstein 1962)

structured materials, categories 1 and 3, were learned more rapidly than their counterparts.

Marks and Miller (1964), as well as other investigators (i.e., Rosenberg 1966a), have confirmed Epstein's findings that syntax makes an important contribution to the retention of contextual material.

In a second experiment (Epstein 1962), the four categories of material used in the first study were presented via a memory drum, and each sentence was learned as a series of individual items. Items were presented at a two-second rate with a six-second intertrial interval. Surprisingly, differences between categories were not obtained. The author suggested that the effect of syntax seems to depend on the perception of the series of items as a unit—i.e., a generalized linguistic form—and that this effect is not dependent upon sequential or semantic associations, which should be present in serial learning as well as in the form of presentation utilized in experiment I.

SEMANTICS

As was indicated at the beginning of this chapter, the second variable investigators have examined in the learning of extended verbal material is semantics. In a study by Marks and Miller (1964), the role of this variable as well as that of syntactic constraint was examined in the memorization of English sentences. The material consisted of five sentences of five words each; the sentences had identical syntactic structures, i.e., adjective-plural noun-verb-adjective-plural noun. A sample sentence would be: *Fatal accidents deter careful drivers.* From these original sentences five additional sentences were constructed by taking the first word from the first sentence, the second word from the second sentence and so on, e.g., *Rapid bouquets deter sudden neighbors.* The syntactic structure of these derivative sentences remained identical to those of the "normal" sentences, but because of the word substitutions, the derivative sentences were semantically anomalous. In addition, two other types of strings of words were derived. The first type, specified as anagram strings, was constructed by taking each of the normal sentences and scrambling its word order; each sentence was scrambled somewhat differently in order to prevent the subjects from noticing any pattern. Thus, nothing was done to the semantic components of these sentences, but the normal syntactic structure was destroyed. Finally, strings of words that the investigators identified as word lists were similarly formed by scrambling the word order of the anomalous sentences. These word lists preserved neither the syntactic structure nor the semantic components of the original sentences.

Five sentences—representing one of the four types of material, i.e., normal sentences, anomalous sentences, anagram strings, or word lists—were presented to the subject, who listened to all of these on a single trial. Two minutes were then provided in which the subject was to write the sentences down (in any order) as accurately as possible. Fig. 8–2 indicates the median percent of words correct for each of the four types of material over the five

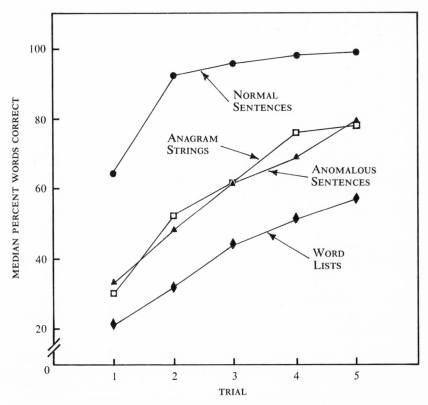

Fig. 8–2. Median percent of words correct for each of the four types of strings over five trials. A word was counted as correct only if it appeared in its correct position in the string.

(Adapted from Marks and Miller 1964)

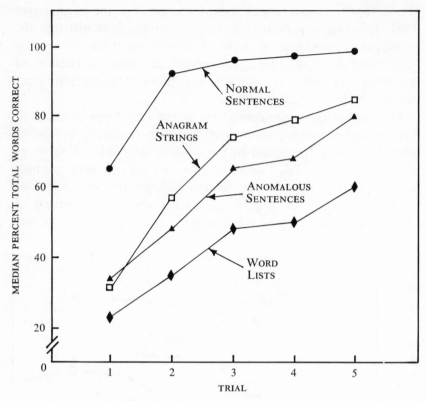

Fig. 8–3. Median percent of total words correct for each of the four types of strings over five trials. A word was counted as correct regardless of its position in the string.

(Adapted from Marks and Miller 1964)

trials when words were counted correct only if they appeared in their correct positions in the string. In a different method of scoring, words were counted correct regardless of their positions in the string. These findings are indicated in Fig. 8–3. Both methods of scoring support the position that both syntactic and semantic structure facilitate learning.

SENTENCE COMPLEXITY

Martin and Roberts (1966) have proposed that "As a listener receives a grammatical string of words, not only does he perceive each word as it arrives, but in addition, upon the arrival of each, he makes an encoding response a major constituent of which is formation of an expectation as to what is coming next" (p. 211). These responses are the result of the experience the listener has had with the sentence structure of the language. The particular responses that are elicited by each word of the "arriving" sentence are dictated by (1) the speaker's choice of word class for that position in the sentence, and his manipulation of pitch, stress, and juncture—in short, the stimulus situation for the listener; and (2) the listener's knowledge of word-word and class-class transition probabilities and his familiarity with what different variations in pitch, stress and juncture signalize in his language—in short, the listener's existing habit structures. Thus, as a sentence is received, the intonation and prosody (tone, accent, voice modulation) of the lengthening string serve as stimuli for anticipatory responses where what is anticipated is a partial ordering of particular word classes. The position taken by Martin and Roberts (1966) is that these anticipatory responses are a major component of what the individual places in memory, and that the likelihood of correct recall is related to the number of such responses the listener makes in attempting to store the sentence in memory.

The authors point out that a parallel analysis can be made for the speaker. Thus, he also must make commitments if he is to complete the sentence in good grammatical form. To provide an example of this point of view, assume that the sentence, "The new club member came early," is read to a listener. Upon hearing the word *the*, the listener responds with the following two anticipations: (1) he expects to hear the rest of the noun phrase begun by *the* and (2) he expects a predicate of some sort. Correspondingly, in uttering the same sentence, the speaker incurs two commitments upon saying *the:* one of them is to finish the noun phrase begun with *the*, the second is to provide a predicate. Thus from psychological considerations, *the* may be said to be structurally embedded to a depth of two—"structurally" because the expectations and commitments are grammatically founded. The word that comes next, *new*, is also indicated to have a depth of two: since *new* elicits in the listener an expectation of completion of a new noun phrase and affirms the already elicited expectation of a predicate. Similarly, *club* also has a depth of two. The noun *member*, however, has a depth of one since the only expectation (commitment) is that of a predicate. With the verb *came*, the expectation of a predicate is partially met, however, its intonation elicits the expectation of an adverb, and hence is itself embedded to a depth of one. Finally, the pitch and stress of the adverb *early* indicates that *early* is the terminal word—thus, it has a depth of zero. The sentence, "The new club member came early," can thus be provided the following set of numbers: 2, 2, 2, 1, 1, 0. As Martin and Roberts (1966) wrote, "These numbers reflect the structural involvement of each word in the sentence from the point of view of both a listener and a speaker" (p. 212). In essence, these numbers also serve to index the load on memory imposed by the sentence.

A formal model for determining such a characterizing set of numbers for any sentence had been provided by Yngve (1960); the hypothesis proposed by Martin and Roberts was that the likelihood of recall of a sentence is inversely related to the mean depth of that sentence.[1]

In an examination of this variable, the authors devised sentences with a mean depth of 1.29, e.g., "They were not prepared for rainy weather," and another set of sentences with a mean depth of 1.71, e.g., "Children are not allowed out after dark." All sentences were seven words long. The general procedure was to read aloud six unrelated sentences, all of which had the same mean depth, in immediate succession; after the last sentence had been read, subjects were asked to write down as many of the sentences as they could remember. As soon as a subject finished writing, the sheet on which he had written the sentences was collected. The same six sentences were again read, in a new order, and the subjects again attempted to reproduce them. In all, six such trials were provided; every sentence was placed in each ordinal position over the six trials. In examining the mean number of sentences recalled for each subject for the six trials, the mean recall score for sentences having a mean depth of 1.29 was 3.86, while mean recall was 3.07 for those sentences having a mean depth of 1.71. Thus, the experiment was

[1] We shall not detail Yngve's (1960) model of sentence production here. However, on the basis of this model, and certain assumptions that relate to the order in which the constituents of the sentence are expanded, as well as on the assumption that the temporary memory of the organism is limited, Yngve proposed a hypothesis of depth limitation in language that leads to a number of specific predictions about the types of syntactic structures to be found in languages.

supportive of the position that structural complexity as indexed by the sentence mean-depth measure is a factor in sentence retention.

Unfortunately, a subsequent study by Martin and Roberts (1967), as well as two other studies by Perfetti (1969, 1969a), did not support the depth measure as a contributor to sentence retention.

LEXICAL DENSITY

Perfetti (1969a) suggested that a semantic variable related to sentence retention is the semantic content load of the sentence, and that a reasonable index for this variable may be lexical density. The index figure itself is obtained by counting the number of lexical words in a sentence and dividing by the total number of words in the sentence.[1]

Perfetti constructed sixty-four ten-word sentences representing two levels of lexical density (as well as two levels of mean depth), with these sentences controlled for word length, articulation length in syllables, and word frequency. Lexical density was indexed by the number of lexical words per ten-word sentence. Thus, nouns, adjectives, adjective and noun verbals, adverbs, and main verbs were counted as lexical; prepositions, conjunctions, pronouns and verb auxiliaries were considered grammatical. An example of a low lexical sentence was: "The family has accepted an offer to purchase the house," while a high lexical sentence was: "The police watched nearly every move of the clever thief."

The general procedure consisted of an oral presentation of the sentences followed by a series of seven numbers. The subjects were instructed to write the sum of the numbers and then the sentence. Results, as measured by perfectly recalled sentences, revealed that those sentences with high lexical density were recalled less frequently than those with low lexical density. As was mentioned previously, sentence depth was not found to be related to retention. A second experiment replicated the findings obtained by the first.

Although lexical density was indicated to play an important role in sentence recall, the author points out that other measures of

[1] The distinction between lexical and grammatical words was defined as follows: lexical words included the open sets of noun, adjective, verb, and adverb, while grammatical words included the closed sets of verb auxiliary, article, pronoun, etc.

meaningfulness or sentence complexity should also be considered. That is, high lexical sentences also contain a greater number of underlying "sentences" or meaningful phrases. Contrast the low lexical density sentence, "The firemen hurried to the factory that was reported burning," with the high lexical density sentence, "The museum is providing free public lectures on modern art." In the first example, the underlying sentences include: (a) firemen hurried to the factory; (b) the factory was burning; (c) someone reported it. On the other hand, the more complex sentence indicates the following: (a) the museum provides lectures; (b) the lectures are free; (c) the lectures are public; (d) the lectures are on art; (e) art is modern. Clearly, the high lexical density sentence also contains more meaningful phrases, which make it more difficult to learn.

GRAMMATICAL TRANSFORMATIONS

Another variable that has been posited to be related to the learning of contextual material is the kind of sentence that the subject is required to learn. Linguists in particular have directed attention to the position that the corpus of English sentences can be divided into kernels and nonkernels. A kernel is an active, affirmative sentence. Negative, passive, passive-negative and interrogative sentences exemplify nonkernels. An example of a kernel sentence would be: "The boy has hit the ball," or "The girl has worn the jewel." A nonkernel, negative would be, "The boy hasn't hit the ball," while the passive transformation would be, "The ball has been hit by the boy." The interrogative sentence would be, "Has the ball been hit by the boy?" A transformation may be applied in combination to produce, for example, a passive-negative question: "Hasn't the ball been hit by the boy?"

In investigating the role of grammatical transformations in the recall of English sentences, Mehler (1963) examined learning as a function of the presentation of kernel sentences and their transformations. In this study, eight kernel sentences, together with their seven transformations (negative, passive, interrogative, negative-interrogative, negative-passive, interrogative-passive, and negative-passive-interrogative), were used. The kernel sentences used were as follows: "The man has bought the house"; "The boy has taken the photograph"; "The biologist has made the discovery"; "The girl has worn the jewel"; "The student has written the essay"; "The car has hit the tree"; "The airplane has carried the passenger"; "The secretary has typed the paper." Sentences representing each of the eight grammatical types (one for each) were presented to subjects for five successive trials, each time in a different order. The sentences were recorded on tape with a separation of two seconds between the end of one sentence and the beginning of the next. After each presentation, subjects attempted to recall the sentences, and wrote their responses in a recall booklet that was composed of five pages, one for each of the five trials. Eight prompting words were listed on each page, one for each sentence. Four of these prompting words were subjects and four were predicates. Thus, one page in the booklet might contain the words *man, boy, biologist, girl, tree, essay, paper,* and *airplane,* listed vertically.

In scoring, a sentence was counted correct if it was a verbatim reproduction of the stimulus sentence or if it differed from the stimulus sentence only by (a) the replacement of a word by a synonym, (b) a change from the definite to the indefinite article, and/or (c) a change in tense.

Fig. 8–4 shows the acquisition curves for each of the various transformations, where percent recalled correctly was plotted as a function of the trial number. The most striking conclusion is the greater facility with which subjects learned the kernel sentences.

The author has suggested that subjects do not recall a sentence verbatim but rather analyze it syntactically and encode it as a kernel sentence with an appropriate transformation. Thus, if the sentence, "The ball has been hit by the boy," is used, presumably the subject codes it as an underlying kernel, with some "mental tag" that indicates that the passive transformation must be applied for recall. Precisely how the kernel is encoded, of course, is not established.

It should be acknowledged, however, that Martin and Roberts (1966) were not able to confirm Mehler's findings. In this study, which was a part of the earlier one described, the following kinds of sentences were employed: kernel, passive, truncated passive, negative, passive negative, and truncated passive negative.[1]

---

[1] A passive is truncated when the agent is not specified. *"We were met by our two children"* is not truncated because the agent (our children) was named; however, "The power was turned off at 5:00" is truncated because the agent who turned off the power is not given.

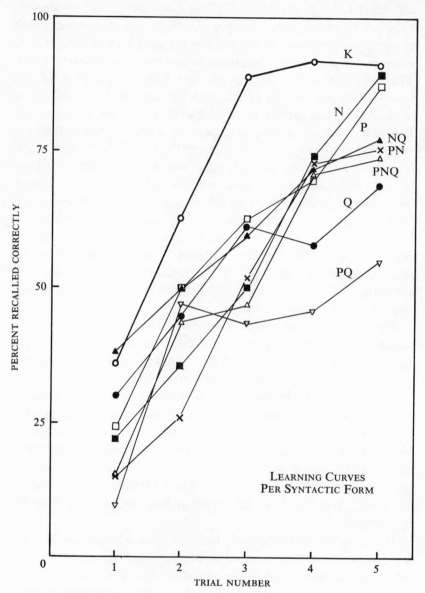

Fig. 8–4. Acquisition curves for each of the transformed sentences. The kernel is learned with greater facility than any of the other sentences. (Adapted from Mehler 1963)

TABLE 8–4

MEAN NUMBER CORRECT RECALLS PER S IN SIX TRIALS

| | Sentence Mean Depth | |
| | 1.29 | 1.71 |
Sentence Kind	Recall	Recall
Kernel	3.27	2.17
Passive	3.99	2.97
Truncated Passive	3.27	2.50
Negative	4.71	3.29
Passive Negative	3.94	4.04
Truncated Passive Negative	3.97	3.46
Mean	3.86	3.07

(Adapted from Martin and Roberts 1966)

The procedure utilized was similar to Mehler's (1963) in that six trials were provided. As can be noted in Table 8–4, the results indicate that recall of kernels is uniformly inferior to recall of non-kernels and, except for this disconfirming regularity, there is no consistent effect on recall attributable to the remaining sentence types.

The authors analyzed Mehler's (1963) study with regard to sentence complexity and found the relationship that emerged between total number of correct recalls and sentence mean depth was a remarkably strong one with the mean depth values of 1.17, 1.38, 1.43, and 1.67, and with the total number of recalls at 300, 243, 234, and 191 respectively for the k, p, n, and pn sentences.

Another consideration related to Mehler's findings was that he did not control for sentence length. As Martin and Roberts (1967) pointed out, "A possible explanation of Mehler's result is the fact that his kernels were shorter sentences than were the corresponding transformations" (p. 535). And in an experiment designed to examine the contribution of sentence length on retention, Martin and Roberts found that sentence length was a highly significant factor in sentence recall. As a result, they concluded that research on sentence retention must control the length of the sentence to be recalled.

ASSOCIATIVE STRENGTH

If the words, *good-bad,* or *hot-cold,* were used in the making up of a paired-associate task, learning to respond with the word *bad* when *good* was presented, or *cold* when *hot* was presented, would probably take place within a single trial. These associative, pre-experimental relationships have been found to play an important role in paired-associate, serial and free-recall learning situations. It is not surprising therefore that some investigators have also been interested in examining the role of association with contextual material.

In one study, Rosenberg (1966), in order to construct sentences with high associative strength, selected four stimulus nouns from free association norms, each of which had elicited two adjectives and a verb with some frequency. Thus, the noun *lion* was noted to have elicited the adjectives *strong* and *fierce,* and the verb *roar.* A plural "s" was added to each noun and the adverb tag "ly" to one of the adjectives so that sentences of the form adjective-noun-verb-adverb could be constructed. The sentences that resulted were: "Shrill whistles blow loudly"; "Good soldiers fight bravely"; "Deep rivers flow swiftly"; and "Strong lions roar fiercely." Sentences with very weak associative relationships between words were constructed by selecting for each of the same nouns, two adjectives and a verb of low frequency of occurrence, as indicated by the association norms. An example of such a sentence would be: "Orange whistles smile harshly." Sentences with moderate associative relationships between words were also constructed by replacing each of the nouns in the high association sentences with a semantically inappropriate noun, one that did not appear as a response to the original noun in the free association norms. The results, it was hoped, would be sentences with three instead of four related words. An example of this type of sentence would be "Good machines fight bravely."

In addition to associative strength, syntax was manipulated by rearranging the order of form classes, with all sentences rearranged in the same manner, i.e., "Loudly whistles shrill blow." In brief, then, the basic design of the study was a 3 x 2 factorial with three levels of associative strength and two levels of syntactic habit. This design resulted in the following groups: (1) high association-grammatical; (2) moderate association-grammatical; (3) low association-grammatical; (4) high association-ungrammatical; (5) moderate association-ungrammatical; (6) low association-ungrammatical.

The experimental procedure consisted of providing four trials; each trial consisted of a presentation of four sentences selected from one of the above-listed categories. Each sentence was presented for six seconds, and the presentation of the four sentences was followed by a two-minute recall period in which the subjects were requested to write down as much of each sentence as they could remember. Three response measures were obtained: (1) number of sentences recalled; (2) number of words correctly recalled in their correct sentence position; and (3) total number of words recalled.

Table 8–5 provides the findings on all three measures; it can be noted that the performances of the groups exposed to grammatical sequences, regardless of associative level, were superior to the performances of the groups exposed to ungrammatical sequences. Although high associative strength sentences were easiest to learn, a surprising finding was that the moderate associative strength sentences were most difficult. Perhaps this was because the operations designed to produce moderate associative strength were different from those utilized with the two other associative strengths.

Although Rosenberg's (1966) study does indicate that associative strength can play a role in the learning of contextual material,

TABLE 8–5

MEANS FOR THREE MEASURES OF RECALL

	Means		
Group	Sentences	Words in Position	Total Word Recall
High association-Grammatical	11.95	55.00	55.00
Low association-Grammatical	7.85	46.90	47.90
Moderate association-Grammatical	6.15	43.70	43.85
High association-Ungrammatical	8.25	47.50	49.85
Low association-Ungrammatical	5.45	38.95	41.70
Moderate association-Ungrammatical	4.80	38.45	41.10

(Adapted from Rosenberg 1966)

most psychologists as well as linguists have generally rejected the position that the learning of contextual material is based upon an associative chaining process.

Almost two decades ago, Lashley (1951) pointed out that language responses, like many other forms of serial behavior, are emitted at such a high rate that it is not plausible to assume that successive elements are dependent upon the stimulus consequences of their predecessors—since the time between elements is too brief. He believed that an essential characteristic of most serially ordered behavior is that it conforms to a kind of "schema of action." If sentences were generated according to the associative bonds between words most sentences would look quite peculiar and meaningless. Because of this, Lashley suggested that any account of serial ordering must also include some kind of central determining event that not only selects the response elements that will occur but at least in part determines the order in which the elements will occur within the response sequence. Thus, for structured and meaningful language sequences, Lashley presented a good case against an associative chaining position.

Johnson (1968) reported an interesting study by Frankart (1964) that bears on this issue. Frankart had subjects learn word sequences that varied in grammaticalness. The lowest degree of grammaticality consisted of random sequences of words, while the sequence representing the highest degree of grammaticality contained only perfectly grammatical sentences. Prior to such learning, however, subjects first learned a paired-associate task that consisted of pairs of words that later occurred adjacently in the to-be-learned grammatical sequences. The rate at which the critical word pairs were integrated during the learning of the sequences was measured by determining the conditional probability that the first word of the pair would occur when the second member did not.

As anticipated, there was an overall facilitating effect of the prior paired-associate learning on the learning of the critical word pairs contained in the sequence. The interesting finding, however, was that as degree of grammaticalness increased, there was a marked decrease in the facilitation from the previous paired-associate learning. Thus, for the two lowest degrees of grammaticalness, there was a sizeable facilitating effect, but there was little or no effect for the two highest degrees of grammaticalness. These experimental findings call into question the extent to which the learning of contextual material can be explained in terms of word-to-word associations; the subject's ability to transfer such specific associations to a sentence learning task would appear to be quite limited.

CONTEXT: ITS ROLE IN THE LEARNING OF PAIRED-ASSOCIATES AND SERIAL LISTS

One of the early studies to examine the role of context on the learning of paired-associates was performed by Epstein, Rock and Zuckerman (1960). In one experiment (VIIa), four lists of six pairs of concrete nouns were constructed. In one list, these nouns were joined by a third word which made up a meaningful phrase; in the second and third lists, the middle word was an irrelevant connective which produced a nonmeaningful phrase; the fourth list was a control in that it simply consisted of the two nouns. Table 8–6 indicates the material used. Instructions indicated that a series

TABLE 8–6

Makeup of the Lists Used

List 1	List 2
cake near road	cake but road
box near cloud	box late cloud
shoe on lake	shoe but lake
bank on roof	bank late roof
lamp in bottle	lamp how bottle
card in sand	card how sand

List 3	List 4
cake and road	cake-road
box and cloud	box-cloud
shoe without lake	shoe-lake
bank or roof	bank-roof
lamp or bottle	lamp-bottle
card without sand	card-sand

(Adapted from Epstein, Rock and Zuckerman 1960)

TABLE 8–7

NUMBER OF PAIRS LEARNED

	N	Number Retained	Mean
List 1	20	76	3.8
List 2	20	54	2.7
List 3	20	46	2.3
List 4	20	48	2.4

(Adapted from Epstein, Rock and Zuckerman 1960)

of six three-word phrases (except in the case of the control), with the first and third words underlined, would be presented. Subjects were asked to read each entire phrase; following presentation of the list for a single trial, they were then given a test trial in which they were asked to indicate what the second word was after having been shown the first. The findings are indicated in Table 8–7, and it can be noted that the presence of a relevant connecting word aided in the learning of the pair.

In a second experiment (VIIb), similar findings were obtained when pictures of objects were used. In this study, six pairs of out-line pictures of familiar objects were used, and the pictures were so drawn that each pair would constitute a unit or consist of isolated items. See Fig. 8–5. Instructions were similar to the previous study in that after the subjects had seen the pictures on a single trial, they were shown one item of the pair and asked to indicate the missing one. Results are indicated in Table 8–8, from which it can be noted that the findings of the previous study can be extended to the use of this type of material.

Jensen and Rohwer, and Rohwer and his associates also conducted a series of studies that examined the role of context (or mediation) in the learning of paired-associates as well as serial lists of material.[1] In the first study of the series, Jensen and Rohwer (1963) made up pictures of common objects, and then used those

---

[1] It is interesting to note that while Epstein et al. considered the variable to be one of context, and in a sense, a task variable, Jensen and Rohwer (1963) conceptualized the concept in terms of a process—mediation. That is, they posited that the providing of context results in a mediating process on the part of the subject.

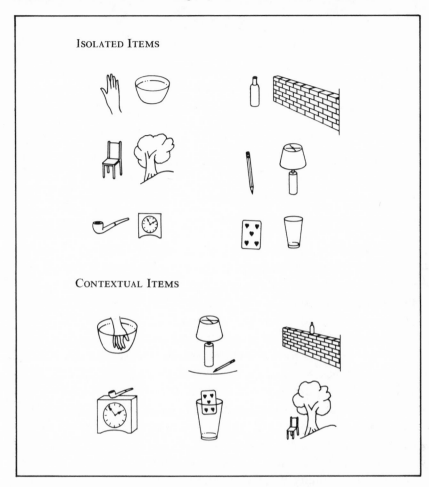

ISOLATED ITEMS

CONTEXTUAL ITEMS

Fig. 8–5. Isolated and contextual pairs of items that were learned.
(Adapted from Epstein, Rock and Zuckerman 1960)

pictures to form paired-associate learning material. The procedure employed was to place one card (stimulus) over a second card (response) and then to point to the top card and ask the subject what picture was underneath it. Mentally retarded adults were used as subjects. A mediation condition was utilized in which the subject was asked on the first trial to make up a sentence or phrase linking the two picture objects. Usually, very simple phrases were constructed, such as, "The hat is on the table." In the nonmediation condition, subjects were asked only to name the objects. Following

TABLE 8–8

PAIRS OF PICTURES LEARNED

Material	Group 1	Group 2
pipe—clock	18	11
card—glass	15	7
chair—tree	18	11
bottle—wall	16	12
pencil—lamp	15	10
bowl—hand	16	11
Total	98	66
Mean	4.9	3.3

(Adapted from Epstein, Rock and Zuckerman 1960)

the first trial, the procedure was identical for both groups in that all subjects were asked to name the object that was underneath the stimulus object card. The task was comprised of eight paired-associates, and all subjects were given ten trials.

The mean errors for the eight paired-associates for the nonmediation group was 43.7, while for the mediation group it was 13.9. This represents a dramatically facilitating effect on paired-associate learning and indicates the importance of the subject's placing the material within a contextual frame—a finding that supports Epstein, Rock and Zuckerman (1960).

In a second experiment, Jensen and Rohwer (1963) were interested in determining whether mediation, or the use of contextual material, would facilitate the learning of a serial list of material. A study similar to the previous one was undertaken. However, in addition to mediation versus nonmediation instructions, subjects were given a serial learning task as well as a paired-associate task. In brief, then, a 2 x 2 design was used, and ten mentally retarded subjects were assigned to each cell. The paired-associate task was comprised of eight pairs of items. For the nonmediation condition, subjects merely named the pictures on the first trial; for the mediation condition, unlike the situation in the previous study, a standard set of mediating verbalizations was provided by the experimenter upon initial presentation of the pairs. These mediators were not repeated by the experimenter after the first trial. Eight items also comprised the serial list, and the nonmediation condition was one in which the subjects went through the list naming the pictures on the first trial. Inasmuch as a different order of pictures was used for all subjects in the serial list-mediating condition, a standard set of mediators was not possible. Different mediating instructions were thus used for each subject. All subjects in each condition were given twenty trials in the learning task.

Results can be found in Table 8–9 and it is interesting to note that the findings are unequivocal in demonstrating that only paired-associate learning was facilitated by the mediation instructions.

In a second study by these investigators (Jensen and Rohwer 1965), the role of mediation was examined as a function of age. As in the earlier experiment, both paired-associate and serial learning lists were used; the general procedure used was similar to that previously utilized. The serial list consisted of ten items while the paired-associate task consisted of ten pairs of items. Subjects were obtained from kindergarten, as well as grades two, four, six, eight, ten and twelve, which provided age populations of five, seven, nine, eleven, thirteen, fifteen, and seventeen years. Subjects were run to a criterion of one errorless trial or a total of fifteen trials, whichever was obtained first. Statistical analysis of the results supported the earlier study, in that the use of mediation produced a significant effect only in the case of paired-associate learning—although it should be noted that such differences were not significant for kindergarten or for the eighth and twelfth grades.

TABLE 8–9

MEANS OF ERROR SCORES AND TOTAL TIME IN LEARNING
SERIAL LISTS AND PAIRED-ASSOCIATES

Instructions	Serial Learning		Paired Associates	
	Errors	Time	Errors	Time
Mediation	33.1	14.37	14.7	12.75
Nonmediation	33.1	16.89	72.7	25.73

(Adapted from Jensen and Rohwer 1963)

In the Epstein, Rock and Zuckerman (1960) study, it was noted that irrelevant connectives did not contribute to better learning, and in the study just cited, there was the suggestion from the work with kindergarten children that the placing of a conjunction between the nouns, i.e., "cow and ball," did not contribute to superior learning. In a subsequent study by Rohwer (1966), the characteristic of the connective defined as: (1) semantic constraint was investigated, as well as two other variables, (2) meaningfulness and (3) syntactic structure. In this study, meaningfulness was manipulated by using strings of English words and also strings of nonsense syllables. Syntactic structure was examined using verbal strings of material, which either were structured according to the rules of English grammar or scrambled with regard to grammatical rules. Finally, semantic constraint was investigated by using either conjunctions, prepositions, or verbs as connectives.

Table 8–10 provides an example of the varying types of material used.

The general procedure consisted of providing the varying groups of subjects with three pretraining trials, in which the different types of materials were presented as indicated in Table 8–10.

Following such training, the two nouns were presented in the standard anticipation method at a 4:4 rate, to a criterion of one perfect trial, or until the list had been presented six times (whichever occurred last).

TABLE 8–10

TYPES OF MATERIAL USED

Examination of Constraint
    The running *cow* and the bouncing *ball*. (conjunction)
    The running *cow* behind the bouncing *ball*. (preposition)
    The running *cow* chases the bouncing *ball*. (verb)

Examination of Syntax
    The running *cow* chases the bouncing *ball*
    bouncing chases *cow* the running the *ball*

Examination of Meaningfulness
    The running *cow* chases the bouncing *ball*.
    The ludding *cow* drases the spraking *ball*.

(Adapted from Rohwer 1966)

TABLE 8–11

ACQUISITION OF THE PAIRED-ASSOCIATE LISTS: MEAN NUMBERS
OF CORRECT RESPONSES ON FIRST SIX TRIALS

| Meaningfulness | Constraint | Correct Responses | |
		Structured	Scrambled
English	Conjunctions	22.38	18.06
	Prepositions	31.75	21.94
	Verbs	36.31	20.62
	Mean	30.15	20.21
Nonsense	Quasi-conjunctions	22.94	18.00
	Quasi-prepositions	19.75	22.38
	Quasi-verbs	18.88	17.75
	Mean	20.52	19.38

(Adapted from Rohwer 1966)

Table 8–11, in which the mean number of correct responses on the first six trials is provided, shows the acquisition of the paired-associate lists.

First, it may be noted that paired-associate learning was facilitated by the preliminary training with syntactically structured, English word strings of material, in contrast to nonsense connectives. Within the English word strings, it may be noted that syntax facilitated learning—a general finding discussed earlier in this chapter. Finally, the constraint variable also provided differences, with findings in keeping with the prediction made by Rohwer that verb strings would produce the fastest rate of learning.

SUMMARY

Although the basic material used in traditional studies of verbal learning is the isolated unit, some investigators have been interested in examining the learning and retention of extended serial or contextual material. One of the early studies in this area was performed by Miller and Selfridge (1950), who proposed that for any given number of words in a verbal passage, there are varying approximations to English—with approximation to English defined as the probability that any one word will follow the second, third, etc. In order to examine the relationship between approximation to English and learning, these investigators constructed ten approximations to English in either ten- or fifty-word groupings. Subjects were instructed to learn these word groups following an oral presentation. Results revealed that learning increased as approximation to English increased, up to the fifth order of approximation. Beyond the fifth order, however, little improvement took place. Subsequent studies have raised questions concerning the methodology and materials used by Miller and Selfridge. These more recent experiments have demonstrated that learning continues to improve with increases in approximation to English beyond the fifth order.

More recent work in the area has emphasized semantics and syntax as two variables that appear to contribute to the learning of contextual materials. Syntax represents the orderly arrangement of words found in prose; semantics is concerned with the meaning of the material. A variety of experimenters have indicated that both variables contribute to learning.

In manipulating the semantic variable, many investigators have been content to demonstrate only that a meaningful sentence is learned more rapidly than a nonmeaningful one. The meaningfulness dimension may be looked at in terms of a continuum of complexity, and recent investigators have directed their attention toward obtaining some basic measure of semantic content. One area of investigation has been concerned with sentence depth, and another, lexical density. Although an early study by Martin and Roberts (1966) was most encouraging in indicating that sentence depth contributed to retention, more recent studies have not been able to replicate this finding. Lexical density appears to hold some promise, although more work will be necessary in order to demonstrate its usefulness.

The role of association strength has also been investigated and it has been discovered that sentences constructed of items with high inter-item associative strength are learned more rapidly than those with low inter-item associative strength. Some question must be raised, however, about relating these findings to ordinary prose, since it is likely that there is little inter-item associative strength among the words that comprise such material.

Finally, some experimenters have been interested in the learning of paired-associates that are placed within a contextual framework. Most studies have supported the position that if a pair of items is to be learned, the placing of these items within a meaningful context will contribute to ease of learning.

9 Verbal Learning Models and Processes

At least two different approaches to the study of learning can be distinguished. The experimenter can interest himself primarily in the identification and/or delineation of variables that contribute to the learning process. In such an investigation, as we have already noted, the researcher may be interested in identifying particular characteristics of verbal material and in determining the influence of those characteristics in particular learning situations. This approach can be described as a functional one, and much of the work in verbal learning has been in this tradition.

In contrast is the theoretical oriented approach, in which the experimenter attempts to infer processes from experimental findings. In working with these processes, the experimenter develops or builds models that have relevance for the learning task (or tasks) at hand, and from which predictions can be made concerning the relative contribution of a number of variables. At this point in time, the models and processes posited by investigators in verbal learning have been limited to relatively specific types of learning situations.

Both approaches have their advantages as well as disadvantages. The functional approach places emphasis upon experimental data and the establishment of a dimensional analysis, or the experimental relationships among demonstrable variables. But the result can be an unexciting collection of data without hierarchical structure. Hilgard and Bower (1966), in commenting on this kind of approach to the study of behavior, wrote, "Dimensional analysis puts data in order for exposition and for verification, but in itself does not connect the data into an economical scientific system. Such a system has to be logically structured as well as empirically sound" (p. 331).

The hypothesizing of processes and building of models, on the other hand, can be an interesting and exciting venture, since a number of experimental findings must be accounted for; moreover, it allows the investigator to make predictions about types of experiments that have not yet been done. A basic problem with this approach, of course, is that of developing a model that can successfully account for the experimental data contained in the literature.

Although the general approach taken in this text is primarily functional in character, it is not wholly so; experimental work in verbal learning has been placing an ever-increasing emphasis upon processes and models. As a result, this chapter shall include a brief survey of some of those processes and models that have been proposed in the paired-associate, serial, and extended serial or contextual situations.

PAIRED-ASSOCIATE LEARNING

As was discussed in Chapter 1, the paired-associate task is one in which the subject is required to associate a stimulus (i.e., nonsense syllable, word, etc.) with a response. A number of models and processes have been proposed in order to account for the learning that takes place in this type of learning situation.

CLASSICAL CONDITIONING MODEL

Classical conditioning has been at times conceptualized as a kind of learning situation with wide generality; in addition, it is an area that has generated many experimental findings. It is not surprising that some investigators have used the classical conditioning situation as a model by which to examine paired-associate learning. This approach was proposed by Goss, Morgan and Golin (1959), who wrote that "learning the correct anticipation for each pair of a list of paired-associates can be considered analogous to classical conditioning" (p. 96). Here, the stimulus member of the pair corresponds to the CS. The presentation of the response member corresponds to the UCS, while the subject's response to the presentation may be considered as the UCR. Finally, the elicitation of the subject's response through the presentation of the stimulus can be considered comparable to the formation of a CS-CR association. Figure 9–1 illustrates this.

A primary reason for the postulation of any model is its heuristic value; that is, its ability to provide the investigator with new insights about conditions or processes found in the learning situation. Two variables, (1) percentage of reinforcement and (2) the CS-UCS interval, have produced reasonably stable findings in

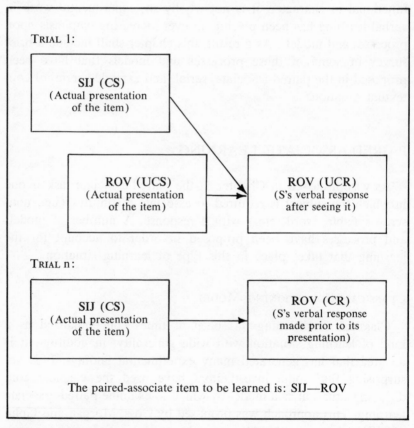

Fig. 9–1. Illustration of the classical conditioning model of paired-associate learning.

classical conditioning. However, Schulz and Runquist (1960), and Kintsch and McCoy (1964) have not been able to obtain analogous findings in manipulating these same variables in the paired-associates learning task.

In order to provide the reader with some general idea concerning this kind of comparison, we should like to briefly present the Schulz and Runquist (1960) study. In this experiment, a paired-associate list was constructed with either 20, 40, 60, 80, or 100 percent occurrence of the response member (ORM) of the pair. With the 20 percent ORM, a response was paired with its stimulus member on only one of each block of five trials. Subjects who were attempting to learn the varying lists were told that the response members of the pairs would be omitted a certain percentage of the time, but to do their best in spite of this handicap. This omission of the presentation of the response item was likened to the partial reinforcement situation in classical conditioning where the UCS is presented intermittently. (It will be recalled that Goss, Morgan and Golin [1959] considered that the presentation of the response term in paired-associate learning could be likened to the UCS.) The criterion for learning was one perfect recitation. Results, similar to those obtained in an earlier study by Goss, Morgan and Golin (1959), indicated that the number of correct responses increased (and the mean number of trials required to reach the learning criterion decreased) as the percentage of occurrences of the response member of the pair (ORM) increased. These findings are, of course, in contrast to those of typical classical conditioning studies, which have indicated that partial reinforcing situations (omission of the UCS) lead to greater response strength (as measured by experimental extinction) rather than less.

In classical conditioning, delayed conditioning procedures have almost always resulted in better conditioning than trace conditioning procedures. Kintsch and McCoy (1964) contrasted these types of procedures using the paired-associate learning situation; they were, however, unable to find a superiority of the delayed conditioning procedure. They have concluded that "the repeated failure to find a delay effect in paired-associate learning questions the relevance of the classical conditioning paradigm for paired-associate learning" (p. 374).

Although these experiments do not provide overwhelming evidence against the value of classical conditioning as a model considerable question must be raised concerning how much this model aids in providing a better understanding of paired-associate learning.

UNDERWOOD AND SCHULZ'S TWO-STAGE MODEL

In 1960 Underwood and Schulz proposed a two-stage model of paired-associate learning that has generated a great deal of interest. Briefly, the Underwood and Schulz model assumes that in the paired-associate learning task there is (1) a response availability stage and (2) an associative or hook-up stage. The response availability stage is one in which the subject acquires the necessary responses, or makes them available in his repertoire of responses. The second stage can be characterized as a hook-up stage, during which the subject learns to associate these available responses to the stimuli presented.

As we shall note, other paired-associate models differ from the Underwood and Schulz (1960) model primarily in terms of the number of additional processes hypothesized to operate in this same type of learning situation. There is general agreement, however, that a response availability stage and an associative stage represent basic processes in paired-associate learning; a variety of experiments have provided support for the existence of these stages. One of the most interesting studies has been performed by McCormack and Haltrecht (1965) who continuously recorded the eye movements of twenty subjects learning seven pairs of CVCs. The data were analyzed frame by frame; the main results are indicated in Fig. 9–2. These findings indicate that the mean number of frames (or amount of time) during which the subject looked at the stimulus remained relatively constant over the learning trials. On the other hand, early in the learning a considerably greater amount of time was spent in looking at the response; the authors have assumed that this reflects the response learning phase. As learning trials continued, it can be noted that there was a systematic decline in the amount of time spent looking at the response. This systematically decreasing ratio of response time to

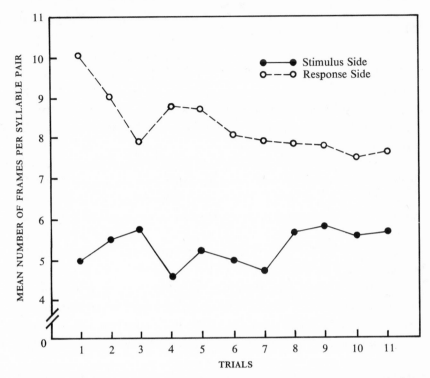

Fig. 9–2. Mean number of frames of stimulus and response as a function of trials.
(Adapted from McCormack and Haltrecht 1965)

stimulus time over trials, the authors point out, is clearly consistent with the two-stage hypothesis, and it reflects the transition from the response availability stage to the hook-up phase.

MEDIATION MODELS

A number of investigators have taken the position that the Underwood and Schulz (1960) model should be supplemented with mediational constructs in order for this model to more adequately mirror the processes taking place in paired-associate learning. As a result, McGuire (1961), Newman (1961, 1964a), and Melton (1967) all have proposed models that emphasize the contribution of mediation to paired-associate learning.

McGuire's Three-Stage Model

McGuire (1961) proposed that an important process in paired-associate learning is associating a mediating stimulus-producing response, r, with each stimulus. This is an encoding process by which the subject discriminates that stimulus from other stimuli in the list and at the same time identifies it, frequently in an idiosyncratic way.

In brief, then, McGuire assumed that learning each S-R pair in the paired-associate task involves three processes or component habits. In the first stage, the subject encodes or transforms the formal stimulus into one he can identify and discriminate from other stimuli in the list. In the second stage, he learns the appropriate responses or makes them available; in the third, he attaches the response (R) to the stimulus (S).

McGuire (1961) examined the operation of this model in the following study. The stimuli and responses used were designed to permit the investigator to manipulate independently the difficulty in learning each of the three processes he had postulated. The stimuli used were two sets of nine solid black circles of varying diameters. In set I, the diameters ranged from .37 to 1.49 in .14 centimeter steps; in set II, .07 centimeter steps were used with a range of .37 to .93. McGuire assumed that the difficulty in learning to discriminate the circles of the second set would be greater than that posed by the first set. Thus, H-1$_E$ refers to the use of set I stimuli, H-1$_D$ to set II stimuli.

The responses were numbers. For one set of responses, the numbers used were 1 through 9. For the second set of responses, the numbers used were three digits in length, randomly obtained. It was assumed that it would be more difficult for subjects to acquire the second set of responses than the first. Here, H-3$_E$ refers to the use of single digit numbers as responses, while H-3$_D$ refers to the use of three digit numbers.

The difficulty of learning to associate the stimulus with the response, or the operation of the associative process, was manipulated by the manner in which the responses were paired with the stimuli. For one set, the stimuli and responses were so assigned that successively larger numbers were assigned to progressively larger circles. For the second set, responses were paired with stimuli randomly. Thus, for the S-R learning, H-2$_E$ refers to the systematic pairing of the stimuli and responses while H-2$_D$ refers to random pairing.

The procedure involved the standard paired-associate learning task, in which the usual 2:2 anticipation method was employed and eighty continuous trials were provided. Six different groups of subjects were utilized, with each group assigned to a different condition. The varying conditions can be noted in Table 9–1. Results, as measured by the proportion of correct anticipations per trial for each of the six conditions, can be noted also in Table 9–1.

In the examination of the role of the stimulus encoding process, condition 1 can be compared with condition 2, and condition 3 with condition 4. In each comparison the only difference between the tasks was that the stimulus discrimination was more difficult in the latter conditions. It can be noted that in each comparison, easier stimulus discriminability results in better learning, and that this difference is statistically significant.

The difficulty of learning the response, or the response availability process, can be examined by comparing conditions 1 vs.

TABLE 9–1

Description of Difficulty Levels of Component Habits in Each of the Six Conditions, Along with the Proportion of Correct Anticipations per Trial in Each of the Six Conditions

Condition		Proportion of Correct Responses/Trial
1	H-1$_E$, H-2$_E$, H-3$_E$	.793
2	H-1$_D$, H-2$_E$, H-3$_E$	.635
3	H-1$_E$, H-2$_E$, H-3$_D$	.618
4	H-1$_D$, H-2$_E$, H-3$_D$	.491
5	H-1$_D$, H-2$_D$, H-3$_E$	.462
6	H-1$_D$, H-2$_D$, H-3$_D$	.340

(Adapted from McGuire 1961)

3, and conditions 2 vs. 4. Here, the only difference between the comparisons is related to whether single-digit or three-digit responses had to be learned. Again the findings indicate that single-digit responses, which were more readily available, led to more rapid learning. Again, differences between groups were statistically significant.

An examination of differences in the associative stage can be made by comparing conditions 2 vs. 5 and 4 vs. 6. The differences are statistically significant, and this strongly implies that the ease of associating the stimulus with the response contributes to improved paired-associate learning.

NEWMAN'S SELECTIVE MEDIATION MODEL

Like McGuire (1961), Newman (1961) also posited that a mediating response is made by the subject when the stimulus item is presented; however, he hypothesized that a mediating response is made to the response item as well. In positing a second mediation response that arises from the overt response, Newman acknowledges a particular distinction: that between a response learning process through which the subject is able to verbalize the response, and a response discrimination process through which a mediating response permits the differentiation of the response from other response terms. The distinction between response availability and response differentiation is also mirrored on the stimulus side, where—at least in some situations—stimulus differentiation can be distinguished from stimulus learning.[1]

In total, then, Newman's (1961) model increases the number of processes to five: (1) stimulus term discrimination, (2) stimulus term learning, (3) response term discrimination, (4) response term learning, and (5) stimulus-response association.

MELTON'S MEDIATIONAL MODEL

Finally, Melton (1967) proposed that McGuire's (1961) model be expanded to provide for the possibility of an alternative mediational route for the connection of the mediated internal repre-

---

[1] The situation that requires a stimulus learning process would be one in which the subject was required to pronounce the stimulus term when it was presented.

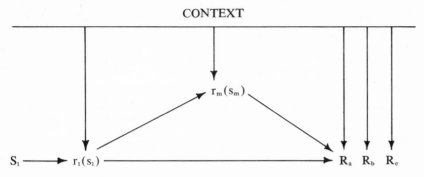

Fig. 9–3. A multi-process model of associative learning.
(Adapted from Melton 1967)

sentative of the physical stimulus (mediated response to the physical stimulus) and the required response. A second addition was the positing of associations that arise between contextual stimuli (i.e., usually unspecified but manipulable environmental and intraorganic stimuli) and all response elements involved in the S-R sequence. Fig. 9–3 presents this Melton multi-process model.

OTHER PAIRED-ASSOCIATE PROCESSES

It is obvious, of course, that the ease of learning a list of paired-associates will depend upon a number of variables. Some of these conditions are related (a) to the characteristics of learning tasks that have been performed prior to the learning task in question, (b) to the kind of procedure that is utilized, (c) to the nature of the stimulus and response material, etc. A number of investigators have recognized that, depending upon these conditions, a number of learning subprocesses may be brought into play that should in turn be identified.

An examination of the influence of intralist similarity has resulted in Underwood, Ekstrand and Keppel's (1965) hypothesizing three such subprocesses. In the paired-associate list in which the stimulus and response terms are similar, the subject will sometimes respond with one of the stimulus items. This type of error indicates a lack of complete differentiation on the part of the subject between these two classes of items. As a result, the authors hypothesized that one subprocess in the learning of paired-associates is the subject's learning to differentiate the stimulus items from those of the response.

In addition, two other subprocesses these authors proposed are derived from types of interference (or kinds of errors) that are found in the learning of highly similar intralist items. In the learning of such material, it is frequently found that the subject has difficulty in discriminating among the stimuli presented. Here, a subprocess was hypothesized that enables the learner to successfully discriminate among the varying stimulus items. Finally, learning protocols frequently reveal incorrect stimulus-response or associative connections, and this led the authors to posit a third subprocess that enables the subject to eventually learn which responses are attached to which stimuli.

Mention should also be made of Battig's (1968) listing of processes (and subprocesses) that he assumed to be present in paired-associate learning. Some of these have been already delineated in this text; others have not been identified.

1. *List differentiation.*

This refers to the identification of the class (or classes) of items that make up the list, and to which particular members or subsets of that class (or those classes) are or are not included in the list. During the learning of a list of paired-associates, the subject seldom makes a response that is outside the set of responses that comprise the paired-associate list. Obviously then, the subject, although not able to attach a specific response to its appropriate stimuli, or perhaps not having available those responses that comprise the list, nonetheless has learned something about the set of responses that make up the task.

2. *Classification of items as stimulus and response terms.*

This early stage of paired-associate learning, frequently overlapping with the list differentiation stage, consists of the identification of the stimulus or response function served by each individual item. As Battig points out, the importance of this stage is maximized when both the stimulus and response terms represent the same class of items.

3. *Discrimination of stimulus and response terms.*

In addition to learning to identify general classes of stimulus and response terms, the subject must also learn to discriminate among the individual members within each class. If the items are very similar within either or both classes, it is obvious that this stage assumes more importance than if the class items are quite dissimilar.

4. *Response learning or integration.*

In this stage, the subject learns the response sufficiently well to be able to produce it in the presence of appropriate stimuli.

5. *Stimulus selection and coding.*

This stage or process has been widely accepted in the analysis of paired-associate learning. Here, in effect, the subject transforms a nominal stimulus into a functional one.

6. *Stimulus-response associations.*

The process whereby the subject learns to associate a specific available response to specific stimuli represents a process widely accepted in paired-associate learning.

7. *Classification of pairs as learned and unlearned.*

Battig also called attention to a process in which a subject is able to identify and provide differential attention to pairs of items that belong to learned as well as unlearned categories. Typically, the subject learns to differentiate those pairs of items that he already knows from those he does not, during the course of learning. As a result, he frequently "pays careful attention" to the pairs he has not already learned.

8. *Additional stimulus learning.*

Battig believed that during and following intermediate stages of paired-associate learning, particularly where intratask interference is at its maximum, there may be substantial learning of stimulus-response associations involving stimulus cues over and above those initially selected or encoded as the functional stimuli.

9. *Mediated and extralist associations.*

In those paired-associate learning situations in which there is considerable intratask interference, individual stimulus-response associations may be buttressed by extralist mediated associations between the stimulus and response terms.

10. *Interpair grouping.*

Battig assumed that advanced stages of paired-associate learning might involve the development of a hierarchical organizational structure in which the total list to be learned is categorized into subsets or groups of pairs connected by some common property or other interrelationship.

Battig (1968) did not suggest that these processes operate independently of one another nor that all of them are importantly involved in any and/or all paired-associate learning tasks. Rather, he suggested that there appeared to be considerable variation in the relative involvement of these processes across the various paired-associate tasks and conditions; there are marked individual differences as to which processes are employed and to what extent. Further research is obviously necessary in order to delineate the conditions that minimize and maximize the operations of these varying hypothesized processes.

AN EXAMINATION OF THE STIMULUS DIFFERENTIATION PROCESS

One step in the direction of making a more specific examination of some of the processes just listed, and in particular, the stimulus differentiation or discrimination process, was undertaken by Martin (1967).

Martin argued that in paired-associate learning, following the presentation of the stimulus, the subject selectively attends or focuses on only certain parts of the stimulus. The subject codes those perceived aspects in various ways in order to obtain a mediator that will facilitate the association between the stimulus and the response. According to Martin, this mediator (or, the intervening response made by the subject following the presentation of the stimulus) must, at least in some sense, remain stable or be invariant over trials, if it is to be able to elicit consistently the appropriate response. He postulated that this stable perceptual mediator could be identified as a recognition process. Martin's (1967) study was designed to test the position that in order for a stimulus to elicit a response, the subject must make an intervening recognition response to the stimulus. It is the nature of this recognition response process, then, that interested him. He further proposed that the notion of stimulus meaningfulness should be varied with the idea that if the two processes—recognition and association formation—proved separable, the locus of stimulus-meaningful effects might be identifiable.

In his experiment, Martin gave each subject twelve study and twelve test trials on a paired-associate list that consisted of eight trigrams (CCC) as stimuli and the digits 1 through 8 as responses. The material was presented aurally at a two-second rate. On each test trial twenty-four trigrams were presented; eight of these were the stimuli used on the study trials, and sixteen were new trigrams that had never appeared on any previous trial, study or test. In order to manipulate stimulus meaningfulness, four trigrams on the study list had low association values, and four high. With regard to the composition of the sixteen filler trigrams used on the test trials, half had low association values while the other half had high association values. The general procedure during the test trials was to present a trigram aurally—upon hearing a trigram, the subject had to press one of two buttons, one marked old and the other new; in this way, the subject indicated whether or not he recognized the trigram as one that had occurred on study trials. If the trigram was designated as "old," the subject had to say aloud the response digit that had been associated with the stimulus. If he thought a given trigram was new, he was to say any one of the eight digits that came in mind.

Trial-by-trial summary of the recognition button-pressing data is indicated in Fig. 9–4. The proportion of correct recognitions (calling old stimuli old) increases to a higher asymptote for the higher meaningful stimuli than for low meaningful stimuli. Over trials, then, high meaningful stimuli proved significantly easier to recognize. On the other hand, the proportion of false positives, that is, calling new stimuli old, was clearly not affected by meaningfulness. Martin concluded that his results indicated that whereas meaningfulness is not a factor in the subject's ability to correctly identify new stimuli, it is a significant factor in the subject's ability to recognize old stimuli.

A trial-by-trial representation of the correct response data is indicated in Fig. 9–5. Given stimulus recognition, the effect of stimulus meaningfulness is significant. When the stimulus is not recognized, the proportion of correct responses does not differ from chance and meaningfulness is no longer a factor.

In commenting upon these findings, Martin pointed out that regardless of the current status of a stimulus-response association, the

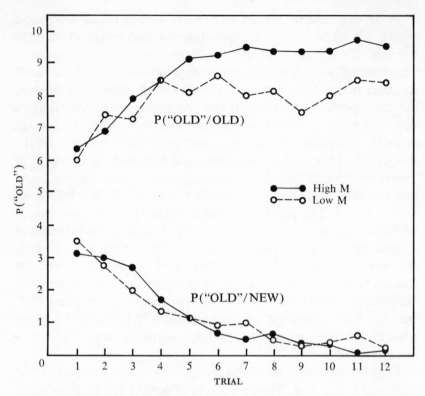

Fig. 9–4. Proportion "old" responses when stimuli are old (recognitions) and new (false positives).
(Adapted from Martin 1967)

activation of that association, and hence the occurrence of the response event, R, has as a necessary antecedent the recognition of the stimulus event, S. The utilization of an associative connection apparently requires a particular perceptual response to the stimulus member of that association—a response that consistently causes the subject to regard that stimulus as identical from one occasion to the next. There is little doubt that all subjects clearly heard all stimuli as they came over the earphones. Each subject therefore made a perceptual response of some sort to each stimulus. That these perceptual responses were variable, especially in early trials, is evidenced by the number of nonrecognitions. Martin concluded that it would not be implausible to assume that a major portion of the paired-associate task is taken up with the establishment of consist-

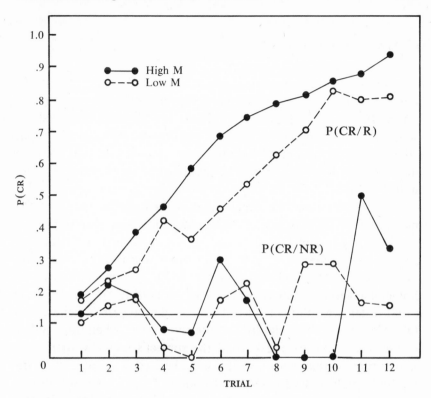

Fig. 9–5. Proportion correct responses (CR) given recognition (R) and nonrecognition (NR) of high- and low-M stimuli. The dashed line is the chance level.

(Adapted from Martin 1967)

ent perceptual responses on which to base overt responses to the stimuli. Moreover, he believed that the formation of such mediating responses is more difficult to low meaningful stimuli than to high, and is distinct from the association-formation process that makes the perceived stimulus the occasion for a given overt response.

In brief, then, Martin's (1967) general position is that the subject makes an intervening recognition response to each stimulus in the paired-associate learning situation before he makes the overt response that is part of his task. Support for this point of view has come from Bernbach (1967), who conducted an experiment similar to Martin's and obtained results that closely parallel Martin's basic findings.

SERIAL LEARNING

Like the two-stage model of paired-associate learning, the learning of a series of items has also been postulated to take place in two
stages. In a study by Hovland and Kurtz (1952) that examined the
serial learning of nonsense syllables, these authors pointed out that
"the process of becoming familiar with the syllable units may be
distinguished from the process of learning the serial order of these
units" (p. 38).

Voss (1966), on the other hand, indicated the necessity for
positing that four processes take place in serial learning. Two
processes, (1) item learning, and (2) serial item placement, are
similar to the familiarity and serial order learning processes hypothesized by Hovland and Kurtz (1952). A third process, (3)
immediate serial memory, is one in which both the items and their
serial order are simultaneously learned; this process is believed to
take place when the serial list is quite short—i.e., when the number
of items does not extend beyond the subject's memory span. The
fourth process that Voss (1966) hypothesized is sequential learning and involves the fundamental notion of the association of adjacent items. Voss (1966) reported that this process is not important when the number of units making up the serial list is short
(i.e., four), but that it does assume importance in an eight-unit list.

However, it must be recognized that these hypotheses concerning
the nature of serial learning have only recently been presented.
Early investigators were interested in the identification of the stimuli
or cues that the subject uses in learning the position of the item—
what Hovland and Kurtz (1952) would designate as the ordering
process, or what would correspond to Voss' (1966) association of
adjacent items. Recent work has continued to focus on this same
problem, although a few investigators (i.e., Horowitz 1961) have
been interested in examining the familiarity or item-learning process
as well.

THE PROCESS OF ASSOCIATIVE CHAINING

The earliest investigation was performed by Ebbinghaus (1885),
whose work with serial learning consisted in conducting a number

of experiments designed to increase the possibility of enlarging our knowledge of memory. Those experiments with primary interest for us at this time can be found in his Chapter 9, "Retention as a Function of the Order of Succession of the Members," which deals with a topic that has frequently been termed the study of "derived lists."

THE EXPERIMENTS OF EBBINGHAUS

Ebbinghaus' experimental procedure consisted of his learning a list of CVCs (he was his own subject) in the following order, 1, 2, 3, 4, 5, 6, 7, 8, 9, and 10; and then learning a second list in which the order of these syllables was changed. Following the learning of the original list, a new list was learned; with one degree of separation (or remoteness), the syllables would be ordered as follows: 1, 3, 5, 7, 9, 2, 4, 6, 8, 10. With two degrees of remoteness, the items would be presented as 1, 4, 7, 10, 2, 5, 8, 3, 6, 9.

The specific experiments undertaken by Ebbinghaus were designed to examine one, two, three, and seven degrees of remoteness. In addition, a fifth condition, designated as a control list, was also examined; here, the position of the first and last syllable remained the same but the positions of the other items were randomly determined. In brief, Ebbinghaus' procedure consisted of learning sixteen items in serial order, and then twenty-four hours later, learning one of the derived lists. The time (in seconds) required to learn the original as well as the second list was recorded.

The specific procedure used by Ebbinghaus, in contrast to the anticipation method, was one in which a series of nonsense syllables were shown to the subject (Ebbinghaus), who then went through the list at a .4-second per item pace, timed first by a metronome and subsequently by the ticking of a watch. When he believed he had learned the list, he attempted to recite it. If he hesitated over a syllable, he went back to studying the list.

Results indicated that the derived list formed by skipping either one, two, three, or seven intermediate members was learned with average savings of 152, 94, 78 and 42 seconds.[1] The random or

---

[1] The savings score was obtained by measuring the difference between the amount of time required to learn the original material and the time required to learn the second list. In the cases cited, the derived list that was formed by skipping every other item required 152 seconds less (on the average) than the original list.

control list was learned with average savings of just 12 seconds.[1]

In accounting for his findings, Ebbinghaus assumed that associations were formed between adjacent items in the serial list. In the learning of a list of items, associations were formed between items 1 and 2, 2 and 3, 3 and 4, etc. In addition, the investigator posited a remote association process in which associations were also formed among other items of the list, and the strength of the association was a function of the number of items or the distance between them. Ebbinghaus wrote: "the associative threads, which hold together a remembered series, are spun not merely between each member and its immediate successor, but beyond intervening members to every member which stands to it in any close temporal relation. The strength of the threads varies with the distance of the members, but even the weaker of them must be considered as relatively of considerable significance" (p. 94).[2]

Ebbinghaus' work gave rise to the position that in serial learning: (1) associations were formed between adjacent items on the list, and (2) associations between each item and items other than the adjacent one were also formed. These latter associations were designated as "remote," and their strength was related to the number of items that intervened between the given item and its associate. In addition, a third assumption, that remote backward associations were formed, was also made.

In brief, and stemming from the Ebbinghaus position, serial learning was conceptualized as the acquisition of a chain of stimulus-response associations; each discrete S-R association was assumed to be comparable to a "paired associate." This chaining hypothesis, it can be noted, assigned both a stimulus as well as a response function to each item in a list. If items 1, 2, and 3 are

---

[1] The reader may be curious as to whether or not the differences among the varying lists were statistically significant. Ebbinghaus could not make an appropriate statistical evaluation of his data, but Young (1968) reported that if the fact that all measures were taken from the same person is ignored, the findings from the derived list study are significant ($F = 5.26$, p. $= <.01$).

[2] It should be noted that a number of contemporary studies have reexamined Ebbinghaus' work, and findings have not always been in accord with those obtained by Ebbinghaus. See Hakes, James and Young (1964); Young, Hakes and Hicks (1965). It is most difficult, however, to compare results. Ebbinghaus used low meaningful items (CVCs) and a span of twenty-four hours between the learning of lists. In both of the Young et al. studies, high meaningful items (adjectives) were used, with two minutes between list learnings.

serially learned, item 2 serves not only as a response to item 1, but also as a cue or stimulus for the next item.[1]

ASSOCIATIVE CHAINING AS MEASURED BY SINGLE AND DOUBLE FUNCTION LISTS

During the early 1960s, there was considerable interest in the chaining hypothesis. Some question was raised at this time regarding the validity of the position that associative chaining makes a major contribution to the learning of a serial list of items.

The type of experimental design most frequently used to investigate the chaining hypothesis has been a transfer situation in which subjects first learn a serial list of items and then are transferred to a list of paired-associates. Following Young (1959, 1961a), the logic of this design has been that if the effective stimulus in the serial learning situation is the preceding item, then that item and the one following it should be learned either faster or slower than

[1] The chaining hypothesis, as well as its remote association corollary, has been a part of the psychology of verbal learning since its original postulation by Ebbinghaus. Lepley (1934), Hull (1935, 1940), Guthrie (1935), and Peters (1935) all proposed hypotheses to account for how remote associations develop. In the most prominent of these (Lepley 1934, and Hull 1935, 1940), the classical conditioning paradigm was used as a model. Briefly, Lepley (1934) hypothesized that adjacent associations could be conceptualized as simultaneous conditioned responses, while the more remote associations between nonadjacent items could be thought of in terms of trace-conditioned responses. These remote response tendencies are suppressed, however, by inhibitory tendencies, which result in the building-up of varying amounts of inhibition between items. Hull (1940) extended this hypothesis by assuming that each item in the series leaves a stimulus trace that continues with diminished strength throughout the remainder of the presentation of material.

No useful purpose would be served in providing an extensive discussion of the Lepley-Hull trace-conditioned hypothesis. This hypothesis appeared to have excellent heuristic value in stimulating individuals to think about the problems of serial learning, but its difficulties were of sufficient magnitude that only an occasional contemporary investigator still believes it to be viable. Fundamentally, of course, there is considerable question as to whether the serial learning situation can be conceptualized as a type of conditioned response learning, since it becomes quite difficult to specify in the serial learning task the varying distinctions among the CS, UCS, CR and UCR that are basic in the conditioned response learning situation. Experimental work with trace-conditioned responses has indicated that the learning of these responses takes place very slowly, and with considerable difficulty; while the remote associations in serial learning, at least as inferred from anticipatory errors, appear to develop quite rapidly.

appropriate control pairs, depending upon how these items are paired in the paired-associate list.

Positive transfer would be presumed to take place if the items in the paired-associate list are so arranged as to duplicate the associations previously formed during the serial learning task. If the experimenter wants each serial item to serve as both a stimulus and a response, as it presumably does in the serial learning situation, a double-function list is constructed. If a serial list of items, 1-2-3-4-5-6, is learned, the paired-associate task would be constructed as follows: 1-2, 2-3, 3-4, 4-5, 5-6. On the other hand, a single-function list is one in which each serial-learned item serves as *either* a stimulus or a response in the paired-associate list. Here, the paired items would be arranged as: 1-2, 3-4, 5-6, etc.

If the pairing of the items is such that the associations formed during serial learning must be rearranged during the paired-associate task, it is presumed that negative transfer will take place. Again, single- or double-function lists can be used in order to examine this function.[1]

A study by Young (1961a) serves to illustrate the operation of the double-function list, as well as indicate Young's own experimental findings. In addition to the use of an experimental design that, according to the chaining hypothesis, would produce positive and negative transfer, Young also manipulated the amount of serial list learning. To the extent that the strength of associations among the varying items in the serial list plays an important role in the subsequent learning of paired-associates, large amounts of serial learning should produce either positive or negative transfer more readily than smaller amounts of such learning.

In this study, groups of subjects were given varying amounts of learning on a nine-item serial learning task. For one group, there was no learning on the relevant serial list; for a second group, the serial list of items was presented until five responses were given

---

[1] Postman and Stark (1967) wrote that "on the assumption that each serial item is both a stimulus and a response, the double-function list provides the most complete measure of associative transfer" (p. 340). At the same time they also point out that a major source of difficulty in the acquisition of a double-function list is heavy interference from backward associations that develop due to the use of the same items as stimuli and responses. Consequently, some question may be raised as to whether or not the double-function list is indeed the best procedure to use.

TABLE 9–2

LISTS OF LEARNING MATERIALS

Serial-List: Predicted Negative Transfer Group	Serial-List: Predicted Positive Transfer Group	PA-List: Both Groups
Entire	Alike	Solvent-Unwell
Icy	Icy	Entire-Rustic
Unwell	Joyous	Icy-Joyous
Rustic	Solvent	Unwell-Clever
Joyous	Unwell	Alike-Icy
Clever	Clever	Clever-Entire
Taboo	Entire	Joyous-Solvent
Alike	Rustic	Rustic-Taboo
Solvent	Taboo	

(Adapted from Young 1961a)

correctly on a single trial; the third group learned the serial list to one perfect trial. Following this, each group was divided in half, so that one half of the subjects were required to learn a paired-associate task in which the items were arranged to provide positive transfer; for the other half, the items were arranged to provide negative transfer.[1]

The specific lists were composed of two-syllable adjectives. These lists can be noted in Table 9–2. The learning of the paired-associate list for all groups under all conditions was carried to one perfect trial; four different orders of presentation were used, to minimize serial learning and thus emphasize learning in pairs.

The mean number of trials to learn the paired-associate list to one perfect recitation for the three conditions for each group is shown in Table 9–3. In the analysis of trials to learn, not a single

[1] Young recognized that the learning of the paired-associate list might be influenced by differences in such general factors as warm-up or learning-to-learn (see Chapter 10 for a description of these variables), which could result from the varying degrees of prior serial learning. In order to make these general factors equivalent for all three conditions, an irrelevant serial list was presented before the relevant serial list a sufficient number of times so that, with the irrelevant and relevant lists combined, the amount of practice and warm-up would be the same for all conditions at the time the subject was transferred to the paired-associate list. For the condition in which the subject was not given trials on the relevant serial list, the irrelevant serial list was learned to one perfect trial.

TABLE 9–3

MEAN TRIALS TO LEARN THE PA-LISTS

	Irrelevant Serial List Learned to One Perfect Trial	Learning on Both Irrelevant and Relevant Serial Lists	Relevant Serial List Learned to One Perfect Trial
Group	Mean No. Trials	Mean No. Trials	Mean No. Trials
Predicted Positive Transfer	28.00	27.75	24.67
Predicted Negative Transfer	24.50	25.20	28.80

(Adapted from Young 1961a)

appropriate statistical test was significant. It can be noted, however, that as the degree of prior serial learning increased, trials to learn decreased in the positive transfer group and increased in the negative transfer group. Although differences were not significant, they were in the direction indicated by the chaining hypothesis.

One interesting finding was that positive transfer occurred early in the paired-associate learning for the Predicted Positive Transfer group. This positive transfer was in evidence until about half the items were learned, after which it decreased; it had disappeared by the time a criterion of one perfect recitation was reached.[1]

An earlier experiment by Young (1959), as well as subsequent studies by that investigator (Young 1962; Erickson, Ingram and Young 1963) and others (Jensen and Rohwer 1965a), confirmed these basic findings; namely, that although positive transfer is obtained early in the paired-associate learning situation, these positive transfer effects disappear during subsequent learning trials so that no overall difference can be noted between experimental and control groups by the time the learning criterion has been reached.

[1] As Postman and Stark (1967) pointed out, the conclusion that associative chaining does not occur in serial learning hinges on the acceptance of the null hypothesis. The question must be raised as to whether the measurement operations used in these tests were sufficiently sensitive to the presence of transfer effects.

In contrast to these negative findings, recent evidence has been obtained to support the chaining hypothesis.

Crowder, Chisholm and Fell (1966), Postman and Stark (1967), Stark (1968), and Crowder (1968), in addition to Horowitz and Izawa (1963), all have provided support for the chaining position. In the Postman and Stark (1967) study subjects first learned eight two-syllable adjectives, which comprised a serial list, following which they were transferred to a double-function, seven paired-associates list. In contrast to most other studies, subjects were given just ten learning trials, rather than learning to a criterion. The reason for this divergence of procedure was that the authors believed that the use of the more severe learning criterion was not an adequate measure of transfer, since it depends upon the "rate of mastery of the most difficult items in the list, and hence will be largely determined by performance in the late rather than in the early stages of acquisition" (p. 341).

The three conditions of transfer, typically found in this type of experiment, were used. In condition P (Positive), the paired-associate list consisted entirely of pairs of adjacent items taken from the serial list, while in condition N (Negative), the paired-associates were composed of nonadjacent members of the serial list. In condition C (Control) there was no overlap between the items used in the serial list and those used in the paired-associate list. Within each condition of transfer, there was (1) an instructed and (2) an uninstructed group. The instructed group was given full information after the end of serial learning about the nature and composition of the transfer list; the uninstructed group received no such information. All subjects served in three experimental cycles in which transfer from serial to paired-associate learning was measured.

Typical serial and paired-associate learning procedures were used. Serial lists were presented at a two-second rate with a two-second intertrial interval; paired-associate lists were presented at a 2:2-second rate, with a four-second intertrial interval.

The mean number of correct responses for the first transfer trial as well as for the full ten trials, as a function of the three presentations (cycles), are indicated in Figures 9–6 and 9–7. Both figures provide clear evidence for associative transfer inasmuch as a reliable difference can be found between the number of correct responses provided by the Positive Transfer groups in contrast to

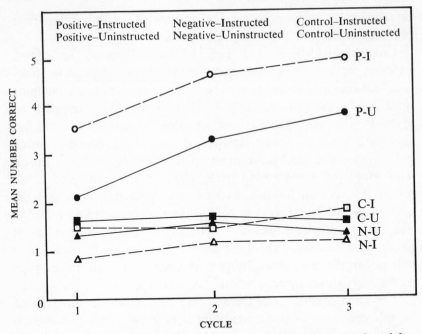

Fig. 9–6. Mean numbers of correct responses on the first transfer trial.
(Adapted from Postman and Stark 1967)

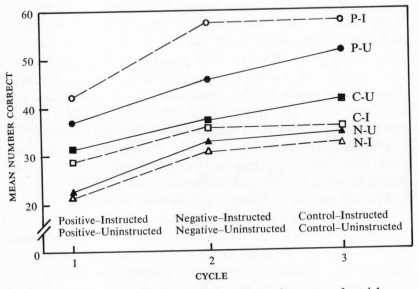

Fig. 9–7. Mean numbers of correct responses in ten transfer trials.
(Adapted from Postman and Stark 1967)

those obtained by the Negative, regardless of whether the first trial or all ten trials were used.

As the authors wrote, the data provide clear evidence for transfer from serial to paired-associate learning; the critical differences among the conditions of transfer present on the first paired-associate trial are brought out fully in the total scores obtained over the ten-trial period. With regard to the role of instructions, information about the relationship between successive tasks appeared to have no apparent effect on the level of negative transfer, but did increase the amount of positive transfer.

Stark (1968) pointed out that the small positive transfer effects that were obtained by many of the earlier investigators might be explained by the fact that the double-function paired-associate list is intrinsically difficult to learn. The reason is that backward (R-S) associations are elicited, since each response in the list also appears as a stimulus. In a list consisting of items, A-B, B-C, etc. B frequently elicits A (backward association) as well as C. These backward associations compete with the to-be-learned forward ones, and must be differentiated from them in order for the list to be mastered. If the experimental subject begins the transfer task with both forward and backward associations, but is unable to differentiate between them, many of the early responses will be incorrect; as a result, he may then reject all serial associations because he does not know which ones are relevant in the transfer list.

In an effort to reduce the effects of competing backward associations, Stark hypothesized that if: (1) subjects were fully informed about the structure of the transfer task (as they had been in the Postman and Stark [1967] study), and (2) the anticipation interval was increased to three seconds, thus permitting the subjects more time for the differentiation and rejection of backward associations, substantial positive transfer should be obtained on the paired-associate task.

Two experiments were conducted that utilized the changes in procedure just outlined; in addition, in experiment I, the meaningfulness of the material (as measured by word frequency) was manipulated, while in experiment II, transfer was investigated as a function of stimulus pronunciation during paired-associate learning.

In experiment I, two experimental and two control groups

learned serial lists of ten words consisting of either high or low frequency items. For the experimental groups, the adjacent words on the originally learned serial lists were used to make up dual-function paired-associate tasks. These same paired-associates were also used for the control groups; however, since these groups had learned different (but comparable) serial lists, the paired-associate items were new.

Following the learning of the serial lists, subjects received general paired-associate instructions and were informed about the structure of the transfer lists. Control groups were given one paired-associate study trial during which both the stimulus and response items were pronounced; this was followed by regular anticipation trials using a 3:2-second rate. Experimental subjects were not given the study trial. All paired-associate learning was carried out to a criterion of one perfect trial.

Measures of transfer list performance are indicated in Table 9–4. It should be noted that transfer does not differ as a function of word frequency; on the other hand, large and significant differences can be noted between the experimental and control groups for either performance measure.

Experiment II was similar to experiment I except that only high frequency three-letter nouns were used as the experimental material; in addition, one experimental and one control group was required to pronounce the stimulus term during the paired-associate learning task; their counterpart groups, however, were not required to do so. Measures of transfer-list performance are indicated in

TABLE 9–4

MEASURES OF TRANSFER-LIST PERFORMANCE
(EXP. I)

Measure	High Frequency		Low Frequency	
	Exper.	Contr.	Exper.	Contr.
Mean correct on Trial 1	6.6	3.4	6.4	2.2
Mean trials to criterion	7.4	20.8	8.7	21.6

(Adapted from Stark 1968)

TABLE 9–5

MEASURES OF TRANSFER-LIST PERFORMANCE
(EXP. II)

Measure	Vocal		Nonvocal	
	Exper.	Contr.	Exper.	Contr.
Mean correct on Trial 1	5.6	2.8	6.0	2.3
Mean trials to criterion	10.3	19.6	11.7	20.8

(Adapted from Stark 1968)

Table 9–5, and although stimulus pronunciation had no significant effects, large and significant differences were again obtained between the experimental and control groups for both performance measures.

The results of both experiments provide consistent findings: positive transfer occurred at all stages of paired-associate learning. Stark (1968) concluded that these findings constitute presumptive support for the importance of the preceding item as a functional stimulus in the serial list.

Finally, Crowder and his associates (Crowder, Chisholm and Fell 1966; Crowder 1968) also obtained evidence for the chaining hypothesis in what has been described as the continuous paired-associate learning situation. This particular task measures short-term retention for individual pairs of items. Crowder (1968) concluded that previous failures to find support for the chaining hypothesis may say more about the complexity of paired-associate learning than about the mechanisms involved in serial learning.

ORDINAL POSITION AS A CUE IN SERIAL LEARNING

With the associative chaining hypothesis unable to account for all of the experimental findings reported (i.e., Young 1959, 1962; Erickson, Ingram and Young 1963), it is not surprising that other hypotheses have been proposed concerning the nature of the functional stimulus in serial learning. Chief among these is the ordinal position hypothesis. This hypothesis states that the position of the item in the list, rather than the previously presented item, is the functional stimulus.

In an early study examining the ordinal position hypothesis, Young (1962, exp. III) had an experimental group learn two serial lists in which the same items were used on each list. In one condition (A), even items held the *same* serial position in both lists while the odd items were randomly rearranged from the first to the second list. For a second condition (B), the odd items held the *same* serial position in both lists while the even items were randomly rearranged from the first to the second list. A control condition (C) was used in which there were no common items from the first list to the second.

Results showed that the mean numbers of trials to learn the test list for conditions A, B, and C were 12.43, 13.86, and 9.71 respectively, thus indicating that the two rearranged lists provided negative transfer. Of primary concern, however, were the learning curves obtained for the items that appeared in the same and different positions in the second list. These can be noted in Fig. 9–8. Items that appeared in the same position in both lists were significantly easier to learn.

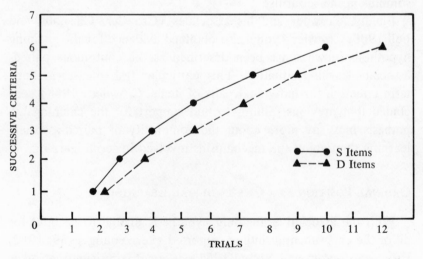

Fig. 9–8. Trials to successive criteria curves for the S- and D-item sublists during test-list learning in experiment III.
(Adapted from Young 1962)

Ebenholtz (1963a, exp. II), using CVCs and employing a slightly different design, confirmed Young's findings. In Ebenholtz's experiment, subjects learned two serial lists. One group found that half (alternate) of the items learned in the first list were also in the second list and in the same position. A second group also found that half (alternate) of the items learned in the first list were also in the second list, but in different positions. For both groups, new items were substituted for those (the half) that had been dropped. A control group learned two different serial lists. Results were similar to those obtained by Young (1962). As Ebenholtz (1963a) wrote,

The learning of repeated items clearly demonstrates positive transfer only for those syllables that are repeated *in position* (Group 1). Syllables repeated at positions which differ from their original list 1 location (Group 2) are learned no earlier than items which are learned for the first time (Group 3). It follows, therefore, that under the present conditions of serial learning, positive transfer is a function of the maintenance of identical serial positions on original and transfer lists (p. 359).

Keppel and Saufley (1964) also obtained findings supporting the ordinal position hypothesis.

Another type of experiment that has been used to examine the ordinal position hypothesis deals with variations in the starting point in the learning of the serial list. If associations are formed between the items on a serial list, it would seem to make little difference at what point any trial was started. Since the position of the item is critical in the ordinal position hypothesis, a new starting point on each trial would produce a change in position of all items in the list from trial to trial; this would result in maximum confusion and difficulty in learning. The studies that have been performed using this type of experimental design have supported the ordinal position hypothesis.

In a second study by Ebenholtz (1963a), ten high association nonsense syllables were used to make up a serial list of items. Each trial consisted of the presentation of thirteen syllables, with the first and last three syllables duplicated. For the Experimental group, the particular syllable that started the list was varied from trial to trial. The sequence of syllables as they appeared for these subjects on trials 1 and 2 can be represented as follows:

Trial 1. A-B-C-D-E-F-G-H-I-J-A-B-C
      2. D-E-F-G-H-I-J-A-B-C-D-E-F

For the Control group, the position of the syllables remained constant from trial to trial. All subjects, using serial anticipation with a two-second rate of presentation, learned the list to a criterion of one perfect trial. As seen from the results, indicated in Figure 9–9, the large difference in learning between the groups is readily apparent. Studies by Bowman and Thurlow (1963), and Winnick and Dornbush (1963) provided similar findings.

Jensen and Rohwer (1965a), in examining the ordinal position hypothesis, pointed out that

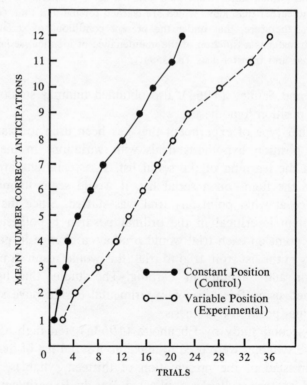

Fig. 9–9. Mean trials to reach successive criteria for constant and variable position groups.

(Adapted from Ebenholtz 1963b)

One difficulty with this conception which is seldom recognized is how *position* acts as the functional stimulus, since in the usual anticipation method of Ser [serial] learning, in which each item appears singly in one window of the memory drum, serial position per se has no objective stimulus characteristics. Therefore, if position is to be regarded as the functional stimulus, one of two assumptions must be made: either absolute temporal position acts directly as the stimulus, or the temporal order gives rise to some symbolically mediated representation of serial position. The first alternative seems highly improbable, since alteration of the pacing interval in the course of Ser learning has not been shown to produce large decremental effects on performance. . . . The second alternative, therefore, seems more tenable. Exactly how temporal order might mediate serial position is an open question. Mediation could take the form of temporal position eliciting the ordinal numerals in the learner; the numerals then serve as the "stimuli" for the "paired-associate" learning of the items in the list (p. 63).

MULTIPLE-CUE HYPOTHESES

Considering the objections that have been raised to both the chaining and the ordinal position hypotheses, it is not surprising that some investigators have suggested a dual process (Jensen and Rohwer 1965a), in which serial learning is presumed to involve both sequential as well as position cues. Young (1962), and Young, Patterson and Benson (1963) posited that chaining is used by subjects to learn the ends of the list, while position learning takes place in the middle. On the other hand, Ebenholtz (1963) concluded just the reverse—that position learning takes place at the ends of the list and chaining occurs in the middle. It must be noted that Jensen and Rohwer (1965a) in an experimental test of their hypothesis, were unsuccessful in confirming the dual-process position.

In the learning of a serial list of items, it is obvious that a variety of cues are present that the subject can use as functional stimuli for appropriate responses. Contrary to the position of some of the earlier investigators, it would be surprising if the subject used only those cues that were of the same general class—which in essence is the point of departure for either a chaining or a position hypothesis. Rather, we would expect that the typical subject might use different cues throughout the list, depending upon what he believed would enable him to learn the different responses most rapidly. Or to put it another way, whether or not the same class of cues is used may depend upon a variety of conditions that make up the learning situation itself.[1]

For example, and in keeping with Ebenholtz's (1963a) point of view, position may serve as an effective cue for the first and last items of a serial list, but at the same time, may be an ineffective cue for items that occur in the middle of the list. Schulz (1955) provided some experimental support for this position. In his study, subjects learned serially a ten-item list of CVCs and immediately upon reaching a given criterion of learning, they were asked to give the number of the position occupied by each syllable in the list. Performance was measured as a function of two parameters: (1) intralist similarity (high and low) and (2) severity of the criterion (five correct responses; one perfect trial plus five additional trials; one perfect trial plus twenty additional trials). The results indicated quite conclusively that a subject's ability to designate the ordinal number of an item's position in a serial list depended largely upon the particular position that that item occupied during learning. Items in the center of the list were most difficult to designate, with items adjacent to these next in difficulty. Items at or near the end or the beginning were easiest to name. Figure 9–10 illustrates these findings. It should be also pointed out that neither the variation in intralist similarity nor the differing levels of list mastery appeared to alter appreciably the subject's relative accuracy in position-naming with respect to any particular position.

On the other hand, and under certain circumstances, subjects may use mediators or previously learned associations in an effort to link together some of the items in the list. Horowitz and Izawa (1963) demonstrated that, if a serial list is composed of adjacent items deliberately selected as strong associates—i.e., black-white-woman-child-table-chair-hard-soft, etc.—it is plausible to assume that the effective stimulus for a given item may be the single preceding item.

The general position that a subject may use different cues in the

[1] Battig, Brown and Nelson (1963), in examining constant versus serial order in paired-associate learning, report that in the postexperimental questioning of subjects who were learning a list of paired-associates in a constant serial order, subjects reported that they had noticed the constant serial order. The subjects further stated that they had attempted to use that order as a cue in their learning of the paired-associate list, but had eventually rejected it in favor of stimulus terms as a basis for learning.

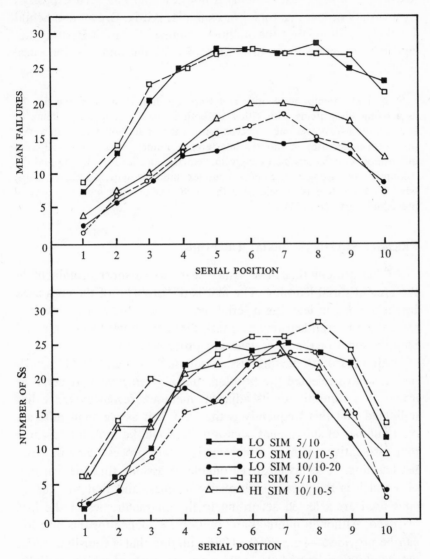

Fig. 9–10. Upper half: Serial position curves based on failures at each position during learning divided by mean trials to learn. Lower half: Difficulty in position-naming as a function of serial position. Each point on the graph represents number of *S*s who incorrectly named the position on the abscissa.

(Adapted from Schulz 1955)

learning of a serial list of items is not new and has been expressed
by a variety of investigators. For example, Battig, Brown and Schild
(1964), in discussing the findings obtained from their study designed to examine the contribution of chaining and position cues,
wrote:

> Ss initially attempt to identify and learn the first item(s) in the list, by
> associating these items with either or both immediately adjacent items or
> serial positions. As learning proceeds toward the middle of the list, however,
> progressive increases in intralist interference render either simple-adjacent
> or position associations increasingly inadequate, and lead to the gradual de-
> velopment of stronger and more complex multiple-item associative units,
> whereby each item is associated with a complex of cues including several
> preceding items (p. 455).

PRESENT STATUS OF SERIAL LEARNING

At the present time, two issues seem to be most prominent in
the area of serial learning. The first is the problem of the cues used
by the subject in learning a serial list of items; the second involves
the value of serial learning as a task that can be used to isolate and
identify some of the basic learning processes.

With regard to the first issue, although a number of experimenters have rejected the position that a given item may serve as
a cue or a stimulus for its adjacent member, recent evidence has
indicated that this frequently is the case. But as we shall reiterate
on a number of subsequent occasions, it would be foolish to assume
that associative chaining represents the *only* process used in serial
list learning. It seems most reasonable to assume that the learning
of serial lists involves a multiplicity of cues, and that the cue or
cues used are selected according to the characteristics of the lists
involved. Although minimal and tentative evidence for this position
can be provided—i.e., Voss' (1966) finding that a four-item serial
list involves an immediate serial memory process, while an eight-
item list involves the association of adjacent items—much more
evidence will be needed to put flesh on this skeleton.

The second issue concerns the usefulness of serial learning as
a learning situation that can be used to identify the operations involved in the basic learning processes. It must be acknowledged
that, largely as a result of the difficulty of sharply delineating the

stimulus in the serial learning situation, there has been progressive disillusionment with the idea that this task can serve this function.

Underwood (1964a) wrote that "the frequency of use of serial learning as a 'standard' vehicle for studying verbal learning will further diminish unless a more precise analysis of stimulus and response functions in this task is accomplished soon" (p. 55), while Young (1968) also pointed out:

the serial learning task by itself does not constitute a good vehicle to investigate processes which are assumed to underlie verbal behavior and learning . . . the usual criticism of the use of serial learning as a technique for the analysis of processes in verbal learning has been that stimulus and response functions are confounded, since the same items serve both as stimulus and response and thus make analysis of response processes independent of stimulus processes impossible. While this is undoubtedly true, . . . it is also true simply because the stimulus in serial learning has not been identified (p. 145).

FREE-RECALL LEARNING

In the two previous sections, certain processes were hypothesized to account for serial and/or paired-associate learning. In contrast, the free-recall learning task has often been used as an analytical tool to aid in the better understanding of memory processes.

As discussed in Chapter 1, some investigators believed that a single item is "learned" when it is first presented, regardless of whether it occurs alone or in a series of other items, because the probability of recall increases from a value near zero immediately prior to the presentation of the item to unity immediately after presentation. So defined, the learning of individual items is equivalent to their perception. This assumed equivalence of learning and perception has led some researchers to direct their attention to the construct of remembering or memory. Tulving (1968) wrote, "single-trial free recall experiments are experiments concerned with *remembering of perceived items* . . ." (p. 7).

Emphasis upon memory led to the postulation of two constructs as basic in the memory system. The first is storage, sometimes designated as availability. This refers to the placing of items in the individual's memory bank. The second construct, retrieval or, as it has been sometimes termed, accessibility, is defined as the ability of the subject to recall the items that have been placed in storage.

Mandler (1967) drew the succinct distinction between storage and retrieval, or availability and accessibility, in the form of an analogy. Think of a word in a person's vocabulary, he wrote, as equivalent to the books in a library. There is no question that a particular book is available if it is in the library. It is accessible, however, only if one knows where to find it; it is the library classification system that produces accessibility. If the catalogue cards were all lost, it would be extremely difficult for a particular book to be accessible. But the loss of the catalogue would obviously not change the book's availability.

The retrieval process is hypothesized to consist of two subprocesses: (a) search and (b) decision. The subject who attempts to recall an item institutes some type of search process that hopefully results in the accessibility of the stored information. A decision mechanism then compares some property of the material found with a hypothetical entity called the "criterion." Depending upon the results of this comparison, the information obtained is used to produce a corresponding response or it is rejected, whereupon the search process continues until the desired information is found and identified as such.

As indicated in the introduction to this section, free-recall learning tasks have frequently been used by experimenters in examining storage and retrieval processes. In order to demonstrate it is possible for an item to be stored but not retrieved, Tulving (1968) reported an early experiment by Nicolai (1922), in which subjects were shown a simultaneous display of ten small objects. Free-recall tests were given twice: once immediately following the presentation of the items, next, after various intervals up to ninety-six hours. The number of objects correctly recalled was invariably greater in the second test than in the first. Although it might be argued that the first test responses provided additional practice, or that subjects rehearsed the material during the retention interval, it is difficult to explain how the practice or rehearsal of those items the subject could recall on the first test would lead to the recall of items that could not previously be remembered.

A more recent study by Tulving and Pearlstone (1966) provides evidence for the related point of view that a stored item may be retrieved only when certain retrieval cues are present. In this experiment, lists of either twelve, twenty-four, or forty-eight words were constructed, and each list was represented by either one, two, or four categories. A twelve-word, two-category list would consist of the following: four-footed animals: *cow, rat;* weapons: *bomb, cannon;* crimes: *treason, theft;* forms of entertainment: *radio, music;* substances for flavoring food: *cinnamon, pepper;* professions: *engineer, lawyer.* The procedure consisted of instructing the subjects that each group of words to be remembered would be preceded by another word or phrase that described these to-be-recalled words. After such instructions, the words were presented orally, followed by a test for immediate recall, either in the presence or absence of category names as retrieval cues. As can be observed in Fig. 9–11,

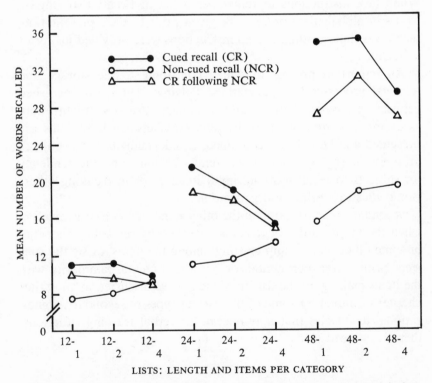

Fig. 9–11. Mean number of words recalled in the first recall test (circles) and the second recall test (triangles) as a function of list length and number of items per category.

(Adapted from Tulving and Pearlstone 1966)

the findings revealed that cued-recall was higher than noncued-recall in all comparisons; in addition, it can be noted that the influence of cueing was greater as the length of the list increased. Within lists of any length, cued-recall was superior when there was only one item per category.

The contribution of retrieval cues has been demonstrated in studies by Deese (1957) and Earhard (1969), who demonstrated that such cues are more effective (in promoting recall) if they are presented to the subject prior to the presentation of the to-be-recalled items than at some later time. For example, Deese (1957) provided serial recall instructions prior to or after the first presentation of items to-be-recalled and found that when instructions were given before the presentation of the items, serial recall was superior. Earhard (1969) obtained similar findings in a free-recall study. When task instructions to remember a list of twenty-two English words in alphabetical order were given prior to their presentation, recall was superior than if such instructions were provided just prior to recall.

An important process that may contribute to the storage and retrieval processes is organization. Tulving (1968) distinguished between two types: primary and secondary. Primary organization, as exemplified by consistent discrepancies between how items are presented and how they are recalled, is independent of the subject's prior familiarity with the input items. To illustrate, the tendency for subjects to recall terminal input items prior to recalling others would illustrate primary organization.

Secondary organization, on the other hand, refers to organization when the output order of items is governed by semantic, phonetic, or some other relationship existing among the items, or by the subjects' prior extraexperimental, or intraexperimental familiarity with the items making up the list. Inasmuch as we discussed in an earlier chapter (Chapter 7) some of the various types of secondary organizational tendencies that may operate in verbal learning situations, there is no need to discuss these here.

CONTEXTUAL MATERIAL OR CONNECTED DISCOURSE

Psychologists have done relatively little toward establishing a model for, or discovering those processes involved in, the learning of contextual material or connected discourse. Two approaches to the problem, however, should be indicated.

In the first of a series of studies by King (1960), contextual material in the form of two short stories was utilized. One of these was the *War of the Ghosts* (Bartlett 1932), while the second was *Who Shall Go,* a science fiction story written by King and concerned with the problem of who would be the first to go aloft in a space-ship. The general procedure was to have the subjects first read the story once or twice, and then attempt to duplicate it as closely as they could from memory. Unlimited time was provided for this task.

King obtained a variety of learning measures from this task. These were as follows:

(1) Idea group: the number of ideas present in the written recall. All of the essentials of an idea had to be present in order for it to be scored as correct.

(2) "Cloze" procedure: every tenth word, if not an article or a conjunction, was eliminated from the original study, and the number of missing words that the subject was capable of filling in was then determined.

(3) Number of sentences recalled.

(4) Content words: the number of content words used by the subjects. Form words, articles, prepositions, and conjunctions were not counted.

(5) Total number of words written.

(6) Identical words: this measure was the same as (4) except that all words were counted.

(7) Criterion scores: each set of recalled material was scaled by judges as to the excellence of recall.

King then correlated each measure against all other measures and subjected the data to a factor analysis. Two factors emerged from this procedure. One of these was identified as a quantitative dimension with heavy loadings on such dependent variables as the number of words produced by the subject. The second was identified as essentially a qualitative or organizational dimension with high loadings on the number of idea units, and sequences of words. A number of subsequent studies (King 1961, 1966; King and Russell 1966; King and Schultz 1960; King and Yu 1962) have essentially replicated the first study and obtained similar findings. Including the original study, twenty-seven factor analyses have been done, and all but one resulted in the two-factor solution.

In a more recent approach, Lachman and his associates (Pompi and Lachman 1967; Lachman and Dooling 1968) took the position that three processes underlie the learning of connected discourse. One, similar to the quantitative process proposed by King, involves the learning of individual lexical units (i.e., words, common phrases, etc.). The second process corresponds to King's organizational dimension—these investigators posited that meaningful verbal material itself provides a theme or schema, and the subject's knowledge of this governs his word choice in the subsequent recall of the material. The third process involves the subject's knowledge of grammatical rules of language, which permits reconstruction of syntactical function words, inflectional suffixes, and intrasentence word orders.

Elaborating upon the second process, Lachman et al. state that the fundamental characteristic of meaningfully connected discourse is that it generates within the individual a schema, abstract, summary or some surrogate structure that is independent of the semantics of the individual words that comprise the material.

One investigation undertaken by Pompi and Lachman (1967) attempted to demonstrate that a unified theme in meaningful discourse initiates these surrogate processes, in that the subject stores some arrangement of words, visual images, and schemata that reflects the essential ideas of the passage. Moreover, they contended, the presentation of the same words randomly arranged will not produce these basic surrogate processes.

In their first study (experiment 1), the learning material consisted of a seventy-nine-word paragraph (seventy-five different words) that read as follows: CHIEF RESIDENT JONES ADJUSTED HIS FACE MASK WHILE ANXIOUSLY SURVEYING A PALE FIGURE SECURED TO THE LONG GLEAMING TABLE BEFORE HIM ONE SWIFT STROKE OF HIS SMALL SHARP INSTRUMENT AND A THIN RED LINE APPEARED THEN AN EAGER YOUNG ASSISTANT CAREFULLY EXTENDED THE OPENING AS ANOTHER AIDE PUSHED ASIDE GLISTENING SURFACE FAT SO THAT VITAL PARTS WERE LAID BARE EVERYONE PRESENT STARED

IN HORROR AT UGLY GROWTH TOO LARGE FOR RE-
MOVAL HE NOW KNEW IT WAS POINTLESS TO CON-
TINUE. The material was presented in the above (meaningful)
order to one group of subjects and in random order to a second
group. Presentation consisted of exposing each word individually
for 1.5 seconds. Following training, the 75 training words, as well
as 150 different distractor words, were randomly intermixed and
presented to the subjects, who sorted them in terms of belonging
or not belonging to the group of words previously presented.

An important consideration in this study was the nature of the
distractor words. Seventy-five of the distractors were words that
selected individuals (judges) believed could blend with or be a part
of the "story." The paragraph had been presented to the judges as
an outline of a short story. Each judge had been instructed to write
down thirty words that were not a part of the paragraph but nonetheless could easily be included in the short story to which the
paragraph allegedly referred. From the varying protocols, the
seventy-five distractor words (high thematic associates) had been
obtained. In essence, then, these seventy-five distractor words could
be conceptualized as part of the theme or schema generated by the
paragraph. Seventy-five other words (low thematic associates)—
which were obtained the same way but from another paragraph with
an entirely different theme—completed the distractor word list.

In order to test the consistency of the findings, a second seventy-
nine-word paragraph was used with which the same procedure was
followed.

The findings, as indicated in Table 9–6, show the number of
words correctly recognized as well as the number of false-positive
errors. It can be noted that the syntactic order failed to produce significantly superior retention, although for both paragraphs, the direction of difference favored syntactic order. The interesting findings,
however, are noted in the mean false-positive errors. The difference
between the high thematic associates and low thematic associates
error scores is significantly greater for material in syntactic order
than in random order. For both materials, the difference is not
significant under the random order condition, a significantly greater
number of high thematic associate errors were produced under
syntactic order. These findings lend support to the investigators'
position that the subjects appear to be storing summary ideas, visual

TABLE 9–6

MEAN NUMBER OF WORDS CORRECT AND MEAN FALSE
POSITIVE ERRORS

	Word Order			
	List 1		List 2	
	Random	Syntactic	Random	Syntactic
Mean Words Correct	43.5	49.7	45.5	50.2
Mean False-Positive Errors				
High TA	6.73	10.47	10.07	21.67
Low TA	8.47	3.20	8.67	3.87

(Adapted from Pompi and Lachman 1967)

images, or themes, and that inasmuch as the high thematic associates were part of the general theme provided by the paragraph, the probability was much higher that these associates would be falsely recognized as part of the previously presented paragraph.

In a second experiment by these authors the materials, instructions, and training procedure utilized were identical to those of experiment I. However, subjects had to recall the words rather than recognize them; the general pattern of findings obtained in experiment I was duplicated.

SUMMARY

Some experimenters have been interested in developing models that will aid in the understanding of how certain types of verbal tasks are learned.

In paired-associate learning, a two-stage model proposed by Underwood and Schulz (1960) has attracted considerable attention. This model proposes that paired-associate learning consists of (1) a response availability stage and (2) an associative or hook-up stage. In the response availability stage, the subject acquires the necessary responses, or makes them available in his repertoire of responses. The second stage can be characterized as one during which the subject learns to associate available responses to the stimuli presented.

Some individuals have taken the position that the Underwood and Schulz two-stage model should be supplemented with mediational constructs, in order for the model to more adequately mirror the processes that are involved in paired-associate learning. McGuire (1961) proposed a three-stage model to accomplish this, while Newman (1964) postulated five stages.

Two significant hypotheses have been proposed to account for serial learning. The first, stemming from the work of Ebbinghaus (1885), was the chaining hypothesis, in which serial learning was conceptualized as the acquisition of a chain of stimulus-response associations. In this chain, each item on the list served as a response for the preceding item and as a stimulus for the next one. The type of experimental design most frequently used to investigate this hypothesis has been a transfer situation, in which the subject first learns a serial list of items and then is transferred to the task of learning a list of paired-associates. The logic of this design has been that if the effective stimulus in the serial learning situation is the preceding item, then that item and the one following it should be learned either faster or slower than control pairs, depending upon how these items are paired in the paired-associate list. Although a number of early studies did not support the chaining hypothesis, recent evidence has demonstrated its validity.

The second hypothesis concerning the learning of serial tasks has been to assume that the stimulus is in actuality the ordinal position of the item on the list, rather than the preceding item. A number of studies have indicated that position can play an important role in serial learning. It seems reasonable to assume, however, that the subject uses a variety of cues in the learning of a serial list of items and that any attempt to isolate only a single cue used throughout the entire learning process will probably fail.

Free-recall learning tasks have been often conceptualized in terms of storage and retrieval processes—a conceptually different point of view from the stimulus-response approach prevalent in paired-associate and serial learning tasks. Storage refers to the placing of items within the memory, while retrieval is concerned with the subject's recalling those items upon being instructed to do so. The distinction between storage and retrieval has been experimentally demonstrated by a variety of investigators.

Work with contextual material or extended serial learning situations led King (1960) to posit two significant factors in the learning of such material. The first might be thought of as a verbatim factor related to such dependent variables as the number of words produced by a subject. The second factor is an organizational factor, which emphasizes the number of idea units, word sequence, etc. Another point of view, that of Lachman and his associates, posits three processes. One is similar to the verbatim or quantitative process proposed by King; the second is related to King's organizational dimension; the third involves the subject's knowledge of grammatical rules of language that permit the reconstruction of syntactical function words, inflectional suffixes, and intrasentence word orders.

10 Transfer of Training

We readily expect an individual who has learned to drive an automobile using a gear shift and clutch to have little difficulty in learning to drive a car with automatic transmission. In such a situation, a previously learned task contributes to the learning of a second. The area of learning that examines the influence of the learning of one task on the learning of a second is designated transfer of training, and is generally acknowledged to be of great practical importance. In fact, our Western culture has been responsible for creating and developing a variety of schools, institutions, etc., with the aim of providing precisely the kind of training that will result in maximizing transfer.

When the learning of one task (task 1) aids in the learning of a second (task 2) we have an example of positive transfer; negative transfer, on the other hand, is obtained when the learning of task 1 hinders the learning of task 2. It could be, of course, that the learning of the first task has no influence on the learning of the second. Although this situation is frequently designated as one of zero transfer, it should actually be classified as indeterminate, since the statement that one task has no influence on the other (or that there is no difference between the tasks) requires the acceptance of the null hypothesis.

Many of the early transfer experiments had their origins in the examination of the concept of "formal discipline." Early educators assumed that the student's mental faculties could be developed in much the same way that a muscle can be strengthened by exercise.

These educators felt that memory, reasoning power, and perception were examples of faculties that could be strengthened with one type of material and thus become more adequate for subsequent tasks. The study of geometry was presumed to develop the student's reasoning power and thus make him a better "reasoner" regardless of the characteristics of the tasks put before him.[1]

The early work of Thorndike and Woodworth (1901, 1901a, 1901b) was monumental in challenging this position. And the experimental findings obtained by these investigators led Thorndike (1914) some years later to conclude that

no careful observer would assert that the influence upon the other mental traits is comparable in amount to that upon the direct object of training. By doubling a boy's reasoning power in arithmetical problems we do not double it for formal grammar or chess or economic history or theories of evolution. By tripling the accuracy of movement in fingering exercises we do not triple it for typewriting, playing billiards or painting. The gain in courage in the game of football is never equaled by the gain in moral courage or resistance to intellectual obstacles (p. 268).

We should now like to turn from the early experimental history of transfer to a discussion of some of the methodological problems involved in the area.

Transfer Design and Measurement

The design and measurement of transfer experiments is obviously basic to our understanding of this area. Although a number of transfer designs have been used, the one most frequently employed is indicated below:

Experimental Group	Learn Task 1	Learn Task 2
Control Group	Learn Task 1'	Learn Task 2
	(or rest)	

[1] Quotations from Roark's *Psychology in Education* (1895) and Morgan's *Psychology for Teachers* (1906) aptly describe the formal discipline position. Roark wrote that *"faculties, like muscles, grow strong by use: therefore, do nothing for the pupil that he can do for himself"* (p. 278). Similarly, Morgan wrote that it is "as a means of training the faculties of comparison and generalisation, that the study of such a language as Latin side by side with English is so valuable" (p. 192).

Although some investigators have permitted their control subjects to "rest" prior to learning task 2, such a procedure ignores the problem that any difference obtained in the learning of the second task by the experimental vs. the control group may have arisen from general transfer factors such as warm-up, or learning-to-learn. That is, by virtue of the fact that the experimental group participated in some type of learning situation prior to the learning of task 2, some general skills or postural adjustments may have been acquired that enabled this group to learn the second task more rapidly. Most experimenters, however, are interested in differentiating transfer effects attributable to these general transfer conditions from those that arise as a result of specific stimulus and response relationships; as a result, most frequently, some type of task 1 learning is provided for the control group in the above design.

A second type of transfer design is indicated as follows:

Experimental Group	Learn Task 1	Learn Task 2
Control Group	Learn Task 1	Learn Task 2'

When this type of design is used, it is necessary to insure that tasks 2 and 2' are equivalent. That is, tasks 2 and 2' should prove equally difficult to learn; if this were not the case, any difference between the performance of the groups would simply reflect differences in task difficulty.

This type of design is used only infrequently, although a good example is found in a study by Russell and Storms (1955). In this experiment, all subjects first learned a paired-associate task that consisted of a CVC and a word, e.g., CEF-stem. The transfer task consisted of learning a second paired-associate list that contained the same stimulus words as the first list. One group, however, had to learn responses that were a part of the associative chain that arose from the first-list response words, while the second group had to learn response words that were not a part of this associative chain. Table 10–1 illustrates the material used.

Although other designs have been used (Hall 1966; Ellis 1969), the use of such designs has been so infrequent that little would be gained by presenting them at this time.

TABLE 10–1

AN EXAMPLE OF ONE TYPE OF TRANSFER DESIGN

	List 1		List 2	
	Stimulus	Response	Stimulus	Response
Experimental Group:	CEF	stem	CEF	smell
Control Group:	CEF	stem	CEF	joy

Positive transfer was predicted in this situation since the learning of list 2 by the experimental group was facilitated by the associative chain: *stem-flower-smell.*

TRANSFER MEASUREMENT

In measuring transfer, most investigators use raw scores as measured by trials to a criterion, number of errors, or number of correct responses. The direction and amount of transfer is obtained by subtracting the lower score of one group on task 2 from the higher score of the second group on the same task. The use of a raw score measure has the advantage of providing precision of meaning but does not enable the investigator to compare the amount of transfer obtained in one experiment with that of another.

The traditional transfer measurement that will enable an investigator to make comparisons among experiments has been to convert the raw scores into a percentage. This is done by the following formula:

$$\text{Percentage of Transfer} = \frac{\begin{array}{c}\text{Experimental Score} - \text{Control Score} \\ \text{or} \\ \text{Control Score} - \text{Experimental Score}\end{array}}{\text{Control Score}} \times 100$$

A second method for examining transfer, also using a percentage measure, is to compare the amount of transfer that has occurred with the maximum amount of improvement possible. This latter value is determined by computing the difference between the total possible score on task 2 and the actual performance of the control group on task 2. If correct responses represent the response measure, the formula would be as follows:

$$\text{Percentage of Transfer} = \frac{\begin{array}{c}\text{Control Score} - \text{Experimental Score}\\ \text{or}\\ \text{Experimental Score} - \text{Control Score}\end{array}}{\text{Total Possible Score} - \text{Control Score}} \times 100$$

Although Gagne, Foster and Crowley (1948) supported the examination of transfer based upon this formula, Murdock (1957) gave a number of reasons why the use of this formula may not always be satisfactory. One difficulty is that determination of the maximum amount of improvement possible in a given learning task may be difficult or impossible to ascertain. Assume, for example, that speed of responding was the response measure. It would be impossible to indicate what the maximum amount of improvement should be with such a measure. A second problem with this formula is that it is generally unsatisfactory for examining negative transfer. Although the upper limit for positive transfer is a value of plus-100 percent, the lower limit is not minus-100 percent but rather, minus infinity. In addition, a minus-100 percent transfer value is not comparable to a plus-100 percent transfer value.

Murdock instead suggested the following percentage of transfer formula.

$$\text{Percentage of Transfer} = \frac{\begin{array}{c}\text{Experimental Score} - \text{Control Score}\\ \text{or}\\ \text{Control Score} - \text{Experimental Score}\end{array}}{\text{Experimental Score} + \text{Control Score}} \times 100$$

It may be noted that the denominator includes the performance of the experimental group as well as the performance of the control group, thus providing a formula in which positive and negative transfer are symmetrical and the upper and lower limits are 100 percent.

THE STIMULUS AND RESPONSE ANALYSIS OF TRANSFER

Much of the experimental work that followed the pioneer studies of Thorndike and Woodworth (1901, 1901a, 1901b) was molar

TABLE 10-2
VARYING TRANSFER PARADIGMS

Description of Transfer Paradigm	Notation				Example (Each List Consists of Two Pairs)			
	List 1		List 2		List 1		List 2	
	Stimulus	Response	Stimulus	Response	Stimulus	Response	Stimulus	Response
Identical Stimuli Unrelated Responses	A —	B	*A —	C	Precise Boastful	Secret Modest	Precise Boastful	Modern Absurd
Similar (Synonymous) Stimuli Unrelated Reponses	A —	B	A' —	C	Precise Boastful	Secret Modest	Exact Bragging	Modern Absurd
Unrelated Stimuli Identical Responses	A —	B	C —	B	Precise Boastful	Rocky Empty	Double Entire	Rocky Empty
Unrelated Stimuli Similar Reponses	A —	B	C —	B'	Precise Boastful	Rocky Empty	Double Entire	Stony Vacant
Similar Stimuli Similar Responses	A —	B	A' —	B'	Precise Boastful	Rocky Empty	Exact Bragging	Stony Vacant
Re-pairing of Stimulus and Reponse Items	A —	B	A —	Br	Precise Boastful	Secret Modest	Precise Boastful	Modest Secret
Unrelated and Control	A —	B	C —	D	Precise Boastful	Secret Modest	Fatal Famous	Modern Absurd

* Sometimes described as A—D.

and unanalyzed in the sense that the investigators were interested only in determining whether a given experiment provided positive or negative transfer. Sleight (1911) and Reed (1917) were interested in examining the influence of memorizing one type of material on the memorizing of a second type; similarly, Martin (1915) was interested in seeing whether training in cancelling certain letters (a letter cancellation task) had an effect on cancelling specific numbers (a number cancellation task).

In the early thirties, the work of Yum (1931) and Bruce (1933) was instrumental in encouraging investigators to examine transfer from a stimulus-response point of view, using the paired-associate learning situation. The transfer variable manipulated in these experiments was similarity, which has continued to be regarded as basic in producing transfer effects. Since the concept of similarity has been used so frequently in research, psychologists have adopted specific notations to indicate the nature of the varying similarity paradigms. These are indicated in Table 10–2. It should be noted, however, that the next-to-last item on the table indicates a type of paradigm in which similarity of either stimulus or response is not manipulated. Instead, this item consists of the re-pairing of the original stimulus with response items to form the transfer task. As was indicated in Table 10–2, this paradigm is one of an A-B, A-Br variety.

MIXED VS. UNMIXED LISTS

We will now discuss one final methodological problem—the mixed vs. the unmixed list design. From our earlier discussion in Chapter 2, it will be recalled that with the mixed list design, the experimental procedure consists of placing varying types of materials (or conditions) within the same list. Each subject acts as his own control since all of the conditions are included within the same list. With the unmixed list design, each of the varying kinds of material or conditions are represented by different lists; this means that varying groups of subjects each learn different sets of material.

An example of the two designs can be found in Table 10–3. Here, the investigator following the learning of A-B examined the

TABLE 10–3

MIXED VS. UNMIXED TRANSFER PARADIGMS

Unmixed List

List 1	:	List 2	or	List 2	or	List 2
A_1-B_1		C_1-B_1		A_1-C_1		C_1-D_1
A_2-B_2		C_2-B_2		A_2-C_2		C_2-D_2
A_3-B_3		C_3-B_3		A_3-C_3		C_3-D_3

Mixed List

List 1	:	List 2
A_1-B_1		C_1-B_1
A_2-B_2		A_2-C_2
A_3-B_3		C_3-D_3

following transfer paradigms: A-C, C-B, and C-D. A basic methodological question is whether different findings are obtained as a function of the use of these different experimental methods.

In an early study by Twedt and Underwood (1959), four transfer paradigms were investigated using both the unmixed and mixed list designs. Following the learning of A-B, the transfer lists were as follows: A-C, A-Br, C-B, and C-D. Twelve pairs of two-syllable adjectives were used; the learning of the first list was carried out to a criterion of one errorless trial. The transfer list, either A-C, A-Br, C-B, or C-D, was presented for just ten trials. With the mixed list design, each of these four transfer conditions was represented by three pairs of items. With the unmixed list design, four groups of subjects were used, and each group learned a list of twelve items representing one of the paradigms listed above.

The results can be noted in Fig. 10–1, which provides the mean total correct responses on the ten transfer trials for both the unmixed and mixed list materials. It can be noted that the difference in results between the two designs is quite small. With the C-D paradigm serving as the control, the three other paradigms provided negative transfer, increasing from C-B to A-C to A-Br. The findings of these investigators suggest, then, that experimenters may use either type of design without being seriously concerned that the transfer effects will be different.

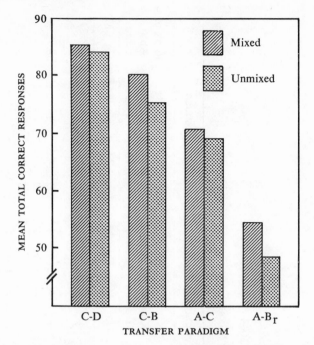

Fig. 10–1. Total correct responses over ten transfer trials as a function of mixed and unmixed lists and four transfer paradigms.
(Adapted from Twedt and Underwood 1959)

Subsequent studies by Postman (1966), Slamecka (1967), and Wickens and Cermak (1967) have not, however, demonstrated a one-to-one correspondence between the findings obtained with the mixed and the unmixed lists.

When we examine transfer obtained with the varying paradigms, using either the mixed or unmixed list design, two types of analyses can be made. The first concerns whether or not a specific paradigm provides positive or negative transfer. This conclusion is determined by comparing the findings obtained with a given paradigm with the C-D (or control) condition. It is readily apparent that differences in the difficulty of learning the C-D items in the two lists may produce differential types of transfer even though absolute performance measures obtained with the paradigms under investigation are similar. A good example of this type of contradictory finding is evidenced by Slamecka's (1967) study. An examination of the A-Br condition in Table 10–4 reveals that the total correct

TABLE 10–4

EXPERIMENTAL FINDINGS OBTAINED WITH MIXED AND UNMIXED LIST DESIGNS

	Twedt and Underwood						Slamecka						Postman					
Paradigm	*Total Cor. Resp. (10 Trials)		Kind of Trans.		Rank of Absol. Scores		Total Cor. Resp. (1st Trial)		Kind of Trans.		Rank of Absol. Scores		Mean No. Cor. (Trial 1)		Kind of Trans.		Rank of Absol. Scores	
	Un	M	Un	M	Un	M	Un	M	Un	M	Un	M	Un	M	Un	M	Un	M
A-B							200	178	+	+	5	5						
A-B'																		
Synonym							146	134	+	+	4	4						
Antonym							123	124	+	+	3	3						
A-C or A-D	69	70	−	−	2	2							5.3	4.0	+	+	4	4
A-Br	49	53	−	−	1	1	63	61	+	−	2	1	1.3	1.1	−	−	1	1
C-B	75	80	−	−	3	3							3.3	2.2	+	−	3	2
C-D	84	85			4	4	35	66			1	2	3.0	2.6			2	3

Paradigm	Wickens and Cermak Exp. I						Wickens and Cermak Exp. II					
	Correct Resp. (8 trials)		Kind of Trans.		Rank of Absol. Scores		Mean No. Cor. (8 trials)		Kind of Trans.		Rank of Absol. Scores	
	Un	M	Un	M	Un	M	Un	M	Un	M	Un	M
A-B												
A-B'												
Synonym	4.72	4.97	+	+	3	4	5.39	5.23	+	+	3	4
Antonym	5.40	4.33	+	−	4	2	5.43	4.82	+	+	4	3
A-C or A-D	3.55	3.60	−	−	1	1	3.85	3.62	+	−	2	1
A-Br												
C-B												
C-D	3.94	4.60			2	3	3.67	4.27			1	2

* Values Estimated from Twedt and Underwood (1959), Fig. 1.

responses for the unmixed list were sixty-three; for the mixed list, the total was sixty-one. Yet with the unmixed list, the A-Br condition resulted in positive transfer while transfer was negative with the mixed list. In general, when the unmixed list design is used, it is more likely for the varying transfer paradigms to provide positive transfer. Slamecka (1967) pointed out that this effect is understandable if it is remembered that under the unmixed list condition, the C-D task requires the learning of many more completely new and unrelated pairs whereas under the mixed list condition, only a relatively few new pairs are learned.

A second kind of analysis involves a comparison of absolute measures of transfer obtained with the mixed and unmixed list designs. In Table 10–4, we have provided absolute measures taken from the experimental studies cited earlier. In order to facilitate a comparison between the mixed and unmixed list designs, these values have been converted into rank orders. It may be noted that the rank orders obtained by the varying paradigms with the mixed and unmixed list are identical in the Twedt and Underwood (1959) study. The studies of Postman (1966) and Slamecka (1967) reveal some divergence between the two rank orders for the mixed and unmixed lists; while the experiments by Wickens and Cermak (1967) reveal even more.

What conclusions can be drawn from the experimental work that has been done in the area? Although there appears to be reasonable agreement in the findings provided by either the mixed or unmixed list designs—particularly with reference to whether or not a given paradigm will provide positive or negative transfer, as well as to the relative amount of transfer provided by a particular paradigm—Postman's (1966) statement that "it cannot be taken for granted that UL and ML will yield equivalent measures of learning or transfer under all conditions" (p. 247) remains valid, and caution must be exercised when experimental studies using these different designs are compared.

Moreover, some question may be raised as to whether or not a comparison between the mixed vs. unmixed list design is meaningful. Although the experimental material used with both types of designs is identical, the different make-up of the transfer lists may (and frequently does) result in the adoption of different learning strategies by the subject. With different strategies used, there is little reason to assume that identical findings should be achieved.

Let us try to illustrate what is meant by the statement that the make-up of the unmixed list represents a different learning task for the subject than does the learning of the mixed list. With the unmixed list, subjects have an opportunity to employ a single strategy that presumably aids in learning. For example, when the transfer list is of the A-B′ variety, the subject may learn that the new responses are synonyms of the old responses found in list 1. Therefore, some strategy may be adopted that enables the subject to use this information to maximize his learning of the second list. Since there is frequently an associative relationship between the responses of the first list and their synonyms, found on the second, the original responses may serve as mediators that facilitate the learning of list 2. When the mixed list is used, on the other hand, no single strategy can be employed, since different relationships exist among the groups of responses found on list 1 and those of list 2. Any attempt to adopt a number of different strategies, each of which corresponds to a different group of items, will undoubtedly result in considerable confusion and the possibility that learning will be inhibited. As a result, it seems likely that the type of strategy used by subjects in learning list 1 is not used by those subjects learning list 2, and that some alternative strategy is utilized.

EMPIRICAL FINDINGS AND THE OSGOOD TRANSFER SURFACE

An examination of Table 10–2 leads to the question, what kinds of experimental findings have been obtained with these varying transfer paradigms? A partial answer to this question has been provided in our examination of the paradigms of mixed and un-mixed lists. It should be acknowledged that those paradigms that have manipulated similarity have traditionally been grouped into two major categories: (1) attaching an old response to a new stimulus, i.e., A-B, C-B; and (2) attaching a new response to an old stimulus, i.e., A-B, A-C.

ATTACHING OLD RESPONSES TO NEW STIMULI (A-B, C-B)

Wylie (1919), Bruce (1933), and Hamilton (1943), as well as other investigators, concluded that when an old response is attached to a new stimulus (A-B, C-B), positive transfer is obtained. As the new stimulus, C, increases in similarity to the old, A, the amount of positive transfer increases. Osgood (1949) concluded that this formulation was one of three empirical laws that govern transfer.

A number of recent investigations, however, have been at variance with this general position. For example, it can be noted from Fig. 10–1, that the C-B condition resulted in fewer mean total correct responses than the C-D (control) condition, indicating negative transfer. Subsequent findings obtained by Postman (1962a), Jung (1962), and Dallett (1962) were in agreement with the Twedt and Underwood results. Postman (1962a), for example, was interested in examining the A-B, C-B paradigm as a function of the degree of first-list learning. Ten two-syllable adjectives were used to make up each list and the degree of first-list learning was varied by having subjects learn the first-list to a criterion of (a) six correct responses on a single trial, (b) ten correct responses on a single trial, and (c) ten correct responses on a single trial plus 50 percent overlearning.[1] When compared to an appropriate control group (A-B, C-D), the A-B, C-B condition yielded negative transfer; the amount of transfer did not change, at least at a statistically significant level, as a function of the degree of first-list learning.

Jung (1963) has provided experimental findings that appear to reconcile the divergent results obtained by the early vs. the later investigators. This experimenter found that the positive or negative transfer obtained with the A-B, C-B paradigm may be a function of the meaningfulness of the material used. In his study, paired-associate lists were used in which two-syllable adjectives served as stimuli and trigrams as responses. Six pairs of items made up each list, and two levels of response meaningfulness (as inferred from measures of trigram frequency) were employed. After the first list had been learned to a criterion of one perfect trial, the second

[1] Overlearning refers to additional trials provided the subject after he reaches the learning criterion set by the experimenter.

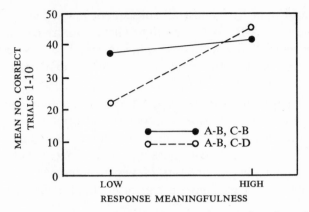

Fig. 10–2. Mean number of correct responses as a function of response meaningfulness.

(Adapted from Jung 1963)

list was presented for ten trials. Results, as measured by the mean number of correct responses for these trials, are indicated in Fig. 10–2. It may be observed that if low meaningful responses are employed, the A-B, C-B condition is superior to the control (A-B, C-D) condition, indicating positive transfer. On the other hand, with high meaningful responses, the conditions are reversed, with the A-B, C-B condition yielding negative transfer. A study by Merikle and Battig (1963) also revealed that negative transfer increased with increased meaningfulness of the material.

In summary, it would appear that the A-B, C-B condition does at times produce small amounts of negative transfer, depending upon the kind of response material employed. Thus, Osgood's empirical law can be modified to indicate that where old responses are attached to new stimuli, positive *or* negative transfer may be obtained, depending upon the meaningfulness of the items used as responses.

ATTACHING NEW RESPONSES TO OLD STIMULI (A-B, A-C)

This paradigm has traditionally been classified as one of associative inhibition. Müller and Schumann (1894), more than half a century ago, formulated the law of associative inhibition, which stated that when any two terms, such as A and B, have been associated, it is more difficult to form an association between either and a third item K. Almost all subsequent investigators who have examined the A-B, A-C paradigm have confirmed these early findings, which indicate that learning to attach a new response to an old stimulus leads to negative transfer. It can be noted from Fig. 10–1 that in the Twedt and Underwood (1959) experiment the A-C paradigm produced a substantial amount of negative transfer as contrasted with the control condition. It can be also observed in that figure that when the amount of negative transfer produced by the A-B, A-C paradigm is compared with the A-B, C-B paradigm, larger amounts of negative transfer are provided by the A-B, A-C paradigm—a typical finding for this type of comparison.

An extension of the A-B, A-C paradigm would be to examine transfer as a function of the similarity of the responses between the two tasks. In one such study, Osgood (1946) used a paired-associate task in which two letters served as stimuli (i.e., c.n., f.s.) and adjectives served as responses. On the transfer task, the stimuli remained the same, but the responses were varied in that they were either (1) similar, (2) neutral, or (3) opposed to the original adjectives. It should be indicated that the similar response words used with the transfer task were not synonyms, nor were the opposed words antonyms of the adjectives used in the original list. Rather, the words used in the transfer list were similar or opposed in terms of the "feeling tone" they yielded. Thus, the word *low* was regarded as similar to *dejected,* while the opposed word for *dejected* was *high.* Osgood employed a mixed list design, in which subjects learned the original list to a criterion of one perfect trial and the transfer task to a criterion of two perfect trials. Results indicated negative transfer under all conditions, although such transfer was least for the identical stimulus-similar response condition. There appeared to be no difference in the amount of negative transfer generated by the identical stimulus-neutral response and by the identical stimulus-opposed response conditions.

As a result of the findings obtained in this study, Osgood (1949) proposed a second empirical law, which stated that where stimuli are functionally identical and responses are varied, negative transfer will be obtained, and the magnitude of such transfer decreases as the similarity between the responses increased.

A further variation of the A-B, A-C paradigm would be to

employ a transfer task in which stimuli similar to those used in the original task were paired with different responses. Gibson (1941) conducted this type of study. First, she made up a number of nonsense forms that resembled standard forms in varying degrees. Fig. 10–3 illustrates some of the standard forms, as well as forms of varying degrees of similarity to the standard, that were used. For the original task, the subject learned to attach a CVC to each of twelve standard forms. A criterion of eight out of twelve correct was used. Following this training, a transfer task was employed in which the variant forms were used as stimuli, and CVCs different from those used in the original training served as responses. The results indicated that maximum negative transfer was obtained when stimuli identical to those used in the original training were paired with the new responses. It will be recalled that this is the A-B, A-C paradigm and therefore Gibson's findings are in keeping

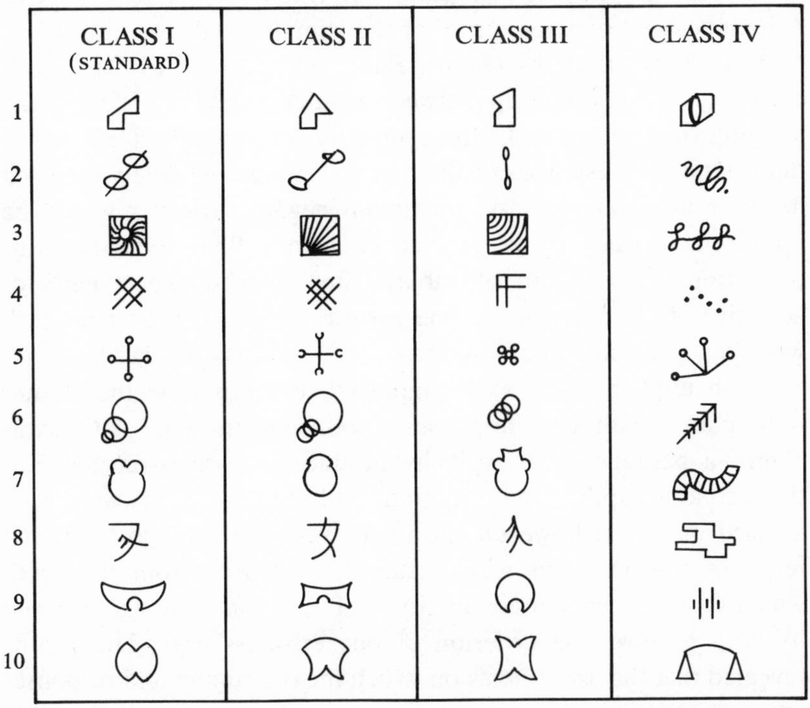

	CLASS I (STANDARD)	CLASS II	CLASS III	CLASS IV
1				
2				
3				
4				
5				
6				
7				
8				
9				
10				

Fig. 10–3. Stimulus forms grouped in classes as a function of their similarity to the standard.

(Adapted from Gibson 1941)

with results obtained by a number of other experimenters. As the similarity of the stimuli decreased, negative transfer also decreased; zero transfer was approximated when neutral stimuli were paired with different responses.

Largely as a result of Gibson's (1941) findings, Osgood (1949) proposed his third transfer principle, which stated that when both stimulus and response members are simultaneously varied, negative transfer is obtained; the magnitude of such transfer increases as stimulus similarity increases.

THE RE-PAIRING OF STIMULI AND RESPONSES (A-B, A-BR)

The transfer paradigms that we have discussed and with which most investigators have been concerned involve the influence of similarity of stimulus and response. On Table 10–2, it will be re-called that the next-to-last paradigm listed, designated as A-B, A-Br, consisted of a re-pairing of the stimulus and response items.

In an early article by Gagne, Baker and Foster (1950), which examined the relationship between similarity and transfer in the learning of a motor task, these investigators hypothesized that if the stimuli and responses of the first task were completely reversed to make up a second task, maximum negative transfer would be produced. A study by Porter and Duncan (1953) examined this prediction. Two groups of subjects first learned twelve pairs of adjectives to a criterion of one errorless trial. The transfer task was then presented. For one group of subjects, the same stimuli as those used in list 1 were employed, but this time the stimuli were paired with new responses, producing an A-B, A-C para-digm—a paradigm that typically produces negative transfer. For the second group, the same stimulus and response words were used as used on list 1; however, the items were re-paired so that each response was matched with a stimulus different from that with which it had been paired on list 1. The second list was learned by both groups to a criterion of one errorless trial. The results revealed that the list of items on which the old stimuli and responses were re-paired (thus forming new pairs), provided significantly greater amounts of negative transfer than the A-B, A-C condition. These findings were subsequently confirmed by a whole host of experimenters, i.e., Besch and Reynolds (1958), Twedt and Underwood (1959), Postman (1962a), Jung (1962), Besch, Thompson and Wetzel (1962), Keppel and Underwood (1962), and Kausler and Kanoti (1963). Some question must be raised about the complete generality of these findings however, since Mandler and Heinemann (1956), using low meaningful material (consonant syllables for responses) in contrast to the high meaningful material used by other investigators, found positive transfer with the same paradigm.

Merikle and Battig (1963) demonstrated that the conflicting findings may be a function of the material used. These investigators employed three levels of meaningful material; common CVC words represented one end of the meaningfulness continuum and consonant syllables (CCCs) represented the other. Subjects learned one of the three lists to a criterion of one errorless trial. A second list containing A-Br, A-C, and C-D (control) pairs was then learned to a criterion of two errorless trials or a maximum of twenty trials. Note that this experiment utilized the mixed list design. Our primary concern is with the A-Br paradigm; Merikle and Battig's results indicated that when the material to be learned had high meaningfulness, negative transfer was obtained—a finding in keeping with those we have just reported. On the other hand, when low meaningful material was used, Mandler and Heinemann's (1956) findings of positive transfer were confirmed. Whether or not the re-pairing of old stimuli and responses to provide new pairs produces positive or negative transfer appears to depend upon whether high or low meaningful material is used.

OSGOOD'S TRANSFER SURFACE

We have noted that Osgood proposed three empirical laws to summarize the contribution of stimulus and/or response similarity in the transfer task. He used these laws to generate a three-demensional transfer surface, which is presented in Fig. 10–4. It may be observed that separate axes were used for the (1) stimulus, (2) response, and (3) kind and amount of transfer. A number of experimenters have attempted to replicate Osgood's transfer surface; unfortunately, these studies have not provided consistent findings. For example, although a study by Dallett (1962) is in essential agreement with Osgood's surface, the experiments of Bugelski and Cadwallader (1956), and Wimer (1964) are not.

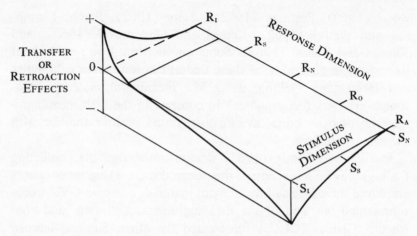

Fig. 10–4. The transfer and retroaction surface: medial plane represents transfer effects of zero magnitude; response relations distributed along length of solid and stimulus relations along its width. The I, S, N, O, and A represent dimensions of similarity; namely, identity, similarity, antagonistic, and opposed relationships, respectively.

(Adapted from Osgood 1949)

Wimer's findings indicated "that only relatively small amounts of transfer could be produced by the very numerous and sometimes extreme combinations of interlist similarity relations used" (p. 278). Bugelski and Cadwallader's (1956) results, on the other hand, indicate partial agreement with the Osgood surface. In their study, the transfer task consisted of four different stimulus conditions (identical, similar, less similar, and neutral), each of which was paired with one of four different responses (identical, similar, neutral, and opposed). Sixteen different experimental conditions were examined. The specific stimuli employed were the nonsense forms used in Gibson's (1941) study, cited earlier, while the responses were obtained from lists which Osgood (1946) had used. The procedure consisted of providing the subject with learning trials until he correctly anticipated a given response on two successive trials, after which the stimulus-response pair was dropped from the list. Learning continued until all of the responses were learned to this criterion. A similar procedure and criterion was used in the learning of the transfer list. The curves depicting the findings obtained in this study are compared with those formulated by Osgood (1949), and are presented in Fig. 10–5.

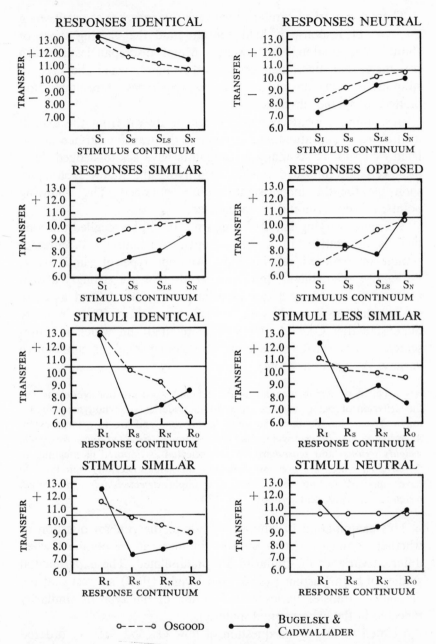

Fig. 10–5. The experimental findings of Bugelski and Cadwallader compared with Osgood's theoretical values.

(Figures have been prepared from data supplied by Bugelski and Cadwallader 1956)

There is a marked similarity between the curves that result when the type of response is held constant and the varying types of stimuli plotted along the abscissa. Major discrepancies between the curves can be noted, on the other hand, when the type of stimulus is held constant and the varying types of responses are plotted along the abscissa.

In summary, what conclusions can be drawn from the experimental work that attempted to confirm the transfer surface postulated by Osgood? As many investigators have acknowledged, little has been accomplished toward identifying the major factors responsible for the inconsistent findings obtained. The following points, however, should be recognized.

There are varying kinds of similarity. It will be recalled that one type is denotative, in which synonyms or antonyms represent similar or opposed relationships. Another type of similarity is associative relatedness. Here, two words that are strongly associated, as measured by a free association test, are defined as more similar than two words with a weak association. The similarity dimension that Osgood (1948) manipulated and which is represented in his transfer surface is of a "feeling tone" or connotative variety. As Osgood wrote,

words called *similar* in meaning to the original word are not synonyms (by the criterion of being listed as such in dictionaries of synonyms and antonyms), but they do have the same feeling-tone and are to a large extent interchangeable descriptively, as for example, *dejected-low, free-open, weighty-serious,* and *tense-hard.* Words selected as opposed in meaning to the original words are not antonyms (by the same criterion), but they do have opposed feeling tone, as for example *dejected-high, free-closed, weighty-humorous,* and *tense-soft* (p. 134).

This examination of similarity leads to the general question of whether or not consistent transfer findings can be obtained when different varieties of similarity are manipulated. The experimental studies of both Bastian (1956) and Ryan (1960) suggest that the amount of transfer varies as a function of the type of similarity reflected in the experimental material.

Related to this is the question of how Osgood (1949) ordered the similarity dimension along the response axis of his transfer surface. It will be recalled, as can be noted from Fig. 10–4, that on the response similarity continuum, Osgood placed these categories in the following order: identity, similarity, neutral, opposed, and antagonistic. The antagonistic category, which Osgood (1948) indicated should provide maximum amounts of negative transfer, was admittedly hypothetical. Most investigators, however, have ignored this response category, since the distinction between an antagonistic and an opposed category was not clear. In addition, at least as measured by associative similarity, there is good reason to reposition the "opposed" category. Martin (1965) commented, "if two items are judged opposite in meaning, they must perforce be related; otherwise, opposition could not be established" (p. 329). As a result, he suggested that the opposition category be placed at points on the axes between identity and complete dissimilarity, instead of beyond the complete dissimilarity point.

OTHER CONSIDERATIONS OF OSGOOD'S SURFACE

One development generated from Osgood's transfer surface was the attempt by a few investigators to provide transfer surfaces for relationships among stimuli and responses not specified by Osgood. For example, Houston (1964) pointed out that two unexamined loci of similarity may be described as the similarity between first-list stimuli and second-list responses (S_1-R_2), and the similarity between second-list stimuli and first-list responses (S_2-R_1). An example of some of the paradigms that can be generated from these two basic situations are indicated in Table 10–5. On the basis of the available experimental evidence, Houston (1964) was able to construct a transfer surface that reflected these relationships. This surface can be observed in Fig. 10–6.

It was also recognized that Osgood's transfer surface did not include the A-B, A-Br paradigm. Dallett (1965) proposed a surface that reflected variations in this paradigm. That is, in addition to the A-B, A-Br paradigm, the re-pairing procedure can be also carried out when similar stimuli and responses are used in the transfer task. Dallett designated all of these re-paired paradigms as noncorresponding (NC); Table 10–6 provides examples of these relationships. It must be recognized that the re-pairing paradigms cannot be extended to situations employing neutral stimuli or responses, since in such cases, there is no way of telling whether the items were meant to be re-paired.

TABLE 10–5

SIMILARITY RELATIONSHIPS IN TRANSFER

| Task 1 | | Task 2 | | |
Stimulus	Response	Stimulus	Response	Type of Transfer Predicted
A (black	B pretty)	B (pretty	A black)	Max. Positive
A (black	B pretty)	B (pretty	A′ dark)	Positive
A (black	B pretty)	B (pretty	C large)	Max. Negative
A (black	B pretty)	B′ (beautiful	A black)	Positive
A (black	B pretty)	C (large	A black)	Zero

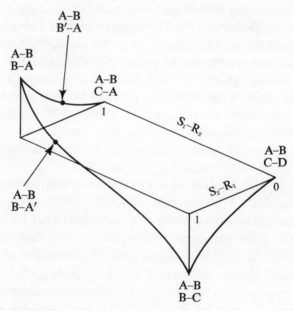

Fig. 10–6. Transfer as a function of S_1-R_2 and S_2-R_1 similarity.
(Adapted from Houston 1964)

TABLE 10–6

NONCORRESPONDING TRANSFER PARADIGMS

		Original S-R List 1		Re-paired S-R List 2	
		Stimulus	Response	Stimulus	Response
$S_{Ident.}$—$R_{Ident.}$	NC	Precise	Stony	Precise	Empty
		Boastful	Empty	Boastful	Stony
$S_{Ident.}$—$R_{Sim.}$	NC	Precise	Stony	Precise	Vacant
		Boastful	Empty	Boastful	Rocky
$S_{Sim.}$—$R_{Ident.}$	NC	Precise	Stony	Exact	Empty
		Boastful	Empty	Bragging	Stony
$S_{Sim.}$—$R_{Sim.}$	NC	Precise	Stony	Exact	Vacant
		Boastful	Empty	Bragging	Rocky

Dallett's proposed transfer surface for these noncorresponding paradigms, along with the original Osgood surface, is indicated in Fig. 10–7. Here we can note that the $S_{Identical}$—$R_{Identical}$ NC condition is hypothesized to produce maximum negative transfer, while the re-pairing of similar stimuli and similar responses produces negative transfer also, although not maximal amounts. When neutral stimuli and responses are used, the experimental findings obtained with these paradigms are assumed to be identical to the findings with the Osgood surface. Thus, along the $S_{neutral}$ and $R_{neutral}$ edges, the Osgood surface and Dallett's proposed surface coincide.

In an experiment in which the four noncorresponding paradigms were combined with seven other paradigms taken from Osgood's surface, Dallett (1965) found that the results generally conformed to Osgood's surface as well as to the noncorresponding surface that Dallett proposed.

The extension of Osgood's surface to reflect transfer paradigms not included in the original formulation has not generated very much experimental interest, perhaps because there is some question about the advisability of doing so until the problem of similarity among materials is solved. Battig (1966) wrote that a concentration on the problems of scaling similarity appears more profit-

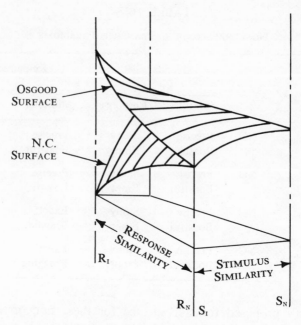

Fig. 10–7. The Osgood transfer surface and the proposed surface for NC paradigms.
(Adapted from Dallett 1965)

able "than continued efforts directed toward precise quantitative specification of intertask similarity effects on transfer without adequate tools for the job" (p. 222).

THE STAGE ANALYSIS OF PAIRED-ASSOCIATE LEARNING AND OSGOOD'S TRANSFER SURFACE

On a number of previous occasions we have indicated that paired-associate learning is generally conceived of as occurring in two stages: (1) a response availability stage and (2) a hook-up or associative stage. Martin (1965) analyzed Osgood's transfer surface in terms of these two stages. He posited that "there are three components to that which is transferred from one paired-associate task to another, namely, response availability, forward associations, and backward associations" (p. 332). (It is interesting to note that Martin has considered the hook-up or associative stage as consisting of forward as well as backward associations.) Martin has pointed out that Osgood's transfer surface is one which reflects net transfer—that is, the amount of transfer that is indicated by the surface results from an algebraic summation of both positive and negative transfer effects arising from the contribution of the three hypothesized paired-associate learning components. This means, then, that since three effects are being transferred, there should be three transfer surfaces, each describing how a particular effect is transferred as a function of the stimulus and response relationships between the original learning and the transfer task.

In Table 10–7, Martin indicated the kind of transfer provided by the three components for four different types of transfer paradigms, namely, (1) A-B, A-B; (2) A-B, C-B; (3) A-B, A-D (or A-C); and (4) A-B, C-D. As can be noted, the response availability component produces positive transfer in two of these paradigms, namely A-B and C-B. In both instances, the same responses are used in both the original and transfer lists, and hence the subject has the responses already available when list 2 is to be learned. With the A-D and C-D paradigms, new responses are demanded in the learning of list 2; thus, no transfer is obtained for the response availability component.

With the forward association component, the A-B transfer paradigm obviously produces positive transfer while the A-D paradigm results in negative transfer. In this latter case, there is a tendency for the old stimulus to elicit the previously learned response, B,

TABLE 10–7

DIRECTION OF COMPONENT TRANSFER EFFECTS

	Component Effect		
Paradigm	R (Response availability)	F (Forward associations)	B (Backward associations)
A-B, A-B	+	+	+
A-B, C-B	+	0	−
A-B, A-D	0	−	0
A-B, C-D	0	0	0

(Adapted from Martin 1965)

rather than D, which is demanded by list 2. As a result, negative transfer is obtained. With the other two paradigms, zero transfer is noted.

With the backward association component, the A-B paradigm again produces positive transfer, while the C-B paradigm is negative. As Martin wrote, "if the backward B-A associations of the first task are elicited during transfer-task learning, then the acquisition of the backward B-C associations will be impeded. Thus the surface representing the transfer of backward associations must be negative at the A-B, C-B position" (p. 334).

Martin carried his analysis one step further by indicating that other learning variables, such as meaningfulness or degree of first-list learning, will influence the amount of total transfer that results from these varying components. For example, if only a few trials of first-list learning are provided, the A-B, C-B transfer paradigm should produce greater amounts of positive transfer than if the learning of the first list is strong. What is the logic involved in this prediction? An examination of the kind of component transfer effects for the A-B, C-B paradigm indicates that the response availability component will produce positive transfer while the backward association component will result in negative transfer. Since the response availability stage during first-list learning takes place earlier than the learning of backward associations, a low degree of first-list learning will have the result that responses will be available but backward associations will be quite weak. As a result, more positive transfer will be produced by the response availability component than negative transfer produced by backward associations; the net effect will be positive transfer. On the other hand, when the learning of the original list is quite strong, although the response availability component will produce a maximum amount of positive transfer, the backward association component will also produce a maximum amount of negative transfer. The net effect, in this case, will be less positive transfer (possibly negative) than that obtained when the original learning was minimal.

A somewhat similar analysis can be made with regard to the role of meaningfulness. If the responses to be learned for list 1, as well as list 2, are of low meaningfulness, list 1 is primarily geared to response learning and only secondarily to association formation. On the other hand, if high meaningful responses are used, such an extensive response learning phase is not necessary; this permits more emphasis on the formation of the backward associations, which in turn will cause interference in the subsequent transfer task. Martin hypothesized that "an increase in response M [meaningfulness], then, means an increased opportunity for the development of negative B [backward association] effects, hence either a decrease in positive transfer or an increase in negative transfer, depending on the given degree of L_1 [learning of list 1]" (p. 337). It will be recalled that an earlier study by Jung (1963) provided experimental support for this prediction.

Martin's analysis of transfer in terms of individual components of the paired-associate task is an approach that we shall undoubtedly see more of in the future. A basic consideration that must arise, however, is the need to obtain response measures that reflect the varying stages or components of paired-associate learning independent of other components that also contribute to the learning.

THE ROLE OF EXTRAEXPERIMENTAL LEARNING

The laboratory examination of transfer typically demands that both the original as well as transfer task be learned in order to enable the experimenter to determine the influence the original learning task has on the learning of the second. This is the most direct and usually easiest way to determine if a given variable has any influence on the transfer task. Recently, a number of experimenters used a different method to examine transfer. They attempted to assess the subject's learning outside of the experimental situation, and then measured the influence of such learning on the acquisition of material provided in the experimental situation.

In their examination of such extraexperimental learning, Underwood and Postman (1960) delineated two types of verbal habits that may influence the learning of verbal material in the laboratory. These habits are of the (1) unit sequence and (2) letter sequence varieties. By "unit sequence habit," these authors refer to connections between verbal items that have been learned with varying degrees of strength. It has been generally accepted that one way of assessing the strengths of these varying unit sequence habits is to use a free-association procedure. For example, if a subject's continuous associations to the word *hard* are *easy, soft, egg, wood,* and *rock,* in that order, it would be assumed that the *hard-easy* relationship represents the strongest association of the items listed, whereas *hard-rock* represents a weak association. There would appear to be no reason why these previously learned associations should not either facilitate or interfere with the learning of paired-associates in the laboratory, depending of course upon the specific nature of the material to be learned. The paired-associate *hard-easy* should be easy to learn since the preexisting association and the association to be learned in the laboratory are identical. On the other hand, if the paired-associate was *hard-devil,* it would be expected that the stronger associations to *hard* would interfere with the learning of the *hard-devil* pair. Thus, the subject would have to extinguish or inhibit these stronger associates before learning could take place.

By "letter sequence habit," Underwood and Postman (1960) mean that the individual has learned that certain letters (rather than words) will follow others with varying degrees of probability. Most individuals in the United States have learned that U almost invariably follows Q and that the probability that any other letter follows Q is quite low. Following the earlier argument, when a subject attempts to learn the bigram QJ, the previously learned habit that U follows Q will provide interference to such learning; this previously established habit will have to be inhibited or extinguished before the new bigram can be learned.

Experiments by a variety of investigators (Underwood and Postman 1960, Underwood and Schulz 1960, Postman 1962, Spence 1963, and Coleman 1963a) have demonstrated the contribution of these previously learned habits to the learning of material provided in the laboratory. In Coleman's (1963a) study, subjects were first required to continuously associate adjectives to eighty different nouns. For example, the words *"doughnut is"* were presented to the subject, who was required to respond with adjectives in a continuous association manner in order to make a sensible associate to the word *doughnut*. Thus, a subject might first respond with *round* and then *sweet, sugary, powdery,* and *crusty*. Similarly, the words, *"coffee is"* might elicit *brown, bitter, good, black,* and *sweet,* in that order. Association hierarchies were then compiled for each noun on a subject-by-subject basis. It was assumed that adjectives given early in the series represented strong associations for the subject and that words given late represented weak associations. Thirteen responses were then so selected that they were preceded by a number of stronger associates. For example, *doughnut-crusty* might be used since it was preceded by *round, sweet, sugary,* and *powdery*. For thirteen other pairs, each response was preceded by only one or two stronger associates. *Coffee-bitter* might be used since it would be exceeded in associative strength only by *coffee-brown*. It may be noted, then, that for thirteen pairs of words, there was strong extraexperimental interference, but for thirteen other pairs, such interference was minimal. The list was presented until each subject had learned at least twenty responses. Coleman found that the paired-associates that seemed to be subject to strong extra-experimental interference, as indicated by the association test, were more difficult to learn than associates subject to minimal interference. Most of the incorrect responses made by the subjects in learning the material could be traced back to the association hierarchies provided by the subject in the association test.

MEDIATION AND TRANSFER

In Chapter 7 we discussed mediation as an organizational process used by individuals to facilitate the learning of verbal material.

It may be also pointed out that the mediation process has interested psychologists for some time, since mediated associations can help explain (1) how a stimulus can elicit a response although the two have never been previously paired; (2) how two different stimuli can elicit the same response, in which case we have an instance of stimulus equivalence, and (3) how two different responses can be elicited by the same stimulus, thus providing an instance of response equivalence. As we noted, experimenters have almost invariably used some kind of mediation paradigm—i.e., stage I: Learn A-B; stage II: Learn B-C; stage III: Learn A-C—in order to investigate the characteristics of the mediation process. Also, relevant to our consideration of mediation in this chapter, it may be observed that the varying stages of the mediation paradigm provide a kind of paired-associates transfer of training situation.

MEDIATION PARADIGMS

It must be acknowledged that the chaining or A-B, B-C, A-C mediation paradigm described in Chapter 7 is just one of a number of three-element or three-stage paradigms that have been used to examine mediation. In fact, three different types of three-stage mediation paradigms have been investigated.[1] As Table 10–8 indi-

TABLE 10–8

THREE-STAGE MEDIATION PARADIGMS

		I	II	
Stage 1	Learning	A-B	B-C	Simple Chain
Stage 2	Learning	B-C	A-B	
Stage 3	Test	A-C	A-C	
		III	IV	
Stage 1	Learning	B-A	C-B	Reverse Chain
Stage 2	Learning	C-B	B-A	
Stage 3	Test	A-C	A-C	
		V	VI	
Stage 1	Learning	A-B	C-B	Stimulus Equivalence
Stage 2	Learning	C-B	A-B	
Stage 3	Test	A-C	A-C	
		VII	VIII	
Stage 1	Learning	B-A	B-C	Response Equivalence
Stage 2	Learning	B-C	B-A	
Stage 3	Test	A-C	A-C	

[1] Four-stage paradigms have also been examined; we shall not discuss these, but the interested reader may consult Jenkins (1963a) and Kjeldergaard (1968).

cates, these have been identified as: (1) the simple and reverse chain, (2) stimulus equivalence, and (3) response equivalence.

The A-B, B-C, and A-C paradigm has been termed "forward chaining." The term is derived from the fact that the direction of the A-C association is forward, inasmuch as A served as a stimulus in the first learning task, and C as a response in the second.

A second chaining paradigm is backward or reverse chaining, with a B-A, C-B and A-C relationship. Note that in this situation, the A item served as a response and the B item as a stimulus during the first two learning stages; hence it is necessary to assume that a backward association was learned, in order to account for the facilitation of learning the A-C association.

The second mediating paradigm, A-B, C-B, A-C, is known as stimulus equivalence, while the third, which involves a B-A, B-C, A-C relationship, is classified as response equivalence. As Table 10–8 indicates, it is possible by reversing the first and second learning stages to provide a second series of forward and reverse chaining, stimulus and response equivalence paradigms.

A basic question that has been asked is whether all of the paradigms described above facilitate learning? The classic study in the area was done by Horton and Kjeldergaard (1961). Their experimental material consisted of eight pairs of low frequency, five-letter words. The learning of the first two lists (stages 1 and 2) was carried out to a criterion of three successive errorless trials, while just five trials were provided for the learning of list 3. A mixed list design was used, in which each subject learned four pairs of items, each of which represented one of the eight mediation paradigms and four control pairs. The total correct responses for the experimental and control pairs of words for each of the eight paradigms are indicated in Table 10–9. Statistical analysis indicated that all differences between the experimental and control pairs were significant except for one of the chaining paradigms.[1]

Although the various mediation paradigms are usually assumed to provide positive transfer, it is possible to so arrange conditions that negative transfer is obtained. This kind of situation has been

[1] The authors pointed out that the lack of a significant difference between pairs for this paradigm was probably due to chance since performance on the control pairs of items was substantially higher than that obtained with any of the other paradigms.

TABLE 10–9

TOTAL CORRECT RESPONSES ON EXPERIMENTAL AND CONTROL
PAIRS FOR EACH OF THE EIGHT PARADIGMS

| | Paradigm | | | | | | | |
| | Response chaining | | | | Stimulus equivalence | | Response equivalence | |
Pair	I	II	III	IV	V	VI	VII	VIII
Experimental	188	149	151	147	146	180	192	178
Control	133	108	143	114	103	108	127	121

(Adapted from Horton and Kjeldergaard 1961)

only infrequently investigated; however, a study by Norcross and
Spiker (1958) illustrates such an effect. In this study (experiment
II), first grade children were used as subjects. Three lists of six
paired-associates per list were constructed, and pictures of familiar
objects, i.e., dog, horse, etc., served as stimuli and responses. Three
pairs of items were arranged so as to provide chaining, while three
other pairs were used as control pairs. It was predicted that the
three chaining pairs would produce interference, since the responses
used on list 3 had been rearranged. This relationship is indicated in
Table 10–10. Subjects were run over three days, with list 1 and
list 2 being learned on day 1 and day 2 respectively. On the third
day, five trials were provided on list 3. Results revealed that the
learning of the control pairs of items was significantly better than
that of the experimental pairs, which supported the position that
the mediation process in this situation produced negative transfer.

TABLE 10–10

CHAINING PARADIGM USED TO PROVIDE INTERFERENCE

List 1	List 2	List 3
A_1-B_1	B_1-C_1	A_1-C_2
A_2-B_2	B_2-C_2	A_2-C_3
A_3-B_3	B_3-C_3	A_3-C_1

CONTEMPORARY RESEARCH IN MEDIATION

Contemporary research in mediation has been directed toward an examination of those variables that investigators believe contribute to the mediation process. One such consideration involves the examination of the characteristics of the mediators.

We would expect that the learning of mediators could be traced to the formal learning situation of the laboratory, as well as to the subject's everyday language experiences (or his natural language history). The comparison of mediators learned in the laboratory and those revealed in the natural language history of the individual was made in studies by Bugelski and Scharlock (1952), Sacks and Russell (as reported by Jenkins 1963a), and Russell and Storms (1955).

In the Bugelski and Scharlock study, lists of sixteen paired-associate CVCs per list were so constructed to provide a forward chaining paradigm (A-B, B-C, A-C), as well as an appropriate control (A-B, B-C, A-D).[1] College students served as subjects, each as their own control. Results indicated that the experimental list, A-C, was learned more rapidly than the A-D list, and the findings provided a clear demonstration of the role of a laboratory learned mediator in the acquiring of verbal material. An interesting aspect of this study is that none of the subjects who were interrogated after they had learned the A-C list reported being conscious of using the mediating B syllable in the learning of the A-C list.

An experiment by Sacks and Russell reported by Jenkins (1963a) provides an example of the use of natural language mediators (NLM). In this study the A-B relationship was obtained from free association norms and was characterized by such pairs of items as *table-chair, king-queen,* etc. Experimental subjects first learned to associate a CVC with one of these terms, i.e., XOJ-*king.* Following this, they were asked to learn a second list which consisted of

[1] The A-B, B-C, A-D control condition is not the most adequate since (1) the experimental subjects who learn the A-B, B-C, A-C lists are more familiar with the response terms, C, found in stage 3 learning, than the control subjects who must learn an A-D relationship, and (2) the two stage 3 learning lists, A-C and A-D, are assumed to be of equal difficulty. As a result, most contemporary investigators use an A-B, D-C, A-C control condition that controls both for response familiarity and list difficulty.

the same stimulus associated with the other member of the natural pair, i.e., XOJ-*queen*. Control subjects were required to learn only the second list. Results indicated that the experimental group learned the second list significantly more rapidly than the controls; in fact, Jenkins (1963a) reports that the experimental subjects learned the list in virtually one trial.

This type of experiment, however, has been criticized on the grounds that the experimental subjects were "aware" of the relationship existing between the responses in the first and second lists. Although Jenkins has admitted the validity of the criticism, he points out that it is irrelevant since there is nothing in the construct of mediation to indicate that the subject must not be aware of the mediators.

A subsequent experiment by Russell and Storms (1955) extended the mediation chain by another link. The design they used was similar to that used by Bugelski and Scharlock (1952), except that two implicit words rather than one linked the pairs on the stage 3 learning trials. List 1 consisted of pairing a CVC with a response word obtained from the Kent-Rosanoff Association Test. Russell and Storms had obtained norms for responses on this test that made it possible to infer a B-C and C-D association without establishing those associations experimentally. With this arrangement, C was a very frequent free association response to B, and D the most frequent free associate of C; however, D was not found among the ten most frequent responses to B. The test for the mediation effect was then made by requiring the subjects to learn a list of A-D pairings. A control group was provided with similar training except that the response on the test list consisted of A-X pairings. The manner in which these investigators hypothesized that the associative chains facilitated the learning of the A-D pairs is schematically illustrated in Table 10–11, while the CVCs, associative chains, and control words used in forming the paired-associate lists are indicated in Table 10–12. As might be anticipated, Russell and Storms found that learning was facilitated for the A-D pairs as contrasted with the A-X pairs. McGehee and Schulz (1961) confirmed this finding.

One mediation variable that has been extensively studied is meaningfulness. In an early study by Horton (1964), two media-

TABLE 10–11

AN ILLUSTRATION OF THE CHAINING AND CONTROL PARADIGMS

	LIST 1	ASSOCIATIONS INFERRED FROM NORMS	LIST 2 (TEST LIST)
Chaining Paradigm	$A_1\ldots>B_1$	$(B_1\to C_1\to D_1)$	$A_1\ldots\ldots\ldots>D_1$ $\searrow(B_1\to C_1)\nearrow$
Control Paradigm	$A_2\ldots>B_2$	$(B_2\to C_2\to D_2)$	$A_2\ldots\ldots\ldots\ldots>X_2$ $\searrow(B_2\to C_2\to D_2)$

(Adapted from Russell and Storms 1955)

tion paradigms, simple chaining and response equivalence, were examined as a function of the meaningfulness of the mediator. A paired-associate task was used in which the A and C items were CVCs of high association value, while high and low meaningful mediating B terms were selected from Noble's (1952) list of ninety-six paralogs. High meaningful B terms were represented by such words as *office, money, army,* etc., while some of the low meaning-

TABLE 10–12

NONSENSE SYLLABLES, ASSOCIATIVE CHAINS, AND CONTROL WORDS USED IN FORMING THE PAIRED-ASSOCIATE LISTS

A Nonsense Syllable	B First Chained Word	C Second Chained Word	D Final Chained Word	X Control Word
CEF	Stem	Flower	Smell	Joy
DAX	Memory	Mind	Matter	Afraid
YOV	Soldier	Army	Navy	Cheese
VUX	Trouble	Bad	Good	Music
WUB	Wish	Want	Need	Table
GEX	Justice	Peace	War	House
JID	Thief	Steal	Take	Sleep
ZIL	Ocean	Water	Drink	Doctor
LAJ	Command	Order	Disorder	Cabbage
MYV	Fruit	Apple	Red	Hand

(Adapted from Russell and Storms 1955)

ful B items were *davit, welkin,* and *polef.* One experiment was conducted using a mixed list design while the second employed separate groups for the varying conditions. Subjects in both experiments learned the list in the first two stages to a criterion of two errorless trials while the third list was presented for just five trials. The results from both studies indicated statistically significant effects in favor of the experimental groups (or pairs of items) containing the high meaningful mediators.

The findings of Peterson, Colavita, Sheahan and Blattner (1964) are interesting since these investigators examined the role of meaningfulness over all eight of the three-stage mediation paradigms. Their general procedure, however, departed from the usual experimental methodology that had typically been used. One of these procedural modifications was to present the three pairs of items that defined a particular mediation paradigm, i.e., A-B, B-C, A-C, in succession. This would be followed by a second group of three pairs of items, then a third group, etc. A second modification was that the A-C test trial consisted of a multiple-choice test in which A was presented along with items C, D, and E. The subject was instructed to indicate the response alternative that "seemed right or made the best pair" with the A item. The first experiment used CCC trigrams as the experimental material, while the second study employed 100 percent association value CVCs. The results for the two studies are indicated in Table 10–13, where it may be noted that when less meaningful material is used, just one stimulus equivalence and two response equivalence models revealed facilitation. When high meaningful items were used, facilitation was noted in all but three paradigms.

How does meaningfulness produce its effect? It is possible that the more meaningful mediator produces stronger associative connections between the A-B, B-C pairs during the first two learning stages; or it may be that the greater meaningfulness of the mediator results in greater response learning of the mediator. In either event, the mediating response should be more readily available to the subject during stage 3, which should facilitate the learning taking place at this time.

A second variable that has been investigated for its possible contribution to mediation effects has been a temporal one. It may be assumed that with certain kinds of learning situations, long de-

TABLE 10–13

MEAN NUMBERS OF SELECTIONS OF C ON TEST
TRIALS; EXPERIMENTS I AND II

Paradigm	Exp. I, CCCs		Exp. II, CVCs	
	Med.	Cont.	Med.	Cont.
I	2.55	2.38	2.95	2.86
II	2.00	1.92	3.08	2.73 [b]
III	1.92	1.84	2.91	2.75 [a]
IV	1.94	1.77	2.61	2.61
V	1.84	1.84	2.95	2.80
VI	1.94	1.69 [b]	2.53	2.23 [b]
VII	2.72	2.36 [b]	3.14	2.91 [b]
VIII	2.25	1.81 [b]	2.89	2.39 [b]

[a] $p < 0.05$
[b] $p < 0.01$

(Adapted from Peterson, Colavita, Sheahan and
Blattner 1964)

lays between the learning stages could result in some forgetting of
the associations, which in turn would reduce the mediation effect.
In an examination of the length of the delay interval interpolated
between (a) stage 1 and stage 2 learning, and (b) stage 2 and
stage 3 learning, Peterson (1965) examined delays of zero, two, or
eight seconds, as well as the meaningfulness of the material. The
general procedure used was similar to the earlier Peterson, et al.
(1964) study. It will be recalled that this procedure consisted of
presenting the three pairs of items defining a particular mediation
paradigm, followed by a second group of three, etc. In addition, the
A-C test trial consisted of a multiple-choice test in which A was
presented along with items C, D, and E; the subject was instructed
to indicate the response alternative that completed the best pair.
It should be noted that when the two- or eight-second interval interpolated between learning stages was used, the subject was asked to
name colors in the interval. The results indicated that increases in
the length of the delay interval were associated with a reliable decrease in learning (number of selections of the C item on the test
trials). The mean number of test trial C selections, corresponding to

the delay intervals of zero, two, and eight seconds that separated the two acquisition stages, were 1.85, 1.75, and 1.60; while the means for the same delay intervals occurring between the second acquisition stage and the test stage were 1.79, 1.73, and 1.67. When comparing the results obtained from the experimental group with those of the control, it was noted that with low meaningful material, mediated facilitation was obtained with zero- and two-second delays, but not with an eight-second delay, for both positions of interpolation of the delay interval. When the high meaningful material was examined, mediated facilitation was noted with the eight-second delay interval as well.[1]

A second temporal interval that has been examined within the mediation paradigm has been the length of time that is provided in stage 3 learning. And if the learning of stage 3 uses a study-test procedure, it is possible to vary the length of the study time as well as the testing period. Schulz and his associates (Schulz and Lovelace 1964, Schulz and Weaver 1968) pointed out that it may be fruitful to distinguish between the "discovery" of mediating responses and their "utilization." These experimenters suggested that the discovery process may be a function of the length of stage 3 study time, while the utilization of the responses may be related to the length of the stage 3 test trials.

In an examination of this position, Schulz and Weaver (1968) manipulated the length of the study interval (1.0 or 2.5 seconds) and the length of the test interval (1.5 or 3.0 seconds) on third stage (A-C) learning. The general procedure was one in which usual recall procedures were utilized for stage 1 test trials, while the test trials on stages 2 and 3 took the form of a four-alternative multiple-choice test for each pair of items. An examination of the number of correct responses on the fifteen A-C trials was a function of the length of the study interval as well as the test interval. Fig. 10–8 provides this data. In brief, it would appear that increasing the time that subjects have to discover as well as utilize the mediators appears to be an important consideration in the facilitation of the A-C learning task.

A final variable that has interested some investigators has been

---

[1] It may seem unusual that delay periods measured in seconds are capable of producing forgetting; however, as we shall note in a subsequent chapter (see Chapter 11), studies of short term memory have indicated this to be a bona fide phenomenon.

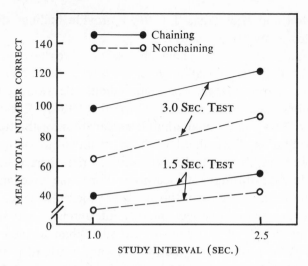

Fig. 10–8. Mean total numbers of correct responses during fifteen trials of stage III performance.
(Adapted from Schulz and Weaver 1968)

the subjects' awareness of the existence of the mediating item. In Horton's (1964) study investigating meaningfulness (to which we referred previously) an evaluation of the subjects' awareness was made following their completion of the A-C task. Subjects were asked whether they noticed any relationship between the stage 3 pairs of items they had just learned and the pairs they had learned during stages 1 and 2. Subjects' reports were categorized according to one of three levels of awareness: (1) the subject was unaware of any relationship between the pairs; (2) the subject indicated he was aware of some relationship but was unable to be very specific about its nature; (3) the subject was aware of the relationship and was able to specify it. Horton's findings indicated that significant increases in mediation score accompanied increases in awareness. That this was not an unusual finding is indicated by the fact that Runquist and Farley (1964) also found a positive relationship between ease of learning and reported mediators.

Although it may be tempting to assume that increases in mediation accompany increases in awareness, it could as logically be assumed that mediation occurs prior to and contributes to awareness. In any event, it should not be assumed that mediation cannot take place without awareness, as Bugelski and Scharlock (1952) and Horton and Kjeldergaard (1961) provide findings that contradict this assumption.

One final word. Throughout this section we have made the assumption that the mediation process makes a basic contribution to the A-C learning stage. The reader should be aware that some investigators, i.e., Mandler and Earhard (1964), Earhard and Mandler (1965), have an alternative explanation for the frequently found facilitating effects that have been attributed to the mediation process. In brief, these investigators assumed that there is less interlist interference during A-C learning. Thus, the mechanism for facilitation in the learning of this list is not the presence of a mediating process, but rather less interlist interference. We shall not go into the details of this controversy other than to indicate that Jenkins' (1965) analysis of the Mandler and Earhard position, as well as an experimental study by Schulz, Weaver, and Ginsberg (1965), appears to place the construct of mediation on firm ground. As these latter authors wrote, "it seems clear from the present results that, given appropriate conditions, the inference that mediating associations facilitate performance . . . is not based on an 'artifact' " (p. 170).

GENERAL FACTORS IN TRANSFER

A well-known phenomenon found in the verbal learning laboratory is a tendency on the part of subjects learning a number of lists of items to show progressive increases in performance. It is frequently difficult to account for these performance increases in terms of the transfer of specific associative habits, and as a result, non-associative or general transfer effects have been postulated. These have been indicated to be: (1) warm-up and (2) learning-to-learn.

Is it possible to distinguish between these two constructs? Postman and Schwartz (1964), addressing themselves to this problem, wrote that

Warm-up refers to the development of a set which maximizes S's efficiency in the performance of a rote-learning task. An effective set presumably involves such factors as postural adjustments and the adoption of an optimal rhythm for observing stimuli and giving overt responses. Learning to learn, on the other hand, has been taken to imply the acquisition of instrumental habits which facilitate the mastery of new tasks, e.g., the development of successful techniques of mediation. The basic criterion used for distinguishing between warm-up and learning to learn has been the degree of temporal persistence of the practice effects. The postural and attitudinal adjustments which constitute an effective response set may be expected to be lost after S leaves the experimental situation. . . . Under conditions of daily practice, gains are considerably greater within sessions than between sessions. Thus, warm-up would appear both to grow and to decline more rapidly than the effects of learning to learn (p. 37).[1]

THE CONTRIBUTION OF WARM-UP

As we have just reported, warm-up can be defined as the establishment of an effective set for the performance of the learning task; this set would include appropriate postural adjustments as well as an optimal rhythm of responding. The contribution of warm-up to verbal learning has not been extensively investigated. In one of the early studies, Heron (1928) had subjects learn two different paired-associate lists of CVCs each day on three different days. He found that the first list learned on the second day required significantly more trials to learn than did the second list on the first day. Moreover, the first list that was learned on the third day was learned less rapidly than was the second list learned on either of the two preceding days. It was assumed that the learning of the first list on any given day provided the subjects with an opportunity to "warm-up," which resulted in their being able to learn the second lists more rapidly.

Thune (1950), Hamilton (1950), and more recently Schwenn and Postman (1967) have provided contemporary examinations of warm-up effects.

Using the paired-associate learning situation, with lists consisting of fifteen pairs of words each, Thune (1950) examined the influence of different amounts as well as different types of warm-up activities

---

[1] This distinction is not an absolute one. The authors have acknowledged that: The criterion of temporal persistence provides an uncertain basis for the distinction between warm-up and learning to learn. The instrumental habits which constitute learning to learn are undoubtedly subject to interference and hence may be forgotten between experimental sessions. On the other hand, some of the adjustments which enter into an effective response set may be conditioned to the experimental situation and have long term effects on performance (pp. 37–38).

upon subsequent learning. In experiment 1 subjects were given six trials on a practice list following which a second list (list A) was presented to six groups of subjects who received either zero, two, four, six, eight, or ten trials. On day 2, list A was again presented; the varying groups received either ten, eight, six, four, two, or zero additional trials. It may be noted that the total number of trials for each group was ten, and that the number of trials on day 2 was contingent upon the number of trials provided on day 1. Thus, the group given two trials on day 1 received eight trials on day 2; the group given six trials on day 1 received four trials on day 2, etc. Following the second day's trials on list A, a ten-minute cartoon sorting task was provided, followed by the learning of a second list (list B) of paired-associates. Ten trials were provided. The varying conditions are indicated in Table 10–14. All lists were so constructed that formal or meaningful similarities or associations between stimulus and response words within the same list and between the varying lists were minimized. The results, indicating the mean number of correct anticipations on the ten trials of list B are presented in Fig. 10–9. Here, it can be noted that as the number of trials on list A during day 2 increased, the mean number of correct anticipations also increased—an effect interpreted in terms of warm-up.

TABLE 10–14

SEQUENCE OF EXPERIMENTAL EVENTS USED TO MEASURE THE EFFECT OF 0, 2, 4, 6, 8, AND 10 PAIRED–ASSOCIATE LEARNING TRIALS UPON SUBSEQUENT LEARNING OF NEW PAIRED–ASSOCIATE MATERIAL

	Day 1			Day 2		
Condition	Practice List	Rest	List A	List A	Cartoon Sorting	List B
0	6 trials	1′	10 trials	0 trials	10′	10 trials
2	6 trials	1′	8 trials	2 trials	10′	10 trials
4	6 trials	1′	6 trials	4 trials	10′	10 trials
6	6 trials	1′	4 trials	6 trials	10′	10 trials
8	6 trials	1′	2 trials	8 trials	10′	10 trials
10	6 trials	—	—	10 trials	10′	10 trials

(Adapted from Thune 1950)

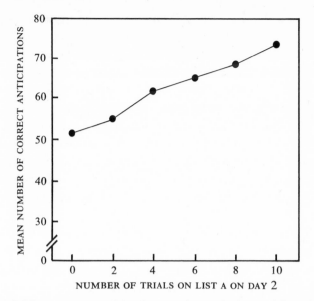

Fig. 10–9. Mean correct anticipations on the total of ten trials on List B. (Adapted from Thune 1950)

Inasmuch as the first experiment utilized an *associative* learning situation (trials on task A)to provide warm-up, experiment 2 was undertaken to examine warm-up as influenced by a nonassociative task—color guessing. In this task, the subjects attempted to guess, presumably through the use of "extra-sensory perception" which one of five colors (red, yellow, blue, green, or black) would be presented. In keeping with findings obtained in the first experiment, Thune found that the presentation of color-guessing trials just prior to the learning of the test list resulted in the list's being learned significantly more rapidly than if the color-guessing trials were given the day previously. A comparison of the appropriate groups from the two experiments yielded the unusual finding that "paired-associate verbal learning and nonassociative color-guessing are approximately equal in effectiveness in facilitating subsequent learning of a new paired-associate list after a brief interval" (p. 432).

If the warm-up state is believed to consist of appropriate attitudinal and postural adjustments adopted by subjects in order to accomplish their task, it would seem likely that such adjustments are acquired over a number of trials rather than instantly. In addition, such adjustments should be lost gradually, rather than suddenly during the rest period. Thus, after practice on one task, the learning of a second task should be an inverse function of the amount of time that separates the two tasks. Hamilton's (1950) study was designed to examine this hypothesis. Thus, the experimental procedure consisted of employing nine groups of subjects, each of which received ten trials on a list of paired adjectives, followed by a rest interval of either 8 seconds or 5, 10, 20, 40, 60, 120, 180, or 240 minutes. This in turn was followed by ten trials on a second list made up of paired one syllable nouns. Hamilton's findings can be noted in Fig. 10–10, in which performance on the second list is shown as an exponential decay function of the rest interval.

In a recent examination of the role of warm-up, Schwenn and Postman (1967) were interested in further examining Thune's (1950) rather unusual finding that a nonassociative task would provide the subject with as much warm-up benefit as an associative

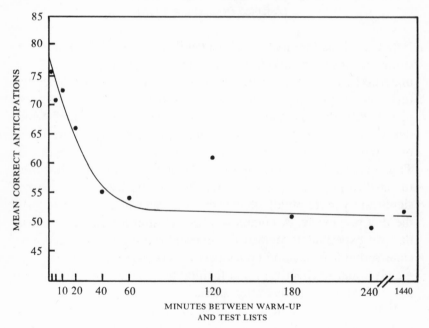

Fig. 10–10. Mean correct anticipations during ten trials on the test list following different intervals of rest between test and warm-up lists. The point above 1440 min. is taken from a previous study by Thune (1950).

(Adapted from Hamilton 1950)

one. The Schwenn-Postman experimental groups represented the factorial combinations of two types of training tasks and two levels of practice. Warm-up consisted of either a paired-associate learning task (LT) or a nonlearning task (NLT)—number guessing—and consisted of four or ten trials. A control group received no warm-up of any type. The learning of a paired-associate two-syllable adjective test list was begun 2.5 minutes following warm-up and was continued for ten trials. The mean number of correct responses for the five groups over these learning trials is indicated in Fig. 10–11. It can be noted that these results do not support Thune's (1950) earlier conclusions, since the performance of the groups receiving the learning or associative warm-up tasks was superior to that of all other groups.

Rather, the findings of the Schwenn and Postman study support the position that test-list performance shows considerably greater

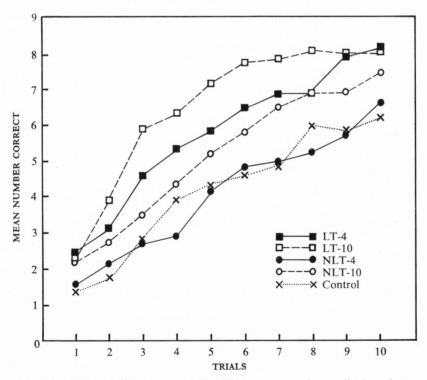

Fig. 10–11. Acquisition curves of the different groups in test-list learning. (Adapted from Schwenn and Postman 1967)

improvement after prior paired-associate practice than after an
equal number of trials on a nonassociative task. The authors point
out that

It is likely that the critical difference between the two studies lies in the fact
that Thune's Ss had prior experience with the learning task whereas the Ss
in the present experiment were naive. For a naive S familiarization with the
verbal requirements of the task is more essential than warm-up per se; for
experienced S both a learning and a nonlearning activity may serve primarily
a warm-up function (p. 573).

In summary, there appears to be little doubt that warm-up is a
bona fide phenomenon, at least with the paired-associate learning
task. It should be acknowledged, however, that Murdock (1960)
was unable to find a warm-up effect with the free-recall learning
situation. In one of Murdock's experiments (experiment 2), subjects learned six successive thirty-word lists in one two-hour session, and facilitation of performance was not found to be a function
of the number of lists learned. A basic problem, however, is that
forgetting (proactive inhibition) was undoubtedly present, which
could easily offset any positive benefits accruing from warm-up.

LEARNING-TO-LEARN

It will be recalled from our introduction to this general area that
learning-to-learn refers to the acquisition of certain types of habits
that facilitate the mastery of new tasks.

One of the early verbal learning studies demonstrating the learning-to-learn phenomenon was performed by Ward (1937), who
had subjects learn serial lists of twelve CVCs by the anticipation
method. The average number of trials taken to reach the criterion
of one perfect recitation as a function of the number of lists learned
is indicated in Fig. 10–12. Melton and Von Lackum (1941) also
reported a similar effect with subjects who had served for twenty-
eight days in an experiment in which lists of CVCs, words, and
numbers represented the experimental material.

A basic question not answered by these studies, however, is, how
long does learning proficiency continue to improve? A recent study
by Keppel, Postman and Zavortink (1968) attempted to deal with
this. In this study, paired-associate lists consisting of ten-word pairs

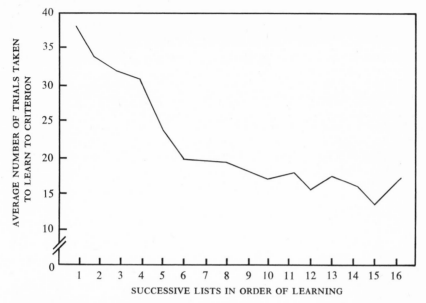

Fig. 10–12. A curve indicating the changes in rate of learning sixteen successive lists of twelve nonsense syllables.
(Adapted from Ward 1937)

were constructed, drawn from a pool of approximately 1,000 common English words. Alternating study and recall trials were provided, and each list was learned to a criterion of one perfect trial. One such list was learned every forty-eight hours, with five subjects learning thirty-six lists. The basic learning data are presented in Fig. 10–13. It is evident, although there were marked fluctuations in performance on the early learned lists, that learning proficiency continued to improve over the course of the experiment. One question that can be raised here is whether further improvement occurred beyond the learning of the thirty-six lists. Inasmuch as four subjects completed forty-four learning lists, the authors examined these additional data points to determine the course of further improvement. The mean trials to criterion for the last eight lists, blocked in groups of three—except for lists 43 and 44 which make up block 15—was 4.50, 5.00, and 4.75 (blocks 13 through 15 respectively). These values provided no statistical support for further improvement. Thus, the authors concluded that the learning-to-learn function is negatively accelerated and that the asymp-

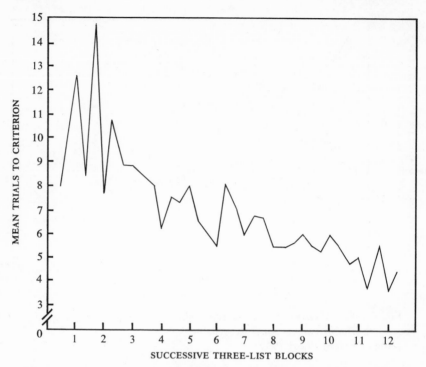

Fig. 10–13. Mean trials to criterion as a function of successive blocks of three lists.

(Adapted from Keppel, Postman and Zavortink 1968)

tote is not reached until a great deal of practice has taken place. The actual magnitude of improvement was an approximate halving of the learning rate from the first to the last block of lists; this value compares favorably with that reported by Ward (1937) for serial learning—although a bona fide comparison between the experiments is not possible because of differences in materials as well as list length.[1]

Postman and his associates undertook a series of studies designed to examine in somewhat greater detail the learning-to-learn mechan-

[1] A somewhat similar study was conducted by Webb (1962)—subjects learned lists of six English-Russian pairs to a criterion of one perfect trial. After one list was learned to a criterion, a new list was immediately introduced and learned to the same criterion. Learning continued for six hours without interruption or until 111 lists had been learned. Some learning-to-learn was in evidence; however, the contribution of fatigue and boredom arising from such a prolonged learning period appeared to negate any clear indication of the learning-to-learn phenomenon.

ism. In one of the early studies, Postman and Schwartz (1964) were interested in determining how (1) the class of verbal material which is employed, as well as (2) the type of learning situation (paired-associate or serial learning) contribute to learning-to-learn. In the procedure used, experimental subjects first learned list 1 to a criterion of one perfect trial. This list consisted of one of four different kinds of tasks: (1) paired-associate adjectives, (2) serial adjectives, (3) paired-associate trigrams, (4) serial trigrams. Two control groups were not given first list learning. Following the learning of list 1, all groups learned one test list to a criterion of one perfect recitation or for ten trials, whichever took longer. The test list consisted of a (a) paired-associate or (b) serial learning task in which adjectives comprised the experimental material.

The findings obtained for the varying groups can be noted in Table 10–15. These results indicate that improvement in performance was greater when the method of practice was the same on both lists; the difference reached statistical significance in the case of the paired-associate learning test list, and fell just short of significance with serial learning. Differences in performance as a function of the type of material used, however, did not approach significance.

In summary, these findings point to three general conclusions. First, since all conditions of pretraining produced substantial im-

TABLE 10–15

MEAN NUMBERS OF TRIALS TO CRITERION AND OF CORRECT RESPONSES
ON FIRST TEN TRIALS

Acquisition of Paired-Associate Test List		Acquisition of Serial Test List	
Condition	Mean Trials to Criterion	Condition	Mean Trials to Criterion
Control	16.75	Control	15.50
PA(A)-PA(A)	7.38	S(A)-S(A)	9.31
PA(T)-PA(A)	9.62	S(T)-S(A)	9.75
S(A)-PA(A)	11.25	PA(A)-S(A)	12.44
S(T)-PA(A)	13.00	PA(T)-S(A)	11.44

(Adapted from Postman and Schwartz 1964)

provement in performance on the test list, the authors concluded that much of interlist transfer must be general, at least in the sense of being independent both of the specific method of practice and of the class of verbal materials used in the prior learning task. Secondly, the results also provide some evidence for transfer effects specific to the method of practice; presumably, specific instrumental habits related to practice methods are carried over from one task to another. The authors speculated that the acquisition of these specific skills, at least in the case of paired-associate learning, include the ability to form stable associative links between the members of a pair and to differentiate stimulus and response terms within a list. Finally, transfer effects do not seem to be related to the class of materials used. One reason for this may be that the beneficial effects of prior experience with the class of materials used in the test list may be counteracted by associative interference that occurs because of uncontrolled similarities between the items in the two lists.

It should be recognized, however, that this last conclusion does not have generality for all types of materials. In a subsequent study, Postman, Keppel and Zacks (1968) found that a paired-associate task using response terms consisting of low meaningful trigrams, which thus required considerable integration on the part of the subject, produced greater transfer effects in learning a test list also consisting of low meaningful trigrams, than when the first paired-associate task consisted of highly integrated responses (days of the week). Thus, the authors pointed out that in a test list with trigram responses, the practice effects are greater when the responses in the prior list are also trigrams than when they are highly familiar and available English words.

LEARNING-TO-LEARN AND TRANSFER

In most learning-to-learn studies, there is a deliberate attempt on the part of the investigator to control the interlist similarity of the items used. Such a procedure is employed in order to minimize specific transfer effects so that any general transfer effects are more readily apparent.

It is possible, however, for general transfer effects or learning-to-learn to operate within the framework of specific transfer paradigms. That is, the question may be asked, what influence does learning-to-learn have on specific transfer paradigms?

In an early study examining this problem, Postman (1964) used four transfer situations: (1) attaching a similar response to an identical stimulus, A-B:AB′; (2) attaching a new response to an identical stimulus, A-B:A-C; (3) re-pairing the stimulus and response items of the first list to form new S-R pairs, A-B:A-Br; and (4) a control condition, employing unrelated stimuli and unrelated responses, A-B:CD. Separate groups were assigned to the learning of each paradigm. All groups of subjects learned three sets; each set consisted of two lists of paired-associates. Each list was made up of eight pairs of two-syllable adjectives. The first list in each set was learned to a criterion of seven correct items out of the eight items presented, while the second list was presented for just five trials.

Fig. 10–14 indicates the mean number of correct responses dur-

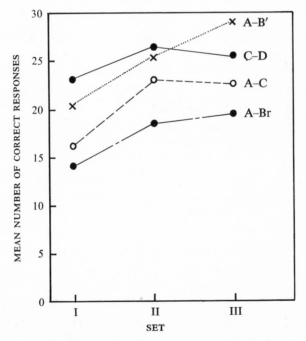

Fig. 10–14. Mean numbers of correct responses in five trials of list-2 learning as a function of set and paradigm.

(Adapted from Postman 1964)

ing the five trials of list 2 learning, as a function of successive sets and the paradigm employed.

It can be noted that all experimental paradigms revealed greater improvement in list 2 learning over the course of learning than did the control or reference conditions. The most pronounced change occurred in condition A-B′, in which there was a progressive development of positive transfer. The amount of negative transfer decreased for both A-C and A-Br; however, the divergence from the control condition was significant only in the case of A-C.

Postman (1964) wrote that

The major result of this study is the finding that the rate at which performance on the transfer tests improves with practice is a function of paradigm. The present design does not make it possible to determine, however, to what extent these differences in improvement reflect (a) learning skills specific to each paradigm which differ in effectiveness, and (b) general transfer skills acquired as a result of practice, e.g., the ability to respond appropriately to similarity relations between lists, which are applied with varying degrees of success depending on the specific paradigm (p. 447).

In attempting to answer this question, a subsequent study by Keppel and Postman (1966) was not successful in supporting the position that experience with different transfer paradigms has any differential effect on the learning of the test list. As these investigators pointed out, the important variable appears to be the transfer paradigm presented, rather than previous experience with other paradigms or the same paradigm.

SUMMARY

Transfer of training refers to the influence that the learning of one task has on the learning of a second; transfer is thus conceptualized as positive, negative, or indeterminate. Many of the early transfer experiments had their origins in the examination of "formal discipline," which assumed that the mental faculties of the individual could be developed in much the same way that a muscle could be strengthened by exercise. The pioneer experiments of Thorndike and Woodworth (1901, 1901a, 1901b) however, effectively challenged this position.

Most contemporary experimenters examining transfer use a paired-associates task since this permits manipulation of the stimulus items independent of response items. A basic variable that has interested investigators has been the amount of similarity between the two stimuli and two responses that comprise two tasks. Within this framework, two basic transfer paradigms have been examined: (1) where responses in the two tasks are identical, the similarity of the stimuli has been varied from being very similar to completely dissimilar; (2) where the stimuli in the two tasks are identical, response similarity has been manipulated from similar to completely dissimilar.

Osgood (1949) constructed a three-dimensional surface effectively drawing together much of the empirical research that has examined stimulus and response similarity to kind and amount of transfer. The findings indicate that attaching an old response to a new stimulus will provide positive transfer, while attaching a new response to an old stimulus will produce negative transfer. There have been a sufficient number of divergent findings from these "laws," however, which indicates the necessity for additional research.

A recent and important development has been the examination of the relationship between transfer and the stage analysis of paired-associate learning. Martin (1965) pointed out that typical transfer studies reflect only the net amount of transfer that has taken place; if paired-associate learning takes place in stages, however, one may ask how these stages have been influenced by the experimental variable under consideration. By conceptualizing paired-associate learning to be made up of a response availability process, as well as forward and backward associative relationships, and by relating transfer to each of these components, Martin provided an important analytic step that should go far in providing a better understanding of the transfer task.

It has been recently recognized that the language habits learned by individuals in their everyday lives play an important role in determining the ease of learning laboratory tasks. Whether such laboratory tasks are easy or difficult depends upon the kind of transfer these extraexperimental learning habits provide. Two of the extraexperimental language habits were postulated by Underwood and Postman (1960) to be of a (1) unit sequence or (2) letter sequence variety. A unit sequence habit is defined as the connection between verbal items (words) that have been learned with varying degrees of strength. If the individual has a letter sequence habit, he has learned that certain letters will follow others with varying degrees of probability. For example, learning the bigram QW will provide some difficulty since the previous acquisition of QU, an old and well-established letter sequence habit, will probably interfere with the learning of the new habit. A variety of experimenters obtained findings that support the position that these extraexperimental habits influence learning.

Another variable that has interested investigators has been mediation, which is generally assumed to be a source of positive transfer. That is, if the subject is asked to learn A-B, B-C, and then A-C, it is assumed that the rapid learning of A-C is a result of the fact that B serves as a mediator in the establishment of the A-C relationship. Early investigators were interested in examining transfer effects as related to a variety of three-stage mediation paradigms: e.g., simple chaining (A-B, B-C, A-C); reverse chaining (B-A, C-B, A-C); stimulus equivalence (A-B, C-B, A-C); and response equivalence (B-A, B-C, A-C). Contemporary research, on the other hand, has been directed toward examining how specific variables, e.g., kind of material, influence the mediation process.

At times it is difficult to account for increased (or decreased) learning efficiency on the basis of specific associative habits, and as a result, general transfer effects have been postulated. These are (1) learning-to-learn, or the concept of a learning set, and (2) warm-up. This latter construct refers to the subject's development of a set that maximizes his efficiency; an effective set would involve such factors as postural adjustments, the maintenance of a particular rhythm, etc. The other general transfer variable, learning-to-learn, has been defined as the acquisition of instrumental habits that facilitate the mastery of new tasks. Sufficient experimental work has been done to indicate that both of these variables make basic contributions to verbal learning.

11 Long and Short Term Retention

As was indicated in Chapter 2, there is an obvious difficulty in making any absolute distinction between learning and retention. Traditionally, however, and following Melton's (1963) point of view, retention has referred to an examination of changes arising from Trial n to Trial $n + 1$, when the variable of interest was the interval itself and/or the events that fill this interval.

The operations involved in traditional or long term retention studies consist of interpolating varying periods of time, usually measured in minutes or hours, between the reaching of some learning criterion and the subsequent test for retention. As an example, Luh (1922) had subjects learn a list of CVCs to a criterion of one perfect trial, and following intervals of twenty minutes or one, four, twenty-four or forty-eight hours, measured the recall of the material.

In the late fifties, the experimental work of Brown (1958), and Peterson and Peterson (1959) generated considerable interest in the area of what is now termed short term retention. In the procedure utilized by Peterson and Peterson (1959), subjects were presented with a single trigram for approximately one second. A three-digit number was then exposed and subjects were asked to count backwards from that number by threes or fours for a period ranging from three to eighteen seconds, following which they were asked to recall the trigram.

The operations, although not necessarily the processes, involved in the measurement of short term and long term retention are continuous, so that any distinction between these two constructs must be arbitrary. Nonetheless, most investigators have agreed that the study of short term retention involves: (1) the presentation of material that is within the memory span of the subject, (2) for only a single trial, (3) with a time period, measured in seconds, intervening between the presentation of the material and the test for retention. Conversely, long term retention involves multiple presentation of material beyond the memory span of the subject, with a period of time, usually minutes or hours, placed between the last learning trial and the test for retention.

The experimental work in the area of short term retention during the last decade has been so extensive that it is necessary here to consider this area apart from traditional long term retention studies. Before proceeding, we should like to provide the reader with a few words about response measures—a topic with relevance for both areas.

RESPONSE MEASURES

As we discussed in Chapter 2, response measures used in learning should not be differentiated from those employed in retention. Response indicants for both long and short term retention can be grouped into those employing (1) probability, as well as (2) latency measures. Most investigators generally employ probability measures, and in particular (a) recall and/or (b) recognition. To these, we should like to add a third measure, which, however, can be used only when previous learning has taken place (thus, it has applicability primarily in long term retention-type situations). This is the savings or relearning measure.

(1) *Recall*—it will be recalled that with this response measure the subject is asked to reproduce or recall the material that was presented. Typically, the specific measure is in terms of number of correct responses or number of errors.

(2) *Recognition*—with this response measure the subject must identify the material that had been presented previously. The most familiar procedure is one in which the subject is provided with a number of alternatives from which to choose a previously "learned" item. It will be recalled that in our earlier discussion of this measure, we pointed out that a more recently employed method of

measuring recognition was to present the subject with a series of items, with instructions to respond to those items in terms of whether or not the material previously had been presented. For example, in a study by Shepard and Teghtsoonian (1961) subjects were presented with a series of three-digit numbers, some of which were duplicates of numbers presented earlier. The subject was to respond in terms of whether or not each item had been seen previously (thus making it an "old" item) or had not been seen before (making it a "new" item). Subjects were permitted to proceed through the deck of items at their own rate but were not allowed to look back at any earlier item.

One interesting development in the use of this type of recognition measure has been to apply a theory of signal-detection. In the signal-detection study (i.e., Swets, Tanner and Birdsall 1961) the probability of the subject's responding "old" to an old item was identified as the "hit" rate, while the probability of labeling a new item "old" was identified as the "false alarm" rate. These two probabilities have been shown to co-vary systematically and have provided what has been called the "receiver operating characteristics" or ROC curve.

Applying this model to the recognition response, it may be assumed that the presentation of a particular test item results in a "recognition" response on the part of the subject that varies from certainty—in which case the subject unequivocally knows whether or not a given test item had been presented previously—to the other end of the continuum, where the individual has no knowledge as to whether or not the item had been presented. The characteristics of the typical recognition test measure demand, however, that the subject provide a dichotomous response of either "old" or "new." Thus the subject must partition the familiarity continuum just discussed into a region of acceptance and a region of rejection. He can do this by establishing a subjective criterion and then classifying a presented item as "old" only if its familiarity exceeds the subjective criterion he has set.

The basic assumptions that have been made with this theoretical model are indicated in Fig. 11–1, which notes the different distributions of events when the subject looks at an old item or when he inspects a new one.

Depending on the nature of the task, the instructions that have

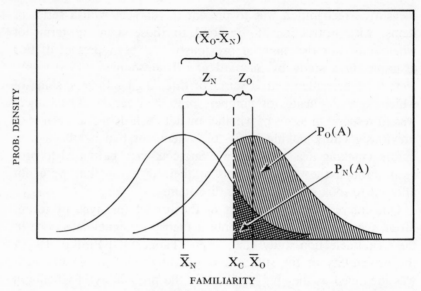

Fig. 11–1. Basic assumptions: $f_O(X)$, the curve to the right, represents the distribution of events that occurs on those occasions when the subject inspects an old item; $f_N(X)$, the curve to the left, represents the distribution of events that occurs when new items are inspected. (Assuming that the subject sets his cutoff at (X_C) and responds "old item" if and only if (X_i) exceeds (X_C), then $(P_O(A))$ represents the probability that the subject will respond "old" when in fact the item is an old item. $(P_N(A))$ represents the probability that the subject will report "old" when in fact the item is a new item.)

(Adapted from Parks 1966)

been provided, etc., the subject must make some decision regarding what degree of familiarity an item must possess in order for a particular item to be identified as "old" or "new." This given level of familiarity, or point on the familiarity continuum, has been identified as the cutoff point. A given item will be identified by the subject as "old" if it falls on the one side of this point, and "new" if it falls on the other side.

For most tasks, the distributions will overlap, so that—in accordance with the cutoff point—on some occasions the individual will identify old responses as new and new ones as old, in addition to correctly identifying items.

This kind of a model has been quite useful in identifying certain variables that, at least from an intuitive point of view, would appear to play an important role in recognition. For example, the difference (d') between the distribution of old and new items on the familiarity continuum should depend on the similarity of the items. A second variable could be the amount of study time provided, which might result in better learning of the old items. The kinds of rewards and penalties that would be attached to making correct and incorrect responses would be another variable. Finally some knowledge about the number of old items presented in contrast to new should also play a role. That is, if the subject believes that the number of old items presented is large relative to the number of new ones, he will set his criterion low, so that he makes the decision "old" when he is uncertain about a particular item. This low criterion of course insures a high hit rate—the probability of labeling an old item old is high—but it also insures a high false alarm rate, since there is a high probability of labeling a new item old. Conversely if the number of new items presented is large relative to the number of old items, the subject will probably set his criterion at a high value, so that when he is uncertain about a particular item he will respond "new." This increases the probability that he will reject new items but it also decreases the probability that old items will be "recognized."

(3) *Savings or Relearning*—as we indicated, this measure has particular reference to situations in which previous learning has taken place. Here, the subject learns the original material to a specified criterion and, following a retention interval, is required to relearn the material to the same criterion. The difference between the number of trials required to learn the material and then relearn it is represented by a savings score. This score may be converted to a percentage value by the following formula:

$$\frac{\text{Number original learning trials} - \text{New learning trials}}{\text{Original learning trials}} \times 100 = \% \text{ savings}$$

LONG TERM RETENTION: SOME METHODOLOGICAL CONSIDERATIONS

In the next several sections, we will examine a number of topics that fall primarily within the province of long term retention.

RETENTION CURVES AND RESPONSE MEASUREMENT

For a long time the only systematic comparison of retention curves resulting from different response measures had been made in an early study by Luh (1922), who had subjects learn a list of CVCs to a criterion of one perfect recitation and then, following intervals of twenty minutes, one, four, twenty-four, or forty-eight hours, measured the retention of the material. Relearning, recognition, recall as measured by anticipation, written reproduction, and the reconstruction method, were used to measure retention.[1]

Luh's results indicated that for all of the retention intervals, the reconstruction measure provided the highest retention score, reconstruction next, and then written reproduction. The anticipation method resulted in the smallest amount of retention. The relearning measure produced variable findings and provided next to the poorest value when the retention interval was twenty minutes, one hour or four hours. At the forty-eight hour retention interval, however, only the recognition measure provided a higher retention score.

This study suffers from several methodological difficulties. Three of the retention tests used by Luh were given in succession to the same subjects, and it is possible that performance on the latter two tests was influenced by the previous ones. In addition, the same subjects served repeatedly under each of the experimental conditions, and some served as many as five times in each condition. Such a procedure meant that the subjects became highly practiced learners, which would probably result in higher retention scores. At the same time, however, the learning of successive lists of CVCs could also provide increasing amounts of interference that could reduce retention scores. It is difficult to assess the net effect of these facilitating and inhibitory factors.

Recognizing that these difficulties may have produced anomalies in Luh's (1922) findings, Postman and Rau (1957) performed a similar study in which they examined the retention of words as well as CVCs. Twelve-item serial lists of (a) CVCs and (b) words

[1] The written reproduction method was a type of free-recall situation whereby subjects were asked to recall all the items they could without regard to order. The reconstruction method consisted of furnishing the subjects with the original material and requiring them to arrange the items in the correct serial order.

were each learned to a criterion of one perfect recitation by the anticipation method. After reaching the criterion, retention was measured after either twenty minutes, twenty-four hours, or forty-eight hours, and four response measures were used: (1) recognition, (2) free recall, (3) anticipation and (4) relearning. In measuring recognition, twelve-item multiple-choice tests were employed in which each multiple-choice item consisted of four alternatives, one of which was correct. For the measurement of free recall, the subject was instructed to write down as many of the items as he could remember, not necessarily in the order of presentation. The measure for the anticipation method was the score obtained on the first trial of the relearning series, while the relearning score was obtained from the number of trials the subject required to reach the same criterion as was employed in the original learning. The findings from the two types of material, as indicated in Fig. 11–2, in general confirm the results of Luh (1922), who also found that recognition produced best retention, and free recall and anticipation the poorest.

Luh's finding, confirmed by Postman and Rau (1957), resulted in the general position that recognition invariably produced higher retention scores and recall. Thus, one of Postman and Rau's conclusions was that there was substantial experimental evidence to support the position that tests of recognition yield higher scores than do tests of recall. The theoretical explanation for this difference was that "active recall depends on stronger, more 'available' associations than recognition" (Postman, Jenkins and Postman 1948, p. 516).

There is now, however, recognition of the fact that differences among response measures used in retention studies are a function of the conditions under which these measures are obtained. Bahrick (1964) has provided an excellent summary of the evidence supporting this position.[1]

First, there is little doubt that the *number* of the distractors used plays an important role in determining recognition test scores. Studies by Postman (1950), Teghtsoonian (1958), Davis, Sutherland and Judd (1961), Schwartz (1961), Murdock (1963),

---

[1] Some of the experiments that will be cited would more frequently be categorized as learning than as retention studies; nonetheless, their findings have relevance to this issue.

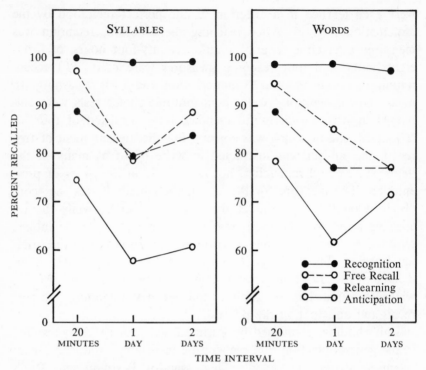

Fig. 11–2. Retention curves for nonsense syllables and words as a function of the method of measurement.

(Adapted from Postman and Rau 1957)

Bahrick and Bahrick (1964), Bruce and Cofer (1967) provide only a sampling of the many experiments that have supported this position.

For example, in an early study by Postman (1950) thirty-six CVCs were read to subjects five times each, with each item spelled out. Following the fifth presentation of the material, groups of subjects received one of four recognition tests. These tests differed only on the basis of the number of incorrect alternatives provided. More specifically, either one, three, six, or nine incorrect alternatives for each correct response was provided. Postman found that as the number of alternatives increased, recognition performance became progressively poorer. Or, in a more recent study, Murdock (1963) gave subjects thirty seconds in which to study lists of twenty words. This was followed by a recognition test in which the number of distractors was 20, 60,

100, or 140. The mean proportion of correct responses as a function of these varying numbers of distractors, after correction for chance, was .56, .54, .44 and .42.

It has been also shown that the *characteristics* of the distractors play an important role in elevating or depressing recognition test scores. More than twenty years ago, Underwood (1949) wrote,

if we require S to learn a list of adjectives and then place the adjectives among a group of nonsense syllables, S would probably show a very small loss in retention. Obviously the similarity of the test material to the other material is an important variable which determines the recognition scores (p. 512).

A large number of experimental studies have supported Underwood's position (Postman, Jenkins and Postman 1948, Bahrick and Bahrick 1964, McNulty 1965).

In the Postman, Jenkins and Postman (1948) study, forty-eight CVCs were read to groups of subjects for six presentations. Following the last presentation, a recall as well as recognition test was provided. In order to control for order, the presentation of the tests was counterbalanced. Of particular concern was the nature of the recognition test. Each test item consisted of three distractors, in addition, of course, to the correct item. One of the distractors represented a one-letter change from the correct item, while the two other distractors were entirely new but differed from each other by just a single letter. Thus, if JIV was the correct item, the four multiple-choice items might be as follows: JIX, QUN, JIV, MUN. Results indicated that the incorrect similar syllable (e.g., JIX) was chosen significantly more frequently as the correct item than would be indicated by chance.

A somewhat different facet of the problem has been pointed to by McNulty (1965) who notes that a "partial learning" process may contribute to the fact that recognition yields higher scores than recall. That is, with recall measures it is necessary to produce the "whole" item in order for it to be scored as correct; however, it may be that the recall of only a single letter or two enables the subject either to recognize the correct whole item or to eliminate distractors. McNulty reasoned that the higher the order of English approximation of an item, the greater the size of the unit (in number of letters) learned by the subject. Thus, he hypothesized, if the superiority of recognition over recall depends on partial learning, and if higher-order items tend to be learned as whole units rather than in parts, differences between recognition and recall should decrease as approximation to English increases. The experimental materials consisted of three lists; two of these consisted of eight-letter paralogs of first- and third-order approximations to English. The third list consisted of eight-letter words which mostly had a relatively low Thorndike-Lorge frequency count. Each item was presented at a three-second rate for four learning trials. Following each trial, a retention test was administered. The unaided recall measure consisted of having the subject write down as many of the items as he could recall. Two recognition tests were also used, in which sixteen incorrect alternatives were provided along with the sixteen correct ones. The primary difference between the recognition tests was in terms of the similarity of the incorrect alternatives to the correct ones. Table 11–1 provides an example of the three types of approximations to English along with the correct and incorrect alternatives.

TABLE 11–1

EIGHT-LETTER SEQUENCES USED

| | First-Order Approximation to English | |
Original Items	Incorrect Alternatives Recognition II	Incorrect Alternatives Recognition I
larrgtti	darrgtti	vsedeewn
btseiosr	baseiosr	eduietee
eiehtecs	eithtecs	rctamerl
	Third-Order Approximation to English	
onsedure	insedure	diassall
wersuble	warsuble	hangiste
ivessent	ivassent	seentyll
	Words	
boldness	coldness	variable
flagrant	fragrant	coupling
interior	inferior	previous

(Adapted from McNulty 1965)

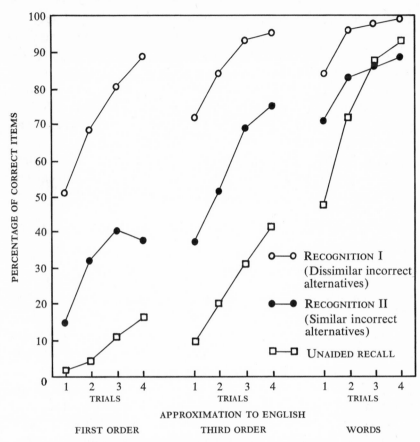

Fig. 11–3. Percentage of items correctly remembered under the three methods of measurement. Data are plotted as a function of trials and approximation to English.
(Adapted from McNulty 1965)

The percentage of items correctly remembered under each of the three methods of measurement is indicated in Fig. 11–3, in which scores have been corrected for guessing. In keeping with McNulty's hypothesis, it may be noted that the difference between recognition and recall decreased as a function of approximation to English. In fact, it can be observed that on trials 3 and 4 recognition provided a lower percentage of correct items than unaided recall when words were used as the experimental material.

A final point to which we would like to call attention is that in making the comparison between recognition and recall measures, most experimenters have not controlled the degree of original learning. That is, subjects should be trained to the same criterion, using the same measure as that on which a subsequent retention test is provided. In the Postman and Rau (1957) study, for example, all subjects first learned the original material by the anticipation method; subsequently, varying groups were tested for retention by a variety of measures, i.e., recall, recognition, etc. The issue raised by Bahrick (1964) is that the reaching of a given criterion by the anticipation method results in an overlearning effect when measured by recognition. Thus, in the subsequent test of retention, better recognition performance reflects this original learning difference.

This point was demonstrated experimentally in a study by Bahrick and Bahrick (1964). In that study the learning material consisted of seven paired-associates. The stimulus member of each pair was an 8x8 matrix with one of the sixty-four cells filled in black and the remainder left blank. The position of the single black cell was chosen randomly from cells that did not comprise the perimeter of the matrix. The response member was a randomly chosen three-digit number. The anticipation method of learning was used with a 4:4-second presentation. Following each anticipation trial, two of the groups also received recognition tests. Each test item consisted of five stimulus matrices and five three-digit numbers. One set of recognition test items, in which each set of distractor responses shared no digits in common with the correct response numbers while incorrect stimulus positions were three cells removed from the correct position, was designated as easy. In the difficult test items, all incorrect response numbers shared two of the three digits with the correct number; incorrect stimulus positions were only one cell removed from the correct position. The third group did not receive any type of recognition testing after each trial. In keeping with the Bahrick-Bahrick position, each recognition group was trained until subjects gave seven correct recognition responses, while the anticipation group was trained until subjects gave seven correct anticipation responses. It should be noted that each group had reached the same level of learning as measured by the subsequent retention test. Two hours, two days, or two weeks later, subjects were given anticipation or recognition tests.

A second study replicated the first except that modified Jap-

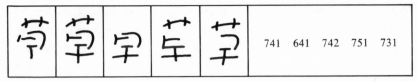

(DIFFICULT)

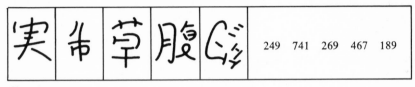

(EASY)

Fig. 11–4. One row from the difficult and easy recognition test for characters.

(Adapted from Bahrick and Bahrick 1964)

anese characters were used as the stimulus material. A sample row of the difficult and easy recognition test used in this second study is indicated in Fig. 11–4.

Table 11–2 reveals the mean number of trials it took each group in both experiments to reach their learning criterion; this same table indicates the mean percentage of items retained by the recognition and anticipation groups over the three retention inter-

TABLE 11–2

LEARNING AND RETENTION DATA

Condition	Mean Trials to Learn	Mean Percentage Retained		
		2 hours	2 days	2 weeks
Experiment I				
Easy Recognition	8.0	83.7	79.2	56.9
Anticipation	9.3	80.0	72.8	38.6
Difficult Recognition	11.5	74.7	68.8	31.7
Experiment II				
Easy Recognition	6.9	82.2	81.0	64.3
Anticipation	14.2	71.4	64.3	21.4
Difficult Recognition	15.4	67.4	56.9	36.1

(Adapted from Bahrick and Bahrick 1964)

vals. An inspection of the retention scores reveals that the frequently held dictum that recognition scores are higher than recall scores does not hold. In both experiments, difficult recognition performance ranks below performance using an anticipation test. It may be noted that if the easy recognition group had been given training equivalent to that of the anticipation group during the original learning, recognition learning would have been overlearned.

THE LEARNING AND RETENTION OF INDIVIDUAL ITEMS

The learning of the varying items that comprise a paired-associate or serial list takes place at different rates and to different terminal levels. That is, it cannot be assumed that when a list of paired-associates is learned to a criterion of one errorless trial, all of the items of that list have been learned equally well. A number of investigators believe that such unequal learning of items may seriously distort retention processes; these investigators have given serious attention to means of correcting this difficulty.

The problem of unequal learning of individual items has been attacked by using the "method of adjusted learning," as suggested by Gillette (1936) and more recently by Battig (1965). Following an early suggestion by Woodworth (1914), Gillette's technique was to drop each item from the list upon the attainment of a specified criterion (i.e., one correct anticipation for that item). As a result of this procedure, the length of the list varies from trial to trial. Some years later, Madden, Adams and Spence (1950) suggested a somewhat different procedure. Here, these experimenters held the list length constant by presenting only half of the pairs on any given trial; correct pairs were removed and replaced from a pool of unused pairs after each trial. After all pairs had been used, subsequent replacements for correct pairs were previously correct pairs, substituted in the order in which they had been learned. This procedure was continued until three correct responses were given for each individual pair; after this, all pairs were presented together for a single, final criterion trial.

Some question has been raised, however, as to whether or not even such procedures as these result in equal learning for individual pairs of items. Underwood's (1954) analysis of Gillette's procedure indicated that this technique does not always lead to identical associative strengths for all items on a list. Moreover, Battig (1965) has quoted a study by Merikle (1964) in which there was evidence that the first pairs of items learned and then dropped were better learned than were the last learned pair, even though these latter pairs of items had been presented more frequently as well as more recently. As Battig (1965) wrote, "that the first-learned pairs still yield better performance after having been dropped from the list points up the even more sizable magnitude of this discrepancy when they remain in the list, as under the usual paired-associate procedure" (p. 5). As an alternative to these methods, Battig suggested a procedure in which each trial begins with the presentation of all pairs in the list, followed by a recall test for each, exactly as in any trial under the typical study-test or recall procedure. Each correctly recalled pair is then removed, so the next time only the previously incorrect pairs are presented and subsequently tested for recall. Following the second presentation, correct pairs are once again eliminated and the procedure is repeated until each individual pair of items has been recalled correctly. This total procedure defines the first trial, and each subsequent trial proceeds in exactly the same manner. Trials can be continued, either to a specified number of trials or to such a list-based criterion as the correct recall of all pairs in the list following the initial presentation of the complete list at the beginning of the trial. Inasmuch as the definition of a complete trial under this procedure is one in which each item is recalled correctly once, Battig (1965) termed it a correction procedure after the closely analogous method used in discrimination learning experiments. Montague and Kiess' (1966) study examining Battig's procedure raised some question as to whether this technique provides the hoped-for equivalence of learned items.

In summary, it must be pointed out that adjusted learning techniques have not had widespread use. In many instances, and particularly in those studies in which learning was examined as a function of a particular variable, interpair differences in learning have little relevance to the experimental problem. In those experiments in which it would be desirable to hold interpair differences to a minimum, a basic problem is in the programming of such a procedure. The typical memory drum or other exposure device almost invariably demands that the materials be prearranged in a fixed and unalterable sequence for presentation. The dropping of different items on each trial provides procedural difficulties that cannot usually be surmounted by facilities available to the typical investigator, although some recent experimenters have utilized computer devices that can solve the problem.

Finally, a few studies have been directed toward an examination of this problem, but experimental findings demonstrating that the use of adjusted learning techniques provide different results than regular procedures are lacking. Thus, in the Madden, Adams and Spence (1950) study to which we have referred previously, identical amounts of retroactive inhibition were obtained under the adjusted learning and conventional anticipation learning procedures.

LONG TERM RETENTION: THE ROLE OF LEARNING VARIABLES

As we noted earlier, the operations involved in the study of long term retention frequently consist of first having the subjects reach a learning criterion, at which time it is tacitly assumed that the learning process is completed. A period of time is then interpolated between the last learning trial and the test for retention. Contemporary interest in retention has frequently been directed toward determining whether those variables that resulted in differential learning functions would similarly contribute to differences in retention.

THE ROLE OF OVERLEARNING

Inasmuch as the distinction between a learning trial and a retention trial is arbitrary, it would be expected that when the amount or degree of original learning varies, such differences will be reflected on the retention test. In an early study demonstrating such an effect, Underwood (1954a) had one group of subjects learn a serial list of twelve CVCs to a criterion of seven correct responses on a single trial. A second group of subjects was given trials until one perfect recitation was obtained. Paired-associate lists were also utilized, with one group learning a ten-pair list until five correct responses were made on a single trial, while a second group learned the list to a criterion of one perfect trial. Recall scores obtained twenty-four hours later by the two learning groups for both serial and paired-associate lists reflected the differences between these groups at the end of the training period.

One question that follows from this general finding relates to the influence of learning trials beyond a criterion of one perfect recitation. That is, once perfect recitation is achieved, what can be achieved by providing additional learning trials? Contemporary investigators consider this problem as merely an extension of the one we have just discussed. That is, it is recognized that the criterion of learning is arbitrary; consequently, so-called overlearning trials merely provide the subject with the opportunity to achieve a more stringent criterion.

Although the classical study of the influence of overlearning was performed by Krueger (1929), we will return now to the previously discussed Underwood study. In addition to the two degrees of learning employed in the learning of the two tasks, a third degree of learning was also utilized. Here, paired-associate and serial lists were learned to a criterion of one perfect trial plus seven additional trials. Findings indicated that the group receiving the overlearning trial recalled more items twenty-four hours later than the groups that had learned to a criterion of only one perfect trial.

In Krueger's (1929) classic study, groups of subjects either learned lists of monosyllabic nouns to one perfect recitation or were provided additional trials amounting to 50 percent or 100 percent of those taken to reach criterion. These degrees of learning have been designated as 100 percent, 150 percent, and 200 percent. Following such learning, one, two, four, seven, fourteen, or twenty-eight days later, relearning trials were given in which the first trial provided a recall score. Table 11–3 reveals the scores obtained as a function of the degree of learning and the interval between the last learning trial and the test for retention. It may be noted here that overlearning trials significantly aided retention, and that the increased retention scores were smaller from 150 percent to 200 percent, than from 100 percent to 150 percent. Postman (1962b) replicated Krueger's study and confirmed his findings.

TABLE 11–3

RECALL SCORES AS A FUNCTION OF DEGREE
OF LEARNING

Interval (Days)	Mean Words Recalled, Degree of Learning		
	100	150	200
1	3.10	4.60	5.83
2	1.80	3.60	4.65
4	.50	2.05	3.30
7	.20	1.30	1.65
14	.15	.65	.90
28	.00	.25	.40

(Adapted from Krueger, 1929)

Most investigators, however, have not been interested in examining retention differences when different degrees of learning are present at the end of the learning trials, since any difference in retention merely reflects the difference present at the end of the original training. Rather, interest has been directed toward determining whether different materials or procedures result in differential amounts of retention when original learning has (presumably) been held constant.

In order to hold original learning constant for groups that have undergone different experimental treatments, the most frequently used procedure has been to have all of the experimental groups achieve the same criterion. If the experimental variable does influence the rate of learning, such a procedure means that the different experimental groups will receive varying numbers of trials prior to reaching the criterion. For example, if the experimenter wishes to examine the influence of meaningfulness of material on retention, and if he uses CVCs of varying association values, it would be expected that the list containing the low association value CVCs would require significantly more trials to reach a criterion of one perfect recitation than a list containing high association CVCs. Most investigators have assumed, however, that once the criterion has been reached, the degree of learning for the varying experimental groups is equivalent.

Underwood (1964) believed that there was a major difficulty with this assumption. His argument falls into two parts. First, he claimed, any criterion trial does not reflect the true amount of learning that has taken place. This is the case because the trial not only measures the learning that has taken place up to that time, but also provides the subject with additional learning that is not measured. For example, when the anticipation method is used, if the subject fails to respond to a given stimulus on the criterion trial, the correct response member is exposed and the subject has the opportunity to learn the response at that time. But any performance measure taken on the trial does not reflect this additional learning.

The second part of Underwood's argument is that if learning is taking place at different rates as a function of the independent variable, i.e., high versus low meaningful material, the additional nonmeasured learning on the criterion trial will be greater for the group with the higher rate, thus resulting in an inequality of true learning for the two groups. Fig. 11–5 illustrates the hypothetical growth of learning easy and difficult items as a function of the number of trials provided. Although a criterion of 100 percent has been achieved in each case, it is assumed that the associative

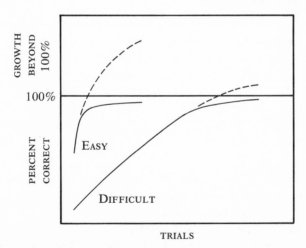

TRIALS

Fig. 11–5. Hypothetical growth of degree of learning beyond 100 percent as a function of continued trials after reaching asymptote for easy and difficult items.

(Adapted from Underwood 1964)

strength of the easy and difficult items continues to grow, and that the strength of the easy items increases at a faster rate.

Although Underwood dealt primarily with the anticipation method of learning, he did not confine his analysis just to this method but believed it had relevance for all types of learning situations. Thus, he wrote,

> the use of alternate study and test trials [rather than anticipation] does not avoid this problem, for most assuredly some change in performance must occur as a consequence of a test trial even without knowledge of the correctness of performance (p. 114).[1]

Underwood suggested a number of solutions to this problem. An obvious one is to use a control group that is given an extra trial; the mean score for this group can then be used in estimating the last learning trial scores. Other solutions suggested by Underwood have been designated as single- and multiple-entry projection. Although we cannot discuss these methods in detail at this time, the procedures involve an estimation or a projection of the expected performance on a hypothetical trial following the last learning trial. These projected scores are then used as a base learning score from which to measure the amount of retention, after an appropriate interval.

RETENTION AS A FUNCTION OF SPEED OF LEARNING

An examination of retention as a function of speed of learning provides an example of Underwood's multiple entry projection technique. In an early study in which an adjusted learning procedure was used, Gillette (1936) concluded that "the slow learner when given sufficient time to learn the *same amount* as the fast learner, but not allowed to *overlearn* the material, is not able to retain as much as the fast learner" (p. 50). In the adjusted learning technique used by Gillette, the items in the list were "dropped out" after being learned to some specified criterion. Thus, if one correct anticipation was used as the criterion, the first time that the subject correctly anticipated the response that simulus response

---

[1] Battig (1965) rejected this point of view, citing a study by Richardson and Gropper (1964) that indicates that such learning during recall trials is quite small in magnitude.

pair was dropped from the list. The subject continued to be given trials on those items he had not correctly anticipated. In this way, all items of the list were given the same number of "reinforcements." The basic assumption made here was that the associative strength for all items at the end of the learning trial was the same for fast and for slow subjects.

Analyzing the findings obtained from a series of earlier studies, Underwood (1954) confirmed Gillette's conclusions. That is, when items were equated for number of "reinforcements" during learning, retention proved consistently superior for the fast learner. But Underwood pointed out that this conclusion was based on the assumption that reinforcement (defined as making a correct response) for a slow learner results in the same associative strength as reinforcement for the fast learner. It is possible, Underwood suggested, that one reinforcement adds more strength to an association acquired by a fast learner than it does to an association for a slow learner; the result is that the degree of learning of the material is not equal prior to the introduction of the retention interval.

In order to make an appropriate comparison of the retention of the fast and slow learners, Underwood indicated that it is essential that the response strength of the items for each be equated at the end of the learning trials. The adjusted learning technique does not ensure this to be the case and the solution Underwood provided was a successive probability analysis of learning that he later termed multiple-entry projection.

Using experimental data obtained from earlier studies, Underwood (1954) obtained a population of ninety fast and ninety slow learners, of which each group learned and recalled three lists of paired-associates. Two hundred seventy lists were thus available for each group. Since each list consisted of ten stimulus-response pairs of items, 2,700 responses per group were available for examination. Analysis consisted of determining the growth of the associative strength for each item. This was accomplished by observing when a response was first correctly anticipated. It was then noted whether that response was anticipated correctly or incorrectly on the next trial, the trial following that, and so on, until the last learning trial. With such an analysis made for each item for a large number of subjects, the experimenter was in a position to predict the probability of the subject's making a correct response on a succeeding trial when this response had been correctly anticipated on previous trials once, twice, three times, etc. Successive probability curves for fast and slow subjects based on this method of analysis are plotted in Fig. 11–6. Thus for the slow learner, the probability of making the correct response on the trial following one reinforcement was .50. After nine reinforcements, the probability of obtaining the correct response on the next trial increased to approximately .85. Probability of securing a correct response for the fast learners after one reinforcement was approximately .62 and after nine reinforcements it increased to approximately .91. It is clear, then, that reinforcement does not result in equal probability that a response will be correct on the next trial for fast and

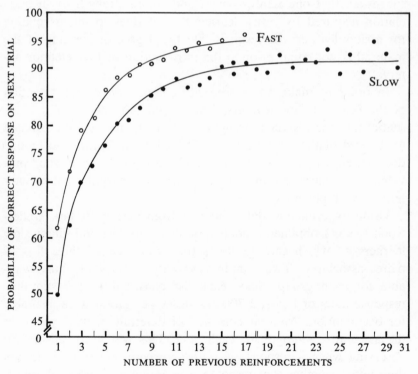

Fig. 11–6. The relationship between number of reinforcements during learning and the probability of correct response on next trial for fast and slow learners.

(Adapted from Underwood 1954)

slow learners. It is equally clear that the studies that matched fast and slow learners by equating the number of reinforcements had not equated these learners for associative strength. In order to provide such equality more reinforcements would have to be provided for slow learners than for fast ones. Thus, as Fig. 11–6 indicates, six reinforcements for slow learners provide about the same associative strength as three reinforcements provide for fast learners. When the proportion of items recalled after twenty-four hours for fast and slow learners for each level of associative strength was plotted, as has been done in Fig. 11–7, no consistent differences were shown to exist between the groups. Underwood (1954) thus concluded that when associative strength at the end of learning is equivalent for fast and slow learners, no difference in retention can be expected.

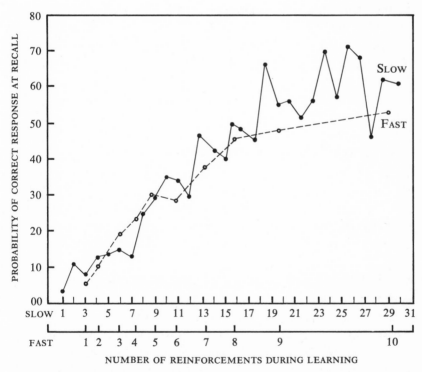

Fig. 11–7. Retention of fast and slow learners after twenty-four hours when associations are equated for strength at the end of learning.
(Adapted from Underwood 1954)

The Role of Warm-up in Retention

In the chapter on transfer (Chapter 10), we examined the construct of warm-up and reviewed some of the studies that investigated the influence of this variable within the transfer situation. Another area of inquiry is the contribution of warm-up to retention.

One of the early studies examining warm-up effects on the recall of verbal material was performed by Irion (1949). In this study (experiment 2) subjects were required to learn a fifteen-unit list of paired two-syllable adjectives. All groups were given ten trials of original learning. Group A was then given twenty-four hours of rest followed by one trial of color-naming. Color-naming was designated as the warm-up task so that the colors were arranged in paired-associate fashion and presented on the memory drum at the same rate of presentation as the adjectives. Subjects were instructed not to attempt to learn the colors but merely to name the second color of each pair as it appeared in the window of the drum. Thus the task provided was similar to the learning task but would not, it was believed, increase the degree of learning of the originally learned activity. Ten relearning trials were then provided. Group B was also given a twenty-four hour rest period but the color-naming task was not provided prior to the ten relearning trials. Finally, Group C was given the ten relearning trials immediately following the first ten. Using the total number of correct anticipations during the first ten learning trials as the initial measure, three analyses of covariance were conducted on the scores obtained on the first relearning trial. The first of these compared Group C (no rest condition) with Group B (twenty-four hour rest without warm-up). This analysis revealed that the no rest condition was significantly superior on this trial. The second analysis compared Group C with Group A (twenty-four hour rest and one warm-up trial) and revealed a nonsignificant difference. A comparison of Group B (twenty-four hour rest without warm-up) with Group A (twenty-four hour rest with warm-up) revealed a significantly superior retention score for Group A. From these findings, Irion (1949) concluded that a significant amount of forgetting had taken place over the twenty-four hour rest period without warm-up before recall, and that the warming-up technique had produced a significant reduction in the amount of this forgetting.

In a second study, Irion and Wham (1951) examined the influence of the amount of warm-up activity on recall and predicted that the greater the amount of such warm-up, the higher the level of recall performance. Six groups of subjects were first given twenty trials to learn a list of nine CVCs in rote serial fashion. One group was then given ten additional relearning trials. The remaining groups were provided rest intervals of varying lengths and varying numbers of warm-up trials, just before undergoing ten relearning trials. The specific length of the rest periods, along with the number of warm-up trials, is presented in Table 11–4. The warm-up task consisted of reciting a list of nine three-digit numbers, where the presentation of the digits was similar to the presentation of the original learning material. In order to minimize the possibility that learning would take place during this period, the digits were arranged in order: 1-2-3, 4-5-6, 7-8-9, 1-2-3, etc. Since the subjects were informed of this arrangement, it was possible for all subjects to anticipate each number correctly, beginning with the first warm-up trial. The general findings are indicated in Table 11–5. Again, warm-up had a facilitating effect, and all three warm-up conditions produced recall scores on the first relearning trial that were superior to those obtained without warm-up.

TABLE 11–4

PLAN OF EXPERIMENT

Condition	No. Trials Original Learning	Length of Rest	No. Trials Warming Up	No. Trials Relearning
I	20	no rest	0	10
II	20	35'0"	0	10
III	20	34'50"	0.5	10
IV	20	34'36"	1	10
V	20	34'12"	2	10
VI	20	33'24"	4	10

(Adapted from Irion and Wham 1951)

TABLE 11–5

MEAN CORRECT ANTICIPATIONS ON TRIALS
TWENTY AND TWENTY-ONE

Condition	Warming-Up Trials	Mean Correct Anticipations		Difference
		Trial 20	Trial 21	
I	—	6.00	6.00	0.00
II	0	6.07	4.40	−1.62
III	0.5	6.00	5.67	−0.33
IV	1	6.20	5.46	−0.74
V	2	5.87	5.53	−0.34
VI	4	4.53	5.87	+1.34

(Adapted from Irion and Wham 1951)

Some investigators (Rockway and Duncan 1952, Dinner and Duncan 1959) were unable to replicate the Irion (1949), and Irion and Wham (1951) experimental findings; however Adams (1961), in an extensive review of the literature, concluded that the experimental evidence demonstrates that the warm-up effect, particularly in the area of verbal learning and recall, is a bona fide phenomenon. As he noted, however, there are a disconcerting number of negative findings so that we cannot be sure what variables are contributing to the discrepant results.

RETENTION IN RELATION TO OTHER LEARNING VARIABLES

A survey of retention studies reveals that a number of early investigators were interested in examining retention as a function of a variety of variables. Davis (1935) examined eighteen studies using meaningless material and twenty-four studies using meaningful material; he concluded that meaningful material was retained better than meaningless material. This finding was echoed by McGeoch and Irion (1952), who wrote that "there is good ground for concluding that meaningful materials . . . are usually much better retained than are nonsense materials and others learned by rote" (p. 383). Serial list position and distribution of practice, as well as the similarity of the materials used, have also been examined by a variety of investigators in order to determine the influence these variables have on retention (Hovland 1940, 1940a; Underwood 1952, 1952a, 1953, 1953a, 1953b; Underwood and Richardson 1955).

The basic problem with these studies, however, is that the associative strengths of the varying types of experimental material have not been held constant. The typical procedure has been to have the experimental groups learn the material to some criterion, following which a retention test is provided, some minutes or hours later. As we noted earlier, the associative strengths of the different types of experimental materials are not equal upon reaching the learning criterion, so such differences continue to be reflected in measures of retention.

More recent studies have found that when the associative strengths of the varying types of experimental material are held constant, the amount of material retained is also constant. For example, Underwood and Richardson (1956) were interested in examining retention as a function of intralist similarity, meaningfulness, and serial position. When these investigators adjusted associative strengths so that, at the conclusion of the learning trials, the expected probabilities of immediate recall were the same for all items, they concluded that there was no evidence that any of these variables contributed to superior retention.

Similarly, Postman and Rau (1957), in examining the retention of nonsense syllables and words, found no difference between these two types of material when their associative strengths at the end of the learning trials were equated.

SHORT TERM RETENTION

As we noted in the introduction to this chapter, considerable interest has been generated in short term retention during this past decade. A survey of this ocean of literature reveals that most of the experimental work has been directed toward an examination of the theoretical mechanisms that appear to be involved in retention decrement (or forgetting)—we shall discuss this topic in Chapter 12. In this section, we should like to delineate the variety of operations that have been used to investigate short term memory, and then briefly discuss how some specific variables influence short term retention performance.

MEMORY SPAN

The development of those operations involved in the measurement of the memory span cannot be said to be recent since they were introduced by Jacobs in 1887. In the typical procedure used, the experimenter tells the subject that a series of numbers (or letters) will be presented and instructs the subject to then recall the numbers in the same order. A short list is used first, to which single items are added until the subject can no longer reproduce the items. It has been acknowledged that a subject does not have a fixed memory span, that is, he is not limited to remembering one quantity of items; but rather, his performance may vary from one trial to the next. Although there is a reasonable degree of constancy in an individual's memory span there is some variation; as a result, the memory span is defined as a statistical average—the number of items that have a probability of .50 of being correctly reproduced. The average adult is able to recall about seven digits or letters accurately 50 percent of the time.

For a long time, the memory span attracted attention as (1) a fundamental aspect of an organism's mental ability and (2) representing a process that could be investigated as a function of a variety of variables, i.e., sensory, modality, etc., but at the same time as independent of other types of memory. Recently, there has been increasing recognition that memory span operations are on the same continuum as other memory operations. Thus, some investigators who examined memory span, i.e., Pollack, Johnson and Knaff (1959), indicated the continuity of memory span and long term retention, by indicating that an important consideration in memory span performance is related to interference effects provided by the material presented.

SHORT TERM RETENTION METHODS

Although the operations defining memory span have had a long history, the procedures involved in the measurement of short term memory or retention have not. As we indicated earlier, short term retention studies were introduced by Brown (1958), and Peterson and Peterson (1959) at the end of the fifties. It will be recalled that Peterson and Peterson's procedure consisted of orally presenting three consonants immediately followed by the exposure of a three-digit number. The subject counted backward by threes or fours from that number until a cue was received to recall the consonants.

This procedure, in which the retention interval is filled with a kind of activity that is unlike the original task, has been called the distractor technique, since the primary objective is to distract the subject so that rehearsal of the material does not take place.

A second method utilized in the study of short term memory is the probe technique. Although it was Waugh and Norman (1965) who were responsible for naming this procedure, Anderson (1960) and Sperling (1960) were among the early investigators who used the method. Here, the retention interval is filled, not with material dissimilar to the original items but with items similar to those used in the original presentation. In Anderson's (1960) study, lists of twelve digits were presented in groups of four. Thus, the subject would hear, 4, 5, 3, 9, pause, 2, 1, 6, 8, pause, 3, 2, 7, 4. Zero, five or thirty seconds after the last digit had been read, the subjects were instructed to recall the first, second, or third grouping of numbers. About the same time, Sperling (1960) used the tachistoscopic presentation of letters with similar type of task instructions following the presentation. The procedure of instructing the subject what part of the total stimulus presentation to recall following its exposure has been termed "post-stimulus cueing."

Murdock (1961, 1963a) also used the probe technique in examining the short term retention of serial lists or paired-associates. As used in these early studies, a paired-associate list is presented once, following which the subject is immediately tested for the recall of just one of the pairs. Presentation of the stimulus serves as a cue for the recall of the response. A fixed rate of presentation is used so that the number of pairs following the pair to be recalled determines the length of the retention interval. If a serial learning task is employed, recall is signalled by the presentation of an item that appeared previously in the list; the response is the item that followed.

The probe technique, unlike the distractor technique, does not permit the experimenter to distinguish between the effects of interference generated by the additional items that are presented and the effects of elapsed time per se. On the other hand, this procedure has the advantage of making rehearsal difficult, inasmuch as the subject does not know which items to rehearse. In contrast to Keppel (1965), who indicated that much more forgetting takes place when the probe technique is used in contrast to the distraction procedure, Murdock (1967) obtained experimental evidence that supports the position that it is the number of items to be remembered rather than the nature of the interpolated task that determines the retention function. Murdock (1967) wrote, "the same retention function appears under both conditions; the rate constants apparently differ but the function itself does not" (p. 33).

Short term memory has been examined also in a continuous or sequential task situation. One such experimental procedure, utilized by Lloyd, Reid and Feallock (1960), and Yntema and Mueser (1960) consists of presentation of a long series of items, during which the experimenter interrupts from time to time to request the subject to recall a previously presented item. In the Lloyd, Reid and Feallock (1960) study, for example, the subjects might hear the words: *pine, tin, polo, METAL, copper, TREE,* etc. With the presentation of the word *METAL,* the subject would be expected to recall the word denoted by metal, i.e., *tin,* and when *TREE* was presented the subject would be expected to recall *pine.* A somewhat similar procedure employing the recognition response was introduced by Shepard and Teghtsoonian (1961). Here, three-digit numbers were placed on index cards; the subject was given a pack of cards and instructed to examine the number on each card and indicate whether that number was "old" or "new," depending on whether he remembered having seen the number on a card presented earlier. Subjects were permitted to proceed through the deck at their own rate but were not permitted to look back to earlier cards. Feedback concerning the correctness of responses was not provided.

VARIABLES INFLUENCING SHORT TERM RETENTION

Some investigators, like their counterparts who examined long term retention, have been interested in determining how a variety of variables influence short term retention.

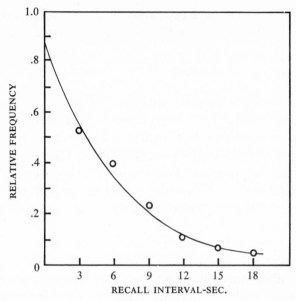

Fig. 11–8. Correct recalls with latencies below 2.83 sec. as a function of recall interval.

(Adapted from Peterson and Peterson 1959)

THE LENGTH OF THE DELAY INTERVAL

In Peterson and Peterson's (1959) early study, the basic variable examined was the time interval that was interpolated between the presentation of the material and the cue for recall. It will be recalled that the experimental procedure consisted of orally presenting to each subject a single CCC followed by a three-digit number. The subject then counted backward by threes or fours from this number until a cue for the recall of the trigram was provided. Each subject was tested eight times at three, six, nine, twelve, fifteen or eighteen seconds. Responses made during a fifteen-second interval following the signal for recall were recorded. Correct recalls with latencies below 2.83 seconds as a function of the recall interval are indicated in Fig. 11–8.[1] These findings, which indicate that short term retention is a function of the length

[1] It would have been possible to use any number of other latency values but the recall function would not have materially changed. The 2.83 value was used since the mean latency of all correct responses was 2.83.

of the recall interval, have been replicated by a whole host of subsequent investigators, i.e., Hellyer (1962), Talland (1967), etc.

NUMBER OF PRESENTATIONS

Although it is a common procedure to present short term retention material for only a single trial, early investigators were interested in examining how such retention varied as a function of number of presentations. Although Peterson and Peterson (1959) reported evidence of a progressive improvement in recall with an increase in the number of repetitions of the material, Hellyer's (1962) study examining this variable was somewhat more extensive.

In this experiment, each consonant syllable was presented either one, two, four, or eight times. Following the last presentation, intervals of either three, nine, eighteen, or twenty-seven seconds were provided prior to the recall of the syllable. The proportion of items correctly recalled as a function of number of presentations as well as recall delay intervals is presented in Table 11–6.

CHARACTERISTICS OF THE DELAY INTERVAL

An important issue facing experimenters who examine short term retention is how the retention interval will be filled. A frequently employed activity is the backward number counting task devised by Peterson and Peterson (1959). Subsequent investigators have used a variety of other procedures such as number adding

TABLE 11–6

PROPORTIONS OF ITEMS CORRECTLY RECALLED

Number of Presentations	Recall Delay Interval (Sec.)			
	3	9	18	27
8	.99	.89	.74	.66
4	.94	.73	.56	.46
2	.92	.54	.31	.22
1	.89	.38	.21	.14

(Adapted from Hellyer 1962)

or subtracting, number reading, color-naming, etc. The rationale for the use of a particular type of activity is rarely provided, other than that it presumably prevents rehearsal. It is the opinion of most investigators, however, that it would be most unlikely if any task completely suppressed rehearsal. For example, Wickens, Born and Allen (1963) report that some subjects were heard rehearsing during a color-naming task. These investigators also noted a tendency for latencies of color-naming to increase over trials; thus, one might infer from these lengthened latencies some tendency on the part of the subject to rehearse.

It might be anticipated that any activity that encourages re-hearsal or practice would also increase recall. Brelsford and At-kinson (1968) had subjects repeat their originally presented ma-terial twice, in contrast to a condition in which the subject was instructed to study the material silently. Results indicated the su-periority of recall for the overt rehearsal condition.

Another facet of how the retention interval will be filled has to do with the characteristics of the task itself.

Studies by Talland (1967), and Dillon and Reid (1969) have demonstrated that retention is related to the difficulty of the task provided during the retention interval. In Talland's study, follow-ing the presentation of a series of consonants, the delay interval for one group of subjects was filled by a subtraction task (diffi-cult); for the second group, a reading (easy) task was used. This latter group read the same numbers that were verbalized by the first experimental group in performing their subtraction task. Two other variables were examined—the number of consonants pre-sented in the original task, three, four, or five, and the length of the retention interval, which was either three, six, nine, twelve, fifteen or eighteen seconds. Talland found that the reading of numbers in contrast to the subtraction task during the recall inter-val resulted in increased recall of the consonants. He also obtained the interesting finding that recall was not influenced by the ac-curacy with which the subtraction task was performed. As might be anticipated, the amount of recall was inversely related to the other two variables manipulated—the number of consonants that made up the original task, and the length of the recall interval.

In the Dillon and Reid (1969) study, four experiments were run, in which the general procedure consisted of presentation of a trigram, after which the subject performed an easy or difficult task, or combination of these, for 15 seconds. For the easy task, the subject read two digits aloud; for the difficult task, the subject had to report the sum of these digits as well as to indicate whether their sum was odd or even.

As would be expected from Talland's (1967) findings, recall of the trigrams when the easy task filled the retention interval was superior to recall when a difficult task filled this interval. One interesting result was that if equal amounts of time in the retention interval were devoted to both an easy and difficult task, the presentation of the difficult task first resulted in greater forgetting than if the easy task was presented first.

The studies of both Talland (1967), and Dillon and Reid (1969) support the position that the presentation of the easier task during the recall interval permits more time for rehearsal of the to-be-recalled material. At a theoretical level, it has been proposed that the short term memory system of the individual has limited capacity that in turn limits the amount of information that can be processed. The forgetting of the original material results because the demands placed on the central processing system of the individual exceed the capacity required to perform the interpolated task and rehearse the recall items.

But does the rehearsal task consist of nothing more than a kind of automatic repetition of the material to be recalled? Sanders (1961) and Neisser (1967) suggested that whether increased recall results from rehearsal appears to depend upon the assimilation of the material by means of interpretation, imposition of rhythms, findings of rules, etc., rather than mere automatic repetition. In a sense, then, there is the suggestion that "rehearsal" is a process bearing a marked similarity to coding.

MEANINGFULNESS

Since meaningfulness has been demonstrated to play an important role in the multiple trial learning of verbal material, it is not surprising that a variety of dimensions of this variable, i.e., association value, word frequency, pronunciability, abstractness, etc., have been investigated using the short term retention paradigm. One of the early studies was performed by Peterson, Peterson and Miller (1961), who investigated association value. In their first experiment, three-letter words, as well as high and low association trigrams, were used as experimental material. Each three-letter item was presented for 1.1 seconds following which the subject was asked to count backwards for six seconds. The subjects were then asked to recall the original item. Results indicated that the proportion of items recalled was a function of the meaningfulness of the material; thus, low association trigrams were recalled 58 percent of the time, high association trigrams 64 percent of the time, and words were recalled 85 percent of the time. In a second experiment, for which just words and low association trigrams were used, one- and six-second recall intervals were investigated. No difference in recall for the two types of material at the one-second recall interval was obtained; at six seconds, however, the proportion of items recalled for the two types of material approximated the findings obtained in experiment 1.

Lindley's (1963a) experimental material consisted of three-letter words, syllables, or low association value trigrams. Following the presentation of a single item, retention intervals of either three, thirteen, or thirty-nine seconds were provided, following which the subject was asked to recall the item presented. During the retention interval, the subject read rows of random digits. Findings were similar to those obtained by Peterson, Peterson and Miller (1961), in that retention was found to be a function of the meaningfulness of the material. Moreover, the retention of each type of material decreased as a function of the length of the retention interval. Fig. 11–9 illustrates these findings.

In a more recent study, Turnage (1967) was interested in the role of word frequency. Twenty high frequency and twenty low frequency two-syllable nouns made up the experimental material. In addition to word frequency, retention intervals of two, five, fifteen and thirty seconds were also examined. In keeping with the Peterson and Peterson (1959) procedure, each subject was shown a single word and then required to count backwards until receiving the cue for recall. Results indicated that at the short retention intervals, high frequency words were better recalled than low.[1]

[1] An unusual finding of this study was that at the thirty-second retention interval, low frequency words were better recalled than high. Since recall of the low frequency words did not reveal a retention decrement—low frequency

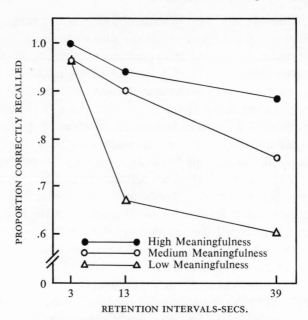

Fig. 11–9. Proportions correctly recalled.
(Adapted from Lindley 1963a)

In a study examining pronunciability, Gorfein and Stone (1967) hypothesized that if each trigram in a short term memory study were presented so that the interval of presentation was adjusted to the pronunciation latency, differences among trigrams in ease of recall would be significantly reduced. Using easy-to-pronounce and difficult-to-pronounce trigrams (as indicated by the pronunciation latencies of these syllables provided by Lindley and Stone 1966), these investigators utilized a standard presentation condition (control) that consisted of presenting all items for 2.05 seconds—the average presentation interval for the trigrams of condition 1. In the experimental condition, the interval of presentation for the trigrams was varied to correspond to the mean pronunciation latencies of the syllables.

Results supported the investigators' hypothesis in that in the control condition, where the intervals of presentation were con-

words were recalled as well after a thirty-second interval as after one or two seconds—as has been typically demonstrated when retention intervals have been lengthened, the reliability of Turnage's findings should be established before any attempt is made to "explain" them.

stant, there was a large and significant effect of pronunciability on recall of the original items. On the other hand, in the experimental condition that controlled for the pronunciation latency, no differences were found.

In summary, these authors found that shortening the presentation interval for easy-to-pronounce syllables did not increase recall errors for those syllables; lengthening the presentation intervals for the difficult-to-pronounce trigrams, however, did improve recall.

Laughery and Pinkus (1968) examined the role of pronunciability as well as meaningfulness when the material used was beyond the memory span of their subjects. Sequences of twelve letters served as the experimental material. Each sequence was composed of four three-letter units in which meaningfulness and pronunciability were manipulated as follows:

(1) the units were three-letter words providing a pronounceable and meaningful sequence, i.e., FUNPEGPUTJAB;

(2) meaningful and familiar three-letter abbreviations used formed nonpronounceable twelve-letter sequences, i.e., CIAB-TUCIODDS;

(3) three-letter CVCs used were pronounceable but meaningless, i.e., NUFGEPTUPTIB;

(4) three-letter groupings used produced a meaningless as well as unpronounceable unit, i.e., WGWIATMPCTOU.

In brief, then, four kinds of items were used: (1) meaningful and pronounceable; (2) meaningful and unpronounceable, (3) meaningless and pronounceable; and (4) meaningless and unpronounceable.

Those subjects who were to be presented with one of these four kinds of material were given information indicating the nature of the material. Thus, one group was instructed that the twelve-item sequences could be grouped into four three-letter words. A second group was told that the sequence could be divided into three-letter abbreviations, while a third group was told that the sequence could be broken up into pronounceable but meaningless syllables. The group that was given the meaningless and unpronounceable items was told only that the sequences would contain twelve items.

In addition to the characteristics of the material, these investigators were interested also in presentation rate; thus each twelve-letter sequence was presented for either .3, .6, 1.0, 2.0, or 3.0 seconds. Immediately following such presentation, subjects recorded their responses on answer sheets. The mean number of letters correct per sequence for the various experimental conditions is plotted in Fig. 11–10. Although it may appear surprising that the memory for meaningful, unpronounceable items is poorer than for those that were meaningless and pronounceable, the authors indicated that a likely explanation for this effect is based on the efficiency of implicit rehearsal. They have suggested that in the typical memory-span task most subjects report using the inter-item intervals to rehearse those items that have already been presented, and since the time required to pronounce a CVC syllable is less

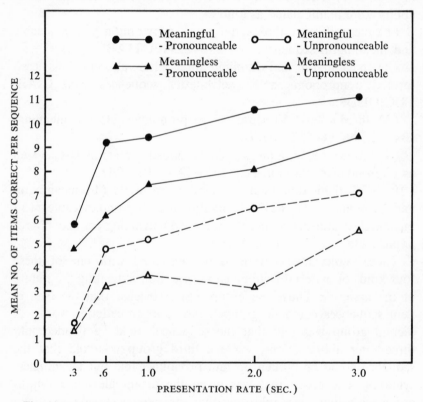

Fig. 11–10. Mean number of items correct for various experimental conditions.

(Adapted from Laughery and Pinkus 1968)

than the time needed to pronounce the individual letters, rehearsal is maximized in the meaningless-pronounceable condition.

A subsequent study by Stanners and Meunier (1969) also supported the position that rehearsal efficiency is higher with easy-to-pronounce than with difficult-to-pronounce items.

Finally, Borkowski and Eisner (1968) examined the influence of abstractness and meaningfulness, defining meaningfulness in terms of Noble's (1952) *m*. A measure of abstractness was obtained by using an abstraction scale developed by Spreen and Schulz (1966). One-syllable nouns, with similar Thorndike-Lorge (1944) frequency counts, were selected so that two groups of nouns differed with regard to *m* but were equated on abstractness; two other groups of nouns were equated on *m* but differed on abstractness. Three experiments were run, and the general procedure consisted of presenting sets of either four or five words for three seconds, followed by a short (three- or four-second) or long eighteen- or twenty-second) retention interval. During this interval, subjects were instructed to count forward by ones from a three-digit number. A six-second recall period was then provided. The findings obtained from these experiments indicated that abstractness is an important determinant of retention when varied independently of *m*. Meaningfulness, on the other hand, appeared to be significant only if abstractness is not controlled.

In the previous section on long term retention, we discussed Underwood's (1964) position that because differing types of material have been learned to the same criterion, it cannot be assumed that they are equivalent with regard to associative strength. A similar situation occurs in some of the short term retention studies we have just examined. That is, although items of differential meaningfulness or pronunciability, etc. are capable of being reproduced perfectly by the subject immediately following their presentation, it cannot be assumed that such items have been "learned" equally well. Keppel (1965) concluded that most experimental findings indicating that one type of material provides better short term retention than another are suspect since it is likely that the associative strengths of the items have not been equated.

One possible solution to the problem proposed by Keppel (1965) and Underwood (1964) is that the latency of the individ-

ual's responding might be used as a more sensitive index of associative strengths at immediate recall. But there are problems with
this solution since the correlation between latency and correctness
of recall is not very high. Adams (1967) ventured the opinion that
there is

no good solution at this time to the control of associative strength. . . .
When different types of items enter each treatment condition, the experimenter must face the problem that differences at recall may be as much an
effect of differences in associative strength as of other variables being manipulated (p. 143).

SERIAL POSITION EFFECTS

An examination of the influence of serial position using the
short term retention paradigm was made by Peterson and Peterson
(1962). In one study, two paired-associates were presented. Thus,
a stimulus word was followed by the presentation of a response
word; this procedure was repeated for the second pair. Following
the presentation of the second response, a retention interval of
either four, eight, or sixteen seconds was provided, during which
subjects were instructed to count backward. In one condition following an appropriate time interval, the subject was asked to recall
the response associated with the first stimulus word, whereas in a
second condition, the subject was asked to recall the response associated with the second stimulus word. Recall scores revealed that
performance was superior when the response of the first pair rather
than that of the second pair was required. This is somewhat unusual since the presentation of the second response was closer in
time to the recall period than was the first response. Current investigators have called this a primacy effect and its influence was
examined in a second experiment using three paired-associates. In
this study, three pairs of items were presented, and following a
retention interval of twelve seconds, one of the three stimuli appeared to cue the subject's response. The results revealed that the
primacy effect continued to be present. In general the response to
the first stimulus was recalled most frequently, followed by the response to the second stimulus, while the response to the third
stimulus was recalled least frequently.

Coding and the Concept of Chunks

In our discussion of the memory span it was pointed out that the average adult is able to recall about seven digits or letters accurately 50 percent of the time.[1] Thus, the probability of recall is related to the number of units presented.

There is a problem, however, in determining what constitutes a unit. It is obvious that although the memory span for the average individual may be seven unrelated letters, if those seven letters make up a word, the individual's memory span would go well beyond it. It was Miller (1956) who was responsible for calling attention to the fact that within the immediate memory span, the individual groups the items into familiar units. Miller called these units "chunks." The important point made by Miller is that although the span for immediate memory appears to be relatively fixed at about seven chunks, the amount of material that is recalled can be increased effectively by building larger and larger chunks. That is, by appropriate coding operations the individual can combine a number of small chunks into a larger one and thus increase the amount of material that can be recalled.

An excellent example he uses to illustrate this phenomenon is that of a man just beginning to learn telegraphic code. At first the man hears each dit and dah as a separate chunk, but soon he is able to organize these sounds into letters so that he deals with letters as chunks. After some practice, the letters organize themselves into words, which become larger chunks. Following this, the operator begins to hear whole phrases as chunks. We see, then, that as larger and larger chunks emerge in the learning of the code, the amount of the message that the operator can remember increases accordingly.

An early study by Murdock (1961) indicated that the number

---

[1] Ross (1969) assumed however that when items must be retained in exact sequential order, an average of only four or five items is retained. Digit span, both because of previous item familiarity and the manner in which it is measured, working up to the longest sequence by practice on shorter ones, gives a considerable overestimate of the number of items an individual typically retains when he has no preconceptions to aid him (p. 339). An experimental study by Ross (1969) indicated the reliability of this assumption, since it found that the adult's average span for items in an unpatterned series was about four.

of chunks of material presented during the short term memory procedure was an important consideration. In one study of a series, the Peterson and Peterson (1959) procedure was replicated, except that the duration of the interpolated activity was zero, three, six, nine, twelve, or eighteen seconds, so that a zero-second interval was substituted for the fifteen-second interval. Three different types of material were used: (a) CCC trigrams, (b) monosyllabic high frequency words, and (c) three monosyllabic words. The findings indicated in Table 11–7 show the mean proportion of correct recalls at each retention interval. It can be noted that although single words were recalled significantly better than the CCC trigrams, there is a marked similarity between the correct recalls of the word triads and the CCC trigrams. The authors argued that the constant syllables and word triads consist of three items (or chunks) to be remembered, while an individual word is only a single item.

It is possible for coding to influence short term retention. In one study demonstrating the role of coding, Lindley (1963a) used trigrams that differed in level of meaningfulness. High meaningful trigrams were words, medium meaningful trigrams were syllables, and low meaningful trigrams were nonsyllables. Three retention intervals, of either three, thirteen, or thirty-nine seconds, were

TABLE 11–7

MEAN PROPORTION OF CORRECT RECALLS AT EACH
RETENTION INTERVAL: EXPERIMENT I

Retention Interval	Session 1 CCC Trigrams		Session 2 Words		Session 3 Word Triads	
	Mean	SD	Mean	SD	Mean	SD
0 sec.	.94	.11	.98	.04	.93	.10
3 sec.	.77	.15	.99	.03	.73	.21
6 sec.	.40	.18	.96	.07	.39	.23
9 sec.	.26	.19	.91	.10	.30	.21
12 sec.	.24	.14	.86	.11	.31	.22
18 sec.	.16	.12	.84	.14	.23	.16

(Adapted from Murdock 1961)

utilized. Recording cues consisted of having the trigram to be recalled typed in capital letters and then providing additional lower case letters in appropriate positions to make a complete English word. Thus, the trigram CQU was coded by presenting the additional lower case letters necessary to make the word *acquire*. When word trigrams were used, these were coded into different words by providing additional letters; i.e., *wash*. As with typical short term retention studies, only a single item was presented, followed by a retention interval, followed by recall. During the retention interval, the subject was requested to read a row of random digits; he was instructed to perform this task as rapidly as possible and not to rehearse the items that had been presented. Results revealed that the proportion of items correctly recalled decreased as a function of the retention interval. With regard to the coding function, an interaction was found between recoding cues and meaningfulness. In brief, then, the presence of coding cues facilitated the recall of low meaningful items but interfered with the retention of high meaningful items.

SUMMARY

Contemporary investigations of retention can be divided into (1) long term and (2) short term operations. In traditional or long term retention studies, all subjects are given learning trials until they reach some criterion. A retention interval, usually measured in minutes or hours, is then provided, following which a retention test is given. Short term retention studies involved the single-trial presentation of an amount of material that is within the memory span of the subject; a recall interval measured in seconds is then provided, followed by a retention test.

The most frequently used retention measures are recall and recognition. Although it has been generally accepted that the recognition measure yields a higher score than recall, there is now awareness of the fact that any difference between these response measures is a function of the conditions under which these measures are obtained. It has been experimentally demonstrated that recognition scores are related to the number and characteristics of the distractors used. Moreover, studies in which these measures have been compared have not controlled for the degree of original learning.

Contemporary interest in long term retention has been directed toward determining whether those variables that result in differential learning scores make a similar contribution to differences in retention. The general procedure has been to have the varying experimental groups (e.g., groups learning material differing in meaningfulness) reach the same criterion. A retention test is then provided following some interval measured in minutes or hours. A common assumption with this type of design has been that once the criterion is reached, the degree of learning or associative strength for the varying experimental groups is equivalent.

Underwood (1964) pointed to what he believes is a major difficulty with this position. He reasoned that the criterion trial provides the varying groups with differential amounts of learning that is not measured. This, in turn, confounds retention scores. In order to remedy this difficulty, Underwood proposed a projection method that involves an estimation or a projection of the performance that would be expected following the criterion trial. Experimental studies examining the contribution of a variety of learning variables, e.g., meaningfulness, intralist similarity, etc., in which associative strengths have been adjusted so that the varying groups are equivalent in associative strength at the conclusion of the learning trials, have been unable to provide any support for the position that any of these variables contribute to superior retention.

Typical short term retention studies have consisted of presenting a trigram followed by the exposure of a three-digit number. The subject is requested to count backwards by threes or fours from this number until a signal is given for him to recall the trigram. This type of procedure has been termed the distractor technique, since the major objective of the backward counting procedure is to prevent the subject from rehearsing the to-be-recalled item. A second short term retention method, the probe technique, consists of filling the retention interval with items similar to those used in the original presentation. The subject is then instructed as to what part of the total stimulus presentation he should recall. In comparing the two procedures, the probe technique does not permit the experimenter to distinguish between the effects of interference generated by the additional items presented and the effects of elapsed time per se. On the other hand, this procedure has the advantage of making rehearsal difficult, inasmuch as the subject does not know which item to rehearse.

Investigators have been interested in a variety of variables that influence short term retention. Many studies have examined the length and characteristics of the delay interval, number of presentations, and the meaningfulness of the material used; superior retention has been found when the delay interval is short and more meaningful material is used.

12 Forgetting Processes and Dual Theories of Memory

Forgetting is obviously the other side of retention. While retention refers to the amount of previously learned material that persists or has been retained by the subject, forgetting refers to the amount the subject has lost or has not retained. Although one may use "retention decrement" synonymously with the construct of forgetting, the term forgetting has frequently been used when investigators have been interested in directing attention to those processes or mechanisms they believe can account for retention loss. Thus, a theory of forgetting refers to the postulation of a process (or processes) that can account for a loss in retention over a period of time.

In Chapter 11, we considered long term retention apart from short term retention. Current theoretical formulations demand that we make this same distinction in our examination of forgetting.

LONG TERM FORGETTING

The psychology of learning and retention from the time of Ebbinghaus (1885) until the late 1950s was primarily concerned with multiple-trial learning—beyond memory span material—and retention intervals measured in minutes, hours, or days. It is not surprising, therefore, that theoretical formulations of forgetting were generated to handle the retention decrement that would be found in this kind of situation. Accordingly, we may designate these as long term forgetting theories.

458

Over a period of time, measured in hours or days, a subject will typically forget some of the material he originally learned; some investigators have focused on this time period as providing the reason why people forget. That is, since time appears to be the common denominator in virtually all instances of forgetting, it is not surprising that time has been looked on by some as the basic contributor to forgetting.

A second point of view has been to emphasize time-related variables. Thus, some early experimenters hypothesized disuse as the important variable. During the time between the learning and the attempted recall, the material has not been used; hence, it has been forgotten.

A related point of view has been to emphasize physiological factors. Here, forgetting has been explained in terms of a spontaneous decay of the memory trace. As time passes, normal bodily processes result in a fading of the trace; this is mirrored in the behavioral changes we term forgetting.

Although many early psychologists supported disuse as a primary explanation of forgetting, the experimental work of Jenkins and Dallenbach (1924), and a replication of this study by Van Ormer (1932) were important attacks against this position. In the Jenkins and Dallenbach experiment, subjects first learned a list of ten CVCs to a criterion of one perfect trial. After one, two, four, or eight hours of either (a) ordinary waking activity, or (b) sleeping, subjects were asked to recall the material. The results, as indicated in Fig. 12–1, indicated that CVCs were retained better after intervals of sleeping than after corresponding periods of wakefulness. Since the same amount of time, or interval during which the material was not used, occurred between the original learning and the test for recall, it is difficult to account for the differential forgetting using time or disuse as an explanation. Ekstrand (1967) recently obtained similar results.

These experimental findings were used by McGeoch (1932) in his now classic paper attacking disuse or time as a fundamental variable in forgetting. A basic point made by McGeoch was that time should be thought of merely as a conceptual framework within which events take place. The iron bar that is tossed in the field does not rust because of time; rather, oxygen from the air combines with the iron to produce rust, and this process takes place

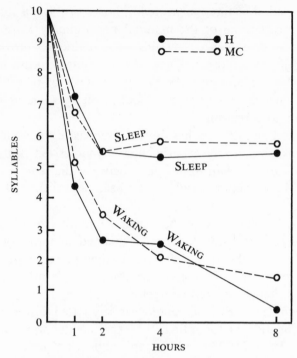

Fig. 12–1. Average number of syllables recalled after intervals of sleeping and waking.

(Adapted from Jenkins and Dallenbach 1924)

within a time interval. Further, a bar placed in a vacuum does not accumulate rust regardless of the amount of time it remains there. In short, environmental events themselves, rather than time intervals alone, must be considered in order to account for forgetting. McGeoch (1932) believed that if the interval of time interpolated between learning and recall was entirely devoid of activity, retention would be perfect. He wrote, "recall after sleep is sufficiently high to support the inference that, could an interval be rendered absolutely empty of events, a vacuum mentally, and the conditions of learning and of recall equated, there would be no forgetting" pp. 361–362.[1]

[1] Another point of view was expressed by Adams (1967), who wrote that McGeoch was wrong in discounting trace theory because time is the independent variable. A measure of time is a perfectly respectable independent variable and

RETROACTIVE AND PROACTIVE INHIBITION

McGeoch (1932) believed that the basic factor contributing to forgetting was the activity interpolated between the original learning and the test for retention. This condition has been given the name "retroactive inhibition," following the usage of Müller and Pilzecker (1900). The term thus refers to a retention decrement resulting from activity interpolated between the original learning and the test for retention. The experimental design that typically has been utilized is as follows:

Retroactive inhibition

Experimental group	learn A	learn B	recall A
Control group	learn A	rest	recall A

It has been also acknowledged that learning that has taken place prior to the learning and recall of material may inhibit recall. The interference that such activity provides has been designated proactive inhibition and the experimental design employed is as follows:

Proactive inhibition

Experimental group	learn B	learn A	recall A
Control group	rest	learn A	recall A

has been throughout the history of science. Certainly it is unnecessary for a scientific law to say *why* time has the effects it does. In general terms, lawfulness only requires that (1) a dependent variable be a specifiable function of one or more independent variables, and (2) the variables be defined objectively so that any scientist can manipulate them. Time, in this general sense, is as defensible an independent variable as one could name. . . . Time deserves an unquestioned role in science as long as it can be shown to be a reliable determinant of dependent variables. Other processes working in time may be uncovered eventually and lead to new laws and a science may come to regard these new laws as more fundamental for explanation (p. 25).

Adams' position is reasonable providing that "time . . . can be shown to be a reliable determinant of dependent variables." It would appear, however, that time frequently does not have such reliability since as the early Jenkins and Dallenbach (1924), and Van Ormer (1932) studies showed, differential activities taking place over identical time intervals produce differences in the dependent variable.

It should be recognized that these designs may result in retro-active or proactive facilitation as well as inhibition; investigators interested in forgetting have, of course, been concerned with in-hibition-related variables.

VARIABLES THAT CONTRIBUTE TO PROACTIVE AND RETROACTIVE INHIBITION

A variety of experimental variables have been examined in order to determine their influence on proactive and retroactive inhibition. Two of these, (a) similarity and (b) degree of learning, have been investigated extensively.

SIMILARITY

SIMILARITY OF STIMULUS AND RESPONSE

It will be recalled that in our chapter on transfer, we mentioned that Osgood (1949) had constructed a three-dimensional surface relating similarity of stimuli and responses to kind and amount of transfer. Osgood stated that the general relationships reflected by this transfer surface could also be used to predict proaction and retroaction effects; this position is generally accepted. Some sup-port for this point of view comes from an experiment by Bugelski and Cadwallader (1956), who reported a correlation of $-.85$ between trials to learn interpolated material (transfer) and recall of the original material (retroaction).

In the examination of that part of Osgood's (1949) surface that has primary relevance for this chapter—those stimulus and response relationships that result in negative transfer—we can note that when neutral or opposed responses are attached to identi-cal stimuli and used as sources of interference, retroactive (or pro-active) inhibition should be obtained. As was noted in Chapter 10, Bugelski and Cadwallader (1956) obtained retroactive in-hibition effects when either similar, neutral, or opposed responses were attached to identical stimuli and were used as the interpolated material. But, as revealed in Fig. 10–5, the specific curve form obtained by these investigators is somewhat different from that formulated by Osgood. In contrast, Young (1955), and Gladis and Braun (1958) confirmed that portion of Osgood's surface that posited that inhibitory effects should increase as the interfering responses go from similarity through neutrality.

Saltz and Hamilton (1967) obtained retroactive inhibition when the stimuli in the original and interpolated lists were similar rather than identical. In this study, subjects were trained on an A-B, A'-C paradigm and were then compared with a control group to which a D-C list had been presented during the interpolated learning period. The paired-associate task consisted of CVCs and similarity of stimuli was manipulated by changing one letter of the three, i.e., BIH, BIY. Ten trials were provided on list 1 and eight trials on list 2. Following the last trial of the interpolated material, a one-minute, or one-, five-, or twenty-four-hour rest period was provided, followed by the recall of list 1. The findings can be noted in Fig. 12–2, from which we can see that there is much greater

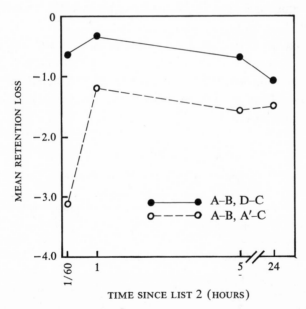

TIME SINCE LIST 2 (HOURS)

Fig. 12–2. Mean retention loss of List 1 for the A-B, A'-C and the A-B, D-C conditions as a function of the interval between List 2 acquisition and subsequent recall of List 1.

(Adapted from Saltz and Hamilton 1967)

retention loss over all of the time intervals for the experimental group that was provided similar stimuli during the learning of the interpolated list. An interesting result is the significant recovery of list 1 items as a function of time following the learning of list 2— an effect that appears to be a function of the similiarity variable, inasmuch as equivalent recovery could not be observed in the A-B, D-C condition.

Studies by a number of investigators, i.e., Morgan and Underwood (1950) and Dallett (1962a), have also demonstrated proactive inhibition effects as a function of the similarity of first- and second-list responses with identical stimuli. In the Morgan and Underwood study, varying groups of subjects learned lists of twelve pairs of two-syllable adjectives; the stimuli on the two lists were identical while the degree of synonymity among the response items was varied through five levels. The first level utilized dissimilar responses, the second only slightly similar, and so on, to the fifth condition, in which the responses employed in the two lists were highly similar. Each list was learned to a criterion of seven correct anticipations on a single trial, following which the second list was relearned to a criterion of one perfect trial. These investigators found that proactive inhibition tended to increase as response similarity decreased. As Table 12–1 reveals, although the function is not a smooth one, there is the tendency for increased proactive inhibition effects to be associated with decreasing amounts of response similarity.

TABLE 12–1

SECOND-LIST RELEARNING SCORES

	Mean Trials to Criterion
List A (Dissimilar responses)	7.42
B	7.88
C	7.63
D	8.12
E	8.21
List F (Very similar responses)	7.71

(Adapted from Morgan and Underwood 1950)

SIMILARITY OF ORGANIZATION

In an earlier chapter, we indicated that organizational cues, i.e., categories, particularly in the free-recall learning task, could play an important role in learning. Shuell (1968) has indicated that the similarity of organizational processes also contribute to retroactive inhibition effects. More specifically, this experimenter hypothesized that retroactive inhibition should be obtained whenever similar organizational cues were used in successive lists in the free-recall situation. In such a situation, an A-B, A-C paradigm could be conceptulized, where A would represent the organizational cues, and B and C terms the words in each of the two lists.

The experimental material consisted of two lists of thirty-five words per list, with each list consisting of seven conceptual categories. For one experimental condition, identical categories were represented in both the original and interpolated lists—the words in each list were, of course, different. For a second experimental condition, the two lists had no categories in common. A control group was not given second-list learning trials. Findings revealed that there was significantly greater forgetting for the experimental groups in contrast to the control; when the two experimental groups were compared, significantly greater retroactive inhibition was present for the group learning the lists that had identical categories.

SIMILARITY OF FORM CLASS

Most studies investigating similarity have employed proactive or retroactive inhibition paradigms in which the material used is of the same form class; that is, the same type of material (CVC, nouns, adjectives, etc.) serves as stimuli and/or responses in the lists to be learned. Recently, some investigators have been interested in manipulating form class in order to determine the influence of this variable on retroactive inhibition.

In one early study, Postman, Keppel and Stark (1965) varied response class in an A-B, A-C paradigm by using adjectives as responses for one of the lists and letters as responses for the other. The stimuli in all instances were single-digit numbers, 2 through

9; the experimental group was provided with two-syllable adjectives as responses in one list and repeated letters, e.g., GG, ZZ, etc., in the other. (Two letters were used so that pronunciation time for the adjectives and letters would be similar.) For the control groups, the responses for both lists were either adjectives or letters. The procedure consisted of having the first list learned to a criterion of one perfect recitation, following which the second list was presented for twenty trials. Following the last learning trial of the second list, a free-recall test was given in which the stimulus terms were presented and the subjects were asked to recall first-list responses; second-list responses were listed for the subjects to see during this test period. Results indicated significantly greater amounts of retroactive inhibition for control groups that had the same type of response or form class in both lists.

Another retroactive inhibition study by Friedman and Reynolds (1967) confirmed as well as extended these findings. In this study an A-B, A-C paradigm was used. The interpolated material consisted of three variations of response class similarity. List 1 responses consisted of CVCs while second-list responses were either (1) CVCs, (2) CCCs, (3) CVs, or (4) three-digit numbers. A control group was asked to fill out a personality inventory during the time required for second-list learning. The stimuli in both lists consisted of small colored disks.

The first list was learned to a criterion of one perfect trial, while second-list items were presented for just twenty trials. Following the last trial, subjects were instructed to recall the appropriate response terms from the first list. These investigators found that the mean number of correct responses for the varying groups was as follows: control 7.7; 3 three-digit numbers 6.7; CVs 5.1; CCCs 5.0; CVCs 3.4.

These general findings indicate a positive relationship between the similarity of response class and amount of retroactive inhibition, and represent an interesting contradiction to Osgood's three-dimensional surface, which indicates that retroactive inhibition should increase as successive responses to the same stimuli become more dissimilar. Thus, if form class is conceptualized as a response made to the specific stimuli that appear on the list, the Osgood formulation does not apply and a new principle is suggested: the more dissimilar the classes of responses attached to the same stimuli, the more likely it becomes that successive response classes will maintain their strength independently of each other.

SIMILARITY OF SET AND THE LEARNING ENVIRONMENT

Our examination of similarity has been confined to specific stimulus-response relationships, as well as to the organization and form class of the experimental material. There is no reason, however, why the study of similarity cannot be extended to: (1) the learner's set, as well as (2) his learning environment.

Although set is a difficult construct to define with precision, a number of studies have been conducted that have examined retroactive inhibition as a function of this variable. In an early study by Postman and Postman (1948), set was defined as the subject's expectation to form associations that embody a given type of logical relationship. Pairs of meaningful words were used as the experimental material, and were so chosen that members of the pair were either compatible or incompatible with each other vis-à-vis meaning and connotation. An example of a compatible pair would be *doctor-heal,* or *war-bloodshed,* while an incompatible pair would be *doctor-harm,* or *war-peaceful.* Four groups of subjects were used with the following original and interpolated learning situations:

TABLE 12–2

EXPERIMENTAL DESIGN EXAMINING RETROACTIVE INHIBITION AS A
FUNCTION OF SET

Group	Original Learning	Interpolated Learning
1	Compatible pairs	Compatible pairs
2	Incompatible pairs	Incompatible pairs
3	Compatible pairs	Incompatible pairs
4	Incompatible pairs	Compatible pairs

(Adapted from Postman and Postman 1948)

Following the learning of both the original and interpolated tasks by the method of anticipation, all subjects were retested on the original list. In analyzing the results, groups 1 and 2 were combined, since the same set was present during the original and interpolated learning; groups 3 and 4 were also combined, since the set present during the interpolated learning task was different from that of the original learning and the test for retention. Results revealed that if the same set was present, the percentage of the materials retained was significantly lower than if different sets were used during the original and interpolated learning sessions.

Jenkins and Postman (1949) demonstrated a similar finding when the subject's set was manipulated by varying the testing procedures employed during the original and interpolated learning. The original learning task consisted of serially presenting a list of twenty-five adjectives for five trials. Following the fifth presentation, either an anticipation method or a recognition test was used to measure recall. With the latter measure subjects were instructed to select twenty-five items from a list containing one hundred alphabetized adjectives. Interpolated learning took place immediately after the original learning. Twenty-five adjectives made up the second list. This list was also presented for five trials, followed by either a recognition or anticipation test. Recall of the original material immediately followed the interpolated learning; again, either an anticipation or recognition test was employed. The varying experimental conditions for the four groups of subjects are presented in Table 12–3; results were in keeping with the Postman and Postman's (1948) earlier findings. When original, inter-

TABLE 12–3

EXPERIMENTAL DESIGN EXAMINING RETROACTIVE INHIBITION
AS A FUNCTION OF SET

Group	Test for Original Learning	Test for Interpolated Learning	Rest	
1	Anticipation	Anticipation	Anticipation	Same Set
2	Recognition	Recognition	Recognition	
3	Anticipation	Recognition	Anticipation	Same Set
4	Recognition	Anticipation	Recognition	

(Adapted from Jenkins and Postman 1949)

polated, and relearning activities were carried out under the same set, a greater amount of forgetting resulted than when the original learning and interpolated learning took place under different sets.

The investigation of similarity has been extended also to an examination of the learner's environment. Studies by both Bilodeau and Schlosberg (1951), and Greenspoon and Ranyard (1957) have demonstrated that when the acquisition of the original and interpolated material takes place within the same learning environment, larger amounts of forgetting of the original materials are obtained than if varying environments are associated with the learning of the different lists.

In the Bilodeau and Schlosberg (1951) study, the original task consisted of learning ten pairs of adjectives by the anticipation method. In the first experiment, all original learning took place in what the investigators described as a "drum room"—a dingy storeroom filled with old apparatus. The subject stood as he attempted to learn the material presented on a memory drum. The learning of a second list of paired-adjectives for the first experimental group was done in a room identified as the "card room"— a room made as different as possible from the room in which the original learning took place. The card room was a large basement classroom in which the subject was seated and the material was presented on a card-flipping device similar to a desk calendar. A second experimental group learned their second list in the room where the original learning took place. The (control) group's interpolated activity consisted of doing long division problems for eight minutes, also in the original learning room. Following the interpolated activity, all groups relearned the original material in the drum room. In a second experiment, the original learning took place in the card room, while the drum room was used for the interpolated learning of one of the experimental groups. The findings indicated that the control group showed the best recall. Our primary concern, however, is with the findings of the experimental groups. The first experimental group, which learned the interpolated material in an environmental setting different from that in which the original material was learned, recalled the original material significantly better than the second experimental group, which learned the original and interpolated material in the same room. Greenspoon and Ranyard (1957) have confirmed the Bilodeau and Schlosberg (1951) findings.

DEGREE OF LEARNING

A second area of interest has been retroactive and proactive inhibition effects when the degree or strength of original learning, as well as the degree of learning of the interfering material, has been manipulated. Before continuing, we should like to call the reader's attention to the fact that proactive and retroactive inhibition values may be expressed in relative as well as absolute terms. An absolute difference refers to the numerical difference obtained by subtracting the experimental group's retention score from that of the control group. Relative proactive or retroactive inhibition values, however, represent a percentage difference between these scores and are expressed by the following:

$$\frac{\text{Control group retention score} - \text{experimental group retention score}}{\text{Control Group Retention Score}} \times 100 = $$

$$\text{Percent PI or RI}$$

In most experimental situations, the findings obtained by using an absolute measure of proactive or retroactive inhibition will parallel those obtained by a relative measure. Such parallelism does not always hold, however, when inhibition effects are examined as a function of the degree of original learning. As Slamecka and Ceraso (1960) have indicated, when the degree of original learning is small, the control group's retention score is also small and slight departures from this base line on the part of the experimental group will result in a substantial percentage difference. On the other hand, when a large number of original training trials has been provided, thus producing large retention values in the control group, the same absolute difference between the control and experimental groups will reflect a smaller percentage change. Although relative proactive or retroactive inhibition values will have decreased, the absolute amount of inhibition will have remained the same. When the degree of original learning is manipulated, relative proactive or retroactive inhibition scores generally provide the most appropriate kinds of analysis, although the experimenters might do well to provide both values.

DEGREE OF LEARNING AND RETROACTIVE INHIBITION

Logically, it would follow that increases in the original learning, with the degree of interpolated learning held constant, should result in decreasing the amount of retroactive inhibition. One of the early investigations in this area was a serial learning study by McGeoch (1929), who used lists of nine CVCs as the material to be learned. Either six, eleven, sixteen, twenty-one, or twenty-six presentations of the original list were provided; the number of interpolated lists presentations was held constant at eleven. The original list was then relearned to a criterion of one perfect recitation, with the first relearning trial providing a measure of recall. McGeoch found that relative retroactive inhibition values decreased with increases in the degree of original learning.

A second consideration relates to the degree of interpolated learning. It would seem to follow here that as the degree of interpolated learning increases, with the degree of original learning held constant, the amount of retroactive inhibition should increase. A second serial learning study by McGeoch (1932) demonstrated this. The materials and conditions were the same as in the previous study except that the original material was presented for just eleven trials and the interpolated material was presented for either six, eleven, sixteen, twenty-one, or twenty-six trials. Recall scores obtained on the first relearning trial of the original material provided the basic data. Both absolute and relative amounts of retroactive inhibition increased as the interpolated learning trials increased from six to eleven trials—further increases in the degree of interpolated learning had no additional effects. Similar serial list findings were obtained by Melton and Irwin (1940) a few years later.

Thune and Underwood (1943) extended McGeoch's (1932), and Melton and Irwin's (1940) findings to the paired-associate learning situation. The original and interpolated lists, comprising an A-B, A-C paradigm, consisted of ten paired-associates that were learned by the anticipation method.

Five original learning trials were provided, followed by either two, five, ten, or twenty trials of interpolated learning. The original list was then relearned to a criterion of two perfect trials. The findings closely paralleled the results obtained by previous investigators in that increasing the amount of interpolated learning up to a particular point (ten trials) resulted in increased retroactive inhibition, as measured in recall scores. After ten trials, additional interpolated learning (twenty trials) did not produce increased retroactive inhibition.

A variety of contemporary investigators (Richardson 1956, Briggs 1957, and Postman and Riley 1959), using both serial and paired-associate learning tasks, and examining retroactive inhibition as a function of the degree of original as well as interpolated learning, obtained findings in accord with those cited.

Underwood (1945) demonstrated that increases in retroactive inhibition take place as a function of the number of interpolated *lists* learned, as well as the number of trials that previous experimenters have used. In this study, ten pairs of two-syllable adjectives made up the learning material, and the original list was learned to a criterion of six correct responses. Following this, subjects learned either zero, two, four, or six interpolated lists; each list was presented for just four trials. Each interpolated list contained the same stimulus words as the original list; responses, however, varied. Following the presentation of the appropriate number of interpolated lists, subjects relearned the original list to a criterion of two successive errorless trials. The results, seen in Fig. 12–3, indicated that retroactive inhibition—as measured by the mean number of correct responses on the first relearning trial—increased as a function of the number of interpolated lists presented.

In the studies that we have cited, the experimental findings were based upon serial or paired-associate learning situations. Postman and Keppel (1967) recently examined the influence of degree of interpolated learning on free recall. In this study, experimental groups learned two twenty-word (two-syllable noun) lists in succession. Four study-test trials were provided for the first list; for the second list, separate groups were given either two, four, or six study-test trials. Following the last test trial for the second list, subjects were instructed to write all of the words they could remember in any order they wished. They were then asked to identify the list membership of the words they had written. A control group worked a series of mathematical problems for a period of time equal to that provided the group given the six study-test trials on the interpolated material. The findings are indicated in Fig. 12–4,

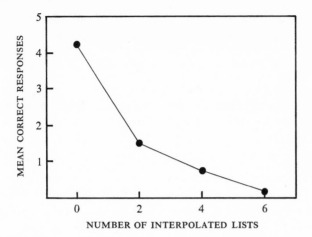

Fig. 12–3. Mean correct responses on the first relearning trial with 0, 2, 4, and 6 interpolated lists presented for four trials each.
(Adapted from Underwood 1945)

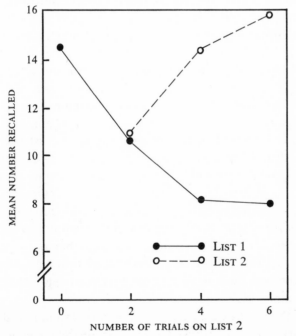

Fig. 12–4. Mean number of items recalled from the two lists on the terminal test of retention.
(Adapted from Postman and Keppel 1967)

which provides the mean number of items recalled from the two lists on the retention test. These findings parallel those observed with serial and paired-associate learning situations, in that there was a negatively accelerated decrease in the number of items recalled as a function of the amount or degree of interpolated learning. An increasing tendency for list 2 words to precede list 1 words during recall was also noted.

DEGREE OF LEARNING AND PROACTIVE INHIBITION

In one of the early studies examining proactive inhibition as a function of degree of first-list learning, Underwood (1949a) had subjects learn lists of ten pairs of two-syllable adjectives using an A-B, A-C paradigm. For one condition, the first list was presented until three or more responses were anticipated correctly on a single trial, while for a second condition, the first list was presented until eight or more responses were correctly anticipated on one trial. In a third condition, the first list was presented until all ten items had been anticipated correctly on a single trial, following which five additional trials were provided. A control group was not given any trials on the first list. Following presentation of the first list for the experimental conditions, the second list was presented until six or more responses were anticipated on a single trial. Either twenty minutes (experiment 1) or seventy-five minutes (experiment 2) after first-list learning, the second list was recalled. Underwood found that proactive inhibition increased as the degree of first learning increased; thus significant amounts of proactive inhibition were produced by the two highest degrees of first-list learning when retention was measured twenty minutes after the learning of the second list. When proactive inhibition was measured after seventy-five minutes, results indicated that only the highest degree of first-list learning produced a significant amount of proactive inhibition. A subsequent study by Atwater (1953) confirmed Underwood's findings.

One of the most extensive factorial studies examining the degree of both first- and second-list learning on proactive inhibition was performed by Postman and Riley (1959). Serial lists of CVCs served as the material to be learned. Subjects were given either five, ten, twenty, or forty trials on the first list followed by five, ten, twenty, or forty trials on the second list. Twenty minutes after the last trial on the second list, the second list was relearned to a criterion of two perfect recitations; recall scores were provided by the first relearning trial. The results are found in Table 12–4. Using relative proactive inhibition scores, the findings parallel those obtained by previous investigators. Thus, by increasing the number of first-list learning trials, and keeping the number of second-list learning trials constant, increasing amounts of proactive inhibition are obtained. There is some indication that when the number of second-list learning trials are minimal, increases in the number of first-list learning trials result in increases of proactive inhibition only up to a point. Beyond this, further increases in first-list learning trials produce a decrement in proactive inhibition. When first-list learning trials are held constant, and second-list learning trials are varied, a curvilinear relationship is obtained, in which small and large amounts of second-list learning provide maximum amounts of proactive inhibition within each first-list learning trial condition.

Underwood (1945) examined proactive inhibition when the material to be learned consisted of a number of different lists rather than when the number of trials on a single list was manipulated. In this experiment, similar to the one by Underwood (1945) that was examined in the retroactive inhibition section, either zero, two, four, or six lists of ten paired-adjectives were presented;

TABLE 12–4

RELATIVE AMOUNTS OF PROACTIVE INHIBITION
(IN PERCENT)

First-List Learning Trials	Second-List Learning Trials			
	5	10	20	40
5	32.4	−11.9 *	−7.9 *	16.5
10	38.2	−7.1 *	−3.2 *	26.8
20	50.0	−4.5 *	25.4	30.9
40	32.4	2.4	17.5	33.0

* Minus values reflect facilitation
(Adapted from Postman and Riley 1959)

four trials were provided on each list. A second list was then learned to a criterion of six correct responses. Following twenty-five minutes of rest, the second list was relearned to a criterion of two successive errorless trials. The results, presented in Fig. 12–5, reveal that proactive inhibition increased as a function of the number of prior lists learned—a finding in keeping with the results of other investigators who manipulated learning trials.

In summary, the experimental evidence supports the position that when the degree of first-list learning is increased and that of second-list learning held constant, the relative amount of proactive inhibition increases. This finding is in keeping with the studies on retroactive inhibition and can be stated more generally: as interfering responses—whether arising from prior or interpolated learning—increase in strength, retention decreases.

The second finding with proactive inhibition studies has been that as the degree of second-list learning increases, with first-list learning held constant, the amount of proactive inhibition first increases, but then decreases as greater degrees of second-list learning are provided. There appears to be some disparity between these findings and those obtained from the retroactive inhibition studies. In summary, holding the strength of interfering responses constant, and increasing the strength of the original list responses appears

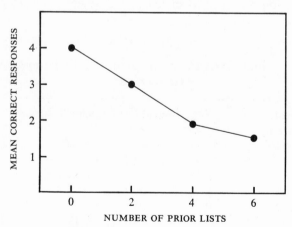

Fig. 12–5. Mean correct responses on the first relearning trial with 0, 2, 4, and 6 prior lists presented for four trials each.
(Adapted from Underwood 1945)

to result in decreasing the amount of retroactive inhibition but increasing and then decreasing the amount of proactive inhibition. Inasmuch as the proactive inhibition findings are based upon only a single study (Postman and Riley 1959), verification of this finding must await further experimental tests.

RETROACTIVE INHIBITION OF CONNECTED DISCOURSE

In contrast to the many investigators who have found proactive and retroactive inhibition using the serial list or paired-associate learning situation, a number of early investigators were unable to demonstrate retroactive inhibition effects when prose or connected discourse was used as the material to be learned and recalled (McGeoch and McKinney 1934, Deese and Hardman 1954, Hall 1955, Ausubel, Robbins and Blake 1957).

The more recent studies of Slamecka (1959, 1960, 1960a, 1961, 1962) have shown, however, that retention of passages of connected discourse is subject to retroactive as well as proactive inhibition effects. In one study (1960), a single sentence consisting of twenty words served as the original material. An example of such a sentence was as follows: *"We must postulate that from strictly semantic points of vantage, most confusions in communication revolve about inadequate stipulation of meaning."* Sentences of either high, intermediate, or low similarity to the original material were utilized as the interpolated material. The high similarity passage also dealt with the topic of semantics, the intermediate similarity passage was concerned with mathematics, and the low similarity passage dealt with government. In contrast to most prose learning situations, a serial anticipation procedure was used; each word was presented for three seconds and subjects were told to anticipate the next word. Both the original and interpolated passages were learned to a criterion of one perfect trial. The time between the end of the original learning and the start of the relearning of the original passage was held constant at twelve minutes, six seconds.

Absolute retroactive inhibition effects were obtained for all work groups. The group given the highest similarity of interpolated ma-

terial revealed the poorest recall scores, followed by the intermediate group, and then the low. In a second study, Slamecka
(1961) demonstrated that this type of material was also susceptible
to proactive inhibition effects, while in a third study (1960a) he
examined retroactive inhibition effects as a function of the degree
of interpolated and original learning. All of the findings supported
the results obtained when more traditional verbal learning materials were utilized. King and Tannenbaum (1963) confirmed
the findings of Slamecka, extending them to group learning situations in which there was unlimited time available for written recall.

THE ANALYSIS OF RETROACTIVE
AND PROACTIVE INHIBITION

RESPONSE COMPETITION, UNLEARNING,
AND SPONTANEOUS RECOVERY

Many contemporary investigators account for retention decrement in terms of proactive and retroactive inhibition; the use of
these constructs make up what has been commonly referred to
as an interference theory of forgetting.

An early formulation of interference theory was provided by
McGeoch (1942) who, primarily concerned with retroactive inhibition, assumed that the forgetting produced by interpolated material could be accounted for in terms of competition between responses. That is, the responses acquired during the original and
interpolated learning situations and attached to identical or similar
stimuli remained available and competed with each other during
the recall of the original material. As already noted, the similarity
variable appeared to be a significant factor in producing inhibitory
effects—a finding in keeping with the response competition
position.

In 1940 Melton and Irwin postulated a second factor that they
believed also made an important contribution to retroactive inhibition. Their primary purpose in the study cited earlier in this
chapter, was to examine retroactive inhibition as a function of
the amount of interpolated activity. It will be recalled that their

original learning material consisted of a list of eighteen CVCs presented in serial order for five trials. An interpolated eighteen-item list of CVCs was then presented for either five, ten, twenty, or forty trials, followed by the relearning of the original list. In addition to examining the total amount of retroactive inhibition produced by the varying interpolated learning trials, these investigators looked at the number of responses that could be identified as belonging to the interpolated list—that is, overt interpolated list intrusions. Melton and Irwin (1940) believed that this measure would provide an index of the amount of competition between the original and the interpolated responses at recall. The findings are plotted in Fig. 12–6.

No consistent relationship between the number of such interlist intrusions and the total amount of retroactive inhibition, however, could be observed. Since the total amount of retroactive inhibition increased to an asymptote at approximately twenty trials of inter-polated learning and then remained relatively constant, Melton and Irwin reasoned that some variable other than response compe-tition must be contributing to the recall decrement. This variable, designated as factor X, was tentatively identified as the unlearning of the original responses. In brief, these investigators suggested that when the original responses intruded during the learning of

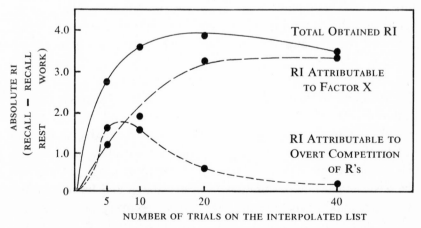

Fig. 12–6. Relationship between the amount of retroactive inhibition and the degree of learning of the interpolated material.

(Adapted from Melton and Irwin 1940)

the interpolated list, they were not reinforced; this occurred because those responses were incorrect in the new context, which in turn led to their being unlearned or extinguished.

As a result of these findings, the authors posited a two-factor theory of retroactive inhibition in which competition between responses was one factor and unlearning was the second. Note, of course, that the unlearning process is not operative in proactive inhibition since there is no opportunity for the second-list responses that are subsequently to be recalled, to be unlearned.

Two studies by Underwood (1948, 1948a) were important in furthering understanding of the operation of the unlearning factor. In the first of these studies, Underwood (1948) had subjects learn each of two lists of paired-adjectives (A-B, A-C paradigm) to a criterion of one perfect trial. Recall of either the first or second list took place under the following conditions: (1) list 1 recalled after five hours (RI); (2) list 2 recalled after five hours (PI); (3) list 1 recalled after forty-eight hours (RI); and (4) list 2 recalled after forty-eight hours (PI).

Underwood found that after a five-hour retention interval, the recall of the first list (RI paradigm) was significantly less than the recall of the second list (PI paradigm). This general result is in keeping with the two-factor theory since retroactive inhibition, which arises from both unlearning and response competition factors, should be greater than proactive inhibition, which is presumed to arise as a result of response competition alone. An earlier study by Melton and von Lackum (1941) had obtained similar findings.

A surprising finding, however, was that after forty-eight hours there was no difference in the recall of the two lists. An examination of Fig. 12–7, which shows the experimental findings, indicates an increase in the recall score for the retroactive inhibition condition from five to forty-eight hours, and a decline in recall for the proactive inhibition condition. Underwood suggested that if the basic unlearning postulate posited by Melton and Irwin (1940) was broadened to include the spontaneous recovery of the associations that were unlearned during the presentation of the second list, this increase in recall could be adequately explained.

In Underwood's (1948a) second study, in which the spontaneous

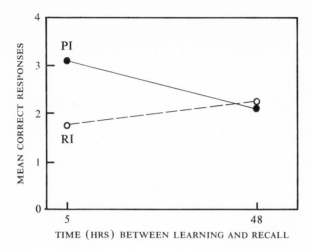

Fig. 12–7. Mean number of correct anticipations on the first relearning trial after five and forty-eight hours. RI refers to the recall of the first list; PI to the recall of the second.

(Adapted from Underwood 1948)

recovery of verbal associations was investigated further, an interesting feature was used, which has become known as a modified free-recall (MFR) procedure. The experiment consisted of subjects' learning two lists (A-B, A-C paradigm) of ten paired two-syllable adjectives to a criterion of one perfect recitation. Following the learning of the second list and after an interval of either one minute, or five, twenty-four, or forty-eight hours, the modified free-recall procedure was used. This consisted of presenting the subject with each common stimulus word and asking him to say the first of the two response words that came to mind. If no response was provided by the end of ten seconds, the subject was asked, "What response does the stimulus word make you think of?" If no response was provided by the end of thirty seconds, the subject was instructed to "Give any word which occurs to you." The mean frequency of the different types of responses on the modified free-recall trial over the four time intervals is indicated in Fig. 12–8. As the time interval increased between the learning of the second list and the modified free-recall test, it may be noted that there was a consistent decline in the frequency of responses from the list that was learned second; in contrast, frequency of responses from the first list remained relatively constant—a result

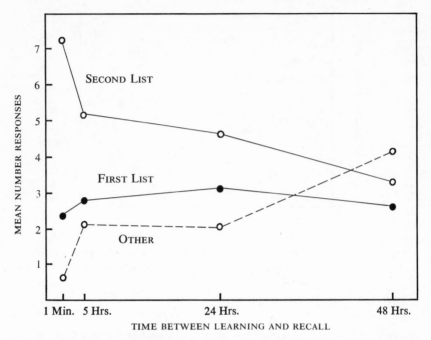

Fig. 12–8. Mean frequency of response on the free-recall trial for the four different time intervals.

(Adapted from Underwood 1948a)

that Underwood (1948a) believed further indicated the viability of the unlearning-spontaneous recovery process.

A subsequent study by Briggs (1954), also using the modified free-recall procedure to examine the relative strength of competing response systems in the retroactive inhibition situation, confirmed Underwood's findings.

The "fate" of first-list associations during the learning of a second list was further examined in a study by Barnes and Underwood (1959). Their experimental procedure was one in which subjects first learned a paired-associate list in which CVCs served as stimuli and two-syllable adjectives served as responses. Following the learning of the first list, a second list was presented for either one, five, ten, or twenty trials. The second list consisted of identical stimuli and unrelated responses, thus providing the frequently used A-B, A-C paradigm. Following the appropriate number of interpolated trials, the memory drum was stopped and the subject was given a piece of paper on which the stimulus words were printed. He was then asked to write down the two responses that had been associated with each stimulus. This operation of asking the subject to indicate *both* responses was a modification of the MFR procedure and has been designated as MMFR.

The results are presented in Fig. 12–9. Here it can be noted that as the number of trials on the second list increased, the number of correct responses from this list also increased, while the responses from the first list showed a gradual decline. Since subjects were instructed to recall first-list responses if possible, it is as if the A-B associations were extinguished or unlearned during the learning of the A-C pairs.

Finally, an important study examining the unlearning process is found in an experiment by McGovern (1964), who hypothesized that unlearning effects could be broken down into (1) specific and (2) contextual components. With regard to the specific component, McGovern posited that there is an unlearning of backward associations (B-A), in addition to the unlearning of forward associations (A-B), with both of these processes, of course, taking place during the learning of the second list.

In addition to the unlearning of the specific components, con-

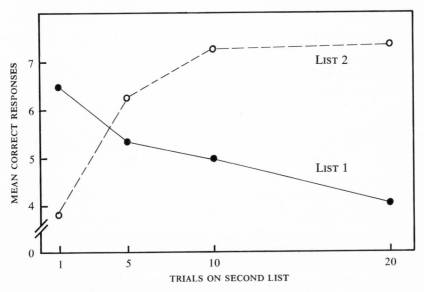

Fig. 12–9. Mean number of responses correctly recalled and identified with stimulus and list in the A-B, A-C paradigm.
(Adapted from Barnes and Underwood 1959)

textual stimulus-response relationships may also be unlearned. That is, in the typical paired-associate learning situation, contextual or environmental stimuli (the characteristics of the experimental room, memory drum, etc.) have been posited to be associated with the to-be-learned verbal responses. Thus, in the learning of two completely different paired-associate lists—exemplified by the A-B, C-D paradigm—an A-B, A-D relationship is also established, in which the stimuli (A) involved are of a contextual or environmental variety. McGovern (1964) believed that it was possible for contextual stimuli-verbal response relationships to be unlearned during second-list learning just as it is possible that specific components may be unlearned.

McGovern (1964) attempted to examine the contribution of these unlearning factors as they applied to four basic transfer paradigms, i.e., A-B, C-D; A-B, C-B; A-B, A-C; A-B, A-Br. More specifically, this investigator hypothesized that:

(1) The A-B, C-D paradigm involves only the unlearning of contextual associations. That is, since the specific stimuli and responses are different in second-list learning, there can be no unlearning of either forward or backward associations acquired during the learning of the first list. On the other hand, since response B has been attached to the contextual stimuli during first-list learning and response D has been attached to the same contextual stimuli in list 2 learning, both of these first-list associations should be unlearned.

(2) The A-B, C-B paradigm involves the extinction of backward associations. Here we may note that if a backward association, B-A, is learned during first-list learning, the learning of C-B in the second list would result in the unlearning of the backward association.

(3) The A-B, A-C paradigm involves the unlearning of forward as well as contextual associations.

(4) The A-B, A-Br paradigm involves the unlearning of forward as well as backward associations.

Inasmuch as the last two paradigms have two sources of unlearning to reduce recall, in contrast to only one source for the first two, McGovern predicted that retroactive inhibition should be greatest for the A-B, A-C and A-B, A-Br conditions.

The experimental procedure consisted of having four groups of subjects learn the varying transfer paradigms just delineated. The first list was learned to a criterion of one perfect trial while just fifteen trials were provided on the second list. Following the fifteenth trial on list 2, all subjects were given a list of the stimuli used on list 1. One-half of the subjects in each transfer group were given a free-recall test in which they had to recall the first-list responses and pair them with their appropriate stimuli, whereas the other half of the subjects in each group were given list 1 stimuli and responses and instructed to match them to form list 1 pairs. It was believed that the value of this matching procedure was that it neutralized the contextual factor so that recall was primarily influenced by the contribution of specific forward and backward associations. It should also be pointed out that a control group was used. These subjects, following the learning of the A-B list, were given a wooden puzzle to solve, followed by appropriate recall measures.

The results are indicated in Fig. 12-10. It may be noted that the A-C and A-Br conditions provided poorest recall of A-B, thus

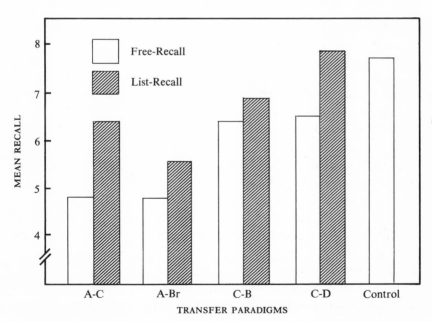

Fig. 12–10. Mean recall in the free- and list-recall subgroups of the four transfer paradigms.

(Adapted from McGovern 1964)

supporting one aspect of McGovern's hypothesis. McGovern's analysis of the source and locus of the varying unlearning factors she hypothesized to operate during second-list learning is too complex to discuss in detail, since it involved comparisons not only among the varying transfer paradigms but also between the retention values obtained with free-recall and matching tasks. In brief, however, her hypotheses, enumerated above, were confirmed. In addition, the comparison between the retention measures confirmed the Underwood and Schulz (1960) two-stage theory of paired-associate learning, by demonstrating that a loss of retention in one stage may occur independently of a loss in the other.

OTHER VARIABLES INFLUENCING FORGETTING

Some investigators have recognized that, in the learning of lists of items and their subsequent retention, variables or processes other than those related to specific stimulus-response relationships may contribute to the forgetting process. Generalized response competition and list differentiation have been posited as two such processes.

GENERALIZED RESPONSE COMPETITION

McGeoch's (1942) early formulation of an interference theory of forgetting stressed response competition arising from the specific verbal responses found on the lists that made up the retroactive inhibition experiment.

Newton and Wickens (1959) hypothesized the existence of a second-response competition process, "generalized response competition." They defined this latter process as the subject's set or tendency to give responses from the last learned list at the time of recall. Such a set should tend to increase retroactive inhibition, since the subject would continue to provide second-list responses at the time of first-list recall. On the other hand, proactive inhibition should decrease, since the tendency to provide responses from the second list during the recall period is appropriate for this task.

Postman and Riley (1959) also inferred a generalized response

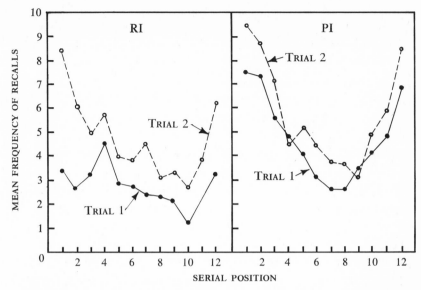

Fig. 12–11. Average serial-position curves of retroactive inhibition and proactive inhibition work groups at recall.
(Adapted from Postman and Riley 1959)

competition process from findings they obtained in their examination of proactive and retroactive inhibition in the recall of serial lists of CVCs. Fig. 12–11 presents their serial position curves for the proactive and retroactive inhibition groups at recall. A flattening of the curve may be noted at the beginning of the list for the retroactive inhibition group—a finding not obtained with the proactive inhibition group. On the second trial, however, the retroactive inhibition group's recall curve has recovered its typical bow-shaped appearance. The retention decrement found in the first portion of the list for the retroactive inhibition group was attributed to generalized competition that is substantially reduced or eliminated once the context of the original list is reestablished.

Keppel and Zavortink (1968) also obtained evidence of a flattening effect of their serial position curve in a more recent examination of retroactive inhibition in serial learning.

It would appear to follow from the nature of the generalized response competition process that if different and distinct sets were established during the learning of the first and second lists in the retroactive inhibition experiment, there would be a reduction in the amount of such competition, with a resultant decrement in forgetting. The studies cited earlier—in which investigators manipulated the similarity of the subject's set, with a resultant decrease in retroactive inhibition as similarity was reduced—are in keeping with this position.

List Differentiation

It will be recalled that Melton and Irwin's (1940) failure to find a consistent relationship between the number of overt interlist intrusions and the total amount of retroactive inhibition suggested that an unlearning factor was contributing to the decrement of recall. As Postman (1961) pointed out, however, this lack of correlation between the amount of retroactive inhibition and the number of intrusions is capable of being explained in terms other than the hypothesizing of an unlearning process. In one alternative explanation, a list differentiation factor was postulated. Underwood (1945) hypothesized that this concept is related to the subject's verbally reported experience of "knowing" that the responses from one list are inappropriate during the attempted recall of the other. The degree of differentiation, in this sense, is an indication of the degree to which the subject has identified the list to which each response belongs.

As a result of two experimental studies, Underwood (1945, 1949a) posited that the amount of list differentiation was dependent upon two conditions: (1) the relative strengths of the two lists that were learned, and (2) the time interval between the end of learning the second list and the test for recall. With regard to the first condition, Underwood (1949a) stated that "differentiation is postulated to be low when two response systems are of near equal strength" (p. 32), although he noted that further elaboration of this point was necessary, in that absolute strength of the two lists would also have to be considered. With regard to temporal influences, Underwood (1949a) suggested that differentiation "decreases as some function of the interval between learning and recall" (p. 32).

Although list differentiation may represent an alternative explanation for the unlearning process, it is now generally agreed that acceptance of this concept does not negate acceptance of the unlearning process. As Postman (1961) wrote, "acceptance of the differentiation hypothesis does not, however, in any sense contradict the assumption of unlearning" (p. 155). That is to say, unlearning may serve to change the relative strengths of competing items, which in turn may influence the list differentiation process.

There is a surprising lack of empirical work reported on the list differentiation construct, perhaps because there is substantial agreement on its functional properties. A recent series of studies by Winograd (1968), however, confirmed the general postulations of Underwood (1949a) that this process is minimal where both lists are equal in strength, and that there is a loss of differentiation with time. Winograd (1968a) further found that if subjects were asked to indicate list membership, when the lists were made up of either similar or different categories, list differentiation was clearly poorer for words that belong to categories appearing on both lists. Thus, confusion of list membership is greater when the same category appears on both lists than when it does not.

RECENT DEVELOPMENTS

Much of the recent experimental work in interference theory has centered on an examination of the unlearning process. This interest has been due, at least in part, to the use of certain kinds of procedures in the recall test that are assumed to minimize the influence of response competition, so that any decrement shown in recall as compared with results from a control group is attributed to unlearning. For example, use of the MMFR procedure gives the subject unlimited time to recall both of the response terms. If the subject is unable to recall one or both of these, it is assumed that these responses are unavailable—this unavailability presumably arises from the operation of an unlearning process.

UNLEARNING AND INTERLIST INTRUSIONS

Inasmuch as the unlearning process has been likened to experimental extinction, investigators have often assumed that intrusions of first-list responses taking place during second-list learning are a necessary prerequisite for unlearning. As we noted earlier, Melton and Irwin (1940) were unable to find any relationship between the number of interlist overt intrusions and the total amount of retroactive inhibition; nonetheless, most investigators have assumed that if covert intrusions were included in this total, such a relationship would be evident.

But how can such covert intrusions be brought to the surface? One procedure designed to increase the number of first-list intrusions has been to instruct subjects to guess during second-list learning—a technique examined both by Keppel and Rauch (1966), and Houston and Johnson (1967). In the latter study, subjects learned an A-B, A-C paradigm in which CVCs served as stimuli and adjectives as responses. During the learning of the second list, one group of subjects were instructed to guess each time they saw a syllable but could not remember the correct response, while a second group was asked to refrain from guessing when they were not sure of the appropriate response. Although the results indicated that the group given the guessing instructions provided eight times as many first-list responses as the second group, there was no difference in retention of first-list responses. (An interesting result, however, was that the "no guess" group learned the second list better than the "guess" group.) Thus, the principal findings of the study revealed significant effects of the guessing technique upon second-list performance but not upon first list recall. This finding, that the making of overt, first-list responses during second-list learning has no influence on subsequent first list forgetting, parallels the results previously obtained by Keppel and Rauch (1966).

Paul and Silverstein (1968) used a somewhat different experimental technique to get at this problem. Two experiments were run, and the findings from both studies were similar. The procedure consisted of having three groups of subjects learn an A-B paired-associate list consisting of twelve single-consonant letters as stimuli and two-syllable adjectives as responses. Second-list learning for one group consisted of learning a homogeneous A-C list while a second group learned a mixed list of A-B and A-C items. The third (control) group worked on simple arithmetic problems. Following second-list learning, the retention of the six first-list A-B items, which were present in both the homogeneous and mixed lists, was measured by presenting the subjects with the six critical stimulus items and asking them to recall responses from both lists (MMFR). An examination of performance on these six critical pairs of items during second-list learning revealed that the number of intrusions provided by the mixed list was significantly greater than that for the group learning the homogeneous list. Thus, the mean number of interlist intrusions for the homogeneous group was .55, while it was 3.25 for the mixed list. Presumably these latter first-list responses, which were made during second-list learning, should have undergone greater extinction. The recall of first-list responses, however, revealed better retention with the mixed list.

In summary, the results of the Keppel and Rauch (1966), Houston and Johnson (1967), and Paul and Silverstein (1968) studies argue against the use of interlist intrusions as an indicant of extinction of specific stimulus-response associations and subsequent poorer recall.[1]

Unlearning and Degree of Dominance

One hypothesis generated from the unlearning position is that the frequency with which old habits (list 1 responses) are elicited and subjected to extinction depend upon the degree of dominance achieved by the new habits. As the new response to a given stimulus increases in strength, it becomes less likely that the old response will occur either as an explicit or implicit intrusion. It is assumed that during a constant period of interpolated learning, the level of dominance attained by the new habits should vary inversely with the number of different (new) responses attached to each of the old stimuli. That is, the larger the number of different responses, the longer the original response should continue to be elicited as an error during the interpolated learning. It follows, then, that the degree to which first list associations are unlearned

[1] One discordant note in this experimental area is found in a retroactive inhibition study by Goggin (1967), who discovered that learning of the interpolated list by the anticipation method, in contrast to the prompting method, resulted in significantly more forgetting of first-list responses. She hypothesized that the greater amount of retroactive inhibition provided by the anticipation group could be attributed to the greater opportunity for this group to make erroneous responses during second-list learning.

should increase with the number of new lists practiced during a given period of interpolated learning.

Postman (1965) examined this position. His procedure consisted of having subjects learn a list consisting of twelve pairs of items with CVC-trigrams serving as stimuli and adjectives as responses. The interpolated task consisted of sixteen trials in which new responses were attached to the stimuli used in the first list. For one group, a single list was practiced for all sixteen trials; for a second group, two lists were given for eight trials each; while for a third group, four lists were provided for four trials each. A control condition learned and recalled only the first list. Two methods of measuring retention were used: (1) MMFR and (2) an S-R matching task, in which the subject was supplied with a list of correct responses and was required to match them to the appropriate stimuli. Postman found that retroactive inhibition increased in both methods of recall in proportion to the number of interpolated lists. Inasmuch as both recall procedures were believed to minimize response competition, the conclusion was drawn that unlearning is influenced by successive list interpolations. Birnbaum (1968) also obtained results supporting Postman's findings.

SPONTANEOUS RECOVERY

Spontaneous recovery has been posited as a second aspect of the unlearning process. It will be noted that in Underwood's (1948, 1948a) studies, to which we referred earlier, recall of first-list responses increased as a function of the retention interval, although recall of second-list responses revealed the typical retention decrement. The increment in recall of the first-list responses has been used to infer a spontaneous recovery process, which in turn has been hypothesized as an important correlate of unlearning.

It must be noted, however, that recent studies investigating the spontaneous recovery of unlearned associations using the modified free-recall procedure (MMFR) have provided contradictory findings. Koppenaal (1963), Ceraso and Henderson (1965, 1966), Slamecka (1966), and Silverstein (1967), like Underwood (1948, 1948a), obtained increases in the recall of first-list responses as a function of the retention interval; but in all instances differences between experimental and control groups have not been statistically reliable. On the other hand, Birnbaum (1965), Houston (1966), and Howe (1967) were unable to obtain such supportive evidence.

In reviewing many of these experiments, Postman, Stark and Fraser (1968) suggested that one source of the discrepancies obtained among the experimental findings may be due to differences in the level of retention at the time of the test for spontaneous recovery. These experimenters pointed out that if conditions are such that there is a good deal of forgetting, an absolute increase in first-list recall is unlikely even if there is spontaneous recovery of extinguished associations. Thus, the smaller the amount of forgetting, the more sensitive the delayed test should be to the recovery process. They also pointed out that spontaneous recovery of these first-list responses becomes less likely as the retention interval is lengthened—those studies that have provided positive findings have used retention intervals of twenty-four hours or less.

In their extensive examination of the spontaneous recovery process, Postman, Stark and Fraser (1968) conducted five experiments examining the temporal changes in proactive as well as retroactive inhibition. In the experimental procedure, subjects learned successive lists of paired-associates conforming to the A-B, A-C paradigm. CVCs served as stimuli, and adjectives were used as responses; the number of learning trials did not go beyond seven. We cannot detail the variety of conditions manipulated by these investigators; the results, however, were straightforward in demonstrating absolute increases in first-list recall—a finding in agreement with some of the earlier studies cited.

A REEXAMINATION OF UNLEARNING AND SPONTANEOUS RECOVERY

The experimental studies that have examined unlearning and spontaneous recovery mechanisms have not been entirely convincing in demonstrating the viability of these mechanisms in accounting for retention decrement. As a result of the experimental studies to which we have just referred, Postman, Stark and Fraser (1968) provided a somewhat different point of view regarding the functioning of the unlearning and spontaneous recovery mechanisms.

These authors hypothesized that spontaneous recovery of first-list responses results from the dissipation of "response-set inter-ference"—a mechanism that exerts its primary effect on the entire class of first-list responses, rather than on any specific stimulus-response associations.

(At this point, however, we will digress for a paragraph to acquaint the reader with a selector mechanism that is presumed to operate during the learning of a list of items and bears an intimate relationship to the concept of response-set interference. The operation of a selector mechanism was first hypothesized by Underwood and Schulz (1960), who noted a dependable tendency on the part of subjects learning a list of verbal items to restrict their overt responses to items from within the list. When a new list is learned, as in the transfer task, the subject quickly restricts himself to the responses contained only in the second list. This new selection criteria begins to regulate the subject's responses immediately upon exposure to the transfer task, and is evident from the few interlist intrusions obtained.)

The basic question raised by Postman, Stark and Fraser was, how might the action of the selector mechanism result in the un-learning of first-list responses? They posited the following:

(1) The exposure of the subjects to the list of items found in the first list leads to the selective arousal of a repertoire of pre-scribed responses. The recency of the presentation of these items provides an immediately effective criterion of selective arousal. Other effective criteria, however, may be also used—formal or se-mantic similarities among the items, membership in common taxonomic categories, etc. also serve this function.

(2) When there is a change in the responses to be learned, as in the A-C list of the A-B, A-C paradigm, the readiness with which new criteria of selective arousal become effective depends upon the distinctiveness of the words in the two lists. Relative recency again provides one basis for discriminating items on the second list from those on the first, but other criteria may be used as well. The greater the interlist stimulus similarity, however, the

more likely it becomes that first-list responses will be elicited as overt or covert errors during second-list learning. The probability that the subject will make these errors is reduced as the criteria of selection become more and more specific to the currently correct repertoire of responses. The establishment of such increasingly restrictive criteria of selection is tantamount to the suppression of the class of first-list responses. The extent to which such suppression will occur is a function of the degree of associative interference during second-list learning.

(3) When an individual thinks of a response in a learning or retention situation, a scanning process comes into play that has the function of matching the response against the selection criteria. Such a process is inferred because there is every reason to believe that a substantial portion of interlist and extralist intrusions are recognized as errors, but that the subject withholds these responses from overt expression. Thus, much of the interference in transfer is of a covert variety. The hypothetical sequence of events in the operation of the selector mechanism, the authors posit, is activation, scanning, matching, and editing of responses. It is the latter phases of scanning, matching, and editing that are implied by the mechanism of list differentiation discussed earlier.

(4) One of the characteristics of the selector mechanism is its inertia. That is, the most recently established selection criteria continues to influence response activation and output after the termination of practice. On a test of recall after interpolated learning, a shift back to the first-list criteria of selection is difficult to the extent that the second-list criteria, which have been in continuous operation during the immediately preceding period, remain dominant.

The inertia that characterizes the selector mechanism is assumed to be, however, of limited duration. That is, the degree of dominance of the most recent criteria of selection diminishes over time. Thus, effects that the inertia of the selector mechanism has on output are reversible. The last assumption bears directly of course on the explanation of absolute rises in first-list recall obtained by Postman, Stark and Fraser (1968) as well as earlier investigators. That is, response-set interference reflects dominance at the time of recall of the second-list criteria of selection; as the degree of dominance declines, response-set interference dissipates.[1]

THE RELATIVE CONTRIBUTIONS OF PROACTIVE AND RETROACTIVE INHIBITION TO FORGETTING

Most of the early investigators who supported an interference theory of forgetting assumed that retroactive inhibition was of greater importance than proactive inhibition. Logically, however, this position is weak, since the amount of material available to interfere with new learning in proactive inhibition is all that acquired during the subject's lifetime; while the interfering material in the retroactive inhibition experiment must be assumed to arise only in the experimental situation, in the interval between the time of original learning and the subsequent test for recall.

In an extremely important paper, Underwood (1957a) attempted to demonstrate that proactive inhibition makes a much greater contribution to forgetting than had previously been believed.

The problem, as conceptualized by Underwood, was as follows: A subject learns a list of adjectives, and, after a period of twenty-four hours, is tested for retention of the material. An examination of many of the early rote learning studies indicated that approximately 75 percent of the material learned was forgotten during this twenty-four hour period. For example, if a twelve-item list was learned to a criterion of one perfect trial, twenty-four hours later only three of the items would be recalled. The usual interference explanation for such forgetting was that subjects learned interpolated material, during the twenty-four hour interval, that interfered with recall of the items. But, as Underwood reasoned, it seems an incredible extension of an interference hypothesis to hold that this degree of forgetting was caused by material the subject learned outside the laboratory during this twenty-four hour period. Moreover, if CVCs represented the items learned, what kind of material could have been learned during the retention interval to provide interfering responses?

[1] The authors point out that this interpretation is closely related to the generalized response competition process proposed by Newton and Wickens (1956), discussed earlier.

The basic point made by Underwood was that those studies that examined retention over a twenty-four hour period and that indicated 75 percent forgetting, used subjects who had learned many previous lists in the experimental situation. When the percentage of recall was plotted as a function of the number of previous lists learned, Underwood (1957a) obtained the relationship indicated in Fig. 12–12.

Underwood's examination of the retention performance of naive subjects led him to estimate that the amount of forgetting over a twenty-four hour period would be approximately 25 percent. He interpreted these findings as indicating that the major factor in forgetting in many of the early studies arose from proactive rather than retroactive inhibition.

An earlier study by Greenberg and Underwood (1950) supported this interpretation. These investigators examined the learning and recall of paired-adjectives as a function of the number of

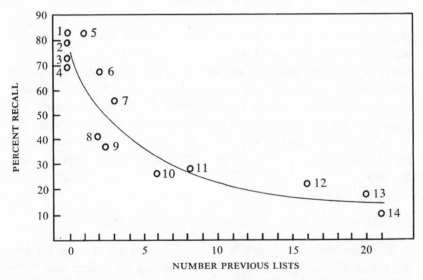

Fig. 12–12. Recall as a function of number of previous lists learned as determined from a number of studies. (1) Weiss and Margolius (1954); (2) Gibson (1942); (3) Belmont and Birch (1951); (4) Underwood and Richardson (1955); (5) Williams (1950); (6) Williams (1950); (7) Johnson (1939); (8) Underwood (1952a, 1953, 1953a, 1953b); (9) Lester (1932); (10) Krueger (1929); (11) Cheng (1929); (12) Hovland (1940); (13) Luh (1922); and (14) Youtz (1941).

(Adapted from Underwood 1957a)

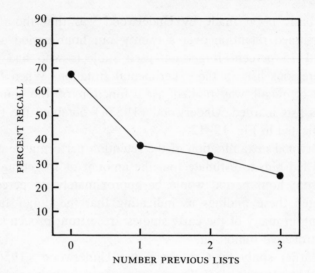

Fig. 12–13. Recall of paired-adjectives as a function of number of previous lists learned.
(Adapted from Greenberg and Underwood 1950)

previous lists learned. Their subjects learned a list of ten paired-adjectives to a criterion of eight out of ten correct on a single trial. Forty-eight hours later the list was recalled. The following day a new list was learned to the same criterion, and this list was also recalled after a forty-eight hour interval. The same procedure was continued for the learning and recalling of two additional lists. The findings, as indicated in Fig. 12–13, revealed that the amount of recall diminishes as a function of the number of previous lists learned.

EXTRAEXPERIMENTAL SOURCES OF INTERFERENCE

If an interference theory is to be viable in accounting for forgetting, it must also account for the retention decrement that takes place in situations in which formal interfering tasks have not been provided. Single-list retention studies represent one such situation. In an attempt to handle the forgetting that takes place in such cases, Underwood and Postman (1960) suggested that the interference here is of an extraexperimental source. That is, interfering responses arise not from the formal learning situation, but from verbal habits learned outside of the laboratory. These they have termed extraexperimental. These authors have asserted that "the evidence from the formal proactive and retroactive operations leads to an interference conception of forgetting which in turn leads to the assertion that when *no* formal interfering task is given the forgetting observed must be due to extraexperimental sources of interference" (p. 74). Two sources of extraexperimental interference suggested by these authors consist of: (1) letter sequence habits and (2) unit sequence habits.

Letter sequence habits indicate habits developed through the normal course of learning the language. For example these investigators would assume that if the two-letter combination QJ was presented, (1) previously learned letter sequence habits, i.e., QU, would make this particular sequence difficult to learn, since the earlier habit would have to be extinguished. Moreover, (2) with the passage of time, the older habit would recover in strength and interfere with the recall of these letters. However, if letter sequence habits produce such interference at recall, the magnitude of such interference will decrease as the letter sequences more and more closely approximate the most frequently used sequences in the language. Thus, a gradient of interference is hypothesized that diminishes in amount as the letter sequences being tested correspond more and more closely to those sequences more frequently used in the language.

"Unit sequence habits" refers to words or sequences of letters that appear in a given list as independent units. Let us assume that the word *over* is a unit in a serial list. Because of long-established language habits, there is a strong tendency for *over* to elicit *there*. It is presumed that this association would have to be extinguished before a new association could be established; with the passage of time, however, the original association recovers and provides interference at recall. It follows from this position that the more frequently a word occurs in the language, the greater the number of words with which it is associatively connected. Thus, if a high frequency word were used in a serial list, a large number of preexperimental associations could be assumed to exist among the items, many of which would have to be extinguished in order for the subject to achieve the particular order of items required by the experimenter. It would be anticipated, therefore, that the recovery of these preexperimental associations over a retention interval would result in considerable interference at the time of the retention test.

In short, the unit sequence conception of interference posits that maximum interference is present with high frequency words, but that such interference decreases as word frequency decreases.

The operation of letter sequence and unit sequence habits can be summarized as follows: Letter sequence interference will be at a maximum when the preexperimental associative strength between letters is low; the amount of such interference decreases as the preexperimental associative connection between letters increases. With the unit sequence gradient, the amount of interference will increase up to the point at which very high frequency words are presented.

Although the experimental evidence supports the position that extraexperimental associations play a role in the learning of material provided in the laboratory situation, a series of studies by Underwood and Postman (1960), Postman (1961a), Underwood and Keppel (1963b), Ekstrand and Underwood (1965), and Underwood and Ekstrand (1966, 1968), using a variety of learning situations, failed to verify the role of extraexperimental interference in retention.

Two types of experiments illustrate the nature of these negative findings. In a study by Postman (1961a), three experiments were conducted in which lists of high and low frequency words were serially learned to a criterion of one perfect recitation. Thirty seconds, two days, or seven days following the end of the original learning, retention was tested. In one experiment, retention was examined by having the subjects relearn the material to the same criterion. Although the unit interference position would predict more rapid relearning (smaller amounts of forgetting) for the low frequency words, differences in retention as a function of word frequency were not obtained.

In a second study, Underwood and Ekstrand (1968) conducted two paired-associate experiments in which the stimuli and responses consisted of high (or low) crossed paired-associates. That is, the response terms for the list of high crossed associates were all primary responses to the stimulus terms, but were so arranged that no high associative strengths existed between any stimulus response pairs. For example, the word *table,* serving as a stimulus, would be paired with the response word *nail,* while the stimulus word *hammer* would be paired with the response word *chair*. Thus *table-nail, hammer-chair* are examples of the paired-associates learned. It was anticipated that, following learning, a recall test would show this group to recall fewer responses, since the previously learned, strong associates, i.e., *table-chair, hammer-nail,* should interfere with the to-be-remembered response, e.g., *table-nail*. Results, however, indicated that the high crossed paired-associates had *superior* recall to control lists. The results of this study, along with those of a second and similar one, indicated a lack of support for differential forgetting based on assumed differential interference from linguistic sources.

In their summary, the authors wrote that

a wide enough variety of situations has now been explored to make very strong the possibility that the relative constancy of the forgetting of single lists, lists with widely different characteristics, must be accepted. This does not mean, of course, that the forgetting shown is not due to interference, but, if so, it must be due to competition of a general nature . . . (p. 170).

THE ROLE OF INTERFERENCE THEORY IN PREDICTING FORGETTING

We will conclude this section with one further consideration. In spite of the average adult's strong letter sequence and unit sequence habits, we have noted a variety of experimental findings in which the amount of forgetting is far less than would be predicted by an interference theory. Postman (1963), in addressing himself to this problem, concluded that the basic assumptions of interference theory remain tenable, but must be supplemented from time to time by "principles of conservation" that systematically reduce the amount of forgetting produced by the competition of habits. The principles of conservation delineated by Postman were:

1. *Differentiation*. This refers to the subject's ability to discriminate between correct and incorrect responses and thus to reject errors at the time of recall.

2. *The Selector Mechanism*. This mechanism, which we discussed earlier, also operates to reduce interference. Here the subject confines himself to the class of items, such as words or trigrams, that makes up the experimental material. It appears that the criteria of selection become part of the subject's long term

memory. Postman points out that in recalling a rote series of high frequency words one week after learning, subjects rarely introduce new items even though each word has strong associates outside the list. As a result, interference at recall is produced primarily by the recovery of competing associations from within the list. As long as the contextual cues remain intact, as they do in most standard experiments on retention, the persistent operation of the selector mechanism severely restricts the population of interfering associations that compete with correct responses at recall.

3. *Nominal vs. Functional Conditions of Transfer.* The experimental evidence indicates that normative classifications of stimulus and response relationships do not always predict direction and amount of transfer effects that develop during learning and recall. What appears to take place is that subjects adopt methods of practice that substantially alter the conditions of transfer from those predictable on the basis of population norms; the probability that subjects will do this varies systematically with both the nature of the materials and the experimental setting. There has been increasing recognition of the need to distinguish between nominal and functional stimuli in learning; Postman points out that a parallel distinction between nominal and functional conditions of transfer and interference may prove equally essential.

4. *Recording and Interference.* There is little doubt that it is possible to enhance the amount of retention by introducing sequential dependencies, recoding, and other nonrandom rules of formation into the learning materials. Thus, no matter how carefully one constructs a series of unrelated items, there always remains a multiplicity of formal, grammatical and semantic dimensions that provide a basis for sequential linkages. The net effect on recall will depend not only on the appropriateness of the rules for recoding but also on the efficiency of the process of decoding.

SHORT TERM RETENTION AND DUAL THEORIES OF MEMORY

SHORT TERM RETENTION AND INTERFERENCE THEORY

A basic issue about which there is considerable controversy is whether short term retention decrement occurs because of a decay of the memory trace, or whether it takes place because of interfering associations. Decay theorists have assumed that short term retention depends on continuous rehearsal, and that retention decrement is due to decay that starts as soon as rehearsal is terminated.

Interference theorists, on the other hand—taking their cue from long term retention tradition—hypothesize that short term remembering continues unchecked so long as interfering associations are not present; forgetting is the direct result of competition between the original learning and interfering associations. In fact, some supporters of an interference theory even reject the position that short term memory should be differentiated from long term memory. As Melton (1963) so eloquently argued, both types of memory represent points on a retention continuum and similar processes operate in both situations.

In summary, both the decay and interference points of view predict rapid forgetting of short term memory as a result of interpolated activity; but they arrive at this conclusion by different routes. Decay theory posits that interfering associations prevent rehearsal and that this permits the decay process to operate; interference theory posits that either interpolated or previously learned material interferes with the to-be-recalled material.

The literature that has been published in this area during the past decade has been so extensive that we can do little more than present a small sample of the research findings. Let us begin with Peterson and Peterson's (1959) early study.

It will be recalled that these investigators obtained a declining retention curve, with recall intervals measured in seconds. These findings provided a kind of tentative support for the position that short term memory could be correlated with the establishment of a memory trace that decayed rapidly over time. Moreover, although Peterson and Peterson's (1959) experimental procedure was one in which each subject was tested eight times at the varying recall intervals, thus resulting in the exposure of each subject to forty-eight syllables during the course of the experiment, Peterson and Peterson reported no evidence of proactive inhibition—a second finding that would seem to provide support for the position that interference theory could not be used as an explanation for short term forgetting.

More to this latter point, it would be assumed by an interference theorist that items learned late in the experimental session should be subject to a greater number of potentially interfering associations than should those items presented early. However, when the number of correct responses within each successive block of twelve presentations was analyzed, with short recall intervals (three and six seconds) analyzed separately from long recall intervals (fifteen and eighteen seconds), the findings indicated that the proportions of correct responses for the short recall interval were .57, .66, .70 and .74, with the difference between the first and last blocks statistically significant. The proportions of correct responses for the long recall interval were .08, .15, .09, and .12, and the gain from the first to the last blocks was not significant. These findings support the authors' contention that proactive inhibition effects were not present.

A number of individuals, however, have pointed to the difficulty of assessing the role of proactive inhibition with this type of study. As the subject proceeds through the experiment, there is a learning-to-learn effect that may serve to counteract any retention decrement taking place as a function of the increasing number of potentially interfering associations.

Keppel and Underwood (1962), in keeping with this point of view, hypothesized that with short retention intervals, the learning-to-learn or practice effect should more than compensate for the increased interference provided by the increasing number of items presented. With long retention intervals, however, the interference is of sufficient magnitude to mask this effect. In one study, these investigators demonstrated the validity of their hypothesis. The Peterson and Peterson (1959) short term retention procedure was used, with single consonant trigrams employed as the material to be learned. One subgroup received retention intervals in the order of three-eighteen-three-eighteen, etc. whereas for the other subgroup, the intervals were presented in the reverse order. This procedure permitted an examination of retention of the items after three and eighteen seconds following zero, one, two, three, four, and five presentations. The proportions of correct responses for both intervals are presented in Fig. 12–14. As can be noted, with eighteen-second intervals, retention declined with successive tests, but this did not occur with three-second intervals. The authors

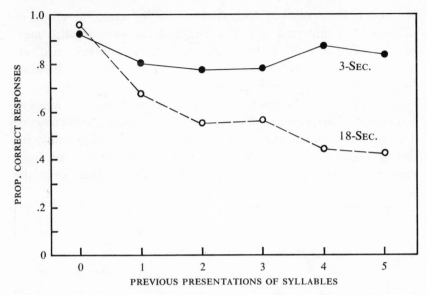

Fig. 12–14. Retention as a function of number of prior syllables and length of retention interval.
(Adapted from Keppel and Underwood 1962)

interpreted their findings as both indicating that short term memory was subject to proactive inhibition as well as supporting their hypothesis of an interaction between the amount of interference and the length of the retention interval.

Keppel and Underwood's (1962) findings, in addition to a similar study conducted by Loess (1964), suggest, however, that maximal interference, at least with Peterson and Peterson's (1959) type of experimental procedure, is provided after presentation of only a relatively small number of prior items.

A variety of other investigations have also testified to the in-fluence of inhibition effects on short term memory situations. In one experiment (experiment 2) of a series, Pollack, Johnson and Knaff (1959) demonstrated the influence of proactive inhibition on running memory span. In this study, subjects were orally pre-sented with varying lengths of randomly selected digits, and follow-ing this presentation, were asked to write down as many of the last numbers in the group as they could remember. Thus, it was necessary for the subjects to write under a column marked "Last Digit" the last number that they heard, then the next-to-last num-

ber in a column marked "Next-to-Last Digit," etc. One group of
subjects were informed as to the length of the to-be-recalled message, while a second group of subjects were not so informed, although all subjects were told that the messages would be between
four and forty digits in length.

Figure 12–15 indicates that auditory memory span decreases as
a function of message length, particularly for uninformed subjects.
The authors assumed that proactive inhibition was responsible for
this decrease, since the subjects' ability to remember the last digits
grew poorer as a function of the length of the message, once the

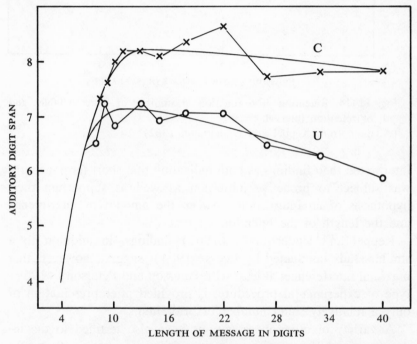

Fig. 12–15. Auditory memory span as a function of message length.
The abscissa is the length of the presented message. The ordinate is the
digital span in terms of the number of digits successively correct from the
end of the message. The curve marked (C) is associated with messages of
known or certain length; the curves marked (U) are associated with messages of unknown or uncertain length. Each point is based upon 160
messages (five subjects, eight blocks, four rates of presentation). The
points associated with message lengths of four to seven digits fall on the
smooth curves.

(Adapted from Pollock, Johnson and Knaff 1959)

number of digits presented was larger than the subjects' memory span.

In a second series of experiments, Pollack (1963), again using digits as his experimental material, demonstrated retroactive inhibition effects in a short term retention task. His general procedure was to have subjects view six-digit sequences of the numbers one through eight, randomly arranged. An interpolated task was then provided in which the subjects were required to recite aloud random sequences of either (a) the numbers zero and nine, or (b) the numbers one and eight. The number of interpolated interfering digits (one, two, four or sixteen) presented was varied, as was the rate at which they were presented (one, two, or three digits per second). Following the presentation of the intervening activity, the subjects were asked to recite the items that had been presented initially. Subjects were told how many interfering digits would be presented, and were encouraged to actively rehearse the originally presented sequence during each available opportunity. Results revealed that as the number of interfering digits increased, with the rate of presentation held constant, correct recall declined—a finding that clearly indicates the importance of inhibitory effects in short term retention.

In keeping with the long term retention studies, which indicate that the amount of forgetting can be related to the similarity between the original and interfering materials, Wickens and his associates have demonstrated almost the same effect in a proactive inhibition, short term retention experiment. In the first study of the series (Wickens, Born and Allen 1963), consonant trigrams (CCCs) and three digit numbers (NNNs) were used as the experimental material. A Peterson and Peterson (1959) procedure was utilized, with single items read to the subject, followed by an eleven-second retention interval filled with color-naming. Two major groups were employed; one group was presented with a series of CCCs and the other group with a series of NNNs. The general procedure consisted of presenting one type of material (either CCCs or NNNs) for a given number of trials (three, six, or nine) followed by a shift to the other type of material for the next trial. Thus, one group received three trials of CCC (or NNN) presentation, but was then shifted to the presentation of an NNN (or CCC) for the fourth trial. A second group received six trials of CCCs (or NNNs) but was then shifted to an NNN (or CCC) on the seventh. A third group received nine trials of CCCs (or NNNs) but was then shifted to the presentation of an NNN (or CCC) for the tenth trial. Control groups were run and received only CCCs or NNNs for ten trials. The results are presented in Fig. 12–16, which reveals the percent correct recall as a function of the number of previous items of the same or different classes.

First it may be noted that there is a clear and significant tendency for higher recall scores to be achieved with numbers; a basic question exists as to whether this type of material is freer of interfering effects than consonants, or whether the sample of items for the number class was easier than that for the consonant sample. The authors believed this latter explanation to be the correct one. In any event, the difference in recall as a function of the kind of material used was not of major concern. What was of interest, of course, was the marked improvement in recall when a group had been shifted to a new kind of material. Thus, it was found that

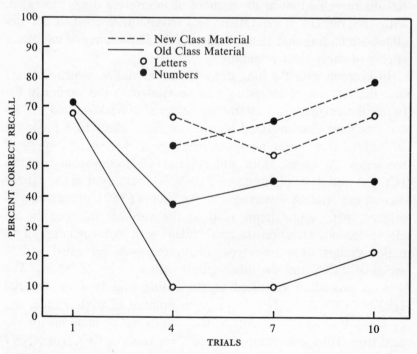

Fig. 12–16. Percent correct recall as a function of the number of previous items of the same and of a different class.

(Adapted from Wickens, Born and Allen 1961)

successive presentation of the same (or similar) type(s) of material results in a rapid build-up of proactive inhibition—a finding similar to that obtained by Keppel and Underwood (1962). When a different or nonsimilar type of material is presented, recall increases to a level not significantly different from that achieved by the control group on the first trial. In summary, the authors believed that

the experiment offers support for interference theory as a means of accounting for the forgetting which occurs in the STM situation: it does so because it demonstrates, as does the study of Keppel and Underwood, a decrement in recall as a consequence of the presentation of previous items, and that this decline is statistically identifiable only if the previous items are drawn from the same class of material as the test item (p. 444).

A subsequent study by Loess (1967) showed the same kind of proactive inhibition build-up, with subsequent release when subjects were shifted from a homogeneous class of word triads (such as a species of birds) to a new class of word triads (species of trees).

Wickens (1970) believes that in the short term memory situation, items presented seem to be encoded not only as unique items, but also as members of a given conceptual class. If items are from the same conceptual class, competition among the items results in recall decrement; on the other hand, if a different conceptual class of items is used, competition no longer occurs, or at least is minimal.

Studies by Wickens and Clark (1968), and Wickens, Clark, Hill and Wittlinger (1968) examined proactive inhibition effects as related to a variety of conceptual categories, with findings frequently, although not always, supporting the original Wickens, Born and Allen (1963) study.

The similarity variable—in this instance acoustic similarity—has also been shown to play a role in determining retroactive inhibition effects. Wickelgren (1965), using a Peterson and Peterson (1959) procedure, presented a list of four letters, followed immediately by a second list of eight letters. Subjects were instructed to write down all second-list letters as they were presented. The presentation rate was two letters per second, and the written task was followed by the immediate recall of the first four letters. Wickelgren found that recall of the original four-letter list was a function of the acoustic similarity of the intervening list to the original list. Thus an interfering list whose letters were pronounced similarly to those of the original list produced greater amounts of retroactive inhibition than an interfering list whose letters had a very different pronunciation. As might be anticipated, if the interfering list was composed of letters identical to those of the original list, but presented in a different order, there was less forgetting of the letters themselves, but more forgetting of their correct positions.

We have reviewed only a few of the many studies that have indicated that proactive and retroactive inhibition effects can be obtained with short term memory; it would appear that any theoretical formulation of short term memory must take into account the contribution of interfering associations.

Conrad (1967), however, proposed a modified decay model; "The modification proposes that during the retention interval, decay involves those characteristics of an item that make it discriminable, along the coding dimensions used in short term storage, from other items in an available set" (p. 52). From this model, he hypothesized that at very short recall intervals, items that are acoustically similar to the originally presented material will lead to greater confusion than acoustically dissimilar items. As the retention interval and decay increase, and the material loses its identifying characteristics, the number of erroneous alternative responses increase, with errors tending more and more toward chance. In an experiment by Conrad (1967), similar and dissimilar groups of consonants were used as the experimental material in a short term retention study. After the individual presentation of four consonants, i.e., BCFM, a short (2.4 seconds) or long (7.2 seconds) retention interval was provided during which the subjects read digits aloud, following which the four items were recalled. Results supporting Conrad's position indicated a significant difference in error distribution between the short and long intervals. At the short interval, errors tended to be acoustically similar to the correct letter, while at the long interval, errors tended more toward chance.[1]

[1] Some question must be raised as to whether the occurrence of overt errors is correlated with interference processes. Obviously Conrad (1967) believes this to be the case. We noted earlier in the chapter, however, in our examination of long term retention, that some question can be raised concerning the nature of this relationship.

DUAL THEORIES OF MEMORY

In the late 1950s, beginning with Broadbent's (1958) *Perception and Communication,* and continuing to the present time, a number of investigators working in the area of human information processing observed the need to formulate a theory of memory that would encompass their own experimental findings as well as those obtained with traditional long term retention operations. The general result has been the postulation of a variety of theories of memory, all of which hypothesize two basic systems of storage mechanism. Broadbent (1958), Waugh and Norman (1965), Glanzer and Cunitz (1966), Neisser (1967), and Atkinson and Shiffrin (1968) are some of the investigators who have posited theoretical models of memory that incorporate both long and short term mechanisms.[1] We cannot provide individual descriptions of the points of view expressed by all of these investigators. However, a composite view would indicate the following:

Neisser (1967), and Atkinson and Shiffrin (1968) hypothesized a mechanism that holds incoming sensory information while it is being initially processed. Atkinson and Shiffrin (1968) termed this the "sensory register," while Neisser (1967) referred to "iconic" (visual), and "echoic" (auditory) storage mechanisms. The experimental work of Sperling (1960), and Averbach and Coriell (1961) have been used to support the existence of this transient memory storage system. In Sperling's (1960) study, a 3x3 array of letters was tachistoscopically exposed for fifty milliseconds. In one part of the experiment, by means of a prearranged signal that was provided immediately after presentation of the letters, the subject was instructed to recall only a single row of the display. Under these circumstances, the subjects were almost 100 percent accurate in their reports of the critical row. If the signal was delayed, however, for even a fraction of a second, there was a marked decrease in accuracy.

---

[1] It should not be assumed that the dual theories of memory that have been posited during the past decade represent a new approach to this area. As early as 1890, William James conceptualized man's memory as consisting of a primary and a secondary system. Primary memory was a faithful record of events perceived by the individual in the psychological present, whereas secondary memory was related to the recalling of material from the past, and was characterized by omissions, gaps and distortions.

Information that is placed in the sensory register passes on to a memory system that has been known by a variety of names. Primary memory or working memory are two of these, although the term short term memory is most frequently employed. The sensory register mechanism was not included in the models of some theorists, so that short term or primary memory represents the first part of their two-part memory system. Waugh and Norman (1965) conceptualized primary memory in the same way that James (1890) did eighty years ago. An event in primary memory never leaves the organism's consciousness and is a part of his psychological present. Waugh and Norman believe that primary memory is illustrated in the individual's ability to recall verbatim the last few words in a sentence that he has heard even when he was barely paying attention to what was being said. Experimentally, the ability of a subject to immediately recall the last four or five words in a list also presumably illustrates the operation of this mechanism.

According to Shiffrin and Atkinson (1969), the short term memory system serves a number of useful functions. It decouples the memory system from the external environment and relieves the system from the responsibility of moment to moment attention to environmental changes. In addition, it provides the individual with a working memory in which manipulations of information may take place on a temporary basis.

What are the characteristics of short term memory? First, most investigators believe that short term memory has a very limited capacity. Atkinson and Shiffrin (1968) conceived of the short term store in terms of a buffer or fixed number of bins, or slots. As each new item comes into the system, it enters a bin and knocks out the item already there. This displaced item is either permanently lost or makes its way to the long term store.

Miller's (1956) work, which we reviewed previously and which indicates that the immediate memory span is limited to approximately seven chunks, has formed a basis for theorists who hold that short term memory storage is of very limited capacity.

A second aspect of short term memory, suggested by the work of Conrad (1962, 1964), is that this process involves acoustical representation of the information that is stored. In Conrad's (1964) most comprehensive study, two groups of letters that had been used earlier (Conrad 1962) were employed, since these letters had high within-group but low between-group acoustic confusability. The letters in the two groups were: B C P T V and F M N S X. In the first part of the study, these ten letters were divided into 120 six-letter sequences, i.e., B F V T S N. The letter order was random, although no letter occurred more than once in any six-letter sequence, and within each block of twenty sequences each of the ten letters occurred equally often in each serial position. The six letters were exposed individually at a .75-second rate, with subjects instructed to write down the letters in the order in which they were exposed following the presentation. Subjects were told to guess rather than leave blank spaces; the ten-letter vocabulary was written on the blackboard and thus was available for reference throughout the proceedings.

In the second part of the study, the auditory confusability of the twenty-six letters of the alphabet was determined. Subjects were instructed to listen carefully to the auditory presentation of each letter, which was partially masked by white noise, and to write down the letter they thought they heard. Again instructions emphasized that the subjects should guess rather than leave blanks. When the confusability of the ten visually presented letters of the first part of the study was compared with that of the same ten auditorily presented letters, there was substantial agreement between the two confusability matrices. See Table 12–5. The rank order correlation between errors in the two studies was .64, thus establishing the point that although the material had been visually presented, recall errors were similar in nature to hearing errors.

A third assumed characteristic is that short term memory can hold an item for only a short period of time without rehearsal, perhaps thirty seconds or less. The forgetting curve of single CCCs obtained by Peterson and Peterson (1959) has been used to describe the course of short term retention over periods of time measured in seconds, when the original item has not been rehearsed. The process of rehearsal is believed to play an important role in enabling an item to remain in short term memory, or in transferring it into long term memory.

Inasmuch as material cannot stay in the short term store for a prolonged period of time, it must be transferred to a long term store—the second component of a dual theory of memory. The process or mechanism involved in the transfer from short term to long term store is unknown, although many assume that practice or rehearsal is one variable that plays an important role in this

TABLE 12–5

LISTENING CONFUSIONS
Stimulus letter

		B	C	P	T	V	F	M	N	S	X
Response letter	B	.	171	75	84	168	2	11	10	2	2
	C	32	.	35	42	20	4	4	5	2	5
	P	162	350	.	505	91	11	31	23	5	5
	T	143	232	281	.	50	14	12	11	8	5
	V	122	61	34	22	.	1	8	11	1	0
	F	6	4	2	4	3	.	13	8	336	238
	M	10	14	2	3	4	22	.	334	21	9
	N	13	21	6	9	20	32	512	.	38	14
	S	2	18	2	7	3	488	23	11	.	391
	X	1	6	2	2	1	245	2	1	184	.

RECALL CONFUSIONS
Stimulus letter

		B	C	P	T	V	F	M	N	S	X
Response letter	B	.	18	62	5	83	12	9	3	2	0
	C	13	.	27	18	55	15	3	12	35	7
	P	102	18	.	24	40	15	8	8	7	7
	T	30	46	79	.	38	18	14	14	8	10
	V	56	32	30	14	.	21	15	11	11	5
	F	6	8	14	5	31	.	12	13	131	16
	M	12	6	8	5	20	16	.	146	15	5
	N	11	7	5	1	19	28	167	.	24	5
	S	7	21	11	2	9	37	4	12	.	16
	X	3	7	2	2	11	30	10	11	59	.

(Adapted from Conrad 1964)

process. Once material has been transferred into a long term memory, some investigators have assumed that a permanent trace is laid down, and that forgetting takes place because of an inability on the part of the individual to retrieve the information.

Penfield (1958), a neurosurgeon, provided some interesting physiological evidence to support the position that long term memory is permanent. Penfield's surgical procedure consisted of exposing a patient's cerebral cortex under local anesthesia. These patients had been afflicted by recurring attacks of focal epilepsy, and surgical excision of an abnormal area of cortex in which epileptogenic discharge arises appeared to relieve such patients of their attacks approximately 50 percent of the time. Before such excisions were carried out, Penfield explored the exposed cortex, applying a gentle electrical current to it from place to place in an effort to reproduce the beginning of a patient's attack and thus verify the position of the epileptogenic focus. He noted that stimulation of the temporal lobes frequently produced in the patient what he has called a psychical response—a meaningful integrated experience on the part of the patient. These psychical responses "include many different elements of thought, made up of auditory, visual, somatic and labyrinthine information, as well as interpretations, perceptions, comparisons, emotions" (p. 59).

Penfield likened these psychical responses to a stream of consciousness and attempted to indicate their nature by means of a parable:

Among the millions and millions of nerve cells that clothe certain parts of the temporal lobe on each side, there runs a thread. It is the thread of time, the thread that has run through each succeeding wakeful hour of the individual's past life. Think of this thread, if you like, as a pathway through an unending sequence of nerve cells, nerve fibers and synapses. It is a pathway which can be followed again because of the continuing facilitation that has been created in the cell contacts.

When, by chance, the neurosurgeon's electrode activates some portion of that thread, there is a response as though that thread were a wire recorder, or a strip of cinematographic film, on which are registered all those things of which the individual was once aware, the things he selected for his attention in that interval of time. Absent from it are the sensory impulses he ignored, the talk he did not heed (pp. 67–68).

Regardless of whether long term memories are temporary or permanent, any complete account of the processes involved must be speculative, as Shiffrin and Atkinson's (1969) recent treatment of this area has indicated.

In summary, a dual theory of memory has frequently been assumed to consist of a sensory register, a short term memory store, and a long term memory store. Shiffrin and Atkinson's (1969) model, to which we have frequently referred, is indicated in Fig. 12–17.

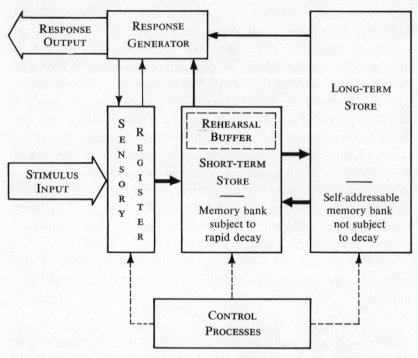

Fig. 12–17. A flow chart of the memory system. (Solid lines indicate paths of information transfer. Dashed lines indicate connections which permit comparison of information arrays residing in different parts of the system; they also indicate paths along which control signals may be sent which activate information transfer rehearsal mechanisms, etc.)

(Adapted from Shiffrin and Atkinson 1969)

EVIDENCE FOR A DUAL THEORY OF MEMORY

A variety of different types of evidence, some of which we have reviewed, have been used to support the position that memory can be divided into short term and long term stores. Glanzer and Cunitz (1966), supporters of a dual position, proposed that the U-shaped serial position curve found in free-recall studies is actually made up of two curves, with each curve representing output from a separate storage mechanism. The recall of items from the beginning of the list represents output from long term memory, while the recall of items from the end of the list is from short term storage. In a test of their position, the authors' strategy was to manipulate variables that should produce one effect on one end of the curve and a different effect (either no effect or an opposed effect) on the other end.

In their first experiment, presentation rate and number of presentations were varied, since both of these variables had been shown to play a role in long term retention studies. Twenty monosyllabic nouns were presented to three groups of subjects at a rate of either three, six, or nine seconds per word. In addition, presentation was varied for two other groups by presenting each word twice in succession at a three-second rate, or three times in succession, also at a three-second rate. Following presentation of the material, subjects had two minutes to write down all the words they could recall. An examination of the findings, as revealed in the recall of the beginning items of the list, indicated a clear and systematic effect from varying rates of presentation, and a similar but less clear effect from number of presentations. The rate of presentation effect is in keeping with findings of an earlier study by Murdock (1962). Inasmuch as the last items presented were unaffected, these findings were in keeping with the authors' hypothesis. The authors found surprising, however, the inability to secure a varying presentations effect, and they attempted to account for this by suggesting that the effect of repetition was cancelled by a covert rehearsal of unrepeated items.

In the second experiment, designed to investigate a variable that would influence short term but not long term retention, the authors manipulated the length of the delay between the end of the list and the beginning of the recall period. Subjects were given lists composed of fifteen high frequency nouns, presented at a rate of one word per second. They were then asked to recall freely the items in each list after retention intervals of either zero, ten, or thirty seconds. Subjects in the two delay conditions performed a counting task during the delay interval. As Fig. 12–18 reveals, increasing the delay prior to recall decreased the retention of items at the end of the list (short term memory function), but had no influence upon recall of items at the beginning of the list (long term memory function).

In summary, the differential serial position curves, obtained as a function of manipulating short term and long term retention variables, has been in keeping with Glanzer and Cunitz's (1966)

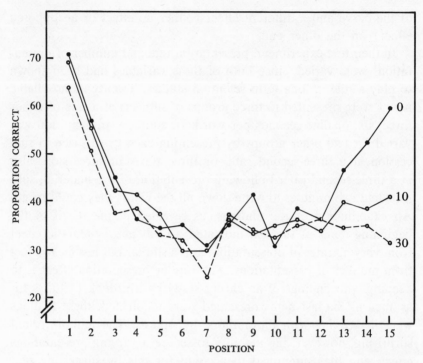

Fig. 12–18. Serial position curves for 0-, 10-, and 30-sec. delays. Each point represents the mean for five lists and forty-six Ss.
(Adapted from Glanzer and Cunitz 1966)

position that man's memory system can be conceptualized in terms of long term and short term mechanisms.

An earlier study by Sumby (1963), although not conducted with a view toward examining Glanzer and Cunitz's hypothesis, is in keeping with this position. As one part of Sumby's study, lists of fifteen words that varied in frequency were presented at a rate of two seconds per word, with a thirty-second free-recall period following each trial. Serial position curves were plotted as a function of high and low frequency words. For words presented at the end of the list there was no difference between high and low frequency words, as measured by percent correctly recalled. On the other hand, for words presented at the beginning of the list, high frequency words were recalled more easily than low. We find, then, that word frequency, which has frequently been demonstrated to be an important variable in learning studies, had no influence on recall for items at the end of the list—presumably short term memory was unaffected by this variable. On the other hand, long term memory, as inferred from performance at the beginning of the list, was influenced by this variable.[1]

Physiological Evidence for a Dual Theory of Memory

A number of memory theorists have used physiological evidence to support the position that the distinction between short term and long term memory is a valid one.

One of the early studies was undertaken by Moore (1919), who was interested in seeing whether perception, immediate memory, and long term memory could be related to different localizable cortical centers. The approach used was to examine subjects who had a history of cortical involvement so that it might be possible to find some individuals in whom one function could be seriously affected without the other being involved. In the part of the study that has primary relevance for us, a task was employed in which subjects were exposed to eight individual items—one about every two seconds. The items were pictures, printed words, spoken words, and actual objects. Following a single presentation of the material, the subject was called upon to repeat as many of the items as he could without regard to the original order of presentation. When he was unable to recall any more items, he was engaged in solving a series of simple arithmetical problems for one minute. After this, he was again asked to indicate the items that had been presented. Two measures of memory were obtained from these tests: (1) the number of items that were immediately recalled, and (2) the ratio of what was remembered after one minute to the value obtained for immediate memory.

The subjects who were tested were diagnosed as suffering from dementia paralytica, dementia senilis, or chronic alcoholism. It was assumed that all of these conditions would produce diffuse although not identical cortical impairment. Analysis of the performance measures led Moore (1919) to conclude that the evidence supported the distinction of immediate memory and the

[1] A basic problem, of course, is that some of the short term retention studies reviewed in the last chapter indicated that high frequency words were better recalled than low frequency words after very short recall intervals.

power of retention as two separate and distinct mental functions.

In the studies we have reported, cerebral deficit was inferred from the behavior of the patient, but anatomical localization of the deficit was not determined. Studies by Penfield and Milner (1958), Penfield (1959), and Drachman and Arbit (1966) were more precise in their identification of the location of the cerebral insult. Earlier in this chapter we discussed the neurological work of Penfield, who used the procedure of removing a portion of the temporal lobes for relief of epilepsy. Penfield and Milner (1958) reported that *bilateral* removal of the hippocampus and hippo-campalgyrus in man results in a loss of recent memory. As these authors wrote,

as soon as he has turned his attention to something else, the patient is unable to remember what was happening a moment earlier. It is as though he had made no record of present experience. . . . Psychological study of our patients shows that, in spite of the above-noted deficiencies, memory for the distant past is not lost, nor is there corresponding loss of attention, concentration, reasoning ability, or previously acquired skills. The intelligence quotient shows no drop when compared with preoperative testing. There is no interference with speech, and the memory of words is unimpaired (p. 495).

These authors reported that their findings confirmed an earlier report by Glees and Griffith (1952), who had written that the hippocampal formation of the adult appears to be essential for recent memory.

A more analytic presentation of the nature of this dual function of memory is found in a paper by Milner (1968), as reported by Atkinson and Shiffrin (1968). On the basis of her work with Penfield, Milner wrote,

Bilateral surgical lesions in the hippocampal region, on the mesial aspect of the temporal lobes, produce a remarkably severe and persistent memory disorder in human patients, the pattern of breakdown providing valuable clues to the cerebral organization of memory. Patients with these lesions show no loss of preoperatively acquired skills, and intelligence as measured by formal tests is unimpaired, but, with the possible exception of acquiring motor skill, they seemed largely incapable of adding new information to the long-term store. This is true whether acquisition is measured by free recall, recognition, or learning with savings. Nevertheless the immediate registration of new input (as measured, for example, by digit span and dichotic listening tests) appears to take place normally and material which can be encompassed by verbal rehearsal is held for many minutes without further loss than that entailed in the initial verbalization. Interruption of rehearsal, regardless of the nature of the distracting task, produces immediate forgetting of what went before and some quite simple material which cannot be categorized in verbal terms decays in 30 seconds or so, even without an interpolated distraction. Material already in long-term store is unaffected by the lesion, except for a certain amount of retrograde amnesia for preoperative events [as quoted by Atkinson and Shiffrin 1968, p. 97].

Drachman and Arbit (1966) compared patients with bilateral hippocampal lesions to normals in a somewhat more systematic study. Their approach was to examine "immediate memory span" and then extend the material to be recalled beyond this so that it would be necessary for subjects to take a number of trials before being able to recall the material perfectly. They believed that this procedure would separate pure memory "storage" from immediate memory span of the individual. Five patients with bilateral lesions of the hippocampal regions were studied along with twenty controls. The digit span task began with five digits that the subjects had to immediately recall following presentation; the task then continued with the addition of a single digit each time the subjects recalled the previous span perfectly. Once the number was increased beyond the memory span, additional trials were provided in order to enable the subjects to reach the criterion of one perfect trial. In addition, a paired-light span was also used that was conceptually similar to the digit span task. Results obtained from both tasks were similar. Findings of the extended digit span task are indicated in Fig. 12–19, where it can be noted that the digit storage capacity for the control group was twenty digits or greater for normal subjects, while no patient had a digit storage capacity of greater than twelve digits; the mean digit storage capacity score for the patient group was 8.60. Similar differences between the two groups were obtained for the extended paired-light span task.

In commenting upon these findings, the authors wrote that when subspan items are used, the subject requires only a single trial for perfect recall. Some kind of "holding mechanism" enables him to recall and repeat the items contained in the list. Although there is no way of preventing some more lasting storage from taking place, such storage is not needed for successful recall of material that is

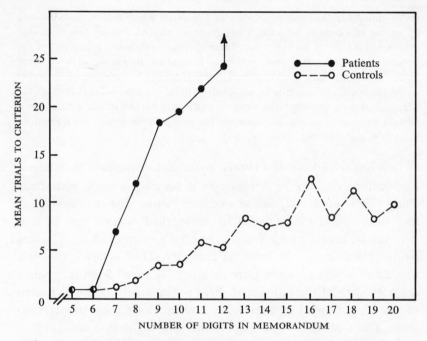

Fig. 12–19. Extended digit span: mean trials to criterion for subspan and supraspan memoranda. Patients with hippocampal lesions require many more trials than controls to achieve criterion with supraspan memoranda; no patient successfully recalled more than twelve digits.

(Adapted from Drachman and Arbit 1966)

presented within the organism's memory span. When the material is beyond the immediate memory span, however, the subject requires multiple repetitions to achieve perfect recall. Thus, he must accumulate information with successive exposures so that some memory storage must take place from trial to trial, enduring at least throughout the series of trials until the final correct recall is provided. When such material was used, with multiple repetitions provided, normal subjects were able to recall as many as twenty digits and ten paired lights; by contrast, all of the patients had great difficulty in recalling the items in excess of their immediate memory span and none succeeded beyond twelve digits or six paired lights. The authors concluded that it appears to be quite clear that patients with bilateral hippocampal lesions show a marked deficit of storage ability, while their holding mechanisms or immediate memory span were unimpaired.

Penfield and Milner (1958) reported that unilateral partial temporal lobectomy, including the hippocampus and hippocamal-gyrus, is a reasonably successful method of treating focal epilepsy, and that this operation does not cause any serious psychological impairment—provided the opposite temporal lobe is functioning normally. They found that unilateral operations do not normally cause a generalized memory disturbance, although with lesions of the dominant temporal lobe there may be difficulty in learning and retention specific to verbal material. They pointed out two cases, however, in which a unilateral operation did result in an unexpected and generalized loss of recent memory, from which subsequent recovery was only slight. They found, however, that these patients had impairment of the other lobe, which presumably caused these results. Such a factor may account for Walker's (1957) and Victor, Angevine, Mancall and Fisher's (1961) reports of cases in which unilateral excision did result in a memory deficit.

SUMMARY

Early experimental work suggested that long term forgetting could be accounted for in terms of interfering responses that were acquired either prior to the original learning (proactive inhibition) or between the original learning and the subsequent test for retention (retroactive inhibition). In either case, it was assumed that during the test for the retention of the original material, these responses interfered with those that were to be recalled, and this in turn resulted in retention decrement.

Investigators examining proactive and retroactive inhibition effects have demonstrated that similarity of the stimuli comprising the original and interfering material is an important contributor to the amount of forgetting. A second variable, degree of learning, has also been shown to play an important role in retention decrement; the experimental evidence indicates that as interfering responses increase in strength, whether they arise from prior or interpolated learning, retention of the original material declines.

A second factor that has been postulated as an important contributor to retroactive inhibition is unlearning. Researchers postulate that as the subject reacts with first-list responses during the learning of the interpolated material, these responses extinguish or are unlearned. However, such unlearning is believed to recover in strength over time, much as extinguished conditioned responses reveal spontaneous recovery.

Recent developments have centered around an examination of the unlearning process, since it has been generally accepted that by using a modified free-recall test—asking the subject to give both first- and second-list responses—during the retention test period, response competition or the role of interfering responses can be minimized. A variety of experimental studies have investigated the characteristics of the unlearning process, but have not been entirely convincing in demonstrating the viability of this construct. Recent consideration of this problem by Postman, Stark and Fraser (1968) resulted in an emphasis by these investigators on what they termed "response set interference" as an important variable in forgetting.

Many investigators have assumed that interference must also play an important role in short term forgetting, and a large number of experiments have shown this assumption to be tenable. It has been further demonstrated that the degree of similarity of the interfering material to the original material is an important factor in determining the amount of such forgetting.

A number of theorists have posited that memory consists of both a short term and a long term store. According to these theorists, short term memory has a very limited capacity, and can hold an item for only a short period of time without rehearsal. Inasmuch as material cannot stay in the short term store for a prolonged period of time, it must be transferred to a long term store, where some investigators have posited that a permanent trace is established. The postulation of such a dual system has been supported by behavioral as well as physiological evidence.

Bibliography

Adams, J. A. The second facet of forgetting: A review of warm-up decrement. *Psychological Bulletin,* 1961, **58,** 257–273.

Adams, J. A. *Human memory.* New York: McGraw-Hill, 1967.

Allan, M. D. Memorizing, recoding, and perceptual organization. *British Journal of Psychology,* 1961, **52,** 25–30.

Anderson, N. S. Poststimulus cuing to immediate memory. *Journal of Experimental Psychology,* 1960, **60,** 216–221.

Archer, E. J. A re-evaluation of the meaningfulness of all possible CVC trigrams. *Psychological Monographs,* 1960, **74,** No. 10.

Archer, E. J. Some comments on Noble's "measurement of association value (a), etc. . . ." *Psychological Reports,* 1961, **9,** 679–680.

Atkinson, R. C., and Shiffrin, R. M. Human memory: A proposed system and its control processes. In Spence, K. W., and Spence, J. T., Eds., *The psychology of learning and motivation.* New York: Academic Press, 1968.

Atwater, S. K. Proactive inhibition and associative facilitation as affected by degree of prior learning. *Journal of Experimental Psychology,* 1953, **46,** 400–404.

Ausubel, D., Robbins, K., and Blake, F., Jr. Retroactive inhibition and facilitation in the learning of school materials. *Journal of Educational Psychology,* 1957, **48,** 334–343.

Avant, L. L., and Bevan, W. The role of stimulus variation in learning to name stimulus classes and their individual cases. *Journal of General Psychology,* 1969, **80,** 47–55.

Averbach, E., and Coriell, A. S. Short-term memory in vision. *Bell System Technical Journal,* 1961, **40,** 309–328.

Bahrick, H. P. Retention curves: Facts or artifacts? *Psychological Bulletin,* 1964, **61,** 188–194.

Bahrick, H. P., and Bahrick, P. O. A re-examination of the interrelations among measures of retention. *Quarterly Journal of Experimental Psychology,* 1964, **16,** 318–324.

Bakan, D. A generalization of Sidman's results on group and individual functions and criterion. *Psychological Bulletin,* 1954, **51,** 63–64.

Barnes, J. M., and Underwood, B. J. "Fate" of first-list associations in transfer theory. *Journal of Experimental Psychology,* 1959, **58,** 97–105.

Barraud, E. M. The development of behaviour in some young passerines. *Bird Study,* 1961, **8,** 111–118.

Bartlett, F. C. *Remembering.* Cambridge: Cambridge University Press, 1932.

Barton, D. E., and David, F. N. Multiple runs. *Biometrika,* 1957, **44,** 168–178.

Bastian, J. R. Response chaining in verbal transfer. Unpublished doctoral dissertation, University of Minnesota, 1956.

Battig, W. F. Procedural problems in paired-associate learning research. *Psychonomic Monograph Supplements,* 1965, **1.**

Battig, W. F. Facilitation and interference. In Bilodeau, E. A., Ed., *Acquisition of skill.* New York: Academic Press, 1966.

Battig, W. F. Paired-associate learning. In Dixon, T. R., and Horton, D. L., Eds., *Verbal behavior and general behavior theory.* Englewood Cliffs, N.J.: Prentice-Hall, 1968.

Battig, W. F., and Brackett, H. R. Comparison of anticipation and recall methods in paired-associate learning. *Psychological Reports,* 1961, **9,** 59–65.

Battig, W. F., Brown, S. C., and Nelson, D. Constant vs. varied serial order in paired-associate learning. *Psychological Reports,* 1963, **12,** 695–721.

Battig, W. F., Brown, S. C., and Schild, M. E. Serial position and sequential associations in serial learning. *Journal of Experimental Psychology,* 1964, **67,** 449–457.

Battig, W. F., and Lawrence, P. S. The greater sensitivity of the serial recall than anticipation procedure to variations in serial order. *Journal of Experimental Psychology,* 1967, **73,** 172–178.

Battig, W. F., and Montague, W. E. Category norms for verbal items in 56 categories: A replication and extension of the Connecticut category norms. *Journal of Experimental Psychology, Monograph,* 1969, **80.**

Battig, W. F., and Spera, A. J. Rated association values of numbers from 0–100. *Journal of Verbal Learning and Verbal Behavior,* 1962, **1,** 200–202.

Battig, W. F., and Wu, R. D. Comparison of recall and anticipation paired-associate procedures within mixed aurally-presented lists. *Psychonomic Science,* 1965, **3**, 233–234.

Baumeister, A. A., and Hawkins, W. F. Stimulus-response durations in paired-associate learning. *Psychonomic Science,* 1966, **4**, 167.

Belmont, L., and Birch, H. G. Re-individualizing and the repression hypothesis. *Journal of Abnormal and Social Psychology,* 1951, **46**, 226–235.

Berlyne, D. E., Borsa, D. M., Craw, M. A., Gelman, R. S., and Mandell, E. E. Effects of stimulus complexity and induced arousal on paired-associate learning. *Journal of Verbal Learning and Verbal Behavior,* 1965, **4**, 291–299.

Berlyne, D. E., Borsa, D. M., Hamacher, J. H., and Koenig, I. D. V. Paired-associate learning and the timing of arousal. *Journal of Experimental Psychology,* 1966, **72**, 1–6.

Bernbach, H. A. Stimulus learning and recognition in paired-associate learning. *Journal of Experimental Psychology,* 1967, **75**, 513–519.

Berry, R. N. Skin conductance levels and verbal recall. *Journal of Experimental Psychology,* 1962, **63**, 275–277.

Besch, N. F., and Reynolds, W. F. Associative interference in verbal paired-associate learning. *Journal of Experimental Psychology,* 1958, **55**, 554–558.

Besch, N. F., Thompson, V. E., and Wetzel, A. B. Studies in associative interference. *Journal of Experimental Psychology,* 1962, **63**, 342–352.

Bevan, W., and Dukes, W. F. Stimulus variation and recall: The role of belongingness. *American Journal of Psychology,* 1967, **80**, 309–312.

Bevan, W., Dukes, W. F., and Avant, L. L. The effect of variation in specific stimuli on memory for their superordinates. *American Journal of Psychology,* 1966, **79**, 250–257.

Bilodeau, I. McD., and Schlosberg, H. Similarity in stimulating conditions as a variable in retroactive inhibition. *Journal of Experimental Psychology,* 1951, **41**, 199–204.

Birnbaum, I. Long-term retention of first-list associations in the A-B, A-C paradigm. *Journal of Verbal Learning and Verbal Behavior,* 1965, **4**, 515–520.

Birnbaum, I. M. Unlearning as a function of second-list dominance. *Journal of Verbal Learning and Verbal Behavior,* 1968, **7**, 257–259.

Bone, R. N., and Goulet, L. R. Serial position and the von Restorff isolation effect. *Journal of Experimental Psychology,* 1968, **76**, 494–496.

Borkowski, J. G., and Eisner, H. C. Meaningfulness and abstractness in short-term memory. *Journal of Experimental Psychology,* 1968, **76**, 57–61.

Bourne, L. E., Jr. An evaluation of the effect of induced tension on performance. *Journal of Experimental Psychology,* 1955, **49,** 418–422.

Bourne, L. E., Jr., and Parker, B. K. Interitem relationships, list structure, and verbal learning. *Canadian Journal of Psychology,* 1964, **18,** 52–61.

Bousfield, W. A. The occurrence of clustering in the recall of randomly arranged associates. *Journal of General Psychology,* 1953, **49,** 229–240.

Bousfield, W. A., and Cohen, B. H. The occurrence of clustering in the recall of randomly arranged words of different frequencies of usage. *Journal of General Psychology,* 1955, **52,** 83–95.

Bousfield, W. A., and Cohen, B. H. Clustering in recall as a function of the number of word categories in stimulus-word lists. *Journal of General Psychology,* 1956, **54,** 95–106.

Bousfield, W. A., Cohen, B. H., and Whitmarsh, G. A. Associative clustering in the recall of words of different taxonomic frequencies of occurrence. *Psychological Reports,* 1958, **4,** 39–44.

Bousfield, W. A., and Puff, C. R. Clustering as a function of response dominance. *Journal of Experimental Psychology,* 1964, **67,** 76–79.

Bousfield, W. A., Puff, C. R., and Cowan, T. M. The development of constancies in sequential organization during repeated free recall. *Journal of Verbal Learning and Verbal Behavior,* 1964, **3,** 489–495.

Bousfield, W. A., Steward, J. R., and Cowan, T. M. The use of free associational norms for the predictions of clustering. *Journal of General Psychology,* 1964, **70,** 205–214.

Bousfield, W. A., Whitmarsh, G. A., and Berkowitz, H. Partial response identities in associative clustering. *Journal of General Psychology,* 1960, **63,** 233–238.

Bousfield, W. A., Whitmarsh, G. A., and Esterson, J. Serial position effects and the "Marbe effect" in the free recall of meaningful words. *Journal of General Psychology,* 1958, **59,** 255–262.

Bowers, H. Memory and mental imagery. An experimental study. *British Journal of Psychology,* 1931, **21,** 271–282.

Bowers, H. Factors influencing visual imagery for letter groups. *American Journal of Psychology,* 1932, **44,** 775–779.

Bowman, R. E., and Thurlow, W. R. Determinants of the effect of position in serial learning. *American Journal of Psychology,* 1963, **76,** 436–445.

Braud, W. G., Tolin, P., and Holborn, S. W. Pronunciability rating and learning of doubly homogeneous paired-associate lists. *Psychonomic Science,* 1966, **6,** 457–458.

Braun, H. W., and Heymann, S. P. Meaningfulness of material, distribution of practice, and serial-position curves. *Journal of Experimental Psychology,* 1958, **56,** 146–150.

Bregman, A. S. Distribution of practice and between-trials interference. *Canadian Journal of Psychology,* 1967, **21,** 1–14.

Brelsford, J. W., Jr., and Atkinson, R. C. Recall of paired-associates as a function of overt and covert rehearsal procedures. *Journal of Verbal Learning and Verbal Behavior,* 1968, **7,** 730–736.

Brewer, C. L. Presentation time, trials to criterion, and total time in verbal learning. *Journal of Experimental Psychology,* 1967, **73,** 159–162.

Briggs, G. E. Acquisition, extinction, and recovery functions in retroactive inhibition. *Journal of Experimental Psychology,* 1954, **47,** 285–293.

Briggs, G. E. Retroactive inhibition as a function of degree of original and interpolated activity. *Journal of Experimental Psychology,* 1957, **53,** 60–67.

Broadbent, D. E. *Perception and communication.* New York: Pergamon Press, 1958.

Brown, J. Some tests of the decay theory of immediate memory. *Quarterly Journal of Experimental Psychology,* 1958, **10,** 12–21.

Brown, J., and Huda, M. Response latencies produced by massed and spaced learning of a paired-associates list. *Journal of Experimental Psychology,* 1961, **61,** 360–364.

Bruce, D., and Cofer, C. N. An examination of recognition and free recall as measures of acquisition and long-term retention. *Journal of Experimental Psychology,* 1967, **75,** 283–289.

Bruce, R. W. Conditions of transfer of training. *Journal of Experimental Psychology,* 1933, **16,** 343–361.

Bruder, G. A. Effects of method of presentation on paired-associate learning. *Journal of Experimental Psychology,* 1969, **79,** 383–384.

Bugelski, B. R. Presentation time, total time, and mediation in paired-associate learning. *Journal of Experimental Psychology,* 1962, **63,** 409–412.

Bugelski, B. R. Images as mediators in one-trial paired-associate learning II: Self-timing in successive lists. *Journal of Experimental Psychology,* 1968, **77,** 328–334.

Bugelski, B. R., and Cadwallader, T. C. A reappraisal of the transfer and retroaction surface. *Journal of Experimental Psychology,* 1956, **52,** 360–365.

Bugelski, B. R., Kidd, E., and Segmen, J. Image as a mediator in one-trial paired-associate learning. *Journal of Experimental Psychology,* 1968, **76,** 69–73.

Bugelski, B. R., and Rickwood, J. Presentation time, total time, and mediation in paired-associate learning: Self-pacing. *Journal of Experimental Psychology,* 1963, **65,** 616–617.

Bugelski, B. R., and Scharlock, D. P. An experimental demonstration of unconscious mediated association. *Journal of Experimental Psychology,* 1952, **44,** 334–338.

Calkins, M. W. Association. *Psychological Review,* 1894, **1,** 476–483.

Calkins, M. W. Association: An essay analytic and experimental. *Psychological Review Monograph Supplements,* 1896, **2.**

Ceraso, J., and Henderson, A. Unavailability and associative loss in RI and PI. *Journal of Experimental Psychology,* 1965, **70,** 300–303.

Ceraso, J., and Henderson, A. Unavailability and associative loss in RI and PI: Second try. *Journal of Experimental Psychology,* 1966, **72,** 314–316.

Cheng, N. Y. Retroactive effect and degree of similarity. *Journal of Experimental Psychology,* 1929, **12,** 444–449.

Cieutat, V. J. Differential familiarity with stimulus and response in paired-associate learning. *Perceptual and Motor Skills,* 1960, **11,** 269–275.

Cieutat, V. J., Stockwell, F. E., and Noble, C. E. The interaction of ability and amount of practice with stimulus and response meaningfulness (m, m') in paired-associate learning. *Journal of Experimental Psychology,* 1958, **56,** 193–202.

Clark, L. L., Lansford, T. G., and Dallenbach, K. M. Repetition and associative learning. *American Journal of Psychology,* 1960, **73,** 22–40.

Cochran, S. W. Rated association values of 251 colors. *Journal of Verbal Learning and Verbal Behavior,* 1968, **7,** 14–15.

Cochran, S. W., and Wickens, D. D. Supplementary report: Rated association values of numbers from 0–100. *Journal of Verbal Learning and Verbal Behavior,* 1963, **2,** 373–374.

Cofer, C. N. A study of clustering in free recall based on synonyms. *Journal of General Psychology,* 1959, **60,** 3–10.

Cofer, C. N. On some factors in the organizational characteristics of free recall. *American Psychologist,* 1965, **20,** 261–272.

Cofer, C. N. Learning of content and function words in nonsense syllable frames: A replication and extension of Glanzer's experiment. *Journal of Verbal Learning and Verbal Behavior,* 1967, **6,** 198–202.

Cofer, C. N., Bruce, D. R., and Reicher, G. M. Clustering in free recall as a function of certain methodological variations. *Journal of Experimental Psychology,* 1966, **71,** 858–877.

Cofer, C. N., Diamond, F., Olsen, R. A., Stein, J. S., and Walker, H. Comparison of anticipation and recall methods in paired-associate learning. *Journal of Experimental Psychology,* 1967, **75,** 545–558.

Cohen, B. H. Recall of categorized word lists. *Journal of Experimental Psychology,* 1963, **66,** 227–234.

Cohen, B. H., Bousfield, W. A., and Whitmarsh, G. A. Cultural norms for verbal items in 43 categories. Technical Report No. 22, Contract Nonr 631(00), Office of Naval Research and University of Connecticut, 1957.

Cohen, J. C., and Musgrave, B. S. Effect of meaningfulness on cue selection in verbal paired-associate learning. *Journal of Experimental Psychology,* 1964, **68,** 284–291.

Coleman, E. B. Approximations to English. *American Journal of Psychology,* 1963, **76,** 239–247

Coleman, E. B. The association hierarchy as an indicator of extra-experimental interference. *Journal of Verbal Learning and Verbal Behavior,* 1963, **2,** 417–421. (a)

Conrad, R. An association between memory errors and errors due to acoustic masking of speech. *Nature,* 1962, **193,** 1314–1315.

Conrad, R. Acoustic confusions in immediate memory. *British Journal of Psychology,* 1964, **55,** 75–84.

Conrad, R. Interference or decay over short retention intervals? *Journal of Verbal Learning and Verbal Behavior,* 1967, **6,** 49–54.

Cook, J. O. Supplementary report: Processes underlying learning a single paired-associate item. *Journal of Experimental Psychology,* 1958, **56,** 455.

Cook, J. O., and Kendler, T. S. A theoretical model to explain some paired-associate learning data. In G. Finch and F. Cameron, Eds., *Symposium on Air Force human engineering, personnel, and training research.* Washington, D.C.: National Academy of Sciences—National Research Council Publication 455, 1956.

Cook, J. O., and Spitzer, M. E. Supplementary report: Prompting versus confirmation in paired-associate learning. *Journal of Experimental Psychology,* 1960, **59,** 275–276.

Cooper, E. H., and Pantle, A. J. The total-time hypothesis in verbal learning. *Psychological Bulletin,* 1967, **68,** 221–234.

Costantini, A. F., and Blackwood, R. O. CCC trigrams of low association value: A re-evaluation. *Psychonomic Science,* 1968, **12,** 67–68.

Crowder, R. G. Evidence for the chaining hypothesis of serial verbal learning. *Journal of Experimental Psychology,* 1968, **76,** 497–500.

Crowder, R. G., Chisholm, D. D., and Fell, D. A. Transfer from serial to continuous paired-associate learning. *Psychonomic Science,* 1966, **6,** 455–456.

Dallett, K. M. The transfer surface re-examined. *Journal of Verbal Learning and Verbal Behavior,* 1962, **1,** 91–94.

Dallett, K. M. The role of response similarity in proactive inhibition. *Journal of Experimental Psychology,* 1962, **64,** 364–372. (a)

Dallett, K. M. Number of categories and category information in free recall. *Journal of Experimental Psychology,* 1964, **68,** 1–12.

Dallett, K. M. Implicit mediators in paired-associate learning. *Journal of Verbal Learning and Verbal Behavior,* 1964, **3,** 209–214. (a)

Dallett, K. M. A transfer surface for paradigms in which second-list S-R pairings do not correspond to first-list pairings. *Journal of Verbal Learning and Verbal Behavior,* 1965, **4,** 528–534.

Daves, W. F., and Adkins, M. Stimulus variation and free recall: A confirmation. *American Journal of Psychology,* 1969, **82,** 122–124.

Davis, F. C. The relative reliability of words and nonsense syllables. *Journal of Experimental Psychology,* 1930, **13,** 221–234.

Davis, R., Sutherland, N. S., and Judd, B. R. Information content in recognition and recall. *Journal of Experimental Psychology,* 1961, **61,** 422–429.

Davis, R. A. *Psychology of learning.* New York: McGraw-Hill, 1935.

Davis, W. L., Brown, S. C., and Ritchie, E. Cue selection as a function of degree of learning and response similarity. *Journal of Experimental Psychology,* 1968, **78,** 323–328.

Deese, J. Serial organization in the recall of disconnected items. *Psychological Reports,* 1957, **3,** 577–582.

Deese, J. Influence of inter-item associative strength upon immediate free recall. *Psychological Reports,* 1959, **5,** 305–312.

Deese, J. Frequency of usage and number of words in free recall: The role of associations. *Psychological Reports,* 1960, **7,** 337–344.

Deese, J. From the isolated verbal unit to connected discourse. In Cofer, C. N., Ed., *Verbal learning and verbal behavior.* New York: McGraw-Hill, 1961.

Deese, J., and Hardman, G. W., Jr. An analysis of errors in retroactive inhibition of rote verbal learning. *American Journal of Psychology,* 1954, **67,** 299–307.

Deese, J., and Kaufman, R. A. Serial effects in recall of unorganized and sequentially organized verbal material. *Journal of Experimental Psychology,* 1957, **54,** 180–187.

Deese, J., Lazarus, R. S., and Keenan, J. Anxiety, anxiety reduction, and stress in learning. *Journal of Experimental Psychology,* 1953, **46,** 55–60.

Dillon, R. F., and Reid, L. S. Short-term memory as a function of information processing during the retention interval. *Journal of Experimental Psychology,* 1969, **81,** 261–269.

Dinner, J., and Duncan, C. P. Warm-up in retention as a function of degree of verbal learning. *Journal of Experimental Psychology,* 1959, **57,** 257–261.

DiVesta, F. J., and Ingersoll, G. M. Influence of pronounceability, articulation, and test mode on paired-associate learning by the study-recall procedure. *Journal of Experimental Psychology,* 1969, **79,** 104–108.

Dowling, R. M., and Braun, H. W. Retention and meaningfulness of material. *Journal of Experimental Psychology,* 1957, **54,** 213–217.

Drachman, D. A., and Arbit, J. A. Memory and the hippocampal complex: II. Is memory a multiple process? *Archives of Neurology,* 1966, **15,** 52–61.

Dukes, W. F., and Bastian, J. Recall of abstract and concrete words equated for meaningfulness. *Journal of Verbal Learning and Verbal Behavior,* 1966, **5,** 455–458.

Dukes, W. F., and Bevan, W. Stimulus variation and repetition in the acquisition of naming responses. *Journal of Experimental Psychology,* 1967, **74,** 178–181.

Earhard, B., and Mandler, G. Pseudomediation: A reply and more data. *Psychonomic Science,* 1965, **3,** 137–138.

Earhard, M. Cued recall and free recall as a function of the number of items per cue. *Journal of Verbal Learning and Verbal Behavior,* 1967, **6,** 257–263.

Earhard, M. Storage and retrieval of words encoded in memory. *Journal of Experimental Psychology,* 1969, **80,** 412–418.

Ebbinghaus, H. *Memory: A contribution to experimental psychology,* H. A. Ruger and C. E. Bussenius, trans. 1913. New York: Teachers College, Columbia University, 1885.

Ebenholtz, S. M. Position mediated transfer between serial learning and a spatial discrimination task. *Journal of Experimental Psychology,* 1963, **65,** 603–608.

Ebenholtz, S. M. Serial learning: Position learning and sequential associations. *Journal of Experimental Psychology,* 1963, **66,** 353–362. (a)

Ekstrand, B. R. Effect of sleep on memory. *Journal of Experimental Psychology,* 1967, **75,** 64–72.

Ekstrand, B., and Underwood, B. J. Paced versus unpaced recall in free learning. *Journal of Verbal Learning and Verbal Behavior,* 1963, **2,** 288–290.

Ekstrand, B. R., and Underwood, B. J. Free learning and recall as a function of unit-sequence and letter-sequence interference. *Journal of Verbal Learning and Verbal Behavior,* 1965, **4,** 390–396.

Ellis, H. C. Transfer and retention. In Marx, M. H., Ed., *Learning: Processes*. Toronto: Macmillan, 1969.

Epstein, W. The influence of syntactical structure on learning. *American Journal of Psychology,* 1961, **74,** 80–85.

Epstein, W. A further study of the influence of syntactical structure on learning. *American Journal of Psychology,* 1962, **75,** 121–126.

Epstein, W. Temporal schemata in syntactically structured material. *Journal of General Psychology,* 1963, **68,** 157–164.

Epstein, W. Some conditions of the influence of syntactical structure on learning: Grammatical transformation, learning instructions, and "chunking." *Journal of Verbal Learning and Verbal Behavior,* 1967, **6,** 415–419.

Epstein, W., Rock, I., and Zuckerman, C. B. Meaning and familiarity in verbal learning. *Psychological Monographs,* 1960, **74,** No. 491.

Erickson, C. C., Ingram, R. D., and Young, R. K. Paired-associate learning as a function of rate of presentation and prior serial learning. *American Journal of Psychology,* 1963, **76,** 458–463.

Erickson, R. L. Relational isolation as a means of producing the von Restorff effect in paired-associate learning. *Journal of Experimental Psychology,* 1963, **66,** 111–119.

Erickson, R. L. Differential effects of stimulus and response isolation in paired-associate learning. *Journal of Experimental Psychology,* 1965, **69,** 317–323.

Erickson, R. L. Role of associative learning in the production of differential stimulus-response isolation effects. *Journal of Verbal Learning and Verbal Behavior,* 1968, **7,** 225–229.

Estes, W. K. The problem of inference from curves based on group data. *Psychological Bulletin,* 1956, **53,** 134–140.

Feldman, S. M., and Underwood, B. J. Stimulus recall following paired-associate learning. *Journal of Experimental Psychology,* 1957, **53,** 11–15.

Frankart, J. The relationship between grammaticalness and utilization of short-range associations. Unpublished doctoral dissertation, Ohio State University, 1964.

Friedman, M. J., and Reynolds, J. H. Retroactive inhibition as a function of response-class similarity. *Journal of Experimental Psychology,* 1967, **74,** 351–355.

Frincke, G. Word characteristics, associative-relatedness, and the free-recall of nouns. *Journal of Verbal Learning and Verbal Behavior,* 1968, **7,** 366–372.

Gagne, R. M. *The conditions of learning.* New York: Holt, Rinehart and Winston, 1965.

Gagne, R. M., Baker, K. E., and Foster, H. On the relation between similarity and transfer of training in the learning of discriminative motor tasks. *Psychological Review,* 1950, **57,** 67–79.

Gagne, R. M., Foster, H., and Crowley, M. E. The measurement of transfer of training. *Psychological Bulletin,* 1948, **45,** 97–130.

Gannon, D. R., and Noble, C. E. Familiarization (*n*) as a stimulus factor in paired-associate verbal learning. *Journal of Experimental Psychology,* 1961, **62,** 14–23.

Garskof, B. E., and Houston, J. P. Measurement of verbal relatedness: An idiographic approach. *Psychological Review,* 1963, **70,** 277–288.

Gates, A. I. Recitation as a factor in memorizing. *Archives of Psychology,* 1917, **6,** No. 40.

Gentile, J. R., and Seibel, R. A rating scale measure of word relatedness. *Journal of Verbal Learning and Verbal Behavior,* 1969, **8,** 252–256.

Gibson, E. J. Retroactive inhibition as a function of degree of generalization between tasks. *Journal of Experimental Psychology,* 1941, **28,** 93–115.

Gibson, E. J. Intra-list generalization as a factor in verbal learning. *Journal of Experimental Psychology,* 1942, **30,** 185–200.

Gibson, E. J., Bishop, C. H., Schiff, W., and Smith, J. Comparison of meaningfulness and pronunciability as grouping principles in the perception and retention of verbal material. *Journal of Experimental Psychology,* 1964, **67,** 173–182.

Gillette, A. L. Learning and retention: A comparison of three experimental procedures. *Archives of Psychology,* 1936, **28.**

Gladis, M., and Abbey, O. Relationship between whole and part methods of learning and degree of meaningfulness of serial lists. *Journal of Experimental Psychology,* 1969, **81,** 194–196.

Gladis, M., and Braun, H. W. Age differences in transfer and retroaction as a function of intertask response similarity. *Journal of Experimental Psychology,* 1958, **55,** 25–30.

Glanzer, M. Grammatical category: A rote learning and word association analysis. *Journal of Verbal Learning and Verbal Behavior,* 1962, **1,** 31–41.

Glanzer, M., and Cunitz, A. R. Two storage mechanisms in free recall. *Journal of Verbal Learning and Verbal Behavior,* 1966, **5,** 351–360.

Glaze, J. A. The association value of nonsense syllables. *Journal of Genetic Psychology,* 1928, **35,** 255–269.

Glees, P., and Griffith, H. B. Bilateral destruction of the hippocampus (Cornu ammonis) in a case of dementia. *Monatsschrift Psychiatry and Neurology,* 1952, **129,** 193–204.

Goggin, J. First-list recall as a function of second-list learning method. *Journal of Verbal Learning and Verbal Behavior,* 1967, **6,** 423–427.

Gorfein, D. S., and Stone, W. G. Encoding interval in short-term memory. *Journal of Verbal Learning and Verbal Behavior,* 1967, **6,** 520–522.

Gorman, A. M. Recognition memory for nouns as a function of abstractness and frequency. *Journal of Experimental Psychology,* 1961, **61,** 23–29.

Goss, A. E., Morgan, C. H., and Golin, S. J. Paired-associates learned as a function of percentage of occurrence of response members (reinforcement). *Journal of Experimental Psychology,* 1959, **57,** 96–104.

Goss, A. E., and Nodine, C. *Paired-associates learning: The role of meaningfulness, similarity, and familiarization.* New York: Academic Press, 1965.

Goss, A. E., Nodine, C. F., Gregory, B., Taub, H., and Kennedy, K. Stimulus characteristics and percentage of occurrence of response members in paired-associate learning. *Psychological Monographs,* 1962, **76.**

Goulet, L. R. Anxiety (Drive) and verbal learning: Implications for research and some methodological considerations. *Psychological Bulletin,* 1968, **69,** 235–247.

Greenberg, R., and Underwood, B. J. Retention as a function of stage of practice. *Journal of Experimental Psychology,* 1950, **40,** 452–457.

Greeno, J. G. Paired-associate learning with massed and distributed repetitions of items. *Journal of Experimental Psychology,* 1964, **67,** 286–295.

Greenspoon, J., and Ranyard, R. Stimulus conditions and retroactive inhibition. *Journal of Experimental Psychology,* 1957, **53,** 55–59.

Gumenik, W. E., and Levitt, J. The von Restorff effect as a function of difference of the isolated item. *American Journal of Psychology,* 1968, **81,** 247–252.

Guthrie, E. R. *The psychology of learning.* New York: Harper and Row, 1935.

Haagen, C. H. Synonymity, vividness, familiarity, and association value ratings of 400 pairs of common adjectives. *Journal of Psychology,* 1949, **27,** 453–463.

Hakes, D. T., James, C. T., and Young, R. K. A re-examination of the Ebbinghaus derived list paradigm. *Journal of Experimental Psychology,* 1964, **68,** 508–514.

Hall, J. F. Learning as a function of word-frequency. *American Journal of Psychology,* 1954, **67,** 138–140.

Hall, J. F. Retroactive inhibition in meaningful material. *Journal of Educational Psychology,* 1955, **46,** 47–52.

Hall, J. F. *Psychology of learning.* Philadelphia: J. B. Lippincott Co., 1966.

Hall, J. F. Relationships among a number of measures of meaningfulness. *American Journal of Psychology,* 1967, **80,** 291–293.

Hall, J. F. A note on the relationship between the Thorndike-Lorge and Underwood-Schulz frequency counts. *Journal of Verbal Learning and Verbal Behavior,* 1967, **6,** 771–772. (a)

Hall, J. F. Paired-associate learning as related to "pronunciability" and word frequency. *Canadian Journal of Psychology,* 1968, **22,** 212–216.

Hamilton, C. E. The relationship between length of interval separating two learning tasks and performance on the second task. *Journal of Experimental Psychology,* 1950, **40,** 613–621.

Hamilton, R. J. Retroactive facilitation as a function of degree of similarity between tasks. *Journal of Experimental Psychology,* 1943, **32,** 363–376.

Harrington, A. L. Effects of component emphasis on stimulus selection in paired-associate learning. *Journal of Experimental Psychology,* 1969, **79,** 412–418.

Haun, K. W. Measures of association and verbal learning. *Psychological Reports,* 1960, **7,** 451–460.

Hawker, J. R. The influence of training procedure and other task variables in paired-associate learning. *Journal of Verbal Learning and Verbal Behavior,* 1964, **3,** 70–76.

Hayes, K. J. The backward curve: A method for the study of learning. *Psychological Review,* 1953, **60,** 269–275.

Hebb, D. O. Drives and the C.N.S. (Conceptual nervous system). *Psychological Review,* 1955, **62,** 243–254.

Hellyer, S. Supplementary report: Frequency of stimulus presentation and short-term decrement in recall. *Journal of Experimental Psychology,* 1962, **64,** 650.

Heron, W. T. The warming-up effect in learning nonsense syllables. *Journal of Genetic Psychology,* 1928, **35,** 219–228.

Hilgard, E. R. Methods and procedures in the study of learning. In Stevens, S. S., Ed., *Handbook of experimental psychology.* New York: Wiley, 1951.

Hilgard, E. R., and Bower, G. H. *Theories of learning* (3rd ed.). New York: Appleton-Century-Crofts, 1966.

Hilgard, E. R., and Campbell, A. A. The course of acquisition and retention of conditioned eyelid responses in man. *Journal of Experimental Psychology,* 1936, **21,** 310–319.

Hinde, R. A. *Animal behaviour.* New York: McGraw-Hill, 1966.

Horowitz, L. M. Free recall and ordering of trigrams. *Journal of Experimental Psychology,* 1961, **62,** 51–57.

Horowitz, L. M., and Izawa, C. Comparison of serial and paired-associate learning. *Journal of Experimental Psychology,* 1963, **65,** 352–361.

Horton, D. L. The effects of meaningfulness, awareness, and type of design in verbal mediation. *Journal of Verbal Learning and Verbal Behavior,* 1964, **3,** 187–194.

Horton, D. L., and Kjeldergaard, P. M. An experimental analysis of associative factors in mediated generalization. *Psychological Monographs,* 1961, **75.**

Houston, J. P. Verbal transfer and interlist similarities. *Psychological Review,* 1964, **71,** 412–416.

Houston, J. P. First-list retention and time and method of recall. *Journal of Experimental Psychology,* 1966, **71,** 839–843.

Houston, J. P. Stimulus selection as influenced by degrees of learning, attention, prior associations, and experience with the stimulus components. *Journal of Experimental Psychology,* 1967, **73,** 509–516.

Houston, J. P., and Johnson, O. Unlearning and the unreinforced evocation of first-list responses. *Journal of Verbal Learning and Verbal Behavior,* 1967, **6,** 451–453.

Hovland, C. I. Experimental studies in rote-learning theory: III. Distribution of practice with varying speeds of syllable presentation. *Journal of Experimental Psychology,* 1938, **23,** 172–190.

Hovland, C. I. Experimental studies in rote-learning theory: V. Comparison of distribution of practice in serial and paired-associate learning. *Journal of Experimental Psychology,* 1939, **25,** 622–633.

Hovland, C. I. Experimental studies in rote-learning theory: VI. Comparison of retention following learning to same criterion by massed and distributed practice. *Journal of Experimental Psychology,* 1940, **26,** 568–587.

Hovland, C. I. Experimental studies in rote-learning theory: VII. Distribution of practice with varying lengths of list. *Journal of Experimental Psychology,* 1943, **27,** 271–284. (a)

Hovland, C. I. Experimental studies in rote-learning theory: VIII. Distributed practice of paired-associates with varying rates of presentation. *Journal of Experimental Psychology,* 1949, **39,** 714–718.

Hovland, C. I., and Kurtz, K. H. Experimental studies in rote learning: X. Pre-syllable familiarization and the length-difficulty relationship. *Journal of Experimental Psychology,* 1952, **44,** 31–39.

Howe, T. S. Unlearning and competition in List-1 recall. *Journal of Experimental Psychology,* 1967, **75,** 559–565.

Howes, D. A word count of spoken English. *Journal of Verbal Learning and Verbal Behavior,* 1966, **5,** 572–604.

Hudson, R. L. Category clustering as a function of level of information and number of stimulus presentations. *Journal of Verbal Learning and Verbal Behavior,* 1968, **7,** 1106–1122.

Hull, C. L. The meaningfulness of 320 selected nonsense syllables. *American Journal of Psychology,* 1933, **45,** 730–734.

Hull, C. L. The conflicting psychologies of learning—a way out. *Psychological Review,* 1935, **42,** 491–516.

Hull, C. L. *Mathematico-deductive theory of rote learning: A study in scientific methodology.* New Haven: Yale University Press, 1940.

Hull, C. L. *Principles of behavior.* New York: Appleton-Century-Crofts, 1943.

Hull, C. L. *Essentials of behavior.* New Haven: Yale University Press, 1951.

Hull, C. L. *A behavior system.* New Haven: Yale University Press, 1952.

Hume, D. An enquiry concerning human understanding. In Burtt, E. A., Ed., *The English philosophers from Bacon to Mill.* New York: Modern Library, 1939.

Hunter, W. S. Experimental studies in learning. In Murchison, C., Ed., *Foundations of experimental psychology.* Worcester: Clark University Press, 1929.

Irion, A. L. Retention and warming-up effects in paired-associate learning. *Journal of Experimental Psychology,* 1949, **39,** 669–675.

Irion, A. L., and Wham, D. S. Recovery from retention loss as a function of amount of pre-recall warm-up. *Journal of Experimental Psychology,* 1951, **41,** 242–247.

Jacobs, A. Formation of new associations to words selected on the basis of reaction-time-GSR combinations. *Journal of Abnormal and Social Psychology,* 1955, **51,** 371–377.

Jacobs, J. Experiments on "prehension." *Mind,* 1887, **12,** 75–79.

Jahnke, J. C. Serial position effects in immediate serial recall. *Journal of Verbal Learning and Verbal Behavior,* 1963, **2,** 284–287.

James, C. T., and Greeno, J. G. Stimulus selection at different stages of paired-associate learning. *Journal of Experimental Psychology,* 1967, **74,** 75–83.

James, W. *Principles of psychology.* New York: Holt, Rinehart and Winston, 1890.

Jenkins, J. G., and Dallenbach, K. M. Obliviscence during sleep and waking. *American Journal of Psychology,* 1924, **35,** 605–612.

Jenkins, J. J. Stimulus "fractionation" in paired-associate learning. *Psychological Reports,* 1963, **13,** 409–410.

Jenkins, J. J. Mediated associates: Paradigms and situations. In Cofer, C. N., and Musgrave, B. S., Eds., *Verbal behavior and learning.* New York: McGraw-Hill, 1963. (a)

Jenkins, J. J., and Bailey, V. C. Cue selection and mediated transfer in paired-associates learning. *Journal of Experimental Psychology,* 1964, **67,** 101–102.

Jenkins, J. J., Mink, W. D., and Russell, W. A. Associative clustering as a function of verbal association strength. *Psychological Reports,* 1958, **4,** 127–136.

Jenkins, J. J., and Russell, W. A. Associative clustering during recall. *Journal of Abnormal and Social Psychology,* 1952, **47,** 818–821.

Jenkins, P. M., and Cofer, C. N. An exploratory study of discrete free association to compound verbal stimuli. *Psychological Reports,* 1957, **3,** 599–602.

Jenkins, W. O., and Postman, L. An experimental analysis of set in rote learning: Retroactive inhibition as a function of changing set. *Journal of Experimental Psychology,* 1949, **39,** 69–72.

Jensen, A. R. The von Restorff isolation effect with minimal response learning. *Journal of Experimental Psychology,* 1962, **64,** 123–125.

Jensen, A. R., and Rohwer, W. D., Jr. Verbal mediation in paired-associate and serial learning. *Journal of Verbal Learning and Verbal Behavior,* 1963, **1,** 346–352.

Jensen, A. R., and Rohwer, W. D., Jr. Syntactical mediation of serial and paired-associate learning as a function of age. *Child Development,* 1965, **36,** 601–608.

Jensen, A. R., and Rohwer, W. D., Jr. What is learned in serial learning? *Journal of Verbal Learning and Verbal Behavior,* 1965, **4,** 62–72. (a)

Jersild, A. Primacy, recency, frequency, and vividness. *Journal of Experimental Psychology,* 1929, **12,** 58–70.

Johnson, L. M. The relative effect of a time interval upon learning and retention. *Journal of Experimental Psychology,* 1939, **24,** 169–179.

Johnson, N. F. The functional relationship between amount learned and frequency vs. rate vs. total time of exposure of verbal materials. *Journal of Verbal Learning and Verbal Behavior,* 1964, **3,** 502–504.

Johnson, N. F. The influence of grammatical units on learning. *Journal of Verbal Learning and Verbal Behavior,* 1968, **7,** 236–240.

Johnson, R. C. Reanalysis of "meaningfulness and verbal learning." *Psychological Review,* 1962, **69,** 233–238.

Jones, F. M., and Jones, M. H. Vividness as a factor in learning lists of nonsense syllables. *American Journal of Psychology,* 1942, **55,** 96–101.

Jung, J. Transfer of training as a function of degree of first-list learning. *Journal of Verbal Learning and Verbal Behavior,* 1962, **1,** 197–199.

Jung, J. Effects of response meaningfulness (*m*) on transfer of training under two different paradigms. *Journal of Experimental Psychology,* 1963, **65,** 377–384.

Jung, J. Transfer analysis of familiarization effects. *Psychological Review,* 1967, **74,** 523–29.

Jung, J. *Verbal learning.* New York: Holt, Rinehart and Winston, 1968.

Kalish, H. I., Garmezy, N., Rodnick, E. H., and Bleke, R. C. The effects of anxiety and experimentally-induced stress on verbal learning. *Journal of General Psychology,* 1958, **59,** 87–95.

Kanungo, R. N. Learning of content, function, and nonsense words: An extension of Glanzer's experiment. *Journal of Verbal Learning and Verbal Behavior,* 1969, **8,** 262–265.

Kaplan, S., and Kaplan, R. Arousal and memory: A comment. *Psychonomic Science,* 1968, **10,** 291–292.

Kausler, D. A., and Kanoti, G. A. R-S learning and negative transfer effects with a mixed list. *Journal of Experimental Psychology,* 1963, **65,** 201–205.

Keppel, G. Problems of method in the study of short-term memory. *Psychological Bulletin,* 1965, **63,** 1–13.

Keppel, G., and Postman, L. Studies of learning to learn: III. Conditions of improvement in successive transfer tasks. *Journal of Verbal Learning and Verbal Behavior,* 1966, **5,** 260–267.

Keppel, G., Postman, L., and Zavortink, B. Studies of learning to learn: VIII. The influence of massive amounts of training upon the learning and retention of paired-associate lists. *Journal of Verbal Learning and Verbal Behavior,* 1968, **7,** 790–796.

Keppel, G., and Rauch, D. S. Unlearning as a function of second-list error instructions. *Journal of Verbal Learning and Verbal Behavior,* 1966, **5,** 50–58.

Keppel, G., and Rehula, R. J. Rate of presentation in serial learning. *Journal of Experimental Psychology,* 1965, **69,** 121–125.

Keppel, G., and Saufley, W. A., Jr. Serial position as a stimulus in serial learning. *Journal of Verbal Learning and Verbal Behavior,* 1964, **3,** 335–343.

Keppel, G., and Underwood, B. J. Proactive inhibition in short-term retention and single items. *Journal of Verbal Learning and Verbal Behavior,* 1962, **1,** 153–161.

Keppel, G., and Zavortink, B. Unlearning and competition in serial learning. *Journal of Verbal Learning and Verbal Behavior,* 1968, **7,** 142–147.

Kimble, G. A. *Hilgard and Marquis' Conditioning and learning.* New York: Appleton-Century-Crofts, 1961.

Kimble, G. A., and Dufort, R. H. Meaningfulness and isolation as factors in verbal learning. *Journal of Experimental Psychology,* 1955, **50,** 361–368.

King, D. J. On the accuracy of written recall: A scaling and factor analytic study. *Psychological Record,* 1960, **10,** 113–122.

King, D. J. Scaling the accuracy of recall of stories in the absence of objective criteria. *Psychological Record,* 1961, **11,** 87–90.

King, D. J. Contextual constraint and retroaction in verbal material. *Journal of General Psychology,* 1966, **75,** 39–63.

King, D. J., and Russell, G. W. A comparison of rote and meaningful learning of connected meaningful material. *Journal of Verbal Learning and Verbal Behavior,* 1966, **5,** 478–483.

King, D. J., and Schultz, D. P. Additional observations on scoring the accuracy of written recall. *Psychological Record,* 1960, **10,** 203–209.

King, D. J., and Tanenbaum, S. Comparison of two procedures in the study of retroactive interference in connected meaningful material. *Journal of Experimental Psychology,* 1963, **65,** 420–421.

King, D. J., and Yu, K. C. The effects of reducing the variability of length of written recalls on the rank order scale of the recalls. *Psychological Record,* 1962, **12,** 39–44.

Kintsch, W., and McCoy, D. F. Delay of informative feedback in paired-associate learning. *Journal of Experimental Psychology,* 1964, **68,** 372–375.

Kjeldergaard, P. M. Transfer and mediation in verbal learning. In Dixon, T. R., and Horton, D. L., Eds., *Verbal behavior and general behavior theory.* Englewood Cliffs, N.J.: Prentice-Hall, 1968.

Kjerstad, C. L. The form of the learning curves for memory. *Psychological Monographs,* 1919, **26.**

Kleinsmith, L. J., and Kaplan, S. Paired-associate learning as a function of arousal and interpolated interval. *Journal of Experimental Psychology,* 1963, **65,** 190–193.

Kleinsmith, L. J., and Kaplan, S. Interaction of arousal and recall interval in nonsense syllable paired-associate learning. *Journal of Experimental Psychology,* 1964, **67,** 124–126.

Kleinsmith, L. J., Kaplan, S., and Tarte, R. D. The relationship of arousal to short- and long-term verbal recall. *Canadian Journal of Psychology,* 1963, **17,** 393–397.

Koppenaal, R. J. Time changes in strengths of A-B, A-C lists; spontaneous recovery? *Journal of Verbal Learning and Verbal Behavior,* 1963, **2,** 310–319.

Kothurkar, V. K. Effect of stimulus-response meaningfulness on paired-associate learning and retention. *Journal of Experimental Psychology,* 1963, **65,** 305–308.

Krueger, W. C. F. The effect of overlearning on retention. *Journal of Experimental Psychology,* 1929, **12,** 71–78.

Krueger, W. C. F. The relative difficulty of nonsense syllables. *Journal of Experimental Psychology,* 1934, **17,** 145–153.

Kučera, H., and Francis, W. N. *Computational analysis of present-day American English.* Providence, R.I.: Brown University Press, 1967.

Kuiken, D., and Schulz, R. W. Response familiarization and the associative phase of paired-associate learning. *Journal of Verbal Learning and Verbal Behavior,* 1968, **7,** 106–109.

L'Abate, L. Manifest anxiety and the learning of syllables with different associative values. *American Journal of Psychology,* 1959, **72,** 107–110.

Lachman, R., and Dooling, D. J. Connected discourse and random strings: Effects of number of inputs on recognition and recall. *Journal of Experimental Psychology,* 1968, **77,** 517–522.

Lambert, W. E., and Paivio, A. The influence of noun-adjective order on learning. *Canadian Journal of Psychology,* 1956, **10,** 9–12.

Lashley, K. S. The problem of serial order in behavior. In Jeffress, L. A., Ed., *Cerebral mechanisms in behavior: The Hixon symposium.* New York: Wiley, 1951.

Laughery, K. R., and Pinkus, A. L. Recoding and presentation rate in short-term memory. *Journal of Experimental Psychology,* 1968, **76,** 636–641.

Laurence, M. W. Age differences in performance and subjective organization in the free-recall learning of pictorial material. *Canadian Journal of Psychology,* 1966, **20,** 388–399.

Lazarus, R. S., Deese, J., and Hamilton, R. Anxiety and stress in learning: The role of intra-serial duplication. *Journal of Experimental Psychology,* 1954, **47,** 111–114.

Lepley, W. M. Serial reactions considered as conditioned reactions. *Psychological Monographs,* 1934, **46.**

Lester, O. F. Mental set in relation to retroactive inhibition. *Journal of Experimental Psychology,* 1932, **15,** 681–699.

Levonian, E. Attention and consolidation as factors in learning. *Psychonomic Science,* 1966, **6,** 275–276.

Lindley, R. H. Association value and familiarity in serial verbal learning. *Journal of Experimental Psychology,* 1960, **59,** 366–370.

Lindley, R. H. Association value, familiarity, and pronunciability ratings as predictors of serial verbal learning. *Journal of Experimental Psychology,* 1963, **65,** 347–351.

Lindley, R. H. Effects of controlled coding cues in short-term memory. *Journal of Experimental Psychology,* 1963, **66,** 580–587. (a)

Lindley, R. H., and Stone, W. G. Measures of meaningfulness and ease of free recall. *Journal of Verbal Learning and Verbal Behavior,* 1967, **6,** 264–267.

Lloyd, K. E., Reid, L. S., and Feallock, J. B. Short-term retention as a function of the average number of items presented. *Journal of Experimental Psychology,* 1960, **60,** 201–207.

Lockhart, R. S. Stimulus selection and meaningfulness in paired-associate learning with stimulus items of high formal similarity. *Journal of Experimental Psychology,* 1968, **78,** 242–246.

Lockhead, G. R. Methods of presenting paired associates. *Journal of Verbal Learning and Verbal Behavior,* 1962, **1,** 62–65.

Loess, H. Proactive inhibition in short-term memory. *Journal of Verbal Learning and Verbal Behavior,* 1964, **3,** 362–367.

Loess, H. Short-term memory, word class, and sequence of items. *Journal of Experimental Psychology,* 1967, **74,** 556–561.

Logan, F. A. *Learning and motivation.* Dubuque, Iowa: W. C. Brown Co., 1969.

Lovelace, E. A., and Blass, E. M. Utilization of stimulus elements in paired associate learning. *Journal of Experimental Psychology,* 1968, **76,** 596–600.

Lucas, J. D. The interactive effects of anxiety, failure, and intra-serial duplication. *American Journal of Psychology,* 1952, **65,** 59–66.

Luh, C. W. The conditions of retention. *Psychological Monographs,* 1922, **31.**

Lyon, D. O. The relation of length of material to time taken for learning and the optimum distribution of time. *Journal of Educational Psychology,* 1914, 5, I. 1–9, II. 85–91, III. 155–163.

Madden, M. S., Adams, J. A., and Spence, S. A. Memory-drum vs. adjusted-learning techniques in the study of associative interference in learning by paired associates. *American Journal of Psychology,* 1950, **63,** 186–195.

Maltzman, I., Kantor, W., and Langdon, B. Immediate and delayed retention, arousal, and the orienting and defense reflexes. *Psychonomic Science,* 1966, **6,** 445–446.

Mandler, G. Response factors in human learning. *Psychological Review,* 1954, **61,** 235–244.

Mandler, G. Associative frequency and associative prepotency as measures of response to nonsense syllables. *American Journal of Psychology,* 1955, **68,** 662–665.

Mandler, G. Organization and memory. In Spence, K. W., and Spence, J. T., Eds., *The psychology of learning and motivation.* New York: Academic Press, 1967.

Mandler, G. Association and organization: Facts, fancies, and theories. In Dixon, T. R., and Horton, D. L., Eds., *Verbal behavior and general behavior theory.* Englewood Cliffs, N.J.: Prentice-Hall, 1968.

Mandler, G., and Earhard, B. Pseudomediation: Is chaining an artifact? *Psychonomic Science,* 1964, **1,** 247–248.

Mandler, G., and Heinemann, S. H. Effect of overlearning of a verbal response on transfer of training. *Journal of Experimental Psychology,* 1956, **52,** 39–46.

Mandler, G., and Huttenlocher, J. The relation between associative frequency, associative ability, and paired-associate learning. *American Journal of Psychology,* 1956, **69,** 424–428.

Marks, L. E., and Miller, G. A. The role of semantic and syntactic constraints in the memorization of English sentences. *Journal of Verbal Learning and Verbal Behavior,* 1964, **3,** 1–5.

Marks, M. R., and Jack, O. Verbal context and memory span for meaningful material. *American Journal of Psychology,* 1952, **65,** 298–300.

Marshall, G. R., and Cofer, C. N. Associative indices as measures of word relatedness: A summary and comparison of ten methods. *Journal of Verbal Learning and Verbal Behavior,* 1963, **1,** 408–421.

Martin, C. J., and Saltz, E. Serial versus random presentation of paired associates. *Journal of Experimental Psychology,* 1963, **65,** 609–615.

Martin, E. Transfer of verbal paired associates. *Psychological Review,* 1965, **72,** 327–343.

Martin, E. Stimulus recognition in aural paired-associate learning. *Journal of Verbal Learning and Verbal Behavior,* 1967, **6,** 272–276.

Martin, E. Stimulus meaningfulness and paired-associate transfer: An encoding variability hypothesis. *Psychological Review,* 1968, **75,** 421–441.

Martin, E., and Roberts, K. H. Grammatical factors in sentence retention. *Journal of Verbal Learning and Verbal Behavior,* 1966, **5,** 211–218.

Martin, E., and Roberts, K. H. Sentence length and sentence retention in the free-learning situation. *Psychonomic Science,* 1967, **8,** 535–536.

Martin, J. G. Associative strength and word frequency in paired-associative learning. *Journal of Verbal Learning and Verbal Behavior,* 1964, **3,** 317–320.

Martin, M. A. The transfer effects of practice in cancellation tests. *Archives of Psychology,* 1915, **4,** No. 32.

Marx, M. H. Learning processes. In Marx, M. H., Ed., *Learning: Processes.* Toronto: Macmillan, 1969.

Mathews, R. Recall as a function of the number of classificatory categories. *Journal of Experimental Psychology,* 1954, **47,** 241–247.

McCormack, P. D., and Haltrecht, E. J. Two-stage paired-associate learning and eye movements. *Science,* 1965, **148,** 1749–1750.

McCrary, J. W., and Hunter, W. S. Serial position curves in verbal learning. *Science,* 1953, **117,** 131–134.

McGehee, N. E., and Schulz, R. W. Mediation in paired-associate learning. *Journal of Experimental Psychology,* 1961, **62,** 565–570.

McGeoch, J. A. The influence of degree of learning upon retroactive inhibition. *American Journal of Psychology,* 1929, **41,** 252–262.

McGeoch, J. A. The influence of associative value upon the difficulty of non-sense syllable lists. *Journal of Genetic Psychology,* 1930, **37,** 421–426.

McGeoch, J. A. Forgetting and the law of disuse. *Psychological Review,* 1932, **39,** 352–370.

McGeoch, J. A. *The psychology of human learning.* New York: David McKay, 1942.

McGeoch, J. A., and Irion, A. L. *The psychology of human learning* (2d ed.). New York: David McKay, 1952.

McGeoch, J. A., and McKinney, F. The susceptibility of prose to retroactive inhibition. *American Journal of Psychology,* 1934, **46,** 429–436.

McGeoch, J. A., and McKinney, F. Studies in retroactive inhibition: VIII. The influence of the relative order of presentation on original and interpolated paired associates. *Journal of Experimental Psychology,* 1937, **20,** 60–83.

McGeoch, J. A., and Underwood, B. J. Tests of the two-factor theory of retroactive inhibition. *Journal of Experimental Psychology,* 1943, **32,** 1–16.

McGovern, J. B. Extinction of associations in four transfer paradigms. *Psychological Monographs,* 1964, **78,** No. 16.

McGuire, W. J. A multiprocess model for paired-associate learning. *Journal of Experimental Psychology,* 1961, **62,** 335–347.

McLaughlin, J. P. The von Restorff effect in serial learning: Serial position of the isolate and length of list. *Journal of Experimental Psychology,* 1966, **72,** 603–609.

McManis, D. L. Relative errors with three lengths of serial list. *Psychological Reports,* 1965, **16,** 1086–1088.

McNulty, J. A. An analysis of recall and recognition processes in verbal learning. *Journal of Verbal Learning and Verbal Behavior,* 1965, **4,** 430–436.

Meehl, P. E. On the circularity of the law of effect. *Psychological Bulletin,* 1950, **47,** 52–75.

Mehler, J. Some effects of grammatical transformations on the recall of English sentences. *Journal of Verbal Learning and Verbal Behavior,* 1963, **2,** 346–351.

Melton, A. W. A comparative study of the materials employed in experimental investigations of memory. Unpublished M.A. thesis, Yale University, 1929.

Melton, A. W. The end-spurt in memorization curves as an artifact of the averaging of individual curves. *Psychological Monographs,* 1936, **47,** No. 212.

Melton, A. W. Implications of short-term memory for a general theory of memory. *Journal of Verbal Learning and Verbal Behavior,* 1963, **2,** 1–21.

Melton, A. W. Individual differences and theoretical process variables: General comments on the conference. In Gagne, R. M., Ed., *Learning and individual differences.* Columbus, Ohio: Charles E. Merrill, 1967.

Melton, A. W., and Irwin, J. M. The influence of degree of interpolated learning on retroactive inhibition and the overt transfer of specific responses. *American Journal of Psychology,* 1940, **53,** 173–203.

Melton, A. W., and Von Lackum, W. J. Retroactive and proactive inhibition in retention: evidence for a two-factor theory of retroactive inhibition. *American Journal of Psychology,* 1941, **54,** 157–173.

Merikle, P. M. The effects of stimulus and response meaningfulness in four paired-associate transfer paradigms. Unpublished M.A. thesis, University of Virginia, 1964.

Merikle, P. M., and Battig, W. F. Transfer of training as a function of experimental paradigm and meaningfulness. *Journal of Verbal Learning and Verbal Behavior,* 1963, **2,** 485–488.

Merrill, M. The relationship of individual growth to average growth. *Human Biology,* 1931, **3,** 37–70.

Meyer, D. R. On the interaction of simultaneous responses. *Psychological Bulletin,* 1953, **50,** 204–220.

Michelson, N. I. Meaningfulness (*m*) indices for 120 nouns for children aged nine years. *Journal of Verbal Learning and Verbal Behavior,* 1969, **8**, 80–82.

Miller, G. A. Magical number 7, plus or minus two. *Psychological Review,* 1956, **63**, 81–97.

Miller, G. A., Galanter, E., and Pribram, K. *Plans and the structure of behavior.* New York: Holt, Rinehart and Winston, 1960.

Miller, G. A., and Isard, S. Some perceptual consequences of linguistic rules. *Journal of Verbal Learning and Verbal Behavior,* 1963, **2**, 217–228.

Miller, G. A., and Selfridge, J. A. Verbal context and the recall of meaningful material. *American Journal of Psychology,* 1950, **63**, 176–185.

Millward, R. Latency in a modified paired-associate learning experiment. *Journal of Verbal Learning and Verbal Behavior,* 1964, **3**, 309–316.

Milner, B. *Neuropsychological evidence for differing memory processes.* Abstract for the symposium on short-term and long-term memory. Proceedings of the 18th International Congress of Psychology, Moscow, 1966. Amsterdam: North-Holland Publications, 1968.

Modigliani, V., and Saltz, E. Evaluation of a model relating Thorndike-Lorge frequency and *m* to learning. *Journal of Experimental Psychology,* 1969, **82**, 584–586.

Montague, E. K. The role of anxiety in serial rote learning. *Journal of Experimental Psychology,* 1953, **45**, 91–96.

Montague, W. E., Adams, J. A., and Kiess, H. O. Forgetting and natural language mediation. *Journal of Experimental Psychology,* 1966, **72**, 829–833.

Montague, W. E., and Kiess, H. O. Test of a procedure to control interpair learning and the effect of repeated, post-criterion test trials on retention. *Psychonomic Science,* 1966, **6**, 191–192.

Moore, T. V. The correlation between memory and perception in the presence of diffuse cortical degeneration. *Psychological Monographs,* 1919, **27**, 297–345.

Morgan, C. L. *Psychology for teachers.* New York: Scribner, 1906.

Morgan, R. L., and Underwood, B. J. Proactive inhibition as a function of response similarity. *Journal of Experimental Psychology,* 1950, **40**, 592–603.

Müller, G. E., and Pilzecker, A. Experimentelle Beiträge zur Lehre vom Gedächtnis. *Zeitschrift für Psychologie,* Ergbd. **1**, 1900, 1–300.

Müller, G. E., and Schumann, F. Experimentelle Beiträge zur Untersuchung des Gedächtnisses. *Zeitschrift für Psychologie,* 1894, **6**, 81–90.

Murdock, B. B., Jr. Transfer designs and formulas. *Psychological Bulletin,* 1957, **54,** 313–326.

Murdock, B. B., Jr. The immediate retention of unrelated words. *Journal of Experimental Psychology,* 1960, **60,** 222–234.

Murdock, B. B., Jr. The retention of individual items. *Journal of Experimental Psychology,* 1961, **62,** 618–625.

Murdock, B. B., Jr. The serial position effect of free recall. *Journal of Experimental Psychology,* 1962, **64,** 482–488.

Murdock, B. B., Jr. An analysis of the recognition process. In Cofer, C. N., and Musgrave, B. S., Eds., *Verbal behavior and learning.* New York: McGraw-Hill, 1963.

Murdock, B. B., Jr. Short-term retention of single paired associates. *Journal of Experimental Psychology,* 1963, **65,** 433–443. (a)

Murdock, B. B., Jr. Signal-detection theory and short-term memory. *Journal of Experimental Psychology,* 1965, **70,** 443–447.

Murdock, B. B., Jr. Distractor and probe techniques in short-term memory. *Canadian Journal of Psychology,* 1967, **21,** 25–36.

Murdock, B. B., Jr., and Babick, A. J. The effect of repetition on the retention of individual words. *American Journal of Psychology,* 1961, **74,** 596–601.

Nachmias, J., Gleitman, H., and McKenna, V. V. The effect of isolation of stimuli and responses in paired associates. *American Journal of Psychology,* 1961, **74,** 452–456.

Neisser, U. *Cognitive psychology.* New York: Appleton-Century-Crofts, 1967.

Nelson, D. L. Paired-associate acquisition as a function of association value, degree, and location of similarity. *Journal of Experimental Psychology,* 1968, **77,** 364–369.

Newman, S. E. A mediation model for paired-associate learning. Technical Report No. 1, North Carolina State College, Contr. Nonr 486(08) Office of Naval Research, 1961.

Newman, S. E. Effect of pairing time and test time on performance during and after paired-associate training. *American Journal of Psychology,* 1964, **77,** 634–637.

Newman, S. E. A mediation model for paired-associate learning. In DeCecco, J. P., Ed., *Educational technology.* New York: Holt, Rinehart and Winston, 1964. (a)

Newman, S. E. Serial position as a cue in learning: The effect of test rate. *Journal of Experimental Psychology,* 1966, **71,** 319–320.

Newman, S. E., and Buckhout, R. S-R and R-S learning as functions of intralist similarity. *American Journal of Psychology,* 1962, **75,** 429–436.

Newman, S. E., and Saltz, E. Isolation effects: Stimulus and response generalization as explanatory concepts. *Journal of Experimental Psychology,* 1958, **55,** 467–472.

Newman, S. E., and Saltz, E. Serial position as a cue in learning. *American Journal of Psychology,* 1962, **75,** 102–108.

Newton, J. M., and Wickens, D. D. Retroactive inhibition as a function of the temporal position of the interpolated learning. *Journal of Experimental Psychology,* 1956, **51,** 149–154.

Nice, M. M. Studies in the life-history of the Song Sparrow: II. *Transactions of the Linnæan Society,* 1943; N.Y., **6,** 1–328.

Nicholson, W. M. The influence of anxiety upon learning. *Journal of Personality,* 1958, **26,** 303–319.

Nicolai, F. Experimentelle untersuchungen über das haften von gesichtseindrucken und dessen zeitlichen verlauf. *Archives geschichtes Psychologie,* 1922, **42,** 132–149.

Noble, C. E. An analysis of meaning. *Psychological Review,* 1952, **59,** 421–430.

Noble, C. E. The role of stimulus meaning (m) in serial verbal learning. *Journal of Experimental Psychology,* 1952, **43,** 437–446. (a)

Noble, C. E. The meaning-familiarity relationship. *Psychological Review,* 1953, **60,** 89–98.

Noble, C. E. The familiarity-frequency relationship. *Journal of Experimental Psychology,* 1954, **47,** 13–16.

Noble, C. E. The effect of familiarization upon serial verbal learning. *Journal of Experimental Psychology,* 1955, **49,** 333–338.

Noble, C. E. Emotionality (e) and meaningfulness (m). *Psychological Reports,* 1958, **4,** 16.

Noble, C. E. Measurements of association value (a), rated associations (a'), and scaled meaningfulness (m') for the 2100 CVC combinations of the English alphabet. *Psychological Reports,* 1961, **8,** 487–521.

Noble, C. E. Meaningfulness and familiarity. In Cofer, C. N., and Musgrave, B. S., Eds., *Verbal behavior and learning.* New York: McGraw-Hill, 1963.

Noble, C. E., and Fuchs, J. E. Serial errors in human learning: A test of the McCrary-Hunter hypothesis. *Science,* 1959, **129,** 570–571.

Noble, C. E., and McNeely, D. A. The role of meaningfulness (m) in paired-associate verbal learning. *Journal of Experimental Psychology,* 1957, **53,** 16–22.

Noble, C. E., and Parker, G. V. C. The Montana scale of meaningfulness (m). *Psychological Reports,* 1960, **7,** 325–331.

Noble, C. E., Showell, F. A., and Jones, H. R. Serial CVC learning with varied m' but equal a values. *Psychonomic Science,* 1966, **4,** 217–218.

Noble, C. E., Stockwell, F. E., and Pryer, M. W. Meaningfulness (*m'*) and association value (a) in paired-associate syllable learning. *Psychological Reports,* 1957, **3,** 441–452.

Noble, C. E., Sutker, P. B., and Jones, H. R. On the sigmoidal law relating association value (a) and scaled meaningfulness (*m'*). *Perception and Motor Skills,* 1968, **26,** 375–386.

Nodine, C. F. Stimulus durations and stimulus characteristics in paired-associate learning. *Journal of Experimental Psychology,* 1963, **66,** 100–106.

Nodine, C. F. Stimulus durations and stimulus characteristics in paired-associate learning. *Journal of Experimental Psychology,* 1965, **69,** 534–536.

Norcross, K. J., and Spiker, C. C. Effects of mediated associations on transfer in paired-associate learning. *Journal of Experimental Psychology,* 1958, **55,** 129–134.

Obrist, P. A. Some autonomic correlates of serial learning. *Journal of Verbal Learning and Verbal Behavior,* 1962, **1,** 100–104.

Osgood, C. E. Meaningful similarity and interference in learning. *Journal of Experimental Psychology,* 1946, **36,** 277–301.

Osgood, C. E. An investigation into the causes of retroactive interference. *Journal of Experimental Psychology,* 1948, **38,** 132–154.

Osgood, C. E. The similarity paradox in human learning: A resolution. *Psychological Review,* 1949, **56,** 132–143.

Paivio, A. Learning of adjective-noun paired associates as a function of adjective-noun word order and noun abstractness. *Canadian Journal of Psychology,* 1963, **17,** 370–379.

Paivio, A. Abstractness, imagery, and meaningfulness in paired-associate learning. *Journal of Verbal Learning and Verbal Behavior,* 1965, **4,** 32–38.

Paivio, A. Latency of verbal associations and imagery to noun stimuli as a function of abstractness and generality. *Canadian Journal of Psychology,* 1966, **20,** 378–387.

Paivio, A. Paired-associate learning and free recall of nouns as a function of concreteness, specificity, imagery, and meaningfulness. *Psychological Reports,* 1967, **20,** 239–245.

Paivio, A. A factor-analytic study of word attributes and verbal learning. *Journal of Verbal Learning and Verbal Behavior,* 1968, **7,** 41–49.

Paivio, A. Mental imagery in associative learning and memory. *Psychological Review,* 1969, **76,** 241–263.

Paivio, A., and Olver, M. Denotative-generality, imagery, and meaningfulness in paired-associate learning of nouns. *Psychonomic Science,* 1964, **5,** 55–56.

Paivio, A., Smythe, P. C., and Yuille, J. C. Imagery versus meaningfulness of nouns in paired-associate learning. *Canadian Journal of Psychology,* 1968, **22,** 427–441.

Paivio, A., Yuille, J. C., and Madigan, S. A. Concreteness, imagery, and meaningfulness values for 925 nouns. *Journal of Experimental Psychology Monograph Supplement,* 1968, **76,** 1–25.

Paivio, A., Yuille, J. C., and Rogers, T. B. Noun imagery and meaningfulness in free and serial recall. *Journal of Experimental Psychology,* 1969, **79,** 509–514.

Paivio, A., Yuille, J. C., and Smythe, P. C. Stimulus and response abstractness, imagery, and meaningfulness, and reported mediators in paired-associate learning. *Canadian Journal of Psychology,* 1966, **20,** 362–377.

Palermo, D. S., and Jenkins, J. J. *Word association norms.* Minneapolis: University of Minnesota Press, 1964.

Parks, T. E. Signal-detectability theory of recognition-memory performance. *Psychological Review,* 1966, **73,** 44–58.

Patten, E. F. The influence of distribution of repetitions on certain rote learning phenomena. *Journal of Psychology,* 1938, **5,** 359–374.

Paul, C., and Silverstein, A. Relation of experimentally produced interlist intrusions to unlearning and retroactive inhibition. *Journal of Experimental Psychology,* 1968, **76,** 480–485.

Penfield, W. *The permanent record of the stream of consciousness.* Proceedings of the 14th International Congress of Psychology. Amsterdam: North Holland Publications, 1954.

Penfield, W., and Milner, B. Memory deficits produced by bilateral lesions in the hippocampal zone. *AMA Archives of Neurology and Psychiatry,* 1958, **79,** 475–597.

Perfetti, C. A. Sentence retention and the depth hypothesis. *Journal of Verbal Learning and Verbal Behavior,* 1969, **8,** 101–104.

Perfetti, C. A. Lexical density and phrase structure depth as variables in sentence retention. *Journal of Verbal Learning and Verbal Behavior,* 1969, **8,** 719–724. (a)

Peters, H. N. Mediate association. *Journal of Experimental Psychology,* 1935, **18,** 20–48.

Peters, H. N. The relationship between familiarity of words and their memory value. *American Journal of Psychology,* 1936, **48,** 572–585.

Peterson, L. R. Paired-associate latencies after the last error. *Psychonomic Science,* 1965, **2,** 167–168.

Peterson, L. R., and Brewer, C. L. Confirmation, correction, and contiguity. *Journal of Verbal Learning and Verbal Behavior,* 1963, **1,** 365–371.

Peterson, L. R., and Peterson, M. J. Short-term retention of individual items. *Journal of Experimental Psychology,* 1959, **58,** 193–198.

Peterson, L. R., and Peterson, M. J. Minimal paired-associate learning. *Journal of Experimental Psychology,* 1962, **63,** 521–527.

Peterson, L. R., Peterson, M. J., and Miller, A. Short-term retention and meaningfulness. *Canadian Journal of Psychology,* 1961, **15,** 143–147.

Peterson, M. J. Effects of delay intervals and meaningfulness on verbal mediating responses. *Journal of Experimental Psychology,* 1965, **69,** 60–66.

Peterson, M. J., Colavita, F. B., Sheahan, D. B., III, and Blattner, K. C. Verbal mediating chains and response availability as a function of the acquisition paradigm. *Journal of Verbal Learning and Verbal Behavior,* 1964, **3,** 11–18.

Pollack, I. Interference, rehearsal, and short-term retention of digits. *Canadian Journal of Psychology,* 1963, **17,** 380–392.

Pollack, I., Johnson, L. B., and Knaff, P. R. Running memory span. *Journal of Experimental Psychology,* 1959, **57,** 137–146.

Pompi, K. F., and Lachman, R. Surrogate processes in the short-term retention of connected discourse. *Journal of Experimental Psychology,* 1967, **75,** 143–150.

Porter, L. W., and Duncan, C. P. Negative transfer in verbal learning. *Journal of Experimental Psychology,* 1953, **46,** 61–64.

Postman, L. Choice behavior and the process of recognition. *American Journal of Psychology,* 1950, **63,** 576–583.

Postman, L. The present status of interference theory. In Cofer, C. N., Ed., *Verbal learning and verbal behavior.* New York: McGraw-Hill, 1961.

Postman, L. Extra-experimental interference and the retention of words. *Journal of Experimental Psychology,* 1961, **61,** 97–110. (a)

Postman, L. The effects of language habits on the acquisition and retention of verbal associations. *Journal of Experimental Psychology,* 1962, **64,** 7–19.

Postman, L. Transfer of training as a function of experimental paradigm and degree of first-list learning. *Journal of Verbal Learning and Verbal Behavior,* 1962, **1,** 109–118. (a)

Postman, L. Retention as a function of degree of overlearning. *Science,* 1962, **135,** 666–667. (b)

Postman, L. Does interference theory predict too much forgetting? *Journal of Verbal Learning and Verbal Behavior,* 1963, **2,** 40–48.

Postman, L. Studies of learning to learn. II. Changes in transfer as a function of practice. *Journal of Verbal Learning and Verbal Behavior,* 1964, **3,** 437–447.

Postman, L. Unlearning under conditions of successive interpolation. *Journal of Experimental Psychology,* 1965, **70,** 237–245.

Postman, L. Differences between unmixed and mixed transfer designs as a function of paradigm. *Journal of Verbal Learning and Verbal Behavior,* 1966, **5,** 240–248.

Postman, L. The effect of interitem associative strength on the acquisition and retention of serial lists. *Journal of Verbal Learning and Verbal Behavior,* 1967, **6,** 721–728.

Postman, L. Association and performance in the analysis of verbal learning. In Dixon, T. R., and Horton, D. L., Eds., *Verbal behavior and general behavior theory.* Englewood Cliffs, N. J.: Prentice-Hall, 1968.

Postman, L., and Adams, P. A. Studies in incidental learning: Effects of contextual determination. *Journal of Experimental Psychology,* 1960, **59,** 153–164.

Postman, L., and Goggin, J. Whole versus part learning of serial lists as a function of meaningfulness and intralist similarity. *Journal of Experimental Psychology,* 1964, **68,** 140–150.

Postman, L., and Goggin, J. Whole versus part learning of paired-associate lists. *Journal of Experimental Psychology,* 1966, **71,** 867–877.

Postman, L., and Greenbloom, R. Conditions of cue selection in the acquisition of paired-associate lists. *Journal of Experimental Psychology,* 1967, **73,** 91–100.

Postman, L., Jenkins, W. O., and Postman, D. L. An experimental comparison of active recall and recognition. *American Journal of Psychology,* 1948, **61,** 511–520.

Postman, L., and Keppel, G. Retroactive inhibition in free recall. *Journal of Experimental Psychology,* 1967, **74,** 203–211.

Postman, L., Keppel, G., and Stark, K. Unlearning as a function of the relationship between successive response classes. *Journal of Experimental Psychology,* 1965, **69,** 111–118.

Postman, L., Keppel, G., and Zacks, R. Studies of learning to learn: VII. The effects of practice on response integration. *Journal of Verbal Learning and Verbal Behavior,* 1968, **7,** 776–784.

Postman, L., and Postman, D. L. Change in set as a determinant of retroactive inhibition. *American Journal of Psychology,* 1948, **61,** 236–242.

Postman, L., and Rau, L. Retention as a function of the method of measurement. *University of California Publication in Psychology,* 1957, **8,** 217–270.

Postman, L., and Riley, D. A. Degree of learning and interserial interference in retention. *University of California Publication in Psychology,* 1959, **8,** 271–396.

Postman, L., and Schwartz, M. Studies of learning to learn. I. Transfer as a function of method of practice and class of verbal materials. *Journal of Verbal Learning and Verbal Behavior,* 1964, **3,** 37–49.

Postman, L., and Stark, K. Studies of learning to learn. IV. Transfer from serial to paired-associate learning. *Journal of Verbal Learning and Verbal Behavior,* 1967, **6,** 339–353.

Postman, L., Stark, K., and Fraser, J. Temporal changes in interference. *Journal of Verbal Learning and Verbal Behavior,* 1968, **7,** 672–694.

Puff, C. R. Clustering as a function of the sequential organization of stimulus word lists. *Journal of Verbal Learning and Verbal Behavior,* 1966, **5,** 503–506.

Rabinowitz, F. M., and Witte, K. L. Stimulus selection as a function of letter color. *Journal of Verbal Learning and Verbal Behavior,* 1967, **6,** 167–168.

Reed, H. B. A repetition of Ebert and Meumann's practice experiment on memory. *Journal of Experimental Psychology,* 1917, **2,** 315–346.

Reed, H. B. Associative aids: I. Their relation to learning, retention, and other associations. *Psychological Review,* 1918, **25,** 128–155.

Restorff, H. von. Uber die Wirkung von Bereichsbildungen im Spurenfeld (Analyse von Vorgangen in Spurenfeld). *Psychologie Forschung,* 1933, **18,** 299–342.

Reynolds, J. H. Effects of non-anticipation and anticipation procedures upon paired-associate learning in unmixed and mixed list designs. *Psychological Reports,* 1964, **15,** 795–801.

Reynolds, J. H. Confirmation, contiguity, and response practice in paired-associate learning. *Journal of Experimental Psychology,* 1967, **73,** 394–400

Richardson, J. Retention of concepts as a function of degree of original and interpolated learning. *Journal of Experimental Psychology,* 1956, **51,** 358–364.

Richardson, J., and Gropper, M. S. Learning during recall trials. *Psychological Reports,* 1964, **15,** 551–560.

Richardson, P., and Voss, J. F. Replication report: Verbal context and the recall of meaningful material. *Journal of Experimental Psychology,* 1960, **60,** 417–418.

Riley, D. A., and Phillips, L. W. The effects of syllable familiarization on rote learning, association value, and reminiscence. *Journal of Experimental Psychology,* 1959, **57,** 372–379.

Roark, R. N. *Psychology in education.* New York: American Book Co., 1895.

Roberts, W. A. A further test of the effect of isolation in serial learning. *American Journal of Psychology,* 1962, **75,** 134–139.

Robinson, E. S. *Association theory today.* New York: Century House, Inc., 1932.

Robinson, J. A. Category clustering in free recall. *Journal of Psychology,* 1966, **62,** 279–285.

Rocklyn, E. H., Hessert, R. B., and Braun, H. W. Calibrated materials for verbal learning with middle- and old-aged subjects. *American Journal of Psychology,* 1957, **70,** 628–630.

Rockway, M. R., and Duncan, C. P. Pre-recall warming-up in verbal retention. *Journal of Experimental Psychology,* 1952, **43,** 305–312.

Rohwer, W. D., Jr. Constraint, syntax and meaning in paired-associate learning. *Journal of Verbal Learning and Verbal Behavior,* 1966, **5,** 541–547.

Rosenberg, S. Associative clustering and repeated trials. *Journal of General Psychology,* 1966, **74,** 89–96.

Rosenberg, S. Recall of sentences as a function of syntactic and associative habit. *Journal of Verbal Learning and Verbal Behavior,* 1966, **5,** 392–396. (a)

Rosenzweig, M. R., and McNeill, D. Inaccuracies in the semantic count of Lorge and Thorndike. *American Journal of Psychology,* 1962, **75,** 316–319.

Ross, B. M. Sequential visual memory and the limited magic of the number seven. *Journal of Experimental Psychology,* 1969, **80,** 339–347.

Rubin, E. D., and Brown, S. C. Constant versus varied serial order in paired-associate learning: The effect of formal intralist similarity. *Journal of Experimental Psychology,* 1967, **73,** 257–262.

Runquist, W. N. Verbal behavior. In Sidowski, J. B., Ed., *Experimental methods and instrumentation in psychology.* New York: McGraw-Hill, 1966.

Runquist, W. N. Functions relating intralist stimulus similarity to acquisition performance with a variety of materials. *Journal of Verbal Learning and Verbal Behavior,* 1968, **7,** 549–553.

Runquist, W. N. Rated similarity of high *m* CVC trigrams and words and low *m* CCC trigrams. *Journal of Verbal Learning and Verbal Behavior,* 1968, **7,** 967–968. (a)

Runquist, W. N., and Farley, F. H. The use of mediation in the learning of verbal paired-associates. *Journal of Verbal Learning and Verbal Behavior,* 1964, **3,** 280–285.

Runquist, W. N., and Joinson, P. The rated similarity of low *m* trigrams. *Journal of Verbal Learning and Verbal Behavior,* 1968, **7,** 317–320.

Russell, W. A., and Storms, L. H. Implicit verbal chaining in paired-associate learning. *Journal of Experimental Psychology,* 1955, **49,** 287–293.

Ryan, J. J. Comparison of verbal response transfer mediated by meaningfully similar and associated stimuli. *Journal of Experimental Psychology,* 1960, **60,** 408–415.

Saltz, E. Thorndike-Lorge frequency and m of stimuli as separate factors in paired associates learning. *Journal of Experimental Psychology,* 1967, **73,** 473–478.

Saltz, E., and Ager, J. W. Issues in scaling meaningfulness: Noble's revised CVC norms. *Psychological Reports,* 1962, **10,** 25–26.

Saltz, E., and Hamilton, H. Spontaneous recovery of List 1 responses in the A-B, A'-C paradigm. *Journal of Experimental Psychology,* 1967, **75,** 267–273.

Saltz, E., and Hoehn, A. J. A test of the Taylor-Spence theory of anxiety. *Journal of Abnormal and Social Psychology,* 1957, **54,** 114–117.

Saltz, E., and Modigliani, V. Response meaningfulness in paired associates: T-L frequency, m, and number of meanings (dm). *Journal of Experimental Psychology,* 1967, **75,** 313–320.

Saltz, E., and Newman, S. E. The von Restorff isolation effect: Test of the intralist association assumption. *Journal of Experimental Psychology,* 1959, **58,** 445–451.

Sanders, A. F. Rehearsal and recall in immediate memory. *Ergonomics,* 1961, **4,** 25–34.

Sarason, I. G. The effect of associative value and differential motivating instructions on serial learning. *American Journal of Psychology,* 1957, **70,** 620–623.

Sarason, I. G. Effects on verbal learning of anxiety, reassurance, and meaningfulness of material. *Journal of Experimental Psychology,* 1958, **56,** 472–477.

Sarason, I. G. Empirical findings and theoretical problems in the use of anxiety scales. *Psychological Bulletin,* 1960, **57,** 403–415.

Sarason, I. G., and Palola, E. G. The relationship of test and general anxiety, difficulty of task, and experimental instructions to performance. *Journal of Experimental Psychology,* 1960, **59,** 185–191.

Sauer, F. M. The relative variability of nonsense syllables and words. *Journal of Experimental Psychology,* 1930, **13,** 235–246.

Schlosberg, H. Three dimensions of emotion. *Psychological Review,* 1954, **61,** 81–88.

Schulz, R. W. Generalization of serial position in rote serial learning. *Journal of Experimental Psychology,* 1955, **49,** 267–272.

Schulz, R. W., and Kasschau, R. A. Serial learning as a function of meaningfulness and mode of presentation with audio and visual stimuli of equivalent duration. *Journal of Experimental Psychology,* 1966, **71,** 350–354.

Schulz, R. W., and Lovelace, E. A. Mediation in verbal paired-associate learning: The role of temporal factors. *Psychonomic Science,* 1964, **1,** 95–96.

Schulz, R. W., and Martin, E. Aural paired-associate learning: Stimulus familiarization, response familiarization, and pronunciability. *Journal of Verbal Learning and Verbal Behavior,* 1964, **3,** 139–145.

Schulz, R. W., and Runquist, W. N. Learning and retention of paired adjectives as a function of percentage occurrence of response members. *Journal of Experimental Psychology,* 1960, **59,** 409–413.

Schulz, R. W., and Thysell, R. The effect of familiarization on meaningfulness. *Journal of Verbal Learning and Verbal Behavior,* 1965, **4,** 409–413.

Schulz, R. W., and Tucker, I. F. Supplementary report: Stimulus familiarization in paired-associate learning. *Journal of Experimental Psychology,* 1962, **64,** 549–550.

Schulz, R. W., and Tucker, I. F. Stimulus familiarization and length of the anticipation interval in paired-associate learning. *Psychological Record,* 1962, **12,** 341–344. (a)

Schulz, R. W., and Weaver, G. E. The A-B, B-C, A-C mediation paradigm: The effects of variation in A-C study- and test-interval lengths and strength of A-B or B-C. *Journal of Experimental Psychology,* 1968, **76,** 303–311.

Schulz, R. W., Weaver, G. E., and Ginsberg, S. Chaining is not an artifact! *Psychonomic Science,* 1965, **2,** 169–170.

Schwartz, F. *Immediate memory and amount of information.* Paper presented at Eastern Psychological Association meeting, Philadelphia, 1961.

Schwartz, M. Instructions to use verbal mediators in paired-associate learning. *Journal of Experimental Psychology,* 1969, **79,** 1–5.

Schwenn, E., and Postman, L. Studies of learning to learn. V. Gains in performance as a function of warm-up and associative practice. *Journal of Verbal Learning and Verbal Behavior,* 1967, **6,** 565–573.

Schwenn, E. A., and Underwood, B. J. The effect of formal and associative similarity on paired-associate and free-recall learning. *Journal of Verbal Learning and Verbal Behavior,* 1968, **7,** 817–824.

Shapiro, S. I. Paired-associate response latencies as a function of free association strength. *Journal of Experimental Psychology,* 1968, **77,** 223–231.

Shapiro, S. I. Response word frequency in paired-associates learning. *Psychonomic Science,* 1969, **16,** 308–309.

Shapiro, S. I., and Palermo, D. S. Mediated clustering in free recall. *Journal of Experimental Psychology,* 1967, **75,** 365–371.

Shapiro, S. S. Word associations and meaningfulness values for grade-school-aged children. *Psychological Reports,* 1964, **15,** 447–455.

Sharp, H. C. Effect of contextual constraint upon recall of verbal passages. *American Journal of Psychology,* 1958, **71,** 568–572.

Shepard, R. N., and Teghtsoonian, M. Retention of information under conditions approaching a steady state. *Journal of Experimental Psychology,* 1961, **62,** 302–309.

Shiffrin, R. M., and Atkinson, R. C. Storage and retrieval processes in long-term memory. *Psychological Review,* 1969, **76,** 179–193.

Shuell, T. J. Retroactive inhibition in free-recall learning of categorized lists. *Journal of Verbal Learning and Verbal Behavior,* 1968, **7,** 797–805.

Shuell, T. J. Clustering and organization in free recall. *Psychological Bulletin,* 1969, **72,** 353–374.

Sidman, M. A note on functional relations obtained from group data. *Psychological Bulletin,* 1952, **49,** 263–269.

Sidowski, J. B., Kopstein, F. F., and Shillestad, I. J. Prompting and confirmation variables in verbal learning. *Psychological Reports,* 1961, **8,** 401–406.

Sidowski, J. B., and Nuthmann, C. Induced muscular tension, incentive, and blink rate in a verbal learning task. *Journal of Experimental Psychology,* 1961, **61,** 295–299.

Silberman, H. F., Melaragno, R. J., and Coulson, J. E. Confirmation and prompting with connected discourse material. *Psychological Reports,* 1961, **9,** 235–238.

Silverstein, A. Unlearning, spontaneous recovery, and the partial-reinforcement effect in paired-associate learning. *Journal of Experimental Psychology,* 1967, **73,** 15–21.

Silverstein, A., and Dienstbier, R. A. Rated pleasantness and association value of 101 English nouns. *Journal of Verbal Learning and Verbal Behavior,* 1968, **7,** 81–86.

Simpson, W. E. Effects of approximation to sentence word-order and grammatical class upon the serial learning of word lists. *Journal of Verbal Learning and Verbal Behavior,* 1965, **4,** 510–514.

Simpson, W. E. Error versus correct responses in the serial learning of word lists. *Psychonomic Science,* 1967, **7,** 213–214.

Skinner, B. F. *The behavior of organisms; an experimental analysis.* New York: Appleton-Century-Crofts, 1938.

Slamecka, N. J. Studies of retention of connected discourse. *American Journal of Psychology,* 1959, **72,** 409–416.

Slamecka, N. J. Retroactive inhibition of connected discourse as a function of similarity of topic. *Journal of Experimental Psychology,* 1960, **60,** 245–249.

Slamecka, N. J. Retroactive inhibition of connected discourse as a function of practice level. *Journal of Experimental Psychology,* 1960, **59,** 104–108. (a)

Slamecka, N. J. Proactive inhibition of connected discourse. *Journal of Experimental Psychology,* 1961, **62,** 295–301.

Slamecka, N. J. Retention of connected discourse as a function of duration of interpolated learning. *Journal of Experimental Psychology,* 1962, **63,** 480–486.

Slamecka, N. J. A search for spontaneous recovery of verbal associations. *Journal of Verbal Learning and Verbal Behavior,* 1966, **5,** 205–207.

Slamecka, N. J. Transfer with mixed and unmixed lists as a function of semantic relations. *Journal of Experimental Psychology,* 1967, **73,** 405–410.

Slamecka, N. J., and Ceraso, J. Retroactive and proactive inhibition of verbal learning. *Psychological Bulletin,* 1960, **57,** 449–475.

Sleight, W. G. Memory and formal training. *British Journal of Psychology,* 1911, **4,** 386–457.

Smith, M. H., Jr. The influence of isolation on immediate memory. *American Journal of Psychology,* 1949, **62,** 405–411.

Smith, M. H., Jr., and Stearns, E. G. The influence of isolation on the learning of surrounding materials. *American Journal of Psychology,* 1949, **62,** 369–381.

Smythe, P. C., and Paivio, A. A comparison of the effectiveness of word imagery and meaningfulness in paired-associate learning of nouns. *Psychonomic Science,* 1968, **10,** 49–50.

Spence, J. T. Associative interference on paired-associate lists from extraexperimental learning. *Journal of Verbal Learning and Verbal Behavior,* 1963, **2,** 329–338.

Spence, K. W. Mathematical theories of learning. *Journal of General Psychology,* 1952, **49,** 283–291.

Spence, K. W. *Behavior theory and conditioning.* New Haven: Yale University Press, 1956.

Spence, K. W. A theory of emotionally based drive (D) and its relation to performance in simple learning situations. *American Psychology,* 1958, **13,** 131–141.

Spence, K. W. Anxiety (Drive) level and performance in eyelid conditioning. *Psychological Bulletin,* 1964, **61,** 129–139.

Spence, K. W., Farber, I. E., and McFann, H. H. The relation of anxiety (drive) level to performance in competitional and noncompetitional paired-associates learning. *Journal of Experimental Psychology,* 1956, **52,** 296–305.

Sperling, G. The information available in brief visual presentations. *Psychological Monographs,* 1960, **74.**

Spielberger, C. D., and Smith, L. H. Anxiety (drive), stress, and serial position effects in serial-verbal learning. *Journal of Experimental Psychology,* 1966, **72,** 589–595.

Spreen, O., and Schulz, R. W. Parameters of abstraction, meaningfulness, and pronunciability for 329 nouns. *Journal of Verbal Learning and Verbal Behavior,* 1966, **5,** 459–468.

Stanners, R. F., and Meunier, G. F. Pronunciability and rehearsal time in short-term memory with controlled acquisition. *Journal of Experimental Psychology,* 1969, **80,** 359–363.

Stark, K. Transfer from serial to paired-associate learning: A reappraisal. *Journal of Verbal Learning and Verbal Behavior,* 1968, **7,** 20–30.

Stein, B. Random versus constant presentation of S-R pairs: Effects of associative value and test rate. *Journal of Experimental Psychology,* 1969, **80,** 401–402.

Steiner, T. E., and Sobel, R. Intercomponent association formation during paired-associate training with compound stimuli. *Journal of Experimental Psychology,* 1968, **77,** 275–280.

Stennett, R. G. The relationship of performance level to level of arousal. *Journal of Experimental Psychology,* 1957, **54,** 54–61.

Stimmel, D. T., and Stimmel, N. S. Free recall as a function of intralist similarity and order of presentation constraints. *Psychological Reports,* 1967, **21,** 541–544.

Stimmel, D. T., and Stimmel, N. S. Free recall of low meaningfulness trigrams as a function of four levels of intralist similarity. *Psychological Reports,* 1968, **23,** 895–898.

Stoke, S. M. Memory for onomatopes. *Journal of Genetic Psychology,* 1929, **36,** 594–596.

Stolurow, L. M., Jacobs, P. I., and Blomme, R. W. Tables of estimated letter and letter combinations (bigrams and trigrams) frequencies in printed English. *AF Project: 33(616)—5965 Memorandum Report No. 13,* 1960.

Sumby, W. H. Word frequency and serial position effects. *Journal of Verbal Learning and Verbal Behavior,* 1963, **1,** 443–450.

Swets, J. A., Tanner, W. P., and Birdsall, T. G. Decision processes in perception. *Psychological Review,* 1961, **68,** 301–340.

Talland, G. A. Short-term memory with interpolated activity. *Journal of Verbal Learning and Verbal Behavior,* 1967, **6,** 144–150.

Taylor, J. A. The relationship of anxiety to the conditioned eyelid response. *Journal of Experimental Psychology,* 1951, **41,** 81–92.

Taylor, J. A. The effects of anxiety level and psychological stress on verbal learning. *Journal of Abnormal and Social Psychology,* 1958, **57,** 55–60.

Taylor, J. A., and Spence, K. W. The relationship of anxiety level to performance in serial learning. *Journal of Experimental Psychology,* 1952, **44,** 61–64.

Taylor, J. D., and Kimble, G. A. The association value of 320 selected words and paralogs. *Journal of Verbal Learning and Verbal Behavior,* 1967, **6,** 744–752.

Teghtsoonian, R. The influence of amount of information on performance in a recognition test of verbal learning. Unpublished doctoral dissertation, Harvard University, 1958.

Thorndike, E. L. *Educational psychology: briefer course.* New York: Columbia University Press, 1914.

Thorndike, E. L. *The fundamentals of learning.* New York: Teachers College, Columbia University, 1932.

Thorndike, E. L., and Lorge, I. *The teacher's word book of 30,000 words.* New York: Columbia University Press, 1944.

Thorndike, E. L., and Woodworth, R. S. The influence of improvement in one mental function upon the efficiency of other functions. I. *Psychological Review,* 1901, **8,** 247–261.

Thorndike, E. L., and Woodworth, R. S. The influence of improvement in one mental function upon the efficiency of other functions. II. The estimation of magnitudes. *Psychological Review,* 1901, **8,** 384–395. (a)

Thorndike, E. L., and Woodworth, R. S. The influence of improvement in one mental function upon the efficiency of other functions. III. Functions involving attention, observation, and discrimination. *Psychological Review,* 1901, **8,** 553–564. (b)

Thune, L. E. The effect of different types of preliminary activities on subsequent learning of paired-associate material. *Journal of Experimental Psychology,* 1950, **40,** 423–438.

Thune, L. E., and Underwood, B. J. Retroactive inhibition as a function of degree of interpolated learning. *Journal of Experimental Psychology,* 1943, **32,** 185–200.

Titchener, E. B. *A text-book of psychology.* New York: Macmillan, 1919.

Tragash, H. J., and Newman, S. E. Effects of pairing- and test-order constancy on performance during and after paired-associate training. *Journal of Verbal Learning and Verbal Behavior,* 1967, **6,** 762–765.

Tryk, H. E. Subjective scaling of word frequency. *American Journal of Psychology,* 1968, **81,** 170–177.

Tulving, E. Subjective organization in free recall of "unrelated" words. *Psychological Review,* 1962, **69,** 344–354.

Tulving, E. The effect of alphabetical subjective organization on memorizing unrelated words. *Canadian Journal of Psychology,* 1962, **16,** 185–191. (a)

Tulving, E. Theoretical issues in free recall. In Dixon, T. R., and Horton, D. L., Eds., *Verbal behavior and general behavior theory.* Englewood Cliffs, N.J.: Prentice-Hall, 1968.

Tulving, E., McNulty, J. A., and Ozier, M. Vividness of words and learning to learn in free-recall learning. *Canadian Journal of Psychology,* 1965, **19,** 242–252.

Tulving, E., and Pearlstone, Z. Availability versus accessibility of information in memory for words. *Journal of Verbal Learning and Verbal Behavior,* 1966, **5,** 381–391.

Turnage, T. W. Unit-sequence interference in short-term memory. *Journal of Verbal Learning and Verbal Behavior,* 1967, **6,** 61–65.

Twedt, H. M., and Underwood, B. J. Mixed vs. unmixed lists in transfer studies. *Journal of Experimental Psychology,* 1959, **58,** 111–116.

Uehling, B., and Sprinkle, R. Recall of a serial list as a function of arousal and retention interval. *Journal of Experimental Psychology,* 1968, **78,** 103–106.

Umemoto, T., and Hilgard, E. R. Paired-associate learning as a function of similarity: Common stimulus and response items within the list. *Journal of Experimental Psychology,* 1961, **62,** 97–104.

Underwood, B. J. The effect of successive interpolations on retroactive and proactive inhibition. *Psychological Monographs,* 1945, **59.**

Underwood, B. J. Retroactive and proactive inhibition after five and forty-eight hours. *Journal of Experimental Psychology,* 1948, **38,** 29–38.

Underwood, B. J. "Spontaneous recovery" of verbal associations. *Journal of Experimental Psychology,* 1948, **38,** 429–439. (a)

Underwood, B. J. *Experimental psychology.* New York: Appleton-Century-Crofts, 1949.

Underwood, B. J. Proactive inhibition as a function of time and degree of prior learning. *Journal of Experimental Psychology,* 1949, **39,** 24–34. (a)

Underwood, B. J. Studies of distributed practice: II. Learning and retention of paired-adjective lists with two levels of intralist similarity. *Journal of Experimental Psychology,* 1951, **42,** 153–161.

Underwood, B. J. Studies of distributed practice: III. The influence of stage of practice in serial learning. *Journal of Experimental Psychology,* 1951, **42,** 291–295. (a)

Underwood, B. J. Studies of distributed practice: VI. The influence of rest-interval activity in serial learning. *Journal of Experimental Psychology,* 1952, **43,** 329–340.

Underwood, B. J. Studies of distributed practice: VII. Learning and retention of paired nonsense syllables as a function of intralist similarity. *Journal of Experimental Psychology,* 1952, **44,** 80–87. (a)

Underwood, B. J. Studies of distributed practice: VIII. Learning and retention of paired nonsense syllables as a function of intralist similarity. *Journal of Experimental Psychology,* 1953, **45,** 133–142.

Underwood, B. J. Studies of distributed practice: IX. Learning and retention of paired adjectives as a function of intralist similarity. *Journal of Experimental Psychology,* 1953, **45,** 143–149. (a)

Underwood, B. J. Studies of distributed practice: X. The influence of intralist similarity on learning and retention of serial adjective lists. *Journal of Experimental Psychology,* 1953, **45,** 253–259. (b)

Underwood, B. J. Studies in distributed practice: XI. An attempt to resolve conflicting facts on retention of serial nonsense lists. *Journal of Experimental Psychology,* 1953, **45,** 355–359. (c)

Underwood, B. J. Speed of learning and amount retained: A consideration of methodology. *Psychological Bulletin,* 1954, **51,** 276–282.

Underwood, B. J. Studies of distributed practice: XII. Retention following varying degrees of original learning. *Journal of Experimental Psychology,* 1954, **47,** 294–300. (a)

Underwood, B. J. A graphical description of rote learning. *Psychological Review,* 1957, **64,** 119–122.

Underwood, B. J. Interference and forgetting. *Psychological Review,* 1957, **64,** 49–60. (a)

Underwood, B. J. Ten years of massed practice on distributed practice. *Psychological Review,* 1961, **68,** 229–247.

Underwood, B. J. Stimulus selection in verbal learning. In Cofer, C. N., Musgrave, B. S., Eds., *Verbal behavior and learning.* New York: McGraw-Hill, 1963.

Underwood, B. J. Degree of learning and the measurement of forgetting. *Journal of Verbal Learning and Verbal Behavior,* 1964, **3,** 112–129.

Underwood, B. J. The representativeness of rote verbal learning. In Melton, A. W., Ed., *Categories of human learning.* New York: Academic Press, 1964. (a)

Underwood, B. J. Experimental psychology, 2d edition. New York: Appleton-Century-Crofts, 1966.

Underwood, B. J. Motor-skills learning and verbal learning: Some observations. In Bilodeau, E. A., Ed., *Acquisition of skill.* New York: Academic Press, 1966. (a)

Underwood, B. J., and Archer, E. J. Studies of distributed practice: XIV. Intralist similarity and presentation rate in verbal discrimination learning of consonant syllables. *Journal of Experimental Psychology,* 1955, **50,** 120–124.

Underwood, B. J., and Ekstrand, B. R. An analysis of some shortcomings in the interference theory of forgetting. *Psychological Review,* 1966, **73,** 540–549.

Underwood, B. J., and Ekstrand, B. R. Effect of distributed practice on paired-associate learning. *Journal of Experimental Psychology Monograph, Supplement,* 1967, **73,** 1–21.

Underwood, B. J., and Ekstrand, B. R. Response-term integration. *Journal of Verbal Learning and Verbal Behavior,* 1967, **6,** 432–438. (a)

Underwood, B. J., and Ekstrand, B. R. Linguistic associations and retention. *Journal of Verbal Learning and Verbal Behavior,* 1968, **7,** 162–171.

Underwood, B. J., Ekstrand, B. R., and Keppel, G. Studies of distributed practice: XXIII. Variations in response-term interference. *Journal of Experimental Psychology,* 1964, **68,** 201–212.

Underwood, B. J., Ekstrand, B. R., and Keppel, G. An analysis of intralist similarity in verbal learning with experiments on conceptual similarity. *Journal of Verbal Learning and Verbal Behavior,* 1965, **4,** 447–462.

Underwood, B. J., and Erlebacher, A. H. Studies of coding in verbal behavior. *Psychological Monographs,* 1965, **79.**

Underwood, B. J., and Freund, J. S. Further studies on conceptual similarity in free-recall learning. *Journal of Verbal Learning and Verbal Behavior,* 1969, **8,** 30–35.

Underwood, B. J., and Goad, D. Studies of distributed practice: I. The influence of intralist similarity in serial learning. *Journal of Experimental Psychology,* 1951, **42,** 125–134.

Underwood, B. J., Ham, M., and Ekstrand, B. Cue selection in paired-associate learning. *Journal of Experimental Psychology,* 1962, **64,** 405–409.

Underwood, B. J., and Keppel, G. Bidirectional paired-associate learning. *American Journal of Psychology,* 1963, **76,** 470–474.

Underwood, B. J., and Keppel, G. Coding processes in verbal learning. *Journal of Verbal Learning and Verbal Behavior,* 1963, **1,** 250–257. (a)

Underwood, B. J., and Keppel, G. Retention as a function of degree of learning and letter-sequence interference. *Psychological Monographs,* 1963, **77.** (b)

Underwood, B. J., and Postman, L. Extraexperimental sources of interference in forgetting. *Psychological Review,* 1960, **67,** 73–95.

Underwood, B. J., and Richardson, J. Studies of distributed practice: XIII. Interlist interference and the retention of serial nonsense lists. *Journal of Experimental Psychology,* 1955, **50,** 39–46.

Underwood, B. J., and Richardson, J. The influence of meaningfulness, intralist similarity, and serial position on retention. *Journal of Experimental Psychology,* 1956, **52,** 119–126.

Underwood, B. J., Runquist, W. N., and Schulz, R. W. Response learning in paired-associate lists as a function of intralist similarity. *Journal of Experimental Psychology,* 1959, **58,** 70–78.

Underwood, B. J., and Schulz, R. W. Studies of distributed practice: XIX. The influence of intralist similarity with lists of low meaningfulness. *Journal of Experimental Psychology,* 1959, **58,** 106–110.

Underwood, B. J., and Schulz, R. W. *Meaningfulness and verbal learning.* Philadelphia: J. B. Lippincott Co., 1960.

Underwood, B. J., and Schulz, R. W. Studies of distributed practice: XX. Sources of interference associated with differences in learning and retention. *Journal of Experimental Psychology,* 1961, **61,** 228–235.

Underwood, B. J., and Schulz, R. W. Studies of distributed practice: XXI. Effect of interference from language habits. *Journal of Experimental Psychology,* 1961, **62,** 571–575. (a)

Underwood, B. J., and Viterna, R. O. Studies of distributed practice: IV. The effect of similarity and rate of presentation in verbal-discrimination learning. *Journal of Experimental Psychology,* 1951, **42,** 296–299.

Van Buskirk, W. L. An experimental study of vividness in learning and retention. *Journal of Experimental Psychology,* 1932, **15,** 563–573.

Van Ormer, E. B. Sleep and retention. *Psychological Bulletin,* 1932, **30,** 415–439.

Vicory, A. C., and Asher, J. J. A simplified associative-frequency measure of meaningfulness in verbal learning. *Journal of Verbal Learning and Verbal Behavior,* 1966, **5,** 507–513.

Victor, M., Angevine, J. B., Jr., Mancall, E. L., and Fisher, C. M. Memory loss with lesions of hippocampal formation. *Archives of Neurology,* 1961, **5,** 244–263.

Vincent, S. B. The function of the vibrissae in the behavior of the white rat. *Behavioral Monographs,* 1912, **1,** No. 5.

Voss, J. F. Serial acquisition as a function of item probability and sequential probability. *Journal of Experimental Psychology,* 1966, **71,** 304–313.

Walker, A. E. Recent memory impairment in unilateral temporal lesions. *AMA Archives of Neurology and Psychiatry,* 1957, **78,** 543–552.

Walker, E. L. The duration and course of reaction decrement and the influence of reward. *Journal of Comparative and Physiological Psychology,* 1956, **49,** 167–176.

Walker, E. L. Action decrement and its relation to learning. *Psychological Review,* 1958, **65,** 129–142.

Walker, E. L., and Motoyoshi, R. The effects of amount of reward and distribution of practice on active and inactive memory traces. *Journal of Comparative and Physiological Psychology,* 1962, **55,** 32–36.

Walker, E. L., and Paradise, N. A positive correlation between action decrement and learning. *Journal of Experimental Psychology,* 1958, **56,** 45–47.

Walker, E. L., and Tarte, R. D. Memory storage as a function of arousal and time with homogeneous and heterogeneous lists. *Journal of Verbal Learning and Verbal Behavior,* 1963, **2,** 113–119.

Wallace, W. Review of the historical, empirical and theoretical status of the von Restorff phenomenon. *Psychological Bulletin,* 1965, **63,** 410–424.

Wallach, M. A. On psychological similarity. *Psychological Review,* 1958, **65,** 103–116.

Ward, L. B. Reminiscence and rote learning. *Psychological Monographs,* 1937, **49.**

Waters, R. H. The law of acquaintance. *Journal of Experimental Psychology,* 1939, **24,** 180–191.

Waugh, N. C. Two methods for testing serial memorization. *Journal of Experimental Psychology,* 1963, **65,** 215–216.

Waugh, N. C. Presentation time and free recall. *Journal of Experimental Psychology,* 1967, **73,** 39–44.

Waugh, N. C. Free recall of conspicuous items. *Journal of Verbal Learning and Verbal Behavior,* 1969, **8,** 448–456.

Waugh, N. C., and Norman, D. A. Primary memory. *Psychological Review,* 1965, **72,** 89–104.

Webb, W. B. The effects of prolonged learning on learning. *Journal of Verbal Learning and Verbal Behavior,* 1962, **1,** 173–182.

Webster's new collegiate dictionary. Springfield, Mass.: G. & C. Merriam, 1959.

Weingartner, H. The free recall of sets of associatively related words. *Journal of Verbal Learning and Verbal Behavior,* 1964, **3,** 6–10.

Weiss, W., and Margolius, G. The effect of context stimuli on learning and retention. *Journal of Experimental Psychology,* 1954, **48,** 318–322.

Wickelgren, Wayne A. Acoustic similarity and retroactive interference in short-term memory. *Journal of Verbal Learning and Verbal Behavior,* 1965, **4,** 53–61.

Wickens, D. D. Encoding categories of words: An empirical approach to meaning. *Psychological Review,* 1970, **77,** 1–15.

Wickens, D. D., Born, D. G., and Allen, C. K. Proactive inhibition and item similarity in short-term memory. *Journal of Verbal Learning and Verbal Behavior,* 1963, **2,** 440–445.

Wickens, D. D., and Cermak, L. S. Transfer effects of synonyms and antonyms in mixed and unmixed lists. *Journal of Verbal Learning and Verbal Behavior,* 1967, **6,** 832–839.

Wickens, D. D., and Clark, S. Osgood dimensions as an encoding class in short-term memory. *Journal of Experimental Psychology,* 1968, **78,** 580–584.

Wickens, D. D., Clark, S. E., Hill, F. A., and Wittlinger, R. P. Investigation of grammatical class as an encoding category in short-term memory. *Journal of Experimental Psychology,* 1968, **78,** 599–604.

Wicklund, D. A., Palermo, D. S., and Jenkins, J. J. Associative clustering in the recall of children as a function of verbal association strength. *Journal of Experimental Child Psychology,* 1965, **2,** 58–66.

Wilcoxon, H. C., Wilson, W. R., and Wise, D. A. Paired-associate learning as a function of percentage of occurrence of response members and other factors. *Journal of Experimental Psychology,* 1961, **61,** 283–289.

Williams, M. The effects of experimentally induced needs upon retention. *Journal of Experimental Psychology,* 1950, **40,** 139–151.

Wimer, R. Osgood's transfer surface: Extension and test. *Journal of Verbal Learning and Verbal Behavior,* 1964, **3,** 274–279.

Winnick, W. A., and Dornbush, R. L. Role of positional cues in serial rote learning. *Journal of Experimental Psychology,* 1963, **66,** 419–421.

Winograd, E. List differentiation as a function of frequency and retention interval. *Journal of Experimental Psychology Monograph Supplement,* 1968, **76,** 1–18.

Winograd, E. List differentiation, recall, and category similarity. *Journal of Experimental Psychology,* 1968, **78,** 510–515. (a)

Witmer, L. R. The association value of three-place consonant syllables. *Journal of Genetic Psychology,* 1935, **47,** 337–360.

Wood, G., and Bolt, M. Mediation and mediation time in paired associate learning. *Journal of Experimental Psychology,* 1968, **78,** 15–20.

Wood, G., and Underwood, B. J. Implicit responses and conceptual similarity. *Journal of Verbal Learning and Verbal Behavior,* 1967, **6,** 1–10.

Woodworth, R. S. A contribution to the question of "quick learning, quick forgetting." *Psychological Bulletin,* 1914, **11,** 58–59.

Woodworth, R. S., and Schlosberg, H. *Experimental psychology.* New York: Holt, Rinehart and Winston, 1954.

Wright, J. H. Effects of stimulus meaningfulness, method of presentation, and list design on the learning of paired associates. *Journal of Experimental Psychology,* 1967, **73,** 72–77.

Wright, J. H., Gescheider, G. A., and Klein, S. B. Effects of constant and varied serial order of presenting paired associates in learning and testing. *Journal of Experimental Psychology,* 1969, **80,** 198–200.

Wylie, H. H. An experimental study of transfer of response in the white rat. *Behavioral Monographs,* 1919, **3,** No. 16.

Yarmey, A. D., and Paivio, A. Further evidence on the effects of word abstractness and meaningfulness in paired-associate learning. *Psychonomic Science,* 1965, **2,** 307–308.

Yngve, V. H. A model and an hypothesis for language structure. *Proceedings of the American Philosophical Society,* 1960, **104,** 444–466.

Yntema, D. B., and Mueser, G. E. Remembering the present states of a number of variables. *Journal of Experimental Psychology,* 1960, **60,** 18–22.

Young, R. K. Retroactive and proactive effects under varying conditions of response similarity. *Journal of Experimental Psychology,* 1955, **50,** 113–119.

Young, R. K. A comparison of two methods of learning serial associations. *American Journal of Psychology,* 1959, **72,** 554–559.

Young, R. K. Paired-associate learning when the same items occur as stimuli and responses. *Journal of Experimental Psychology,* 1961, **61,** 315–318.

Young, R. K. The stimulus in serial verbal learning. *American Journal of Psychology,* 1961, **74,** 517–528. (a)

Young, R. K. Tests of three hypotheses about the effective stimulus in serial learning. *Journal of Experimental Psychology,* 1962, **63,** 307–313.

Young, R. K. Serial learning. In Dixon, T. R., and Horton, D. L., Eds., *Verbal behavior and general behavior theory.* Englewood Cliffs, N.J.: Prentice-Hall, 1968.

Young, R. K., Hakes, D. T., and Hicks, R. Y. Effects of list length in the Ebbinghaus derived-list paradigm. *Journal of Experimental Psychology,* 1965, **70,** 338–341.

Young, R. K., Patterson, J., and Benson, W. M. Backward serial learning. *Journal of Verbal Learning and Verbal Behavior,* 1963, **1,** 335–338.

Youtz, A. C. An experimental evaluation of Jost's laws. *Psychological Monographs,* 1941, **53.**

Yuille, J. C. Concreteness without imagery in PA learning. *Psychonomic Science,* 1968, **11,** 55–56.

Yum, K. S. An experimental test of the law of assimilation. *Journal of Experimental Psychology,* 1931, **14,** 68–82.

Zacks, R. T. Invariance of total learning time under different conditions of practice. *Journal of Experimental Psychology,* 1969, **82,** 441–447.

Zechmeister, E. B. Orthographic distinctiveness. *Journal of Verbal Learning and Verbal Behavior,* 1969, **8,** 754–761.

Name Index

Subject Index